Big Data Computing

A Guide for Business and Technology Managers

Chapman & Hall/CRC
Big Data Series

SERIES EDITOR
Sanjay Ranka

AIMS AND SCOPE

This series aims to present new research and applications in Big Data, along with the computational tools and techniques currently in development. The inclusion of concrete examples and applications is highly encouraged. The scope of the series includes, but is not limited to, titles in the areas of social networks, sensor networks, data-centric computing, astronomy, genomics, medical data analytics, large-scale e-commerce, and other relevant topics that may be proposed by potential contributors.

PUBLISHED TITLES

BIG DATA COMPUTING: A GUIDE FOR BUSINESS AND TECHNOLOGY MANAGERS
Vivek Kale

BIG DATA OF COMPLEX NETWORKS
Matthias Dehmer, Frank Emmert-Streib, Stefan Pickl, and Andreas Holzinger

BIG DATA : ALGORITHMS, ANALYTICS, AND APPLICATIONS
Kuan-Ching Li, Hai Jiang, Laurence T. Yang, and Alfredo Cuzzocrea

NETWORKING FOR BIG DATA
Shui Yu, Xiaodong Lin, Jelena Mišić, and Xuemin (Sherman) Shen

Big Data Computing

A Guide for Business and Technology Managers

Vivek Kale

CRC Press
Taylor & Francis Group
Boca Raton London New York

CRC Press is an imprint of the
Taylor & Francis Group, an **informa** business
A CHAPMAN & HALL BOOK

CRC Press
Taylor & Francis Group
6000 Broken Sound Parkway NW, Suite 300
Boca Raton, FL 33487-2742

Printed on acid-free paper
Version Date: 20160426

International Standard Book Number-13: 978-1-4987-1533-1 (Hardback)

Library of Congress Cataloging-in-Publication Data

Names: Kale, Vivek, author.
Title: Big data computing : a guide for business and technology managers / author, Vivek Kale.
Description: Boca Raton : Taylor & Francis, CRC Press, 2016. | Series: Chapman & Hall/CRC big data series | Includes bibliographical references and index.
Identifiers: LCCN 2016005989 | ISBN 9781498715331
Subjects: LCSH: Big data.
Classification: LCC QA76.9.B45 K35 2016 | DDC 005.7--dc23
LC record available at https://lccn.loc.gov/2016005989

Visit the Taylor & Francis Web site at
http://www.taylorandfrancis.com

and the CRC Press Web site at
http://www.crcpress.com
Printed and bound in the United States of America by Edwards Brothers Malloy on sustainably sourced paper.

To

Nilesh Acharya and family

for unstinted support on

references and research

for my numerous book projects.

Contents

Section II Road to Big Data Computing

Section III Big Data Computing

Section IV Big Data Computing Applications

List of Figures

List of Tables

Preface

The rapid growth of the Internet and World Wide Web has led to vast amounts of information available online. In addition, business and government organizations create large amounts of both structured and unstructured information that need to be processed, analyzed, and linked. It is estimated that the amount of information stored in a digital form in 2007 was 281 exabytes, and the overall compound growth rate has been 57% with information in organizations growing at an even faster rate. It is also estimated that 95% of all current information exists in unstructured form with increased data processing requirements compared to structured information. The storing, managing, accessing, and processing of this vast amount of data represent a fundamental need and an immense challenge in order to satisfy the need to search, analyze, mine, and visualize these data as information. This deluge of data, along with emerging techniques and technologies used to handle it, is commonly referred to today as *big data computing*.

Big data can be defined as volumes of data available in varying degrees of complexity, generated at different velocities and varying degrees of ambiguity, that cannot be processed using traditional technologies, processing methods, algorithms, or any commercial off-the-shelf solutions. Such data include weather, geo-spatial and GIS data, consumer-driven data from social media, enterprise-generated data from legal, sales, marketing, procurement, finance and human-resources departments, and device-generated data from sensor networks, nuclear plants, X-ray and scanning devices, and airplane engines. This book describes the characteristics, challenges, and solutions for enabling such big data computing.

The fundamental challenges of big data computing are managing and processing exponentially growing data volumes, significantly reducing associated data analysis cycles to support practical, timely applications, and developing new algorithms that can scale to search and process massive amounts of data. The answer to these challenges is a scalable, integrated computer systems hardware and software architecture designed for parallel processing of big data computing applications. Cloud computing is a prerequisite to big data computing; cloud computing provides the opportunity for organizations with limited internal resources to implement large-scale big data computing applications in a cost-effective manner.

Relational databases are based on the relational model and provide online transaction processing (OLTP), schema-on-write, and SQL. Data warehouses are based on the relational model and support online analytical processing (OLAP). Data warehouses are designed to optimize data analysis, reporting, and data mining; data are extracted, transformed, and loaded (ETL) from other data sources to load data into the data warehouse. However, today's data environment demands innovations that are faster, extremely scalable, scale cost effectively, and work easily with structured, semistructured, and unstructured data. Hadoop and NoSQL databases are designed to work easily with structured, unstructured, and semistructured data. Hadoop, along with relational databases and data warehouses, increases the strategies and capabilities of leveraging data to increase the accuracy and speed of business decisions. Hadoop plays an important role in the modern data architecture. Organizations that can leverage the capabilities of relational databases, data warehouses and Hadoop, and all the available data sources will have a competitive advantage.

What Makes This Book Different?

This book interprets the 2010s big data computing phenomenon from the point of view of business as well as technology. This book unravels the mystery of big data computing environments and applications and their power and potential to transform the operating contexts of business enterprises. It addresses the key differentiator of big data computing environments, namely, that big data computing systems combine the power of elastic infrastructure (via cloud computing) and information management with the ability to analyze and discern recurring patterns in the colossal pools of operational and transactions data (via big data computing) to leverage and transform them into success patterns for an enterprise's business. These extremes of requirements for storage and processing arose primarily from developments of the past decade in the areas of social networks, mobile computing, location-based systems, and so on.

This book highlights the fact that handling gargantuan amounts of data became possible only because big data computing makes feasible computing beyond the practical limits imposed by Moore's law. Big data achieves this by employing non–Neumann architectures enabling parallel processing on a network of nodes equipped with extremely cost-effective commoditized hardware while simultaneously being more tolerant of fault and failures that are unavoidable in any realistic computing environments.

On April 19, 1965, Gordon Moore, the cofounder of Intel Corporation, published an article in Electronics Magazine titled "Cramming More Components onto Integrated Circuits" in which he identified and conjectured a trend that computing power would double every 2 years (this was termed as Moore's law in 1970 by CalTech professor and VLSI pioneer Calvin Mead). This law has been able to predict reliably both the reduction in costs and the improvements in computing capability of microchips, and those predictions have held true since then. This law effectively is a measure and professes limits on the increase in computing power that can be realistically achieved every couple of years. The requirements of modern applications such as social networks and mobile applications far outstrip what can be delivered by conventional Von Neumann architectures employed since the 1950s.

The phenomenon of big data computing has attained prominence in the context of the heightened interest in business analytics. An inevitable consequence of organizations using the pyramid-shaped hierarchy is that there is a decision-making bottleneck at the top of the organization. The people at the top are overwhelmed by the sheer volume of decisions they have to make; they are too far away from the scene of the action to really understand what's happening; and by the time decisions are made, the actions are usually too little and too late. The need to be responsive to evolving customer needs and desires creates operational structures and systems where business analysis and decision making are pushed out to operating units that are closest to the scene of the action—which, however, lack the expertise and resources to access, process, evaluate, and decide on the course of action. This engenders the significance of analysis systems that are essential for enabling decisive action as close to the customer as possible.

The characteristic features of this book are as follows:

1. It enables IT managers and business decision-makers to get a clear understanding of what big data computing really means, what it might do for them, and when it is practical to use it.
2. It gives an introduction to the database solutions that were a first step toward enabling data-based enterprises. It also gives a detailed description of data warehousing- and data mining-related solutions that paved the road to big data computing solutions.
3. It describes the basics of distributed systems, service-oriented architecture (SOA), web services, and cloud computing that were essential prerequisites to the emergence of big data computing solutions.
4. It provides a very wide treatment of big data computing that covers the functionalities (and features) of NoSQL, MapReduce programming models, Hadoop development ecosystem, and analysis tools environments.
5. It covers most major application areas of interest in big data computing: web, social networks, mobile, and location-based systems (LBS) applications.
6. It is not focused on any particular vendor or service offering. Although there is a good description of the open source Hadoop development ecosystem and related tools and technologies, the text also introduces NoSQL and analytics solutions from commercial vendors.

In the final analysis, big data computing is a realization of the vision of *intelligent infrastructure* that reforms and reconfigures automatically to store and/or process incoming data based on the predefined requirements and predetermined context of the requirements. The intelligent infrastructure itself will automatically capture, store, manage and analyze incoming data, take decisions, and undertake prescribed actions for standard scenarios, whereas nonstandard scenarios would be routed to DevOperators. An extension of this vision also underlies the future potential of Internet of Things (IoT) discussed in the Epilogue. IoT is the next step in the journey that commenced with computing beyond the limits of Moore's law made possible by cloud computing followed by the advent of big data computing technologies (like MapReduce and NoSQL). I wanted to write a book presenting big data computing from this novel perspective of computing beyond the practical limits imposed by Moore's law; the outcome is the book that you are reading now. Thank you!

How This Book Is Organized

This book traces the road to big data computing, the detailed features and characteristics of big data computing solutions and environments, and, in the last section, high-potential application areas of big data.

Section I provides a glimpse of the genesis of big data computing. Chapter 2 provides an overview of traditional database environments.

Section II describes significant milestones on the road to big data computing. Chapters 3 and 4 review the basics of analytics and data warehousing. Chapter 5 presents the standard characteristics of data mining. Chapters 7 and 8 wrap up this part with a detailed discussion on the nature and characteristics of service oriented architecture (SOA) and web services and cloud computing.

Section III presents a detailed discussion on various aspects of a big data computing solution. The approach adopted in this book will be useful to any professional who must present a case for realizing big data computing solutions or to those who could be involved in a big data computing project. It provides a framework that will enable business and technical managers to make the optimal decisions necessary for the successful migration to big data computing environments and applications within their organizations. Chapter 9 introduces the basics of big data computing and gives an introduction to the tools and technologies, including those that are essential for big data computing.

Chapter 10 describes the various technologies employed for realization of big data computing solutions: Hadoop development, NoSQL databases, and YARN. Chapter 11 details the offerings of various big data NoSQL database vendors. Chapter 12 details the Hadoop ecosystem essential for the development of big data applications. Chapter 13 presents details on analysis languages, tools and development environments. Chapter 14 describes big data-related management and operation issues that become critical as the big data computing environments become more complex.

Section IV presents detailed descriptions of major areas of big data computing applications. Chapter 15 discusses now familiar web-based application environments. Chapter 16 addresses popular social network applications such as Facebook and Twitter. Chapter 17 deals with the burgeoning mobile applications such as WhatsApp. Finally, Chapter 18 describes lesser known but more promising areas of location-based applications.

Context-aware applications can significantly enhance the efficiency and effectiveness of even routinely occurring transactions. Chapter 19 introduces the concept of context as constituted by an ensemble of function-specific decision patterns. This chapter highlights the fact that any end-user application's effectiveness and performance can be enhanced by transforming it from a *bare* transaction to a transaction *clothed* by a surrounding context formed as an aggregate of all relevant decision patterns in the past. This generation of an important component of the generalized concept of *context* is critically dependent on employing big data computing techniques and technologies deployed via cloud computing.

Who Should Read This Book?

All stakeholders of a big data project can read this book.

This book presents a detailed discussion on various aspects of a big data computing solution. The approach adopted in this book will be useful to any professional who must present a case for realizing big data computing solutions or to those who could be involved in a big data computing project. It provides a framework to enable business and technical managers to make the optimal decisions necessary for the successful migration to big data computing environments and applications within their organizations.

All readers who are involved with any aspect of a big data computing project will profit by using this book as a road map toward a more meaningful contribution to the success of their big data computing initiative(s).

Following is the minimal recommendations of tracks of chapters that should be read by different categories of stakeholders:

- Executives and business managers should read Chapters 3, 5, 9, 11, and 15 through 19.
- Operational managers should read Chapters 3, 4, 5, 8, 9, 11, and 13 through 19.
- Project managers and module leaders should read Chapters 1 through 11 and 13 through 19.
- Technology managers should read Chapters 1 through 19.
- Professionals interested in big data computing should read Chapters 2 through 19.
- Students of computer courses should read Chapters 1 through 19.
- Students of management courses should read Chapters 3, 4, 5, 9, and 13 through 19.
- General readers interested in the phenomenon of big data computing should read Chapters 1 through 19.

Vivek Kale
Mumbai, India

You may want to get a copy of *Guide to Cloud Computing for Business and Technology Managers* as a companion for this book. The guide is designed to help you better understand the background, characteristics, and applications of cloud computing. Together, these two books form a complete road map for building successful cloud-based analytical applications.

Acknowledgments

I would like to thank all those who have helped me with their clarifications, criticism, and valuable information during the writing of this book.

Thanks again to Aastha Sharma for making this book happen and Ed Curtis for guiding its production to completion.

I would like to thank my family, especially, my wife, Girija, who has suffered the long hours I have dedicated to the book instead of the family and whose love and support is what keeps me going.

Vivek Kale

Author

Vivek Kale has more than two decades of professional IT experience during which he has handled and consulted on various aspects of enterprise-wide information modeling, enterprise architectures, business process redesign, and e-business architectures. He has been Group CIO of Essar Group, the steel/oil and gas major of India, as well as Raymond Ltd., the textile and apparel major of India. He is a seasoned practitioner in transforming the business of IT, facilitating business agility and enhancing IT-enabled enterprise intelligence. He is the author of *Implementing SAP R/3: The Guide for Business and Technology Managers* (Sams 2000) and *Guide to Cloud Computing for Business and Technology Managers: From Distributed Computing to Cloudware Applications* (CRC Press 2015).

1

Computing Beyond the Moore's Law Barrier While Being More Tolerant of Faults and Failures

Since the advent of computer in the 1950s, weather forecasting has been a hugely challenging computational problem. Right since the beginning, weather models ran on a single supercomputer that could fill a gymnasium and contained a couple of fast (for the 1970s) CPUs with very expensive memory. Software in the 1970s was primitive, so most of the performance at that time was in clever hardware engineering. By the 1990s, software had improved to the point where a large program running on monolithic supercomputers could be broken into a hundred smaller programs working simultaneously on a hundred workstations. When all the programs finished running, their results were stitched together to form a weeklong weather simulation. What used to take fifteen days to compute and simulate seven days of weather even in the 90's, today the parallel simulations corresponding to a weeklong forecast can be accomplished in a matter of hours.

There are lots of data involved in weather simulation and prediction, but weather simulation is not considered a representative of "big data" problems because it is computationally intensive rather than being data intensive. Computing problems in science (including meteorology and engineering) are also known as high-performance computing (HPC) or scientific supercomputing because they entail solving millions of equations.

Big data is the commercial equivalent of HPC, which could also be called high-performance commercial computing or commercial supercomputing. Big data can also solve large computing problems, but it is less about equations and more about discovering patterns. Today companies such as Amazon, eBay, and Facebook use commercial supercomputing to solve their Internet-scale business problems. Big data is a type of supercomputing for commercial enterprises and governments that will make it possible to monitor a pandemic as it happens, anticipate where the next bank robbery will occur, optimize fast-food supply chains, predict voter behavior on election day, and forecast the volatility of political uprisings while they are happening.

Big data can be defined as data sets whose size is beyond the ability of typical database software tools to capture, store, manage, and analyze.

Big data is different from the traditional concept of data in terms of the following:

- Bigger volume: There is more than a half-a-trillion pieces of content (photos, notes, blogs, web links, and news stories) shared on Facebook every month and 4 billion hours of video are watched at YouTube every month. It is believed that there will be more than 50 billion connected devices in the world by 2020.
- Higher velocity: At 140 characters per tweet, Twitter-generated data volume is larger than 10 terabytes per day. It is believed that more data were created between 2008 and 2011 than in all history before 2008.

- More data variety: It is estimated that 95% of the world data are unstructured, which makes big data extremely challenging. Big data could exist in various formats, namely, video, image, audio, text/numbers, and so on.
- Different degree of veracity: The degree of authenticity or accuracy of data ranges from objective observations of physical phenomenon to subjective observations or opinions expressed on social media.

Storing, managing, accessing, and processing of this vast amount of data represent a fundamental need and an immense challenge in order to satisfy the need to search, analyze, mine, and visualize these data as information.

1.1 Moore's Law Barrier

On April 19, 1965, Gordon Moore, the cofounder of Intel Corporation, published an article in *Electronics Magazine* titled "Cramming More Components onto Integrated Circuits" in which he identified and conjectured a trend that computing power would double every 2 years (this was termed as Moore's law in 1970 by the CalTech professor and VLSI pioneer, Calvin Mead). This law has been able to predict reliably both the reduction in costs and the improvements in computing capability of microchips, and those predictions have held true (see Figure 1.1).

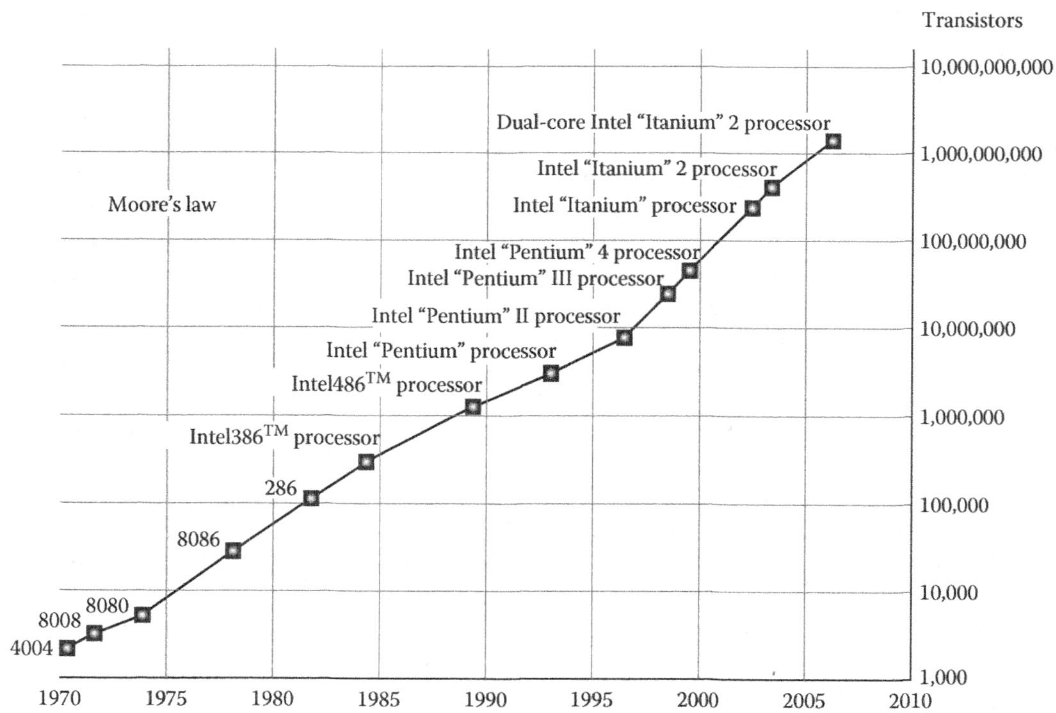

FIGURE 1.1
Increase in the number of transistors on an Intel chip.

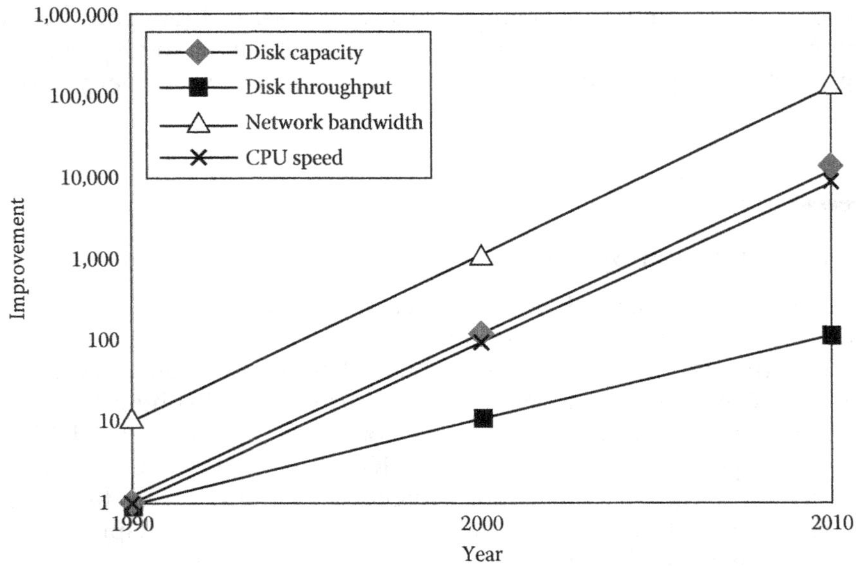

FIGURE 1.2
Hardware trends in the 1990s and the first decade.

In 1965, the amount of transistors that fitted on an integrated circuit could be counted in tens. In 1971, Intel introduced the 4004 microprocessor with 2,300 transistors. In 1978, when Intel introduced the 8086 microprocessor, the IBM PC was effectively born (the first IBM PC used the 8088 chip)—this chip had 29,000 transistors. In 2006, Intel's Itanium 2 processor carried 1.7 billion transistors. In the next couple of years, we will have chips with over 10 billion transistors. While all this was happening, the cost of these transistors was also falling exponentially, as per Moore's prediction (Figure 1.2).

In real terms, this means that a mainframe computer of the 1970s that cost over $1 million had less computing power than the iPhone has today. The next generation of smartphone in the next few years will have GHz processor chips, which will be roughly one million times faster than the Apollo Guidance Computer that put "man on the moon." Theoretically, Moore's law will run out of steam somewhere in the not too distant future. There are a number of possible reasons for this.

First, the ability of a microprocessor silicon-etched track or circuit to carry an electrical charge has a theoretical limit. At some point when these circuits get physically too small and can no longer carry a charge or the electrical charge bleeds, we will have a design limitation problem. Second, as successive generations of chip technology are developed, manufacturing costs increase. In fact, Gordon Moore himself conjectured that as tolerances become tighter, each new generation of chips would require a doubling in cost of the manufacturing facility. At some point, it will theoretically become too costly to develop manufacturing plants that produce these chips.

The usable limit for semiconductor process technology will be reached when chip process geometries shrink to be smaller than 20 nanometers (nm) to 18 nm nodes. At those scales, the industry will start getting to the point where semiconductor manufacturing tools would be too expensive to depreciate with volume production; that is, their costs will be so high that the value of their lifetime productivity can never justify it.

Lastly, the power requirements of chips are also increasing. More power being equivalent to more heat equivalent to bigger batteries implies that at some point, it becomes increasingly difficult to power these chips while putting them on smaller platforms.

1.2 Types of Computer Systems

Today's computer systems come in a variety of sizes, shapes, and computing capabilities. The Apollo 11 spacecraft that enabled landing men on the moon and returning them safely to the earth was equipped with a computer that assisted them in everything from navigation to systems monitoring, and it had a 2.048 MHz CPU built by MIT. Today's standards can be measured in 4 GHz in many home PCs (megahertz [MHz] is 1 million computing cycles per second, while gigahertz [GHz] is 1 billion computing cycles per second). Further, the Apollo 11 computer weighed 70 pounds versus today's powerful laptops weighing as little as 1 pound—we have come a long way. Rapid hardware and software developments and changing end user needs continue to drive the emergence of new models of computers, from the smallest handheld personal digital assistant/cell phone combinations to the largest multiple-CPU mainframes for enterprises. Categories such as microcomputer, midrange, mainframe, and supercomputer systems are still used to help us express the relative processing power and number of end users that can be supported by different types of computers. These are not precise classifications, and they do overlap each other.

1.2.1 Microcomputers

Microcomputers are the most important category of computer systems for both business and household consumers. Although usually called a personal computer, or PC, a microcomputer is much more than a small computer for use by an individual as a communication device. The computing power of microcomputers now exceeds that of the mainframes of previous computer generations, at a fraction of their cost. Thus, they have become powerful networked professional workstations for business professionals.

1.2.2 Midrange Computers

Midrange computers are primarily high-end network servers and other types of servers that can handle the large-scale processing of many business applications. Although not as powerful as mainframe computers, they are less costly to buy, operate, and maintain than mainframe systems and thus meet the computing needs of many organizations. Midrange systems first became popular as minicomputers in scientific research, instrumentation systems, engineering analysis, and industrial process monitoring and control. Minicomputers were able to easily handle such functions because these applications are narrow in scope and do not demand the processing versatility of mainframe systems. Today, midrange systems include servers used in industrial process control and manufacturing plants and play major roles in computer-aided manufacturing (CAM). They can also take the form of powerful technical workstations for computer-aided design (CAD) and other computation and graphics-intensive applications. Midrange systems are also used as front-end servers to assist mainframe computers in telecommunications processing and network management.

Midrange systems have become popular as powerful network servers (computers used to coordinate communications and manage resource sharing in network settings) to help manage large Internet websites, corporate intranets and extranets, and other networks. Internet functions and other applications are popular high-end server applications, as are integrated enterprise-wide manufacturing, distribution, and financial applications. Other applications, such as data warehouse management, data mining, and online analytical processing, are contributing to the demand for high-end server systems.

1.2.3 Mainframe Computers

Mainframe computers are large, fast, and powerful computer systems; they can process thousands of million instructions per second (MIPS). They can also have large primary storage capacities with main memory capacity ranging from hundreds of gigabytes to many terabytes. Mainframes have downsized drastically in the last few years, dramatically reducing their air-conditioning needs, electrical power consumption, and floor space requirements—and thus their acquisition, operating, and ownership costs. Most of these improvements are the result of a move from the cumbersome water-cooled mainframes to a newer air-cooled technology for mainframe systems.

Mainframe computers continue to handle the information processing needs of major corporations and government agencies with high transaction processing volumes or complex computational problems. For example, major international banks, airlines, oil companies, and other large corporations process millions of sales transactions and customer inquiries every day with the help of large mainframe systems. Mainframes are still used for computation-intensive applications, such as analyzing seismic data from oil field explorations or simulating flight conditions in designing aircraft.

Mainframes are also widely used as superservers for large client/server networks and high-volume Internet websites of large companies. Mainframes are becoming a popular business computing platform for data mining and warehousing, as well as electronic commerce applications.

1.2.4 Supercomputers

Supercomputers are a category of extremely powerful computer systems specifically designed for scientific, engineering, and business applications requiring extremely high speeds for massive numeric computations. Supercomputers use parallel processing architectures of interconnected microprocessors (which can execute many parallel instructions). They can easily perform arithmetic calculations at speeds of billions of floating-point operations per second (gigaflops)—a floating point operation is a basic computer arithmetic operation, such as addition, on numbers that include a decimal point. Supercomputers that can calculate in trillions of floating-point operations per second (teraflops), which use massively parallel processing (MPP) designs of thousands of microprocessors, are now in use (see Chapter 1 Sub-section 1.4.4,"Massively Parallel Processing").

The market for supercomputers includes government research agencies, large universities, and major corporations. They use supercomputers for applications such as global weather forecasting, military defence systems, computational cosmology and astronomy, microprocessor research and design, and large-scale data mining.

Interconnecting microprocessors to create minisupercomputers is a reality. The next wave was looking at harnessing the virtually infinite amount of unused computing power that exists in the myriad of desktops and laptops within the boundaries or outside of a modern organization. Distributed or grid or cloud computing in general is a special type of parallel computing that relies on complete or virtual computers (with onboard CPU, storage, power supply, network interface, and so forth) connected to a network (private, public, or the Internet) by a conventional or virtual network interface. This is in contrast to the traditional notion of a supercomputer, which has many processors connected together in a single machine. The primary advantage of distributed computing is that each node can be purchased as commodity hardware; when combined, it can produce computing resources similar to a multiprocessor supercomputer, but at a significantly lower cost. This is due to the economies of scale of producing desktops and laptops, compared with the lower efficiency of designing and constructing a small number of custom supercomputers.

1.3 Parallel Computing

A parallel computer is a set of processors that are able to work cooperatively to solve a computational problem. This definition is broad enough to include parallel supercomputers that have hundreds or thousands of processors, networks of workstations, multiple-processor workstations, and embedded systems. Parallel computers are interesting because they offer the potential to concentrate computational resources—whether processors, memory, or I/O bandwidth—on important computational problems.

The performance of a computer depends directly on the time required to perform a basic operation and the number of these basic operations that can be performed concurrently. The time to perform a basic operation is ultimately determined by the "clock cycle" of the processor, that is, the time required to perform the most primitive operation. However, clock cycle times are decreasing slowly and already approaching physical limits defined, for example, by the speed of light. We cannot depend on faster processors to provide increased computational performance. If a computation can be considered as transfer of information from one side of the square chip with area A to another, the amount of information that can be moved in a time t would be of the order of $\sqrt{At}$.

To decrease the time required to move information by a certain factor, the cross section must be increased by the same factor, and therefore the total area must be increased by the square of that factor. This result means that not only is it difficult to build individual components that operate faster, it may not even be desirable to do so. It may be cheaper to use more, slower components. For example, if we have an area n^2A of silicon to use in a computer, we can either build n^2 components, each of size A and able to perform an operation in time t, or build a single component able to perform the same operation in time t/n. The multicomponent system is potentially n times faster.

Computer designers use a variety of techniques to overcome these limitations on single computer performance, including pipelining (different stages of several instructions execute concurrently) and multiple function units (several multipliers, adders, etc., are controlled by a single instruction stream). Increasingly, designers are incorporating multiple "computers," each with its own processor, memory, and associated interconnection logic. This approach is facilitated by advances in VLSI technology that continue to decrease the number of components required to implement a computer. As the cost of a computer is (very approximately) proportional to the number of components that it contains, increased integration also increases the number of processors that can be included in a computer for a particular cost.

Parallelizing query processing permits to handle larger data sets in reasonable time or to speed up complex operations and, therefore, represents the key to tackle the big data problem. Parallelization implies that the processing work is split and distributed across a number of processors, or processing nodes. "Scale-out" refers to scenarios where the amount of data per node is kept constant, and nodes are added to handle large data volumes while keeping the processing time constant. In contrast, "speedout" means that the data volume is kept constant and nodes are added to speed up the processing time.

The ideal scale-out behavior of a query has a linear relationship between the number of nodes and the amount of data that can processed in a certain time. The theoretical linear scale-out is hardly achieved, because a certain fraction of the query processing is normally not parallelizable, such as the coordinated startup of the processing or exclusive access to shared data structures. The serial part of the computation limits its parallel scalability—this relationship has been formulated as Amdahl's Law: Let f be the portion of the program that is parallelizable, and p be the number of processors (or nodes). The maximal speed up S_{max} is then given by

$$S_{max} = \frac{1}{(1-f)*\frac{f}{p}}$$

It is obvious that for a totally parallelizable program ($f = 1$), the speed up is p. However, since in practice, $f < 1$, the speedup is sublinear and is in fact bounded by a constant, which it approaches an asymptotically increasing number of processors. Effectively, a very high percentage of parallelizable code is imperative for a program to be truly fast: even programs that have 99% parallelizable code running on 100 nodes are only sped up by factor of 50!

Another important trend changing the face of computing is an enormous increase in the capabilities of the networks that connect computers. Not long ago, high-speed networks ran at 1.5 Mbits per second; by the end of the 1990s, bandwidths in excess of 1,000 Mbits per second were commonplace. These trends made it feasible to develop applications that use physically distributed resources as if they were part of the same computer. A typical application of this sort may utilize processors on multiple remote computers, access a selection of remote databases, perform rendering on one or more graphics computers, and provide real-time output and control on a workstation.

Effective and efficient computing power necessitates convergence of parallel and distributed computing:

- Concurrency: Programs will be required to exploit the multiple processors located inside each computer and the additional processors available across a network. Because most existing algorithms are specialized for a single processor, this implies a need for new *concurrent* algorithms and program structures that are able to perform many operations at once.
- Scalability: Software systems will be required to be resilient to stupendous increases in the number of processors.

1.3.1 Von Neumann Architectures

Conventional computers are based on the von Neumann architecture, which processes information serially, one instruction at a time.

The Mauchly–Eckert–von Neumann concept of the stored program computer used the basic technical idea that a binary number system could be directly mapped to the two physical states of a flip-flop electronic circuit. In this circuit, the logical concept of the binary unit "1" could be interpreted as the on (or conducting state) and the binary unit "0" could be interpreted as the off (or not conducting state) of the electric circuit. In this way, the functional concept of numbers (written on the binary base) could be directly mapped into the physical states (physical morphology) of a set of electronic flip-flop circuits. The number of these circuits together would express how large a number could be represented. This is what is meant by word length in the digital computer. Binary numbers must encode not only data but also the instructions that perform the computational operations on the data. One of the points of progress in computer technology has been how long a word length could be built into a computer.

The design of the early computer used a hierarchy of logical operations. The lowest level of logic was the mapping of a set of bistable flip-flop circuits to a binary number system. A next step-up had circuits mapped to a Boolean logic (AND, OR, NOT circuits). A next step-up had these Boolean logic circuits connected together for arithmetic operations (such as add and subtract, multiply and divide). Computational instructions were then encoded as sequences of Boolean logic operations and/or arithmetic operations. Finally, at the highest logic level, von Neumann's stored program concept was expressed as a clocked cycle of fetching and performing computational instructions on data. This is now known as a von Neumann computer architecture—sequential instruction operated as a calculation cycle, timed to an internal clock.

The modern computer has four hierarchical levels of schematic logics mapped to physical morphologies (forms and processes) of transistor circuits:

1. Binary numbers mapped to bistable electronic circuits
2. Boolean logic operations mapped to electronic circuits of bistable circuits
3. Mathematical basic operations mapped (through Boolean constructions) to electronic circuits
4. Program instructions mapped sequentially to temporary electronic circuits (of Boolean and/or arithmetic instructions)

The Neumann architecture was the first modern design for computers based on the stored program concept. Figure 1.3 shows a block diagram of Neumann architecture. The

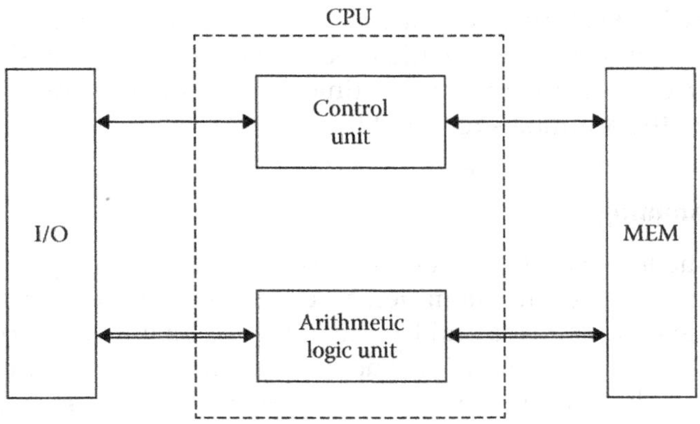

FIGURE 1.3
Von Neumann computer architecture.

arithmetic and logic unit is the place where calculations take place. The control unit interprets the instructions and coordinates the operations. Memory is used to store instructions and data as well as intermediate results. Input and output interfaces are used to read data and write results.

1.3.2 Non-Neumann Architectures

Non-Neumann comprises a number of von Neumann computers, or nodes, linked by an interconnection network. Each computer executes its own program. This program may access local memory and may send and receive messages over the network. Messages are used to communicate with other computers or, equivalently, to read and write remote memories. In the idealized network, the cost of sending a message between two nodes is independent of both node location and other network traffic, but depends only on the length of the message.

Thus, accesses to local (same-node) memory are less expensive than accesses to remote (different-node) memory; in other words, read and write are less costly than send and receive. Therefore, it is desirable that accesses to local data be more frequent than accesses to remote data. This defining attribute of non-Neumann architectures is called *locality*.

1.4 Parallel Processing

Parallel processing is performed by the simultaneous execution of program instructions that have been allocated across multiple processors with the objective of running a program in less time. On the earliest computers, a user could run only one program at a time. This being the case, a computation-intensive program that took X minutes to run, using a tape system for data I/O that took X minutes to run, would take a total of X + X minutes to execute. To improve performance, early forms of parallel processing were developed to allow interleaved execution of both programs simultaneously. The computer would start an I/O operation (which is typically measured in milliseconds), and while it was waiting for the I/O operation to complete, it would execute the processor-intensive program (measured in nanoseconds). The total execution time for the two jobs combined became only slightly longer than the X minutes required for the I/O operations to complete.

1.4.1 Multiprogramming

The next advancement in parallel processing was multiprogramming. In a multiprogramming system, multiple programs submitted by users are all allowed to use the processor for a short time, each taking turns and having exclusive time with the processor in order to execute instructions. This approach is known as round-robin scheduling (RR scheduling). It is one of the oldest, simplest, fairest, and most widely used scheduling algorithms, designed especially for time-sharing systems. In RR scheduling, a small unit of time called a time slice is defined. All executable processes are held in a circular queue. The time slice is defined based on the number of executable processes that are in the queue. For example, if there are five user processes held in the queue and the time slice allocated for the queue to execute in total is 1 s, each user process is allocated 200 ms of process execution time on the CPU before the scheduler begins moving to the next process in the queue. The CPU scheduler manages this queue, allocating the CPU to each process for a time interval of one time slice. New processes are always added to the end of the queue.

The CPU scheduler picks the first process from the queue, sets its timer to interrupt the process after the expiration of the timer, and then dispatches the next process in the queue. The process whose time has expired is placed at the end of the queue. If a process is still running at the end of a time slice, the CPU is interrupted and the process goes to the end of the queue. If the process finishes before the end of the time slice, it releases the CPU voluntarily. In either case, the CPU scheduler assigns the CPU to the next process in the queue. Every time a process is granted the CPU, a context switch occurs, which adds overhead to the process execution time. To users, it appears that all the programs are executing at the same time.

Resource contention problems often arose in those early systems. Explicit requests for resources led to a condition known as deadlock. Competition for resources on machines with no tie-breaking instructions led to the critical section routine. Contention occurs when several processes request access to the same resource. In order to detect deadlock situations, a counter for each processor keeps track of the number of consecutive requests from a process that have been rejected. Once that number reaches a predetermined threshold, a state machine that inhibits other processes from making requests to the main store is initiated until the deadlocked process is successful in gaining access to the resource.

1.4.2 Vector Processing

The next step in the evolution of parallel processing was the introduction of multiprocessing. Here, two or more processors share a common workload. The earliest versions of multiprocessing were designed as a master–slave model, where one processor (the master) was responsible for all the tasks to be performed and it only offloaded tasks to the other processor (the slave) when the master processor determined, based on a predetermined threshold, that work could be shifted to increase performance. This arrangement was necessary because it was not then understood how to program the machines, so they could cooperate in managing the resources of the system. Vector processing was developed to increase processing performance by operating in a multitasking manner. Matrix operations were added to computers to allow a single instruction to manipulate two arrays of numbers performing arithmetic operations. This was valuable in certain types of applications in which data occurred in the form of vectors or matrices. In applications with less well-formed data, vector processing was less valuable.

1.4.3 Symmetric Multiprocessing Systems

The next advancement was the development of symmetric multiprocessing (SMP) systems to address the problem of resource management in master/slave models. In SMP systems, each processor is equally capable and responsible for managing the workflow as it passes through the system. The primary goal is to achieve sequential consistency, in other words, to make SMP systems appear to be exactly the same as a single-processor, multiprogramming platform. Engineers discovered that system performance could be increased nearly 10%–20% by executing some instructions out of order.

However, programmers had to deal with the increased complexity and cope with a situation where two or more programs might read and write the same operands simultaneously. This difficulty, however, is limited to a very few programs, because it only occurs in rare circumstances. To this day, the question of how SMP machines should behave when accessing shared data remains unresolved.

Data propagation time increases in proportion to the number of processors added to SMP systems. After a certain number (usually somewhere around 40–50 processors), performance benefits gained by using even more processors do not justify the additional expense of adding such processors. To solve the problem of long data propagation times, message passing systems were created. In these systems, programs that share data send messages to each other to announce that particular operands have been assigned a new value. Instead of a global message announcing an operand's new value, the message is communicated only to those areas that need to know the change. There is a network designed to support the transfer of messages between applications. This allows a great number of processors (as many as several thousand) to work in tandem in a system. These systems are highly scalable and are called massively parallel processing (MPP) systems.

1.4.4 Massively Parallel Processing

MPP is used in computer architecture circles to refer to a computer system with many independent arithmetic units or entire microprocessors, which run in parallel. Massive connotes hundreds if not thousands of such units. In this form of computing, all the processing elements are interconnected to act as one very large computer. This approach is in contrast to a distributed computing model, where massive numbers of separate computers are used to solve a single problem such as in the search for extraterrestrial intelligence. Early examples of MPP systems were the Distributed Array Processor, the Connection Machine, and the Ultracomputer. In data mining, there is a need to perform multiple searches of a static database. The earliest MPP systems all used serial computers as individual processing units in order to maximize the number of units available for a given size and cost.

Single-chip implementations of MPP arrays are becoming ever more cost-effective due to the advancements in integrated circuit technology.

MPP machines are not easy to program, but for certain applications, such as data mining, they are the best solution.

> Just as the speed of light defines the theoretical limit of how fast we can travel in our universe, Amdahl's law defines the limits of performance gain we can achieve by adding more nodes to clusters. In a nutshell, the law states that if a given solution can be made perfectly parallelizable up to a proportion P (where P ranges from 0 to 1), the maximum performance improvement we can obtain given an infinite number of nodes (a fancy way of saying a lot of nodes in the cluster) is 1/(1–P). Thus, if we have even 1 percent of the execution that cannot be made parallel, the best improvement we can get is only 100 fold. All programs have some serial dependencies, and disk I/O and network I/O will add more. There are limits to how many improvements we can achieve regardless of the methods we use.

1.5 Fault Tolerance

Fault tolerance is the ability of a system to continue performing its intended functions in presence of faults. In a broad sense, fault tolerance is associated with reliability, with successful operation, and with the absence of breakdowns. A fault-tolerant system should be able to handle faults in individual hardware or software components, power failures, or other kinds of unexpected problems and still meet its specification.

Fault tolerance is necessary because it is practically impossible to build a perfect system. The fundamental problem is that, as the complexity of a system grows, its reliability drastically decreases, unless compensatory measures are taken. For example, if the reliability of individual components is 99.99%, then the reliability of a system consisting of 100 nonredundant components is 99.01%, whereas the reliability of a system consisting of 10,000 nonredundant components is just 36.79%. Such a low reliability is unacceptable in most applications. If a 99% reliability is required for a 10,000-component system, individual components with a reliability of at least 99.999% should be used, implying a sharp increase in cost.

Another problem is that although designers do their best to have all the hardware defects and software bugs cleaned out of the system before it goes on the market, history shows that such a goal is not attainable. It is inevitable that some unexpected environmental factor is not taken into account, or some new unexpected environmental factor comes into play, or some potential user mistakes are not foreseen. Thus, even in an unlikely case in which a system is designed and implemented perfectly, faults are likely to be caused by situations outside the control of the designers.

A system is said to fail if it has ceased to perform its intended functions; failure can be a total cessation of function or a performance of some function in a subnormal quality or quantity, like deterioration or instability of operation. System is used in this book in the generic sense of a group of independent but interrelated elements comprising a unified whole. Therefore, the techniques presented are applicable to a variety of products, devices, and subsystems. The aim of fault-tolerant design is to minimize the probability of failures, whether those failures simply annoy the users or result in lost fortunes, human injury, or environmental disaster.

As semiconductor technology progressed, hardware components became intrinsically more reliable and the need for tolerating component defects diminished for general purpose applications. Nevertheless, fault tolerance remained an essential attribute for systems used:

- Safety-critical applications are those where loss of life or environmental disaster must be avoided. Examples are nuclear power plant control systems, computer-controlled radiation therapy machines, heart pacemakers, and flight control systems.
- Mission-critical applications stress mission completion, as in the case of a spacecraft or a satellite.
- Business-critical applications are those in which keeping a business operating continuously is an issue. Examples are bank and stock exchange automated trading systems, web servers, and e-commerce.

During the mid-1990s, the interest in fault tolerance resurged considerably. On the one hand, noise margins were reduced to a critical level as the semiconductor manufacturing process size continuously shrinks, the power supply voltage is lowered, and operating speed increases. This made integrated circuits (ICs) highly sensitive to transient faults caused by crosstalk and environmental upsets such as atmospheric neutrons and alpha particles. It became mandatory to design ICs that are tolerant to these faults in order to maintain an acceptable level of reliability. On the other hand, the rapid development of real-time computing applications that started around the mid-1990s, especially the demand for software-embedded intelligent devices, made software fault tolerance a pressing issue. Software systems offer a compact design and a rich functionality at a competitive cost. Instead of implementing a given functionality in hardware, a set of instructions accomplishing the desired tasks are written and loaded into a processor. If changes in the functionality are required, the instructions can be modified instead of building a different physical device. Software eliminates many of the physical constraints of hardware; for example, it does not suffer from random fabrication defects and does not wear out.

There are various approaches to achieving fault tolerance. Common to all these approaches is a certain amount of redundancy. For our purposes, redundancy is the provision of functional capabilities that would be unnecessary in a fault-free environment. This can be a replicated hardware component, an additional check bit attached to a string of digital data, or a few lines of program code verifying the correctness of the program's results. The idea of incorporating redundancy in order to improve the reliability of a system was pioneered by John von Neumann in the 1950s in his work "Probabilistic Logic and Synthesis of Reliable Organisms from Unreliable Components."

Two kinds of redundancy are possible: space redundancy and time redundancy. Space redundancy provides additional components, functions, or data items that are unnecessary for fault-free operation. Space redundancy is further classified into hardware, software, and information redundancy, depending on the type of redundant resources added to the system. In time redundancy, the computation or data transmission is repeated and the result is compared to a stored copy of the previous result.

1.6 Reliability Conundrum

In all engineering disciplines, reliability is the ability of a system to perform its required functions under stated conditions for a specified period of time. In software, for application reliability, this becomes the ability of a software application and all the components it depends on (operating system, hypervisor, servers, disks, network connections, power supplies, etc.) to execute without faults or halts all the way to completion. But completion is defined by the application designer. Even with perfectly written software and no detected bugs in all underlying software systems, applications that begin to use thousands of servers will run into the "mean time to failure" in some piece of hardware, and some number of those instances will fail. Therefore, the application depending on those instances will also fail.

Many design techniques for achieving high reliability depend upon redundant software, hardware, and data. For redundant software components, this may consist of double- or triple-redundant software components (portions of your application) running in parallel with common validation checks. One idea is to have the components developed by different teams based on the same specifications. This approach costs more, but extreme reliability may require it. Because each component is designed to perform the same function, the failures of concurrent identical components are easily discovered and corrected during quality-assurance testing.

Although redundant software components provide the quality-assurance process with a clever way to validate service accuracy, certain applications may want to deploy component redundancy into the production environment. In such conditions, multiple parallel application processes can provide validity checks on each other and let the majority rule. Although the redundant software components consume extra resource consumption, the trade-off between reliability and the cost of extra hardware may be worth it.

Another redundancy-based design technique is the use of services such as clustering (linking many computers together to act as a single faster computer), load balancing (workloads kept balanced between multiple computers), data replication (making multiple identical copies of data to be processed independently and in parallel), and protecting complex operations with transactions to ensure process integrity. Naturally, when one is using cloud provider services, many of these services are inbuilt in the base infrastructure and services.

Redundant hardware is one of the most popular strategies for providing reliable systems. This includes redundant arrays of independent disks (RAID) for data storage, redundant network interfaces, and redundant power supplies. With this kind of hardware infrastructure, individual component failures can occur without affecting the overall reliability of the application. It is important to use standardized commodity hardware to allow easy installation and replacement.

In 2008, Google had to solve the massive search problem across all content on the web, which was bordering on one trillion unique URLs. They ended up employing loosely coupled distributed computing on a massive scale: clusters of commodity (cheap) computers working in parallel on large data sets. Even with individual server with excellent reliability statistics, with hundreds of thousands of servers, there were still multiple failures per day as one machine or another reached its mean time to failure. Google had no choice but to give up on reliability of the hardware and switch things over to achieve the same with the reliability of the software. The only way to build a reliable system across a group of large number of unreliable computers is to employ suitable software to address those failures. MapReduce was the software framework invented by Google to address this issue; the name MapReduce was inspired by the map and reduce functions of the functional programming language Lisp.

Parallel programming on a massive scale has the potential to not only address the issue of reliability but also deliver a huge boost in performance. This is opportune because, given the problems with large data sets of the web, without massive parallelism, leave aside reliability, the processing itself may not be achievable.

Instituting strategies and mechanisms that accommodate instead of avoiding possibilities of routine faults and failures is not new. TCP/IP that is a grouping of transmission control protocol (TCP) and Internet protocol (IP) are two of the core technology standards on which the Internet is based. TCP/IP is a low-level protocol that ensures that signals can be moved from one place to another. IP moves packets of data from one point to another, with routers helping those packets find their way across networks; this transmission of packets is unreliable. TCP builds reliable connections on top of IP, accepting that not all packets will complete their journeys and resending them as necessary.

1.7 Brewer's CAP Theorem

Techniques for achieving Atomicity, Consistency, Isolation, and Durability (ACID) properties in a database system are explained in the note below. However, applying these techniques in large-scale scenarios such as data services in the cloud leads to scalability problems: the amount of data to be stored and processed and the transaction and query load to be managed are usually too large to run the database services on a single machine. To overcome this data storage bottleneck, the database must be stored on multiple nodes, for which horizontal scaling is the typically chosen approach.

The database is partitioned across the different nodes: either tablewise or by sharding (see Chapter 9 Sub-section 9.2.3, "Row Partitioning or Sharding"). Both cases result in a distributed system for which Eric Brewer has formulated the famous consistency availability partition (CAP) theorem, which characterizes three of the main properties of such a system:

1. Consistency: All clients have the same view, even in the case of updates. For multisite transactions, this requires all-or-nothing semantics. For replicated data, this implies that all replicas have always consistent states.
2. Availability: Availability implies that all clients always find a replica of data even in the presence of failures.
3. Partition tolerance: In the case of network failures that split the nodes into groups (partitions), the system is still able to continue the processing.

The CAP theorem further states that in a distributed, shared-data system, these three properties cannot be achieved simultaneously in the presence of failures. In order to understand the implications, we have to consider possible failures. For scalability reasons, the database is running on two sites S1 and S2 sharing a data object o, for example, a flight booking record. This data sharing should be transparent to client applications, that is, an application AS1 connected to site A and AS2 accessing the database via site S2. Both clients should always see the same state of o even in the presence of an update. Hence, in order to ensure a consistent view, any update performed for instance by AS1 and changing o to a new state o′ has to be propagated by sending a message m to update o at S2 so that AS2 reads o′.

To understand why the CAP theorem holds, we consider the scenario where the network connecting S1 and S2 fails, resulting in a network partitioning and whether all three properties can be simultaneously fulfilled. In this situation, m cannot be delivered resulting in an inconsistent (outdated) value of o at site S2. If we want to avoid this to ensure consistency, m has to be sent synchronously, that is, in an atomic operation with the updates. However, this procedure sacrifices the availability property: if m cannot be delivered, the update on node S1 cannot be performed. However, sending m asynchronously does not solve the problem because then S1 does not know when S2 receives the message. Therefore, any approach trying to achieve a strong consistent view such as locking and centralized management would either violate availability or partition tolerance.

In order to address these restrictions imposed by CAP, the system designer has to choose to relax or give up one of these three properties:

- Consistency: If we want to preserve availability and partition tolerance, the only choice is to give up or relax consistency. The data can be updated on both sites, and both sites will converge to the same state when the connection between them is re-established and a certain time has elapsed.
- Availability: Availability is given up by simply waiting when a partition event occurs until the nodes come back and the data are consistent again. The service is unavailable during the waiting time. Particularly, for large settings with many nodes, this could result in long downtimes.
- Partition tolerance: Basically, this means avoiding network partitioning in the case of link failures. Partition tolerance can be achieved by ensuring that each node is connected to each other or making a single atomically failing unit, but obviously, this limits scalability.

The CAP theorem implies that consistency guarantees in large-scale distributed systems cannot be as strict as those in centralized systems. Specifically, it suggests that distributed systems may need to provide BASE guarantees instead of the ACID guarantees provided by traditional database systems. The CAP theorem states that no distributed system can provide more than two of the following three guarantees: consistency, availability, and partitioning tolerance. Here, consistency is defined as in databases; that is, if multiple operations are performed on the same object (which is actually stored in a distributed system), the results of the operations appear as if the operations were carried out in some definite order on a single system. Availability is defined to be satisfied if each operation on the system (e.g., a query) returns some result. The system provides partitioning tolerance if the system is operational even when the network between two components of the system is down.

A transaction represents a sequence of database operations (insert, update, delete, select) for which the system guarantees four properties also known as ACID:

1. Atomicity: A transaction is executed completely or not at all, thus exhibiting the characteristics of atomicity. As a consequence, all changes to the data made by this transaction become visible only if the transaction reaches a commit successfully. Otherwise, if the transaction was terminated abnormally before reaching a commit, the original state of the data from the beginning is restored.
2. Consistency: The property of consistency guarantees that all defined integrity or consistency constraints are preserved at the end of a transaction, that is, a transaction always moves the database from one consistent state to another consistent state. This has two consequences: In case a consistency constraint is violated, the transaction may be abnormally terminated and secondly, constraints can be temporarily violated during transaction execution but must be preserved upon the commit.
3. Isolation: A transaction behaves as if it runs alone on the database without any concurrent operations. Furthermore, it only sees effects from previously committed transactions.
4. Durability: When a transaction reaches the commit, it is guaranteed that all changes made by this transaction will survive subsequent system and disk failures.

Since distributed systems can satisfy only two of the three properties due to the CAP theorem, there are three types of distributed systems. CA (Consistent, Available) systems provide consistency and availability, but cannot tolerate network partitions. An example of a CA system is a clustered database, where each node stores a subset of the data. Such a database cannot provide availability in the case of network partitioning, since queries to data in the partitioned nodes must fail. CA systems may not be useful for cloud computing, since partitions are likely to occur in medium to large networks (including the case in which latency is very high). If there is no network partitioning, all servers are consistent, and the value seen by both clients is the correct value.

However, if the network is partitioned, it is no longer possible to keep all the servers consistent in the face of updates. There are then two choices. One choice is to keep both servers up and ignore the inconsistency. This leads to AP (Available, Partition-tolerant) systems where the system is always available, but may not return consistent results. The other possible choice is to bring one of the servers down, to avoid inconsistent values. This leads to CP (Consistent, Partition-tolerant) systems where the system always returns consistent results but may be unavailable under partitioning—including the case in which latency is very high. AP systems provide weak consistency. An important subclass of weakly consistent systems is those that provide eventual consistency. A system is defined as being eventually consistent if the system is guaranteed to reach a consistent state in a finite amount of time if there are no failures (e.g., network partitions) and no updates are made. The inconsistency window for such systems is the maximum amount of time that can elapse between the time that the update is made and the time that the update is guaranteed to be visible to all clients. If the inconsistency window is small compared to the update rate, then one method of dealing with stale data is to wait for a period greater than the inconsistency window and then retry the query.

Classic database systems focus on guaranteeing the ACID properties and, therefore, favor consistency over partition tolerance and availability. This is achieved by employing techniques like distributed locking and two-phase commit protocols. In certain circumstances, data needs are not transactionally focused, and at such times, the relational model is not the most appropriate one for what we need to do with the data we are storing. However, giving up availability is often not an option in the web business where users expect a 24 × 7 or always-on operation.

Most traditional RDBMS would guarantee that all the values in all our nodes are identical before it allows another user to read the values. But as we have seen, that is at a significant cost in terms of performance. Relational databases, with their large processing overhead in terms of maintaining the ACID attributes of the data they store and their reliance on potentially processor hungry joins, are not the right tool for the task they have before them: quickly finding relevant data from terabytes of unstructured data (web content) that may be stored across thousands of geographically desperate nodes. In other words, relational model does not scale well for this type of data. Thus, techniques for guaranteeing strong consistency in large distributed systems limit scalability and results in latency issues. To cope with these problems essential for big data, BASE was proposed as an alternative to ACID.

1.8 Summary

This chapter provided an overview of the dominating trend of the last 50 years in the computer industry, namely, computing beyond the Moore's law barrier while becoming more and more tolerant of faults and failures. The first half of the chapter presents a road map of the evolution from parallel computing through parallel processing to MPP using commoditized hardware. The latter part of the chapter highlights aspects of fault tolerance, reliability, and Brewer's CAP theorem. In the following parts, the book presents the genesis, road map, and characteristics of big data computing. The last part of the book describes big data applications in the areas of the web, social networks, mobile, location-based, and the more general context-aware systems.

Section I

Genesis of Big Data Computing

2

Database Basics

The genesis of the big data computing can be traced to the development of databases in the 1960s. For the major part of computing history, database solutions have been focused on capturing, storing, managing, querying, and analyzing structured data. The advent of Internet and the emergence of end-consumer solutions such as web portals, social networks, and mobility solutions have resulted in a deluge of unstructured and real-time data that have to be mined for detecting the patterns of significance critical for the functioning of the digital economy. But the journey commenced with traditional databases-hierarchical, network and relational databases, which subsequently evolved into more refined object-oriented databases. This chapter presents an overview of the characteristics of these traditional databases and lessons learnt from using, developing, and maintaining them.

2.1 Database Management System

A database management system (DBMS) provides the needed organizational approach to flexible storage and retrieval of large amounts of data. A DBMS provides for the organization of the data elements, the representation of relationships among the elements, and the uniform interface for users. A database management system (DBMS) supports the reliable storage of the database, implements the relationship structures, and offers uniform storage/retrieval services to users.

> Actual DBMS implementations are very complicated software systems. The software implementation of each model involves several levels, from the physical structures on disk storage devices through the abstractions (e.g., tables, objects) that describe an application. Variations occur both in the expression of the model structures and in the extra features that distinguish a product from its competitors.

A database is a self-describing collection of data elements, together with relationships among those elements, that presents a uniform service interface. A database management system (DBMS) is a software product that supports the reliable storage of the database, implements the structures for maintaining relationships and constraints, and offers storage and retrieval services to users. Additional features address other issues, such as simultaneous access, security, backup, and recovery. This implies that the data elements reside in a self-describing structure like a table, which confers meaning on them. A database system isolates the computer-related problems of large-volume data storage and retrieval from application oriented issues. It simplifies software development efforts by providing generic services adaptable to varying applications. It also contributes to the efficiency of many interfacing programs dealing with the same data environment by providing self-describing, consistent data to all users. Moreover, a database system provides a general approach for maintaining relationships among data elements.

Database users can be individuals dealing with an interactive interface, or other computer programs requesting services with calls to subprocedures provided by the DBMS. Although some differences distinguish these two modes of service, the DBMS should provide as much uniformity as possible to its users. The user interface module of the DBMS responds to service requests, using the data dictionary to confirm the existence and compatibility of data elements mentioned in the requests. A second module processes storage-retrieval requests, performs optimizations necessary to reduce execution time, and carries out the data operations needed to respond. The DBMS passes the requested data items and any error messages back to the interface module for relay to the user.

Separating data storage and retrieval details into a self-sufficient module represents sound software engineering practice in itself. Still, database systems overcome other deficiencies in the predatabase mode of operation, which use individual programs with their own tailored input/output files. The development of databases helped to avoid the older systems'

1. Unhealthy dependence between data and programs
2. Repetition of data elements
3. Opportunities for inconsistencies
4. Unorganized scattering of related data across many files
5. Distributed ownership of data
6. Decentralized security
7. Unregulated interactions between programs using the same data
8. Inadequate multiuser access
9. Ad hoc approach to error recovery
10. Overdependence on physical considerations, such as disk track and sector addresses

2.1.1 DBMS Benefits

Deficiencies of predatabase information processing include encoded data, interdependence between programs and data files, data repetition and associated inconsistencies, ad hoc representation of relationships among data items, lack of coordination across programs using common data, restricted simultaneous access to data, and nonuniform error recovery methods.

1. Without databases, data and the programs are heavily dependent on each other. A program requires its input files or data in order to execute. But data are meaningful only in the context of the program; you need program to understand the data's meaning.

   Data should not depend on a program to render it understandable and useful. That is, data should be self-describing.
2. Without a central database repository, programs must frequently access data from separate files. A flexible storage and retrieval mechanism should maintain relationships on an equal footing with the individual data elements.

3. In a nondatabase context, each programmer "owns" the data files associated with his program, making these files less accessible to others. By contrast, a database provides more uniform availability of data.
4. Without a centralized database, the security policy must deal with a dispersed collection of files of varying formats; the centralized approach has one uncomfortable security disadvantage: if the central facility is compromised, all the data are exposed.
5. Without databases, programs can interfere with one another. The effects of transactions in one program are not isolated from those in other programs.
6. Data deletions or updates can produce inconsistencies, which are difficult to control in a nondatabase system. A database can coordinate deletion activities, ensuring that no dangling references remain after a deletion.
7. Without databases, data sharing is more difficult. A database can coordinate simultaneous access to the data elements. It allows data sharing at a finer resolution, locking only individual data elements during write operations.
8. Without database oversight, data inconsistencies can arise when a long process terminates with an error. The DBMS rejects a transaction that does not complete, with the state of the database remaining as though the transaction had never started. Because the DBMS handles recovery, individual applications need not deal with failed transactions.
9. Without databases, variations in the physical data representation can cause many problems. Database enables programs to be concerned with manipulating the application objects (e.g., persons, tasks, hours, and accounts), not with storage details.

2.1.2 Defining a Database Management System

A database is a collection of related data with some inherent meaning and a DBMS is a computerized system that enables users to create and maintain a database.

The DBMS is a general-purpose software system that facilitates the processes of defining, creating, manipulating, and sharing databases among various users and applications.

where,

Defining a database involves specifying the data types, structures, and constraints of the data to be stored in the database. The database definition or descriptive information is also stored by the DBMS in the form of a database catalog or dictionary; it is called metadata.

Creating the database is the process of storing the data on some storage medium that is controlled by the DBMS.

Manipulating a database includes functions such as querying the database to retrieve specific data, updating the database to reflect changes in the world, and generating reports from the data.

Sharing a database allows multiple users and programs to access the database simultaneously.

DBMS also provides for querying, protecting, and maintenance of the database. A *query* typically causes some data to be retrieved; a transaction may cause some data to be read, and some data to be written into the database. An application program accesses the database by sending queries or requests for data to the DBMS. *Protection* includes system protection against hardware or software malfunction (or crashes) and security protection against unauthorized or malicious access. Finally, a DBMS must be able to *maintain* the database system by allowing the system to evolve, as requirements change over time.

In traditional file processing, each user defines and implements the files needed for a specific software application as part of programming the application. For example, one user, the performance reporting office may keep files on employees and their performance ratings. Programs to print an employees' appraisal sheet and to enter new ratings are implemented as part of the application. A second user, the accounting office, may keep track of employees' salaries and their logged working hours. Although both users are interested in data about employees, each user maintains separate files—and programs to manipulate these files—because each requires some data that are not available from the other user's files. This redundancy in defining and storing data results in wasted storage space and in redundant efforts to maintain common up-to-date data. By contrast, in the database approach, a single repository maintains data that are defined once and then accessed by various users repeatedly through queries, transactions, and application programs.

The main characteristics of the database approach are the following:

a. *Self-Describing Nature of a Database System:* In traditional file processing, data definition is typically part of the application programs themselves. Hence, these programs are constrained to work with only one specific database, whose structure is declared in the application programs. By contrast, the database system contains not only the database itself, but also a complete definition or description of the database structure and constraints. This definition is stored in the DBMS catalog, which contains information such as the structure of each file, the type and storage format of each data item, and various constraints on the data. The information stored in the catalog is called metadata, and it describes the structure of the primary database.

   The description of a database is called the database schema, which is specified during database design and is not expected to change frequently. However, the actual data in a database may change quite frequently. The data in the database at a particular moment in time is called a database state or snapshot. It is also called the current set of occurrences or instances in the database. In a given database state, each schema construct has its own current set of instances. Many database states can be created to correspond to a particular database schema. Every time we insert or delete a record, or change the value of a data item in a record, we change one state of the database into another state.

b. *Insulation between Programs and Data, and Data Abstraction:* Data abstraction enables program-data and data-operations independence:

   i. *Program-Data Independence:* In traditional file processing, the structure of data files is embedded in the application programs, so any changes to the structure of a file may require changing all programs that access that file. By contrast, DBMS access programs do not require such changes in most cases. The structure of data files is stored in the DBMS catalog separately from the access programs.

   ii. *Program-Operation Independence:* In some types of database systems, such as object-oriented and object-relational systems (see Chapter 12), users can define operations on data as part of the database definitions. An operation (also called a function or method) is specified in two parts. The interface (or signature) of an operation includes the operation name and the data types of its arguments (or parameters). The implementation (or method) of the operation is specified separately and can be changed without affecting the interface. User application programs can operate on the data by invoking these operations through their names and arguments, regardless of how the operations are implemented.

A DBMS provides users with a conceptual representation of data that does not include many of the details of how the data are stored or how the operations are implemented. A data model is a type of data abstraction that is used to provide this conceptual representation. The data model uses logical concepts, such as objects, their properties, and their interrelationships, that may be easier for most users to understand than computer storage concepts. Hence, the data model hides storage and implementation details that are not of interest to most database users.

In the database approach, the detailed structure and organization of each file are stored in the catalog. Database users and application programs refer to the conceptual representation of the files, and the DBMS extracts the details of file storage from the catalog, when these are needed by the DBMS file access modules. Many data models can be used to provide this data abstraction to database users. In object-oriented and object-relational databases, the abstraction process includes not only the data structure but also the operations on the data. Such operations can be invoked by the user queries or application programs without having to know the details of how the operations are implemented.

c. *Support of Multiple Views of the Data:* A database typically has many types of users, each of whom may require a different perspective, or view of the database. A multiuser DBMS whose users have a variety of distinct applications must provide facilities for defining multiple views. A view may be a subset of the database or it may contain virtual data that are derived from the database files, but is not explicitly stored. Some users may not need to be aware of whether the data they refer to are stored or derived.

d. *Sharing of Data and Multiuser Transaction Processing:* A multiuser DBMS, as its name implies, must allow multiple users to access the database at the same time. This is essential if data for multiple applications are to be integrated and maintained in a single database. The DBMS must include concurrency control software to ensure that several users trying to update the same data do so in a controlled manner so that the result of the updates is correct. For example, when several reservation agents try to assign a seat on an airline flight, the DBMS should ensure that each seat can be accessed by only one agent at a time for assignment to a passenger. These type of applications are generally called online transaction processing (OLTP) applications. A fundamental role of multiuser DBMS software is to ensure that concurrent transactions operate correctly and efficiently.

The concept of a transaction has become central to many database applications. A transaction is an executing program or process that includes one or more database accesses, such as reading or updating of database records. Each transaction is supposed to execute a logically correct database access if executed in its entirety without interference from other transactions.

The DBMS must enforce several transaction properties:

- The atomicity property ensures that either all the database operations in a transaction are executed or none of them are executed.
- The consistency property ensures that either all the integrity or consistency constraints are preserved by database operations at the commit of a transaction or it is aborted.
- The isolation property ensures that each transaction appears to execute in isolation from other transactions, even though hundreds of transactions may be executing concurrently.
- The durability property ensures that either all changes affected by a transaction survive subsequent failure or it is rolled back.

In the first decade of the twenty-first century, the proliferation of applications and platforms such as social media websites, large e-commerce companies, web search indexes, and cloud storage or backup led to a surge in the amount of data stored on large databases and massive servers. Some of the requirements of these new systems were not compatible with SQL relational DBMSs; it is quickly apparent that basic relational systems were not very suitable for many of these applications by the following reason:

- More complex data structures were needed for modeling the application than the simple relational representation.
- New data types were needed in addition to the basic numeric and character string types.
- New operations and query language constructs were necessary to manipulate the new data types.
- New storage and indexing structures were needed for efficient searching on the new data types.

New types of database systems were necessary to manage these huge databases—systems that would provide fast search and retrieval as well as reliable and safe storage of nontraditional types of data, such as social media posts and tweets. The term NoSQL is generally interpreted as not only SQL, meaning that in systems that manage large amounts of data, some of the data is stored using SQL systems, whereas other data would be stored using NoSQL, depending on the application requirements.

2.1.2.1 Data Models alias Database Models

One fundamental characteristic of the database approach is that it provides some level of data abstraction. Data abstraction generally refers to the suppression of details of data organization and storage, and the highlighting of the essential features for an improved understanding of data. One of the main characteristics of the database approach is to support data abstraction so that different users can perceive data at their preferred level of detail.

A data model is a collection of concepts that can be used to describe the structure of a database—provides the necessary means to achieve this abstraction. The structure of a database means the data types, relationships, and constraints that apply to the data. Most data models also include a set of basic operations for specifying, retrievals, and updates on the database. Many data models have been proposed, which can be classified according to the types of concepts they use to describe the database structure:

1. High-level or conceptual data models provide concepts that are close to the way many users perceive data. Conceptual data models use concepts such as entities, attributes, and relationships. An entity represents a real world object or concept, such as an employee or a project from the miniworld that is described in the database. An attribute represents some property of interest that further describes an entity, such as the employee's name or salary. A relationship among two or more entities represents an association among the entities, for example, a works-on relationship between an employee and a project. Chapter 3 presents the entity–relationship model—a popular high-level conceptual data model. Chapter 4 describes additional abstractions used for advanced modeling, such as generalization, specialization, and categories (union types).
2. Representational (or implementation) data models provide concepts that may be easily understood by end users, but that are not too far removed from the way data are organized in computer storage. Representational data models hide many details of data storage on disk, but can be implemented on a computer system directly. Representational or implementation data models are the models used most frequently in traditional commercial DBMSs. These include the widely used relational data model, as well as the so-called legacy data models—the network and hierarchical models—that have been widely used in the past. Representational data models represent data by using record structures and hence are sometimes called record-based data models.
3. Low-level or physical data models provide concepts that describe the details of how data are stored on the computer storage media, typically magnetic disks. Concepts provided by physical data models are generally meant for computer specialists, not for end users. Physical data models describe how data are stored as files in the computer by representing information such as record formats, record orderings, and access paths. An access path is a search structure that makes the search for particular database records efficient, such as indexing or hashing. An index is an example of an access path that allows direct access to data using an index term or a keyword. It is similar to the index at the end of textbooks, except that it may be organized in a linear, hierarchical (tree-structured), or some other fashion.

2.2 Database Models

A database model is an organizing principle that specifies particular mechanisms for data storage and retrieval. The model explains, in terms of the services available to an interfacing application, how to access a data element when other related data elements are known.

It also specifies the precise meaning of the term-related data and it provides mappings from particular relationships in an application to the more generic types maintained by the DBMS. In the example above, a relationship exists between each room and the building that houses it, or between each fish and the tank that contains it. The DBMS provides a more general type of relationship in which a container object includes component objects. A database model must allow the representation of a specific building rooms relationship within the more general container-components framework.

A database model is an abstract approach for organizing data elements and their relationships. The relational model is currently the most popular model; the hierarchical and network models represent prerelational technologies, and, the object-oriented model represents postrelational technologies.

The four models examined in this text are hierarchical and network (past), relational (present), and object-oriented and deductive (future). The models differ primarily in the way they represent relationships. The hierarchical model uses a tree format to relate application entities. The tree can be expressed as a linear list, and logical proximity in that linear form implies relations among data elements. The network model provides auxiliary structures, best envisioned as intersecting chains. Navigating along these chains recovers related data elements. The relational model uses common attributes between disjoint tables to relate rows. In one table, the attribute serves to identify the row in question; in the other table the same attribute serves as an embedded reference back to that row. The object-oriented model uses logical containment. Since object attributes can be other objects, related data elements can be found through a recursive search within the attributes of a given data element. Finally, the deductive model uses inference rules to derive related elements.

2.2.1 Relational Database Model

The relational model uses tables to organize the data elements. Each table corresponds to an application entity, and each row represents an instance of that entity. For example, the cat entity in the application corresponds to the Cat table in the database. Each table row represents a different cat. Relationships link rows from two tables by embedding row identifiers from one table as attribute values in another table. For example, the identifier of a cat row (the cat name) appears in a student row, thereby establishing the student as the owner of the cat. Despite complications that arise from relationships involving many rows from many tables, this simple mechanism supports relationships without resorting to auxiliary structures, such as linked lists or indexes. Structured query language (SQL) serves as the uniform interface for users, providing a collection of standard expressions for storing and retrieving data.

Relational DBMS products also derived significant benefits from years of database research. The relational model has a rigorous mathematical base. The concept of a relation itself is a mathematical one. Each attribute has an associated domain, and the relation's body at any time is, except for the attribute order, a subset of the Cartesian product of these domains. The mathematical definition of a relation over a finite collection of domains is essentially the same: a subset of the Cartesian product. The only difference is that the relational definition removes the attribute order that is inherent in the mathematical Cartesian product. The model's name, therefore, comes from its mathematical counterpart.

The definitions of the relational database components also proceed from the following mathematical concepts:

- A relational database is a set of relations, each comprising a schema and a body
- A relational body is a set of tuples over the corresponding relational schema
- A tuple over a relational schema is a set of associations over the corresponding attributes
- A relational schema is a set of attributes
- An association over an attribute is a name-value pair, where the name comes from the attribute and the value comes from the corresponding domain
- An attribute is a name-domain pair
- A domain is a set of values

The relational model was designed to remove the host-language access requirement and to suppress the subsidiary structures for maintaining relationships. From the user's viewpoint, matching values in common attributes implicitly lace together related tuples in disjoint tables. The DBMS can use indices, linked lists, and other structures to enhance performance, but it hides these technical details from the user.

SQL provides a systematic, nonprocedural interface, which removes the need for the user to understand a host programming language. Although SQL itself is a programming language, it is simple compared to the procedural hosts of the hierarchical and network models. Because it is patterned after structured English, SQL is accessible to a wide range of nontechnical users. After writing query solutions for the hierarchical and network models, you can surely appreciate why the relational model received such a warm welcome.

Other strengths of a relational DBMS also arose from relational research, which culminated in Codd's 12 rules including the following important criteria:

1. Only table structures are visible to the user
2. An active catalog stores metadata, which makes the database self-describing
3. The user interface employs a set-oriented language
4. A conceptual schema buffers applications from changes to the underlying physical storage
5. A view mechanism buffers applications from changes in the conceptual schema

In summary, the relational model's advantages over its predecessors are its simple tabular schema, its uncomplicated relationship representation scheme, its comparatively simple access language, SQL, and its strong mathematical foundation for the underlying concepts.

> The relational model has generated its own deficiencies by enabling the exploration of more difficult problem domains, such as databases with pictures and soundtracks. Some difficulties touch on philosophical data modeling issues, such as dispersing an application entity across several tables. Others are simple inconveniences, which seldom provoke practical problems. For example, SQL isn't computationally complete, but this deficiency is barely noticed outside of academic textbooks. The post-relational models do, however, address these issues.

2.2.2 Hierarchical Database Model

The hierarchical model assumes that a tree structure, such as the company organizational chart of Figure 2.1, is the most frequently occurring relationship. The president is at the top, over a reporting structure that branches into vice-presidents, departments, and employees. Several vice-presidents report to the president, and several departments report to each vice-president. At the lowest level, each department contains many employees.

A key feature of this organization is that you can translate it into a linear list, as illustrated below.

President (name = jones, phone = 111-222-3333, etc.)
Vice-president (name = able, ...)
Department (name = Electrical, ...)
Employee (name = doyle, ...)
Employee (name = erikson, ...)
Employee (name = ferris, ...)
Department (name = Mechanical, ...)
Employee (name = gilbert, ...)
Employee (name = hansen, ...)
Vice-president (name = baker, ...)
Department (name = Finance, ...)
Employee (name = jarbo, ...)
Employee (name = karlstrom, ...)
Department (name = Marketing, ...)
Department (name = Accounting, ...)
Employee (name = marchand, ...)

The hierarchical model organizes data elements as tabular rows, one for each instance of an application entity. In this example, a separate row represents the president, each vice-president, each department, and each employee. The row position implies a relationship to

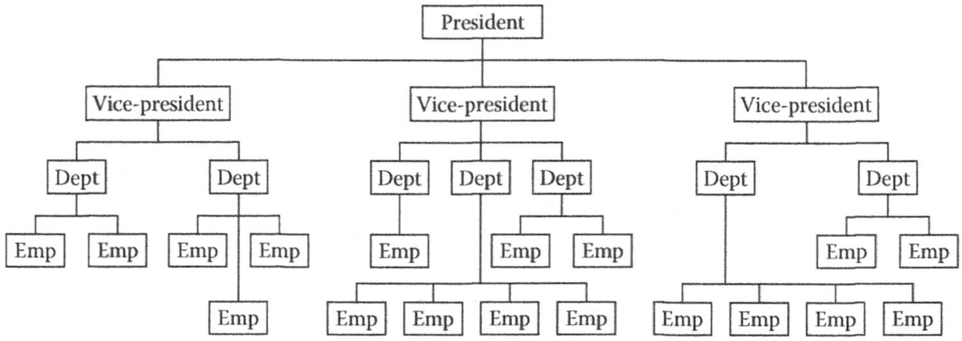

FIGURE 2.1
A hierarchical organization.

other rows. That is, a given employee belongs to the department that is closest above it in the list; a given department reports to the vice-president immediately above it in the list.

The hierarchical model represents relationships with the notion of logical adjacency, or more accurately, with logical proximity, in the linearized tree. You can isolate the set of employees working for departments under vice-president X by first locating vice-president X and then including every employee in the list after X and before the next occurrence of a vice-president (or the end of the list). Because the linearized tree is an abstraction, the term logical proximity is more appropriate. An actual implementation may scatter the data items across various structures and materialize the linearized tree as needed with hashing.

The hierarchical model has overly complicated structures for maintaining relationships. Although logical adjacency is a straightforward organizational principle, it isn't sufficient for multiple parentage situations. In these cases, the hierarchical model introduces a second scheme for maintaining relationships—virtual chains. This solution forces an asymmetry into the model: some relationships use logical adjacency, and some use virtual chains. You must remain constantly aware of the distinction when writing navigational queries. Moreover, the hierarchical model involves database designers in yet more programming details because they must direct the DBMS in constructing the type hierarchies. For instance,

Should the records contain one-way or two-way links?

Should dependent records contain parent pointers?

Should the root records enjoy a fast access path, such as a hash table?

These questions are far from the application domain where the designers should be working.

The hierarchical model actually employs the network set concept, disguised as virtual chains, but doesn't elevate it to full status with appropriate commands for using it. Instead, it mixes database commands with programming language control methods, such as threaded trees. Because the hierarchical model is so tightly bound with a host control language, you must be a capable programmer to use it. Under these conditions, writing database manipulation programs is a difficult and specialized task. The syntax of commercial hierarchical products makes the problem worse because it is typically dense and cryptic, with many references to physical storage details.

The hierarchical and network models share many features.

1. Both represent data as records, and both include navigation commands for moving among related records. Both also express queries and update activities in a host program that makes library procedure calls to transfer information back and forth with the database. These common features lead to common weaknesses.
2. Both the models offset the cumbersome representation of relationships by the relative speed and efficiency. To maintain network sets or virtual relationships, they use pointer chains, which provide direct disk addresses of related records. The application designer can also specify rapid retrieval structures

(Continued)

for the logical adjacency implementation, such as pointer arrays, indices, or hash tables. These devices circumvent the sequential search implied by the physical parent–child relationship in the linearized hierarchy. For relationships that are built into the applications, these methods locate the disk addresses of related records with less overhead than in the relational or post-relational models. The lower-level linkage mechanisms increase efficiency of both these models; they don't make up for the less flexible relationship representation methods. Thus, for ad hoc relationships that appear after the database is in use, however, the prewired disk address links provide no assistance, and the performance degenerates to sequential searches.

3. Both the model's access languages are more powerful than SQL. In particular, you can express recursive queries with unbounded depths. Of course, the price of this flexibility is long and potentially expensive programming. Moreover, the ability to probe recursive relationships is usually wasted in the hierarchical case because a hierarchical DBMS typically doesn't allow recursive relationships.

2.2.3 Network Database Model

The network model replaces the hierarchical tree with a graph, allowing more general connections among the nodes. Suppose in the previous example that an employee works for two departments. Then the strict hierarchical arrangement breaks down, and the tree of Figure 2.1 becomes a more general graph, or network. Logical proximity fails, because you can't place a data item simultaneously in two locations in the list. Although the hierarchical model contains more complicated methods to handle these situations, the syntax becomes difficult to follow. The network database model evolved specifically to handle nonhierarchical relationships.

The network model corrects the hierarchical model's most troublesome oversight—the awkward representation of multiple parentages. It also raises relationships to the status of named database elements, network sets, and it introduces commands for manipulating them. These extensions enable more realistic modeling of real-world situations. They also conform directly with the features of entity–relationship diagrams, which are currently the most popular database design methods. For a user interface, however, the network model still uses database calls from a host language control program. This approach is certainly very flexible because, in theory, you can program any user interface. However, these programs are expensive and involve a lot of duplicated effort. Furthermore, they discourage nontechnical users, who aren't proficient in the host language. The network model also retains a relationship maintenance mechanism (i.e., network sets) that exposes the underlying data structures (i.e., linked chains). Because it requires a familiarity with computer science constructs, this feature further limits the number of potential users.

2.2.4 Object-Oriented Database Models

The object-oriented model represents an application entity as a class. A class captures both the attributes and the behavior of the entity. For example, a Cat class possesses not only cat attributes, such as color, weight, and napTime but also procedures that imitate actions expected of a cat, such as destroyFurniture("sofa"). Instances of the class, called objects, correspond to individual cats. Within an object, the class attributes take specific values, which distinguish, for example, one cat from another. However, the behavior patterns are shared by all cat objects. The object-oriented model does not restrict attribute values to the small set of native data types usually associated with databases and programming languages, such as integer, float, real, decimal, and string. Instead, the values can be other objects. One of the attributes of a cat can be owner, and the value of that attribute can be a student object, corresponding to the student that owns the cat in the application.

In the object-oriented model, the application entities become database classes, and entity instances become objects under the appropriate class. A class corresponds roughly to a table shell in the relational model, and an object corresponds to a row in the table. A class is actually a more expressive modeling feature than a table because it captures the behavior of its objects in addition to their static attributes. Moreover, an object's attribute values aren't limited to the simple strings and numbers of the earlier models: they can be other objects. The DBMS can, therefore, represent an object as a compact structure that contains its related objects; logical inclusion is simpler because it frequently corresponds more naturally with the real-world relationship. By contrast, the relational model visibly maintains related tuples in separate tables. Relationship representation through logical inclusion is at least as straightforward as through common attribute links. Because an application object contains related objects within itself, at some level of recursion, you can construct query solutions by probing the candidate object's attributes. This approach is procedural, so you might suspect it is inferior to the nonprocedural SQL. But the required procedures are, in fact, simple in comparison with the host language programming of the hierarchical and network models. Furthermore, nonprocedural extensions, such as OQL, salvage much of SQL's convenience while still exploiting the model's object-oriented features.

All the strengths of object-oriented modeling are available in an object-oriented database: inheritance, encapsulation, polymorphism, and message-passing among objects. You can insert application classes at appropriate points in an existing class hierarchy. An object instantiated through an application class then contains not only the attributes and methods defined in that class but also the attributes and methods of its superclasses. So you can define a new class incrementally by specifying only how it extends its immediate parent.

The object-oriented models possess the following advantages over its relational predecessor: a class structure, which encapsulates behavior as well as the traditional static attributes; a simple relationship mechanism, logical inclusion, which often corresponds with its real-world equivalent; and application-modeling features adopted from object-oriented software development, such as inheritance and polymorphism. One regression appears to be the reappearance of a host programming language for user access to the database. The object-oriented language syntax is, however, less difficult than the host languages of the earlier models. In any case, a nonprocedural query language, object query language (OQL), is available. OQL retains the flavor of SQL but provides access to the database's object-oriented features.

2.2.5 Comparison of Models

2.2.5.1 Similarities

1. The most obvious similarity is that all five models possess features for storing both application entity descriptions and instances of these entities. Regardless of the database model, an application entity description is an attribute collection; an entity instance is a collection of values under these attributes.

2. To maintain application entities and their instances, all five database models also use some form of table format. Each application entity becomes a separate table. The instances of a given entity become rows in its table. All five database models use some generalization of the table format in this fashion. The relational model, of course, explicitly specifies tables as the storage mechanism.
   a. In a relational schema, you describe a table shell for each application entity. In subsequent processing, you manipulate the table rows as instances of the corresponding application entity.
   b. In a hierarchical schema, you specify a segment for each application entity. Except for the notation, however, a segment description is the same as a network record type description. Both contain a list of named fields and imply a file of records that are compatible with the fields.
   c. In a network schema, you specify a record type for each application entity. A file of records then represents the instances. A file is a generalized table, where the repeating elements are records rather than rows. Each record, however, corresponds exactly to a row because it is a sequence of field values, just as a row is a sequence of attribute values.

   If you broaden the definition of a table to include a file of records, you can conclude that the relational, network, and hierarchical database models all use tables to store the application entities and their instances.

   The object-oriented database models can also use tables. However, this model's philosophies de-emphasize storage structure and leave the choice to a given implementation. In the object-oriented model, an application entity becomes a class; the instances become objects created from the corresponding class. A class encapsulates an attribute collection, and each object from the class provides specific values for the attributes. Although the model provides no further storage details, you can still envision the objects as rows in a table. Each row provides the values for the class attributes, which appear across the top of the table. In this representation, the object identifier (OID) is just another attribute.
3. In addition to using tables to store the application entities and their instances, all five database models also provide some arrangement for navigating through relationships to extract query solutions. The representative structures have evolved from primitive linking schemes that expose the implementation structures to more abstract relationship concepts that suppress implementation detail. In all cases, however, query solutions still exploit the available relationship mechanism to assemble related data elements.

   You always solve an existential query by searching for database paths between a candidate and an anchor.

2.2.5.1.1 Existential Queries

You always solve an existential query by searching for database paths between a candidate and an anchor. Only the details for expressing the path vary from one model to the next.

In the relational model, the path proceeds across one-to-many relationships by linking tuples where the foreign-key value in the dependent entity matches the primary-key value in the dominant entity. In the network model, you construct the path by traversing the record chains of the network sets. This navigation again proceeds across one-to-many relationships because each chain corresponds to a relationship instance, which links a dominant record with its dependent partners. The path can enter on a dominant record and depart from a dependent record, or it can enter on a dependent record and depart from the dominant one. In a hierarchical database, you encounter both physical and virtual one-to-many relationships as you construct the existential path. The process for a virtual relationship is the same as in the network case: you move along linked chains from the dominant to a dependent record or vice versa. For a physical relationship, you move within a linearized hierarchy of records. You move backward to the first record of the proper type to link a dependent record with its dominant partner. You scan forward to obtain the dependents associated with a given dominant record.

In an object-oriented database, an existential path burrows into the candidate's attributes. Because attribute values can be complex objects, this process continually discovers related objects, and it can continue the probe by investigating their attributes. Although the model provides no further implementation detail, you can imagine an existential path passing through table rows, just as in the relational case. Where a relational path jumps from a foreign-key value to a matching primary-key value in a row of a remote table, an object-oriented path jumps from an attribute OID to a matching object in a remote table. This viewpoint, of course, assumes that objects are arrayed in tabular rows as discussed above.

2.2.5.1.2 *Universal Queries*

Solving universal queries is also similar for all five models. You construct two sets: the anchors and the elements reachable from a candidate. If the second set includes the first, the candidate contributes to the answer. Only the details of the set constructions vary across the models. Two approaches are available in the relational model: the set-containment approach and the doubly negated approach. In the former, you explicitly construct the two sets with subqueries and then test for containment. In the doubly negated solution, the set containment is tested one element at a time, without explicitly building the sets. Set A is contained in set B if and only if $(\forall x)(x \in A \Rightarrow x \in B)$. Equivalently, set A is contained in set B if and only if $\neg(\exists x)(x \in A \wedge \neg(x \in B))$. The two negations produce two not-exists subqueries in the structured query language (SQL) expression. In the hierarchical, network, and object-oriented models, you must accumulate the two sets in a host language program, which makes appropriate calls to the database. You also test the set containment with the host language features.

2.2.5.1.3 *Aggregate Queries*

Aggregate queries involve a summarizing computation over a partitioned table. In the hierarchical, network, and object-oriented models, you explicitly program the calculations in a host language program, which calls the database as needed. The process is implicit in the relational and deductive models although the DBMS must set up the same partitioning and summarizing activities that you program in the other models.

2.2.5.2 Dissimilarities

Within a database, an application object or relationship appears as a data element or grouping of data elements. The relational model is value based; it assumes that real-world entity has no identity independent of its attribute values. The content of the database record, rather than its existence, determines the identity of the object represented. If a cat changes its attributes sufficiently to represent a mouse, then it is a mouse.

The object-oriented, network, and hierarchical models assume that the object survives changes of all its attributes; these systems are record based. A record of the real-world entity appears in the database, and even though the record's contents may change completely, the

TABLE 2.1
Characteristics of the Four Database Models

Model	Data Element Organization	Relationship Organization	Identity	Access Language
Relational	Tables	Identifiers for rows of one table are embedded as attribute values in another table	Value-based	Nonprocedural
Object-oriented	Objects—logically encapsulating both attributes and behavior	Logical containment, related objects are found within a given object by recursively examining attributes of an object that are themselves objects	Record-based	Procedural
Deductive	Base facts that can be arranged in tables	Inference rules that permit related facts to be generated on demand	Value-based	Nonprocedural
Hierarchical	Files, records	Logical proximity in a linearized tree	Record-based	Procedural
Network	Files, records	Intersecting chains	Record-based	Procedural

record itself represents the application item. As long as the record remains in the database, the object's identity has not changed. Table 2.1 compares the characteristics of the four database models.

2.3 Database Components

The database provides three layers of abstraction, each buffered to a certain extent from changes in the layers below:

1. The physical layer deals with storage structures. This layer contains low-level data structures (e.g., files, control blocks, search accelerators), and it accommodates the hardware capabilities. The physical layer provides support services for the conceptual layer.
2. The conceptual layer projects the illusion of tables and objects, from which the user fashions the application environment. The DBMS can protect the conceptual layer from certain changes to the physical layer, a feature known as physical data independence.
3. The top layer represents tailored views of the conceptual layer that are suitable for different users. The DBMS can protect the top layer from limited changes to the conceptual schema, a feature known as logical data independence.

A DBMS contains a module for processing the database schema, which is a script describing the application environment in terms of the structures provided by the model, that is, in terms of tables, objects, inference rules, hierarchical trees, or network chains. The DBMS stores this description as a data dictionary, which it uses to resolve references to application entities that appear in service requests. Another component provides a clean interface to users, hiding the computer structures. The user never faces indices, hash tables, file buffers, and the like. Rather, he deals with the tables, objects, axioms, and rules that model the application environment.

2.3.1 External Level

The highest level of Figure 2.2 presents varying external tailored views of the application to different users. For example, one program may consider cat attributes to be simply name and weight, while another program may expect a more complete definition, including eye color, fur color, and associated student owners. Differing external views can use the same conceptual description to satisfy these differing expectations. Moreover, if a program expects an entity to contain certain attributes, it should be unaffected if the conceptual schema changes to add more attributes to the corresponding database object. Of course, certain DBMS parameters may require adjustment to materialize the old external view from a modified conceptual schema. However, the program that uses that old view remains insulated from the change.

2.3.2 Conceptual Level

Isolating these storage details in the lowest level of the DBMS provides a comfortable buffer for the next higher layer of abstraction, the conceptual level. The application objects exist at this level. If the underlying hardware or operating system changes, the consequences are confined to the interface between the physical layer and the conceptual layer immediately above it. If the database designer is controlling the physical schema, he may need to modify and recompile it. In any case, he must retune the DBMS to function efficiently in the new environment. In the worst case, this may involve purchasing a new version of the DBMS. For example, if the platform changes from VAX VMS to UNIX (two operating systems), a new version of the DBMS would probably be necessary. The important point is that all applications constructed over the objects in the conceptual layer remain

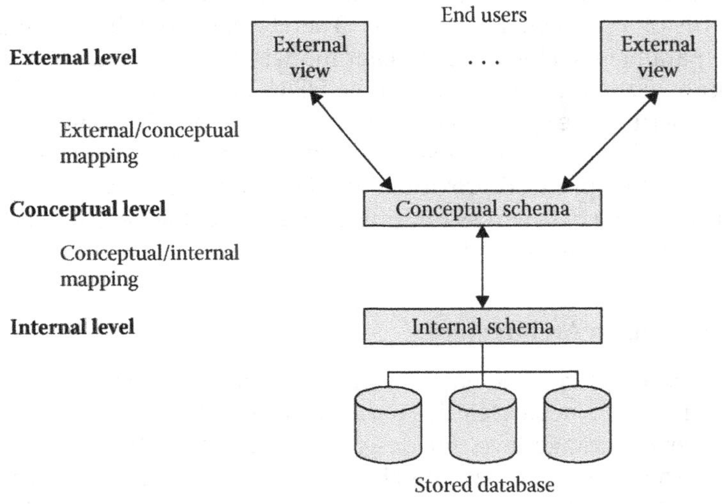

FIGURE 2.2
The three-schema architecture.

TABLE 2.2
Levels of Data Abstraction

Model	Degree of Abstraction	Focus	Independent of
External	High	End-user views	Hardware and software
Conceptual	↑	Global view of data (database model independent)	Hardware and software
Internal	↓	Specific database model	Hardware
Physical	Low	Storage and access methods	Neither hardware nor software

valid. A potentially large investment in application programs that use the database is not affected. The term physical data independence describes this decoupling of the application programs from the underlying hardware and data structures. The three-level diagram of Figure 2.2 illustrates the point.

The center layer of Figure 2.2 describes the complete application environment in terms of the abstractions supported by the DBMS, such as tables, objects, and inference rules. Here reside the entities of interest in the application, together with their relationships, constraints, and security measures. Just as this layer can remain stable in the face of changes in the physical support layer below it, modifications to this conceptual picture can often be hidden from the next higher level.

2.3.3 Physical Level

At the lowest level, farthest removed from the application entities (e.g., cats, students), certain physical components organize and store the raw data. In addition to the hardware, these components include control structures that track which data elements reside on which disks and in which format. Other structures appear here also to accelerate performance, such as buffers for holding frequently used data and information for conducting rapid searches. The physical layer typically has parameters that can be tuned for optimal performance under the access patterns of a particular application. Therefore, the database designer may want to specify these parameters. However, the later models (i.e., relational, object-oriented, and deductive) typically leave the tuning task to the DBMS. If the database designer does have access to these structures, he specifies appropriate values in a physical schema. The physical schema is a second machine-readable script, which addresses such issues as what data elements to store in close physical proximity (on the same disk track or cylinder, for example), how to distribute the data across multiple files and storage devices, and which files to index. Table 2.2 shows the levels of data abstraction.

2.3.4 The Three-Schema Architecture

The three-level ANSI architecture has an important place in database technology development because it clearly separates the users' external level, the database's conceptual level, and the internal storage level for designing a database. In most DBMSs that support user views, external schemas are specified in the same data model that describes the conceptual-level information; for example, a relational DBMS like Oracle or SQLServer uses SQL for fulfilling this requirement. The goal of the three-schema architecture, is to separate the user applications from the physical database.

Schemas can be defined at the following three levels:

1. The external or view level includes a number of external schemas or user views. Each external schema describes the part of the database that a particular user group is interested in and hides the rest of the database from that user group. As in the previous level, each external schema is typically implemented using a representational data model, possibly based on an external schema design in a high-level conceptual data model.
2. The conceptual level has a conceptual schema, which describes the structure of the whole database for a community of users. The conceptual schema hides the details of physical storage structures and concentrates on describing entities, data types, relationships, user operations, and constraints. Usually, a representational data model is used to describe the conceptual schema when a database system is implemented. This implementation conceptual schema is often based on a conceptual schema design in a high-level data model.
3. The internal level has an internal schema, which describes the physical storage structure of the database. The internal schema uses a physical data model and describes the complete details of data storage and access paths for the database.

The three schemas are only descriptions of data; the actual data are stored at the physical level only. In the three-schema architecture, each user group refers to its own external schema. Hence, the DBMS must transform a request specified on an external schema into a request against the conceptual schema, and then in turn into a request on the internal schema for processing over the stored database. If the request is database retrieval, the data extracted from the stored database must be reformatted to match the user's external view. The processes of transforming requests and results between levels are called ***mappings***.

2.3.4.1 Data Independence

The schema is not supposed to change frequently; however, as the application requirements change, the schema may have to be changed occasionally and is known as *schema evolution*. The three-schema architecture can be used to explain the concept of ***data independence***, which can be defined as the capacity to change the schema at one level of a database system without having to change the schema at the next higher level.

Whenever we have a multiple-level DBMS, its catalog must be expanded to include information on how to map requests and data among the various levels. The DBMS uses additional software to accomplish these mappings by referring to the mapping information in the catalog. Data independence occurs because when the schema is changed at some level, the schema at the next higher level remains unchanged; only the mapping between the two levels is changed. Hence, application programs referring to the higher-level schema need not be changed.

Data independence is of two types:

1. Logical data independence is the capacity to change the conceptual schema without having to change external schemas or application programs. The conceptual schema may be changed to expand the database (by adding a record type or data item), to change constraints, or to reduce the database (by removing a record type or data item). In the last case, external schemas that refer only to the remaining

data should not be affected. Only the view definition and the mappings need to be changed in a DBMS that supports logical data independence. After the conceptual schema undergoes a logical reorganization, application pro-grams that reference the external schema constructs must work as before. Changes to constraints can be applied to the conceptual schema without affecting the external schemas or application programs.

2. Physical data independence is the capacity to change the internal schema without having to change the conceptual schema. Hence, the external schemas need not be changed as well. Changes to the internal schema may be needed because some physical files were reorganized—for example, by creating additional access structures—to improve the performance of retrieval or update. If the same data as before remains in the database, we should not have to change the conceptual schema.

Logical data independence is harder to achieve because it allows structural and constraint changes without affecting application programs. In contrast, physical data independence already exists in most databases and file environments where physical details, such as the exact location of data on disk, and hardware details of storage encoding, placement, compression, splitting, merging of records, and so on, are hidden from the user. Applications remain unaware of these details.

2.4 Database Languages and Interfaces

The various languages provided by DBMSs are as follows:

1. Data definition language (DDL) is used to define to specify conceptual and internal schemas for the database and any mappings between the two. The DBMS will have a DDL compiler whose function is to process DDL statements in order to identify descriptions of the schema constructs and to store the schema description in the DBMS catalog.
2. Storage definition language (SDL) is used to specify the internal schema. The mappings between the two schemas may be specified in either one of these languages. However, in most relational DBMSs today, there is no specific language that performs the role of SDL. Instead, the internal schema is specified by a combination of functions, parameters, and specifications related to storage of files.
3. Data manipulation language (DML) is used to provide a set of operations including retrieval, insertion, deletion, and modification of the data.

   High-level DMLs, such as SQL, can specify and retrieve many records in a single DML statement; therefore, they are called set-at-a-time or set-oriented DMLs. A query in a high-level DML often specifies, which data to retrieve rather than how to retrieve it; therefore, such languages are also called declarative.

   A low-level or procedural DML must be embedded in a general-purpose programming language. This type of DML typically retrieves individual records or objects from the database and processes each separately. Therefore, it needs to use programming language constructs, such as looping, to retrieve and process each record from a set of records. Low-level DMLs are also called record-at-a-time DMLs because of this property.

4. View definition language (VDL) is used to specify user views and their mappings to the conceptual schema; however, in most DBMSs the DDL is used to define both conceptual and external schemas.
5. A high-level DML used in a standalone interactive manner is called a query language. Casual end users typically use a high-level query language to specify their requests, whereas programmers use the DML in its embedded form.

In current DBMSs, the preceding types of languages are usually not considered distinct languages; rather, a comprehensive integrated language is used that includes constructs for conceptual schema definition, view definition, and data manipulation. A typical example of a comprehensive database language is the SQL relational database language, which represents a combination of DDL, VDL, and DML, as well as statements for constraint specification, schema evolution, and many other features. A high-level or nonprocedural DML can be used on its own to specify complex database operations concisely.

The various interfaces provided by DBMS are as follows:

1. *Interfaces for the DBA*: Most database systems contain privileged commands that can be used only by the DBA staff. These include commands for creating accounts, setting system parameters, granting account authorization, changing a schema, and reorganizing the storage structures of a database.
2. *Keyword-based database search*: These are somewhat similar to web search engines, which accept strings of natural language (like English or Spanish) words and match them with documents at specific sites (for local search engines) or web pages on the web-at-large (for engines like Google or Ask). They use predefined indexes on words and use ranking functions to retrieve and present resulting documents in a decreasing degree of match. Such *free form* textual query interfaces are not yet common in structured relational databases.
3. *Graphical user interfaces* (GUI): A GUI typically displays a schema to the user in diagrammatic form. The user then can specify a query by manipulating the diagram. In many cases, GUIs utilize both menus and forms.
   a. *Menu-based interfaces for web clients or browsing*: These interfaces present the user with lists of options (called menus) that lead the user through the formulation of a request. Menus do away with the need to memorize the specific commands and syntax of a query language; rather, the query is composed step-by-step by picking options from a menu that is displayed by the system. Pull-down menus are a very popular technique in web-based user interfaces. They are also often used in browsing interfaces, which allow a user to look through the contents of a database in an exploratory and unstructured manner.
   b. *Forms-based interfaces*: A forms-based interface displays a form to each user. Users can fill out all of the form entries to insert new data, or they can fill out only certain entries, in which case the DBMS will retrieve matching data for the remaining entries. Forms are usually designed and programmed for naive users as interfaces to canned transactions. Many DBMSs have forms

specification languages, which are special languages that help programmers specify such forms. SQL*Forms is a form-based language that specifies queries using a form designed in conjunction with the relational database schema. Oracle Forms is a component of the Ora-cle product suite that provides an extensive set of features to design and build applications using forms. Some systems have utilities that define a form by letting the end user interactively construct a sample form on the screen.

4. *Apps for mobile devices*: These interfaces present mobile users with access to their data. For example, banking, reservations, and insurance companies, among many others, provide apps that allow users to access their data through a mobile phone or mobile device. The apps have built-in programmed interfaces that typically allow users to login using their account name and password; the apps then provide a limited menu of options for mobile access to the user data, as well as options such as paying bills (for banks) or making reservations (for reservation websites).
5. *Natural language interfaces*: These interfaces accept requests written in English or some other language and attempt to understand them. A natural language interface usually has its own schema, which is similar to the database conceptual schema, as well as a dictionary of important words. The natural language interface refers to the words in its schema, as well as to the set of standard words in its dictionary, that are used to interpret the request. If the interpretation is successful, the interface generates a high-level query corresponding to the natural language request and submits it to the DBMS for processing; otherwise, a dialog is started with the user to clarify the request.
6. *Speech input and output*: Limited use of speech as an input query and speech as an answer to a question or result of a request is becoming commonplace. Applications with limited vocabularies, such as inquiries for telephone directory, flight arrival or departure, and credit card account information, are allowing speech for input and output to enable customers to access this information. The speech input is detected using a library of predefined words and used to set up the parameters that are supplied to the queries. For output, a similar conversion from text or numbers into speech takes place.

2.5 Categories of Database Management Systems

Database management systems can be categorized on the basis of:

1. *Data Models:* DBMS systems can be categorized into the following based on the data model implemented and employed by them:
   a. The network data model was proposed in the 1971 Database Task Group (DBTG) Report as an extension of the COBOL language. The network model represents data as record types and also represents a limited type of 1:N relationship called a set type. A 1:N, or one-to-many, relationship relates one instance of a record to many record instances using some pointer-linking mechanism in these models. The network model also known as the CODASYL DBTG model14

has an associated record-at-a-time language that must be embedded in a host programming language.

b. The hierarchical model represents data as hierarchical tree structures. Each hierarchy represents a number of related records. There is no standard language for the hierarchical model. A popular hierarchical DML is DL/1 of the IMS system. It dominated the DBMS market for over 20 years between 1965 and 1985. Its DML, called DL/1, was a de facto industry standard for a long time.

c. The relational data model represents a database as a collection of tables, where each table can be stored as a separate file. Most relational databases use the high-level query language called SQL and support a limited form of user views.

d. The object data model defines a database in terms of objects, their properties, and their operations. Objects with the same structure and behavior belong to a class, and classes are organized into hierarchies (or acyclic graphs). The operations of each class are specified in terms of predefined procedures called methods. Relational DBMSs have been extending their models to incorporate object database concepts and other capabilities; these systems are referred to as object-relational or extended-relational systems.

e. The XML (Extensible Markup Language) model is a tree-structured data model; these DBMSs are referred to as native XML DBMSs. Several commercial relational DBMSs have added XML interfaces and storage to their products. The XML model has emerged as a standard for exchanging data over the web and has been used as a basis for implementing several prototype native XML systems. XML uses hierarchical tree structures. It combines database concepts with concepts from document representation models. Data are represented as elements; with the use of tags, data can be nested to create complex tree structures. This model conceptually resembles the object model but uses different terminology. XML capabilities have been added to many commercial DBMS products.

> Big data systems are based on various data models, with the following most common four data models. The key-value data model associates a unique key with each value (which can be a record or object) and provides very fast access to a value given its key. The document data model is based on JSON (Java Script Object Notation) and stores the data as documents, which somewhat resemble complex objects. The graph data model stores objects as graph nodes and relationships among objects as directed-graph edges. Finally, the column-based data models store the columns of rows clustered on disk pages for fast access and allow multiple versions of the data.

2. *Number of sites*: DBMS systems can be categorized based on the number of sites over which the database is distributed:

a. A centralized DBMS has all the data stored at a single computer site. A centralized DBMS can support multiple users, but the DBMS and the database reside totally at a single computer site.

b. A distributed DBMS (DDBMS) can have the actual database and DBMS software distributed over many sites connected by a computer network. Big data systems are often massively distributed with hundreds of sites. The data are often replicated on multiple sites so that failure of a site will not make some data unavailable.
c. A federated DBMS (or multidatabase system) is a group of DBMS, in which the participating DBMSs are loosely coupled and have a degree of local autonomy; specialized middleware software enables access to several autonomous preexisting databases stored under heterogeneous DBMSs. Homogeneous DDBMSs use the same DBMS software at all the sites, whereas heterogeneous DDBMSs can use different DBMS software at each site.

3. *Number of Users:* DBMS systems can be classified based on the number of users supported by them. Single-user systems support only one user at a time and are mostly used with PCs. Multiuser systems, which include the majority of DBMSs, support concurrent multiple users.

2.6 Other Databases

2.6.1 Text Databases

Text databases are databases that contain word descriptions for objects. These word descriptions are usually not simple keywords but rather long sentences or paragraphs, such as product specifications, error or bug reports, warning messages, summary reports, notes, and other documents. Text databases may be highly unstructured (e.g., some web pages on the World Wide Web). Some text databases may be somewhat structured, that is, semistructured (e.g., email messages and many HTML/XML web pages), whereas others are relatively well structured (e.g., library catalogue databases). Text databases with highly regular structures typically can be implemented using relational database systems.

2.6.2 Multimedia Databases

Multimedia databases store image, audio, and video data. They are used in applications such as picture content-based retrieval, voice-mail systems, video-on-demand systems, the World Wide Web, and speech-based user interfaces that recognize spoken commands. Multimedia databases must support large objects, because data objects such as video can require gigabytes of storage. Specialized storage and search techniques are also required. Because video and audio data require real-time retrieval at a steady and predetermined rate in order to avoid picture or sound gaps and system buffer overflows, such data are referred to as continuous-media data.

2.6.3 Temporal Databases

A temporal database typically stores relational data that include time-related attributes. These attributes may involve several timestamps, each having different semantics.

A sequence database stores sequences of ordered events, with or without a concrete notion of time. Examples include customer shopping sequences, web click streams, and biological sequences.

A time-series database stores sequences of values or events obtained over repeated measurements of time (e.g., hourly, daily, weekly). Examples include data collected from the stock exchange, inventory control, and the observation of natural phenomena (like temperature and wind).

2.6.4 Spatial Databases

Spatial databases contain spatial-related information. Examples include geographic (map) databases, very large-scale integration (VLSI) or computer-aided design databases, and medical and satellite image databases. Spatial data may be represented in raster format, consisting of n-dimensional bit maps or pixel maps. For example, a two-dimensional satellite image may be represented as raster data, where each pixel registers the rainfall in a given area. Maps can be represented in vector format, where roads, bridges, buildings, and lakes are represented as unions or overlays of basic geometric constructs, such as points, lines, polygons, and the partitions and networks formed by these components.

Geographic databases have numerous applications, ranging from forestry and ecology planning to providing public service information regarding the location of telephone and electric cables, pipes, and sewage systems. In addition, geographic databases are commonly used in vehicle navigation and dispatching systems. An example of such a system for taxis would store a city map with information regarding one-way streets, suggested routes for moving from region A to region B during rush hour, and the location of restaurants and hospitals, as well as the current location of each driver.

A spatial database that stores spatial objects that change with time is called a spatiotemporal database, from which interesting information can be mined. For example, we may be able to group the trends of moving objects and identify some strangely moving vehicles, or distinguish a bioterrorist attack from a normal outbreak of the flu based on the geographic spread of a disease with time.

2.6.5 Multiple or Heterogeneous Databases

A heterogeneous database consists of a set of interconnected, autonomous component databases. The components communicate in order to exchange information and answer queries. Objects in one component database may differ greatly from objects in other component databases, making it difficult to assimilate their semantics into the overall heterogeneous database.

Many enterprises acquire legacy databases as a result of the long history of information technology development (including the application of different hardware and operating systems). A legacy database is a group of heterogeneous databases that combines different kinds of data systems, such as relational or object-oriented databases, hierarchical databases, network databases, spreadsheets, multimedia databases, and file systems. The heterogeneous databases in a legacy database may be connected by intra- or inter-computer networks.

2.6.6 Stream Databases

Many applications involve the generation and analysis of a new kind of data, called stream data, where data flow in and out of an observation platform (or window) dynamically. Such data streams have the following unique features: huge or possibly infinite volume, dynamically changing, flowing in and out in a fixed order, allowing only one or a small number of scans, and demanding fast (often real-time) response time. Typical examples of data streams include various kinds of scientific and engineering data, time-series data, and data produced in other dynamic environments, such as power supply, network traffic, stock exchange, telecommunications, web click streams, video surveillance, and weather or environment monitoring.

Because data streams are normally not stored in any kind of data repository, effective and efficient management and analysis of stream data pose great challenges to researchers. Currently, many researchers are investigating various issues relating to the development of data stream management systems. A typical query model in such a system is the continuous query model, where predefined queries constantly evaluate incoming streams, collect aggregate data, report the current status of data streams, and respond to their changes.

2.6.7 Web Databases

The World Wide Web and its associated distributed information services, such as Yahoo!, Google, Facebook, Twitter, provide rich, worldwide, online information services, where data objects are linked together to facilitate interactive access. Users seeking information of interest traverse from one object via links to another. Such systems provide ample opportunities and challenges for data mining. For example, understanding user access patterns will not only help improve system design (by providing efficient access between highly correlated objects) but also leads to better marketing decisions (e.g., by placing advertisements in frequently visited documents, or by providing better customer/user classification and behavior analysis). Capturing user access patterns in such distributed information environments is called web usage mining (or weblog mining) or web analytics.

Although web pages may appear fancy and informative to human readers, they can be highly unstructured and lack a predefined schema, type, or pattern. Thus, it is difficult for computers to understand the semantic meaning of diverse web pages and structure them in an organized way for systematic information retrieval and data mining. Web services that provide keyword-based searches without understanding the context behind the web pages can only offer limited help to users. For example, a web search based on a single keyword may return hundreds of web page pointers containing the keyword, but most of the pointers will be very weakly related to what the user wants to find. Web mining or analytics can often provide additional help here than web search services. For example, authoritative web page analysis based on linkages among web pages can help rank web pages based on their importance, influence, and topics. Automated web page clustering and classification help group and arrange web pages in a multidimensional manner based on their contents. Web community analysis helps identify hidden web social networks and communities and observe their evolution. Web mining is the development of scalable and effective web data analysis and mining methods. It may help us learn about the distribution of information on the web in general, characterize and classify web pages, and uncover web dynamics and the association and other relationships among different web pages, users, communities, and web-based activities.

2.7 Evolution of Database Technology

Unlike the monolithic DBMSs available today, in future component database systems will be available, whereby different database services could be combined and used according to the user's needs.

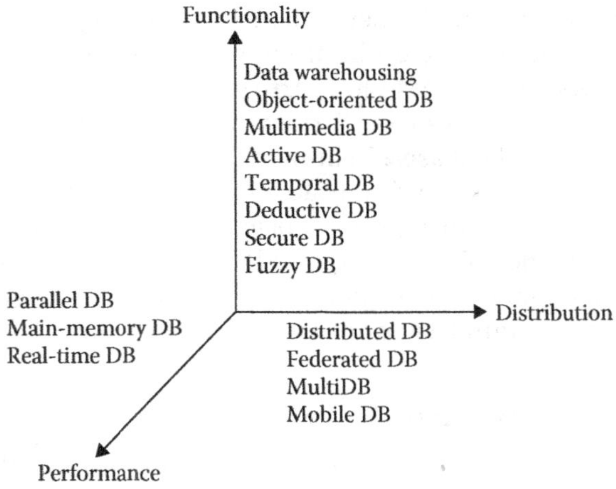

FIGURE 2.3
Evolution of database technology.

Database technology is evolving along three significant dimensions, namely, distribution, performance, and functionality. Figure 2.3 shows the evolution of database technology along these three dimensions.

2.7.1 Distribution

In the past decade, the first distributed DBMSs appeared on the market and have been an important focus of database research and marketing. Some achievements of the early distributed products were two-phase commit, replication, and query optimization.

Distributed databases can be classified into three areas: distribution, heterogeneity, and autonomy. In the last area, federated databases (semiautonomous databases) and multidatabases (completely autonomous) can be found. A higher degree of distribution is offered by mobile databases, which can be considered distributed systems, in which links between nodes change dynamically.

This also implies higher emphasis on the integration of databases, Internet, and the web. The web adds new components to databases, including a new technology for the graphical user interface (GUI), a new client or server model (the hypertext transfer protocol, HTTP), and a hyperlink mechanism between databases. New architectures capable of connecting different software components and allowing the interoperation between them are needed. Database architectures must provide extensibility for distributed environments, allow the integration of legacy mainframe systems, client or server environments, web-based applications, and so on.

Software vendors now offer enough of the integration facilities required to access distributed databases from all types of devices (personal computers, PDAs, palmtops, laptops, etc.) and Internet data.

2.7.2 Performance

To cope with the burgeoning volumes of data, databases are taking advantage of new hardware. Since the mid-1980s, different parallel databases (shared memory, shared disk, and shared nothing) have been implemented, exploiting parallelism as well as strategies like interquery (several queries executed independently in various processors) and intraquery (independent parts of a query executed in different processors). Hardware performance-to-price ratio also allows the database (or part of it) to be stored in the main memory during its execution. Therefore, we can distinguish between new in-memory databases and traditional disk-resident databases. In in-memory databases, several concepts, such as index structures, clustering, locks, and transactions must be restated.

Performance is also important in a given set of applications where response time is critical (e.g., control systems). The ability to respond is of vital importance because it is not so much rapid response as guaranteed response in a specific time. Real time DBMSs, conceived with that objective in mind, set priorities for transactions.

2.7.2.1 Database Design for Multicore Processors

In general, all the query-processing algorithms and even the classical transaction properties of Atomicity, Consistency, Isolation, and Durability (ACID) must be adapted for the new-generation *not only SQL* (NoSQL) databases (see Chapter 10).

Database systems today run on computers with multicore processors. As stated in Chapter 1, as per Moore's Law, processor speed has increased at an exponential rate, doubling every 18–24 months resulting from an exponential growth in the number of transistors that could be fit within a unit area of a silicon chip. Until recently, the increase in the number of transistors and the decrease in their size led to ever-faster processors. Although technological progress continues to behave as predicted by Moore's law, another factor has emerged to slow the growth in processor speed. Fast processors are power inefficient that is problematic in terms of energy consumption and cost, battery life for mobile computers, and heat dissipation (all the power used eventually turns into heat). As a result, modern processors typically are not one single processor but rather consist of several processors on one chip. To maintain a distinction between on-chip multiprocessors and traditional processors, the term core is used for an on-chip processor.

Each core is capable of processing an independent stream of machine instructions. However, because processors are able to process data faster than it can be accessed from main memory, main memory can become a bottleneck that limits overall performance. For this reason, computer designers include one or more levels of cache memory in a computer system. Cache memory is more costly than main memory on a per-byte basis, but offers a faster access time. In multilevel cache designs, the levels are called L1, L2, and so on, with L1 being the fastest cache (and thus the most costly per byte and therefore the smallest), L2 the next fastest, and so on. This result in effectively extending the storage hierarchy to include the various levels of cache below main memory.

Although the database system can control the transfer of data between disk and main memory, the computer hardware maintains control over the transfer of data among the various levels of cache and between the cache and main memory. Despite this lack of direct control, the database system's performance can be affected by how cache is utilized. If a core needs to access a data item that is not in cache, it must be fetched from main memory. Because main memory is so much slower than processors, a significant amount of potential processing speed may be lost while a core waits for data from main memory. These waits are referred to as cache misses.

One way in which computer designers attempt to limit the impact of cache misses is via multithreading. A thread is an execution stream that shares memory with other threads running on the same core. If the thread currently executing on a core suffers a cache miss (or other type of wait), the core proceeds to execute another thread, thereby not wasting computing speed while waiting. Thus, threads introduce yet another source of parallelism beyond the multiplicity of cores. Each new generation of processors supports more cores and more threads.

The architecture trend of slower increase in raw speed accompanied by the growth in the number of cores has significant implications for database system design. Database systems are an ideal application to take advantage of large numbers of cores and threads, since database systems support large numbers of concurrent transactions. However, there are a variety of factors that make optimal use of modern processors challenging; as we allow a higher degree of concurrency to take advantage of the parallelism of modern processors, we increase the amount of data that needs to be in cache. This can result in more cache misses, perhaps so many that even a multithreaded core has to wait for data from memory.

Concurrent transactions need some sort of concurrency control to ensure the ACID properties that were noted in Chapter 1. When concurrent transactions access data in common, some sort of restrictions must be imposed on that concurrent access via the use of locks, timestamps, or validation that may result in waiting or the loss of work due to transaction aborts. To avoid excessive amounts of waiting or lost work, it is ideal that concurrent transactions conflict rarely, but attempting to ensure that can actually increase the amount of data needed in cache, resulting in even more cache misses!

Finally, there are components of a database system shared by all transactions. In a system using locking, the lock table is shared by all transactions and access to it can become a bottleneck. Similar problems exist for other forms of concurrency control. Similarly, the buffer manager, the log manager, and the recovery manager serve all transactions and are potential bottlenecks.

Because having a large number of concurrent transactions may not take optimal advantage of modern processors, it is desirable to find ways to allow multiple cores to work on a single transaction. This requires the database query processor to find effective ways to parallelize queries without creating excessive demands on cache. This can be done by creating pipelines of database operations from queries and by finding ways to parallelize individual database operations.

2.7.3 Functionality

In this dimension, the evolution of information systems (IS) can be summarized as the *functionality migration* from programs to database. With the advent of databases, we have seen the consolidation of a trend toward transferring all possible semantics from programs to the database dictionary-catalog so as to store it together with the data. The migration in semantics and other functionalities have evident advantages, in so far as its centralization releases the applications from having to check integrity constraints within individual programs and, thus, prevents their verification from being repeated in the different application programs.

At a first glance, in a process-oriented IS based on files, there are only data in the *DB* (file)—all other information on the data, constraints, control, and process was incorporated in the program. The location of that information in programs contributed to the classical problems of redundancy, maintenance, and security associated with this kind of IS.

Earlier DBMSs represented a second approach, in which description of data was stored with the data in the database catalog or dictionary. However, in the DBMSs of the 1980s, programs were responsible for the verification of constraints (until the 1990s relational products did not support, e.g., referential integrity or check constraints). Later, with the improvement of the performance-to-cost ratio and optimizers, products incorporated more and more information on constraints in the DBMS catalog, becoming more and more of semantic databases. In the early 1990s, active databases appeared which besides the description of the data and the constraints, also stored part of the control information in the database. Active databases could run applications without the user's intervention by supporting triggers, rules, alerts, daemons, and so on.

Subsequently, this was followed by the appearance of object-oriented and object-relational DBMSs, which allow the definition and management of objects that encapsulate their respective structure and behavior. Objects stored in databases can be of any type: images, audio, video, and so on. Finally, there were multimedia databases which could be the latest step in the evolution of databases along the functionality dimension.

Future DBMSs must manage not only different types of data and objects but also knowledge in an integrated way. In that respect, research into deductive DBMSs has been carried out. Two other important aspects of modern information systems (IS) that are being incorporated into databases are time (temporal databases) and uncertainty (fuzzy databases) both of which are critical in decision-making business processes. Decision support systems (DSS) and executive information systems (EIS) are being incorporated within the wider data warehousing and data mining environments in which database technology plays a decisive role.

2.8 Summary

This chapter presented an overview of the traditional database environments, namely, relational, hierarchical, network, and object-oriented databases. This background would be essential to understand the context and challenges that led to the development of NoSQL and Hadoop development environment. But before embarking on understanding big data computing, Part II presents an overview of other areas that were significant milestones on the road to big data computing, namely, analytics, data warehousing, data mining, service oriented architecture (with web services and enterprise service bus), and cloud computing.

Section II

Road to Big Data Computing

3

Analytics Basics

An inevitable consequence of organizations using the pyramid-shaped hierarchy is that there is a decision-making bottleneck at the top of the organization. The people at the top are overwhelmed by the sheer volume of decisions they have to make; they are too far away from the scene of the action to really understand what is happening; and by the time decisions are made, the actions are usually too little and too late. Consequently, companies suffer by staggering from one bad decision to another. No small group of executives, regardless of their smarts, hard work, or sophisticated computer systems, can make all those decisions in a timely or competent manner. Given the pace of change, companies need something more agile and responsive.

The centralized command and control methods that worked for hierarchies will not work for service delivery networks. Instead of a small group of executives telling everybody else what to do, people need to get the authority to figure out for themselves what to do. The need to be responsive to evolving customer needs and desires creates operational structures and systems where business analysis and decision making are pushed out to operating units that are closest to the scene of the action—which, however, lacks the expertise and resources to access, process, evaluate, and decide on the course of action. This engenders the significance of analysis systems that are essential for enabling decisive action as close to the customer as possible. Closed-loop decision making resulting from combination of ongoing performance management with ongoing business analysis can lead to an effective responsive enterprise; hence, the need for intelligent business analysis.

3.1 Intelligent Analysis

Management decisions differ depending on the level of responsibility on which they are made and who makes them. A brief overview is helpful here to put this into context:

1. Strategic decisions have significant resource allocation impact, set the precedents or tone for decisions further down the organization, and have a potentially material effect on the organization's competitiveness within its marketplace. They are made by top managers and affect the business direction of an organization.

   Strategic intelligence is arguably the most vital form of intelligence because it provides a framework within which other forms of intelligence collection and analysis take place. It helps to discern and make sense of important trends, to identify and extract patterns that would otherwise not be visible, and to provide an overall picture of the evolving opportunity and threat environment. Strategic intelligence also provides guidance for tactical and operational assessments, and work done at these levels, in turn, helps to shape the strategic intelligence focus. As strategic analytic methodologies mature, they will also offer the basis for predictive or anticipatory assessments that can serve to provide warning of potential high-impact activities.

Generic strategic analytical methodologies are as follows:

- Sector/competitor assessments: Focus on emerging or threatening competitors that provide strong potential for impacting the competitive terrain.
- Pattern or trend analyses: Baseline assessments to better recognize deviations from current practice, especially those that shape the industry's future.
- Anti-pattern or anomaly detection: Requires systematic "environmental scanning," as well as the collating of tactical and operational intelligence reports that identify and highlight specific deviations from the norm.
- Opportunity and threat (O&T) assessments: Used to assess the levels of dependence and vulnerabilities of critical issues, competitive changes that could cause significant impact, and the likelihood of such activities taking place.
- Impact assessments: The macrolevel view taken in Strategic Intelligence Analysis (SIA) offers a good approach for assessing probable cascade effects of threatening competitive action and activity.

2. Tactical decisions are less pervasive than strategic ones and involve formulating and implementing policies for the organization. They are usually made by mid-level managers and often materially affect functions such as marketing, accounting, production, a business unit, or product, as opposed to the entire organization. Tactical decisions generally have lower resource implications than strategic decisions and are typically semistructured.

   Tactical Intelligence Analysis (TIA) is a necessary and important complement to work done at the strategic level. It is the natural link between macro- and micro-level analyses. Although SIA provides the framework for TIA, these assessments, in turn, feed SIA. With a dynamic symbiotic relationship between the two, mutual strength is derived.

   Generic tactical analytical initiatives are as follows:

   - Cluster and pattern analysis: Identifies the use of particular marketplace attack methods, commonalities of targets, and attempts to build profiles of competitors.
   - Value constellation analysis: Identifies the key stakeholders, important partners, allies, joint venture prospects, outsourcing potential, and agents that a company could utilize.
   - Stimulus-response analysis: Identifies actions that could be taken by competitors in response to specific events. This analysis could be used both proactively to develop warnings or reactively to design future tactics.

3. Operational decisions support the day-to-day decisions needed to operate the organization and take effect for a few days or weeks. Typically made by a lower-level manager, operational decisions are distinct from tactical and strategic decisions in that they are made frequently and often "on the fly." Operational decisions tend to be highly structured, often with well-defined procedure manuals.

Operational Intelligence Analysis is often event-centric and single case-oriented. It provides more immediate but lesser-lasting benefits, and typically involves technological assessments of methods used for marketplace battles or investigations of competitive threats.

Generic operational analytical initiatives are as follows:

- Competitor analysis helps in planning and executing competitive intelligence efforts at appropriate time and preventing premature disclosures.
- Vulnerability analysis helps in identification of marketplace vulnerabilities and measures that can rectify, minimize, or eliminate them.

3.1.1 Intelligence Maturity Model

Table 3.1 presents the intelligence maturity model (IMM) discussed below.

3.1.1.1 Data

Data have experienced a variety of definitions, largely depending on the context of its use. For example, Information Science defines data as unprocessed information and other domains treat data as a representation of objective facts. Data result from representation of facts, observation, or an event. Data are understood as discrete, atomistic, tiny packets that have no inherent structure or necessary relationship between them. It is discrete, it can be piled-up, captured, and retrieved, or be recorded and manipulated.

Data are recorded (captured and stored) symbols and signal readings: symbols include words (text and/or verbal), numbers, diagrams, and images (still and/or video), which are the building blocks of communication; signals include sensor and/or sensory readings of light, sound, smell, taste, and touch. As symbols, "Data" are the storage of intrinsic meaning, a mere representation. The main purpose of data is to record activities or situations, to attempt to capture the true picture or real event.

Data are a measuring unit of cognition that describes transactions between natural, artificial, or semantic systems. In businesses, data can measure performance characteristics of production, distribution, transportation, or service.

3.1.1.2 Communication

Communication is a method of transmission from a generating source to receiving destination. Communication presumes content, container, and media of communication; thus, communication fidelity is closely connected with architecture, process, protocol, and format of the various components.

TABLE 3.1

Intelligence Maturity Model (IMM)

Data	–	Data file
Communication	Metadata	Data tables, mapping, and transformation
Information	Meaning	Databases, indices, and spreadsheets
Intelligence	Analytics	Data warehouses, OLAPs
Knowledge	Context	Knowledge bases
Wisdom	Heuristics	Expert systems

Characteristics of communication:

- Correct: Is the transmission correct?
- Clear: Is the transmission accompanied by noise?
- Consistent: Is the transmission consistent?
- Complete: Did the transmission complete without disruption or interruption?
- Certain: Is the transmission data source authentic?
- Confirmed: Is the transmission data source authenticity been confirmed?

3.1.1.3 Information

Information is corpuscular, quantifiable, morselized, commoditized, objective and "out there," transferable, interconvertible, transparent, autonomous, and measurable. It has shape and can be processed and accessed, generated and created, transmitted, stored, sent, distributed, produced and consumed, searched for, used, compressed, and duplicated. Information can also be of different types with different attributes. It can be sensitive information, qualitative or quantitative information. Modern uses even extend its use to biological cells using and transmitting information, with cancers, for example, seen as spreading misinformation.

Information is a message that contains relevant meaning, implication, or input for decision and/or action. Information comes from both current (communication) and historical (processed data or "reconstructed picture") sources. In essence, the purpose of information is to aid in making decisions and/or solving problems or realizing an opportunity.

Characteristics of information:

- Reliability: Can the source of the information be trusted to deliver reliable information?
- Accuracy: Have the data inputs been captured "first hand," or have they been filtered? Is there any reason to think that there might be any deception involved? Is the source able to communicate the data precisely? Is the source truly competent and knowledgeable about the information they provide? Do they have a known vested interest, hidden agenda, or other bias that might impact the information's accuracy? Can the source's data be verified by other sources or otherwise triangulated?
- Ease of access: What is the financial opportunity and time cost to access the source? Is this the best use of limited resources, or can equivalent data be gained with lesser expenditure? Does the source speak the right language, or will translation be needed?

It is a comparative unit of cognition that defines a change between the previous and present state of natural, artificial, or semantic systems. Businesses often compare data from two different periods of operations. Accounting systems often compare actual performance with standards.

3.1.1.4 Concept

Existence of concept presumes a language; ontology is defined in terms of concept(s) and relations between the concepts.

It is a perceptive unit of cognition that generates thoughts or ideas that create our intuition and intention—a sense of direction.

3.1.1.5 Knowledge

Knowledge is the cognition or recognition (know-what), capacity to act (know-how), and understanding (know-why) that resides or is contained within the mind or in the brain. The purpose of knowledge is to better our lives. In the context of business, the purpose of knowledge is to create or increase value for the enterprise and all its stakeholders.

Within the field of knowledge management, there exist two quite distinct and widely accepted types of knowledge: tacit and explicit. Tacit knowledge is knowledge that is hard to encode and communicate. It is ephemeral and transitory and "cannot be resolved into information or itemized in the manner characteristic of information." Further, tacit knowledge is personal, context-specific, and hard to formalize. Toward the other end of the scale, explicit knowledge is exactly that kind of knowledge that can be encoded and is transmittable in language, once again, via the conduit metaphor. It is explicit knowledge that most current knowledge management practices try to, and indeed are able to, capture, acquire, create, leverage, retain, codify, store, transfer, and share.

Characteristics of knowledge:

- Assumptions: This is the knowledge that individuals take for granted. These can come in the form of any of the previously described categories and may refer to things that have occurred in the past, present, or can be fairly safely predicted as going to happen in the future. Explicit assumptions are those that are consciously adopted by the analyst, are well understood, and are shared. Implicit assumptions are those that individuals in the analysis process do not consciously elicit, share, or articulate, and may not even be aware of. Valuable as they are, as with perceptions and beliefs, assumptions need to be consistently and constantly challenged to reflect changing situations and a shifting competitive landscape.
- Facts: Verified information, something known to exist or to have occurred. These are unambiguously true statements and are known to be so. Facts come in any form and will be found among virtually any source of data that enters an employee's awareness, or the enterprise's communication and information systems. It is surprising how few enterprises subject their collected data and information to fact checking and verification processes. This becomes even more important for strategy decision-making purposes because many of the facts about competitors and competition are time-sensitive. What may be accurate today may be dangerously incorrect tomorrow.
- Perceptions: Perceptions are impressions or opinions that fall short of being facts, but which are supported to some extent by underlying data or logic. These are often expressed as thoughts or opinions which are put to test to convert them into facts, pending which have to remain as perceptions for the time being. There is nothing wrong in factoring perceptions into the analysis process, just as long as everybody knows that this is what they are. The error comes when perceptions are mistakenly regarded and treated as facts when they are not. The use of perceptions is perhaps the most exciting element to subject to subsequent analysis, especially when using scenario analysis, war-gaming, what-if analysis, and other such future-oriented techniques.
- Beliefs: Beliefs are often drawn from a mix of facts and perceptions and commonly describe cause-effect relationships. They can be either explicit or implicit, but they too need to be subjected to verification and justification. Beliefs often color the way individuals understand their world and the way in which they think about the future. Therefore, it becomes critical in the analysis process for beliefs to be

aired and made transparent to those individuals who are key parts of the process, whether these individuals are data gatherers, analysts, or decision makers.

- Projections: Projections are composed of a mixture of assumptions, facts, perceptions, and beliefs. They are justified or substantiated judgments about the future. It is again important that the analyst be able to powerfully defend or justify their projections as they become a critical part of the knowledge base underlying the decisions made.
- Synthesis: Having identified the type of knowledge in place, the analyst can proceed with greater confidence toward a high-quality output. Qualified inputs are then subjected to the real heart of analysis—the thinking processes, sifting, synthesis, induction, deduction, abduction, experimentation, mathematical conceptualization, experimentation, research, application of methods, techniques, and a vast array of other activities all designed to generate unique and actionable insights.

Knowledge is a reasoning unit of cognition that creates awareness based on facts, rules, coherent inferences, and well-defined methods. Knowledge provides a point of reference, a standard for analyzing data, information, and concepts.

3.1.1.6 Intelligence

Intelligence requires ability to sense the environment, to make decisions, and to control action. Higher levels of intelligence may include the ability to recognize objects and events, to present knowledge in a world model, and to reason about the plan for the future. In advanced forms, intelligence provides the capacity to perceive and understand, to choose wisely, and to act successfully under a large variety of circumstances as to survive, prosper, and reproduce in a complex and often hostile environment.

Intelligence is thought or mental processing capacities:

- Learning—pattern recognition, memorizing, recalling, and correcting mistakes, sense-making
- Conceptualizing—modeling, prioritizing, and categorizing
- Analytical thinking—analyzing, interpretation, understanding, scenario playing, and evaluating
- Critical thinking—logic and reasoning
- Creative thinking—imaging, imagining, supposing, hypothesizing and simulating
- Quick thinking
- Performing—reading, speaking, music, physical activities, and so on
- Problem solving, decision making, and judging
- Affective thinking—emotion handling

3.1.1.7 Wisdom

Wisdom means more than being cultured and well educated; it implies an ethical obligation to improve society and an attitude of caring. While intelligence is related to action, wisdom is related to options and how to judge what we should do. Therefore, wisdom is making (human) sense of data, communication, information, knowledge, and intelligence, and is composed of values and vision.

Characteristics of wisdom:

- Reasoning ability (has the unique ability to look at a problem or situation and solve it; has good problem solving ability; has a logical mind)
- Expeditious use of information (is experienced; seeks out information, especially details; learns and remembers and gains information from past mistakes or successes)
- Sagacity (considers advices; understands people through dealing with a variety of people; feels he or she can always learn from other people; is fair)
- Learning from ideas and environment (attaches importance to ideas; looks at different perspectives; learns from other people's mistakes)
- Judgment (acts within own physical and intellectual limitations; is sensible; has good judgment at all times; thinks before acting or making decisions)
- Perspicacity (can offer solutions that are on the side of right and truth; is able to see through things—read between the lines; has the ability to understand and interpret his or her environment)

Wisdom is a pragmatic unit of cognition that generates volition—a chosen way of acting and communicating. Wisdom is the process of choosing ordered routines, intended to achieve success and eliminate obstacles.

3.2 Decisions

A decision is a choice from multiple alternatives, usually made with a fair degree of rationality. In an enterprise, these decisions may concern the development of a strategic plan and imply therefore substantial investment choices, the definition of marketing initiatives and related sales predictions, and the design of a production plan that allows the available human and technological resources to be employed in an effective and efficient way.

The decision-making process is part of a broader subject usually referred to as problem solving, which refers to the process through which individuals try to bridge the gap between the current operating conditions of a system (as is) and the supposedly better conditions to be achieved in the future (to be). In general, the transition of a system toward the desired state implies overcoming certain obstacles and is not easy to attain. This forces decision makers to devise a set of alternative feasible options to achieve the desired goal, and then choose a decision based on a comparison between the advantages and disadvantages of each option. Hence, the decision selected must be put into practice and then verified to determine if it has enabled the planned objectives to be achieved. When this fails to happen, the problem is reconsidered, according to a recursive logic.

3.2.1 Types of Decisions

Organizational decision problems are of various types, from daily operational decisions to long-term strategy business decisions, from internal single decisions to multilevel decisions or multiorganizational decisions. Decision makers can be at various levels according to their decision problems, such as a product distributor, a supermarket manager, or a head of department. Organizational decision making seeks to find the optimal or most satisfactory solution for a decision problem such as selecting the best from a set of product prototypes, making an optimized resource plan, choosing the most suitable supplier, and determining a product's price. Different decision-making tasks may have different features and therefore are modeled in different forms or presented by different methods, and solved by different decision support techniques.

A classical classification is based on a given problem's degree of complexity:

1. Structured: A structured decision problem can be described by classic mathematical models, such as linear programming or statistics methods. A typical structured decision example is that to select a supplier who has the lowest price of all the suppliers with the same quality/type of products, or determines a product plan that will bring the highest profit of all the possible product plans in a factory. The procedure for obtaining an optimal solution is known by standard solution methods. For example, goal programming can be used to solve a linear programming model when the decision maker provides a goal for their decision objective.
2. Semistructured: Semistructured decision problems fall between structured and unstructured problems, having both structured and unstructured features, and reflecting most real-world situations. Solving semistructured decision problems involves a combination of both standard optimization solution procedures and human judgment, and also needs the support of related intelligent information processing techniques and inference approaches.
3. Unstructured: An unstructured decision problem is fuzzy, uncertain, and vague, for which there is no standard solution method for obtaining an optimal solution, or where such an optimal solution does not exist. Human intuition is often the basis for decision making in an unstructured problem. Typical unstructured problems include planning new services to customers, hiring an executive for a big company, choosing a set of development projects for a long period, or making a set of policies for a social issue.

Multilevel decision-making (MLDM) problems appear in many situations that require compromise between the objectives of two or more interacting entities, and these entities are arranged within a hierarchical structure with independent and perhaps conflicting objectives.

Computer-based decision support techniques can be more useful in structured and semistructured decision problems than unstructured decision problems. In an unstructured decision problem only part of the problem can be assisted by computerized decision support techniques. For semistructured decision problems, a computerized decision support technique can improve the quality of the information on which a decision is based, therefore increasing the decision maker's situation awareness to reach a better decision and improve decision efficiency.

Enterprise Intelligence Characteristics	Scope of Decisions		
Accuracy	High	⟷	Low
Level of detail	Detailed	⟷	Aggregate
Time horizon	Present	⟷	Future
Frequency of use	High	⟷	Low
Source	Internal	⟷	External
Scope of information	Quantitative	⟷	Qualitative
Nature of information	Narrow	⟷	Wide
Age of information	Present	⟷	Past

FIGURE 3.1
Characteristics of enterprise intelligence in terms of the scope of the decisions.

3.2.2 Scope of Decisions

1. Strategic decisions: Decisions are strategic when they affect the entire organization or at least a substantial part of it for a long period of time. Strategic decisions strongly influence the general objectives and policies of an enterprise. As a consequence, strategic decisions are taken at a higher organizational level, usually by the company top management.
2. Managerial decisions: Tactical decisions affect only parts of an enterprise and are usually restricted to a single department. The time span is limited to a medium-term horizon, typically up to a year. Tactical decisions place themselves within the context determined by strategic decisions. In a company hierarchy, tactical decisions are made by middle managers, such as the heads of the company departments.
3. Operational decisions: Operational decisions refer to specific activities carried out within an organization and have a modest impact on the future. Operational decisions are framed within the elements and conditions determined by strategic and tactical decisions. Therefore, they are usually made at a lower organizational level, by knowledge workers responsible for a single activity or task such as subdepartment heads, workshop foremen, and back-office heads.

The characteristics of the intelligence required in a decision-making process will change depending on the scope of the decisions to be supported (Figure 3.1).

3.3 Decision-Making Process

The nature of a decision process depends on many factors, like the characteristics of the organization within which the system is placed; the subjective attitudes of the decision makers; the availability of appropriate problem-solving methodologies; and, the availability of effective decision support tools.

Decision-making process is characterized by the following:

- The decisions made within a public or private enterprise or organization are often interconnected and determine broad effects. Each decision has consequences for many individuals and several parts of the organization.
- Decisions are often devised by a group of individuals instead of a single decision maker.
- The number of alternative actions may be very high, and sometimes unlimited.
- The effects of a given decision usually appear later, not immediately.
- Experiments carried out in a real-world system, according to a trial-and-error scheme, are too costly and risky to be of practical use for decision making.
- The dynamics in which an enterprise operates, is strongly affected by the pressure of a competitive environment, imply that knowledge workers need to address situations and make decisions quickly and in a timely fashion.
- During the decision-making process, knowledge workers are asked to access data and information, and work on them based on a conceptual and analytical framework.
- Feedback plays an important role in providing information and knowledge for future decision-making processes within a given organization.
- In most instances, the decision-making process has multiple goals, with different performance indicators, that might also be in conflict with one another.
- Many decisions are made in a fuzzy context and entail risk factors. The level of propensity or aversion to risk varies significantly among different individuals.

Decision-making processes consist of the following steps:

1. Intelligence: In the intelligence phase, the task of the decision maker is to identify, circumscribe, and explicitly define the problem that emerges in the system under study. The analysis of the context and all the available information may allow decision makers to quickly grasp the signals and symptoms pointing to a corrective action to improve the system performance. For example, during the execution of a project, the intelligence phase may consist of a comparison between the current progress of the activities and the original development plan. In general, it is important not to confuse the problem with the symptoms. For example, suppose that an e-commerce bookseller receives a complaint concerning late delivery of a book order placed online. Such inconvenience may be interpreted as the problem and be tackled by arranging a second delivery by priority shipping to circumvent the dissatisfaction of the customer.
2. Design: In the design phase, actions aimed at solving the identified problem should be developed and planned. At this level, the experience and creativity of the decision makers play a critical role, as they are asked to devise viable solutions that ultimately allow the intended purpose to be achieved. Where the number of available actions is small, decision makers can make an explicit enumeration of the alternatives to identify the best solution. If, however, the number of alternatives is very large, or even unlimited, their identification occurs in an implicit way, usually

through a description of the rules that feasible actions should satisfy. For example, these rules may directly translate into the constraints of an optimization model.

3. Choice: Once the alternative actions have been identified, it is necessary to evaluate them on the basis of the performance criteria deemed significant. Mathematical models and the corresponding solution methods usually play a valuable role during the choice phase. For example, optimization models and methods allow the best solution to be found in very complex situations involving countless or even infinite feasible solutions. However, decision trees can be used to handle decision-making processes influenced by stochastic events.
4. Implementation: When the best alternative has been selected by the decision maker, it is transformed into actions by means of an implementation plan. This involves assigning responsibilities and roles to all those involved into the action plan.
5. Control: Once the action has been implemented, it is finally necessary to verify and check that the original expectations have been satisfied and the effects of the action match the original intentions. In particular, the differences between the values of the performance indicators identified in the choice phase, and the values actually observed at the end of the implementation plan should be measured. In an adequately planned decision support system (DSS), the results of these evaluations translate into experience and information, which are then transferred into the data warehouse to be used during subsequent decision-making processes.

3.4 Decision-Making Techniques

Decision techniques involved in modeling and executing the decision-making process:

3.4.1 Mathematical Programming

Mathematical programming or optimization refers to the study of decision-making problems in which one seeks to minimize or maximize a function by systematically choosing the values of variables from an allowed set (a feasible set). A mathematical programming model includes three sets of elements: decision variables, objective functions, and constraints (constraint conditions), where uncontrollable variables or parameters are within the objective functions and the constraints. Many real-world decision problems can be modeled by mathematical programming models.

Different types of mathematical programming models are as follows:

- Linear programming
- Multiobjective programming
- Bi-level/multilevel programming

Linear programming is an important type of mathematical optimization in which there is only one objective function, and the objective function and constraints are expressions of linear relationships among decision variables. Linear programming is heavily used in various management activities, either to maximize the profit or minimize the cost of an organization.

3.4.2 Multicriteria Decision Making

When we need to select the best option from a list of alternatives based on multiple criteria for a decision problem, it is often necessary to analyze each alternative in the light of its determination of each of these criteria. Multicriteria decision making (MCDM), also called multiattribute decision making (MADM), refers to making preferred decisions (e.g., evaluation, prioritization, and selection) in the presence of multiple and conflicting criteria over the alternatives available. An MCDM utility model combines all the criteria of a given alternative simultaneously through the use of a specific utility formula or utility function. Problems for MCDM may range from those in our daily life, such as the selection of a restaurant, to those affecting entire nations.

3.4.3 Case-Based Reasoning

Many decision problems cannot be modeled by mathematical programming models. Managers often produce a solution for a given problem based on their previous experience and knowledge. Case-based reasoning (CBR) provides an effective methodology for DSS in solving a new problem based on the solutions of similar past problems. The technique of CBR provides a powerful learning ability that uses past experiences as a basis for dealing with new similar problems. A CBR system can, therefore, facilitate the knowledge acquisition process by eliminating the time required to elicit solutions from experts. In dynamically changing situations where the problem cannot be modeled by mathematical models and solutions are not easy to generate, CBR is the preferred method of reasoning.

3.4.4 Data Warehouse and Data Mining

Data warehouse is a repository of an organization's electronically stored data. A data warehouse system involves not only data storage but also the techniques to retrieve and analyze data, to extract, transform, and load data, and to manage the data dictionary. In particular, the data warehouse includes business intelligence tools to implement the above functions to better support business decision making.

Data mining is the process of extracting hidden and undiscovered patterns from data and is commonly used in a wide range of profiling practices and knowledge discovery projects. Rules and patterns are discovered from data with the aim of leading to a set of options or decisions. In most data mining applications, a data file of query results is created from a data warehouse and then analyzed by a specialist using artificial intelligence or statistical tools.

3.4.5 Decision Tree

A decision tree is a graphic description of a set of decision rules and their possible consequences. It can be used to create a plan to reach a goal of decision. A decision tree, as a special form of tree structure, is a predictive model to map observations about an item with conclusions about the item's target value. Each interior node corresponds to a variable and an arc to a child node represents a possible value or splitting condition of that variable. The decision tree approach, as a decision support tool, models a decision problem and its possible consequences in a tree-like graph. It is very suitable for a decision that involves possible chance event outcomes, resource costs, and utility. Decision trees are commonly used in decision analysis to help identify the strategy that is most likely to reach a goal.

In applications, a decision tree or consequences can contain fuzzy numbers or linguistic terms, and are therefore called fuzzy decision trees.

3.4.6 Fuzzy Sets and Systems

Whatever decision techniques are used, a critical issue is to deal with is uncertainty. Decision environments and data sources often have various uncertain factors, resulting in uncertain relations among decision objectives and decision entities. For example, an individual's preference for alternatives and judgment for criteria are often expressed by linguistic terms, such as "low" and "high," which are uncertain expressions. Precise mathematical and inference approaches are not efficient enough to tackle such uncertainty.

Various uncertain information processing techniques have therefore been developed by using fuzzy sets, fuzzy numbers, and fuzzy logic in decision-making activities. Research results include new methodologies and algorithms of fuzzy multiobjective decision making, fuzzy multicriteria decision making, fuzzy case-based reasoning, fuzzy decision trees, fuzzy data retrieval, and fuzzy association rules. Various applications of fuzzy decision making have been developed as well.

3.5 Analytics

Thus, business analytics, or simply analytics, is the use of data, information technology, statistical analysis, quantitative methods, and mathematical or computer-based models to help managers gain improved insight about their business operations and make better, fact-based decisions. Business analytics is a *process of transforming data into actions through analysis and insights in the context of organizational decision-making and problem-solving.* Business analytics has traditionally been supported by various tools such as Microsoft Excel and various Excel add-ins, commercial statistical software packages such as SAS or Minitab, and more-complex business intelligence suites that integrate data with analytical software.

Tools and techniques of business analytics are used across many areas in a wide variety of organizations to improve the management of customer relationships, financial and marketing activities, human capital, supply chains, and many other areas. Leading banks use analytics to predict and prevent credit fraud. Manufacturers use analytics for production planning, purchasing, and inventory management. Retailers use analytics to recommend products to customers and optimize marketing promotions. Pharmaceutical firms use it to get life-saving drugs to market more quickly. The leisure and vacation industries use analytics to analyze historical sales data, understand customer behavior, improve website design, and optimize schedules and bookings. Airlines and hotels use analytics to dynamically set prices over time to maximize revenue. Even sports teams are using business analytics to determine both game strategy and optimal ticket prices.

Top-performing organizations (those that outperform their competitors) are three times more likely to be sophisticated in their use of analytics than lower performers and are more likely to state that their use of analytics differentiates them from competitors. One of the emerging applications of analytics is helping businesses learn from social media and exploit social media data for strategic advantage (see Chapter 15). Using analytics, firms can integrate social media data with traditional data sources such as customer surveys, focus groups, and sales data; understand trends and customer perceptions of their products; and create informative reports to assist marketing managers and product designers.

3.5.1 Descriptive Analytics

Descriptive analytics describes what happened in the past. Descriptive analytics is the most commonly used and most well-understood type of analytics. Most businesses start with descriptive analytics—the use of data to understand past and current business performance and make informed decisions. These techniques categorize, characterize, consolidate, and classify data to convert it into useful information for the purposes of understanding and analyzing business performance. Descriptive analytics summarizes data into meaningful charts and reports, for example, about budgets, sales, revenues, or cost. This process allows managers to obtain standard and customized reports and then drill down into the data and make queries to understand the impact of an advertising campaign. Descriptive analytics also helps companies to classify customers into different segments, which enables them to develop specific marketing campaigns and advertising strategies. For instance, an enterprise manager might want to review business performance to find problems or areas of opportunity and identify patterns and trends in data.

Descriptive analytics involves several techniques such as

1. Visualizing and exploring data
2. Descriptive statistical measures
3. Probability distributions and data modeling
4. Sampling and estimation
5. Statistical inference

> Typical questions that descriptive analytics helps answer are
> "What was our revenue and profit last quarter?"
> "How much did the company sell in each region?"
> "How many and what types of complaints were addressed?"
> "Which factory has the lowest productivity?"

3.5.2 Predictive Analytics

Predictive analytics seeks to predict the future by examining historical data, detecting patterns or relationships in these data, and then extrapolating these relationships forward in time. Predictive analytics models are very popular in predicting the behavior of customers based on the past buying history and perhaps some demographic variables. They typically use multiple variables to predict a particular dependent variable. For example, a marketer might wish to predict the response of different customer segments to an advertising campaign, a T-shirt manufacturer might want to predict next season's demand for T-shirt of a specific color and size, or a commodity trader might wish to predict short-term movements in commodity prices. Predictive analytics can predict risk and find relationships in data not readily apparent with traditional analyses. Using advanced techniques, predictive analytics can help to detect hidden patterns in large quantities of data to segment and group data into coherent sets to predict behavior and detect trends. For instance, a bank manager might want to identify the most profitable customers or predict the chances that a loan applicant will default, or alert a credit-card customer to a potential fraudulent charge.

Predictive analytics involves several techniques such as

1. Trendlines and regression analysis
2. Forecasting techniques
3. Classification techniques using data mining
4. Modeling and analysis using spreadsheet
5. Monte Carlo simulation and risk analysis

> Predictive analytics helps to answer questions such as
> "What will happen if demand falls by 5% or if supplier prices go up 5%?"
> "What are the top 5 products contributing most to profitability?"
> "What do we expect to pay for fuel over the next several months?"
> "What is the risk of losing money in a new business venture?"

3.5.3 Prescriptive Analytics

Prescriptive analytics determine actions to take to make the future happen. Prescriptive analytics is used in many areas of business including operations, marketing, and finance. Many problems, such as aircraft or employee scheduling and supply chain design, for example, simply involve too many choices or alternatives for a human decision-maker to effectively consider. Randomized testing, in which a test group is compared to a control group with random assignment of subjects to each group, is a powerful method to establish cause. On comparison of the groups, if one is better than the other with statistical significance, the thing that's being tested in the test group should be prescribed. Prescriptive analytics uses optimization to identify the best alternatives to minimize or maximize some objective. The mathematical and statistical techniques of predictive analytics can also be combined with optimization to make decisions that take into account the uncertainty in the data. For instance, a manager might want to determine the best pricing and advertising strategy to maximize revenue, the optimal amount of cash to store in ATMs, or the best mix of investments in a retirement portfolio to manage risk.

Prescriptive analytics involves several techniques such as

1. Linear optimization
2. Integer optimization
3. Decision analysis

> Prescriptive analytics addresses questions such as
> "How much should we produce to maximize profit?"
> "What is the best way of shipping goods from our factories to minimize costs?"
> "What are the top 5 products that may contribute the most to profitability by increasing prices by 5% without effecting their respective demands?"
> "Should we change our plans if a natural disaster closes a supplier's factory: if so, by how much?"

3.6 Data Science Techniques

Doing data science means implementing flexible, scalable, extensible systems for data preparation, analysis, visualization, and modeling.

Many firms are moving away from internally owned, centralized computing systems toward distributed cloud-based services. Distributed hardware and software systems, including database systems, can be expanded more easily as the data management needs of organizations grow. Doing data science means being able to gather data from the full range of database systems, relational and nonrelational, commercial and open source. We employ database query and analysis tools, gathering information across distributed systems, collating information, creating contingency tables, and computing indices of relationship across variables of interest. We use information technology and database systems as far as they can take us, and then we do more, applying what we know about statistical inference and the modeling techniques of predictive analytics.

3.6.1 Database Systems

Relational databases have a row-and-column table structure, similar to a spreadsheet. We access and manipulate these data using structured query language (SQL). Because they are transaction-oriented with enforced data integrity, relational databases provide the foundation for sales order processing and financial accounting systems.

Nonrelational databases focus on availability and scalability. They may employ key-value, column-oriented, document-oriented, or graph structures. Some are designed for online or real-time applications, where fast response times are key. Others are well suited for massive storage and offline analysis, with map-reduce providing a key data aggregation tool.

3.6.2 Statistical Inference

Statistics are functions of sample data, and are more credible when samples are representative of the concerned population. Typically, large random samples, small standard errors, and narrow confidence intervals are preferred. Formal scientific method suggests that we construct theories and test those theories with sample data. The process involves drawing statistical inferences as point estimates, interval estimates, or tests of hypotheses about the population. Whatever the form of inference, we need sample data relating to questions of interest.

Classical and Bayesian statistics represent alternative approaches to inference, alternative ways of measuring uncertainty about the world.

1. Classical hypothesis testing involves making null hypotheses about population parameters and then rejecting or not rejecting those hypotheses based on sample data. Typical null hypotheses (as the word null would imply) states that there is no difference between proportions or groups, or no relationship between variables.

   To test a null hypothesis, we compute a special statistic called a test statistic along with its associated p-value. Assuming that the null hypothesis is true, we can derive the theoretical distribution of the test statistic. We obtain a p-value by referring the sample test statistic to this theoretical distribution. The p-value, itself a sample statistic, gives the probability of rejecting the null hypothesis under the assumption that it is true. Let us assume that the conditions for valid inference have been satisfied. Then, when we observe a very low *p*-value (0.05, 0.01, or 0.001, for instance), this indicates that either of the following two things must be true:

a. An event of very low probability has occurred under the assumption that the null hypothesis is true
b. The null hypothesis is false.

A low *p*-value leads us to reject the null hypothesis, and we say the research results are statistically significant. Some results are statistically significant and meaningful.

2. Bayesian approach treats parameters as random variables having probability distributions representing of our uncertainty about the world that can be reduced by collecting relevant sample data. Sample data and Bayes' theorem are used to derive posterior probability distributions for these same parameters, which, in turn, are used to obtain conditional probabilities.

3.6.3 Regression and Classification

Data science involves a search for meaningful relationships between variables. We look for relationships between pairs of continuous variables using scatter plots and correlation coefficients. We look for relationships between categorical variables using contingency tables and the methods of categorical data analysis. We use multivariate methods and multiway contingency tables to examine relationships among many variables. There are two main types of predictive models: regression and classification. Regression is prediction of a response of meaningful magnitude. Classification involves prediction of a class or category.

The most common form of regression is least-squares regression, also called ordinary least-squares regression, linear regression, or multiple regression. When we use ordinary least-squares regression, we estimate regression coefficients so that they minimize the sum of the squared residuals, where residuals are differences between the observed and predicted response values. For regression problems, we think of the response as taking any value along the real number line, although in practice, the response may take a limited number of distinct values. The important thing for regression is that the response values have meaningful magnitude.

Poisson regression is useful for counts. The response has meaningful magnitude but takes discrete (whole number) values with a minimum value of zero. Log-linear models for frequencies, grouped frequencies, and contingency tables for cross-classified observations fall within this domain.

Most traditional modeling techniques involve linear models or linear equations. The response or transformed response is on the left-hand side of the linear model. The linear predictor is on the right-hand side. The linear predictor involves explanatory variables and is linear in its parameters. That is, it involves the addition of coefficients or the multiplication of coefficients by the explanatory variables. The coefficients we fit to linear models represent estimates of population parameters.

Generalized linear models, as their name would imply, are generalizations of the classical linear regression model. They include models for choices and counts, including logistic regression, multinomial logit models, log-linear models, ordinal logistic models, Poisson regression, and survival data models. To introduce the theory behind these important models, we begin by reviewing the classical linear regression model. Generalized linear models help us model what are obvious nonlinear relationships between explanatory variables and responses.

Linear regression is a special generalized linear model. It has normally distributed responses and an identity link relating the expected value of responses to the linear predictor. Linear regression coefficients may be estimated by ordinary least squares. For other members of the family of generalized linear models, we use maximum likelihood estimation. With the classical linear model, we have analysis of variance and F-tests. With generalized linear models, we have analysis of deviance and likelihood ratio tests, which are asymptotic chi-square tests.

The method of logistic regression, although called "regression," is actually a classification method. It involves the prediction of a binary response. Ordinal and multinomial logit models extend logistic regression to problems involving more than two classes. Linear discriminant analysis is another classification method from the domain of traditional statistics.

3.6.4 Data Mining and Machine Learning

Machine learning refers to the methods or algorithms that are used as an alternative to traditional statistical methods. When we apply these methods in the analysis of data, these are termed *data mining*. Recommender systems, collaborative filtering, association rules, optimization methods based on heuristics, as well as a myriad of methods for regression, classification, and clustering are all examples of machine learning. With traditional statistics, we define the model specification prior to working with the data and also make assumptions about the population distributions from which the data have been drawn. Machine learning, however, is data-adaptive: model specification is defined by applying algorithms to the data. With machine learning, a few assumptions are made about the underlying distributions of the data.

Cluster analysis is referred to as unsupervised learning to distinguish it from classification, which is supervised learning, guided by known, coded values of a response variable or class. Association rules modeling, frequent item sets, social network analysis, link analysis, recommender systems, and many multivariate methods employed and data science represent unsupervised learning methods.

An important multivariate method, principal component analysis, draws on linear algebra and provides a way to reduce the number of measures or quantitative features we use to describe domains of interest. Long a staple of measurement experts and a prerequisite of factor analysis, principal component analysis has seen recent applications in latent semantic analysis, a technology for identifying important topics across a document corpus.

3.6.5 Data Visualization

Statistical summaries fail to tell the story of data. To understand data, we must look beyond data tables, regression coefficients, and the results of statistical tests. Visualization tools help us learn from data. We explore data, discover patterns in data, identify groups of observations that go together and unusual observations or outliers. Data visualization is critical to the work of data science in the areas of discovery (exploratory data analysis), diagnostics (statistical modeling), and design (presentation graphics).

R is particularly strong in data visualization.

3.6.6 Text Analytics

Text analytics is an important and growing area of predictive analytics. Text analytics draws from a variety of disciplines, including linguistics, communication and language arts, experimental psychology, political discourse analysis, journalism, computer science, and statistics.

The output from these processes such as crawling, scraping, and parsing is a document collection or text corpus. This document collection or corpus is in the natural language. The two primary ways of analyzing a text corpus are the bag of words approach and natural language processing. We parse the corpus further, creating commonly formatted expressions, indices, keys, and matrices that are more easily analyzed by computer. This additional parsing is sometimes referred to as text annotation. We extract features from the text, and then use those features in subsequent analyses. Natural language processing is more than a collection of individual words: Natural language conveys meaning.

Natural language documents contain paragraphs, paragraphs contain sentences, and sentences contain words. There are grammatical rules, with many ways to convey the same idea, along with exceptions to rules and rules about exceptions. Words used in combination and the rules of grammar comprise the linguistic foundations of text analytics. Linguists study natural language, the words and, the rules that we use to form meaningful utterances. "Generative grammar" is a general term for the rules; "morphology," "syntax," and "semantics" are more specific terms. Computer programs for natural language processing use linguistic rules to mimic human communication and convert natural language into structured text for further analysis.

A key step in text analysis is the creation of a terms-by-documents matrix (sometimes called a lexical table). The rows of this data matrix correspond to words or word stems from the document collection, and the columns correspond to documents in the collection. The entry in each cell of a terms-by-documents matrix could be a binary indicator for the presence or absence of a term in a document, a frequency count of the number of times a term is used in a document, or a weighted frequency indicating the importance of a term in a document. After being created, the terms-by-documents matrix is like an index, a mapping of document identifiers to terms (keywords or stems) and vice versa. For information retrieval systems or search engines, we might also retain information regarding the specific location of terms within documents.

> An alternative system might distinguish among parts of speech, permitting more sophisticated syntactic searches across documents.

Typical text analytics applications:

1. Spam filtering has long been a subject of interest as a classification problem, and many e-mail users have benefitted from the efficient algorithms that have evolved in this area. In the context of information retrieval, search engines classify documents as being relevant to the search or not. Useful modeling techniques for text classification include logistic regression, linear discriminant function analysis, and classification trees, and support vector machines. Various ensemble or committee methods may be employed.

2. Automatic text summarization is an area of research and development that can help with information management. Imagine a text processing program with the ability to read each document in a collection and summarize it in a sentence or two, perhaps quoting from the document itself. Today's search engines are providing partial analysis of documents prior to their being displayed. They create automated summaries for fast information retrieval. They recognize common text strings associated with user requests. These applications of text analysis comprise tools of information search that we take for granted as part of our daily lives.
3. Sentiment analysis is measurement-focused text analysis. Sometimes called opinion mining, one approach to sentiment analysis is to draw on positive and negative word sets (lexicons, dictionaries) that convey human emotion or feeling. These word sets are specific to the language being spoken and the context of application. Another approach to sentiment analysis is to work directly with text samples and human ratings of those samples, developing text scoring methods specific to the task at hand. The objective of sentiment analysis is to score text for affect, feelings, attitudes, or opinions. Sentiment analysis and text measurement in general hold promise as technologies for understanding consumer opinion and markets. Just as political researchers can learn from the words of the public, press, and politicians, business researchers can learn from the words of customers and competitors. There are customer service logs, telephone transcripts, and sales call reports, along with user group, listserv, and blog postings. And we have ubiquitous social media from which to build document collections for text and sentiment analysis.
4. Text measures flow from a measurement model (algorithms for scoring) and a dictionary, both defined by the researcher or analyst. A dictionary in this context is not a traditional dictionary; it is not an alphabetized list of words and their definitions. Rather, the dictionary used to construct text measures is a repository of word lists, such as synonyms and antonyms, positive and negative words, strong and weak sounding words, bipolar adjectives, parts of speech, and so on. The lists come from expert judgments about the meaning of words. A text measure assigns numbers to documents according to rules, with the rules being defined by the word lists, scoring algorithms, and modeling techniques in predictive analytics.

3.6.7 Time Series and Market Research Models

Sales and marketing data are organized by observational unit, time, and space. The observational unit is typically an economic agent (individual or firm) or a group of such agents as in an aggregate analysis. It is common to use geographical areas as a basis for aggregation. Alternatively, space (longitude and latitude) can be used directly in spatial data analyses. Time considerations are especially important in macroeconomic analysis, which focuses upon nationwide economic measures.

The term time-series regression refers to regression analysis in which the organizing unit of analysis is time. We look at relationships among economic measures organized in time. Much economic analysis concerns time-series regression. Special care must be taken to avoid what might be called spurious relationships, as many economic time series are correlated with one another because they depend upon underlying factors, such as population growth or seasonality. In time-series regression, we use standard linear regression methods. We check the residuals from our regression to ensure that they are not correlated in time. If they are correlated in time (autocorrelated), then we use a method such as generalized least squares as an alternative to ordinary least squares. That is, we incorporate an error data model as part of our modeling process. Longitudinal data analysis or panel data analysis is an example of a mixed data method with a focus on data organized by cross-sectional units and time.

Sales forecasts can build on the special structure of sales data as they are found in business. These are data organized by time and location, where location might refer to geographical regions or sales territories, stores, departments within stores, or product lines. Sales forecasts are a critical component of business planning and a first step in the budgeting process. Models and methods that provide accurate forecasts can be of great benefit to management. They help managers to understand the determinants of sales, including promotions, pricing, advertising, and distribution. They reveal competitive position and market share. There are many approaches to forecasting. Some are judgmental, relying on expert opinion or consensus. There are top-down and bottom-up forecasts, and various techniques for combining the views of experts. Other approaches depend on the analysis of past sales data.

1. Forecasting by time periods: These may be days, weeks, months, or whatever intervals make sense for the problem at hand. Time dependencies can be noted in the same manner as in traditional time-series models. Autoregressive terms are useful in many contexts. Time-construed covariates, such as day of the week or month of the year, can be added to provide additional predictive power. An analyst can work with time-series data, using past sales to predict future sales, noting overall trends and cyclical patterns in the data. Exponential smoothing, moving averages, and various regression and econometric methods may be used with time-series data.
2. Forecasting by location: Organizing data by location contributes to a model's predictive power. Location may itself be used as a factor in models. In addition, we can search for explanatory variables tied to location. With geographic regions, for example, we might include consumer and business demographic variables known to relate to sales.

Sales dollars per time period is the typical response variable of interest in sales forecasting studies. Alternative response variables include sales volume and time-to-sale. Related studies of market share require information about the sales of other firms in the same product category.

When we use the term time-series analysis, however, we are not talking about time-series regression. We are talking about methods that start by focusing on one economic measure at a time and its pattern across time. We look for trends, seasonality, and cycles in that individual time series. Then, after working with that single time series, we look at possible relationships with other time series. If we are concerned with forecasting or predicting the future, as we often are in predictive analytics, then we use methods of time-series analysis. Recently, there has been considerable interest in state space models for time series, which provide a convenient mechanism for incorporating regression components into dynamic time-series models.

There are myriad applications of time-series analysis in marketing, including marketing mix models and advertising research models. Along with sales forecasting, these fall under the general class of market response models. Marketing mix models look at the effects of price, promotion, and product placement in retail establishments. These are multiple time-series problems. Advertising research looks for cumulative effectiveness of advertising on brand and product awareness, as well as sales.

Much of this research employs defined measures such as "advertising stock," which attempt to convert advertising impressions or rating points to a single measure in time. The thinking is that messages are most influential immediately after being received, decline in influence with time, but do not decline completely until many units in time later. Viewers or listeners remember advertisements long after initial exposure to those advertisements. Another way of saying this is to note that there is a carry-over effect from one time period to the next. Needless to say, measurement and modeling on the subject of advertising effectiveness presents many challenges for the marketing data scientist.

3.7 Snapshot of Data Analysis Techniques and Tasks

There is no universally accepted best data analysis method; choosing particular data analytic tool(s) or some combination with traditional methods is entirely dependent on the particular application, and it requires human interaction to decide on the suitability of a blended approach. Depending on the desired outcome, several data analysis techniques with different goals may be applied successively to achieve a desired result. For example, to determine which customers are likely to buy a new product, a business analyst may need first to use cluster analysis to segment the customer database, and then apply regression analysis to predict buying behavior for each cluster.

Table 3.2 presents a selection of analysis techniques and tasks.

TABLE 3.2

Analysis Techniques versus Tasks

Data Analysis Techniques	Data Summarization	Segmentation	Classification	Prediction	Dependency Analysis
Descriptive and visualization	♦	♦			♦
Correlation analysis					♦
Cluster analysis		♦			
Discriminant analysis			♦		
Regression analysis				♦	♦
Neural networks		♦	♦	♦	
Case-based reasoning					♦
Decision trees			♦	♦	
Association rules					♦

A useful selection of data analysis techniques:

1. Descriptive and visualization include simple descriptive statistics such as the following:
   a. Averages and measures of variation
   b. Counts and percentages
   c. Cross-tabs and simple correlations

   They are useful for understanding the structure of the data. Visualization is primarily a discovery technique and is useful for interpreting large amounts of data; visualization tools include histograms, box plots, scatter diagrams, and multidimensional surface plots.
2. Correlation analysis measures the relationship between two variables. The resulting correlation coefficient shows if changes in one variable will result in changes in the other. When comparing the correlation between two variables, the goal is to see if a change in the independent variable will result in a change in the dependent variable. This information helps in understanding an independent variable's predictive abilities. Correlation findings, just as regression findings, can be useful in analyzing causal relationships, but they do not by themselves establish causal patterns.
3. Cluster analysis seeks to organize information about variables so that relatively homogeneous groups, or "clusters," can be formed. The clusters formed with this family of methods should be highly internally homogenous (members are similar to one another) and highly externally heterogeneous (members are not like members of other clusters).
4. Discriminant analysis is used to predict membership in two or more mutually exclusive groups from a set of predictors, when there is no natural ordering on the groups. Discriminant analysis can be seen as the inverse of a one-way multivariate analysis of variance (MANOVA) in that the levels of the independent variable (or factor) for MANOVA become the categories of the dependent variable for discriminant analysis, and the dependent variables of the MANOVA become the predictors for discriminant analysis.
5. Regression analysis is a statistical tool that uses the relation between two or more quantitative variables so that one variable (dependent variable) can be predicted from the other(s) (independent variables). But no matter how strong the statistical relations are between the variables, no cause-and-effect pattern is necessarily implied by the regression model. Regression analysis comes in many flavors, including simple linear, multiple linear, curvilinear, and multiple curvilinear regression models, as well as logistic regression, which is discussed next.
6. Neural networks (NN) are a class of systems modeled after the human brain. As the human brain consists of millions of neurons that are interconnected by synapses, NN are formed from large numbers of simulated neurons, connected to each other in a manner similar to brain neurons. As in the human brain, the strength of neuron interconnections may change (or be changed by the learning algorithm) in response to a presented stimulus or an obtained output, which enables the network to "learn."

   A disadvantage of NN is that building the initial neural network model can be especially time-intensive because input processing almost always means that raw data must be transformed. Variable screening and selection requires large amounts of the analysts' time and skill. Also, for the user without a technical background, figuring out how neural networks operate is far from obvious.

7. Case-based reasoning (CBR) is a technology that tries to solve a given problem by making direct use of past experiences and solutions. A case is usually a specific problem that was encountered and solved previously. Given a particular new problem, CBR examines the set of stored cases and finds similar ones. If similar cases exist, their solution is applied to the new problem, and the problem is added to the case base for future reference.

   A disadvantage of CBR is that the solutions included in the case database may not be optimal in any sense because they are limited to what was actually done in the past, not necessarily what should have been done under similar circumstances. Therefore, using them may simply perpetuate earlier mistakes.

8. Decision trees (DT) are like those used in decision analysis where each nonterminal node represents a test or decision on the data item considered. Depending on the outcome of the test, one chooses a certain branch. To classify a particular data item, one would start at the root node and follow the assertions down until a terminal node (or leaf) is reached; at that point, a decision is made. DT can also be interpreted as a special form of a rule set, characterized by their hierarchical organization of rules.

   A disadvantage of DT is that trees use up data very rapidly in the training process. They should never be used with small data sets. They are also highly sensitive to noise in the data, and they try to fit the data exactly, which is referred to as "overfitting." Overfitting means that the model depends too strongly on the details of the particular dataset used to create it. When a model suffers from overfitting, it is unlikely to be externally valid (i.e., it would not hold up when applied to a new data set).

9. Association rules (AR) are statements about relationships between the attributes of a known group of entities and one or more aspects of those entities that enable predictions to be made about aspects of other entities who are not in the group, but who possess the same attributes. More generally, AR state a statistical correlation between the occurrences of certain attributes in a data item, or between certain data items in a data set. The general form of an AR is X1 … Xn => Y [C, S] which means that the attributes X1, …, Xn predict Y with a confidence C and a significance S.

A useful selection of data analysis tasks:

1. Data Summarization gives the user an overview of the structure of the data and is generally carried out in the early stages of a project. This type of initial exploratory data analysis can help to understand the nature of the data and to find potential hypotheses for hidden information. Simple descriptive statistical and visualization techniques generally apply.
2. Segmentation separates the data into interesting and meaningful subgroups or classes. In this case, the analyst can hypothesize certain subgroups as relevant for the business question based on prior knowledge or based on the outcome of data description and summarization. Automatic clustering techniques can detect previously unsuspected and hidden structures in data that allow segmentation. Clustering techniques, visualization, and neural nets generally apply.

3. Classification assumes that a set of objects—characterized by some attributes or features—belongs to different classes. The class label is a discrete qualitative identifier—for example, large, medium, or small. The objective is to build classification models that assign the correct class to previously unseen and unlabeled objects. Classification models are mostly used for predictive modeling. Discriminant analysis, decision tree, rule induction methods, and genetic algorithms generally apply.
4. Prediction is very similar to classification. The difference is that in prediction, the class is not a qualitative discrete attribute but a continuous one. The goal of prediction is to find the numerical value of the target attribute for unseen objects; this problem type is also known as regression, and if the prediction deals with time-series data, then it is often called forecasting. Regression analysis, decision trees, and neural nets generally apply.
5. Dependency analysis deals with finding a model that describes significant dependencies (or associations) between data items or events. Dependencies can be used to predict the value of an item given information on other data items. Dependency analysis has close connections with classification and prediction because the dependencies are implicitly used for the formulation of predictive models. Correlation analysis, regression analysis, association rules, case-based reasoning, and visualization techniques generally apply.

3.8 Summary

The chapter presents the basics of analytics that are an essential component of big data computing. It introduces the intelligence maturity model consisting of the following six stages: data, communication, information, knowledge, intelligence, and wisdom. It discusses the nature, type, and scope of decisions followed by the decision-making process and the associated techniques of making decisions. The chapter then describes the various kinds of analytics like descriptive, predictive, and prescriptive analytics. The last part of the chapter provides an overview of the data science and related techniques.

4

Data Warehousing Basics

Decision support systems are interactive, computer-based information systems that provide data and analysis tools in order to assist managers at various levels of an organization in the process of decision making. Data warehouses have been developed and deployed as an integral part of decision support systems. Data warehouses are increasingly being used by many organizations in many sectors to improve their operations and to better achieve their objectives. For example, a data warehouse application can be used in an organization to analyze customers' behavior; by understanding its customers, the organization is then able to better address their specific needs and expectations.

Data warehouses are databases of a specific kind that periodically collect information about the activities being performed by an organization. This information is then accumulated over a period of time for the purpose of analyzing how it evolves and, thus, for discovering strategic information such as trends, correlations, and the like. A data warehouse is a database that allows the storage of high volumes of historical data required for analytical purposes. This data is extracted from operational databases, transformed into a coherent whole, and loaded into a data warehouse during an extraction-transformation-loading (ETL) process. Data in data warehouses can be dynamically manipulated using online analytical processing (OLAP) systems.

4.1 Relevant Database Concepts

Databases constitute the core component of today's information systems. A database is a shared collection of logically related data, and a description of that data, designed to meet the information needs and support the activities of an organization. A database is deployed on a database management system (DBMS), which is a software system that allows users to define, create, manipulate, and administer a database.

Designing a database system is a complex undertaking that is typically divided into the following four phases:

1. Requirements specification, which collects information about the users' needs with respect to the database system. A large number of approaches for requirements specification have been developed by both academia and practitioners. In general, these techniques help to elicit necessary and desirable system properties from prospective users and/or project managers, to homogenize requirements, and to assign priorities to them, that is, separate necessary from "nice to have" system properties. During this phase, active participation of users will increase customer satisfaction with the delivered system and avoid errors, which can be very expensive to correct if the subsequent phases have already been developed.
2. Conceptual design, which aims at building a user-oriented representation of the database that does not contain any implementation considerations. This is done by

using a conceptual model in order to identify the relevant entities, relationships, and attributes of the application domain. The entity–relationship model is one of the most often used conceptual models for designing database applications. Alternatively, object-oriented modeling techniques can also be applied, based on unified modeling language notation. Conceptual design can be performed using two different approaches, according to the complexity of the system and the developers' experience.

3. Logical design, which aims at translating the conceptual representation of the database obtained in the previous phase into a particular implementation model (or logical model) common to several DBMSs. Currently, the most common logical models are the relational model and the object relational model. Other logical models include the object-oriented model and the semi-structured (or XML-based) model. To ensure an adequate logical representation, suitable mapping rules must be specified. These ensure that the constructs included in the conceptual model can be transformed to the appropriate structures of the logical model.
4. Physical design, which aims at customizing the logical representation of the database obtained in the previous phase to an implementation in a particular DBMS platform. Common DBMSs include structured query language (SQL) Server, Oracle, DB2, and MySQL, among others.

4.1.1 Physical Database Design

The objective of physical database design is to specify how database records are stored, accessed, and related in order to ensure adequate performance of a database application. Physical database design thus requires one to know the specificities of the given application, in particular, the properties of the data and the usage patterns of the database. The latter involves analyzing the transactions or queries that are run frequently and will have a significant impact on performance, the transactions that are critical to the operations of the organization, and the periods of time during which there will be a high demand on the database (called the peak load). This information is used to identify the parts of the database that may cause performance problems.

There are a number of factors that can be used to measure the performance of database applications. Transaction throughput is the number of transactions that can be processed in a given time interval. In some systems, such as electronic payment systems, a high transaction throughput is critical. Response time is the elapsed time for the completion of a single transaction. Minimizing response time is essential from the user's point of view.

Finally, disk storage is the amount of disk space required to store the database files. However, a compromise usually has to be made among these factors. From a general perspective, this compromise implies the following factors:

1. Space–time trade-off: It is often possible to reduce the time taken to perform an operation by using more space, and vice versa. For example, using a compression algorithm allows one to reduce the space occupied by a large file but implies extra time for the decompression process.
2. Query–update trade-off: Access to data can be made more efficient by imposing some structure upon it. However, the more elaborate the structure, the more time is taken to build it and to maintain it when its contents change. For example, sorting the records of a file according to a key field allows them to be located more easily but there is a greater overhead upon insertions.

Further, once an initial physical design has been implemented, it is necessary to monitor the system and to tune it as a result of the observed performance and any changes in requirements. Many DBMSs provide utilities to monitor and tune the operations of the system. As the functionality provided by current DBMSs varies widely, physical design requires one to know the various techniques for storing and finding data that are implemented in the particular DBMS that will be used.

4.2 Data Warehouse

Organizations in all sectors are being required to improve their decision-making processes in order to maintain their competitive advantage. Traditional database systems like the ones studied in Chapter 2 do not satisfy the requirements of data analysis. They are designed and tuned to support the daily operations of an organization, and their primary concern is to ensure fast, concurrent access to data. This requires transaction processing and concurrency control capabilities, as well as recovery techniques that guarantee data consistency. These systems are known as operational databases or online transaction processing (OLTP) systems. The OLTP paradigm is focused on transactions. The OLTP paradigm is focused on transactions.

In a typical database example, a simple transaction could involve entering a new order, reserving the products ordered, and, if the reorder point has been reached, issuing a purchase order for the required products. Eventually, a user may want to know the status of a given order. If a database is indexed following one of the techniques described in the previous chapter, a typical OLTP query like the above would require accessing only a few records of the database (and normally will return a few tuples). Since OLTP systems must support heavy transaction loads, their design should prevent update anomalies, and thus, OLTP databases are highly normalized. But, they perform poorly when executing complex queries that need to join many relational tables together or to aggregate large volumes of data. Besides, typical operational databases contain detailed data and do not include historical data.

The above needs calls for a new paradigm specifically oriented to analyze the data in organizational databases to support decision making. This paradigm is called online analytical processing (OLAP). This paradigm is focused on queries, in particular, analytical queries. OLAP-oriented databases should support a heavy query load. Typical OLAP queries over the Northwind database would ask, for example, for the total sales amount by product and by customer or for the most ordered products by customer. These kinds of queries involve aggregation, and thus, processing them will require, most of the time, traversing all the records in a database table. Indexing techniques aimed at OLTP are not efficient in this case: new indexing and query optimization techniques are required for OLAP. It is easy to see that normalization is not good for these queries, since it partitions the database into many tables. Reconstructing the data would require a high number of joins.

Therefore, the need for a different database model to support OLAP was clear and led to the notion of data warehouses, which are (usually) large repositories that consolidate data from different sources (internal and external to the organization), are updated off-line (although this is not always the case in modern data warehouse systems), and follow the multidimensional data model. Being dedicated analysis databases, data warehouses can be designed and optimized to efficiently support OLAP queries. In addition, data warehouses are also used to support other kinds of analysis tasks, like reporting, data mining, and statistical analysis. Table 4.1 gives a comparison between OLTP and OLAP systems.

TABLE 4.1

Comparison between OLTP and OLAP Systems

Characteristic	OLTP	OLAP
Volatility	Dynamic data	Static data
Timeliness	Current data only	Current and historical data
Time dimension	Implicit and current	Explicit and variant
Granularity	Detailed data	Aggregated and consolidated data
Updating	Continuous and irregular	Periodic and regular
Activities	Repetitive	Unpredictable
Flexibility	Low	High
Performance	High, few seconds per query	May be low for complex queries
Users	Employees	Knowledge workers
Functions	Operational	Analytical
Purpose of use	Transactions	Complex queries and decision support
Priority	High performance	High flexibility
Metrics	Transaction rate	Effective response
Size	Megabytes to gigabytes	Gigabytes to terabytes

A data warehouse is usually defined as a collection of subject-oriented, integrated, nonvolatile, and time-varying data to support management decisions. Thus, salient features of a data warehouse are as follows:

- Subject-oriented means that a data warehouse targets one or several subjects of analysis according to the analytical requirements of managers at various levels of the decision-making process. For example, a data warehouse in a retail company may contain data for the analysis of the purchase, inventory, and sales of products.
- Integrated expresses the fact that the contents of a data warehouse result from the integration of data from various operational and external systems.
- Nonvolatile indicates that a data warehouse accumulates data from operational systems for a long period of time. Thus, data modification and removal are not allowed in data warehouses: The only operation allowed is the purging of obsolete data that is no longer needed.
- Time-varying underlines that a data warehouse keeps track of how its data has evolved over time; for instance, it may allow one to know the evolution of sales or inventory over the last several months or years. Table 4.2 gives a comparison between operational systems and data warehouses.

Operational databases are typically designed using a conceptual model, such as the entity–relationship (ER) model, and normalization for optimizing the corresponding relational schema. These paradigms are not well suited for designing data warehouse applications. Data warehouses must be modelled in a way that ensures a better understanding of the data for analysis purposes and gives better performance for the complex queries needed for typical analysis tasks. In order to meet these expectations, a multidimensional model has been proposed.

TABLE 4.2

Comparison between Operational Databases and Data Warehouses

Description	Operational Databases	Data Warehouses
User type	Operators, office employees	Managers, high-ranking executives
Usage	Predictable, repetitive	Ad hoc, nonstructured
Data content	Current, detailed data	Historical, summarized data
Data organization	According to operational needs	According to the analysis problem
Data structures	Optimized for small transactions	Optimized for complex queries
Access frequency	High	From medium to low
Access type	Read, update, delete, insert	Read, append only
Number of records per access	Few	Many
Response time	Short	Can be long
Concurrency level	High	Low
Lock utilization	Necessary	Not necessary
Update frequency	High	None
Data redundancy	Low (normalized tables)	High (unnormalized tables)
Data modeling	ER model	Multidimensional model
Modeling and implementation	Entire system	Incremental

4.2.1 Multidimensional Model

Data warehouse and OLAP systems rely on a multidimensional model that includes measures, dimensions, and hierarchies:

- Measures are usually numeric values that are used for quantitative evaluation of aspects of an organization
- Dimensions provide various analysis perspectives
- Hierarchies allow measures to be analyzed at various levels of detail

The multidimensional model views data as consisting of facts linked to several dimensions:

1. Fact represents a focus of analysis (e.g., analysis of sales in stores) and typically includes attributes called measures.
2. Measures are usually numeric values that allow quantitative evaluation of various aspects of an organization to be performed. For example, measures such as the amount or quantity of sales might help to analyze sales activities in various stores.
3. Dimensions are used to see the measures from different perspectives. For example, a time dimension can be used for analyzing changes in sales over various periods of time, whereas a location dimension can be used to analyze sales according to the geographic distribution of stores. Users may combine several different analysis perspectives (i.e., dimensions) according to their needs. For example, a user may require information about sales of computer accessories (the product dimension) in June 2016 (the time dimension) in all store locations (the store dimension). Dimensions typically include attributes that form hierarchies, which allow decision-making users to explore measures at various levels of detail. Examples of hierarchies are month–quarter–year in the time dimension and city–state–country in the location dimension.

4. Hierarchies allow measures to be analyzed at various levels of detail; when a hierarchy is traversed, aggregation of measures takes place. For example, moving in a hierarchy from a month level to a year level will yield aggregated values of sales for the various years.

4.2.1.1 Data Cube

A data cube is defined by dimensions and facts. Dimensions are various perspectives that are used to analyze the data. For example, the data cube in Figure 4.1 is used to analyze sales figures and has three dimensions: Store, Time, and Product. Instances of a dimension are called members. For example, Mumbai, Delhi, Kolkatta, and Chennai are members of the Store dimension. Dimensions have associated attributes describing the dimension. For example, the Product dimension could contain attributes such as Product Number, Product Name, Description, and Size, which are not shown in the figure. However, the cells of a data cube, or facts, have associated with them numeric values, called measures. These measures allow quantitative evaluation of various aspects of the analysis problem at hand to be performed. For example, the numbers shown in the data cube in Figure 4.1 represent a measure amount, indicating the total sales amount specified in, for instance, one million Indian Rupees. A data cube typically contains several measures. For example, another measure, not shown in the cube in Figure 4.1, could be quantity, representing the number of units sold.

A data cube may be sparse or dense depending on whether it has measures associated with each combination of dimension values. In the case of Figure 4.1, this depends on whether all products are sold in all stores throughout the period of time considered. The figure shows two empty cells for the sales in Delhi of books and Indicas during the second and the third quarter, respectively. In real-world applications, it is common to have sparse cubes. Adequately managing sparsity allows the required storage space to be reduced and improves query performance.

4.2.1.2 Online Analytical Processing

OLAP analyses are based on hierarchies of concepts to consolidate the data and to create logical views along the dimensions of a data warehouse. A concept hierarchy defines a set of maps from a lower level of concepts to a higher level. For example, the {location} dimension may originate a totally ordered hierarchy developing along the {address, municipality, province, and country} relationship. The temporal dimension, however, originates a partially ordered hierarchy, also shown in Figure 4.2.

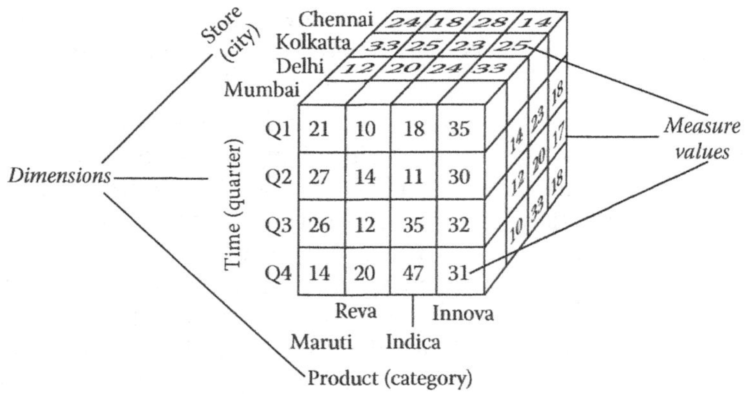

FIGURE 4.1
Cube for sales data having dimensions store, time, and product and a measure amount.

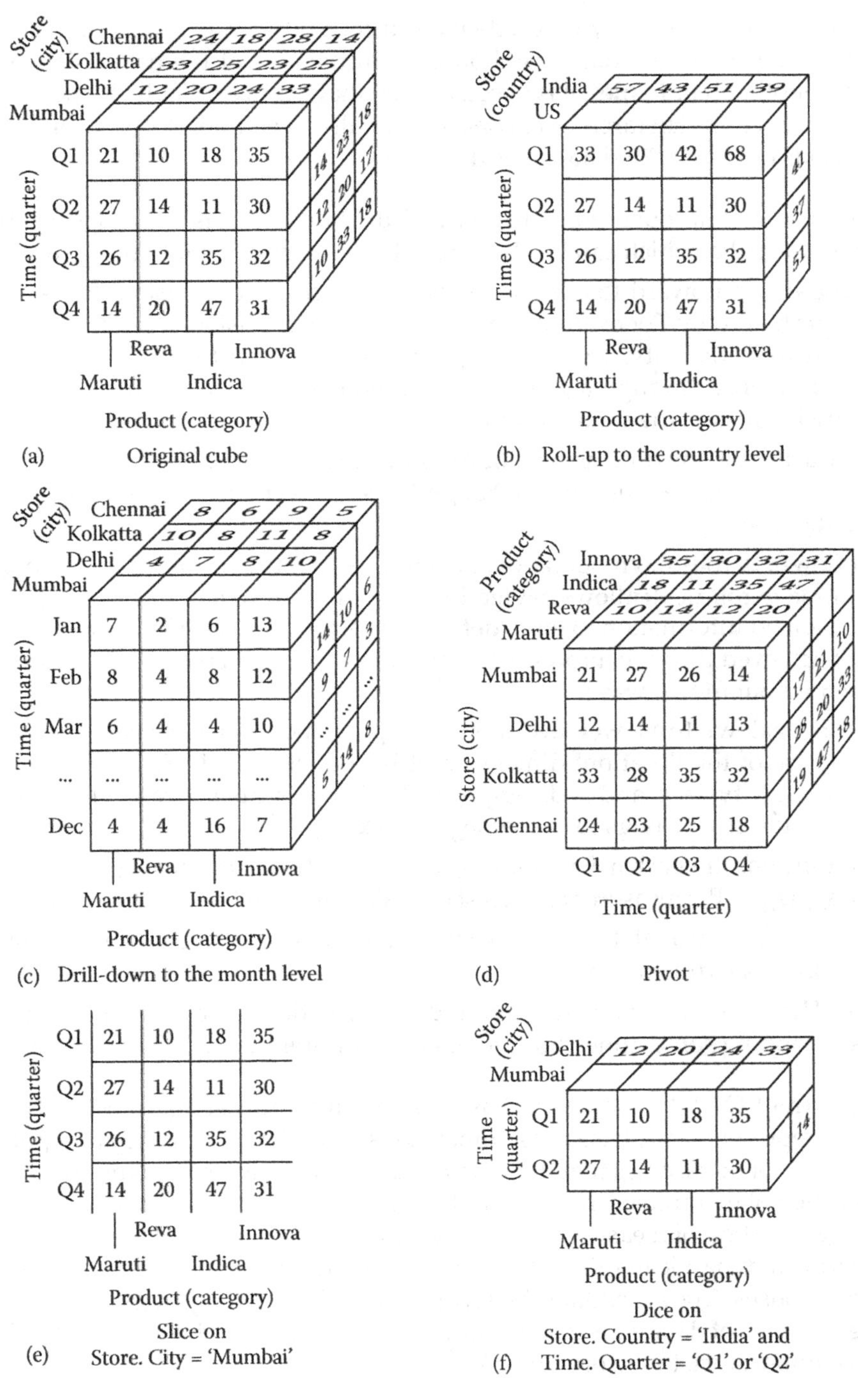

FIGURE 4.2
OLAP Operations. (a) Original Cube (b) Roll-up to the Country level (c) Drill down to the month level (d) Piv (e) Slice on Store.City = 'Mumbai' (f) Dice on Store.Country = 'US' and Time.Quarter = 'Q1' or 'Q2'.

Specific hierarchy types may be predefined in the software platform used for the creation and management of a data warehouse, as in the case of the dimensions shown in Figure 4.2. For other hierarchies, it is necessary for analysts to explicitly define the relationships among concepts. Hierarchies of concepts are also used to perform several visualization operations dealing with data cubes in a data warehouse.

1. Roll-up: A roll-up operation, also termed drill-up, consists of an aggregation of data in the cube, which can be obtained alternatively in the following two ways.

   Proceeding upward to a higher level along a single dimension defined over a concepts hierarchy. For example, for the {location} dimension, it is possible to move upward from the {city} level to the {province} level and to consolidate the measures of interest through a group-by conditioned sum over all records, whereby the city belongs to the same province.

   Reducing by one dimension. For example, the removal of the {time} dimension leads to consolidated measures through the sum over all time periods existing in the data cube.

2. Roll-down: A roll-down operation, also referred to as drill-down, is the opposite operation to roll-up. It allows navigation through a data cube from aggregated and consolidated information to more detailed information. The effect is to reverse the result achieved through a roll-up operation. A drill-down operation can therefore be carried out in two ways.

   Shifting down to a lower level along a single dimension hierarchy. For example, in the case of the {location} dimension, it is possible to shift from the {province} level to the {city} level and to disaggregate the measures of interest over all records, whereby the city belongs to the same province.

   Adding one dimension. For example, the introduction of the {time} dimension leads to disaggregate the measures of interest over all time periods existing in a data cube.

3. Slice and dice: Through the slice operation, the value of an attribute is selected and fixed along one dimension.
4. Pivot: The pivot operation, also referred to as rotation, produces a rotation of the axes, swapping some dimensions to obtain a different view of a data cube.

Although current OLAP systems are based on a multidimensional model, that is, they allow one to represent facts, measures, dimensions, and hierarchies, they are quite restrictive in the types of hierarchies that they can manage. This in an important drawback, since the specification of hierarchies in OLAP systems is important if one is to be able to perform automatic aggregation of measures while traversing hierarchies. OLAP systems allow end users to perform dynamic manipulation and automatic aggregation of the data contained in data warehouses. They facilitate the formulation of complex queries that may involve very large amounts of data. This data is examined and aggregated in order to find patterns or trends of importance to the organization.

OLAP systems have typically been implemented using the following:

1. Relational OLAP (ROLAP)—stores data in a relational database management system
2. Multidimensional OLAP (MOLAP)—uses vendor-specific array data structure
3. Hybrid OLAP (HOLAP) systems—are a combination of ROLAP and MOLAP, for instance, using ROLAP for detailed fact data and MOLAP for aggregated data

4.2.1.3 Relational Schemas

The multidimensional model is usually represented by relational tables organized in specialized structures called star schemas and snowflake schemas. These relational schemas relate a fact table to several dimension tables. Star schemas use a unique table for each dimension, even in the presence of hierarchies, which yields denormalized dimension tables. However, snowflake schemas use normalized tables for dimensions and their hierarchies. These are described as follows:

1. Star schema: Star schema has only one central fact table, and a set of dimension tables, one for each dimension. An example is given in Figure 4.3, where the fact table is depicted in gray and the dimension tables are depicted in white. As shown in the figure, referential integrity constraints are specified between the fact table and each of the dimension tables. In a star schema, the dimension tables may contain redundancy, especially in the presence of hierarchies: The tables are not necessarily normalized. This is the case for the dimensions Product and Store in Figure 4.3. Indeed, all products belonging to the same category will have redundant information for the attributes describing the category and the department. The situation is similar for the dimension Store with respect to the attributes describing the city and the state.
2. Snowflake schema: A snowflake schema avoids the redundancy of star schemas by normalizing the dimension tables. Therefore, a dimension is represented by several tables related by referential integrity constraints. In addition, as in the case of star schemas, referential integrity constraints also relate the fact table and the dimension tables at the finest level of detail. An example of a snowflake schema is given in Figure 4.4, where the dimensions Product and Store are represented by normalized tables. Normalized tables are easy to maintain and allow storage space to be

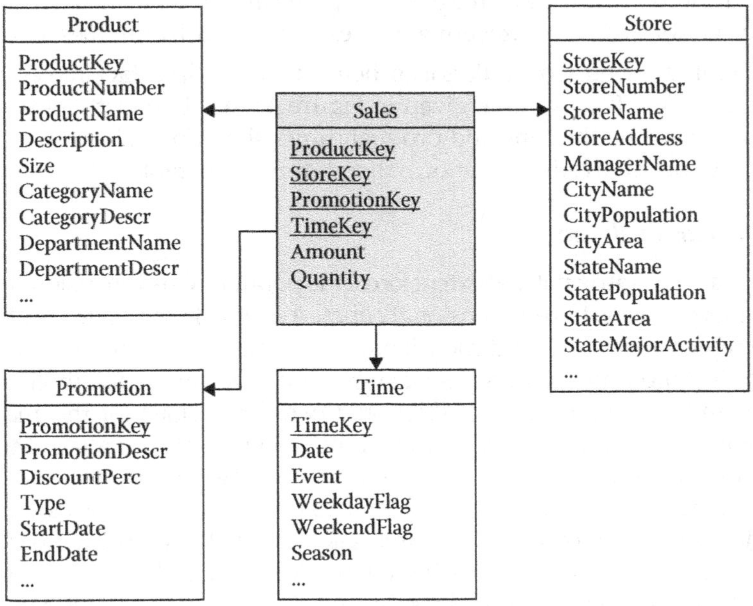

FIGURE 4.3
Example of a star schema.

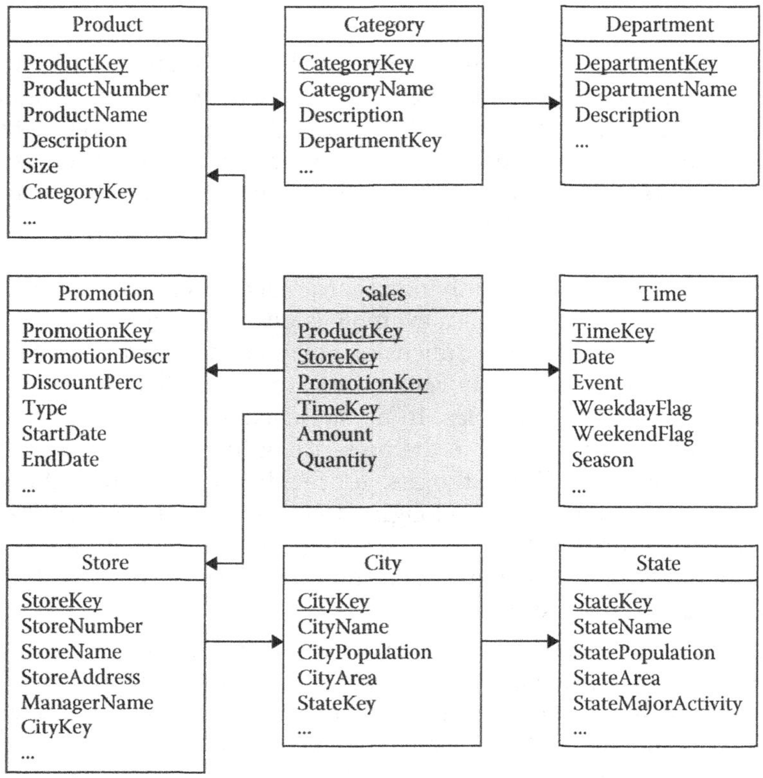

FIGURE 4.4
Example of a snowflake schema.

optimized. However, a disadvantage is that performance is affected since more joins need to be performed when executing queries that require hierarchies to be traversed.

3. Constellation schema Constellation schema has multiple fact tables that share dimension tables: The example given in Figure 4.5 has two fact tables—sales and purchases—sharing the time and product dimension. Constellation schemas may include both normalized and denormalized dimension tables.

4.2.1.4 Multidimensional Cube

Multidimensional cubes are a natural extension of the popular two-dimensional spreadsheets, which can be interpreted as two-dimensional cubes. A fact table connected with n dimension tables may be represented by an n-dimensional data cube where each axis corresponds to a dimension. For instance, consider a sales fact table developed along the three dimensions of {time, product, and city}. Suppose, we select only two dimensions for the analysis, such as {time and product}, having preset the city attribute along the three values {Mumbai, Delhi, and Kolkata}. In this way, we obtain the three two-dimensional tables in which the rows correspond to quarters of a year and the columns to products. The cube shown in Figure 4.1 is a three-dimensional illustration of the same sales fact table. Atomic data are represented by 36 cells that can be obtained by crossing all possible values along the three dimensions: time {Q1, Q2, Q3, and Q4}, city {Mumbai, Delhi, and Kolkata} and product {Reva, Indica, and Innova}. These atomic cells can be supplemented by 44 cells corresponding to the summary values obtained through consolidation along one or more dimensions.

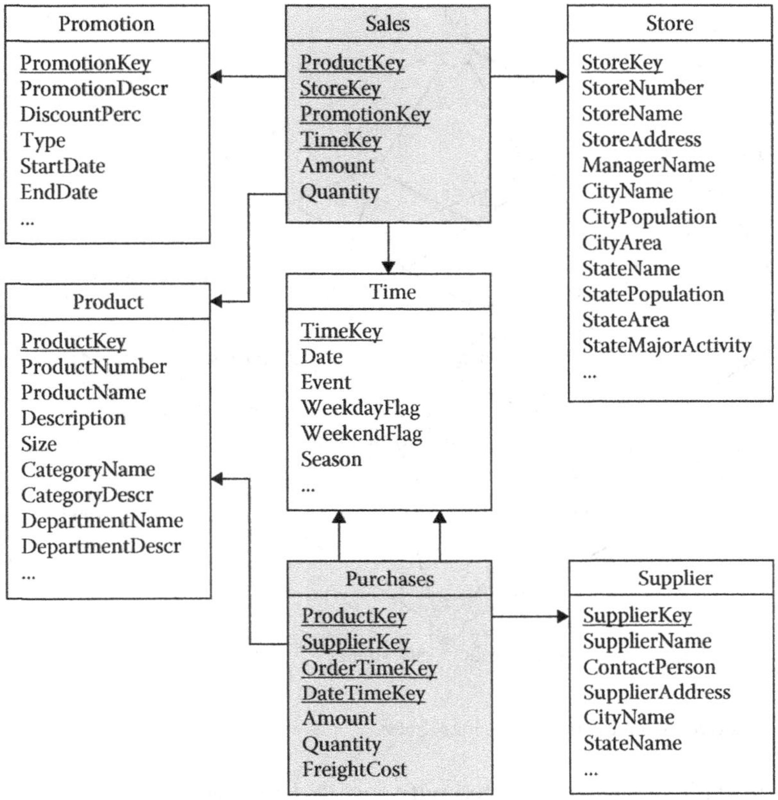

FIGURE 4.5
Example of a constellation schema.

If the sales fact table also contains a fourth dimension represented by the suppliers, the corresponding four-dimensional space cannot be represented graphically; however, this can be achieved by showing four logical views composed of three-dimensional cubes, called cuboids, inside the four-dimensional cube, by fixing the values of one dimension. More generally, starting from a fact table linked to n dimension tables, it is possible to obtain a lattice of cuboids, each of them corresponding to a different level of consolidation along one or more dimensions. This type of aggregation is equivalent in SQL to a query sum derived from a group-by condition. Figure 4.6 illustrates the lattice composed by the cuboids obtained from the data cube defined along the four dimensions {time, product, city, and supplier}.

OLAP analyses developed by knowledge workers may need to access the information associated with several cuboids, based on the specific queries and analyses being carried out. In order to guarantee adequate response time, it might be useful to design a data warehouse where all (or at least a large portion of) values of the measures of interest associated with all possible cuboids are precalculated. This approach is termed full materialization of the information relative to the data cubes.

Observe that where hierarchies of concepts are missing, it is possible to form 2^n distinct cuboids from all possible combinations of n dimensions. The existence of hierarchies along different dimensions makes the number of distinct cuboids even greater. If L_i denotes the

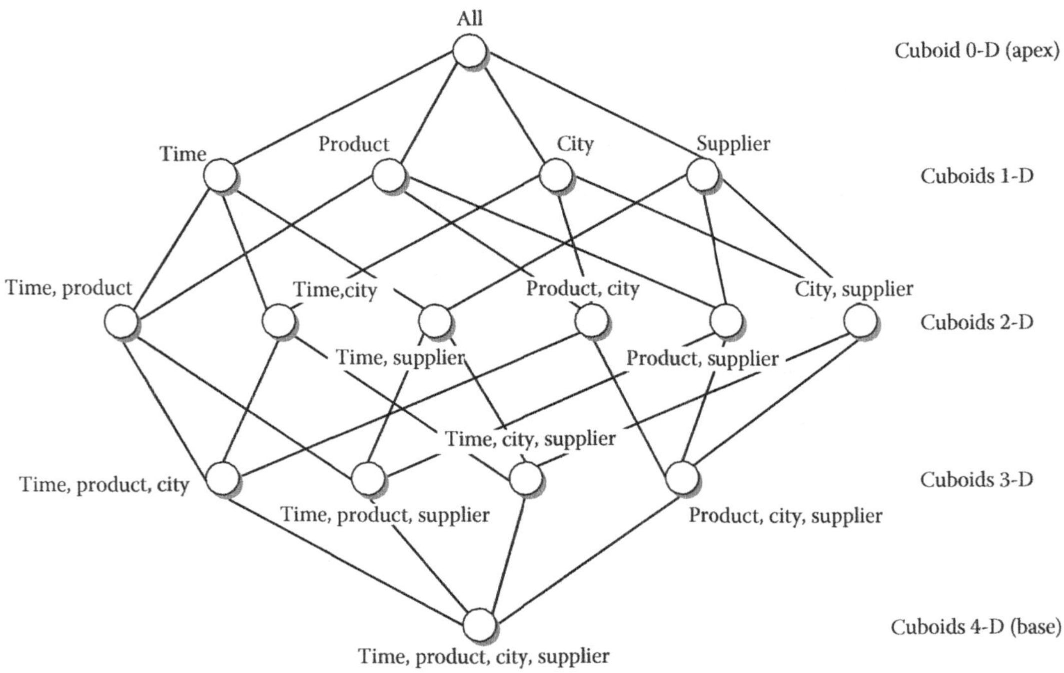

FIGURE 4.6
Lattice of cuboids derived from a four-dimensional cube.

number of hierarchical levels associated with the ith dimension, for an n-dimensional data cube, it is possible to calculate the full number of cuboids, given by the following:

$$T = \prod_{i=1}^{n} (L_i + 1)$$

For example, if a data cube includes five dimensions, and if each of these dimensions includes three hierarchical levels, the number of cuboids is equal to

$$4^5 = 2^{10} \approx 10^3$$

It is clear that the full materialization of the cuboids for all the cubes associated with the fact tables of a data warehouse would impose storage requirements that could be hardly sustained over time, considering the rate at which new records or data get generated.

For all of the above reasons, it is necessary to strike a balance between the need for fast access to information, which would suggest the full materialization of the cuboids, and the need to keep memory use within reasonable limits. As a consequence, preventive materialization should be carried out only for those cuboids that are most frequently accessed, while for the others the computation should be carried out on demand only when actual queries requesting the associated information are performed. This latter approach is referred to as partial materialization of the information relative to the data cubes (See Subsection 4.6, "Data Warehouse Architecture Challenges").

4.3 Data Warehouse Architecture

4.3.1 Architecture Tiers

A typical architecture of a data warehouse system, which consist of several tiers:

4.3.1.1 Back-End Tier

Back-end tier is composed of extraction-transformation-loading (ETL) tools, used to feed data in from operational databases and other data sources, which can be internal or external, and a data staging area, which is an intermediate database where all the data integration and transformation processes are run prior to the loading of the data into the data warehouse.

In the back-end tier, the process commonly known as extraction-transformation-loading is performed. As the name indicates, it is a three-step process as follows:

- Extraction gathers data from multiple, heterogeneous data sources. These sources may be operational databases but may also be files in various formats; they may be internal to the organization or external to it. In order to solve interoperability problems, data are extracted whenever possible using application program interfaces such as open database connection (ODBC), open linking and embedding for databases (OLEDB), and Java database connectivity (JDBC).
- Transformation modifies the data from the format of the data sources to the warehouse format. This includes several aspects: cleaning, which removes errors and inconsistencies in the data and converts these into a standardized format; integration, which reconciles data from different data sources, both at the schema and at the data level; and aggregation, which summarizes the data obtained from data sources according to the level of detail, or granularity, of the data warehouse.
- Loading feeds the data warehouse with the transformed data. This also includes refreshing the data warehouse, that is, propagating updates from the data sources to the data warehouse at a specified frequency in order to provide up-to-date data for the decision-making process. Depending on organizational policies, the refresh frequency may vary from monthly to several times a day, or even to nearly in real time.

The ETL process usually requires a data staging area, that is, a database in which the data extracted from the sources undergoes successive modifications to eventually be ready to be loaded into the data warehouse.

4.3.1.2 Data Warehouse Tier

Data warehouse tier is composed of an enterprise data warehouse and/or several data marts, and a metadata repository storing information about the data warehouse and its contents.

The data warehouse tier in Figure 4.7 depicts an enterprise data warehouse and several data marts.

1. Enterprise data warehouse is a centralized data warehouse that encompasses all functional or departmental areas in an organization.
2. Data mart is a specialized data warehouse targeted toward a particular functional area or user group in an organization. A data mart can be seen as a small, local data warehouse. The data in a data mart can be either derived from an enterprise data warehouse or collected directly from data sources.

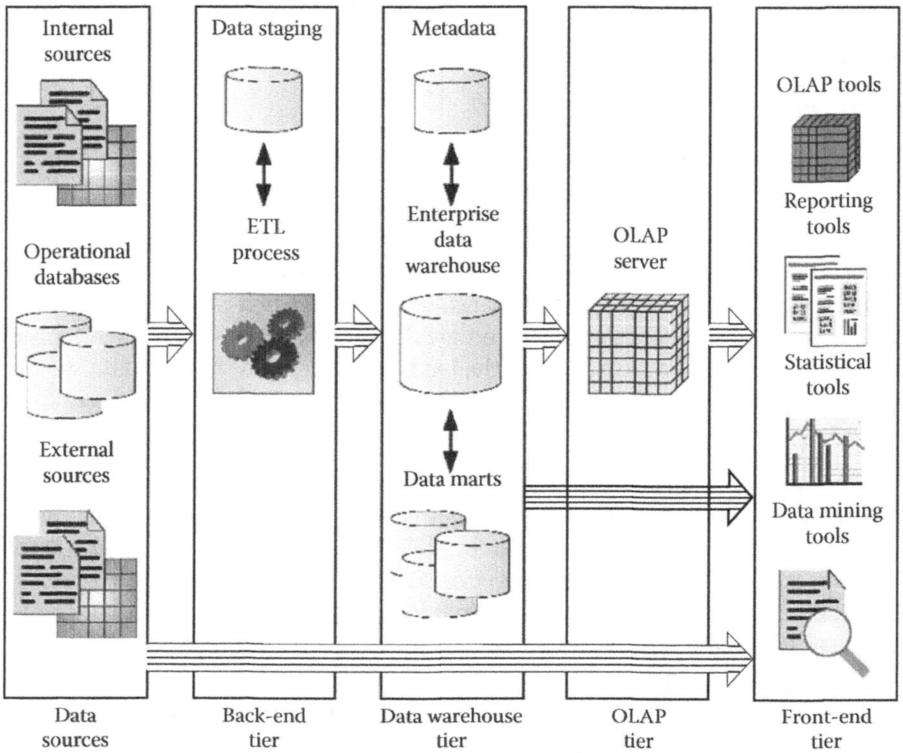

FIGURE 4.7
Reference data warehouse architecture.

Another component of the data warehouse tier is the metadata repository. Metadata can be defined as *data about data.*

1. Business metadata describes the meaning (or semantics) of the data, and organizational rules, policies, and constraints related to the data.
2. Technical metadata describes how data is structured and stored in a computer system, and the applications and processes that manipulate the data.

In the data warehouse context, technical metadata can be of various natures, describing the data warehouse system, the source systems, and the ETL process. In particular, the metadata repository may contain information such as the following:

- Metadata describing the structure of the data warehouse and the data marts, both at the logical level (which includes the facts, dimensions, hierarchies and derived data definitions) and at the physical level (such as indexes, partitions, and replication). In addition, it contains security information (user authorization and access control) and monitoring information (such as usage statistics, error reports, and audit trails).
- Metadata describing the data sources, including their schemas (at the conceptual, logical, and/or physical levels), and descriptive information such as ownership, update frequencies, legal limitations, and access methods.

- Metadata describing the ETL process, including data lineage (i.e., tracing warehouse data back to the source data from which it was derived), data extraction, cleaning, transformation rules and defaults, data refresh and purging rules, and algorithms for summarization.

4.3.1.3 OLAP Tier

OLAP tier is an OLAP server that supports multidimensional data and operations.

The OLAP tier in the architecture of Figure 4.7 is composed of an OLAP server that presents business users with multidimensional data from data warehouses or data marts. As already said, there are several types of OLAP servers depending on the underlying implementation model: ROLAP, MOLAP, and HOLAP.

4.3.1.4 Front-End Tier

Front-end tier deals with data analysis and visualization. It contains client tools such as OLAP tools, reporting tools, statistical tools, and data-mining tools.

The front-end tier in Figure 4.7 contains the client tools that allow users to exploit the contents of the data warehouse. Typical client tools include the following:

- OLAP tools allow interactive exploration and manipulation of the warehouse data in order to find patterns or trends of importance to the organization. They facilitate the formulation of complex queries that may involve large amounts of data. These queries are called ad hoc queries, since the system has no prior knowledge about them.
- Reporting tools enable the production, delivery, and management of reports, which can be paper-based reports or interactive-, web-based reports. Reports use predefined queries, that is, queries asking for specific information in a specific format that are performed on a regular basis.
- Statistical tools are used to analyze and visualize the cube data using statistical methods.
- Data-mining tools allow users to analyze data in order to discover valuable knowledge such as patterns and trends; they also allow predictions to be made on the basis of current data.

4.4 Data Warehouse 1.0

4.4.1 Inmon's Information Factory

Information factory is a model conceived and designed by Bill Inmon. It uses a data modeling approach aligned with the third normal form (3NF) where the data is acquired at its closest form to the source, and subsequent layers are added to the architecture to support analytics, reporting, and other requirements.

In the information factory architecture, the data warehouse is built in a top-down model, starting with multiple source systems across the enterprise sending data to the centralized data warehouse, where a staging area collects the data, and the data quality and cleansing rules are applied. The preprocessed data is finally transformed and loaded to the data warehouse. The 3NF of the data model enables storing the data with minimal transformations into the data warehouse. After loading the data warehouse, depending on the needs of the business intelligence and analytical applications, there are several virtual layers built with views and aggregate tables that can be accessed by the applications. In most cases, a separate data mart is deployed to create further data transformations.

Advantages and disadvantages of information factory approach:

1. Advantages:
    a. Provides an enterprise view of the data
    b. Has centralized architecture
    c. Has central rules and control
    d. Refresh of data happens at one location
    e. Has extremely high performance
    f. Can build in multiple steps
2. Disadvantages:
    a. High risk of failure
    b. Data quality can stall processing data to the data warehouse
    c. Expensive to maintain
    d. Needs more scalable infrastructure

4.4.2 Kimbal's Bus Architecture

Kimball's bus architecture is based on a set of tightly integrated data marts that are based on a dimensional data model approach. The data model allows business to define and build data marts for each line of business and then link the diverse data marts by aligning the common set of dimensions.

This architecture builds a data warehouse from the bottom up. In this technique, we build multiple data marts oriented per subject and join them together using the common bus. The bus is the most common data elements that are shared across the data marts. For instance, customer data is used in sales and call center areas; there will be two distinct data marts—one for sales and one for call center. Using the bus architecture, we can create a data warehouse by consolidating the data marts in a virtual layer. In this architecture, the data marts are based on a dimensional model of dimensions and facts.

Advantages and disadvantages of data mart bus architecture approach:

1. Advantages:
    a. Faster implementation of multiple manageable data marts
    b. Incremental approach to build most important or complex data marts first
    c. Can be deployed in smaller footprint of infrastructure
    d. Simple design at the data mart level
    e. Less risk of failure
2. Disadvantages:
    a. A data mart cannot see outside of its subject area of focus
    b. Needs all requirements to be completed before the start of the project

c. Difficult to manage operational workflows for complex business intelligence requirements
d. Redundant data architecture can become expensive

Shared-everything architecture is an impediment irrespective of whether you design a top-down architecture (Inmon's information factory) or bottom-up architecture (Kimbal's bus architecture).

4.5 Data Warehouse 2.0

The second generation of data warehouses has been designed on more scalable and flexible architecture models, yet in compliance with Codd's rules.

4.5.1 Inmon's DW 2.0

The architecture of DW 2.0 has to address three distinct components:

1. Data architecture—based on information life cycle
2. Infrastructure—based on data architecture and life cycle
3. Unstructured data—new content of text, images, e-mails, and more

Characteristics of DW 2.0 are as follows:

1. Data are divided into four distinct layers, based on the type of data and the business requirements for the data. This concept is similar to information life-cycle management, but extends the metadata layer associated with data across the following different layers:
   a. Interactive sector very current data (e.g., transaction data).
   b. Integrated sector integrated data (e.g., current data that are relative to the business needs, including hourly, daily, or near real time).
   c. Near line sector integrated history (e.g., data older than three to 5 years from the integrated sector).
   d. Archival sector archived data from near line.
2. Metadata is stored in each layer.
3. Each layer has a corresponding unstructured data component.
4. Each layer can be created on different platforms as metadata unites the layers.
5. Data can be integrated across all the layers with metadata.
6. Lower cost compared to DW 1.0.
7. Lower maintenance compared to DW 1.0.
8. Creates platform for strong governance.
9. Provides for flexibility and scalability.

TABLE 4.3
The DSS 2.0 Spectrum

	Strategic BI	Tactical BI	Operational BI
Business focus	Achieve long-term business goals	Manage tactical initiatives to achieve strategic goals	Monitor and optimize operational business processes
Primary users	Executives and business analysts	Business analysts, and LOB managers	LOB managers, operational users and operational processes
Timeframe	Months to years	Days to weeks to months	Intra-day to daily
Data	Historical data	Historical data	Real-time, low-latency and historical data
Mode of operation	User driven Data centric	User driven Data centric	Event driven Process centric

4.5.2 Claudia Imhoff and Colin White's DSS 2.0

The DSS 2.0 model compartmentalizes the workload of the operational and analytical business intelligence (BI) and adds content analytics as a separate module. The three different modules can be harnessed using corporate business rules deployed through a decision support integration platform called decision intelligence (Table 4.3).

While Inmon's DW 2.0 and DSS 2.0 architectures focus on usability and scalability from a user perspective. In contrast, the workload-driven data warehousing architecture is based on functionality and infrastructure scalability, where we can compartmentalize the workloads into discrete architectures. In a sense, the workload-driven architecture can be considered as a combination of Inmon's DW 2.0 and Google's Spanner architecture.

The future evolution of data warehousing will be an integration of different data types and their usage, which will be measured as the workload executed on the data warehouse. The next generation of the data warehouse will be the workload-driven data warehouse, where the architecture and the structure of data warehouse transcends into heterogeneous combinations of data and infrastructure architectures that are based on the underlying workloads.

4.6 Data Warehouse Architecture Challenges

The data warehouse is a collection of transactional data over a period of time and by definition is a larger data set, which will be used for a variety of query and analysis purposes by multiple users in an enterprise. In a shared-services environment, there are several issues that limit the performance and scalability of the data warehouse.

The challenges of a data warehouse can be categorized broadly into the following:

- Dependence on RDBMS: The relational model restricts the ability to create flexible architectures. Enforcing relationships and integrity is needed to keep the quality of the data warehouse, but there is no rule that mandates this as a precursor to build a data warehouse.

- Shared-Everything Architecture: Except for Teradata, all the other databases are built on the shared-everything architecture.
- Explosive growth of data—new data types, volumes, and processing requirements.
- Explosive growth of complexity in querying.
- Evolving performance and scalability demands.
- Unpredictable dynamic workloads.
- Analytical support.
- User evolution from static report consumers to interactive analytical explorers.
- Data management limitations with sharding.

Data warehouse implementations are frequently plagued by performance and scalability issues arising by reason of "share-everything" of resources in the data warehouse layer and the data sources layers (see Figure 4.7):

1. Storage:
    a. The source database is isolated in its own storage, though it is a partition of a larger storage cluster.
    b. The operational data store (if deployed), staging, and enterprise data warehouse (EDW) databases are all normally connected to one storage architecture.
    c. The physical servers for the staging and EDW are the same system and database servers.
    d. This shared infrastructure creates scalability and performance issues:
        - The Input/Output (I/O) is constrained in the same enterprise network pipe.
        - The I/O between the source, staging, and EDW databases needs to travel from source, to staging, to ETL, to storage, to ETL, and to EDW. A lot of system resources and the network are dedicated to managing this dataflow and it introduces natural time latencies.
        - Timeouts on connections, slow-moving transactions, and outages on disk architecture are other common side effects that occur in this environment.
2. Server hardware:
    a. The server hardware can be a set of virtual partitions on a large physical server.
    b. The staging and EDW databases are normally in one server.
    c. Analytical databases are normally installed in their own server environment.

In the share-everything architecture:

1. Memory, CPU, and system bus are shared by all programs running on the systems
2. Storage is shared across the programs
3. Network is a common enterprise network and not a direct tethered connection in most cases

This architecture will scale well and perform with consistency on an OLTP or transaction processing platform, since the transactions are discrete in size and occur in small bursts. The system can be tuned and maintained for optimal performance and managed to accommodate the growth needs of a transactional environment. However, this architecture is not the optimal architecture to handle the large volume of data, the processing complexities, and users defined for the data warehouse.

In a shared-services environment, there are several issues that limit the performance and scalability of the data warehouse. Share-everything architecture is not the optimal architecture to handle the large volume of data, the processing complexities, and users defined for the data warehouse.

4.6.1 Performance

The amount of CPU cycles, memory consumed, and data volume transported between the server and storage can be collectively expressed as a unit of "workload."

For a query action, a particular record in a table will be affected. This activity typically generates a round trip across the different infrastructure layers and does not timeout or abruptly quit processing, since the data activity is performed record by record and each activity is maintained in a buffer until the transaction commit is accomplished.

In the OLTP system, there can be many such small queries that can be processed since the workload performed in this environment is small and discrete. However, the execution of a query on the data warehouse data set would be quite different. Typically, the query will take a longer processing cycle and consume more resources to complete the operation. This can be attributed to the size of the data set and the amount of cycles of transportation of data across the different layers for processing, compiling, and processing the final result set, and presentation of the same to the process or user requesting the query. The data warehouse can handle many such queries and process them, but it needs a more robust workload management design, as the resources to process the data of this size and scale will differ from an OLTP environment.

There is a different class of workload that will be generated when you process data from web applications within the data warehouse environment and another class of workload for analytical query processing.

4.6.2 Scalability

Scalability is another area that has been a significant challenge to the success of data warehouses. Database scalability is commonly used to define improvements in the infrastructure and data structure areas of the data warehouse to accommodate growth. Growth in the data warehouse happens in the following two areas:

a. The volume of data and new data
b. The growth of users across different user hierarchies

Both of these situations affect the performance and the scalability of the database. The performance of a database can be definitely improved by a combination of effective data management strategies, coupled with a boost in additional hardware and storage.

Common techniques to scale up performance in a shared-everything architecture include the following:

1. Adding more server hardware. You need to scale up both the CPU and memory for achieving some benefit; scaling one component does not provide huge benefits.
2. Adding more storage does not help unless the data structures are separated discreetly into their own specific substorage areas.

3. Creating additional indexing strategies normally creates more overhead than help.
4. Compressing data on storage with the available compression algorithms.
5. Creating aggregate tables or materialized views.
6. Implementing a robust data management technique, by reducing the amount of data in the tables by archiving history, can help only if volumes are extremely high.
7. Archiving data based on usage and access. This differs from the traditional archiving techniques where data is archived based on a calendar.

Storage architecture can be managed and improved by using techniques such as the following:

1. Master–slave
   a. Another implementation of multinode concept.
   b. All writes are written to the master.
   c. All reads are performed against the replicated slave databases.
   d. It is a limited success, as large data sets slow down the query performance as the master needs to duplicate data to the slaves.
   e. Master and slave databases are synced on a continuous basis, causing query performance and result set consistency issues.
2. Multimaster replication
   a. Create many nodes or clones.
   b. Each node is a master and connects to peers.
   c. Any node can service a client request.
   d. It did not emerge as a big success for RDBMS:
      - Consistency was loosely coupled.
      - Atomicity consistency isolation and durability principles violated data integrity.
3. Partitioning of data has been a very popular option supported by the database vendors, even though the scalability achieved is limited due to inherent design limitations. With partitioning:
   a. Data can be partitioned across multiple disks for parallel I/O.
   b. Individual relational operations (e.g., sort, join, and aggregation) can be executed in parallel in a partitioned environment, as resources can be bequeathed to the operation.
4. Commonly used partitioning techniques are as follows:
   a. List partitioning:
      - Based on a list of values that are randomly applied.
   b. Range-based partitioning:
      - Applied when a single table cannot sit on a server.
      - Split table onto multiple servers based on ranges of values; commonly used ranges are dates.
   c. Key or hash-based partitioning:

        - In this technique, a key-value pair is used in the hash partitioning and the result set is used in the other servers.

5. Composite partitioning:
    a. Hash: range partitioning:
        - First partition of the table by hash keys.
        - Subpartition by range of values.
    b. Range: hash partitioning:
        - First partition of the table by a range of values.
        - Subpartition by hash keys.

The following are partitioning methods that are used for large tables:

1. Vertical partitioning:
    a. Partition large tables by columns across the database, normally in the same database.
    b. The biggest issue with this technique is that we have to balance the partition when the tables grow in columns.
    c. Queries needing large columns will fail to perform.
    d. The technique will not scale for data warehousing, but lends well for OLTP.
2. Horizontal partitioning:
    a. Tables are partitioned by rows and distributed across servers or nodes in a database.
    b. Queries looking for more than one group of rows will have to read multiple nodes or servers.
    c. Extremely large tables will be heavily skewed in this distribution.
    d. Moderately sized tables will perform well.

4.7 Summary

This chapter presented the basics of data warehousing. It introduced the concept of data warehouse and its characteristics, aspects of data warehouse design including multidimensional models and relational schemas like star, snowflake, and constellation schemas. The later part of the chapter provides the generic architecture of a data warehouse followed by description of Inmon's Information Factory and Kimbal's bus architecture versions for a data warehouse. The chapter ends with the improved versions of these architectures as also the challenges of performance and scalability of the data warehouses that pave the way for exploring big data computing solutions for satisfying these kind of requirements.

5

Data Mining Basics

Data mining is widely used by banking firms in soliciting credit card customers, by insurance and telecommunication companies in detecting fraud, by telephone companies and credit card issuers in identifying those potential customers most likely to churn, by manufacturing firms in quality control, and many other applications. Data mining is being applied to improve food and drug product safety and detection of terrorists or criminals. Data mining involves statistical and/or artificial intelligence (AI) analysis, usually applied to large-scale data sets. Masses of data generated from cash registers, from scanning, and from topic specific databases throughout the company are explored, analyzed, reduced, and reused. Searches are performed across different models proposed for predicting sales, marketing response, and profit. Though automated AI methods are also used, classical statistical approaches are fundamental to data mining.

Data mining tools need to be versatile, scalable, capable of accurately predicting responses between actions and results, and capable of automatic implementation. Versatile refers to the ability of the tool to apply a wide variety of models. Scalable tools imply that if the tools works on a small data set, it should also work on larger data sets. Automation is useful, but its application is relative. Some analytic functions are often automated, but human setup prior to implementing procedures is required. In fact, analyst judgment is critical to successful implementation of data mining. Proper selection of data to include in searches is critical: Too many variables produce too much output, while too few can overlook key relationships in the data. Data transformation also is often required.

> Data mining software products that are being used include Enterprise Miner by SAS, Intelligent Miner by IBM, CLEMENTINE by SPSS, PolyAnalyst by Megaputer. WEKA (from the University of Waikato in New Zealand) is an open source tool with many useful developing methods.

5.1 Data Mining

Traditional statistical analysis involves an approach that is usually directed, in that a specific set of expected outcomes exists. This approach is referred to as supervised (hypothesis development and testing). But, data mining also involves a spirit of knowledge discovery (learning new and useful things). Knowledge discovery is referred to as unsupervised (knowledge discovery). Knowledge discovery by humans can be enhanced by graphical tools and identification of unexpected patterns through a combination of human and computer interaction.

Much of this can be also accomplished through automatic means. A variety of analytic computer models have been used in data mining. The standard models employed in data mining include regression (e.g., normal regression for prediction and logistic regression for classification) and neural networks. This chapter discusses techniques like association rules for initial data exploration, fuzzy data mining approaches, rough set models, and genetic algorithms. Data mining requires identification of a problem, along with collection of data that can lead to better understanding, and computer models to provide statistical or other means of analysis. This may be supported by visualization tools, that display data, or through fundamental statistical analysis, such as correlation analysis.

Data mining aims to extract knowledge and insight through the analysis of large amounts of data using sophisticated modeling techniques; it converts data into knowledge and actionable information. Data mining models consist of a set of rules, equations, or complex functions that can be used to identify useful data patterns, understand, and predict behaviors.

Data mining is a process that uses a variety of data analysis methods to discover the unknown, unexpected, interesting, and relevant patterns and relationships in data that may be used to make valid and accurate predictions. In general, there are two methods of data analysis: supervised and unsupervised. In both cases, a sample of observed data is required. This data may be termed the training sample. The training sample is used by the data mining activities to learn the patterns in the data.

Data mining models are of two kinds:

1. Directed or supervised models: In these models, there are input fields or attributes and an output or target field. Input fields are also called predictors, because they are used by the model to identify a prediction function for the output or target field. The model generates an *input–output* mapping function, which associates predictors with the output so that, given the values of input fields, it predicts the output values. Predictive models themselves are of two types, namely, classification or propensity models and estimation models. Classification models are predictive models with predefined target field or classes or groups, so that the objective is to predict a specific occurrence or event. The model also assigns a propensity score with each of these events that indicates the likelihood of the occurrence of that event. In contrast, estimation models are used to predict a continuum of target values based on the corresponding input values.

   For instance, supervised model is used to estimate an unknown dependency from known input–output data.

   a. Input variables might include the following:

      Quantities of different articles bought by a particular customer

      Date of purchase

      Location

      Price

   b. Output variables might include an indication of whether the customer responds to a sales campaign or not. Output variables are also known as targets in data mining.

   Sample input variables are passed through a learning system, and the subsequent output from the learning system is compared with the output from the sample. In other words, we try to predict who will respond to a sales campaign. The difference between the learning system output and the sample output can be thought of as an error signal. Error signals are used to adjust the learning system. This process is done many times with the data from the sample, and the learning system is adjusted until the output meets a minimal error threshold.

2. Undirected or unsupervised models: In these models, there are input fields or attributes, but no output or target field. The goal of such models is to uncover data patterns in the set of input fields. Undirected models are also of two types, namely, cluster models, and, association and sequence models. Cluster models do not have predefined target field or classes or groups, but the algorithms analyze the input data patterns and identify the natural groupings of cases. In contrast, association or sequence models do not involve or deal with the prediction of a single field. Association models detect associations between discrete events, products, or attributes; sequence models detect associations over time.

> Segmentation is much more complex than it may seem; simplified segmentation models, when tested in real life, seem to imply that people as customers change behavior radically. If this was really true, there would be no trust, no loyalty, and, consequently, no collaboration. The apparent paradox gets resolved only when it is recognized that while people as customers do not possess multiple personalities, they have differing customs and, hence, play differing roles based on different contexts or scenarios. The problem arises on persisting with the stance of one-segment-fits-for-all-contexts-for all-people-on-all-occasions.

Unsupervised data analysis does not involve any fine-tuning. Data mining algorithms search through the data to discover patterns, and there is no target or aim variable. Only input values are presented to the learning system without the need for validation against any output. The goal of unsupervised data analysis is to discover "natural" structures in the input data. In biological systems, perception is a task learnt via an unsupervised technique.

5.1.1 Benefits

Data mining can provide customer insight, which is vital for establishing an effective Customer Relationship Management strategy. It can lead to personalized interactions with customers and hence increased satisfaction and profitable customer relationships through data analysis. It can support an *individualized* and optimized customer management throughout all the phases of the customer life cycle, from the acquisition and establishment of a strong relationship to the prevention of attrition and the winning back of lost customers.

1. Segmentation: It is the process of dividing the customer base into distinct and internally homogeneous groups in order to develop differentiated marketing strategies according to their characteristics. There are many different segmentation types based on the specific criteria or attributes used for segmentation. In behavioral segmentation, customers are grouped by behavioral and usage characteristics. Data mining can uncover groups with distinct profiles and characteristics and lead to rich segmentation schemes with business meaning and value. Clustering algorithms can analyze behavioral data, identify the natural groupings of customers, and suggest a solution founded on observed data patterns.

   Data mining can also be used for the development of segmentation schemes based on the current or expected/estimated value of the customers. These segments are necessary in order to prioritize customer handling and marketing interventions according to the importance of each customer.

2. Direct marketing campaigns: Marketers use direct marketing campaigns to communicate a message to their customers through mail, the Internet, e-mail, telemarketing (phone), and other direct channels in order to prevent churn (attrition) and to drive customer acquisition and purchase of add-on products. More specifically, acquisition campaigns aim at drawing new and potentially valuable customers away from the competition. Cross-/deep-/up-selling campaigns are implemented to sell additional products, more of the same product, or alternative but more profitable products to existing customers. Finally, retention campaigns aim at preventing valuable customers from terminating their relationship with the organization.

   Although potentially effective, this can also lead to a huge waste of resources and to bombarding and annoying customers with unsolicited communications. Data mining and classification (propensity) models, in particular, can support the development of targeted marketing campaigns. They analyze customer characteristics and recognize the profiles or extended-profiles of the target customers.

3. Market basket analysis: Data mining and association models, in particular, can be used to identify related products typically purchased together. These models can be used for market basket analysis and for revealing bundles of products or services that can be sold together.

   However, to succeed with CRM, organizations need to gain insight into customers and their needs and wants through data analysis. This is where analytical CRM comes in. Analytical CRM is about analyzing customer information to better address the CRM objectives and deliver the right message to the right customer. It involves the use of data mining models in order to assess the value of the customers, understand, and predict their behavior. It is about analyzing data patterns to extract knowledge for optimizing the customer relationships. For example,

   a. Data mining can help in customer retention as it enables the timely identification of valuable customers with increased likelihood to leave, allowing time for targeted retention campaigns.
   b. Data mining can support customer development by matching products with customers and better targeting of product promotion campaigns.
   c. Data mining can also help to reveal distinct customer segments, facilitating the development of customized new products and product offerings, which better address the specific preferences and priorities of the customers.

   The results of the analytical CRM procedures should be loaded and integrated into the operational CRM front-line systems so that all customer interactions can be more effectively handled on a more informed and personalized base.

5.2 Data Mining Applications

Data mining can be used by businesses in many ways; two of the most profitable application areas have been the use of customer segmentation by marketing organizations to identify those with marginally greater probabilities of responding to different forms of marketing media, and banks using data mining to more accurately predict the likelihood of people to respond to offers of different services offered.

Table 5.1 shows general application areas of data mining.

TABLE 5.1

Data Mining Application Areas

Application Area	Applications	Specifics
Human management resource	Churn	Identify potential employee turnover
Credit card management	Lift churn	Identify effective market segments
		Identify likely customer turnover
Retailing	Affinity positioning, Cross-selling	Position products effectively
		Find more products for customers
Banking	Customer relationship management	Identify customer value
		Develop programs to maximize revenue
Insurance	Fraud detection	Identify claims meriting investigation
Telecommunications	Churn	Identify likely customer turnover
Telemarketing	Online information	Aid telemarketers with easy data

Many companies are using this data mining to identify their "valuable" customers so that they can provide them the service needed to retain them.

1. Customer Profiling—identifying those subsets of customers most profitable to the business
2. Targeting—determining the characteristics of profitable customers who have been captured by competitors
3. Market Basket Analysis—determining product purchases by consumer, which can be used for product positioning and for cross-selling

The key is to find actionable information, or information that can be utilized in a concrete way to improve profitability. Some of the earliest applications were in retailing, especially in the form of market basket analysis.

Data mining methodologies can be applied to a variety of domains, from marketing and manufacturing process control to the study of risk factors in medical diagnosis, from the evaluation of the effectiveness of new drugs to fraud detection.

a. Relational marketing: It is useful for numerous tasks like identification of customer segments that are most likely to respond to targeted marketing campaigns, such as cross-selling and up-selling; identification of target customer segments for retention campaigns; prediction of the rate of positive responses to marketing campaigns; and, interpretation and understanding of the buying behavior of the customers.
b. Text mining: Data mining can be applied to different kinds of texts, which represent unstructured data, in order to classify articles, books, documents, e-mails, and web pages. Examples are web search engines or the automatic classification of press releases for storing purposes. Other text mining applications include the generation of filters for e-mail messages and newsgroups.
c. Web mining: It is useful for the analysis of so-called clickstreams—the sequences of pages visited and the choices made by a web surfer. They may prove useful for the analysis of e-commerce sites, in offering flexible and customized pages to surfers, in caching the most popular pages, or in evaluating the effectiveness of an e-learning training course.

4. Image recognition: The treatment and classification of digital images, both static and dynamic, are useful to recognize written characters, compare and identify human faces, apply correction filters to photographic equipment, and detect suspicious behaviors through surveillance video cameras.
5. Medical diagnosis: Learning models are an invaluable tool within the medical field for the early detection of diseases using clinical test results.
6. Image analysis: For diagnostic purpose, it is another field of investigation that is currently burgeoning.
7. Fraud detection: Fraud detection is relevant for different industries such as telephony, insurance (false claims), and banking (illegal use of credit cards and bank checks; illegal monetary transactions).
8. Risk evaluation: The purpose of risk analysis is to estimate the risk connected with future decisions. For example, using the past observations available, a bank may develop a predictive model to establish if it is appropriate to grant a monetary loan or a home loan, based on the characteristics of the applicant.

5.3 Data Mining Analysis

5.3.1 Supervised Analysis

5.3.1.1 Exploratory Analysis

This data mining task is primarily conducted by means of exploratory data analysis and therefore, it is based on queries and counts that do not require the development of specific learning models. The information so acquired is usually presented to users in the form of histograms and other types of charts.

Before starting to develop a classification model, it is often useful to carry out an exploratory analysis whose purposes are as follows:

- To achieve a characterization by comparing the distribution of the values of the attributes for the records belonging to the same class
- To detect a difference, through a comparison between the distribution of the values of the attributes for the records of a given class and the records of a different class (or between the records of a given class and all remaining records)

The primary purpose of exploratory data analysis is to highlight the relevant features of each attribute contained in a dataset, using graphical methods and calculating summary statistics, and to identify the intensity of the underlying relationships among the attributes. Exploratory data analysis includes three main phases:

1. Univariate analysis, in which the properties of each single attribute of a dataset are investigated
2. Bivariate analysis, in which pairs of attributes are considered, to measure the intensity of the relationship existing between them (for supervised learning models, it is of particular interest to analyze the relationships between the explanatory attributes and the target variable)
3. Multivariate analysis, in which the relationships holding within a subset of attributes are investigated

5.3.1.2 Classification

In a classification problem, a set of observations is available, usually represented by the records of a dataset, whose target class is known. Observations may correspond, for instance, to mobile phone customers and the binary class may indicate whether a given customer is still active or has churned. Each observation is described by a given number of attributes whose value is known; in the previous example, the attributes may correspond to age, customer seniority, and outgoing telephone traffic distinguished by destination. A classification algorithm can therefore use the available observations relative to the past in order to identify a model that can predict the target class of future observations whose attributes values are known.

> The target attribute, whose value is to be predicted, is categorical in classification problems and therefore takes on a finite and usually rather small number of values. If the target is a binary variable, In most applications the target is even represented by a binary variable. Classification is intended for discrete targets, when the target variable takes on continuous values it is part of regression analysis. Classification models are supervised learning methods for predicting the value of a categorical target attribute, unlike regression models which deal with numerical attributes. Starting from a set of past observations whose target class is known, classification models are used to generate a set of rules that allow the target class of future examples to be predicted.

Classification analysis has many applications in selection of the target customers for a marketing campaign, fraud detection, image recognition, early diagnosis of diseases, text cataloguing, and spam e-mail recognition are just a few examples of real problems that can be framed within the classification paradigm.

5.3.1.3 Regression

If one wishes to predict the sales of a product based on the promotional campaigns mounted and the sale price, the target variable may take on a very high number of discrete values and can be treated as a continuous variable; this would become a case of regression analysis. Based on the available explanatory attributes, the goal is to predict the value of the target variable for each observation. A classification problem may be effectively be turned into a regression problem, and vice versa; for instance, a mobile phone company interested in the classification of customers based on their loyalty may come up with a regression problem by predicting the probability of each customer remaining loyal.

The purpose of regression models is to identify a functional relationship between the target variable and a subset of the remaining attributes contained in the dataset. Regression models

- Serve to interpret the dependency of the target variable on the other variables.
- Are used to predict the future value of the target attribute, based upon the functional relationship identified and the future value of the explanatory attributes.

The development of a regression model allows knowledge workers to acquire a deeper understanding of the phenomenon analyzed and to evaluate the effects determined on the target variable by different combinations of values assigned to the remaining attributes.

This is of great interest particularly for analyzing those attributes that are control levers available to decision makers.

Thus, a regression model may be aimed at interpreting the sales of a product based on investments made in advertising in different media, such as daily newspapers, magazines, TV, and radio. Decision makers may use the model to assess the relative importance of the various communication channels, therefore directing future investments toward those media that appear to be more effective. Moreover, they can also use the model to predict the effects on the sales determined by different marketing policies, so as to design a combination of promotional initiatives that appear to be the most advantageous.

5.3.1.4 Time Series

Sometimes the target attribute evolves over time and is therefore associated with adjacent periods on the time axis. In this case, the sequence of values of the target variable is said to represent a time series. For instance, the weekly sales of a given product observed over 2 years represent a time series containing 104 observations. Models for time-series analysis investigate data characterized by a temporal dynamics and are aimed at predicting the value of the target variable for one or more future periods.

The aim of models for time-series analysis is to identify any regular pattern of observations relative to the past, with the purpose of making predictions for future periods. Time-series analysis has many applications in business, financial, socioeconomic, environmental, and industrial domains—predictions may refer to future sales of products and services, trends in economic and financial indicators, or sequences of measurements relative to ecosystems, for example.

5.3.2 Un-Supervised Analysis

5.3.2.1 Association Rules

Association rules, also known as affinity groupings, are used to identify interesting and recurring associations between groups of records of a dataset. For example, it is possible to determine which products are purchased together in a single transaction, and how frequently. Companies in the retail industry resort to association rules to design the arrangement of products on shelves or in catalogs. Groupings by related elements are also used to promote cross-selling or to devise and promote combinations of products and services.

5.3.2.2 Clustering

The term "cluster" refers to a homogeneous subgroup existing within a population. Clustering techniques are therefore aimed at segmenting a heterogeneous population into a given number of subgroups composed of observations that share similar characteristics; observations included in different clusters have distinctive features. Unlike classification, in clustering, there are no predefined classes or reference examples indicating the target class, so that the objects are grouped together based on their mutual homogeneity.

> By defining appropriate metrics and the induced notions of distance and similarity between pairs of observations, the purpose of clustering methods is the identification of homogeneous groups of records called clusters. With respect to the specific distance selected, the observations belonging to each cluster must be close to one another and far from those included in other clusters.

Sometimes, the identification of clusters represents a preliminary stage in the data mining process, within exploratory data analysis. It may allow homogeneous data to be processed with the most appropriate rules and techniques and the size of the original dataset to be reduced, since the subsequent data mining activities can be developed autonomously on each cluster identified.

5.3.2.3 Description and Visualization

The purpose of a data mining process is sometimes to provide a simple and concise representation of the information stored in a large dataset. Although, in contrast to clustering and association rules, descriptive analysis does not pursue any particular grouping or partition of the records in the dataset, an effective and concise description of information is very helpful, since it may suggest possible explanations of hidden patterns in the data and lead to a better understanding the phenomena to which the data refer. Notice that it is not always easy to obtain a meaningful visualization of the data. However, the effort of representation is justified by the remarkable conciseness of the information achieved through a well-designed chart.

5.4 CRISP-DM Methodology

The cross industry standard process-data mining (CRISP-DM) methodology was initiated in 1996 and represents a generalized pattern applicable to any data mining project. CRISP-DM methodology maps from a general CRISP-DM process into a process with a specific application. In essence, the process model describes the life cycle of the data mining process comprising six basic steps; the model shows phases, the tasks within individual phases, and relations between them. Data mining projects are iterative; once a goal is reached, or new knowledge and insight are discovered that can be useful in one of the previous phases, it is desirable to revisit the earlier phases.

The CRISP-DM process model is constituted of the following six phases:

1. Business understanding
2. Data understanding
3. Data preparation
4. Modeling
5. Model evaluation
6. Model deployment

Figure 5.1 shows a schematic of the CRISP-DM methodology.

The CRISP-DM process can be viewed through four hierarchical levels describing the model at four levels of details, from general to specific. Each specific project passes through the phases at the first level; the first level is, at the same time, the most abstract. At the subsequent level, each stage is broken down into generalized, generic tasks. They are generalized, as they cover all the possible scenarios in the data mining process, depending on the phase the project is in.

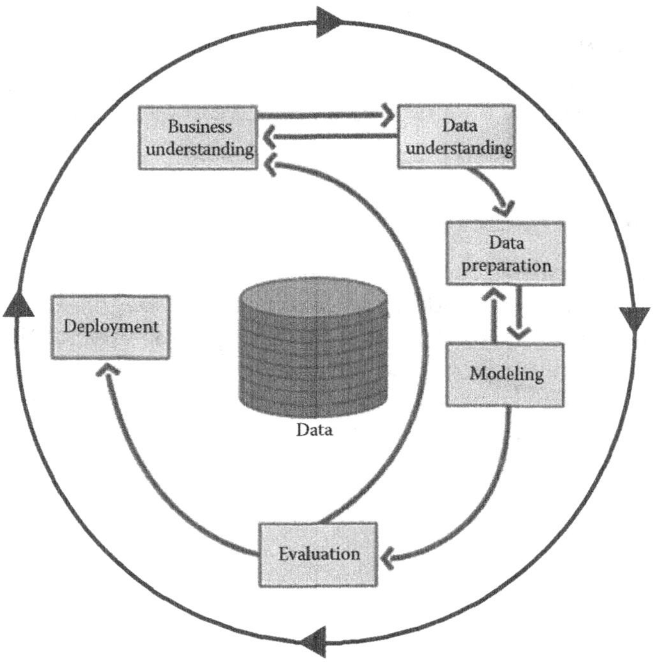

FIGURE 5.1
Schematic of CRISP-DM methodology.

The first level defines the basic phases of the process, that is, the data mining project. The third level defines particular, specialized tasks. They describe how an individual generalized task from the second level is executed in the specific case. For instance, if the second level defines a generic task of data filtering, then the third level describes how this task is executed depending on whether it is a categorical or continuous variable. Finally, the fourth level contains the specific instance of the data mining process, with a range of actions, decisions, and outcomes of the actual knowledge discovery process.

5.4.1 Business Understanding

This phase of the data mining project deals with defining goals and demands from the business point of view. This phase comprises tasks such as the following:

- Determining business objectives
- Situation assessment
- Defining the goals of data mining
- Producing the project plan

It determines the problem domain (marketing, user support, or something similar), as also identifies the organization's business units involved with the project. It also identifies the resources required for this project including the hardware and tools for implementation, as well as the human resources, especially the domain-specific experts required for the project.

At the end of the first phase, a project plan is developed with a list of phases, with constituting tasks and activities, as well as the time and effort estimations; resources for tasks, their interdependencies, inputs, and outputs are also defined. The project plan highlights strategies for issues like risk assessment and quality management.

5.4.2 Data Understanding

This phase of the data mining project deals with getting familiarized with the organization's data through exploratory data analysis, which includes simple statistical characteristics and more complex analyses, that is, setting certain hypotheses on the business problem.

This phase comprises tasks such as the following:

- Collecting initial data
- Describing data
- Exploring data
- Verifying data quality

The data are obtained from identified sources, and the selection criteria are chosen in light of the specific business problem under consideration. Tables are defined, and if the data source is a relational database, or a data warehouse, variations of the tables to be used are also specified.

This is followed by analyzing the basic characteristics of the data, such as quantity and types (e.g., categorical or continuous), then analysis of the correlations between variables, distribution and intervals of values, as well as other simple statistical functions coupled with specialized statistical analysis tools if necessary. It is important to establish the meaning for every variable, especially from the business aspect, and relevance to the specific data mining problem.

The more complex analysis of the data set entails using one of the OLAP or similar visualization tools. This analysis enables on shaping the relevant hypotheses and transforming them into the corresponding mining problem space. In addition, project goals get fine-tuned more precisely.

At the end of this phase, the quality of the data set is ascertained in terms of the completeness and accuracy of data, the frequency of discrepancies or the occurrences of the null-values.

5.4.3 Data Preparation

This phase of the data mining project deals with data preparation for the mining process. It includes choosing the initial data set on which modeling is to begin, that is, the model set.

This phase comprises tasks such as the following:

- Data selection
- Data cleaning
- Data construction
- Data integration
- Data formatting

When defining the set for the subsequent modeling step, one takes into account, among other things, elimination of individual variables based on the results of statistical tests of correlation and significance, that is, values of individual variables. Taking these into account, the number of variables for the subsequence modeling iteration is reduced, with the aim of obtaining an optimum model. Besides this, this is the phase when the sampling (i.e., reducing the size of the initial data set) technique is decided on.

> During a data mining project, the data preparation phase is performed recurrently, as findings from the subsequent modelling phase sometimes require redefining the data set for the next modelling step. A specific example is reducing the number of variables by eliminating low-impact correlations or based on criteria obtained as the outcome for the modelling phase.

At the end of this phase, the issue of data quality is addressed, as well as the manner in which nonexistent values will be managed, as also the strategy for handling particular values. New variables are derived, the values of the existing ones are transformed, and values from different tables are combined in order to obtain new variables values. Finally, individual variables are syntactically adjusted in sync with the modeling tools, without changing their meaning.

5.4.4 Modeling

This phase of the data mining project deals with choosing the data mining technique itself. The choice of the tool, that is, technique to be applied depends on the nature of the problem. Actually, various techniques can always be applied on the same type of problem, but there is always a technique or tool yielding the best results for a specific problem. It is sometimes necessary to model several techniques and algorithms, and then opt for the one yielding the best results. In other words, several models are built in a single iteration of the phase, and the best one is selected.

This phase comprises tasks such as the following:

- Generating test design
- Building the model
- Assessing the model

Before modeling starts, the data (model) set from the previous phase must be divided into subsets for training, testing, and evaluation. The evaluation subset is used for assessing the model's efficiency on unfamiliar data, whereas the test subset is used for achieving model generality, that is, avoiding the over fitting on the training subset.

Division of the data subset is followed by model building. The effectiveness of the obtained model is assessed on the evaluation subset. In the case of predictive models, applying the obtained model on the evaluation subset produces data for the cumulative gains chart showing how well the model predicts on an unfamiliar set. Parameters for the subsequent modeling step are determined based on the obtained graph, the model quality ratio (surface below the graph) and other ratios—such as significance and value factors for individual variables, and correlations between them. If necessary, the developer returns to the previous phase to eliminate noise variables from the model set.

If several models were built in this phase (even those done using different techniques), then models are compared, and the best ones are selected for the next iteration of the modeling phase. Each obtained model is interpreted from the business point of view, as much it is possible in the current phase iteration itself.

At the end of this phase, the developers assess the possibility of model deployment, result reliability, and whether the set goals are met from the business and analytic point-of-view. The modeling phase is repeated until the best, that is, satisfactory model is obtained.

5.4.5 Model Evaluation

This phase of the data mining project deals with the assessment of the final model, that is, the extent to which it meets the goals set in the first phase of the data mining project. The evaluation of the model in the previous phase is more related to the model's technical characteristics (efficiency and generality).

This phase comprises tasks such as the following:

- Evaluating results
- Reviewing the process
- Determining next steps

If the information gained at this point affects the quality of the entire project, this would indicate returning to the first phase and reinitiating the whole process with the newer information. However, if the model meets all the business goals and is considered satisfactory for deployment, a detailed review of the entire data mining process is conducted in order to ascertain the quality of the entire process.

At the end of this phase, project manager decides on moving to the phase of model deployment, or repeating the prior process for improvement.

5.4.6 Model Deployment

This phase of the data mining project deals with model deployment in business, taking into account the way of measuring the model's benefits and its fine-tuning on an ongoing basis.

This phase comprises tasks such as the following:

- Preparing deployment plan
- Monitoring plan
- Maintenance
- Producing final report
- Project review

Because of the changing market conditions and competition, it is necessary to repeat the modeling process periodically to fine-tune or alter the model for sustaining the effectiveness of the insights drawn from data mining.

The application of the model in strategic decision making of a business organization can be used for direct measurement of the benefits of the obtained model, and gather new knowledge for the subsequent iterations for model improvement.

At the end of this phase, the project is concluded by overall review, that is, analysis of its strengths and weaknesses. Final reports and presentations are made. Documentation with experiences usable in possible future projects is also compiled.

5.5 Machine Learning

An intelligent system learns from experience or relevant information on the past happenings. The same is true for machines as well; machines learn from two different ways:

1. They are exposed to past happenings to adaptively learn from whatever they "experience."
2. They are exposed to massive collective data relevant to the past happenings; the machine ingests this data and attempts to learn from it.

Since anticipation of future events is unfeasible, it is not possible to prepare all machines to experience the happenings as they occur, and only the second approach is more feasible. In that case, the larger the data, the better is the scope for learning comprehensively by the machine. The machine when presented with this data carrying hidden facts, rules, and inferences is supposed to discern them so that the next time, if the same data occur, it may identify and compute the correct answer (or solution). The machine summarizes the entire input data into a smaller data set that can be consulted to find outputs to future inputs in a manageable amount of time.

> Clustering is an effective way of limiting the input data. Clustering groups data into various pools; each pool can be represented by a representative element of that group which has average values of the various parameters. Consequently, the entire pool can be replaced by this representative, which conveys the same information as the entire pool. Clustering enables limiting data without appreciable loss of "performance."

The general procedure of working with machine-learning systems consists of the following:

1. Establish the historical database
2. Perform input data acquisition
3. Perform pattern matching
4. Producing output

This procedure is presented in Figure 5.2.

Learning is the process of building a scientific model after discovering knowledge from a sample data set or data sets. Generally, machine learning is considered to be the process of applying a computing-based resource to implement learning algorithms. Formally, machine learning is defined as the complex computation process of automatic pattern recognition and intelligent decision making based on training sample data.

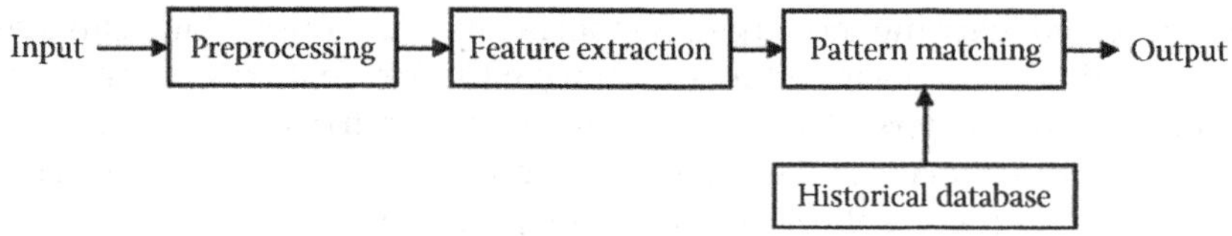

FIGURE 5.2
Architecture of a machine-learning system.

Machine-learning methods can be categorized into four groups of learning activities:

- Symbol-based machine learning has a hypothesis that all knowledge can be represented in symbols and that machine learning can create new symbols and new knowledge, based on the known symbols. In symbol-based machine learning, decisions are deducted using logical inference procedures.
- Connectionist-based machine learning is constructed by imitating neuron net connection systems in the brain. In connectionist machine learning, decisions are made after the systems are trained and patterns are recognized. Behavior-based learning has the assumption that there are solutions to behavior identification, and is designed to find the best solution to solve the problem.
- Immune-system-based approach learns from its encounters with foreign objects and develops the ability to identify patterns in data.

Thus, it is not necessary to select machine-learning methods based on these fundamental distinctions; within the machine-learning process, mathematical models are built to describe the data randomly sampled from an unseen probability distribution.

None of these machine-learning methods has any noticeable advantages over the others. Machine learning has to be evaluated empirically because its performance heavily depends on the type of prior training experience the learning machine has undergone, the performance evaluation metrics, and the strength of the problem definition. Machine-learning methods are evaluated by comparing the learning results of methods applied on the same data set or quantifying the learning results of the same methods applied on sample data sets. Generally, the feasibility of a machine-learning method is acceptable when its computation time is polynomial.

Machine-learning methods use training patterns to learn or estimate the form of a classifier model. The models can be parametric or unparametric. The goal of using machine-learning algorithms is to reduce the classification error on the given training sample data. The training data being finite, the learning theory requires probability bounds on the performance of learning algorithms.

Depending on the availability of training data and the desired outcome of the learning algorithms, machine-learning algorithms are categorized into the following:

1. In supervised learning, pairs of input and target output are given to train a function, and a learning model is trained such that the output of the function can be predicted at a minimum cost. The supervised learning methods are categorized based on the structures and objective functions of learning algorithms. Popular categorizations include artificial neural network (ANN), support vector machine (SVM), and decision trees.

2. In unsupervised learning, no target or label is given in sample data. Unsupervised learning methods are designed to summarize the key features of the data and to form the natural clusters of input patterns given a particular cost function. The most famous unsupervised learning methods include k-means clustering, hierarchical clustering, and self-organization map. Unsupervised learning is difficult to evaluate, because it does not have an explicit teacher and, thus, does not have labeled data for testing.

5.5.1 Cybersecurity Systems

Cybersecurity systems address various cybersecurity threats, including viruses, Trojans, worms, spam, and botnets. These cybersecurity systems combat cybersecurity threats at two levels:

- Host-based defense systems control upcoming data in a workstation by firewall, antivirus, and intrusion detection techniques installed in hosts.
- Network-based defense systems control network flow by network firewall, spam filter, antivirus, and network intrusion detection techniques.

Conventional approaches to cyber defense create a protective shield for cyber infrastructure; they are mechanisms designed in firewalls, authentication tools, and network servers that monitor, track, and block viruses and other malicious cyber attacks. For example, the Microsoft Windows operating system has a built-in Kerberos cryptography system that protects user information. Antivirus software is designed and installed in personal computers and cyber infrastructures to ensure customer information is not used maliciously.

Cybersecurity systems aim to maintain the confidentiality, integrity, and availability of information and information management systems through various cyber defense systems that protect computers and networks from hackers who may want to intrude on a system or steal financial, medical, or other identity-based information. Cyber systems and infrastructure are always vulnerable because of the inherently transient nature of the design and implementation of software and networks. Due to unavoidable design and programming errors, vulnerabilities in common security components, such as firewalls, are inevitable; it is not possible to build a system that has no security vulnerabilities.

Patches are developed continuously to protect the cyber systems, but attackers also continuously exploit newly discovered flaws. Because of the constantly evolving nature of cyber threats, merely building defensive systems for identified attacks is not adequate to protect users; higher-level methodologies are also required to discover overt and covert intrusions and intrusion techniques, so that a more reliable security cyber infrastructure can be ensured.

A high-level defense system consists of the following steps:

1. Information sources: A host-based event originates with log-files; a host-based event includes a sequence of commands executed by a user and a sequence of system calls launched by an application, for example, send mail. A network-based event originates with network traffic; a network-based event includes network traffic data, for example, a sequence of Internet protocol (IP) or transmission control protocol (TCP) network packets.

2. Data capturing tools: Data capturing tools such as Libpcap for Linux or Winpcap for Windows capture events from the audit trails of resource information sources like a host or network.
3. Data preprocessing: The data preprocessing module filters out the attacks for which good signatures have been learned.
4. Feature extraction: A feature extractor derives basic features that are useful in event analysis engines, including a sequence of system calls, start time, duration of a network flow, source IP and source port, destination IP and destination port, protocol, number of bytes, and number of packets.
5. Analysis engines: In an analysis engine, various intrusion detection methods are implemented to investigate the behavior of the cyber infrastructure, which may or may not have appeared before in the record, for example, to detect anomalous traffic.
6. Decision of responses: The decision of responses is generated once a cyber attack has been identified.

The resulting solutions can either be reactive and proactive. Reactive security solutions termed as intrusion detection systems (IDSs) detect intrusions based on the information from log files and network flow, so that the extent of damage can be determined, hackers can be tracked down, and similar attacks can be prevented in the future. However, proactive approaches anticipate and eliminate identified vulnerabilities in the cyber system, while remaining prepared to defend effectively and rapidly against actual attacks. To function correctly, proactive security solutions require user authentication (e.g., user password and biometrics), a system capable of avoiding programming errors, and information protection.

> Privacy-preserving Data Mining (PPDM) protects data from being explored by data-mining techniques in cybersecurity applications.

5.5.1.1 Data Mining for Cybersecurity

Data mining techniques use statistics, artificial intelligence, and pattern recognition of data in order to group or extract behaviors or entities. Data mining uses analysis tools from statistical models, mathematical algorithms, and machine-learning methods to discover previously unknown, valid patterns and relationships in large data sets, which are useful for finding hackers and preserving privacy in cybersecurity. Learning these behaviors is important, as they can identify and describe structural patterns in the data automatically and, as a consequence, theoretically explain data and predict patterns. Automatic and theoretic learning require complex computation that demands stringent machine-learning algorithms.

As discussed in Section 5.3, there are two categories of data mining methods: supervised and unsupervised. Supervised data mining techniques predict a hidden function using training data. The training data have pairs of input variables and output labels or classes. The output of the method can predict a class label of the input variables. Examples of supervised mining are classification and prediction. Unsupervised data mining is an attempt to identify hidden patterns from given data without resorting to training data (i.e., pairs of input and class labels). Typical examples of unsupervised mining are clustering and associative rule mining.

5.6 Soft Computing

Usually the primary considerations of traditional *hard computing* are precision, certainty, and rigor. In contrast, the principal notion in *soft computing* is that precision and certainty carry a cost; and that computation, reasoning, and decision making should exploit (wherever possible) the tolerance for imprecision, uncertainty, approximate reasoning, and partial truth for obtaining low-cost solutions. The corresponding facility in humans leads to the remarkable human ability to understand distorted speech, deciphering sloppy handwriting, comprehending the nuances of natural language, summarizing text, recognizing and classifying images, driving a vehicle in dense traffic, and, more generally, making rational decisions in an environment of uncertainty and imprecision. The challenge, then, is to exploit the tolerance for imprecision by devising methods of computation that lead to an *acceptable solution at low cost*.

Soft computing is a consortium of methodologies that works synergistically and provides, in one form or another, flexible information processing capability for handling real-life ambiguous situations. Its aim is to exploit the tolerance for imprecision, uncertainty, approximate reasoning, and partial truth in order to achieve tractability, robustness, and low-cost solutions. The guiding principle is to devise methods of computation that lead to an acceptable solution at low cost, by seeking for an approximate solution to an imprecisely or precisely formulated problem.

Unlike soft computing, the traditional hard computing deals with precise computation. The rules of hard computing are strict and binding; as inputs, outputs, and procedures are all clearly defined, it generates the same precise answers without any degree of uncertainty—every time that the procedure is applied. Unless the rules or procedures are changed, the output result would never change.

Table 5.2 compares characteristics of soft computing with the traditional hard computing.

The main constituents of soft computing include the following:

- Artificial neural networks (ANNs)
- Fuzzy logic and fuzzy inference systems
- Evolutionary and genetic algorithms
- Rough sets
- Signal processing tools such as wavelets

Though each of them contribute a distinct methodology for addressing problems in its domain, they are complementary to each other and can be blended effectively. The result is

TABLE 5.2

Characteristics of Soft Computing Compared with Traditional Hard Computing

Traditional Hard Computing	Soft Computing
Conventional computing requires a precisely stated analytical model	Soft computing is tolerant of imprecision
Often requires a lot of computation time	Can solve some real world problems in reasonably less time
Not suited for real world problems for which ideal model is not present	Suitable for real world problems
It requires full truth	Can work with partial truth
It is precise and accurate	Imprecise
High cost for solution	Low cost for solution

a more intelligent and robust system providing a human-interpretable, low-cost, approximate solution, as compared to traditional techniques. There is no universally best soft computing method; choosing particular soft computing tool(s) or some combination with traditional methods is entirely dependent on the particular application, and it requires human interaction to decide on the suitability of a blended approach.

Fuzzy sets provide a natural framework for the process in dealing with uncertainty or imprecise data. Generally, they are suitable for handling the issues related to understandability of patterns, incomplete and noisy data, and mixed media information and human interaction and can provide approximate solutions faster. ANNs are nonparametric and robust, and exhibit good learning and generalization capabilities in data-rich environments. Genetic algorithms (GAs) provide efficient search algorithms to optimally select a model, from mixed media data, based on some preference criterion or objective function. Rough sets are suitable for handling different types of uncertainty in data. Neural networks and rough sets are widely used for classification and rule generation. Application of wavelet-based signal processing techniques is new in the area of soft computing. Wavelet transformation of a signal results in decomposition of the original signal in different multiresolution subbands. This is useful in dealing with compression and retrieval of data, particularly images. Other approaches like case-based reasoning and decision trees are also widely used to solve data mining problems.

5.6.1 Artificial Neural Networks

The human brain is composed of an ensemble of millions of small cells or processing units called neurons that work in parallel. Neurons are connected to each other via neuron connections called the synapses. A particular neuron takes its input from a set of neurons, it then processes these inputs and passes on the output to another set of neurons. The brain as a whole is a complex network of such neurons in which connections are established and broken continuously. ANNs have resulted from efforts to imitate the functioning of human brain.

Like the human brain, ANNs are able to learn from historical or sample data; it is able to learn by repeating the learning process for a number of iterations—the performance demonstrates improvement with every completed iteration. Once learned, ANNs can reproduce the same output whenever the same input is applied. The precision and correctness of the answer depends on the learning and nature of the data given: Sometimes, ANN may be able to learn even complex data very quickly, while at other times, it may refuse to learn from another set of data. The precision depends upon on how well the ANN was able to learn from the presented data.

Once ANNs have learned from historical or sample data, they have another extraordinary capability that enables them to predict the outputs of unknown inputs with quite high precision. This capability known as generalization results from the fact that ANNs can emulate any type of simple or complex function. This gives ANNs the power to model almost any problem that is encountered in real world.

> ANNs functioning is highly resistant to disruption or perturbation by noise; Even if there is any noise in the input data, ANNs are still able to perform their normal functions quite appreciably well.

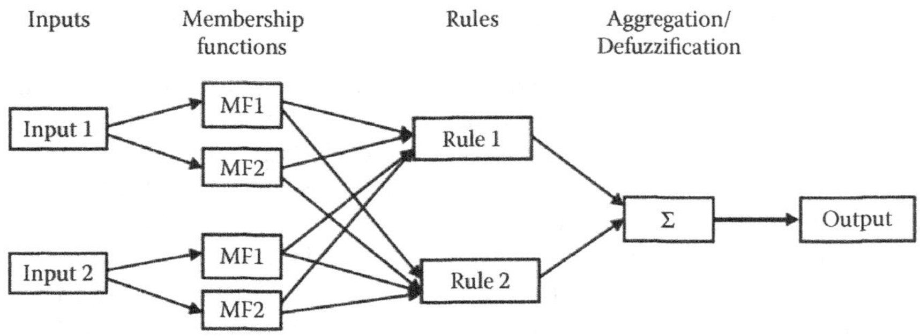

FIGURE 5.3
Architecture of a fuzzy inference system.

5.6.2 Fuzzy Systems

In fuzzy sets, every member of the set does not have a full membership of the set but rather has a degree of belongingness to the set. This degree of membership is termed as the membership degree and the function that determines this membership degree or belongingness is called the membership function. This function associates with each member of the set with a degree or probability of membership: The higher is this degree, the more strongly the member is a part of the set.

Fuzzy systems are implemented by a set of rules called fuzzy rules, which may be defined on the set. A nonfuzzy has a very discreet way of dealing with rules: Either a rule fires fully or does not fire at all, depending on the truth of the expression in the condition specified. However, in the case of fuzzy rules, since the rule is true or false only to a degree, the rule fires to this degree of trueness or falseness. The output of all the rules is aggregated to get the system's final output.

The general procedure of working with fuzzy inference systems consists of the following:

1. Crisp input modeling
2. Membership functions that are applied to obtain the fuzzified inputs
3. Rules that are applied over these inputs to generate the fuzzy outputs
4. Various outputs that are aggregated
5. Aggregated output that is de-fuzzified to produce the crisp output

This procedure is presented in Figure 5.3.

5.6.3 Evolutionary Algorithms

Evolutionary algorithm (EA) is inspired by the success of Darwin's "theory of natural selection" surmised by "survival of the fittest." Natural evolution results from the fusion of male and female chromosomes to generate one or more offspring that have a blend of characteristics from both the male and female counterpart. The offspring may be weaker or fitter than the participating parents and would survive the parents to the degree of its fitness to the surrounding conditions and environment. This process of evolution leads to improvement from one generation to the next one.

EAs work in a similar way. The process is initiated with the generation of a random set of solutions to a given problem resulting in a population of such solutions. These "individual" solutions constituting the population are made to participate in an evolutionary process: From these solutions, a few individuals with high fitness are chosen based on a predetermined method termed as "selection." These pair of individuals are then made to generate offspring guided again by a process termed as "crossover." The system then randomly shortlists some of the newly generated solutions and adds new characteristics to them through another predefined process termed as "mutation;" more similar operations are performed on the shortlisted solutions. The fitness of any one of these mutated solutions is adjudged based on another function termed as the "fitness function."

As the process cycles through newer and newer generations, the quality of the selected solutions continues to improve. This improvement is very rapid over the first few generations but slows down with later generations.

5.6.4 Rough Sets

The purpose of rough sets is to discover knowledge in the form of business rules from imprecise and uncertain data sources. Rough set theory is based on the notion of indiscernibility and the inability to distinguish between objects, and provides an approximation of sets or concepts by means of binary relations, typically constructed from empirical data. As an approach to handling imperfect data, rough set analysis complements other more traditional theories such as probability theory, evidence theory, and fuzzy set theory. The intuition behind the rough set approach is the fact that in real life, when dealing with sets, we often have no means of precisely distinguishing individual set elements from each other due to limited resolution (lack of complete and detailed knowledge) and uncertainty associated with their measurable characteristics.

The rough set philosophy is founded on the assumption that we associate some information (data and knowledge) with every object of the universe of discourse. Objects, which are characterized by the same information, are indiscernible in view of the available information about them. The indiscernibility relation generated in this way is the mathematical basis for the rough set theory. Any set of all indiscernible objects is called an elementary set, and forms a basic granule of knowledge about the universe. Any set of objects being a union of some elementary sets is referred to as crisp or precise set otherwise the set is rough (imprecise or vague). Consequently, each rough set has boundary-line cases (i.e., objects), which cannot be classified with complete certainty as members of the set.

The general procedure for conducting rough set analysis consists of the following:

1. Data preprocessing
2. Data partitioning
3. Discretization
4. Reduct generation
5. Rule generation and rule filtering
6. Applying the discretization cuts to test dataset
7. Score the test dataset on the generated rule set (and measuring the prediction accuracy)
8. Deploying the rules in a production system

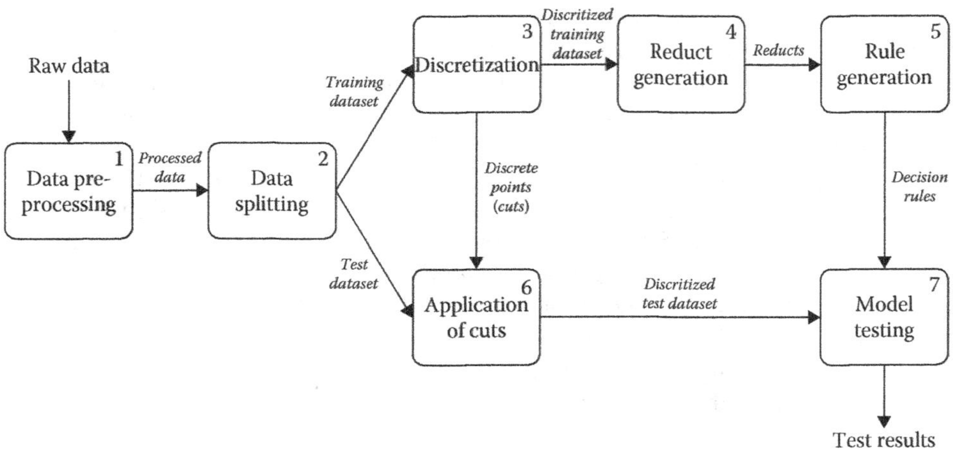

FIGURE 5.4
Architecture of a rough sets system.

This procedure is presented in Figure 5.4.

> Despite their modeling power and wide spread use in complex prediction modeling tasks, artificial neural networks have been criticized for their lack of explanatory power. In other words, it is difficult to trace and explain the way the reasoning is derived from the input variables due to the complexity and nonlinear nature of data transformation conducted within the algorithm. In contrast to neural networks, decision trees and rough sets present their models in the form of business rules, which are intuitively explainable. They connect the input variables (factors) to output variables (conclusions) using IF <condition(s)> THEN <action(s)> structure.

5.7 Summary

This chapter discussed the basics of data mining. It introduced the concept of data mining with its benefits and applications. After describing details of a data mining analysis, it gives an overview of the data mining methodology. The chapter ends with an introduction to the concept of soft computing that is related to the concept of data mining.

6

Distributed Systems Basics

The origins of big data technologies come from database systems and distributed systems, as well as data mining and machine learning algorithms that can process these vast amounts of data to extract needed knowledge. Several distributed database prototype systems were developed in the 1980s and 1990s to address the issues of data distribution, data replication, distributed query and transaction processing, distributed database metadata management, and other topics. More recently, many new technologies have emerged that combine database and distributed technologies. These technologies and systems are being developed for dealing with the storage, analysis, and mining of the vast amounts of data that are being produced and collected, and they are referred to generally as big data technologies (see Chapter 10).

The centralized approach to processing data, in which users access a central database on a central computer through personal computers (PCs) and workstations, dominated organizations from the late 1960s through the mid-1980s because there was no alternative approach to compete with it. The introduction of reasonably priced PCs during the 1980s, however, facilitated the placement of computers at various locations within an organization; users could access a database directly at those locations. Networks connected these computers, so users could access not only data located on their local computers but also data located anywhere across the entire network.

This chapter addresses issues involved in distributed databases where a database is stored on more than one computer.

6.1 Distributed Systems

Distributed systems consist of a collection of heterogeneous but fully autonomous components that can execute on different computers. Although each of these components has full control over its constituent subparts, there is no master component that possesses control over all the components of a distributed system. Thus, for each of these systems to appear as a single and integrated whole, the various components need to be able to interact with each other via predefined interfaces through a computer network.

The characteristic global features of a successful distributed system are as follows:

- Distributed systems are heterogeneous, arising from the need to (say) integrate components on a legacy IBM mainframe, with the components newly created to operate on a UNIX workstation or Windows NT machine.
- Distributed systems are scalable in that when a component becomes overloaded with too many requests or users, another replica of the same component can be

instantiated and added to the distributed system to share the load among them. Moreover, these instantiated components can be located closer to the local users and other interacting components to improve the performance of the overall distributed system.

- Distributed systems execute components concurrently in a multithreaded mode via multiply invoked components, corresponding to the number of simultaneously invoked processes.
- Distributed systems are fault-tolerant in that they duplicate components on different computers so that if one computer fails another can take over without affecting the availability of the overall system.
- Distributed systems are more resilient in that whereas distributed systems have multiple points of failure, the unaffected components are fully operational even though some of the components are not functional or are malfunctioning. Moreover, the distributed system could invoke another instance of the failed components along with the corresponding state of the process (characterized by the program counter, the register variable contents, and the state of the virtual memory used by the process) to continue with the process.
- Distributed systems demonstrate invariance or transparency with reference to the following characteristics:
    - Accessibility, either locally or across networks to the components
    - Physical location of the components
    - Migration of components from one host to another
    - Replication of components including their states
    - Concurrency of components requesting services from shared components
    - Scalability in terms of the actual number of requests or users at any instance
    - Performance in terms of the number and type of available resources
    - Points of failure, be it a failure of the component, network, or response

The terms parallel systems and distributed systems are often used interchangeably; however, the term distributed refers to a wider class of systems, whereas the term parallel implies a subclass of tightly coupled systems. Distributed systems encompasses any architecture or system that allows the computation to be broken down into units and executed concurrently on different computing elements, whether these are processors on different nodes, processors on the same computer, or cores within the same processor. Distributed systems often imply that the locations of all the constituting computing elements are not the same and such elements might be heterogeneous in terms of hardware and software features. Classic examples of distributed computing systems are computing grids or Internet computing systems, which combine together the biggest variety of architectures, systems, and applications in the world.

Parallel systems refer to a model in which the computation is divided among several processors sharing the same memory. The architecture of a parallel computing system is often characterized by the homogeneity of components: each processor is of the same type and it has the same capability as the others. The shared memory has a single address space, which is accessible to all the processors. Parallel programs are then broken down into several units of execution that can be allocated to different processors and can communicate with each other by means of the shared memory.

Originally, parallel systems used to include only those architectures that featured multiple processors sharing the same physical memory and computer. However, by now parallel systems are considered to include all those architectures that are based on the concept of shared memory, regardless of whether this is physically colocated or created with the support of libraries, specific hardware, and a highly efficient networking infrastructure. For example, a cluster of which the nodes are connected through an InfiniBand network and configured with a distributed shared memory system can also be considered a parallel system.

6.1.1 Parallel Computing

Parallel computing involves architecture that is capable of allowing multiple machines to work together. Michael J. Flynn in 1966 created a taxonomy of computer architectures that support parallelism, based on the number of concurrent control and data streams, the architecture can handle. This classification is used extensively to characterize parallel computing architectures.

They are briefly described as follows:

1. *Single instruction, single data stream* (*SISD*): This is a sequential computer that exploits no parallelism, like a PC (single core).
2. *Single instruction, multiple data Stream* (*SIMD*): This architecture supports multiple data streams to be processed simultaneously by replicating the computing hardware. Single instruction means that all the data streams are processed using the same computer logic. Examples of parallel architectures that support this model are array processors or graphics processing unit (GPU).
3. *Multiple instruction, single data stream* (*MISD*): This architecture operates on single data stream but has multiple computing engines using the same data stream. This is not a very common architecture and is sometimes used to provide fault tolerance with heterogeneous systems operating on the same data to provide independent results that are compared with each other.
4. *Multiple instruction, multiple data stream* (*MIMD*): This is the most generic parallel processing architecture where any type of distributed application can be programmed. Multiple autonomous processors executing in parallel, work on independent streams of data. The application logic running on these processors can also be very different. All distributed systems are recognized to be MIMD architectures.

A variant of SIMD is called SPMD for single program, multiple data model, where the same program executes on multiple compute processes. Although SIMD can achieve the same result as SPMD, SIMD systems typically execute in lock step with a central controlling authority for program execution. As can be seen, when multiple instances of the map function are executed in parallel, they work on different data streams using the same map function.

Parallelism within an application can be at several levels as the following:

- Large grain (or task level)
- Medium grain (or data level)
- Fine grain (or instruction level)
- Very fine grain (bit level)

Thus, Flynn's taxonomy is representative of the hardware architecture at many different levels:

1. Task-level parallelism in a multiprocessor system is synonymous with Flynn's MIMD architecture, which occurs when each CPU executes a different process on the same or different data. The varying threads can execute the same or completely different code. In any case, however, varying threads must communicate with one another as they work. Communication takes place usually to pass data from one thread to the next as part of a workflow. Task parallelism emphasizes the distributed (parallelized) nature of the processing (i.e., threads), as opposed to the data (data parallelism). Most real programs fall somewhere on a continuum between task parallelism and data parallelism. Most supercomputers fall into this category.
2. Data-level parallelism is synonymous with Flynn's SIMD architecture—single instruction (all processing units perform identical instruction) and multiple data (each processing unit can operate on varying data elements). Data-level parallelism is accomplished when each processor performs the same task on different data inputs. In some circumstances, one thread may control operations on several different pieces of data. In other situations, threads may control the operation; however, they may execute the same code. Data-level parallelism emphasizes the distributed (parallelized) nature of the data, as opposed to the processing (task parallelism). Most modern computers, particularly those with GPUs, employ SIMD instructions and execution units.
3. Instruction-level parallelism performs many concurrent operations in a single computer program:
    a. R3 <--- R1 + R2
    b. R6 <--- R4 + R5
    c. R7 <--- R3 + R6

    The third operation is dependent on the prior two operations being complete. However, operations a and b are independent operations, so they can be calculated at the same time. The most efficient compiler and processor design would identify and take advantage of as much of this parallelism as possible. Ordinary programs are typically written under a sequential execution model where instructions execute one after the other and in the order specified by the programmer.
4. Bit-level parallelism is a form of parallel computing based on increasing processor word size. It is done by performing the arithmetic on two numbers, bit by bit. The addition, for example, of two 32-bit numbers was performed in 32 machine cycles, by very simple circuitry capable only of adding one bit to another. Quite possibly the earliest use of parallelism in computers was to perform the operations on all bits simultaneously in parallel.

Instruction-level parallelism allows the compiler and the processor to overlap the execution of multiple instructions or even to change the order in which instructions are executed. Pipelining is an excellent example of this form of parallel processing. The idea of pipelining is that as each instruction completes a step, the following instruction

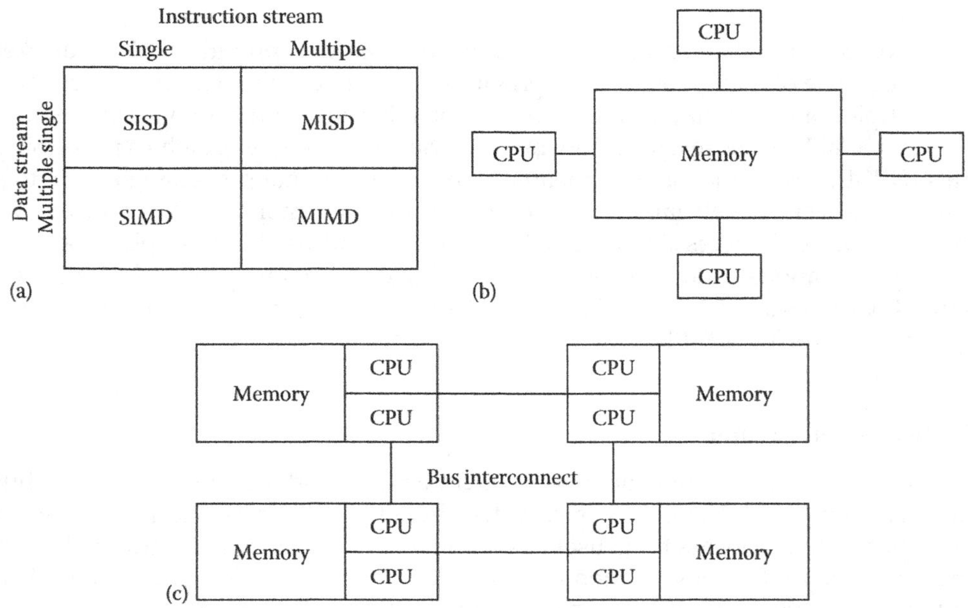

FIGURE 6.1
Parallel computing architectures: (a) Flynn's taxonomy (b) shared memory system, and (c) distributed system.

moves into the stage just vacated. Thus, when the first instruction is completed, the next one is already one stage short of completion. Data hazard occurs when processor fetches data c and f. Since c and f have not been written back, the fetch may access to the wrong data (previously stored in c and f, not the current ones). This is called *read after write* (RAW).

Memory can either be shared or distributed (Figure 6.1b). Shared memory typically is comprised of one of the following two architectures: uniform memory access (UMA) or nonuniform memory access (NUMA). Regardless of the specific architecture, shared memory is generally accessible to all the processors in the system, and multiple processors may operate independently and continue to share the same memory. Figure 6.1b illustrates UMA architecture. Multiple CPUs are capable of accessing one memory resource. This is also referred to as symmetric multiprocessor (SMP). In contrast, NUMA is often made by physically linking two or more SMPs. One SMP is capable of directly accessing the memory of another SMP.

Like shared memory systems, distributed memory systems (Figure 6.1c) vary widely, but share a common characteristic. Distributed memory systems require a communication network to connect interprocessor memory. In this type of architecture, processors have access to their own memory and do not share memory with another SMP. If a processor needs information from another data store, it has to communicate how and when it is to be accessed. This sharing generally comes about through a simple Ethernet connection. Hybrids of this technology have also been developed and are referred to as distributed-shared memory architecture. However, this type of architecture is generally used in supercomputers.

Within parallel computing, there are devices that provide a niche market because of its capabilities. As previously discussed, a system may have multiple cores, but may continue to be limited because of the amount of memory available to those cores. General purpose computing on graphics processing units (GPGPU) is an inexpensive means of adding additional processing ability to a computer. A very beneficial and generous amount of memory is attached to video cards that are only accessible to its GPU. GPGPUs address the multiple cores and memory limitations as an add-on card to a single computer system. As long as a motherboard has available PCI-Express × 16 slot available, it will be capable of hosting a very powerful GPGPU.

6.1.2 Distributed Computing

Distributed computing studies the models, architectures, and algorithms used for building and managing distributed systems. A distributed system is a collection of independent computers that appears to its users as a single coherent system. Distributed systems are primarily focused on aggregation of distributed resources and unified usage. This is accomplished by communicating with other computers only by exchanging messages.

A distributed system is the result of the interaction of several components across the entire computing stack from hardware to software. The hardware and operating system layers make up the bare-bone infrastructure of one or more data centers, where racks of servers are deployed, and connected together through high-speed connectivity. This infrastructure is managed by the operating system, which provides the basic capability of machine and network management. The core logic is then implemented in the middleware that manages the virtualization layer, which is deployed on the physical infrastructure in order to maximize its utilization and provide a customizable runtime environment for applications. The middleware provides different facilities and functionalities per the requirement of the end customers and users. These facilities range from virtual infrastructure building and deployment to application development and runtime environments.

The different layers constituting the distributed system stack are as follows:

1. *Hardware layer*: At the very bottom layer, computer and network hardware constitute the physical infrastructure; these components are directly managed by the operating system, which provides the basic services for interprocess communication (IPC), process scheduling and management, and resource management in terms of file system and local devices. Altogether these two layers become the platform on top of which specialized software is deployed to turn a set of networked computers into a distributed system.
2. *Operating system layer*: The use of well-known standards at the operating system level and even more at the hardware and network levels allows easy harnessing of heterogeneous components and their organization into a coherent and uniform system. For example, network connectivity between different devices is controlled by standards, which allow them to interact seamlessly. At the operating system level, IPC services are implemented on top of standardized communication protocols such as transmission control protocol/Internet protocol (TCP/IP), and user datagram protocol (UDP).

3. *Middleware layer*: The middleware layer leverages such services to build a uniform environment for the development and deployment of distributed applications. This layer supports the programming paradigms for distributed systems, which we will discuss in Chapters 5 and 8 of this book. By relying on the services offered by the operating system, the middleware develops its own protocols, data formats, and programming language, or frameworks for the development of distributed applications. All of them constitute a uniform interface to distributed application developers that is completely independent from the underlying operating system, and hides all the heterogeneities of the bottom layers.
4. *Application layer*: The topmost layer is represented by the applications and services designed and developed to use the middleware. These can serve several purposes and often expose their features in the form of graphical user interfaces (GUIs) accessible locally, or through the Internet via a web browser.

Architectural styles for distributed systems are helpful in understanding the different roles of components in the system and how they are distributed across multiple computers.

Architectural styles are of two types:

- System architectural style
- Software architectural style

6.1.2.1 System Architectural Styles

System architectural styles cover the physical organization of components and processes over a distributed infrastructure. They provide a set of reference models for the deployment of such systems and help engineers not only have a common vocabulary in describing the physical layout of systems, but also quickly identify the major advantages and drawbacks of a given deployment and whether it is applicable for a specific class of applications.

These reference models can be further enhanced or diversified according to the specific needs of the application to be designed and implemented.

6.1.2.1.1 N-Tier Architecture

In the 1980s, the prior monolithic architecture began to be replaced by the client or server architecture, which split applications into two pieces in an attempt to leverage new inexpensive desktop machines. Distributing the processing loads across many inexpensive clients allowed client or server applications to scale more linearly than single host or single process applications could, and the use of off-the-shelf software-like relational database management systems (RDBMS) greatly reduced application development time. Although the client could handle the user interface and data display tasks of the application, and the server could handle all the data management tasks, there was no clear solution for storing the logic corresponding to the business processes being automated. Consequently, the business logic tended to split between the client and the server; typically, the rules for displaying data became embedded inside the user interface, and the rules for integrating several different data sources became stored procedures inside the database. Although this division of logic made it difficult to reuse the user interface code with a different data source, it also made it equally difficult to use the logic stored in the database with a different front-end user interface (like ATM and mobile) without being required to redevelop the logic implemented in the earlier interface. Thus, a customer service system developed for a particular client system (like a 3270 terminal, a PC, or a workstation) would have great difficulty in providing telephony and Internet interfaces with the same business functionality.

The client or server architecture failed to recognize the importance of managing the business rules applicable to an enterprise independent of both the user interface and the storage and management of enterprise data. The three-tier application architecture of the 1990s resolved this problem by subdividing the application into three distinct layers:

1. Data management, which stores and manages data independent of how they are processed and displayed by the other layers
2. Business logic, which implements the business logic to process data independent of how they are stored or displayed by the other two layers
3. Presentation, which formats and displays the data independent of the way they are interpreted or processed and stored by the other two layers

With the advent of the Internet in the past few years, the three tiers were split even further to accommodate the heterogeneity in terms of the user interfaces, processing systems, or databases existing in various parts of an enterprise.

> The power of the n-tier architecture derives from the fact that instead of treating components as integral parts of systems, components are treated as standalone entities, which can provide services for applications. Applications exist only as cooperating constellation of components, and each component in turn can simultaneously be part of many different applications.

6.1.2.1.2 Peer-to-Peer

The peer-to-peer model introduces a symmetric architecture in which all the components, called peers, play the same role and incorporate both client and server capabilities of the client or the server model. More precisely, each peer acts as a server when it processes requests from other peers and as a client when it issues requests to other peers. With respect to the client or server model that partitions the responsibilities of the IPC between server and clients, the peer-to-peer model attributes the same responsibilities to each component. Therefore, this model is quite suitable for highly decentralized architecture, which can scale better along the dimension of the number of peers. The disadvantage of this approach is that the management of the implementation of algorithms is more complex than in the client or server model.

6.1.2.2 Software Architectural Styles

Software architectural styles are based on the logical arrangement of software components. They are helpful because they provide an intuitive view of the whole system, despite its physical deployment.

6.1.2.2.1 Data-Centered Architectures

The repository architectural style is the most relevant reference model in this category. It is characterized by two main components: the central data structure, which represents the current state of the system, and a collection of independent components, which operate on the central data. The ways in which the independent components interact with the central data structure can be very heterogeneous. In particular, repository-based architectures differentiate and specialize further into subcategories according to the choice of control discipline to apply for the shared data structure.

Data-centered architectures are of two types:

1. *Database systems*: In this case, the dynamic of the system is controlled by the independent components, which, by issuing an operation on the central repository, trigger the selection of specific processes that operate on data.
2. *Blackboard systems*: In this case, the central data structure itself is the main trigger for selecting the processes to execute knowledge sources representing the intelligent agents sharing the blackboard, react opportunistically to changes in the knowledge base—almost in the same way that a group of specialists brainstorm in a room in front of a blackboard.

   The blackboard architectural style is characterized by three main components:

   - *Knowledge sources*: These are the entities that update the knowledge base that is maintained in the blackboard.
   - *Blackboard*: This represents the data structure that is shared among the knowledge sources and stores the knowledge base of the application.
   - *Control*: The control is the collection of triggers and procedures that govern the interaction with the blackboard and update the status of the knowledge base.

   Blackboard models have become popular and widely used for artificial intelligent applications in which the blackboard maintains the knowledge about a domain in the form of assertions and rules, which are entered by domain experts. These operate through a control shell that controls the problem-solving activity of the system. Particular and successful applications of this model can be found in the domains of speech recognition and signal processing.

6.1.2.2.2 Data-Flow Architectures

In the case of data-flow architectures, it is the availability of data that controls the computation. With respect to the data-centered styles, in which the access to data is the core feature, data-flow styles explicitly incorporate the pattern of data flow, since their design is determined by an orderly motion of data from component to component, which is the form of communication between them. Styles within this category differ in one of the following ways: how the control is exerted, the degree of concurrency among components, and the topology that describes the flow of data.

Data-flow architectures are optimal when the system to be designed embodies a multistage process, which can be clearly identified as a collection of separate components that need to be orchestrated together. Within this reference scenario, components have well-defined interfaces exposing input and output ports, and the connectors are represented by the data streams between these ports.

1. *Batch sequential style*: The batch sequential style is characterized by an ordered sequence of separate programs executing one after the other. These programs are chained together by providing as an input for the next program and the output generated by the last program after its completion, which is most likely in the form of a file. This design was very popular in the mainframe era of computing and still finds applications today. For example, many distributed applications for scientific computing are defined by jobs expressed as sequences of programs that, for example, prefilter, analyze, and postprocess data. It is very common to compose these phases using the batch-sequential style.
2. *Pipe-and-filter style*: The pipe-and-filter style is a variation of the previous style for expressing the activity of a software system as sequence of data transformations. Each component of the processing chain is called a filter, and the connection between one filter and the next is represented by data stream. With respect to the batch sequential style, data are processed incrementally and each filter processes the data as soon as it is available on the input stream. As soon as one filter produces a consumable amount of data, the next filter can start its processing. Filters generally do not have state, know the identity of neither the previous nor the next filter, and they are connected with in-memory data structures such as first-in or first-out (FIFO) buffers or other structures. This particular sequencing is called pipelining and introduces concurrency in the execution of the filters.

   A classic example of this architecture is the microprocessor pipeline whereby multiple instructions are executed at the same time by completing a different phase of each of them. We can identify the phases of the instructions as the filters, whereas the data streams are represented by the registries that are shared within the processors. Another example is the unix shell pipes (i.e., cat <file-name>| grep<pattern>| wc -l), where the filters are the single shell programs composed together and the connections are their input and output streams that are chained together. Applications of this architecture can also be found in the compiler design (e.g., the lex or yacc model is based on a pipe of the following phases: | scanning | parsing | semantic analysis | code generation), image and signal processing, and voice and video streaming.

6.1.2.2.3 Call and Return Architectures

This category identifies all systems that are organized into components mostly connected together by method calls. The activity of systems modeled in this way is characterized by a chain of method calls whose overall execution and composition identify the execution of one or more operations. The internal organization of components and their connections may vary. Nonetheless, it is possible to identify three major subcategories, which differentiate by the way the system is structured, and how methods are invoked: top-down style, object-oriented style, and layered style.

1. *Top-down style*: This architectural style is quite representative of systems developed with imperative programming, which leads to a divide-and-conquer approach to problem resolution. Systems developed according to this style are composed of one large main program that accomplishes its tasks by invoking subprograms or procedures. The components in this style are procedures and subprograms, and connections are method calls or invocation. The calling program passes information with parameters and receives data from return values or parameters. Method calls can also extend beyond the boundary of a single process by leveraging techniques

for remote method invocation, such as remote procedure call (RPC) and all its descendants. The overall structure of the program execution at any point in time is characterized by a tree, the root of which constitutes the main function of the principal program. This architectural style is quite intuitive from a design point of view, but hard to maintain and manage in large systems.

2. *Layered style*: The layered system style allows the design and implementation of software systems in terms of layers, which provide a different level of abstraction of the system. Each layer generally operates with at most two layers: the one that provides a lower abstraction level and the one that provides a higher abstraction layer. Specific protocols and interfaces define how adjacent layers interact. It is possible to model such systems as a stack of layers, one for each level of abstraction. Therefore, the components are the layers and the connectors are the interfaces and protocols used between adjacent layers. A user or client generally interacts with the layer at the highest abstraction, which, in order to carry its activity, interacts and uses the services of the lower layer. This process is repeated (if necessary) until the lowest layer is reached. It is also possible to have the opposite behavior: events and callbacks from the lower layers can trigger the activity of the higher layer and propagate information up through the stack.

   Following are the advantages of the layered style:

   a. It supports a modular design of systems and allows us to decompose the system according to different levels of abstractions by encapsulating together all the operations that belong to a specific level.
   b. It enables layers to be replaced as long as they are compliant with the expected protocols and interfaces, thus making the system flexible.

   The main disadvantage is constituted by the lack of extensibility, since it is not possible to add layers without changing the protocols and the interfaces between layers. This also makes it complex to add operations. Examples of layered architectures are the modern operating system kernels and the International Standards Organization/Open Systems Interconnection (ISO/OSI) or the TCP or IP stack.

3. *Object-oriented style*: This architectural style encompasses a wide range of systems that have been designed and implemented by leveraging the abstractions of object-oriented programming (OOP). Systems are specified in terms of classes and implemented in terms of objects. Classes define the type of components by specifying the data that represent their state, and the operations that can be done over these data. One of the main advantages over the top-down style is that there is a coupling between data and operations used to manipulate them. Object instances become responsible for hiding their internal state representation and for protecting its integrity while providing operations to other components. This leads to a better decomposition process and more manageable systems. Disadvantages of this style are mainly the following two: each object needs to know the identity of an object if it wants to invoke operations on it, and shared objects need to be carefully designed in order to ensure the consistency of their state.

6.1.2.2.4 Virtual Architectures

The virtual machine class of architectural styles is characterized by the presence of an abstract execution environment (generally referred to as a virtual machine) that simulates features that are not available in the hardware or software. Applications and systems are implemented on top of this layer and become portable over different hardware and software environments as long as there is an implementation of the virtual machine they interface with. The general interaction flow for systems implementing this pattern is the following: the program (or the application) defines its operations and state in an abstract format, which is interpreted by the virtual machine engine. The interpretation of a program constitutes its execution. It is quite common in this scenario that the engine maintains an internal representation of the program state. Very popular examples within this category are rule-based systems, interpreters, and command-language processors.

Virtual machine architectural styles are characterized by an indirection layer between applications and the hosting environment. This design has the major advantage of decoupling applications from the underlying hardware and software environment, but at the same time it introduces some disadvantages, such as a slowdown in performance. Other issues might be related to the fact that, by providing a virtual execution environment, following specific features of the underlying system might not be accessible:

1. *Rule-based style*: This architecture is characterized by representing the abstract execution environment as an inference engine. Programs are expressed in the form of rules or predicates that hold true. The input data for applications are generally represented by a set of assertions or facts that the inference engine uses to activate rules or to apply predicates, thus transforming data. The output can either be the product of the rule activation or a set of assertions that holds true for the given input data. The set of rules or predicates identifies the knowledge base that can be queried to infer properties about the system. This approach is quite peculiar, since it allows expressing a system or a domain, in terms of its behavior rather than in terms of the components. Rule-based systems are very popular in the field of artificial intelligence. Practical applications can be found in the field of process control, where rule-based systems are used to monitor the status of physical devices by being fed from the sensory data collected and processed by programmable logic controllers (PLCs) and by activating alarms when specific conditions on the sensory data apply. Another interesting use of rule-based systems can be found in the networking domain: network intrusion detection systems (NIDS) often rely on a set of rules to identify abnormal behaviors connected to possible intrusions in computing systems
2. *Interpreter style*: The core feature of the interpreter style is the presence of an engine that is used to interpret a pseudo-program expressed in a format acceptable for the interpreter. The interpretation of the pseudo-program constitutes the execution of the program itself. Systems modeled according to this style exhibit the following four main components: the interpretation engine that executes the core activity of this style, an internal memory that contains the pseudo-code to be interpreted, a representation of the current state of the engine, and a representation of the current state of the program being executed. This model is quite useful in designing virtual machines for high-level programming (Java, C#) and scripting languages (Awk, PERL, etc.). Within this scenario, the virtual machine closes the gap between the end-user abstractions and the software or hardware environment in which such abstractions are executed.

6.1.2.2.5 *Independent Components*

This class of architectural style models systems in terms of independent components that have their own life cycles, which interact with each other to perform their activities.

There are two major categories within this class—communicating processes and event systems—which differentiate in the way the interaction among components is managed.

1. *Communicating processes*: In this architectural style, components are represented by independent processes that leverage inter process communication (IPC) facilities for coordination management. This is an abstraction that is quite suitable to modeling distributed systems that, being distributed over a network of computing nodes, are necessarily composed of several concurrent processes. Each of the processes provides other processes with services and can leverage the services exposed by the other processes. The conceptual organization of these processes and the way in which the communication happens vary according to the specific model, used either peer-to-peer or client/server. Connectors are identified by IPC facilities used by these processes to communicate.
2. *Event systems*: In this architectural style, the components of the system are loosely coupled and connected. In addition to exposing operations for data and state manipulation, each component also publishes (or announces) a collection of events with which other components can register. In general, other components provide a callback that will be executed when the event is activated. During the activity of a component, a specific runtime condition can activate one of the exposed events, thus triggering the execution of the callbacks registered with it. Event activation may be accompanied by contextual information that can be used in the callback to handle the event. This information can be passed as an argument to the callback or by using some shared repository between components. Event-based systems have become quite popular, and support for their implementation is provided either at the API level or the programming language level.

   The main advantage of such an architectural style is that it fosters the development of open systems: new modules can be added and easily integrated into the system as long as they have compliant interfaces for registering to the events. This architectural style solves some of the following limitations observed for the top-down and object-oriented styles:

   a. The invocation pattern is implicit, and the connection between the caller and the callee is not hard-coded; this gives a lot of flexibility since addition or removal of a handler to events can be done without changes in the source code of applications.
   b. The event source does not need to know the identity of the event handler in order to invoke the callback.

   The disadvantage of such a style is that it relinquishes control over system computation. When a component triggers an event, it does not know how many event handlers will be invoked and whether there are any registered handlers. This information is available only at runtime and, from a static design point of view, becomes more complex to identify the connections among components and to reason about the correctness of the interactions.

6.1.2.3 Technologies for Distributed Computing

Middleware is system services software that executes between the operating system layer and the application layer and provides services. It connects two or more applications, thus providing connectivity and interoperability to the applications. Middleware is not a silver bullet that will solve all integration problems. Owing to overhype in the 1980s and early 1990s, the term middleware has lost popularity but is coming back in the past few years. The middleware concept, however, is today even more important for integration, and all integration projects will have to use one or many different middleware solutions. Middleware is mainly used to denote products that provide glue between applications, which is distinct from simple data import and export functions that might be built into the applications themselves.

All forms of middleware are helpful in easing the communication between different software applications. The selection of middleware influences the application architecture, because middleware centralizes the software infrastructure and its deployment. Middleware introduces an abstraction layer in the system architecture and thus reduces the complexity considerably. On the other hand, each middleware product introduces a certain communication overhead into the system, which can influence performance, scalability, throughput, and other efficiency factors. This is important to consider when designing the integration architecture, particularly if our systems are mission critical and are used by a large number of concurrent clients.

Middleware is connectivity software that is designed to help manage the complexity and heterogeneity inherent in distributed systems by building a bridge between different systems, thereby enabling communication and transfer of data. Middleware could be defined as a layer of enabling software services that allow application elements to interoperate across network links, despite differences in underlying communications protocols, system architectures, operating systems, databases, and other application services. The role of middleware is to ease the task of designing, programming, and managing distributed applications by providing a simple, consistent, and integrated distributed programming environment. Essentially, middleware is a distributed software layer, or platform, that lives above the operating system and abstracts over the complexity and heterogeneity of the underlying distributed environment with its multitude of network technologies, machine architectures, operating systems, and programming languages.

The middleware layers are interposed between applications and Internet transport protocols. The middleware abstraction comprises of two layers. The bottom layer is concerned with the characteristics of protocols for communicating between processes in a distributed system and how the data objects, for example, a customer order and data structures used in application programs can be translated into a suitable form for sending messages over a communications network, taking into account that different computers may rely on heterogeneous representations for simple data items. Thus, the bottom layer is concerned with interprocess communication mechanisms, whereas the layer above that is concerned with nonmessage- and message-based forms of middleware. Message-based forms of middleware provide asynchronous messaging and event notification mechanisms to exchange messages or react to events over electronic networks. Nonmessage-based forms of middleware provide synchronous communication mechanisms designed to support client–server communication.

Middleware uses two basic modes of message communication:

1. *Synchronous or time-dependent*: The defining characteristic of a synchronous form of execution is that message communication is synchronized between two communicating application systems, which must both be up and running, and that execution flow at the client's side is interrupted, to execute the call. Both sending

and receiving applications must be ready to communicate with each other at all times. A sending application initiates a request (sends a message) to a receiving application. The sending application then blocks its processing until it receives a response from the receiving application. The receiving application continues its processing after it receives the response.

2. *Asynchronous or time-independent*: With asynchronous communication, an application sends (requestor or sender) a request to another while it continues its own processing activities. The sending application does not have to wait for the receiving application to complete and for its reply to come back. Instead, it can continue processing other requests. Unlike the synchronous mode, both application systems (sender and receiver) do not have to be active at the same time for processing to occur.

The basic messaging processes inherently utilize asynchronous communication. There are several benefits to asynchronous messaging:

a. Asynchronous messaging clients can proceed with application processing independently of other applications. Loose coupling of senders and receivers optimizes system processing by not having to block sending client processing while waiting for the receiving client to complete the request.
b. Asynchronous messaging allows batch and parallel processing of messages. The sending client can send as many messages to receiving clients without having to wait for the receiving clients to process previously sent messages. On the receiving end, different receiving clients can process the messages at their own speed and timing.
c. There is less demand on the communication network because the messaging clients do not have to be connected to each other or the message oriented middleware (MOM) while messages are processed. Connections are active only to put messages to the MOM and get messages from the MOM.
d. The network does not have to be available at all times because of timing independence of client processing. Messages can wait in the queue of the receiving client if the network is not available. MOM implements asynchronous message queues at its core. It can concurrently service many sending and receiving applications.

Despite the performance drawbacks, synchronous messaging has several benefits over asynchronous messaging. The tightly coupled nature of synchronous messaging means the sending client can better handle application errors in the receiving client. If an error occurs in the receiving client, the sending client can try to compensate for the error. This is especially important when the sending client requests a transaction to be performed in the receiving client. The better error-handling ability of synchronous messaging means it is easier for programmers to develop synchronous messaging solutions. As both the sending and receiving clients are online and connected, it is easier for programmers to debug errors that might occur during the development stage. Since most developers are also more familiar with programming using synchronous processing, this also facilities the development of synchronous messaging solutions over asynchronous messaging solutions.

When speaking of middleware products, we encompass a large variety of technologies. The most common forms of middleware are as follows:

1. Database access technologies
   a. Microsoft open database connectivity (ODBC)
   b. Java database connectivity (JDBC)
2. Asynchronous middleware
   a. Store and forward messaging
   b. Publish or subscribe messaging
   c. Point-to-point queuing
   d. Event-driven processing mechanism
3. Synchronous middleware
   a. Remote procedure call (RPC)
   b. Remote method invocation (RMI)
4. Message-oriented middleware (MOM)
   a. Integration brokers
   b. Java messaging service (JMS)
5. Request or reply messaging middleware
6. Transaction processing monitors (TPMs)
7. Object request brokers (ORBs)
   a. OMG CORBA ORB compliant
   b. Java RMI and RMI-IIOP (Internet inter-ORB protocol)
   c. Microsoft COM/DCOM/COM+/.NET remoting/WCF
8. Application servers
9. Service oriented architecture
   a. Web services using WSDL, UDDI, SOAP, and XML
   b. RESTful services
10. Enterprise service buses (ESBs)
11. Enterprise systems

For a detailed discussion on the above technologies, refer to Chapter 5 "Integration Technologies" of the companion volume *Guide to Cloud Computing for Business and Technology Managers* (Kale 2015).

6.2 Distributed Databases

A distributed database is a logically interrelated collection of shared data (and a description of these data), physically distributed over a computer network. The distributed database management system (DDBMS) is the software that transparently manages the distributed database.

A DDBMS is distinct from distributed processing, where a centralized DBMS is accessed over a network. It is also distinct from a parallel DBMS, which is a DBMS running across multiple processors and disks and which has been designed to evaluate operations in parallel, whenever possible, in order to improve performance. The advantages of a DDBMS are that it is enabled to reflect the organizational structure; it makes remote data more shareable, it improves reliability, availability, and performance; it may be more economical; and it provides for modular growth, facilitates integration, and helps organizations to remain competitive. The major disadvantages are cost, complexity, lack of standards, and experience.

A DDBMS may be classified as homogeneous or heterogeneous. In a homogeneous system, all sites use the same DBMS product. In a heterogeneous system, sites may run different DBMS products, which need not be based on the same underlying data model, and so the system may be composed of relational, network, hierarchical, and object-oriented DBMSs. A multidatabase system (MDBS) is a distributed DBMS, in which each site maintains complete autonomy. An MDBS resides transparently on top of an existing database and file systems and presents a single database to its users. It maintains a global schema against which users issue queries and updates; an MDBS maintains only the global schema and the local DBMSs themselves maintain all user data.

Communication takes place over a network, which may be a local area network (LAN) or a wide area network (WAN). LANs are intended for short distances and provide faster communication than WANs. A special case of the WAN is a metropolitan area network (MAN), which generally covers a city or suburb. As well as having the standard functionality expected of a centralized DBMS, a DDBMS needs extended communication services, extended system catalog, distributed query processing, and extended security, concurrency, and recovery services.

Network design and performance issues are critical for an efficient operation of a distributed DDBS and are an integral part of the overall solution. The nodes may all be located in the same campus and connected via a LAN, or they may be geographically distributed over large distances and connected via a long haul or WAN. LANs typically use wireless hubs or cables, whereas long haul networks use telephone lines, cables, wireless communication infrastructures, or satellites.

The DDBMS appears like a centralized DBMS by providing a series of transparencies. With distribution transparency, users should not know that the data have been fragmented or replicated. With transaction transparency, the consistency of the global database should be maintained when multiple users are accessing the database concurrently and when failures occur. With performance transparency, the system should be able to efficiently handle queries that reference data do at more than one site.

A relation may be divided into a number of subrelations called fragments, which are allocated to one or more sites. Fragments may be replicated to provide improved availability and performance. There are two main types of fragmentation: horizontal and vertical. Horizontal fragments are subsets of tuples and vertical fragments are subsets of attributes. The definition and allocation of fragments are carried out strategically to achieve locality of reference, improved reliability and availability, acceptable performance, balanced storage capacities and costs, and minimal communication costs.

6.2.1 Characteristics of Distributed Databases

6.2.1.1 *Transparency*

A highly transparent system offers a lot of flexibility to the end user and application developer since it implies being oblivious of the underlying details on their part. The concept of transparency extends the general idea of hiding implementation details from end users. In the case of a traditional centralized database, transparency simply pertains to logical and physical data independence for application developers. However, in a DDB scenario, the data and software are distributed over multiple nodes connected by a computer network, so additional types of transparencies are introduced.

1. *Distribution or network transparency*: This refers to freedom for the user from the operational details of the network and the placement of the data in the distributed system.

   Distribution transparency can be of two types:

   a. Naming transparency implies that once a name is associated with an object, the named objects can be accessed unambiguously without additional specification as to where the data is located.

   b. Location transparency refers to the fact that the command used to perform a task is independent of the location of the data and the location of the node where the command was issued.

2. Fragmentation transparency.

   Fragmentation transparency can be of two types:

   a. Horizontal fragmentation distributes a relation (table) into subrelations that are subsets of the tuples (rows) in the original relation, which is also known as sharding in the newer big data and cloud computing systems.

   b. Vertical fragmentation distributes a relation into subrelations where each subrelation is defined by a subset of the columns of the original relation. Fragmentation transparency makes the user unaware of the existence of fragments.

3. Replication transparency implies that copies of the same data objects may be stored at multiple sites for better availability, performance, and reliability. Replication transparency makes the user unaware of the existence of these copies.

6.2.1.2 *Availability and Reliability*

Reliability and availability are two of the most common potential advantages cited for distributed databases. Reliability is broadly defined as the probability that a system is running (not down) at a certain time point, whereas availability is the probability that the system is continuously available during a time interval. Reliability and availability of the database are directly related to the faults, errors, and failures associated with it. Fault is the cause of an error. Errors constitute that subset of system states that causes the failure. A failure can be described as a deviation of a system's behavior from that which is specified in order to ensure correct execution of operations.

A reliable DDBMS tolerates failures of underlying components, and it processes user requests as long as database consistency is not violated.

A DDBMS system can adopt several strategies to achieve the objective of system reliability:

1. A cure-oriented fault-tolerance strategy recognizes that faults will occur, and it designs mechanisms that can detect and remove faults before they can result in a system failure.
2. A prevention-oriented strategy attempts to ensure that the final system does not contain any faults. This is achieved through an exhaustive design process followed by extensive quality control and testing.

A DDBMS recovery manager deals with failures arising from transactions, hardware, and communication networks. Hardware failures can either be those that result in loss of main memory contents or loss of secondary storage contents. Network failures occur due to errors associated with messages and line failures. Message errors can include their loss, corruption, or out-of-order arrival at destination.

6.2.1.3 Scalability and Partition Tolerance

Scalability determines the extent to which the system can expand its capacity while continuing to operate without interruption.

Scalability can be of two types:

1. *Horizontal scalability*: This refers to expanding the number of nodes in the distributed system. As nodes are added to the system, some of the data and processing loads are distributed from existing nodes to the new nodes.
2. *Vertical scalability*: This refers to expanding the capacity of the individual nodes in the system, such as expanding the storage capacity or the processing power of a node.

The concept of partition tolerance states that the system should have the capacity to continue operating while the network is partitioned. As the system expands its number of nodes, it is possible that the network, which connects the nodes, may have faults that cause the nodes to be partitioned into groups of nodes. The nodes within each partition are still connected by a subnetwork, but communication among the partitions is lost.

6.2.1.4 Autonomy

Autonomy determines the extent to which individual nodes or databases in a connected DDB can operate independently. A high degree of autonomy is desirable for increased flexibility and customized maintenance of an individual node.

Autonomy can be of three types:

1. Design autonomy refers to independence of data model usage and transaction management techniques among nodes.
2. Communication autonomy determines the extent to which each node can decide on sharing of information with other nodes.
3. Execution autonomy refers to independence of users to act as they please.

6.2.2 Advantages and Disadvantages of Distributed Databases

The advantages of distributed databases are as follows:

1. *Improved ease and flexibility of application development*: Developing and maintaining applications at geographically distributed sites of an organization is facilitated due to transparency of data distribution and control.
2. *Increased availability*: This is achieved by the isolation of faults to their site of origin without affecting the other database nodes connected to the network. When the data and DDBMS software are distributed over many sites, one site may fail, whereas other sites continue to operate. Only the data and software that exist at the failed site cannot be accessed. Further improvement is achieved by judiciously replicating data and software at more than one site. In a centralized system, failure at a single site makes the whole system unavailable to all users. In a distributed database, some of the data may be unreachable, but users may still be able to access other parts of the database. If the data in the failed site have been replicated at another site prior to the failure, then the user will not be affected at all. The ability of the system to survive network partitioning also contributes to high availability.
3. *Improved performance*: A distributed DBMS fragments the database by keeping the data closer to where it is needed most. Data localization reduces the contention for CPU and I/O services and simultaneously reduces access delays involved in WANs. When a large database is distributed over multiple sites, smaller databases exist at each site. As a result, local queries and transactions, accessing data at a single site have better performance because of the smaller local databases. In addition, each site has a smaller number of transactions executing than if all transactions are submitted to a single centralized database. Moreover, interquery and intraquery parallelism can be achieved by executing multiple queries at different sites, or by breaking up a query into a number of subqueries that execute in parallel. This contributes to improved performance.
4. *Easier expansion via scalability*: In a distributed environment, expansion of the system in terms of adding more data, increasing database sizes, or adding more nodes is much easier than in centralized (nondistributed) systems.

The disadvantages of distributed databases are as follows:

1. *More Complex Treatment of Concurrent Update:* Concurrent update in a distributed database is treated basically the same way it is treated in nondistributed databases. A user transaction acquires locks, and the locking is two-phase. (Locks are acquired in a growing phase, during which time no locks are released and the DDBMS applies the updates. All locks are released during the shrinking phase.) The DDBMS detects and breaks deadlocks, and then the DDBMS rolls back interrupted transactions. The primary distinction lies not in the kinds of activities that take place but in the additional level of complexity that gets created by the very nature of a distributed database.

   If all the records to be updated by a particular transaction occur at one site, the problem is essentially the same as in a nondistributed database. However, the records in a distributed database might be stored at many different sites. Furthermore, if the data is replicated, each occurrence might be stored at several sites, each requiring the same update to be performed. Assuming each record occurrence has replicas at three different sites, an update that would affect 5 record occurrences in a nondistributed system might affect 20 different record occurrences in a distributed system (each record occurrence together with its three replica occurrences).

Having more record occurrences to update is only part of the problem. Assuming each site keeps its own locks, the DDBMS must send many messages for each record to be updated: a request for a lock, a message indicating that the record is already locked by another user or that the lock has been granted, a message directing that the update be performed, an acknowledgment of the update, and finally a message indicating that the record is to be unlocked. Because all those messages must be sent for each record and its occurrences, the total time for an update can be substantially longer in a distributed database.

A partial solution to minimize the number of messages involves the use of the primary copy mentioned earlier. Recall that one of the replicas of a given record occurrence is designated as the primary copy. Locking the primary copy, rather than all copies, is sufficient and will reduce the number of messages required to lock and unlock records. The number of messages might still be large, however, and the unavailability of the primary copy can cause an entire transaction to fail. Thus, even this partial solution presents problems.

Just as in a nondistributed database, deadlock is a possibility in a distributed database. In a distributed database, however, deadlock is more complicated because two types of deadlocks are possible:

a. Local deadlock is deadlock that occurs at a single site in a distributed database. If each of the two transactions is waiting for a record held by the other at the same site, the local DBMS can detect and resolve the deadlock with a minimum number of messages needed to communicate the situation to the other DBMSs in the distributed system.

b. Global deadlock involves one transaction that requires a record held by a second transaction at one site, whereas the second transaction requires a record held by the first transaction at a different site. In this case, neither site has information individually to allow this deadlock to be detected; this is a global deadlock, and it can be detected and resolved only by sending a large number of messages between the DBMSs at the two sites.

2. *Update of Replicated Data:* Replicating data can improve processing speed and ensure that the overall system remains available even when the database at one site is unavailable. However, replication can cause update problems, most obviously in terms of the extra time needed to update all the copies. Instead of updating a single copy of the data, the DBMS must update several copies. Because most of these copies are at sites other than the site initiating the update, each update transaction requires extra time to update each copy and extra time to communicate all the update messages over the network.

Often a DDBMS designates one copy of the data to be the primary copy. As long as the primary copy is updated, the DDBMS considers the update to be complete. The primary site and the DDBMS must ensure that all the other copies are in sync. The primary site sends update transactions to the other sites and notes whether any sites are currently unavailable. If a site is unavailable, the primary site must try to send the update again at some later time and continue trying until it succeeds. This strategy overcomes the basic problem, but it obviously uses more time. Further, if the primary site is unavailable, the problem would remain unresolved.

3. *More Complex Query Processing:* Processing queries is more complex in a distributed database. The complexity occurs because of the difference in the time it takes to send messages between sites and the time it takes to access a disk.

   Systems that are record-at-a-time-oriented can create severe performance problems in distributed systems. If the only choice is to transmit every record from one site to another site as a message and then examine it at the other site, the communication time required can become unacceptably high. DDBMSs that permit a request for a set of records, as opposed to an individual record, outperform record-at-a-time systems.

4. *More Complex Recovery Measures:* Although the basic recovery process for a distributed database is the same as for centralized database, there is an additional potential problem. To make sure that the database remains consistent, each database update should be made permanent or aborted and undone, in which case, none of its changes will be made. In a distributed database, with an individual transaction updating several local databases, it is possible—because of problems affecting individual sites—for local DBMSs to commit the updates at some sites and undo the updates at other sites, thereby creating an inconsistent state in the distributed database. The DDBMS must not allow this inconsistency to occur.

   A DDBMS usually prevents this potential inconsistency through the use of two-phase commit. The basic idea of two-phase commit is that one site, often the site initiating the update, acts as a coordinator. In the first phase, the coordinator sends messages to all other sites, requesting that they prepare to update the database; in other words, each site acquires all necessary locks. The sites do not update at this point, however, but they do send messages to the coordinator stating that they are ready to update.

   If for any reason any site cannot secure the necessary locks or if any site must abort its updates, the site sends a message to the coordinator that all sites must abort the transaction. The coordinator waits for replies from all sites involved before determining whether to commit the following updates:

   a. If all replies are positive, the coordinator sends a message to each site to commit the update. At this point, each site must proceed with the commit process.
   b. If any reply is negative, the coordinator sends a message to each site to abort the update, and each site must follow this instruction. In this way, the DDBMS guarantees consistency.

   Although a process similar to two-phase commit is essential to the consistency of the database, two problems are associated with it. For one thing, many messages are sent during the process. For another, during the second phase, each site must follow the instructions from the coordinator; otherwise, the process will not accomplish its intended result. This process means that the sites are not as independent as you would like them to be.

5. *More Complicated Security and Backup Requirements:* With a single central database, you need to secure the central physical site, the central database, and the network connecting users to the database at the central site. The security requirements for a distributed database are more demanding, requiring you to secure every physical site and every database, in addition to securing the network. Backing up a distributed database is also more complicated and is best initiated and controlled from a single site.
6. *More Difficult Management of the Data Dictionary:* A distributed database introduces further complexity to the management of the data dictionary or catalog. The choice of storing the data dictionary can have three options:
   a. Choose one site and store the complete data dictionary at this site and this site alone
   b. Store a complete copy of the data dictionary at each site
   c. Distribute, possibly with replication, the data dictionary entries among the various sites

   Although storing the complete data dictionary at a single site is a relatively simple approach to administer, retrieving information in the data dictionary from any other site is more time-consuming because of the communication involved. Storing a complete copy of the data dictionary at every site solves the retrieval problem because a local DBMS can handle any retrieval locally. Because this second approach involves total replication (every data dictionary occurrence is replicated at every site), updates to the data dictionary are more time-consuming. If the data dictionary is updated with any frequency, the extra time needed to update all copies of the data dictionary might be unacceptable.

   One intermediate strategy is to partition the data by storing data dictionary entries at the site at which the data they describe are located. Interestingly, this approach also suffers from a problem. If a user queries the data dictionary to access an entry not stored at the user's site, the system has no way of knowing the entry's location. Satisfying this user's query might involve sending a message to every other site, which involves a considerable amount of network and DDBMS overhead.
7. *More Complex Database Design:* A distributed database adds another level of complexity to database design. Distributing data does not affect the information-level design. During the physical-level design in a nondistributed database, disk activity—both the number of disk accesses and the volumes of data to be transported—is one of the principal concerns. Although disk activity is also a factor in a distributed database, communication activity becomes another concern during the physical-level design. Because transmitting data from one site to another is much slower than transferring data to and from disk, in many situations, communication activity is the most important physical-level design factor. In addition, you must consider possible fragmentation and replication during the physical-level design.

6.2.3 Data Replication and Allocation

Replication is useful in improving the availability of data. The most extreme case is replication of the whole database at every site in the distributed system, thus creating a fully replicated distributed database. This can improve availability remarkably because the system can continue to operate as long as at least one site is up. It also improves performance of retrieval (read performance) for global queries because the results of such queries can be obtained locally from any one site; hence, a retrieval query can be processed at the local site where it is submitted, if that site includes a server module. The disadvantage of full replication is that it can slow down update operations (write performance) drastically, since a single logical update must be performed on every copy of the database to keep the copies consistent. This is especially true if many copies of the database exist. Full replication makes the concurrency control and recovery techniques more expensive than they would be if there was no replication.

The other extreme from full replication involves having no replication—that is, each fragment is stored at exactly one site. In this case, all fragments must be disjoint, except for the repetition of primary keys among vertical (or mixed) fragments. This is also called nonredundant allocation.

Between these two extremes, we have a wide spectrum of partial replication of the data—that is, some fragments of the database may be replicated whereas others may not. The number of copies of each fragment can range from one up to the total number of sites in the distributed system. A special case of partial replication is occurring heavily in applications where mobile workers—such as sales forces, financial planners, and claims adjustors—carry partially replicated databases with them on laptops and PDAs and synchronize them periodically with the server database. A description of the replication of fragments is sometimes called a replication schema.

Each fragment—or each copy of a fragment—must be assigned to a particular site in the distributed system. This process is called data distribution (or data allocation). The choice of sites and the degree of replication depend on the performance and availability goals of the system and on the types and frequencies of transactions submitted at each site. For example, if high availability is required, transactions can be submitted at any site, and most transactions are retrieval only, a fully replicated database is a good choice. However, if certain transactions that access particular parts of the database are mostly submitted at a particular site, the corresponding set of fragments can be allocated at that site only. Data that are accessed at multiple sites can be replicated at those sites. If many updates are performed, it may be useful to limit replication. Finding an optimal or even a good solution to distributed data allocation is a complex optimization problem.

6.2.4 Concurrency Control and Recovery

For concurrency control and recovery purposes, numerous problems arise in a distributed DBMS environment that are not encountered in a centralized DBMS environment. These include the following:

- *Dealing with multiple copies of the data items*: The concurrency control method is responsible for maintaining consistency among these copies. The recovery method is responsible for making a copy consistent with other copies, if the site on which the copy is stored fails and recovers later.

- *Failure of individual sites*: The DDBMS should continue to operate with its running sites, if possible, when one or more individual sites fail. When a site recovers, its local database must be brought up-to-date with the rest of the sites before it rejoins the system.
- *Failure of communication links*: The system must be able to deal with the failure of one or more of the communication links that connect the sites. An extreme case of this problem is that network partitioning may occur. This breaks up the sites into two or more partitions, where the sites within each partition can communicate only with one another and not with sites in other partitions.
- *Distributed commit*: Problems can arise with committing a transaction that is accessing databases stored on multiple sites if some sites fail during the commit process. The two-phase commit protocol (see Section 6.2.6.1) is often used to deal with this problem.
- *Distributed deadlock*: Deadlock may occur among several sites, so techniques for dealing with deadlocks must be extended to take this into account.

Distributed concurrency control and recovery techniques must deal with these and other problems. In the following subsections, we review some of the techniques that have been suggested to deal with recovery and concurrency control in DDBMSs.

To deal with replicated data items in a distributed database, a number of concurrency control methods have been proposed that extend the concurrency control techniques that are used in centralized databases. We discuss these techniques in the context of extending centralized locking. Similar extensions apply to other concurrency control techniques. The idea is to designate a particular copy of each data item as a distinguished copy. The locks for these data item are associated with the distinguished copy, and all locking and unlocking requests are sent to the site that contains that copy.

A number of different methods are based on this idea, but they differ in their method of choosing the distinguished copies. In the primary site technique, all distinguished copies are kept at the same site. A modification of this approach is the primary site with a backup site. Another approach is the primary copy method, where the distinguished copies of the various data items can be stored in different sites. A site that includes a distinguished copy of a data item basically acts as the coordinator site for concurrency control on that item. We discuss these techniques next.

6.2.4.1 Distributed Recovery

The recovery process in distributed databases is quite involved. We give only a very brief idea of some of the issues here. In some cases it is difficult even to determine whether a site is down without exchanging numerous messages with other sites. For example, suppose that site X sends a message to site Y and expects a response from Y, but does not receive it. There are several possible explanations:

- The message was not delivered to Y because of communication failure.
- Site Y is down and could not respond.
- Site Y is running and sent a response, but the response was not delivered.

Without additional information or the sending of additional messages, it is difficult to determine what actually happened.

Another problem with distributed recovery is distributed commit. When a transaction is updating data at several sites, it cannot commit until it is sure that the effect of the transaction on every site cannot be lost. This means that every site must first have recorded the local effects of the transactions permanently in the local site log on disk. The two-phase commit protocol is often used to ensure the correctness of distributed commit (see Section 6.2.6.1).

6.2.5 Query Processing and Optimization

A distributed database query is processed in various stages as follows:

1. *Query mapping*: The input query on distributed data are specified formally using a query language. It is then translated into an algebraic query on global relations. This translation is done by referring to the global conceptual schema and does not take into account the actual distribution and replication of data. Hence, this translation is largely identical to the one performed in a centralized DBMS. It is first normalized, analyzed for semantic errors, simplified, and finally restructured into an algebraic query.
2. *Localization*: In a distributed database, fragmentation results in relations being stored in separate sites, with some fragments possibly being replicated. This stage maps the distributed query on the global schema to separate queries on individual fragments using data distribution and replication information.
3. *Global query optimization*: Optimization consists of selecting a strategy from a list of candidates that is closest to optimal. A list of candidate queries can be obtained by permuting the ordering of operations within a fragment query generated by the previous stage. Time is the preferred unit for measuring cost. The total cost is a weighted combination of costs such as CPU cost, I/O costs, and communication costs. Since DDBs are connected by a network, often the communication costs over the network are the most significant. This is especially true when the sites are connected through a WAN.
4. *Local query optimization*: This stage is common to all sites in the DDB. The techniques are similar to those used in centralized systems.

The first three stages discussed above are performed at a central control site, whereas the last stage is performed locally.

Semijoin is a special operation that is used to optimize some types of queries in a DDBMS. The idea behind distributed query processing using the semijoin operation is to reduce the number of tuples in a relation before transferring it to another site. Intuitively, the idea is to send the joining column of one relation R to the site where the other relation S is located; this column is then joined with S. Following that, the join attributes, along with the attributes required in the result, are projected out, and shipped back to the original site, and joined with R. Hence, only the joining column of R is transferred in one direction, and a subset of S with no extraneous tuples or attributes is transferred in the other direction. If only a small fraction of the tuples in S participate in the join, this can be an efficient solution to minimizing data transfer.

Centralized DBMS were discussed in Chapter 2. In a distributed system, several additional factors further complicate query processing. The first is the cost of transferring data over the network. These data include intermediate files that are transferred to other sites for further processing, as well as the final result files that may have to be transferred to the site where the query result is needed. Although these costs may not be very high if the sites are connected via a high-performance LAN, they become significant in other types of networks. Hence, DDBMS query optimization algorithms consider the goal of reducing the amount of data transfer as an optimization criterion in choosing a distributed query execution strategy.

6.2.6 Transaction Management

The global and local transaction management software modules, along with the concurrency control and recovery manager of a DDBMS, collectively guarantee the ACID properties of transactions (see note on ACID properties in Section 1.7, Chapter 1).

An additional component called the global transaction manager is introduced for supporting distributed transactions. The site where the transaction originated can temporarily assume the role of global transaction manager and coordinate the execution of database operations with transaction managers across multiple sites. Transaction managers export their functionality as an interface to the application programs. The operations exported by this interface are similar to those for database transactions, namely BEGIN_TRANSACTION, READ or WRITE, END_TRANSACTION, COMMIT_TRANSACTION, and ROLLBACK (or ABORT). The manager stores book-keeping information related to each transaction, such as a unique identifier, originating site, name, and so on. For READ operations, it returns a local copy if valid and available. For WRITE operations, it ensures that updates are visible across all sites containing copies (replicas) of the data item. For ABORT operations, the manager ensures that no effects of the transaction are reflected in any site of the distributed database. For COMMIT operations, it ensures that the effects of a write are persistently recorded on all databases containing copies of the data item. Atomic termination (COMMIT or ABORT) of distributed transactions is commonly implemented using the two-phase commit protocol.

The transaction manager passes to the concurrency controller module, the database operations, and associated information. The controller is responsible for acquisition and release of associated locks. If the transaction requires access to a locked resource, it is blocked until the lock is acquired. Once the lock is acquired, the operation is sent to the runtime processor, which handles the actual execution of the database operation. Once the operation is completed, locks are released, and the transaction manager is updated with the result of the operation.

6.2.6.1 Two-Phase Commit Protocol

The net effect of the two-phase commit (2PC) protocol is that either all participating databases commit the effect of the transaction or none of them do. In case any of the participants—or the coordinator—fails, it is always possible to recover to a state where either the transaction is committed or it is rolled back. A failure during or before phase 1 usually requires the transaction to be rolled back, whereas a failure during phase 2 means that a successful transaction can recover and commit.

A global recovery manager, or coordinator, is needed to maintain information needed for recovery, in addition to the local recovery managers, and the information they maintain (log, tables). The two-phase commit protocol consists of the following:

1. *Phase 1*: When all participating databases signal the coordinator that the part of the multidatabase transaction involving each has concluded, the coordinator sends a message prepare for commit to each participant to get ready for committing the transaction. Each participating database receiving that message will force-write all log records and needed information for local recovery to disk and then send a ready to commit or OK signal to the coordinator. If the force-writing to disk fails or the local transaction cannot commit for some reason, the participating database sends a cannot commit or not OK signal to the coordinator. If the coordinator does not receive a reply from the database within a certain time-out interval, it assumes a not OK response.
2. *Phase 2*: If all participating databases reply OK, and the coordinator's vote is also OK, the transaction is successful, and the coordinator sends a commit signal for the transaction to the participating databases. Because all the local effects of the transaction and information needed for local recovery have been recorded in the logs of the participating databases, local recovery from failure is now possible. Each participating database completes transaction commit by writing a [commit] entry for the transaction in the log and permanently updating the database if needed. Conversely, if one or more of the participating databases or the coordinator have a not OK response, the transaction has failed, and the coordinator sends a message to roll back, or UNDO the local effect of the transaction to each participating database. This is done by undoing the local transaction operations, using the log.

6.2.6.2 Three-Phase Commit Protocol

The biggest drawback of 2PC is that it is a blocking protocol. Failure of the coordinator blocks all participating sites, causing them to wait until the coordinator recovers. This can cause performance degradation, especially if participants are holding locks to shared resources. Other types of problems may also occur that make the outcome of the transaction nondeterministic.

These problems are solved by the three-phase commit (3PC) protocol, which essentially divides the second commit phase into two subphases called prepare-to-commit and commit. The prepare-to-commit phase is used to communicate the result of the vote phase to all participants. If all participants vote yes, then the coordinator instructs them to move into the prepare-to-commit state. The commit subphase is identical to its two-phase counterpart. Now, if the coordinator crashes during this subphase, another participant can see the transaction through to completion. It can simply ask a crashed participant if it received a prepare-to-commit message. If it did not, then it safely assumes to abort. Thus the state of the protocol can be recovered irrespective of which participant crashes. Also, by limiting the time required for a transaction to commit or abort to a maximum time-out period, the protocol ensures that a transaction attempting to commit via 3PC releases locks on time-out.

The main idea is to limit the wait time for participants who have prepared to commit and are waiting for a global commit or abort from the coordinator. When a participant receives a precommit message, it knows that the rest of the participants have voted to commit. If a precommit message has not been received, then the participant will abort and release all locks.

6.2.7 Rules for Distributed Databases

C.J. Date (Date, C.J. "Twelve Rules for a Distributed Database." ComputerWorld 21.23, June 8, 1987) formulated 12 rules that distributed databases should follow. The basic goal is that a distributed database should feel like a nondistributed database to users, that is, users should not be aware that the database is distributed. The 12 rules serve as a benchmark against which you can measure DDBMSs. The 12 rules are as follows:

1. *Local autonomy*: No site should depend on another site to perform its database functions.
2. *No reliance on a central site*: The DDBMS should not rely on a single central site to control specific types of operations. These operations include data dictionary management, query processing, update management, database recovery, and concurrent update.
3. *Continuous operation*: Performing functions such as adding sites, changing versions of DBMSs, creating backups, and modifying hardware should not require planned shutdowns of the entire distributed database.
4. *Location transparency*: Users should not be concerned with the location of any specific data in the database. Users should feel as if the entire database is stored at their location.
5. *Fragmentation transparency*: Users should not be aware of any data fragmentation that has occurred in the database. Users should feel as if they are using a single central database.
6. *Replication transparency*: Users should not be aware of any data replication. The DDBMS should perform all the work required to keep the replicas consistent; users should be unaware of the data synchronization work carried out by the DDBMS.
7. *Distributed query processing*: You already learned about the complexities of query processing in a distributed database. The DDBMS must process queries as rapidly as possible.
8. *Distributed transaction management*: You already learned about the complexities of update management in a distributed database and the need for the two-phase commit strategy. The DDBMS must effectively manage transaction updates at multiple sites.
9. *Hardware independence*: Organizations usually have many different types of hardware, and a DDBMS must be able to run on this hardware. Without this capability, users are restricted to accessing data stored only on similar computers, disks, and so on.
10. *Operating system independence*: Even if an organization uses similar hardware, different operating systems might be used within the organization. For the same reason that it is desirable for a DDBMS to support different types of hardware, a DDBMS must be able to run on different operating systems.

11. *Network independence*: Because different sites within an organization might use different communications networks, a DDBMS must run on different types of networks and not be restricted to a single type of network.
12. *DBMS independence*: Another way of stating this requirement is that a DDBMS should be heterogeneous, that is, a DDBMS must support different local DBMSs. Supporting heterogeneous DBMSs is a difficult task. In practice, each local DBMS must *speak* a common language; this common language most likely is SQL.

6.3 Summary

In this chapter, we provided an introduction to parallel and distributed computing as a foundation for better understanding of cloud and big data computing. Parallelism is achieved by leveraging hardware capable of processing multiple instructions in parallel. Different architectures exploit parallelism to increase the performance of a computing system, depending on whether parallelism is realized on data, instructions, or both. The development of parallel applications often requires specific environments and compilers that provide transparent access to the advanced capabilities of the underlying architectures.

Distributed systems constitute a large umbrella, under which several different software systems are classified. Unification of parallel and distributed computing allows one to harness a set of networked and heterogeneous computers and present them as a unified resource. Architectural styles help categorize and provide reference models for distributed systems. More precisely, system architectural styles are more concerned with the physical deployment of such systems, whereas software architectural styles define logical organizations of components and their roles. These two styles are the fundamental deployment blocks of any distributed system. Message-based communication is the most relevant abstraction for IPC and forms the basis for several techniques of IPC, which is a fundamental element in distributed systems; it is the element that ties together separate processes and allows them to be seen as a unified whole.

Section 6.2 in the latter half of the chapter introduced the concepts, characteristics, and issues related to distributed databases. The chapter discussed the use of data replication (to improve system reliability and availability), concurrency control and recovery techniques, query optimization, and transaction management. The chapter ends with Codd's 12 rules for the distributed databases that have been devised on the lines of his rules for the relational database systems.

7

Service-Oriented Architecture Basics

Many motivating factors have led to the emergence of cloud computing. Businesses require services that include both infrastructure and application workload requests while meeting defined service levels for capacity, resource tiering, and availability. IT delivery often necessitates costs and efficiencies that create a perception of IT as a hindrance, not a strategic partner. Issues include underutilized resources, over-provisioning or under-provisioning of resources, lengthy deployment times, and lack of cost visibility. Virtualization is the first step toward addressing some of these challenges by enabling improved utilization through server consolidation, workload mobility through hardware independence, and efficient management of hardware resources.

The virtualization system is a key foundation for the cloud computing system. We stitch together compute resources so as to appear as one large computer behind which the complexity is hidden. By coordinating, managing, and scheduling resources such as CPUs, network, storage, and firewalls in a consistent way across internal and external premises, we create a flexible cloud infrastructure platform. This platform includes security, automation and management, interoperability and openness, self-service, pooling, and dynamic resource allocation. In view of cloud computing, we are advocating, applications can run within an external provider, in internal IT premises, or in combination as a hybrid system—it matters how they are run, not where they are run.

Cloud computing builds on virtualization to create a service-oriented computing model. This is done through the addition of resource abstractions and controls to create dynamic pools of resources that can be consumed through the network. Benefits include economies of scale, elastic resources, self-service provisioning, and cost transparency. Consumption of cloud resources is enforced through resource metering and pricing models that shape user behavior. Consumers benefit through leveraging allocation models such as pay-as-you-go to gain greater cost efficiency, lower barrier to entry, and immediate access to infrastructure resources.

7.1 Service-Oriented Architecture

Integration seems to be one of the most important strategic priorities, mainly because new innovative business solutions demand integration of different business units, business systems, enterprise data, and applications. Integrated information systems improve the competitive advantage with unified and efficient access to the information. Integrated applications make it much easier to access relevant, coordinated information from a variety of sources. It is clear that replacing existing systems with new solutions will often not be a viable proposition. Companies soon realize that the replacement is more complicated, more complex, more time consuming, and costlier than even their worst-case scenarios could have predicted: too much time and money have been invested in them, and there is too much knowledge incorporated in these systems. Therefore, standard ways to reuse existing systems and integrate them into the global, enterprise-wide information system must be defined.

The modern answer to application integration is an SOA with web services; SOA is a style of organizing (services), and web services are its realization. An SOA with web services is a combination of architecture and technology for consistently delivering robust, reusable services that support today's business needs and that can be easily adapted to satisfy changing business requirements. An SOA enables easy integration of IT systems, provides multichannel access to your systems, and automates business processes. When an SOA with its corresponding services is in place, developers can easily reuse existing services in developing new applications and business processes.

A service differs from an object or a procedure because it is defined by the messages that it exchanges with other services. A service's loose coupling to the applications that host it gives it the ability to more easily share data across the department, enterprise, or Internet. An SOA defines the way in which services are deployed and managed. Companies need IT systems with the flexibility to implement specialized operations, to change quickly with the changes in business operations, to respond quickly to internal as well as external changes in conditions, and consequently gain a competitive edge. Using an SOA increases reuse, lowers overall costs, and improves the ability to rapidly change and evolve IT systems, whether old or new.

An SOA also maps IT systems easily and directly to a business's operational processes and supports better division of labor between the business and technical staff. One of the great potential advantages of solutions created using an SOA with SOAP or REST web services is that they can help resolve this perennial problem by providing better separation of concerns between business analysts and service developers. Analysts can take responsibility for defining how services fit together to implement business processes, while the service developers can take responsibility for implementing services that meet business requirements. This will ensure that the business issues are understood well enough to be implemented in technology and the technology issues are understood well enough to meet the business requirements.

Integrating existing and new applications using an SOA involves defining the basic web service interoperability layer to bridge features and functions used in current applications such as security, reliability, transactions, metadata management, and orchestration; it also involves the ability to define automated business process execution flows across the web services after an SOA is in place. An SOA with web services enables the development of services that encapsulate business functions and that are easily accessible from any other service; composite services allow a wide range of options for combining web services and creating new application functionalities.

> As a prerequisite, one will have to deal with a plethora of legacy technologies in order to service-enable them. But the beauty of services and SOA is that the services are developed to achieve interoperability and to hide the details of the execution environments behind them. In particular, for web services, this means the ability to emit and consume data represented as XML, regardless of development platform, middleware, operating system, or hardware type. Thus, an SOA is a way to define and provision an IT infrastructure to allow different applications to exchange data and participate in business processes, regardless of the operating systems or programming languages underlying these applications.

7.1.1 Defining SOA

SOA provides an agile technical architecture that can be quickly and easily reconfigured as business requirements change. The promise of SAO is that it will break down the barriers in IT to implement business process flows in a cost-effective and agile manner that would combine the best of custom solutions and packaged applications while simultaneously reducing lock-in to any single IT vendor.

A Service-oriented architecture (SOA) is a style of organization that guides all aspects of creating and using business services throughout their life cycle (from conception to retirement), as well as defining and provisioning the IT infrastructure that allows different applications to exchange data and participate in business processes regardless of the operating systems or programming languages underlying these applications. The key organizing concept of an SOA itself is a service. The processes, principles, and methods defined by SOA are oriented toward services; the development tools selected by an SOA are oriented toward creating and deploying services; and the runtime infrastructure provided by an SOA is oriented to executing and managing services.

A service is a sum of constituting parts including a description, the implementation, and the mapping layer (termed as transformation layer) between the two. The service implementation, termed as the executable agent, can be any environment for which web service support is available. The description is separated from its executable agent; one description might have multiple different executable agents associated with it and vice versa. The executable agent is responsible for implementing the web service processing model as per the various web service specifications and runs within the execution environment, which is typically a software system or programming language environment. The description is separated from the execution environment using a mapping or transformation layer often implemented using proxies and stubs. The mapping layer is responsible for accepting the message, transforming the XML data to the native format, and dispatching the data to the executable agent.

Web service roles include a requester and a provider; a requester can be a provider and vice versa. The service requester initiates the execution of a service by sending a message to a service provider, which executes the service and returns the results, if any specified, to the requester.

7.1.1.1 Services

Services are coarse-grained, reusable IT assets that have well-defined interfaces (or service contracts) that clearly separate the service accessible interface from the service technical implementation. This separation of interface and implementation serves to decouple the service requesters from the service providers so that both can evolve independently as long as the service contract remains unchanged.

A service is a location on the network that has a machine-readable description of the messages it receives and optionally returns. A service is therefore defined in terms of the message exchange patterns it supports. A schema for the data contained in the message is used as the main part of the contract between a service requester and a service provider; other items of metadata describe the network address for the service, the operations it supports, and its requirements for reliability, security, and transactional integrity. However, developing a service is quite different from developing an object because a service is defined by the message it exchanges with other services, rather than a method signature. A service usually defines a coarse-grained interface that accepts more data in a single invocation than an object because of the need to map to an execution environment, process the XML, and often access it remotely. Services are executed by exchanging messages according to one or more supported message exchange patterns (MEPs), such as request/response, one-way asynchronous, or publish/subscribe. Services are meant to solve interoperability problems between applications and for use in composing new applications or application systems, but not meant like objects to create the detailed business logic for the applications.

From a business perspective, services are IT assets that correspond to real-world business activities or identifiable business functions that can be accessed according to the service policies related to

- Who is authorized to access the service?
- When can the service be accessed?
- What is the cost of using the service?
- What are the reliability levels of using the service?
- What are the performance levels for the service?

A service is normally defined at a higher level of abstraction than an object because it is possible to map a service definition to a procedure-oriented language such as COBOL or PL/1 or to a message queuing system such as JMS or MSMQ, as well as to an object-oriented system such as J2EE or the .NET Framework. Whether the service's execution environment is a stored procedure, message queue, or object does not matter; the data are seen through the filter of a web service, which includes a layer that maps the web service to whatever execution environment is implementing the service. The use of XML in web services provides a clear separation between the definition of a service and its execution so that web services can work with any software system. The XML representation of the data types and structures of a service via the XML schema allows the developer to think solely in terms of the data being passed between the services without having to consider the details of the service's implementation. This is quite in contrast to the traditional nature of the integration problem that involves figuring out the implementation of the service in order to be able to talk to it.

One of the greatest benefits of service abstraction is its ability to easily access a variety of service types, including newly developed services, wrapped legacy applications, and applications composed of other newer and legacy services.

7.2 SOA Benefits

SOA delivers the following business benefits:

1. Increased business agility: SOA improves throughput by dramatically reducing the amount of time required to assemble new business applications, from existing services and IT assets. SOA also makes IT significantly easier and less expensive to reconfigure and adapt services and IT assets to meet new and unanticipated requirements. Thus, the business adapts quickly to new opportunities and competitive threats, while IT quickly changes existing systems.

2. Better business alignment: As SOA services directly support the services that the enterprise provides to customers.
3. Improved customer satisfaction: As SOA services are independent of specific technology, they can readily work with an array of customer-facing systems across all customer touch points that effectively reduce development time, increase customer engagement time, and, hence, increase customer solutioning, enabling enhanced customer satisfaction.
4. Improved ROI of existing assets: SOA dramatically improves the ROI of existing IT assets by reusing them as services in the SOA by identifying the key business capabilities of existing systems and using them as the basis for new services as part of the SOA.
5. Reduced vendor lock-in and switching costs: As SOA is based on loosely coupled services with well-defined, platform-neutral service contracts, it avoids vendor and technology lock-in at all levels, namely, application platform and middleware platform.
6. Reduced integration costs: SOA projects can focus on composing, publishing, and developing web services independently of their execution environments, thus obviating the need to deal with avoidable complexity. Web services and XML simplify integration because they focus on the data being exchanged instead of the underlying programs and execution environments.

Technical benefits of SOA include the following:

1. More reuse: Service reuse lowers development costs and speed.
2. Efficient development: As services are loosely coupled, SOA promotes modularity that enables easier and faster development of composite applications. Once service contracts have been defined, developers can separately and independently design and implement each of the various services. Similarly, service requestors too can be designed and implemented based solely with reference to the published service contracts without any need to contact the concerned developers or without any access to the developers of the service providers.
3. Simplified maintenance: As services are modular and loosely coupled, they simplify maintenance and reduce maintenance costs.
4. Incremental adoption: As services are modular and loosely coupled, they can be developed and deployed in incremental steps.

7.3 Characteristics of SOA

7.3.1 Dynamic, Discoverable, Metadata Driven

Services should be published in a manner by which they can be discovered and consumed without intervention of the provider. Service contracts should use metadata to define service capabilities and constraints, and should be machine readable so that they can be registered and discovered dynamically to lower the cost of locating and using services, reduce corresponding errors, and improve management of services.

7.3.2 Designed for Multiple Invocation Styles

Design and implement service operations that implement business logic that supports multiple invocation styles, including asynchronous queuing, request/response, request/callback, request/polling, batch processing, and event-driven publish/subscribe.

7.3.3 Loosely Coupled

This implies loose coupling of interface and technology; interface coupling implies that the interface should encapsulate all implementation details and make them nontransparent to service requesters, while technology coupling measures the extent to which a service depends on a particular technology, product, or development platform (operating systems, application servers, packaged applications, and middleware).

7.3.4 Well-Defined Service Contracts

A service contract is more important than service implementation because it defines the service capabilities and how to invoke the service in an interoperable manner. A service contract clearly separates the service's externally accessible interface from the service's technical implementation; consequently, the service contract is independent of any single service implementation. The service contract is defined based on the knowledge of the business domain and not so much on service implementation. The service contract is defined and managed as a separate artifact, is the basis for sharing and reuse, and is the primary mechanism for reducing interface coupling.

Changing a service contract is generally more expensive than modifying the implementation of a service because while changing a service implementation is relatively a localized effort, changing a service contract may entail changing hundreds or thousands of service requesters.

7.3.5 Standard Based

Services should be based on open standards as much as possible to the following benefits:

- Minimizing vendor lock-in by isolating from proprietary, vendor-specific technologies and interfaces
- Increasing the choice of service requesters for alternate service providers and vice versa

It is important to base the service-level data and process models on mature business domain standards as and when they become available. This is in addition to complying with technology standards such as SOAP, WSDL, UDDI, and the WS* specification.

7.3.6 Granularity of Services and Service Contracts

Services and service contracts must be defined at a level of abstraction that makes sense to service requesters as also service providers. To achieve this, services should perform discrete tasks and provide simple interfaces to encourage reuse and loose coupling.

An abstract interface at the appropriate level of granularity promotes ready substitutability, which enables any of the existing service providers to be replaced by a new service provider without affecting any of the service requesters.

7.3.7 Stateless

Services should be stateless because they scale more efficiently as any service request can be routed to any service instance. In contrast, stateful interactions do not scale efficiently because the server needs to track which service is serving which client and cannot reuse a service until the conversation is finished or a time-out has occurred.

Thus, services should be implemented so that each invocation is independent and does not depend on the service maintaining client-specific conversations in memory or in persistent state between the invocations.

7.3.8 Predictable Service-Level Agreements (SLAs)

Service delivery platforms must provide service-level management capabilities for defining, monitoring, incident logging, and metering of SLAs for service usage. SLAs should be established early because they affect service design, implementation, and management. There should also be provision for fine-tuning of SLAs based on the feedback of ongoing operations.

Typically, SLAs define metrics for services such as response time, throughput, availability, and meantime between failures. Above all, SLAs are usually tied up to a business model whereby service requesters pay more for higher or more stringent SLAs but charge a penalty when service providers default on their SLA commitments.

7.3.9 Design Services with Performance in Mind

Service invocation should not be modeled on local function calls since local transparency may result in a service that is on another machine on the same LAN or another LAN or WAN.

7.4 SOA Applications

An SOA can be thought of as an approach to building IT systems in which business services are the key organizing principle to align IT systems with the needs of the business. Any business that can implement an IT infrastructure that allows it to change more rapidly than its competitors has an advantage over them. The use of an SOA for integration, business process management, and multichannel access allows any enterprise to create a more strategic environment, one that more closely aligns with the operational characteristics of the business. Earlier approaches to building IT systems resulted in systems that were tied to the features and functions of a particular environment technology (such as CORBA, J2EE, and COM/DCOM) since they employed environment-specific characteristics such as procedure or object or message orientation to provide solutions to business problems. The way in which services are developed aligns them better with the needs of the business than was the case with previous generations of technology. What is new in the concept of SOA is the clear separation of the service interface from execution technology, enabling choice of the best execution environment for any job and tying all of these executional agents together using a consistent architectural approach.

7.4.1 Rapid Application Integration

The combination of web services and SOA provides a rapid integration solution that readily aligns IT investments and corporate strategies by focusing on shared data and reusable services rather than proprietary integration products. These enterprise application integration (EAI) products proved to be expensive, consumed considerable time and effort, and were prone to higher rates of failure. Applications can exchange data more easily by using a web service defined at the business logic layer than by using a different integration technology because web services represent a common standard across all types of software. XML can be used to independently define the data types and structures. Creating a common web service layer or overlay of services into the business logic tiers of application also allows you to use a common service repository in which to store and retrieve service descriptions. If a new application seeks to use an existing service into one of these applications, it can query the repository to obtain the service description to quickly generate (say) SOAP messages to interact with it. Finally, the development of service-oriented entry points at the business logic tier allows a business process management engine to drive an automatic flow of execution across multiple services.

7.4.2 Multichannel Access

Enterprises often use many channels to ensure good service and maintain customer loyalty; therefore, they benefit from being able to deliver customer services over a mixture of access channels. In the past, enterprises often developed monolithic applications that were tied to single access channels, such as a 3270 terminal, a PC interface, or a web browser. The proliferation of access channels represented a significant challenge to IT departments to convert monolithic applications to allow multichannel access. The basic solution is to service-enable these using an SOA with web services that are good for enabling multichannel access because they are accessible from a broad range of clients, including web, Java, C#, and mobile devices. In general, business services change much less frequently than the delivery channels through which they are accessed. Business services refer to operational functions such as vendor management, purchase order management, and billing, which do not vary very often, whereas client devices and access channels are based on new technologies, which tend to change.

7.4.3 Business Process Management

A business process is a real-world activity that consists of a set of logically related tasks that, when performed in an appropriate sequence and in conformity with applicable rules, produce a business outcome. Business process management (BPM) is the name for a set of software systems, tools, and methodologies that enable enterprises to identify, model, develop, deploy, and manage such business processes. BPM systems are designed to help align business processes with desirable business outcomes and ensure that the IT systems support those business processes. BPM systems let business users model their business processes graphically in a way that the IT department can implement; the graphical depiction of a business process can be used to generate an executable specification of the process. Unlike traditional forms of system development, where the process logic is deeply embedded in the application code, BPM explicitly separates the business process logic from other application code. Separating business process logic from other application code renders increased productivity, reduced operational costs, and improved agility. When implemented correctly, enterprises can quickly respond to changing market conditions and seize opportunities for gaining competitive advantage.

SOA with web services can better automate business processes because web services help achieve the goals of BPM more quickly and easily.

7.5 SOA Ingredients

Web services are new standards for creating and delivering cooperative applications over the Internet. Web services allow applications to communicate irrespective of the platform or the operating system.

7.5.1 Objects, Services, and Resources

Any distributed system involves sending messages to some remote entity. Underlying the differences between many systems are the abstractions used to model these entities; they define the architectural qualities of the system. Three abstractions—in particular, object, resource, and service—are commonly used to describe remote entities; their definitions, however, are not always clearly distinguished. Yet the nature of these abstractions has a profound effect on the distributed communication paradigms that result from their use. One approach to identifying the similarities and differences between them is to understand them in terms of their relationship to two properties: state and behavior.

7.5.1.1 Objects

Objects have both state and behavior. The state is maintained through the internal data, and the behavior of the object is defined through the public operations on that data. A primary issue in these systems is the management of object identifiers, which are global pointers to instances of objects. It has been argued that architectures based on global pointers lead to brittle systems if they scale to Internet size because of the proliferation of references and the need to maintain the integrity of the pointers. As a result, these systems are considered to be best suited to medium-sized networks within a single domain, with known latencies and static addressing, and intimate knowledge of the middleware models used.

7.5.1.2 Services

A service is a view of some resource, usually a software asset. Implementation detail is hidden behind the service interface. The interface has well-defined boundaries, providing encapsulation of the resource behind it. Services communicate using messages. The structure of the message and the schema, or form, of its contents are defined by the interface.

Services are stateless. This means all the information needed by a service to perform its function is contained in the messages used to communicate with it.

The service abstraction shares commonalities with the object abstraction but displays crucial differences:

- Similar to an object, a service can have an arbitrary interface.
- Similar to distributed object systems that use an IDL, services usually describe this interface in a description language.
- Unlike objects, services use a message-oriented model for communication. This has quite different semantics and implications to invoking a procedure on a remote object. In the latter, what the remote entity is plays a part. In the case of objects, the class of an object must be known. Once this class is known, behavior based on the class can be inferred by the consumer. Services, however, do not share class. Instead, they share contracts and schema. Therefore, what an entity is has no bearing on communication, and nothing is inferred. Furthermore, communication with an object involves addressing an instance. This is not the case with services, as is discussed in the next item.
- Unlike objects, services do not have state. Object orientation teaches us that data and the logic that acts on that data should be combined, while service orientation suggests that these two things should be separate. Therefore, a service acts upon state but does not expose its own state. Put another way, services do not have instances. You cannot create and destroy a service in the way you can create and destroy an object.

7.5.1.3 Resources

The term resource is used here to specifically refer to the abstraction used by the web and related initiative such as the semantic web. Such a resource is different from a distributed object in a number of ways.

Resource state is not hidden from a client as it is in object systems. Instead, standard representations of state are exposed. In object systems, the public interface of an object gives access to hidden state:

- Unlike distributed objects, resources do not have operations associated with them. Instead, manipulation and retrieval of resource representations rely on the transfer protocol used to dereference the uniform resource identifier (URI).
- As a consequence, a resource can be viewed as an entity that has state, but not the logic to manipulate that state, that is, no behavior.

Because resources have no behavior, they do not define how their state can be manipulated. While this could be viewed as limiting and potentially leading to ad hoc, underspecified interactions, in the case of the web, the opposite is actually true. While an object-oriented system defines proprietary behavioral interfaces for every object, leading to a proliferation of means of manipulating objects, the web uses a single, shared interface: HTTP. The few methods defined by HTTP allow arbitrary resources to be exchanged and manipulated, making interactions between entities far simpler and hence scalable. Imagine, for example, that every web server defined its own interface to accessing the resources in its charge. This would require a browser to digest a new service interface and generate client-side code every time you clicked on a link, a process that would severely influence the scalability of the system as a whole.

7.5.2 SOA and Web Services

Web services are new standards for creating and delivering cooperative applications over the Internet. They allow applications to communicate irrespective of the platform or the operating system. By using web services, developers can eliminate major porting and quality-testing efforts, potentially saving millions of dollars. They will radically change the way that applications are built and deployed in future.

A developer can create an application out of reusable components. But what good is it to have a large library of reusable components if nobody knows that they exist, where they are located, and how to link to and communicate with such programmatic components? Web services are standards for finding and integrating object components over the Internet. They enable a development environment where it is no longer necessary to build complete and monolithic applications for every project. Instead, the core components can be combined from other standard components available on the web to build the complete applications that run as services to the core applications.

Some of the past approaches to enabling program-to-program communication included combinations of program-to-program protocols such as remote procedure call (RPC) and application programming interfaces (APIs), coupled with architectures such as common object model (COM), the distributed common object model (DCOM), and the common object request broker architecture (CORBA). But, without a common underlying network, common protocols for program-to-program communication, and a common architecture to help applications to declare their availability and services, it has proven difficult to implement cross-platform program-to-program communication between application modules. These previous attempts to set up standards for accomplishing these objectives were not very successful because

- They were not functionally rich enough and are difficult to maintain as best of breed.
- They were vendor specific as opposed to using open and cross-vendor standards.
- They were too complex to deploy and use.

The use of web service standards holds the potential for correcting each of these deficiencies. This new approach presents applications as services to each other and enables applications to be rapidly assembled by linking application objects together.

With the advent of the Internet and its protocols, most vendors and enterprises have graduated to a common communication and network protocol—the Internet's TCP/IP. And with the availability of web standards such as Extensible Markup Language (XML); simple object access protocol (SOAP); universal description, discovery and integration (UDDI); and web services description language (WSDL), vendors enable customers to

1. Publish specifications about application modules via WSDL.
2. Find those modules (either on the internal intranet or on the Internet) via the UDDI.
3. Bind the applications together to work seamlessly and cooperatively, and deliver the holistic functionality of composite applications via SOAP and XML.

The significance of web services for the future is by reason of the following:

- Web services will enable enterprises to reduce development costs and expand application functionalities at a fraction of the cost per traditional application development and deployment method.
- Web services will enable independent software vendors (ISVs) to bring products to market more quickly and respond to competitive threats with more flexibility.
- Web services will enable enterprises to reuse existing legacy application functionalities with the latest applications and technologies.
- Web services will obviate the need of porting applications to different hardware platforms and operating systems at great expense.
- Web services enable applications to communicate irrespective of platform or operating system.
- Web services will have the effect of leveling the playing field because it will enable even specialized boutique application firms to compete easily with well-established and resourceful original equipment manufacturers (OEMs).
- Web services will enable only those OEMs to flourish that focus on providing comprehensive implementations and highly productive application development environments for web services.
- Web services will enable applications to be packaged not only as licenses but also as services; this will give a big fillip to ASP services (as discussed in the earlier section) and will consequently expand the overall market size tremendously.
- Web services will enable value-added resellers (VARs) to rapidly add new functionalities to current product offerings or to customize the existing applications of customers.
- Web services will enable enterprises to adapt better to changing market conditions or competitive threats.

Figure 7.1 shows the web services usage model.

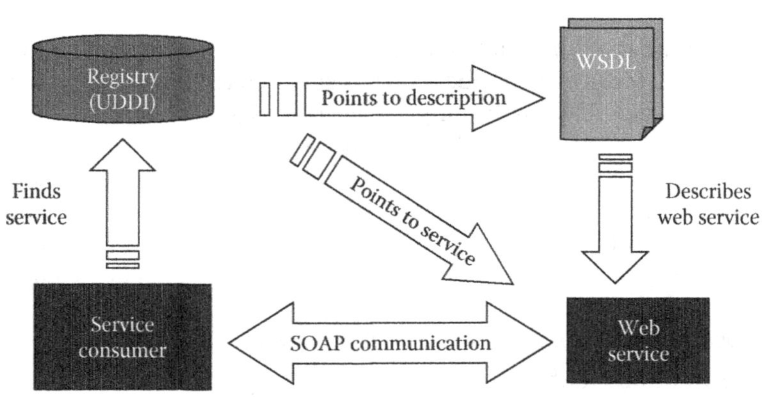

FIGURE 7.1
Web Services usage model.

7.5.2.1 Describing Web Services: Web Services Description Language

The WSDL is an XML-based language used to describe the goods and services that an organization offers and provides a way to access those services electronically.

WSDL is an XML vocabulary that provides a standard way of describing service IDLs. WSDL is the resulting artifact of a convergence of activities between NASSL (IBM) and SDL (Microsoft). It provides a simple way for service providers to describe the format of requests and response Messages for Remote Method Invocations (RMIs). WSDL addresses this topic of service IDLs independent of the underlying protocol and encoding requirements. In general, WSDL provides an abstract language for defining the published operations of a service with their respective parameters and data types. The language also addresses the definition of the locations and binding details of the service.

7.5.2.2 Accessing Web Services: Simple Object Access Protocol

SOAP is an XML-based lightweight protocol for the exchange of information in a decentralized distributed environment. SOAP is a means by which different systems can communicate, based on the HTTP web standard. It specifies how to encode a hypertext transfer protocol (HTTP) header and an XML file so that different applications, running on different systems, can share data. SOAP defines a messaging protocol between requestor and provider objects, such that the requesting objects can perform a remote method invocation on the providing objects in an object-oriented programming fashion. The SOAP specification was coauthored by Microsoft, IBM, Lotus, UserLand, and DevelopMentor. The specification subsequently spawned the creation of W3C XML Protocol Workgroup, which is constituted of over 30 participating companies.

In most vendor implementations of SOA, SOAP forms the basis for distributed object communication. Although SOA does not define a messaging protocol, SOAP has recently been referred to as the SOA protocol due to its common use in SOA implementations. The beauty of SOAP is that it is completely vendor neutral, allowing for independent implementations relative to platform, operating system, object model, and programming language. Additionally, transport and language bindings as well as data-encoding preferences are all implementation dependent.

7.5.2.3 Finding Web Services: Universal Description, Discovery, and Integration

The UDDI is an XML-based registry that enables organizations in a global business-to-business (B2B) environment to locate each other. UDDI specification provides a common set of SOAP APIs that enable the implementation of a service broker. The UDDI specification was outlined by IBM, Microsoft, and Ariba to help facilitate the creation, description, discovery, and integration of web-based services.

UDDI is like a telephone directory that additionally also

- Indicates the suitability of a potential partner.
- Describes the access mechanism by which an enterprise can be interfaced with.

The motivation behind UDDI.org, a partnership and cooperation between more than 70 industry and business leaders, is to define a standard for B2B interoperability.

7.5.3 SOA and RESTful Services

REpresentational state transfer (REST) is a style of software architecture for distributed hypermedia systems such as the World Wide Web. As such, it is not strictly a method for building web services. The terms representational state transfer and REST were introduced in 2000 in the doctoral dissertation of Roy Fielding, one of the principal authors of the HTTP specifications 1.0 and 1.1.

REST refers to a collection of network architecture principles, which outline how resources are defined and addressed. The term is often used in a looser sense to describe any simple interface that transmits domain-specific data over HTTP without an additional messaging layer such as SOAP or session tracking via HTTP cookies. These two meanings can conflict as well as overlap. It is possible to design a software system in accordance with Fielding's REST architectural style without using HTTP and without interacting with the World Wide Web. It is also possible to design simple XML+HTTP interfaces that do not conform to REST principles but instead follow a model of remote procedure call. Systems that follow Fielding's REST principles are often referred to as RESTful.

Proponents of REST argue that the web's scalability and growth are a direct result of a few key design principles. Application state and functionality are abstracted into resources. Every resource is uniquely addressable using a universal syntax for use in hypermedia links, and all resources share a uniform interface for the transfer of state between client and resource. This transfer state consists of a constrained set of well-defined operations and a constrained set of content types, optionally supporting code on demand. State transfer uses a protocol that is client-server based, stateless and cacheable, and layered.

An important concept in REST is the existence of resources, each of which is referenced with a global identifier (e.g., a URI in HTTP). In order to manipulate these resources, components of the network (user agents and origin servers) communicate via a standardized interface (e.g., HTTP) and exchange representations of these resources (the actual documents conveying the information). For example, a resource, which is a circle, may accept and return a representation that specifies a center point and radius, formatted in Scalable Vector Graphics (SVG), but may also accept and return a representation that specifies any three distinct points along the curve as a comma-separated list.

Any number of connectors (clients, servers, caches, tunnels, etc.) can mediate the request, but each does so without seeing past its own request (referred to as layering, another constraint of REST and a common principle in many other parts of information and networking architecture). Thus, an application can interact with a resource by knowing two things: the identifier of the resource and the action required—it does not need to know whether there are caches, proxies, gateways, firewalls, tunnels, or anything else between it and the server actually holding the information. The application does, however, need to understand the format of the information (representation) returned, which is typically an HTML, XML, or JSON document of some kind, although it may be an image, plain text, or any other content.

RESTful web services rely on HTTP as a sufficiently rich protocol to completely meet the needs of web service applications. In the REST model, the HTTP GET, POST, PUT, and DELETE verbs are used to transfer data (often in the form of XML documents) between client and services. These documents are representations of resources that are identified by normal web URIs (uniform resource identifiers). This use of standard HTTP and web technologies means that RESTful web services can leverage the full web infrastructure, such as caching and indexing. The transactional and database integrity requirements of CRUD (create, retrieve, update, and delete) correspond to HTTP's POST, GET, PUT, and DELETE.

One benefit that should be obvious with regard to web-based applications is that a RESTful implementation allows a user to bookmark specific queries (or requests) and allows those to be conveyed to others across e-mail and instant messages or to be injected into wikis, etc. Thus, this representation of a path or entry point into an application state becomes highly portable. A RESTFul web service is a simple web service implemented using HTTP and the principles of REST. Such a web service can be thought of as a collection of resources comprising three aspects:

1. The URI for the web service
2. The MIME type of the data supported by the web service (often JSON, XML, or YAML but can be anything)
3. The set of operations supported by the web service using HTTP methods, including but not limited to POST, GET, PUT, and DELETE

REST provides improved response time and reduced server load due to its support for the caching of representations. REST improves server scalability by reducing the need to maintain session state. This means that different servers can be used to handle different requests in a session.

REST requires less client-side software to be written than other approaches, because a single browser can access any application and any resource. REST depends less on vendor software and mechanisms, which layer additional messaging frameworks on top of HTTP. It provides equivalent functionality when compared to alternative approaches to communication, and it does not require a separate resource discovery mechanism because of the use of hyperlinks in representations. REST also provides better long-term compatibility because of the capability of document types such as HTML to evolve without breaking backward or forward compatibility and the ability of resources to add support for new content types as they are defined without dropping or reducing support for older content types.

SOAs can be built using REST services—an approach sometimes referred to as (ROA) REST-oriented architecture. The main advantage of ROA is ease of implementation, agility of the design, and the lightweight approach. The latest version of WSDL now contains HTTP verbs and is considered an acceptable method of documenting REST services. There is also an alternative known as WADL (web application description language).

7.6 Enterprise Service Bus

The enterprise service bus (ESB) is an open standard-based message backbone designed to enable the implementation, deployment, and management of SOA-based solutions with a focus on assembling, deploying, and managing distributed SOAs. An ESB is a set of infrastructure capabilities implemented by middleware technology that enable an SOA and alleviate disparity problems between applications running on heterogeneous platforms and using diverse data formats. The ESB supports service invocations, message, and event-based interactions with appropriate service levels and manageability. The ESB is designed to provide interoperability between larger-grained applications and other components via standard-based adapters and interfaces. The bus functions as both transport and transformation facilitator to allow distribution of these services over disparate systems and computing environments.

Conceptually, the ESB has evolved from the store and forward mechanism found in middleware products and now is a combination of EAI, web services, XSLT, and orchestration technologies, such as BPEL. To achieve its operational objectives, the ESB draws from traditional EAI broker functionality in that it provides integration services such as connectivity and routing of messages based on business rules, data transformation, and adapters to applications. These capabilities are themselves SOA based in that they are spread out across the bus in a highly distributed fashion and hosted in separately deployable service containers. This is a crucial difference from traditional integration brokers, which are usually heavyweight, highly centralized, and monolithic in nature. The ESB approach allows for the selective deployment of integration broker functionality exactly where it is needed with no additional overbloating where it is not required.

To surmount problems of system heterogeneity and information model mismatches in an SOA implementation, an EAI middleware supporting hub-and-spoke integration patterns could be used. The hub-and-spoke approach introduces an integration layer between the client and server modules that must support interoperability among and coexist with deployed infrastructure and applications, and makes no attempt to replace them. However, this approach has its own drawbacks as a hub can be a central point of failure and can quickly become a bottleneck.

Communication through a bus connection reduces complexity, which is considered a common problem within an enterprise. Integration through point-to-point connections can often become very complex when a company grows. As a result, they acquire more software. The applications are all directly connected with each other, which result in a "spider web like" image. Applications are therefore more difficult to manage (Figure 7.2).

Using an enterprise service bus, the software components are integrated by only connecting to the bus. The bus will then further establish the link between the components.

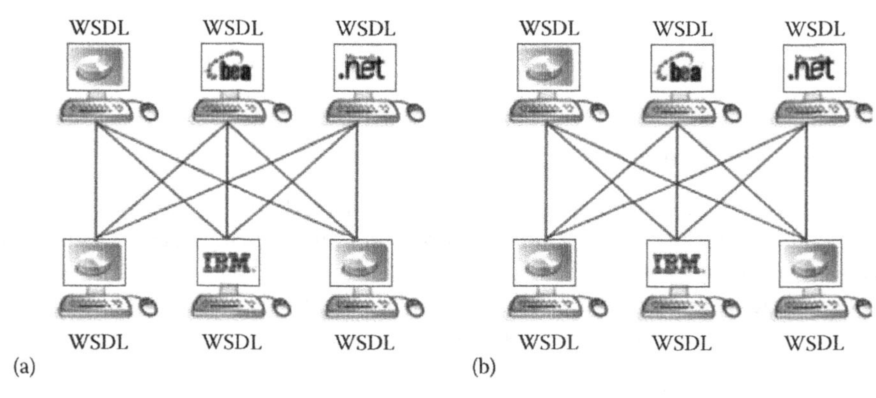

FIGURE 7.2
ESB reducing connection complexity (a) Direct point-to-point connections (n*n) and (b) Connecting through the bus (n).

A scalable distributed architecture such as an SOA needs to employ a constellation of hubs. The requirements to provide an appropriately capable and manageable integration infrastructure for web services and SOA are coalescing into the concept of the ESB, which will be the subject of this section. The two key ideas behind this approach are to loosely couple the systems taking part in the integration and break up the integration logic into distinct, easily manageable pieces.

Figure 7.3 below shows a simplified view of an ESB that integrates a J2EE application using JMS, a .NET application using a C# client, an MQ application that interfaces with legacy applications, and external applications and data sources using web services. In an ESB application, development tools allow new or existing distributed applications to be exposed as web services and be accessed via a portal. In general, resources in the ESB are modeled as services that offer one or more business operations. Technologies like J2EE connector architecture (JCA) may also be used to create services by integrating packaged applications (like ERP systems), which would then be exposed as web services.

The ESB-distributed processing infrastructure is aware of applications and services, and uses content-based routing facilities to make informed decisions about how to communicate with them. In essence, the ESB provides docking stations for hosting services that can be assembled and orchestrated, and are available for use to any other service on the bus. Once a service is deployed into a service container, it becomes an integral part of the ESB and can be used by any application or service connected to it. The service container hosts, manages, and dynamically deploys services and binds them to external resources, for example, data sources, enterprise, and multiplatform applications, such as shown in Figure 7.3.

The distributed nature of the ESB container model allows individual event-driven services to be plugged into the ESB backbone on an as-needed basis. It allows them to be highly decentralized and work together in a highly distributed fashion, while they are scaled independently from one another. Applications running on different platforms are abstractly decoupled from each other and can be connected together through the bus as logical endpoints that are exposed as event-driven services.

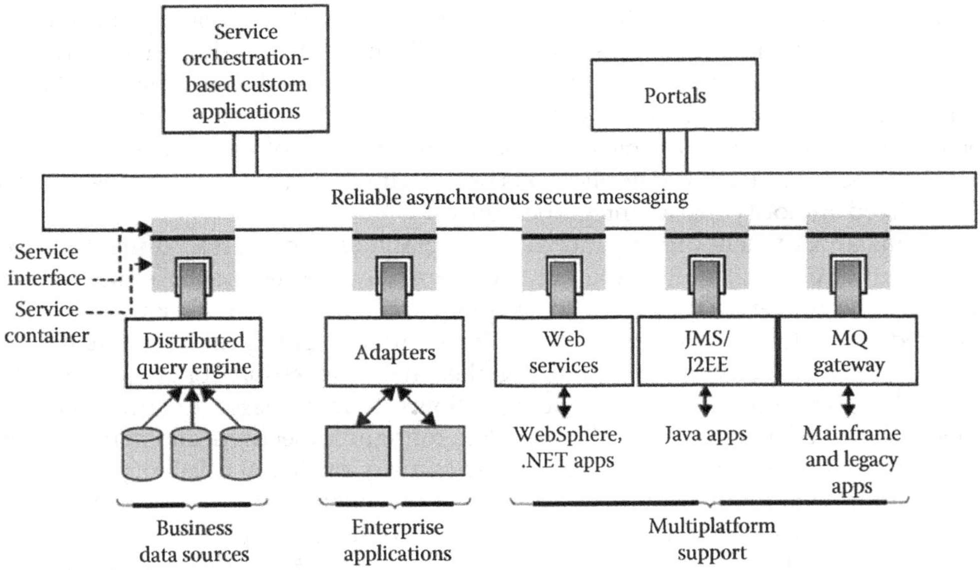

FIGURE 7.3
Enterprise service bus (ESB) linking disparate systems and computing environments.

Endpoints in the ESB depicted in the Figure 7.3 above provide abstraction of physical destination and connection information (like TCP/IP host name and port number). In addition, they facilitate asynchronous and highly reliable communication between service containers using reliable messaging conventions. Endpoints allow services to communicate using logical connection names, which an ESB will map to actual physical network destinations at runtime. This destination independence gives the services that are part of the ESB the ability to be upgraded, moved, or replaced without having to modify code and disrupting existing ESB applications. For instance, an existing ESB invoicing service could be easily upgraded or replaced with a new service without disrupting other applications. Additionally, duplicate processes can be set up to handle failover if a service is not available. The endpoints can be configured to use several levels of QoS, which guarantee communication despite network failures and outages.

7.6.1 Characteristics of an ESB Solution

There are alternative ways to implement an ESB. The ESB itself can be a single centralized service or even a distributed system consisting of peer and subpeer ESBs—in the form of an ESB federation—all working in tandem to keep the SOA system operational. In small-scale implementations of integration solutions, the physical ESB infrastructure is likely to be a centralized ESB topology. A centralized ESB topology is concentrated on a single cluster, or hub, of servers. This solution is reminiscent of hub-and-spoke middleware topologies, which use a central node that manages all interactions between applications and prevent an application having to integrate multiple times with several other applications (Kale 2015). The hub-and-spoke approach simply carries out one integration process on the central node, which is a central point of control responsible for integration/translation activities, maintaining routing information, service naming, and so forth. The most popular hub-and-spoke EAI solution for the inter-enterprise arena is integration brokering.

Even though a hub-and-spoke solution is capable of being stretched out across organizational boundaries, it still does not allow the local autonomy that individual business units require to operate semi-independently of each other. This is usually caused by the integration broker's inability to easily span firewalls and network domains. However, as explained earlier in this chapter, the most serious drawback of this approach is that hub-and-spoke solutions can quickly become a point of contention for large-scale implementations. In an environment of loosely coupled units, it does not make sense for business process flow between localized applications or security domains to be managed by a single centralized authority like an integration broker.

In circumstances where organizational or geographically dispersed units need to act independently from one another, the infrastructure may become more physically distributed while retaining at least logically the central control over configuration. This calls for a federated hub solution. A federated ESB allows different enterprises such as manufacturers, suppliers, and customers to plug together their integration domains into a larger federated integration network. This topology allows for local message traffic, integration components, and adapters to be locally installed, configured, secured, and managed while allowing for a single integrated transaction and security model. In this figure, a federated ESB solution is used to form a virtual network of trading partners across industries and services able to take advantage of the wider range of options and partnering models.

The physical deployment of the ESB depends on candidate ESB technologies such as specialized MOM, integration brokers, and application servers. The use and combination of different candidate ESB technologies result in a variety of ESB patterns, each having its own requirements and constraints in connection with its physical deployment. Some ESB configurations might be suited to very widespread distribution to support integration over large geographic areas, while others might be more suited to deployment in localized clusters to support high availability and scalability. Matching the requirements for physical distribution to the capabilities of candidate technologies is an important aspect of ESB design. Also important is the ability to incrementally extend the initial deployment to reflect evolving requirements to integrate additional systems, or to extend the geographic reach of the ESB infrastructure.

Irrespective of its implementation topology, the main aim of the ESB is to provide virtualization of the enterprise resources, allowing the business logic of the enterprise to be developed and managed independently of the infrastructure, network, and provision of those business services. Implementing an ESB requires an integrated set of middleware facilities that support the following interrelated architectural styles:

- SOAs, where distributed applications are composed of granular reusable services with well-defined, published, and standard-compliant interfaces
- Message-driven architectures, where applications send messages through the ESB to receiving applications
- Event-driven architectures, where applications generate and consume messages independently of one another

The ESB supports these architectural styles and service interaction capabilities, and provides the integrated communication, messaging, and event infrastructure to enable them, as explained in the previous section. To achieve its stated objectives, the ESB amalgamates functional capabilities of application servers, integration brokers, and business process management technologies and product sets into a single integrated infrastructure.

7.6.1.1 Key Capabilities of an ESB

In order to implement an SOA, both applications and infrastructure must support SOA principles. Enabling an application for SOA involves the creation of service interfaces to existing or new functions, either directly or through the use of adapters. Enabling the infrastructure, at the most basic level, involves the provision of the capabilities to route and deliver secure service requests to the correct service provider. However, it is also vital that the infrastructure supports the substitution of one service implementation by another with no effect on the clients of that service. This requires not only that the service interfaces be specified according to SOA principles but also that the infrastructure allow client code to invoke services irrespective of the service location and the communication protocol involved. Such service routing and substitution are among the many capabilities of the ESB. Additional capabilities can be found in the following list that describes detailed functional requirements of an ESB. It should be noted that not all of the capabilities described in the following are offered by current commercial ESB systems:

1. Dynamic connectivity capabilities: Dynamic connectivity is the ability to connect to web services dynamically without using a separate static API or proxy for each service. Most enterprise applications today operate on a static connectivity mode, requiring some static piece of code for each service. Dynamic service connectivity is a key capability for a successful ESB implementation. The dynamic

connectivity API is the same regardless of the service implementation protocol (web services, JMS, EJB/RMI, etc.).

2. Reliable messaging capabilities: Reliable messaging can be used primarily to ensure guaranteed delivery of these messages to their destination and for handling events. This capability is crucial for responding to clients in an asynchronous manner and for a successful ESB implementation.
3. Topic- and content-based routing capabilities: The ESB should be equipped with routing mechanisms to facilitate not only topic-based routing but also more sophisticated content-based routing. Topic-based routing assumes that messages can be grouped into fixed, topical classes so that subscribers can explicate interest in a topic and, as a consequence, receive messages associated with that topic. Content-based routing, on the other hand, allows subscriptions on constraints of actual properties (attributes) of business events. Content-based routing forwards messages to their destination based on the context or content of the service. Content-based routing is usually implemented using techniques that can examine the content of a message and apply a set of rules to its content to determine which endpoints in the ESB infrastructure it may need to be routed to next.
4. Transformation capabilities: A critical ability of the ESB is the ability to route service interactions through a variety of transport protocols and to transform from one protocol to another where necessary. Another important aspect of an ESB implementation is the ability to support service messaging models and data formats consistent with the SOA interfaces. A major source of value in an ESB is that it shields any individual component from any knowledge of the implementation details of any other component. The ESB transformation services make it possible to ensure that messages and data received by any component are in the format it expects, thereby removing the need to make changes. The ESB plays a major role in transforming between differing data formats and messaging models, whether between basic XML formats and web service messages or between different XML formats (e.g., transforming an industry-standard XML message to a proprietary or custom XML format).
5. Service enablement capabilities: Service enablement includes the ability to access already existing resources such as legacy systems—technically obsolete mission-critical elements of an organization's infrastructure—and includes them in an SOA implementation. Tactically, legacy assets must be leveraged, service enabled, and integrated with modern service technologies and applications.
6. Endpoint discovery with multiple QoS capabilities: The ESB should support the basic SOA need to discover, locate, and bind to services. As many network endpoints can implement the same service contract, the ESB should make it possible for the client to select the best endpoint at runtime, rather than hard-coding endpoints at build time. The ESB should, therefore, be capable of supporting various QoSs and allow clients to discover the best service instance with which to interact based on QoS properties. Such capabilities should be controlled by declarative policies associated with the services involved using a policy standard such as the WS-Policy framework.
7. Long-running process and transaction capabilities: Service orientation, as opposed to distributed object architectures such as .NET or J2EE, more closely reflects real-world processes and relationships. Hence, SOA represents a much more natural way to model and build software that solves real-world business processing needs.

Accordingly, the ESB should provide the ability to support business processes and long-running services—services that tend to run for long duration, exchanging messages (conversation) as they progress. Typical examples are an online reservation system, which interacts with the user as well as various service providers (airline ticketing, insurance claims, mortgage and credit product applications, etc.). In addition, in order to be successful in business environments, it is extremely important that the ESB provides certain transactional guarantees. More specifically, the ESB needs to be able to ensure that complex transactions are handled in a highly reliable manner, and if failure should occur, transactions should be capable of rolling back processing to the original, pre-request state. Long-duration transactional conversations could be made possible if implemented on the basis of messaging patterns using asynchrony, store and forward, and itinerary-based routing techniques.

8. Security capabilities: Generically handling and enforcing security is a key success factor for ESB implementations. The ESB needs both to provide a security model to service consumers and to integrate with the (potentially varied) security models of service providers. Both point-to-point (e.g., SSL encryption) and end-to-end security capabilities will be required. These end-to-end security capabilities include federated authentication, which intercepts service requests and adds the appropriate user name and credentials, validation of each service request, and authorization to make sure that the sender has the appropriate privilege to access the service, and, lastly, encryption/decryption of XML content at the element level for both message requests and responses. To address these intricate security requirements, the ESB must rely on WS-Security and other security-related standards for web services that have been developed.
9. Integration capabilities: To support SOA in a heterogeneous environment, the ESB needs to integrate with a variety of systems that do not directly support service-style interactions. These may include legacy systems, packaged applications, or other EAI technologies. When assessing the integration requirements for ESB, several types or styles of integration must be considered, for example, process versus data integration.
10. Management and monitoring capabilities: In an SOA environment, applications cross system (and even organizational) boundaries, they overlap, and they can change over time. Managing these applications is a serious challenge. Examples include dynamic load balancing, failover when primary systems go down, and achieving topological or geographic affinity between the client and the service instance. Effective systems and application management in an ESB requires a management framework that is consistent across an increasingly heterogeneous set of participating component systems, while supporting complex aggregate (cross component) management use cases, such as dynamic resource provisioning and demand-based routing, and SLA enforcement in conjunction with policy-based behavior (e.g., the ability to select service providers dynamically based on the quality of service they offer compared to the business value of individual transactions).
11. Scalability capabilities: With a widely distributed SOA, there will be the need to scale some of the services or the entire infrastructure to meet integration demands. For example, transformation services are typically very resource intensive and may require multiple instances across two or more computing nodes. At the same

time, it is necessary to create an infrastructure that can support the large nodes present in a global service network. The loose-coupled nature of an SOA requires that the ESB use a decentralized model to provide a cost-effective solution that promotes flexibility in scaling any aspect of the integration network. A decentralized architecture enables independent scalability of individual services as well as the communications infrastructure itself.

7.6.1.2 ESB Scalability

Scalability is a particularly important issue for any automated business integration solution. Scalability concerns in the case of ESB translate to how well the particular ESB implementation has been designed. The use of asynchronous communications, message itineraries, and message and process definitions allows different parts of the ESB to operate independently of one another. This results in a decentralized model providing complete flexibility in scaling any aspect of the integration network. Such a decentralized architecture enables independent scalability of individual services as well as the communications infrastructure itself. For instance, parallel execution of business operations and itinerary-based routing significantly contribute to the highly distributed nature of the ESB, as there is no centralized rule engine to refer back to for each step in the process.

Typical integration broker technologies handle scalability using a centralized hub-and-spoke model; that is, they handle changes in load and configuration by increasing broker capacity or by adding brokers in a centralized location. A centralized rule engine for the routing of messages can quickly become a bottleneck and also a single point of failure. In contrast, an ESB allows capacity to be added where it is most needed—at the service itself.

When the capacity of a single broker is reached, brokers can be combined into clusters. These may act as a single virtual broker to handle increased demand from users and applications. The ESB's use of integration brokers and broker clusters increases scalability by allowing brokers to communicate and dynamically distribute load on the bus. For example, in the event that an increase in the use of the inventory services has overloaded the capacity of their host machine(s), new machines and new brokers can be added to handle the load without the need to change any of the services themselves and without requiring any additional development or administration changes to the messaging system. The notion of a separately deployable, separately scalable messaging topology, combined with a separately deployable, separately scalable ESB service container model, is what uniquely distinguishes this architectural configuration. The distributed functional pieces are able to work together as one logical piece with a single, globally accessible namespace for locating and invoking services.

7.6.1.3 Event-Driven Nature of ESB

In an ESB-enabled event-driven SOA, applications and services are treated as abstract service endpoints, which can readily respond to asynchronous events. Applications and event-driven services are tied together in an ESB-enabled event-driven SOA in a loosely coupled fashion, which allows them to operate independently from each other while still providing value to a broader business function. An event source typically sends messages through the ESB that publishes the messages to the objects that have subscribed to the events. The event itself encapsulates an activity and is a complete description of a specific action. To achieve its functionality, the ESB must support both the established web service technologies such as SOAP, WSDL, and BPEL, as well as emerging standards such as WS-ReliableMessaging and WS-Notification.

An SOA requires an additional fundamental technology beyond the service aspect to realize its full potential: event-driven computing. Ultimately, the primary objective of most SOA implementations is to automate as much processing as necessary and to provide critical and actionable information to human users when they are required to interact with a business process. This requires the ESB infrastructure itself to recognize meaningful events and respond to them appropriately. The response could be either by automatically initiating new services and business processes or by notifying users of business events of interest, putting the events into topical context and, often, suggesting the best courses of action. In the enterprise context, business events, such as a customer order, the arrival of a shipment at a loading dock, the payment of a bill, and so forth, affect the normal course of a business process and can occur in any order at any point in time. Consequently, applications that use orchestrated processes that exchange messages need to communicate with each other using a broad capability known as an event-driven SOA.

An event-driven SOA is an architectural approach to distributed computing where events trigger asynchronous messages that are then sent between independent software components that need not have any information about each other by abstracting away from the details of underlying service connectivity and protocols. An event-driven SOA provides a more lightweight, straightforward set of technologies to build and maintain the service abstraction for client applications.

7.7 Summary

Services and service-oriented architectures are pragmatic responses to the complexity and interoperability problems encountered by the builders of previous generations of large-scale integrated applications. Although it is possible to design and build service-oriented systems using any distributed computing or integration middleware, only web services technologies can today meet the critical requirement for seamless interoperability that is such an important part of the service-oriented vision. This chapter presented the definition and characteristics of service-oriented architectures along with approaches to realizing the vision of service-oriented systems with web services and RESTful services, respectively. The last part of the chapter shows how, with an ESB SOA implementation, previously isolated ERP, CRM, supply chain management, and financial and other legacy systems, can become SOA enabled and integrated more effectively than when relying on custom, point-to-point coding or proprietary EAI technology. An ESB supporting web services with more established application integration techniques enables an enterprise-wide solution that combines the best of both of these worlds.

8

Cloud Computing Basics

Cloud computing is on-demand access to a shared pool of computing resources. It helps consumers to reduce costs, reduce management responsibilities, and increase business agility. For this reason, it is becoming a popular paradigm, and increasingly more companies are shifting toward IT cloud computing solutions. Advantages are many, but being a new paradigm, there are also challenges and inherent issues. These relate to data governance, service management, process monitoring, infrastructure reliability, information security, data integrity, and business continuity.

Many motivating factors have led to the emergence of cloud computing. Businesses require services that include both infrastructure and application workload requests while meeting defined service levels for capacity, resource tiering, and availability. IT delivery often necessitates costs and efficiencies that create a perception of IT as a hindrance, not a strategic partner. Issues include underutilized resources, over-provisioning or under-provisioning of resources, lengthy deployment times, and lack of cost visibility. Virtualization is the first step toward addressing some of these challenges by enabling improved utilization through server consolidation, workload mobility through hardware independence, and efficient management of hardware resources.

The virtualization system is a key foundation for the cloud computing system. We stitch together compute resources so as to appear as one large computer behind which the complexity is hidden. By coordinating, managing, and scheduling resources such as CPUs, network, storage, and firewalls in a consistent way across internal and external premises, we create a flexible cloud infrastructure platform. This platform includes security, automation and management, interoperability and openness, self-service, pooling, and dynamic resource allocation. In view of cloud computing, we are advocating, applications can run within an external provider, in internal IT premises, or in combination as a hybrid system—it matters how they are run, not where they are run.

Cloud computing builds on virtualization to create a service-oriented computing model. This is done through the addition of resource abstractions and controls to create dynamic pools of resources that can be consumed through the network. Benefits include economies of scale, elastic resources, self-service provisioning, and cost transparency. Consumption of cloud resources is enforced through resource metering and pricing models that shape user behavior. Consumers benefit through leveraging allocation models such as pay-as-you-go to gain greater cost efficiency, lower barrier to entry, and immediate access to infrastructure resources.

8.1 Cloud Definition

Here is the National Institute of Standards and Technology (NIST) working definition.

Cloud computing is a model for enabling convenient, on-demand network access to a shared pool of configurable computing resources (e.g., networks, servers, storage, applications, and services) that can be rapidly provisioned and released with minimal management effort or service provider interaction. This cloud model promotes availability and is composed of five essential characteristics, three delivery models, and four deployment models.

The five essential characteristics are as follows:

- On-demand self-service
- Broad network access
- Resource pooling
- Rapid elasticity
- Measured service

The three delivery models are as follows:

1. Infrastructure as a service (IaaS)
2. Platform as a service (PaaS)
3. Software as a service (SaaS)

The four deployment models are as follows:

1. Public cloud
2. Private cloud
3. Hybrid cloud
4. Community cloud

Cloud computing is the IT foundation for cloud services, and it consists of technologies that enable cloud services. The key attributes of cloud computing are shown in Table 8.1. Key attributes of cloud services are described in Table 8.2.

TABLE 8.1

Key Attributes of Cloud Computing

Attributes	Description
Offsite, third-party provider	In cloud execution, it is assumed that the third party provides services. There is also a possibility of in-house cloud service delivery
Accessed via the Internet	Services are accessed via standard-based, universal network access. It can also include security and quality-of-service options
Minimal or no IT skill required	There is a simplified specification of requirements
Provisioning	It includes self-service requesting, near-real-time deployment, and dynamic and fine-grained scaling
Pricing	Pricing is based on usage-based capability and it is fine grained
User interface	User interface includes browsers for a variety of devices and with rich capabilities
System interface	System interfaces are based on web services APIs providing a standard framework for accessing and integrating among cloud services
Shared resources	Resources are shared among cloud services users; however, via configuration options with the service, there is the ability to customize

TABLE 8.2
Key Attributes of Cloud Services

Attributes	Description
Infrastructure systems	It includes servers, storage, and networks that can scale as per user demand
Application software	It provides web-based user interface, web services APIs, and a rich variety of configurations
Application development and deployment software	It supports the development and integration of cloud application software
System and application management software	It supports rapid self-service provisioning, and configuration and usage monitoring
IP networks	They connect end users to the cloud and the infrastructure components

8.2 Cloud Characteristics

Large organizations such as IBM, Dell, Microsoft, Google, Amazon, and Sun have already started taking strong positions with respect to cloud computing provision. They are so much behind this latest paradigm that success is virtually guaranteed. The essential characteristics of a cloud environment include the following:

1. On-demand self-service that enables users to consume computing capabilities (e.g., applications, server time, and network storage) as and when required.
2. Rapid elasticity and scalability that allow functionalities and resources to be rapidly, elastically, and automatically scaled out or in, as demand rises or drops.

   According to the current demand requirement, automatic services are provided. This is done using software automation, enabling the expansion and contraction of service capability, as needed. This dynamic scaling needs to be done while maintaining high levels of reliability and security.

   These characteristics show the following features:

   a. An economical model of cloud computing that enables consumers to order required services (computing machines and/or storage devices). The requested service could scale rapidly upward or downward on demand.
   b. A machine responsibility that does not require any human to control the requested services. The cloud architecture manages on-demand requests (increase or decrease in service requests), availability, allocation, subscription, and the customer's bill.
3. Broad network access. Capabilities are available over the network and accessed through standard mechanisms that promote use by heterogeneous thin or thick client platforms (e.g., mobile phones, tablets, laptops, and workstations).

   Capabilities are available over the network, and a continuous internet connection is required for a broad range of devices such as PCs, laptops, and mobile devices, using standards-based APIs (for example, ones based on HTTP). Deployments of services in the cloud include everything from using business applications to the latest application on the newest smart phones.

4. Multitenancy and resource pooling that allow for combining heterogeneous computing resources (e.g., hardware, software, processing, servers, and network bandwidth) to serve multiple consumers—such resources being dynamically assigned.

   A virtualized software model is used that enables the sharing of physical services, storage, and networking capabilities. Regardless of deployment model—whether it be a public cloud or private cloud—the cloud infrastructure is shared across a number of users.

   A cloud vendor provides a pool of resources (e.g., computing machines, storage devices, and network) to customers. The cloud architecture manages all available resources via global and local managers for different sites and local sites, respectively.

   This feature allows big data to be distributed on different servers, which is not possible by traditional models, such as supercomputing systems.
5. Measured provision to automatically control and optimize resource allocation, and to provide a metering capability to determine the usage for billing purpose, allowing easy monitoring, controlling, and reporting.

Resource usage can be monitored, controlled, and reported, providing transparency for both the provider and the consumer of the utilized service. Using metering for managing and optimizing the service and to provide reporting and billing information. In this way, consumers are billed for services according to how much they have actually used during the billing period.

Thus, in summation, cloud computing allows for the sharing and scalable deployment of services, as needed, from almost any location, and for which the customer can be billed based on actual usage.

8.2.1 Cloud Storage Infrastructure Requirements

Data is growing at an immense rate, and with the combination of technology trends such as virtualization with increased economic pressures, exploding growth of unstructured data, and regulatory environments that require enterprises to keep data for longer periods of time, it is easy to see the need for a trustworthy and appropriate storage infrastructure. Storage infrastructure is the backbone of every business. Whether a cloud is public or private, the key to success is creating a storage infrastructure in which all resources can be efficiently utilized and shared. Since all data reside on the storage systems, data storage becomes even more crucial in a shared infrastructure model.

The most important cloud infrastructure requirements are as follows:

1. Elasticity: Cloud storage must be elastic so that it can quickly adjust along with underlying infrastructure to the changing requirements of the customer demands and also comply with the service level agreements (SLAs).
2. Automatic: Cloud storage must have the ability to be automated so that policies can be leveraged to make underlying infrastructure changes such as placing user and content management in different storage tiers and geographic locations quickly and without human intervention.

3. Scalability: Cloud storage needs to scale quickly up and down according to the requirements of the customer. This is one of the most important requirements that make cloud so popular.
4. Recovery performance: Cloud storage infrastructure must provide fast and robust data recovery as an essential element of cloud service.
5. Reliability: As more and more users are depending on the services offered by the cloud, reliability becomes increasingly important. Various users of the cloud storage want to make sure that their data is reliably backed up for disaster recovery purposes and cloud should be able to continue to run in the presence of hardware and software failures.
6. Operational efficiency: Operational efficiency is a key to successful business enterprise, which can be ensured by better management of storage capacities and cost benefit. Both these features should be integral parts of cloud storage.
7. Latency: Cloud storage models are not suitable for all applications, especially for real-time applications. It is important to measure and test network latency before committing to a migration. Virtual machines can introduce additional latency through the time-sharing nature of the underlying hardware, and unanticipated sharing and reallocation of machines can significantly affect run times.
8. Data retrieval: Once the data is stored on the cloud, it can be easily accessed from anywhere at any time where network connection is available. Ease of access to data in the cloud is critical in enabling seamless integration of cloud storage into existing enterprise workflows and to minimize the learning curve for cloud storage adoption.
9. Data security: Security is one of the major concerns of cloud users. As different users store more of their own data on the cloud, they want to ensure that their private data is not accessible to other users who are not authorized to see it. If this is the case, then the user can have a private cloud because security is assumed to be tightly controlled in case of a private cloud. But in case of public clouds, data should either be stored on a partition of a shared storage system or cloud storage providers must establish multitenancy policies to allow multiple business units or separate companies to securely share the same storage hardware.

Storage is the most important component of IT infrastructure. Unfortunately, it is almost always managed as a scarce resource because it is relatively expensive and the consequences of running out of storage capacity can be severe. Nobody wants to take the responsibility of a storage manager, and thus storage management suffers from slow provisioning practices.

8.3 Cloud Delivery Models

Cloud computing is not a completely new concept for the development and operation of web applications. It allows for the most cost-effective development of scalable web portals on highly available and fail-safe infrastructures. In the cloud computing system, we have to address different fundamentals such as virtualization, scalability, interoperability, quality of service, failover mechanism, and cloud deployment models (private, public, hybrid) within the context of the taxonomy. The taxonomy of cloud includes the different participants involved in the cloud, along with the attributes and technologies that are coupled to address their needs and the different types of services such as "XaaS" offerings, where X is software, hardware, platform, infrastructure, data, and business.

8.3.1 Infrastructure as a Service (IaaS)

The IaaS model is about providing compute and storage resources as a service. According to NIST, IaaS is defined as follows:

The capability provided to the consumer is to provision processing, storage, networks, and other fundamental computing resources, where the consumer is able to deploy and run arbitrary software, which can include operating systems and applications. The consumer does not manage or control the underlying cloud infrastructure but has control over operating systems, storage, deployed applications, and possibly limited control of select networking components (e.g., host firewalls).

The user of IaaS has single ownership of the hardware infrastructure allotted to him (may be a virtual machine), and can use it as if it is his own machine on a remote network and has control over the operating system and software on it. IaaS is illustrated in Figure 8.1. The IaaS provider has control over the actual hardware, and the cloud user can request allocation of virtual resources, which are then allocated by the IaaS provider on the hardware (generally without any manual intervention). The cloud user can manage the virtual resources as desired, including installing any desired OS, software, and applications. Therefore, IaaS is well suited for users who want complete control over the software stack they run; for example, the user may be using heterogeneous software platforms from different vendors, and they may not like to switch to a PaaS platform where only select middleware is available. Well-known IaaS platforms include Amazon EC2, Rackspace, and Rightscale. Additionally, traditional vendors such as HP, IBM, and Microsoft offer solutions that can be used to build private IaaS.

8.3.2 Platform as a Service (PaaS)

The PaaS model is to provide a system stack or platform for application deployment as a service. NIST defines PaaS as follows:

The capability provided to the consumer is to deploy onto the cloud infrastructure consumer-created or acquired applications created using programming languages and tools supported by the provider. The consumer does not manage or control the underlying cloud infrastructure, including network, servers, operating systems, or storage, but has control over the deployed applications and possibly application-hosting environment configurations.

Figure 8.2 shows a PaaS model diagrammatically. The hardware, as well as any mapping of hardware to virtual resources, such as virtual servers, is controlled by the PaaS provider. Additionally, the PaaS provider supports select middleware, such as a database and web application server, shown in the figure. The cloud user can configure and build on top of this middleware, such as define a new database table in a database. The PaaS provider maps this new table onto its cloud infrastructure. Subsequently, the cloud user can manage the database as needed and develop applications on top of this database. PaaS platforms are well suited to those cloud users who find that the middleware they are using matches the middleware provided by one of the PaaS vendors. This enables them

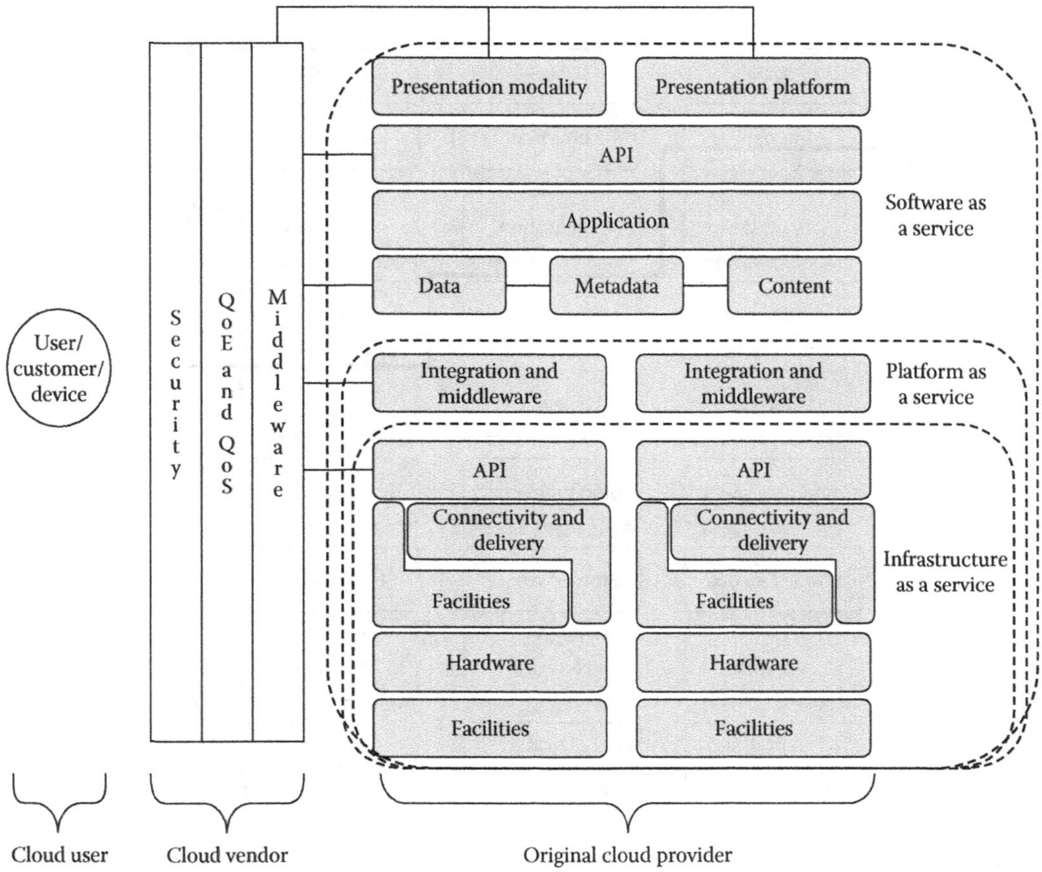

FIGURE 8.1
The cloud reference model.

to focus on the application. Windows Azure, Google App Engine, and Hadoop are some well-known PaaS platforms. As in the case of IaaS, traditional vendors such as HP, IBM, and Microsoft offer solutions that can be used to build private PaaS.

8.3.3 Software as a Service (SaaS)

SaaS is about providing the complete application as a service. SaaS has been defined by NIST as follows:

The capability provided to the consumer is to use the provider's applications running on a cloud infrastructure. The applications are accessible from various client devices through a thin client interface such as a web browser (e.g., web-based email). The consumer does not manage or control the underlying cloud infrastructure, including network, servers, operating systems, storage, or even individual application capabilities, with the possible exception of limited user-specific application configuration settings.

Any application that can be accessed using a web browser can be considered SaaS. These points are illustrated in Figure 8.2. The SaaS provider controls all the layers apart

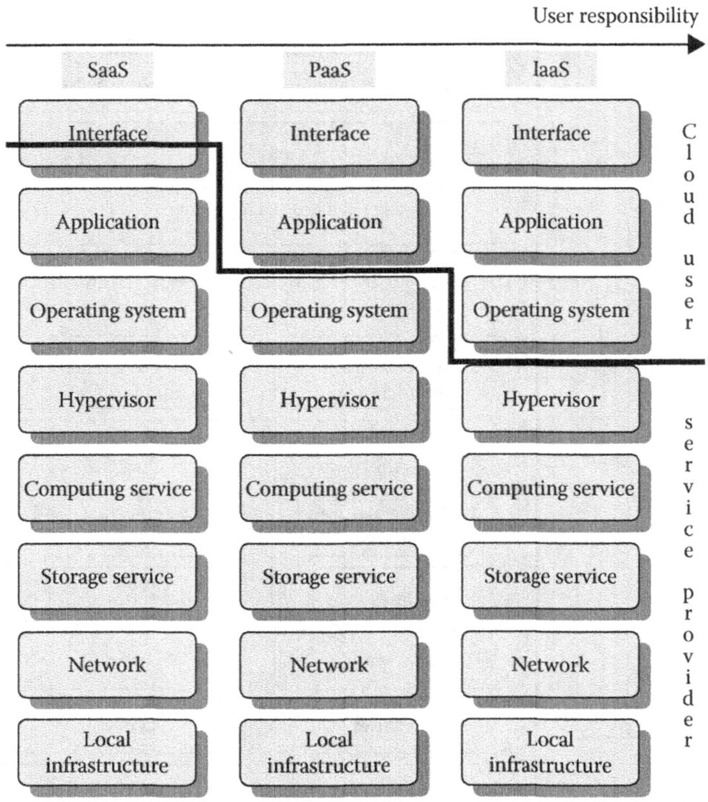

FIGURE 8.2
Portfolio of services for the three cloud delivery models.

from the application. Users who log in to the SaaS service can both use the application and configure the application for their use. For example, users can use Salesforce.com to store their customer data. They can also configure the application, for example, requesting additional space for storage or adding additional fields to the customer data that is already being used. When configuration settings are changed, the SaaS infrastructure performs any management tasks needed (such as allocation of additional storage) to support the changed configuration. SaaS platforms are targeted toward users who want to use the application without any software installation (in fact, the motto of Salesforce.com, one of the prominent SaaS vendors, is "No Software"). However, for advanced usage, some small amount of programming or scripting may be necessary to customize the application for use by the business (for example, adding additional fields to customer data). In fact, SaaS platforms such as Salesforce.com allow many of these customizations to be performed without programming, but by specifying business rules that are simple enough for nonprogrammers to implement. Prominent SaaS applications include Salesforce.com for CRM, Google Docs for document sharing, and web email systems such as Gmail, Hotmail, and Yahoo! Mail. IT vendors such as HP and IBM also sell systems that can be configured to set up SaaS in a private cloud; SAP, for example, can be used as a SaaS offering inside an enterprise.

Table 8.3 presents a comparison of the three cloud delivery models.

TABLE 8.3

Comparison of Cloud Delivery Models

Service Type	IaaS	PaaS	SaaS
Service category	VM rental; online storage	Online operating environment, online database, online message queue	Application and software rental
Service customization	Server template	Logic resource template	Application template
Service provisioning	Automation	Automation	Automation
Service accessing and using	Remote console, Web 2.0	Online development and debugging, integration of offline development tools and cloud	Web 2.0
Service monitoring	Physical resource monitoring	Logic resource monitoring	Application monitoring
Service level management	Dynamic orchestration of physical resources	Dynamic orchestration of logic resources	Dynamic orchestration of application
Service resource optimization	Network virtualization, server visualization, storage visualization	Large-scale distributed file system. Database, middleware, etc.	Multitenancy
Service measurement	Physical resource metering	Logic resource usage metering	Business resource usage metering
Service integration and combination	Load balance	SOA	SOA, mashup
Service security	Storage encryption and isolation, VM isolation, VLAN; SSL/SSH	Data isolation, operating environment isolation, SSL	Data isolation, operating environment isolation, SSL; web authentication and authorization

8.4 Cloud Deployment Models

8.4.1 Private Clouds

A private cloud has an exclusive purpose for a particular organization. The cloud resources may be located on or off premise, and could be owned and managed by the consuming organization or a third party. This may be an example of an organization that has decided to adopt the infrastructure-cost-saving potential of a virtualized architecture on top of existing hardware. The organization feels unable to remotely host its data, so it is looking to the cloud to improve its resource utilization and automate the management of such resources. Alternatively an organization may wish to extend its current IT capability by using an exclusive, private cloud that is remotely accessible and provisioned by a third party. Such an organization may feel uncomfortable with its data being held alongside a potential competitor's data in the multitenancy model.

8.4.2 Public Clouds

A public cloud, as its name implies, is available to the general public and is managed by an organization. The organization may be a business (such as Google), academic institution, or a government department. The cloud computing provider owns and manages the cloud infrastructure. The existence of many different consumers within one cloud architecture is referred to as a multitenancy model.

8.4.3 Hybrid Clouds

Hybrid clouds are formed when more than one type of cloud infrastructure is used for a particular situation. For instance, an organization may use a public cloud for some aspect of its business, yet also have a private cloud on premise for data that is sensitive. As organizations start to exploit cloud service models, it is increasingly likely that a hybrid model is adopted as the specific characteristics of each of the different service models are harnessed. The key enabler here is the open standards by which data and applications are implemented, since if portability does not exist, then vendor lock-in to a particular cloud computing provider becomes likely. Lack of data and application portability has been a major hindrance for the widespread uptake of grid computing, and this is one aspect of cloud computing that can facilitate much more flexible, abstract architectures.

8.4.4 Community Clouds

Community clouds are a model of cloud computing where the resources exist for a number of parties who have a shared interest or cause. This model is very similar to the single-purpose grids that collaborating research and academic organizations have created to conduct large-scale scientific experiments (e-science). The cloud is owned and managed by one or more of the collaborators in the community, and it may exist either on or off premise.

8.5 Cloud Benefits

Cloud Computing is an attractive paradigm that promises numerous benefits, inherent in the characteristics, as mentioned above. These include the following:

- Optimization of a company's capital investment by reducing costs of purchasing hardware and software, resulting in a much lower total cost of ownership and, ultimately, a whole new way of looking at the economies of scale and operational IT
- Simplicity and agility of operations and use, requiring minimal time and effort to provision additional resources
- Enabling an enterprise to tap into a talent pool, as and when needed, for a fraction of the cost of hiring staff or retaining the existing staff and, thus, enabling the key personnel in the organization to focus more on producing value and innovation for the business
- Enabling small organizations to access the IT services and resources that would otherwise be out of their reach, thus placing large organizations and small businesses on a level-playing field
- Providing novel and complex computing architectures and innovation potential
- Providing mechanisms for disaster recovery and business continuity through a variety of fully outsourced ICT services and resources

Cloud computing can be massively scalable, and there are built-in benefits of efficiency, availability, and high utilization that, in turn, result in reduced capital expenditure and reduced operational costs. It permits seamless sharing and collaboration through virtualization. In general, cloud computing promises cost savings, agility, innovation, flexibility, and simplicity. The offerings from vendors, in terms of services of the application, platform, and infrastructure nature, are continuing to mature, and the cost savings are becoming particularly attractive in the current competitive economic climate. Another broader aim of cloud technology is to make supercomputing available to the enterprises, in particular, and the public, in general.

The major benefits of the cloud paradigm can be distilled to its inherent flexibility and resiliency, the potential for reducing costs, availability of very large amounts of centralized data storage, means to rapidly deploy computing resources and scalability.

1. Flexibility and resiliency: A major benefit of cloud computing is flexibility, though cloud providers cannot provide infinite configuration and provisioning flexibility, and will seek to offer structured alternatives. They might offer a choice among a number of computing and storage resource configurations at different capabilities and costs, and the cloud customer will have to adjust his or her requirements to fit one of those models.

   The flexibility offered by cloud computing can be in terms of the following:

   a. Automated provisioning of new services and technologies
   b. Acquiring increased resources on an as-needed basis
   c. Ability to focus on innovation instead of maintenance details
   d. Device independence
   e. Freedom from having to install software patches
   f. Freedom from concerns about updating servers

   Resiliency is achieved through the availability of multiple redundant resources and locations. As autonomic computing becomes more mature, self-management and self-healing mechanisms can ensure increased reliability and robustness of cloud resources. Also, disaster recovery and business continuity planning are inherent in using the provider's cloud computing platforms.

2. Reduced costs: Cloud computing offers reductions in system administration, provisioning expenses, energy costs, software licensing fees, and hardware costs. The cloud paradigm, in general, is a basis for cost savings because capability and resources can be paid for incrementally without the need for large investments in computing infrastructure. This model is especially true for adding storage costs for large database applications. Therefore, capital costs are reduced and replaced by manageable, scalable operating expenses.

There might be some instances, particularly for long-term, stable computing configuration usage, where cloud computation might not have a cost advantage over using one's internal resources or directly leasing equipment. For example, if the volume of data storage and computational resources required are essentially constant, and there is no need for rapid provisioning and flexibility, an organization's local computational capabilities might be more cost effective than using a cloud.

Resources are used more efficiently in cloud computing, resulting in substantial support and energy cost savings. The need for highly trained and expensive IT personnel is also reduced; client organizational support and maintenance costs are reduced dramatically because these expenses are transferred to the cloud provider, including 24/7 support, which, in turn, is spread onto a much larger base of multiple tenants or clients.

Another reason for migrating to the cloud is the drastic reduction in the cost of power and energy consumption.

3. Centralized data storage: Many data centers are an ensemble of legacy applications, operating systems, hardware, and software, and are a support and maintenance nightmare. This situation requires more specialized maintenance personnel, increased costs because of lack of standardization, and a higher risk of crashes. The cloud not only offers a larger number of data storage resources than are normally available in local, corporate computing systems, but also enables a decrease or increase in the resources used per requirements—with corresponding adjustments in operating cost. This centralization of storage infrastructure results in cost efficiencies in utilities, real estate, and trained personnel. Also, data protection mechanisms are much easier to implement and monitor in a centralized system than on large numbers of computing platforms that might be widely distributed geographically in different parts of an organization.
4. Reduced time to deployment: In a competitive environment where rapid evaluation, development, and deployment of new approaches, processes, solutions, or offerings is critical, the cloud offers the means to use powerful computational or large storage resources on short-notice without requiring sizeable initial investments of finances, efforts, or time (in hardware, software, and personnel). Thus, this rapid provisioning of latest technologically upgraded and enhanced resources can be accomplished at a relatively small cost (with minimal cost of replacing discontinued resources) and offers the client access to advanced technologies that are constantly being acquired by the cloud provider. Improved delivery of services obtained by rapid cloud provisioning improves time to market and, hence, market growth.
5. Scalability: Cloud computing provides the means, within limits, for a client to rapidly provision computational resources to meet increases or decreases in demand. Cloud scalability provides for optimal resources so that computing resources are provisioned per requirements, seamlessly ensuring maximum cost benefit to the clients. Since, the cloud provider operates a multitenancy utility model, the client organization has to pay only for the resources it is using at any particular time.

Table 8.4 presents a comparison of cloud benefits for small and medium-sized enterprises (SMEs) and large enterprises.

TABLE 8.4

Comparison of Cloud Benefits for Small and Medium Enterprises (SMEs) and Large Enterprises

Economic Benefits	Small and Medium Enterprises (SMEs)	Large Enterprises
Strategic flexibility	Critical in getting quickly to market. Cloud services allow startups to rapidly develop and deploy their products as long as they can use the open source or proprietary development platforms of the cloud providers. As the cloud market offerings mature, there will be many more platform options available	Cloud services can provide large enterprises the same strategic benefits as startups for new initiatives as long as legacy software integration and data issues are not significant. With appropriate software development talent, operating units can rapidly develop and market test new innovations without putting additional strain on IT budgets, staff, or hardware. Longstanding internal IT management policies and standards may have to be re-examined and modified to allow this to happen
Cost reduction	Pay-as-you-go pricing may be critical if operating capital or venture capital funding is not available. With cloud services, growth can more easily be funded through operating revenues and there may be tax advantages to converting what would have been longer-term depreciation expenses to fully loaded current expenses	Cloud services provide the same cost benefits for isolated and exploratory initiatives. Instant availability and low setup costs for new development and deployment environments allow operating units to explore new initiatives quickly at low cost without increasing internal IT hardware or staff overheads. For high data-traffic volumes, it may become more economical to bring the operations in-house. Because maintaining legacy hardware and software absorb the majority of IT costs, large corporations may see significant cost savings by selectively moving noncritical applications and processes to external clouds
Software availability	Software as a Service (SaaS) and Platform as a Service (PaaS) provide necessary software and infrastructure at low entry cost. Limited online version functionality may be more than offset by dramatic cost savings	Existing volume licensing of legacy desktop and process-integrated enterprise software may make the status quo more attractive if end-user retraining, process modifications, and other change costs are high. Legacy desktop software may have more features and functionality than is currently available in SaaS versions. But the legacy software licensing costs may dramatically increase if it is hosted in a private cloud environment
Scalability	One of the most dramatic benefits for SMEs and startups. If successful, applications designed to autoscale can scale endlessly in a cloud environment to meet the growing demand	Large enterprises with significant hardware, legacy software, and staff resources can benefit from cloud scalability by identifying CPU-intensive processes such as image processing, PDF conversion, and video encoding that would benefit from the massively scalable parallel processing available in clouds. While this may require modifying legacy applications, the speed benefits and reduced local hardware requirements may far outweigh the software modification costs

(Continued)

TABLE 8.4 (*Continued*)

Comparison of Cloud Benefits for Small and Medium Enterprises (SMEs) and Large Enterprises

Economic Benefits	Small and Medium Enterprises (SMEs)	Large Enterprises
Skills and staffing	While the proper design of cloud applications requires high-level software development skills, their maintenance and support is vastly simplified in the cloud environment. Cloud providers handle all maintenance and support issues for both hardware and platform software at costs that are either bundled into the usage fees or available in various configurations as premium services. This allows significant cost savings through reduced staff overheads	Because the majority of enterprise IT costs go to support legacy applications and hardware, the greatest staffing benefits will be seen in new cloud initiatives that do not add to the staffing burden. Longer term, as the enterprise begins to analyze cloud technology potential for its legacy operations, retraining of existing staff or bringing in new staff with cloud technology skills will be necessary to take advantage of the new paradigm. Thus, some investment will have to be made before large-scale or long-term benefits will be seen. The staffing investment may be significant if the enterprise is attempting to create a private cloud to handle dynamic resource allocation and scalability across its operating units. In this case, it may face significant staff investment as well as the required hardware, software, and network investment to implement and maintain their private cloud
Energy efficiency	Because SMEs can dramatically reduce or eliminate local servers, cloud computing provides direct utility cost savings as well as environmental benefits	Even very large enterprise IT data centers cannot achieve the energy efficiencies found in the massive facilities of public cloud providers even with aggressive high-density server and virtualization strategies. In periods of economic downturns, green initiatives typically cannot compete for scarce capital funds. By employing a mixed strategy that off-loads applications and processing to external clouds when feasible, IT managers are able to minimize their energy costs and carbon footprint
System redundancy and data backup	This is a large benefit for SMEs, the majority of which are poorly prepared for hardware failures and disaster recovery [3]. Cloud storage can reduce downside risks at low cost	Because cloud technologies distribute both data storage and data processing across potentially large number of servers, the likelihood of data loss due to hardware failure is much lower than in most large private data centers. The cloud data storage can provide a cost-effective supplemental back-up strategy

8.6 Cloud Challenges

There are multiple technical challenges that any cloud platform or application needs to address in order to truly provide a utility-like computing infrastructure. The three key challenges are as follows:

- Scalability: Ability to scale to millions of clients simultaneously accessing the cloud service

- Multitenancy: Ability to provide isolation and good performance to multiple tenants using the cloud infrastructure
- Availability: Ability to ensure that the infrastructure and the applications are highly available regardless of hardware and software faults

8.6.1 Scalability

On-demand scaling (and de-scaling) of computation is one of the critical needs of any cloud computing platform. Compute scaling can be done either at the infrastructure level or at the platform level. At the infrastructure level, it is about increasing the capacity of the compute power, while at the platform level, the techniques are mainly to intelligently manage the different client requests in a manner that best utilizes the compute infrastructure without requiring the clients to do anything special during peaks in demand.

1. Scale-up or vertical scaling is about adding more resources to a single node or a single system to improve performance—such as addition of CPUs, use of multicore systems instead of single-core, or adding additional memory. In order to support on-demand scaling of the cloud infrastructure, the system should be able to increase its compute power dynamically without impacting the platform or the application executing over it. Unless a system is virtualized, it is generally not possible to increase the capacity of a compute system dynamically without bringing down the system. More powerful compute resources can now be effectively used by a virtualization layer to support more processes or more virtual machines—enabling scaling up to many more clients. The advantage of scale-up systems is that the programming paradigm is simpler, since it does not involve distributed programming, unlike scale-out systems.
2. Scale-out or horizontal scaling, on the other hand, is about expanding the compute resources by adding a new computer system or node to a distributed application. A web server (such as Apache) is a typical example for such a system. In fact, given that most cloud applications are service enabled, they need to be developed to expand on demand using scaling-out techniques. The advantage of scale-out systems is that commodity hardware, such as disk and memory, can be used for delivering high performance. A scale-out system such as interconnected compute nodes forming a cluster can be more powerful than a traditional supercomputer, especially with faster interconnect technologies. Scale-out systems will essentially be distributed systems with a shared high-performance disk storage used for common data. Unlike scale-up systems, in order to leverage full power of scale-out systems, there should be an effort from the programmer to design applications differently. Many design patterns exist for applications designed for scale-out systems such as MapReduce.

Scale-out solutions have much better performance and price/performance over scale-up systems. This is because a search application essentially consists of independent parallel searches, which can easily be deployed on multiple processors. Scale-out techniques can be employed at the application level too. For example, a typical web search service is scalable where two client query requests can be processed completely as parallel threads. The challenge in scale-out systems, however, is the complex management of the infrastructure, especially when the infrastructure caters to dynamic scaling of resources.

The CAP theorem implies that consistency guarantees in large-scale distributed systems cannot be as strict as those in centralized systems. Specifically, it suggests that distributed systems may need to provide BASE guarantees instead of the ACID guarantees provided by traditional database systems. The CAP theorem states that no distributed system can provide more than two of the following three guarantees: consistency, availability, and partitioning-tolerance. Here, consistency is defined as in databases; that is if multiple operations are performed on the same object (which is actually stored in a distributed system), the results of the operations appear as if the operations were carried out in some definite order on a single system. Availability is defined to be satisfied if each operation on the system (for example, a query) returns some result. The system provides partitioning-tolerance if the system is operational even when the network between two components of the system is down.

Since distributed systems can satisfy only two of the three properties due to the CAP theorem, there are three types of distributed systems. CA (Consistent, Available) systems provide consistency and availability, but cannot tolerate network partitions. An example of a CA system is a clustered database, where each node stores a subset of the data. Such a database cannot provide availability in the case of network partitioning, since queries to data in the partitioned nodes must fail. CA systems may not be useful for cloud computing, since partitions are likely to occur in medium to large networks (including the case where latency is very high). If there is no network partitioning, all servers are consistent, and the value seen by both clients is the correct value. However, if the network is partitioned, it is no longer possible to keep all the servers consistent in the face of updates. There are then two choices. One choice is to keep both servers up and ignore the inconsistency. This leads to AP (Available, Partition-tolerant) systems, where the system is always available, but may not return consistent results. The other possible choice is to bring one of the servers down to avoid inconsistent values. This leads to CP (Consistent, Partition-tolerant) systems, where the system always returns consistent results, but may be unavailable under partitioning—including the case where latency is very high.

AP systems provide weak consistency. An important subclass of weakly consistent systems is those that provide eventual consistency. A system is defined as eventually consistent if the system is guaranteed to reach a consistent state in a finite amount of time if there are no failures (e.g., network partitions) and no updates are made. The inconsistency window for such systems is the maximum amount of time that can elapse between the time that the update is made and the time that the update is guaranteed to be visible to all clients. If the inconsistency window is small compared to the update rate, then one method of dealing with stale data is to wait for a period greater than the inconsistency window and then re-try the query.

Additionally, as noted, applications that do not consist of independent computations are difficult to scale out.

8.6.2 Multitenancy

This deals with the implementation of multitenancy with fine grained resource sharing while ensuring security and isolation between customers and also allowing customers to customize the database.

1. Ad hoc/Custom instances: At this lowest level, each customer has its own custom version of the software. This represents the situation currently in most enterprise data centers, where there are multiple instances and versions of the software. It was also typical of the earlier ASP model that represented the first attempt to offer software for rent over the Internet (see Chapter 12). The ASP model was similar to the SaaS model in that ASP customers (normally businesses), upon logging in to the ASP portal, would be able to rent use of a software application like CRM. However, each customer would typically have its own instance of the software being supported. This would imply that each customer would have its own binaries, as well as its own dedicated processes for the implementation of the application. This makes management extremely difficult, since each customer would need its own management support.
2. Configurable instances: At this level, all customers share the same version of the program. However, customization is possible through configuration and other options. Customization could include the ability to put the customer's logo on the screen, tailoring of workflows to the customer's processes, and so on. At this level, there are significant manageability savings over the previous level, since there is only one copy of the software that needs to be maintained and administered. For instance, upgrades are seamless and simple.
3. Configurable, multitenant efficient instances: Cloud systems at this level, in addition to sharing the same version of the program, also have only one instance of the program running which is shared among all the customers. This leads to additional efficiency since there is only one running instance of the program.
4. Scalable, configurable, multitenant efficient instances: In addition to the attributes of the previous level, the software is also hosted on a cluster of computers, allowing the capacity of the system to scale almost limitlessly. Thus, the number of customers can scale from a small number to a very large number, and the capacity used by each customer can range from small to very large. Performance bottlenecks and capacity limitations that may have been present at the earlier level are eliminated. For instance, in a cloud email service like Gmail or Yahoo! Mail, multiple users share the same physical email server and the same email server processes. Additionally, the emails from different users are stored in the same set of storage devices and perhaps the same set of files. This results in management efficiencies; on the contrary, if each user had to have a dedicated set of disks for storing email, the space allocation for each user would have to be managed separately. However, the drawback of shared storage devices is that security requirements are greater; if the email server has vulnerabilities and can be hacked, it is possible for one user to access the emails of another.

8.6.3 Availability

Cloud services also need special techniques to reach high levels of availability. Mission-critical enterprise services generally have availability in the 99.999% range. This corresponds to a downtime of 5 min in an entire year! Clearly, sophisticated techniques are needed to reach such high levels of reliability. Even for nonmission-critical applications, downtime implies loss of revenue. It is, therefore, extremely important to ensure high availability for both mission-critical and nonmission-critical cloud services. There are basically two approaches to ensuring availability. The first approach is to ensure high availability for the underlying application upon which the cloud service is built. This generally involves one of three techniques: infrastructure availability ensuring redundancy in infrastructure, such as servers, so that new servers are always ready to replace failed servers; middleware availability achieved with middleware redundancy; and, application availability achieved via application redundancy.

"To the 9s": measures of application availability Service-level agreements (SLAs) on availability are often measured in 9s. This describes the target percent of unplanned availability to be achieved, typically on a monthly or annual basis. Each 9 corresponds to a 10-fold decrease in the amount of downtime. For an important application, such as email or a CRM system, three 9s might be a reasonable target, whereas critical services such as public utilities would tend to target five 9s.

The following table describes the amount of acceptable downtime per year for the corresponding level of availability:

# of 9s	*SLA target*	*Maximum downtime per year*
2	99%	3 days, 15 hours, and 40 minutes
3	99.9%	8 hours and 46 minutes
4	99.99%	52 minutes and 36 seconds
5	99.999%	5 minutes and 16 seconds
6	99.9999%	31.56 seconds

The other approach is to build support for high availability into the cloud infrastructure, which is of the following two types:

- Failure detection: where the cloud infrastructure detects failed application instances and avoids routing requests to such instances
- Application recovery: where failed instances of application are restarted

8.6.3.1 Failure Detection

Many cloud providers, such as Amazon Web Services' Elastic Beanstalk, detect when an application instance fails and avoid sending new requests to the failed instance. In order to detect failures, one needs to monitor for failures.

- Failure monitoring: There are two techniques of failure monitoring. The first method is heartbeats, where each application instance periodically sends a signal (called a heartbeat) to a monitoring service in the cloud. If the monitoring service does not receive a specified number of consecutive heartbeats, it may declare the application instance as failed. The second is the method of probes. Here, the monitoring service periodically sends a probe, which is a lightweight service request, to the application instance. If the instance does not respond to a specified number of probes, it may be considered failed. There is a trade-off between speed and accuracy of detecting failures. To detect failures rapidly, it may be desirable to set a low value for the number of missed heartbeats or probes. However, this could lead to an increase in the number of false failures.

An application instance may not respond due to a momentary overload or some other transient condition. Since the consequences of falsely declaring an application instance failed are severe, generally a high threshold is set for the number of missed heartbeats or probes to virtually eliminate the likelihood of falsely declaring an instance failed.

- Redirection: After identifying failed instances, it is necessary to avoid routing new requests to these instances. A common mechanism used for this in HTTP-based protocols is HTTP redirection.

8.6.3.2 Application Recovery

In addition to directing new requests to a server that is up, it is necessary to recover old requests. An application independent method of doing this is checkpoint/restart. Here, the cloud infrastructure periodically saves the state of the application. If the application is determined to have failed, the most recent checkpoint can be activated, and the application can resume from that state.

- Checkpoint/restart paradigm: Checkpoint/restart can give rise to a number of complexities. First, the infrastructure should checkpoint all resources, such as system memory, otherwise the memory of the restarted application may not be consistent with the rest of the restarted application. Checkpointing storage will normally require support from the storage or file system, since any updates that were performed have to be rolled back. This could be complex in a distributed application, since updates by a failed instance could be intermingled with updates from running instances. Also, it is difficult to capture and reproduce activity on the network between distributed processes.

  In a distributed checkpoint/restart, all processes of distributed application instances are checkpointed, and all instances are restarted from a common checkpoint if any instance fails. This has obvious scalability limitations and also suffers from correctness issues if any inter-process communication data is in-transit at the time of failure. For instance, Ubuntu Linux has support for checkpoint/restart of distributed programs. Even sequential applications can be transparently checkpointed if linked with the right libraries, using the Berkeley Lab Checkpoint/Restart Library. It can also invoke application-specific code (that may send out a message to the users, write something in a log file, etc.) during checkpointing and restart.
- Transactional paradigm: When an application instance fails, some signal (e.g., closing of network connections) is sent to the other instances, which abort all work in progress for the failed instance. When the failed instance restarts, it restarts all transactions in progress. Additionally, other instances restart any requests they made to the failed instance.

8.7 Cloud Technologies

Virtualization is widely used to deliver customizable computing environments on demand. Virtualization technology is one of the fundamental components of cloud computing. Virtualization allows the creation of a secure, customizable, and isolated execution environment for running applications without affecting other users' applications. The basis of this technology is the ability of a computer program—or a combination of software and hardware—to emulate an executing environment separate from the one that hosts such programs. For instance, we can run Windows OS on top of a virtual machine, which itself is running on Linux OS. Virtualization provides a great opportunity to build elastically scalable systems that can provision additional capability with minimum costs.

8.7.1 Virtualization

Resource virtualization is at the heart of most cloud architectures. The concept of virtualization allows an abstract, logical view on the physical resources and includes servers, data stores, networks, and software. The basic idea is to pool physical resources and manage them as a whole. Individual requests can then be served as required from these resource pools. For instance, it is possible to dynamically generate a certain platform for a specific application at the very moment when it is needed—instead of a real machine, a virtual machine is instituted.

Resource management grows increasingly complex as the scale of a system, as well as the number of users and the diversity of applications using the system, increases. Resource management for a community of users with a wide range of applications running under different operating systems is a very difficult problem. Resource management becomes even more complex when resources are oversubscribed and users are uncooperative. In addition to external factors, resource management is affected by internal factors such as the heterogeneity of the hardware and software systems, the ability to approximate the global state of the system and to redistribute the load, and the failure rates of different components. The traditional solution for these in a data center is to install standard operating systems on individual systems and rely on conventional OS techniques to ensure resource sharing, application protection, and performance isolation. System administration, accounting, security, and resource management are very challenging for the providers of service in this setup; application development and performance optimization are equally challenging for the users.

The alternative is resource virtualization, a technique analyzed in this chapter. Virtualization is a basic tenet of cloud computing, which simplifies some of the resource management tasks. For instance, the state of a virtual machine (VM) running under a virtual machine monitor (VMM) can be saved and migrated to another server to balance the load. At the same time, virtualization allows users to operate in environments with which they are familiar rather than forcing them to work in idiosyncratic environments. Resource sharing in a virtual machine environment requires not only ample hardware support and, in particular, powerful processors but also architectural support for multilevel control. Indeed, resources such as CPU cycles, memory, secondary storage, and I/O and communication bandwidth are shared among several virtual machines; for each VM, resources must be shared among multiple instances of an application. There are two distinct approaches for virtualization:

- Full virtualization: Full virtualization is feasible when the hardware abstraction provided by the VMM is an exact replica of the physical hardware. In this case, any operating system running on the hardware will run without modifications under the VMM.
- Paravirtualization: Paravirtualization requires some modifications of the guest operating systems because the hardware abstraction provided by the VMM does not support all the functions the hardware does.

One of the primary reasons that companies have implemented virtualization is to improve the performance and efficiency of processing of a diverse mix of workloads.

Rather than assigning a dedicated set of physical resources to each set of tasks, a pooled set of virtual resources can be quickly allocated as needed across all workloads. Reliance on the pool of virtual resources allows companies to improve latency. This increase in service delivery speed and efficiency is a function of the distributed nature of virtualized environments and helps improve the overall time-to-realize value. Using a distributed set of physical resources, such as servers, in a more flexible and efficient way delivers significant benefits in terms of cost savings and improvements in productivity:

1. Virtualization of physical resources (such as servers, storage, and networks) enables substantial improvement in the utilization of these resources.
2. Virtualization enables improved control over the usage and performance of the IT resources.
3. Virtualization provides a level of automation and standardization to optimize your computing environment.
4. Virtualization provides a foundation for cloud computing.

Virtualization increases the efficiency of the cloud that makes many complex systems easier to optimize. As a result, organizations have been able to achieve the performance and optimization to be able to access data that were previously either unavailable or very hard to collect. Big data platforms are increasingly used as sources of enormous amounts of data about customer preferences, sentiment, and behaviors (see Section 8.1.1). Companies can integrate this information with internal sales and product data to gain insight into customer preferences to make more targeted and personalized offers.

8.7.1.1 Characteristics of Virtualized Environment

In a virtualized environment, there are three major components: guest, host, and virtualization layer. The guest represents the system component that interacts with the virtualization layer rather than with the host, as would normally happen. The host represents the original environment where the guest is supposed to be managed. The virtualization layer is responsible for recreating the same or a different environment where the guest will operate.

Virtualization has three characteristics that support the scalability and operating efficiency required for big data environments:

1. Partitioning: In virtualization, many applications and operating systems are supported in a single physical system by partitioning (separating) the available resources.
2. Isolation: Each virtual machine is isolated from its host physical system and other virtualized machines. Because of this isolation, if one virtual instance crashes, the other virtual machines and the host system are not affected. In addition, data are not shared between one virtual instance and another.
3. Encapsulation: A virtual machine can be represented (and even stored) as a single file, so you can identify it easily based on the services it provides. For example, the file containing the encapsulated process could be a complete business service. This encapsulated virtual machine could be presented to an application as a complete entity. Thus, encapsulation could protect each application so that it does not interfere with another application.

Virtualization abstracts the underlying resources and simplifies their use, isolates users from one another, and supports replication, which, in turn, increases the elasticity of the system. Virtualization is a critical aspect of cloud computing, equally important to the providers and consumers of cloud services, and plays an important role in

- System security because it allows isolation of services running on the same hardware.
- Portable performance and reliability because it allows applications to migrate from one platform to another.
- Development and management of services offered by a provider.
- Performance isolation.

8.7.1.1.1 Virtualization Advantages

Virtualization—the process of using computer resources to imitate other resources—is valued for its capability to increase IT resource utilization, efficiency, and scalability. One obvious application of virtualization is server virtualization, which helps organizations to increase the utilization of physical servers and potentially save on infrastructure costs; companies are increasingly finding that virtualization is not limited only to servers but is valid and applicable across the entire IT infrastructure, including networks, storage, and software. For instance, one of the most important requirements for success with big data is having the right level of performance to support the analysis of large volumes and varied types of data. If a company virtualizes only the servers, it may experience bottlenecks from other infrastructure elements such as storage and networks; furthermore, it is less likely to achieve the latency and efficiency that it needs and is more likely to expose the company to higher costs and increased security risks. As a result, a company's entire IT environment needs to be optimized at every layer, from the network to the databases, storage, and servers—virtualization adds efficiency at every layer of the IT infrastructure.

For a provider of IT services, the use of virtualization techniques has a number of advantages:

1. Resource usage: Physical servers rarely work to capacity because their operators usually allow for sufficient computing resources to cover peak usage. If virtual machines are used, any load requirement can be satisfied from the resource pool. In case the demand increases, it is possible to delay or even avoid the purchase of new capacities.
2. Management: It is possible to automate resource pool management. Virtual machines can be created and configured automatically as required.
3. Consolidation: Different application classes can be consolidated to run on a smaller number of physical components. Besides server or storage consolidation, it is also possible to include entire system landscapes, data and databases, networks, and desktops. Consolidation leads to increased efficiency and thus to cost reduction.
4. Energy consumption: Supplying large data centers with electric power has become increasingly difficult, and seen over its lifetime, the cost of energy required to operate a server is higher than its purchase price. Consolidation reduces the number of physical components. This, in turn, reduces the expenses for energy supply.

5. Less space required: Each and every square yard of data center space is scarce and expensive. With consolidation, the same performance can be obtained on a smaller footprint and the costly expansion of an existing data center might possibly be avoided.
6. Emergency planning: It is possible to move virtual machines from one resource pool to another. This ensures better availability of the services and makes it easier to comply with service-level agreements. Hardware maintenance windows are inherently no longer required.

8.7.1.1.2 Virtualization Benefits

Since the providers of cloud services tend to build very large resource centers, virtualization leads not only to a size advantage but also to a more favorable cost situation. This results in the following benefits for the customer:

1. Dynamic behavior: Any request can be satisfied just in time and without any delays. In case of bottlenecks, a virtual machine can draw on additional resources (such as storage space and I/O capabilities).
2. Availability: Services are highly available and can be used day and night without stop. In the event of technology upgrades, it is possible to hot-migrate applications because virtual machines can easily be moved to an up-to-date system.
3. Access: The virtualization layer isolates each virtual machine from the others and from the physical infrastructure. This way, virtual systems feature multitenant capabilities and, using a roles concept, it is possible to safely delegate management functionality to the customer. Customers can purchase IT capabilities from a self-service portal (customer emancipation).

The most direct benefit from virtualization is to ensure that MapReduce engines work better. Virtualization will result in better scale and performance for MapReduce. Each one of the map and reduce tasks needs to be executed independently. If the MapReduce engine is parallelized and configured to run in a virtual environment, you can reduce management overhead, and allow for expansions and contractions in the task workloads. MapReduce itself is inherently parallel and distributed. By encapsulating the MapReduce engine in a virtual container, you can run what you need whenever you need it. With virtualization, you can increase your utilization of the assets you have already paid for by turning them into generic pools of resources (see Chapter 10, Section 10.2 "Google MapReduce").

8.7.1.1.3 Virtualization Challenges

There are side effects of virtualization, notably the performance penalty and the hardware costs. All privileged operations of a VM must be trapped and validated by the VMM, which ultimately controls system behavior; the increased overhead has a negative impact on performance. The cost of the hardware for a VM is higher than the cost for a system running a traditional operating system because the physical hardware is shared among a set of guest operating systems and it is typically configured with faster and/or multicore processors, more memory, larger disks, and additional network interfaces compared with a system running a traditional operating system.

A drawback of virtualization is the fact that the operation of the abstraction layer itself requires resources. Modern virtualization techniques, however, are so sophisticated that this overhead is not too significant: due to the particularly effective interaction of current multicore systems with virtualization technology, this performance loss plays only a minor role in today's systems. In view of possible savings and the quality benefits perceived by the customers, the use of virtualization pays off in nearly all cases.

8.7.2 Service-Oriented Computing

SOA introduces a flexible architectural style that provides an integration framework through which software architects can build applications using a collection of reusable functional units (services) with well-defined interfaces, which it combines in a logical flow. Applications are integrated at the interface (contract) and not at the implementation level. This allows greater flexibility since applications are built to work with any implementation of a contract, rather than take advantage of a feature or idiosyncrasy of a particular system or implementation. For example, different service providers (of the same interface) can be dynamically chosen based on policies such as price, performance, or other QoS guarantees, current transaction volume, and so on.

Another important characteristic of an SOA is that it allows many-to-many integration; that is, a variety of consumers across an enterprise can use and reuse applications in a variety of ways. This ability can dramatically reduce the cost/complexity of integrating incompatible applications and increase the ability of developers to quickly create, reconfigure, and repurpose applications as business needs arise. Benefits include reduced IT administration costs, ease of business process integration across organizational departments and with trading partners, and increased business adaptability.

SOA is a logical way of designing a software system to provide services to either end-user applications or to other services distributed in a network, via published and discoverable interfaces. To achieve this, SOA reorganizes a portfolio of previously siloed software applications and support infrastructure in an organization into an interconnected collection of services, each of which is discoverable and accessible through standard interfaces and messaging protocols. Once all the elements of an SOA are in place, existing and future applications can access the SOA-based services as necessary. This architectural approach is particularly applicable when multiple applications running on varied technologies and platforms need to communicate with each other.

The essential goal of an SOA is to enable general-purpose interoperability among existing technologies and extensibility to future purposes and architectures. SOA lowers interoperability hurdles by converting monolithic and static systems into modular and flexible components, which it represents as services that can be requested through an industry-standard protocol. Much of SOA's power and flexibility derives from its ability to leverage standards-based functional services, calling them when needed on an individual basis or aggregating them to create composite applications or multistage business processes. The building-block services might employ pre-existing components that are reused and can also be updated or replaced without affecting the functionality or integrity of other independent services. In this latter regard, the services model offers numerous advantages over large monolithic applications, in which modifications to some portions of the code can have unintended and unpredictable effects on the rest of the code to which it is tightly bundled. Simply put, an SOA is an architectural style, inspired by the service-oriented approach to computing, for enabling extensible interoperability.

SOA as a design philosophy is independent of any specific technology, for example, web services or J2EE. Although the concept of SOA is often discussed in conjunction with web services, these two are not synonymous. In fact, SOA can be implemented without the use of web services, for example, using Java, C#, or J2EE. However, web services should be seen as a primary example of a message delivery model that makes it much easier to deploy an SOA. Web services standards are key to enabling interoperability as well as key issues including quality of system (QoS), system semantics, security, management, and reliable messaging.

8.7.2.1 Advantages of SOA

Enterprises may use SOA for the following:

Implementing end-to-end collaborative business processes: The term end-to-end business process signifies that a succession of automated business processes and information systems in different enterprises (which are typically involved in intercompany business transactions) are successfully integrated. The aim is to provide seamless interoperation and interactive links between all the relevant members in an extended enterprise—ranging from product designers, suppliers, trading partners, and logistics providers to end customers. At this stage, an organization moves into the highest strategic level of SOA implementation. Deployment of services becomes ubiquitous, and federated services collaborate across enterprise boundaries to create complex products and services. Individual services in this extended enterprise may originate from many providers, irrespective of company-specific systems or applications.

Implementing enterprise service orchestrations: This basic SOA entry point focuses on a typical implementation within a department or between a small number of departments and enterprise assets, and comprises two steps: The first step is transforming enterprise assets and applications into an SOA implementation. This can start by service enabling existing individual applications or creating new applications using web services technology. This can begin by specifying a web service interface into an individual application or application element (including legacy systems). The next step after this basic web service implementation is implementing service orchestrations out of the service-enabled assets or newly created service applications.

Service enabling the entire enterprise: The next stage in the SOA entry point hierarchy is when an enterprise seeks to provide a set of common services based on SOA components that can be used across the organization. Enterprise-wide service integration is achieved on the basis of commonly accepted standards. This results in achieving service consistency across departmental boundaries and is a precursor to integrating an organization with its partners and suppliers. Consistency is an important factor for this configuration as it provides both a uniform view to the enterprise and its customers, as well as ensures compliance with statutory or business policy requirements.

One problem when implementing an SOA at the enterprise level or implementing a cross-enterprise collaborative SOA is how to manage the SOA model, how to categorize the elements in this model, and how to organize them in such a way that the different stakeholders reviewing the model can understand it. Toward this end, it is often convenient to think of the SOA as comprising a number of distinct layers of abstraction that emphasize service interfaces, service realizations, and compositions of services into higher-level business processes. Each of these describes a logical separation of concerns by defining a set of common enterprise elements; each layer uses the functionality of the layer below it, adding new functionality, to accomplish its objective. The logical flow employed in the layered SOA development model may focus on a top-down development approach, which emphasizes how business processes are decomposed into a collection of business services and how these services are implemented in terms of pre-existing enterprise assets.

8.7.2.2 Layers in SOA

SOA can considered to be comprised of the following six distinct layers:

1. Domains: A business domain is a functional domain comprising a set of current and future business processes that share common capabilities and functionality, and can collaborate with each other to accomplish a higher-level business objective, such as loans, insurance, banking, finance, manufacturing, marketing, and human resources.
2. Business processes: This layer is formed by subdividing a business domain, such as distribution, into a small number of core business processes, such as purchasing, order management, and inventory, which are made entirely standard for use throughout the enterprise; having a large number of fine-grained processes leads to tremendous overhead and inefficiency, and hence, having a small collection of coarser-grained processes that are usable in multiple scenarios is a better option.
3. Business services: For any process, the right business services is to subdivide it into increasingly smaller subprocesses until the process cannot be divided any further. The resulting subprocesses then become candidate indivisible (singular) business services for implementation. Business services automate generic business tasks that provide value to an enterprise and are part of standard business process. The more processes that an enterprise decomposes in this way, the more commonality across these subprocesses can be achieved. In this way, an enterprise has the chance of building an appropriate set of reusable business services.

   This layer relies on the orchestration interface of a collection of business-aligned services to realize reconfigurable end-to-end business processes. Individual services or collections of services that exhibit various levels of granularity are combined and orchestrated to produce new composite services that not only introduce new levels of reuse but also allow the reconfiguration of business processes.

   The interfaces get exported as service descriptions in this layer using a service description language, such as WSDL. The service description can be implemented by a number of service providers, each offering various choices of qualities of service based on technical requirements in the areas of availability, performance, scalability, and security.

> During the exercise of defining business services, it is also important to take existing utility logic, ingrained in code, and expose it as services, which themselves become candidate services that specify not the overall business process but rather the mechanism for implementing the process. This exercise should thus yield two categories of services: business functionality services that are reusable across multiple processes and a collection of fine-grained utility (or commodity) services, which provide value to and are shared by business services across the organization. Examples of utility services include services implementing calculations, algorithms, and directory management services.

4. Infrastructure services: Infrastructure services are subdivided into technical utility services, access services, management and monitoring services, and interaction services; these are not specific to a single line of business but are reusable across multiple lines of business. They also include mechanisms that seamlessly interlink services that span enterprises. This can, for example, include the policies, constraints, and specific industry messages and interchange standards (such as the need to conform to specific industry message and interchange standards such as EDIFACT, SWIFT, xCBL, ebXML BPSS, or RosettaNet) that an enterprise, say within a particular vertical marketplace, must conform to in order to work with other similar processes. Access services are dedicated to transforming data and integrating legacy applications and functions into the SOA environment. This includes the wrapping and service enablement of legacy functions.
5. Service realizations: This layer is the component realization layer that uses components for implementing services out of pre-existing applications and systems found in the operational systems layer. Components comprise autonomous units of software that may provide a useful service or a set of functionalities to a client (business service) and have meaning in isolation from other components with which they interoperate.
6. Operational systems: This layer is used by components to implement business services and processes. This layer contains existing enterprise systems or applications, including customer relationship management (CRM) and ERP systems and applications, legacy applications, database systems and applications, and other packaged applications. These systems are usually known as enterprise information systems.

8.8 Summary

This chapter introduces the concept of cloud computing. It describes its definition, presents the cloud delivery and deployment models, and highlights its benefits for enterprises. In the last part of the chapter, we discussed the primary challenges faced while provisioning for cloud services, namely, scalability, multitenancy, and availability. The later part of the chapter describes virtualization technology, which is one of the fundamental components of cloud computing. Virtualization allows for the creation of a secure, customizable, and isolated execution environment for running applications without affecting other users' applications. One of the primary reasons companies implement virtualization is to improve the performance and efficiency of processing of a diverse mix of workloads. Rather than assigning a dedicated set of physical resources to each set of tasks, a pooled set of virtual resources can be quickly allocated as needed across all workloads. Virtualization provides a great opportunity to build elastically scalable systems that can provide additional capability with minimum costs.

Section III

Big Data Computing

9

Introducing Big Data Computing

The rapid growth of the Internet and World Wide Web has led to the vast amounts of information available online. In addition, business and government organizations create large amounts of both structured and unstructured information that needs to be processed, analyzed, and linked. It is estimated that the amount of information currently stored in a digital form in 2007 at 281 exabytes and the overall compound growth rate at 57% with information in organizations are growing at even a faster rate. It is also estimated that 95% of all current information exists in unstructured form with increased data processing requirements compared to structured information. The storing, managing, accessing, and processing of this vast amount of data represent a fundamental need and an immense challenge in order to satisfy needs to search, analyze, mine, and visualize this data as information.

The web is believed to have well over a trillion web pages, of which at least 50 billion have been catalogued and indexed by search engines such as Google, making them searchable by all of us. This massive web content spans well over 100 million domains (i.e., locations where we point our browsers, such as <http://www.wikipedia.org>). These are themselves growing at a rate of more than 20,000 net domain additions daily. Facebook and Twitter each has over 900 million users, who between them generate over 300 million posts a day (roughly 250 million tweets and over 60 million Facebook updates). Added to this are over 10,000 credit-card payments made per second, well over 30 billion point-of-sale transactions per year (via dial-up POS devices), and finally over 6 billion mobile phones, of which almost 1 billion are smartphones, many of which are GPS-enabled, which access the Internet for e-commerce, tweets, and to post updates on Facebook. Finally, and last but not least, there are the images and videos on YouTube and other sites, which by themselves outstrip all these put together in terms of the sheer volume of data they represent.

9.1 Big Data

This deluge of data, along with emerging techniques and technologies used to handle it, is commonly referred to today as "big data." Such big data is both valuable and challenging, because of its sheer volume. So much so that the volume of data being created in the current 5 years from 2010 to 2015 will far exceed all the data generated in human history. The web, where all this data is being produced and resides, consists of millions of servers, with data storage soon to be measured in zettabytes.

Cloud computing provides the opportunity for organizations with limited internal resources to implement large-scale big data computing applications in a cost-effective manner. The fundamental challenges of big data computing are managing and processing exponentially growing data volumes, significantly reducing associated data analysis cycles to support practical, timely applications, and developing new algorithms that can scale to search and process massive amounts of data. The answer to these challenges is a scalable, integrated computer systems hardware and software architecture designed for parallel processing of big data computing applications. This chapter explores the challenges of big data computing.

9.1.1 What Is Big Data?

Big data can be defined as volumes of data available in varying degrees of complexity, generated at different velocities and varying degrees of ambiguity that cannot be processed using traditional technologies, processing methods, algorithms, or any commercial off-the-shelf solutions.

Data defined as big data includes weather, geospatial, and geographic information system (GIS) data; consumer-driven data from social media; enterprise-generated data from legal, sales, marketing, procurement, finance and human-resources department; and device-generated data from sensor networks, nuclear plants, X-ray and scanning devices, and airplane engines (Figures 9.1 and 9.2).

9.1.1.1 Data Volume

The most interesting data for any organization to tap into today is social media data. The amount of data generated by consumers every minute provides extremely important insights into choices, opinions, influences, connections, brand loyalty, brand management, and much more. Social media sites not only provide consumer perspectives but also competitive positioning, trends, and access to communities formed by common interest. Organizations today leverage the social media pages to personalize marketing of products and services to each customer.

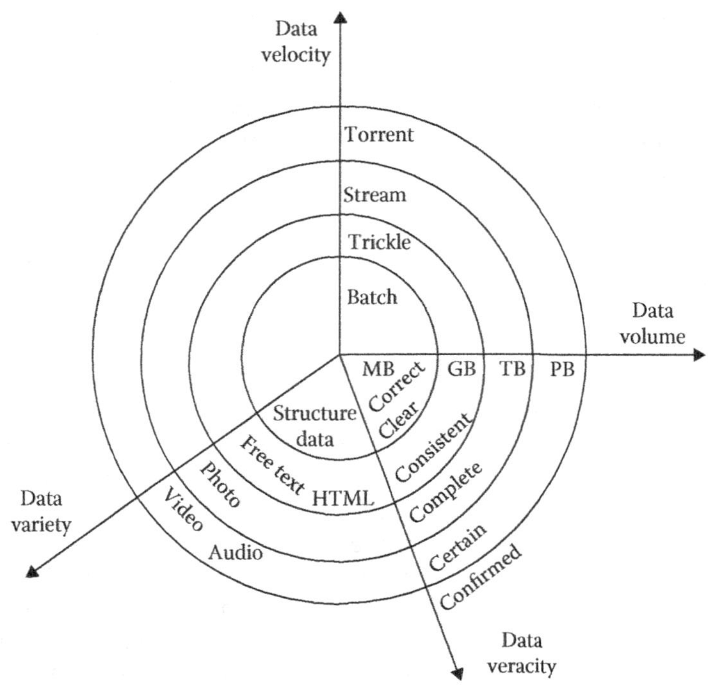

FIGURE 9.1
4V characteristics of big data.

Many additional applications are being developed and are slowly becoming a reality. These applications include using remote sensing to detect underground sources of energy, environmental monitoring, traffic monitoring, and regulation by automatic sensors mounted on vehicles and roads, remote monitoring of patients using special scanners and equipment, and tighter control and replenishment of inventories using radio-frequency identification (RFID) and other technologies. All these developments will have associated with them a large volume of data. Social networks such as Twitter and Facebook have hundreds of millions of subscribers worldwide who generate new data with every message they send or post they make.

Every enterprise has massive amounts of emails that are generated by its employees, customers, and executives on a daily basis. These emails are all considered an asset of the corporation and need to be managed as such. After Enron and the collapse of many audits in enterprises, the U.S. government mandated that all enterprises should have a clear life-cycle management of emails, and that emails should be available and auditable on a case-by-case basis. There are several examples that come to mind like insider trading, intellectual property, competitive analysis, and much more, to justify governance and management of emails.

If companies can analyze petabytes of data (equivalent to 20 million four-drawer file cabinets filled with text files or 13.3 years of HDTV content) with acceptable performance to discern patterns and anomalies, businesses can begin to make sense of data in new ways. Table 9.1 indicates the escalating scale of data.

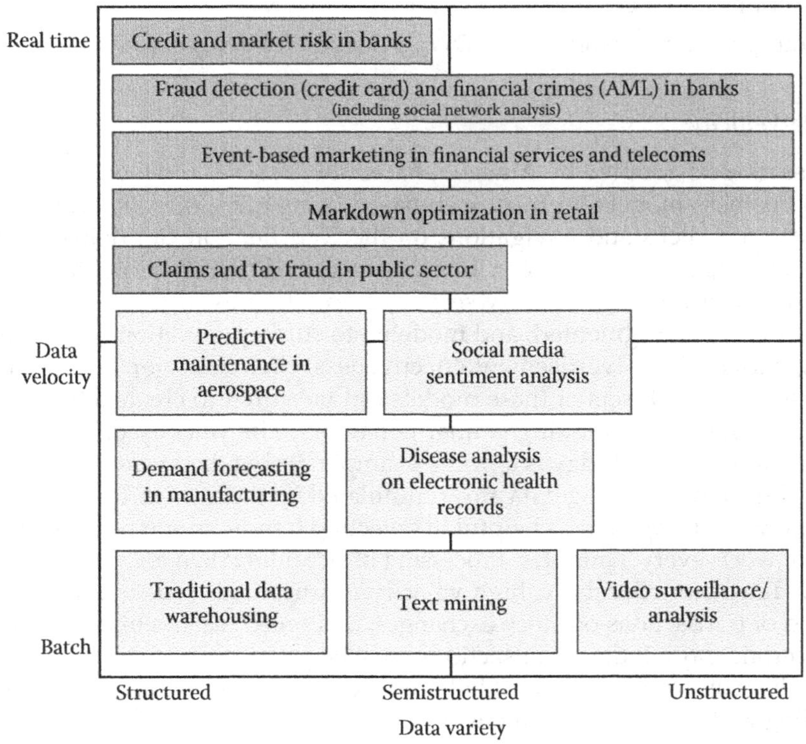

FIGURE 9.2
Use cases for big data computing.

TABLE 9.1
Scale of Data

Size of Data	Scale of Data
1,000 megabytes	1 gigabyte (GB)
1,000 gigabytes	1 terabyte (TB)
1,000 terabytes	1 petabyte (PB)
1,000 petabytes	1 exabyte (EB)
1,000 exabytes	1 zettabyte (ZB)
1,000 zettabytes	1 yottabyte (YB)

The list of features for handling data volume included the following:

- Nontraditional and unorthodox data processing techniques need to be innovated for processing this data type.
- Metadata is essential for processing this data successfully.
- Metrics and key performance indicators (KPIs) are key to provide visualization.
- Raw data do not need to be stored online for access.
- Processed output is needed to be integrated into an enterprise level analytical ecosystem to provide better insights and visibility into the trends and outcomes of business exercises including customer relationship management (CRM), optimization of inventory, clickstream analysis, and more.
- The enterprise data warehouse (EDW) is needed for analytics and reporting.

9.1.1.2 Data Velocity

The business models adopted by Amazon, Facebook, Yahoo!, and Google, which became the defacto business models for most web-based companies, operate on the fact that by tracking customer clicks and navigations on the website, you can deliver personalized browsing and shopping experiences. In this process of clickstreams, there are millions of clicks gathered from users at every second, amounting to large volumes of data. This data can be processed, segmented, and modeled to study population behaviors based on time of day, geography, advertisement effectiveness, click behavior, and guided navigation response. The result sets of these models can be stored to create a better experience for the next set of clicks exhibiting similar behaviors. The velocity of data produced by user clicks on any website today is a prime example for big data velocity.

Real-time data and streaming data are accumulated by the likes of Twitter and Facebook at a very high velocity. Velocity is helpful in detecting trends among people that are tweeting a million tweets every 3 minutes. Processing of streaming data for analysis also involves the velocity dimension. Similarly, high velocity is attributed to data associated with the typical speed of transactions on stock exchanges; this speed reaches billions of transactions per day on certain days. If these transactions must be processed to detect potential fraud or billions of call records on cell phones daily must be processed to detect malicious activity, we are dealing with the velocity dimension.

The most popular way to share pictures, music, and data today is via mobile devices. The sheer volume of data that is transmitted by mobile networks provides insights to the providers on the performance of their network, the amount of data processed at each tower, the time of day, the associated geographies, user demographics, location, latencies, and much more. The velocity of data movement is unpredictable, and sometimes can cause a network to crash. The data movement and its study have enabled mobile service providers to improve the QoS (quality of service), and associating this data with social media inputs has enabled insights into competitive intelligence.

The list of features for handling data velocity included the following:

- System must be elastic for handling data velocity along with volume
- System must scale up and scale down as needed without increasing costs
- System must be able to process data across the infrastructure in the least processing time
- System throughput should remain stable independent of data velocity
- System should be able to process data on a distributed platform

9.1.1.3 Data Variety

Data comes in multiple formats as it ranges from emails to tweets to social media and sensor data. There is no control over the input data format or the structure of the data. The processing complexity associated with a variety of formats is the availability of appropriate metadata for identifying what is contained in the actual data. This is critical when we process images, audio, video, and large chunks of text. The absence of metadata or partial metadata means processing delays from the ingestion of data to producing the final metrics, and, more importantly, in integrating the results with the data warehouse (Table 9.2 and 9.3).

Sources of data in traditional applications were mainly transactions involving financial, insurance, travel, healthcare, retail industries, and governmental and judicial processing. The types of sources have expanded dramatically and include Internet data (e.g., clickstream and social media), research data (e.g., surveys and industry reports), location data (e.g., mobile device data and geospatial data), images (e.g., surveillance, satellites,

TABLE 9.2

Value of Big Data across Industries

	Volume of Data	Velocity of Data	Variety of Data	Underutilized Data (*Dark Data*)	Big Data Value Potential
Banking and securities	High	High	Low	Medium	High
Communications and media services	High	High	High	Medium	High
Education	Very low	Very low	Very low	High	Medium
Government	High	Medium	High	High	High
Health-care providers	Medium	High	Medium	Medium	High
Insurance	Medium	Medium	Medium	Medium	Medium
Manufacturing	High	High	High	High	High
Chemicals and natural resources	High	High	High	High	Medium
Retail	High	High	High	Low	High
Transportation	Medium	Medium	Medium	High	Medium
Utilities	Medium	Medium	Medium	Medium	Medium

TABLE 9.3
Industry Use Cases for Big Data

Manufacturing	Retail
Product research	Customer relationship management
Engineering analysis	Store location and layout
Predictive maintenance	Fraud detection and prevention
Process and quality metrics	Supply-chain optimization
Distribution optimization	Dynamic pricing
Media and telecommunications	*Financial services*
Network optimization	Algorithmic trading
Customer scoring	Risk analysis
Churn prevention	Fraud detection
Fraud prevention	Portfolio analysis
Energy	*Advertising and public relations*
Smart grid	Demand signaling
Exploration	Targeted advertising
Operational modeling	Sentiment analysis
Power-line sensors	Customer acquisition
Health care and life sciences	*Government*
Pharmacogenomics	Market governance
Bioinformatics	Weapon systems and counter terrorism
Pharmaceutical research	Econometrics
Clinical outcomes research	Health informatics

and medical scanning), emails, supply chain data (e.g., EDI—electronic data interchange, vendor catalogs), signal data (e.g., sensors and RFID devices), and videos (YouTube enters hundreds of minutes of video every minute). Big data includes structured, semistructured, and unstructured data in different proportions based on context.

The list of features for handling data variety included the following:

- Scalability
- Distributed processing capabilities
- Image processing capabilities
- Graph processing capabilities
- Video and audio processing capabilities

9.1.1.4 Data Veracity

The veracity dimension of big data is a more recent addition than the advent of the Internet. Veracity has two built-in features: the credibility of the source and the suitability of data for its target audience. It is closely related to trust; listing veracity as one of the dimensions of big data amounts to saying that data coming into the so-called big data applications have a variety of trustworthiness, and therefore before we accept the data for analytical or other applications, it must go through some degree of quality testing and credibility analysis. Many sources of data generate data that is uncertain, incomplete, and inaccurate, therefore making its veracity questionable.

9.1.2 Common Characteristics of Big Data Computing Systems

There are several important common characteristics of big data computing systems that distinguish them from other forms of computing.

1. Principle of co-location of the data and programs or algorithms to perform the computation: To achieve high performance in big data computing, it is important to minimize the movement of data. This principle—"move the code to the data"—that was designed into the data-parallel processing architecture implemented by Seisint in 2003 is extremely effective since program size is usually small in comparison to the large datasets processed by big data systems and results in much less network traffic since data can be read locally instead of across the network. In direct contrast to other types of computing and supercomputing that utilize data stored in a separate repository or servers and transfer the data to the processing system for computation, big data computing uses distributed data and distributed file systems in which data is located across a cluster of processing nodes, and instead of moving the data, the program or algorithm is transferred to the nodes with the data that needs to be processed. This characteristic allows processing algorithms to execute on the nodes where the data resides reducing system overhead and increasing performance.
2. Programming model utilized: Big data computing systems utilize a machine-independent approach in which applications are expressed in terms of high-level operations on data, and the runtime system transparently controls the scheduling, execution, load balancing, communications, and movement of programs and data across the distributed computing cluster. The programming abstraction and language tools allow the processing to be expressed in terms of data flows and transformations incorporating new dataflow programming languages and shared libraries of common data manipulation algorithms such as sorting. Conventional supercomputing and distributed computing systems typically utilize machine-dependent programming models that can require low-level programmer control of processing and node communications using conventional imperative programming languages and specialized software packages that add complexity to the parallel programming task and reduce programmer productivity. A machine-dependent programming model also requires significant tuning and is more susceptible to single points of failure.
3. Focus on reliability and availability: Large-scale systems with hundreds or thousands of processing nodes are inherently more susceptible to hardware failures, communications errors, and software bugs. Big data computing systems are designed to be fault resilient. This includes redundant copies of all data files on disk, storage of intermediate processing results on disk, automatic detection of node or processing failures, and selective recomputation of results. A processing cluster configured for big data computing is typically able to continue operation with a reduced number of nodes following a node failure with automatic and transparent recovery of incomplete processing.

A final important characteristic of big data computing systems is the inherent scalability of the underlying hardware and software architecture. Big data computing systems can typically be scaled in a linear fashion to accommodate virtually any amount of data, or to meet time-critical performance requirements by simply adding additional processing nodes to a system configuration in order to achieve billions of records per second processing rates (BORPS). The number of nodes and processing tasks assigned for a specific application can be variable or fixed

One of the key characteristics of the cloud is elastic scalability: Users can add or subtract resources in almost real time based on changing requirements. The cloud plays an important role within the big data world. Dramatic changes happen when these infrastructure components are combined with the advances in data management. Horizontally expandable and optimized infrastructure supports the practical implementation of big data. Cloudware technologies like virtualization increase the efficiency of the cloud that makes many complex systems easier to optimize. As a result, organizations have the performance and optimization to be able to access data that was previously either unavailable or very hard to collect. Big data platforms are increasingly used as sources of enormous amounts of data about customer preferences, sentiment, and behaviors. Companies can integrate this information with internal sales and product data to gain insight into customer preferences to make more targeted and personalized offers.

depending on the hardware, software, communications, and distributed file system architecture. This scalability allows computing problems once considered to be intractable due to the amount of data required or amount of processing time required to now be feasible and affords opportunities for new breakthroughs in data analysis and information processing.

9.1.3 Big Data Appliances

Big data analytics applications combine the means for developing and implementing algorithms that must access, consume, and manage data. In essence, the framework relies on a technology ecosystem of components that must be combined in a variety of ways to address each application's requirements, which can range from general information technology (IT) performance scalability to detailed performance improvement objectives associated with specific algorithmic demands. For example, some algorithms expect that massive amounts of data are immediately available quickly, necessitating large amounts of core memory. Other applications may need numerous iterative exchanges of data between different computing nodes, which would require high-speed networks.

The big data technology ecosystem stack may include the following:

1. Scalable storage systems that are used for capturing, manipulating, and analyzing massive datasets.
2. A computing platform, sometimes configured specifically for large-scale analytics, often composed of multiple (typically multicore) processing nodes connected via a high-speed network to memory and disk storage subsystems. These are often referred to as appliances.
3. A data management environment, whose configurations may range from a traditional database management system scaled to massive parallelism to databases configured with alternative distributions and layouts, to newer graph-based or other NoSQL data management schemes.
4. An application development framework to simplify the process of developing, executing, testing, and debugging new application code. This framework should include programming models, development tools, program execution and scheduling, and system configuration and management capabilities.

5. Methods of scalable analytics (including statistical and data mining models) that can be configured by the analysts and other business consumers to help improve the ability to design and build analytical and predictive models.
6. Management processes and tools that are necessary to ensure alignment with the enterprise analytics infrastructure and collaboration among the developers, analysts, and other business users.

9.2 Tools and Techniques of Big Data

9.2.1 Processing Approach

Current big data computing platforms use a "divide and conquer" parallel processing approach combining multiple processors and disks in large computing clusters connected using high-speed communications switches and networks that allow the data to be partitioned among the available computing resources and processed independently to achieve performance and scalability based on the amount of data. We define a cluster as "a type of parallel and distributed system, which consists of a collection of interconnected stand-alone computers working together as a single integrated computing resource."

This approach to parallel processing is often referred to as a "shared nothing" approach since each node consisting of processor, local memory, and disk resources shares nothing with other nodes in the cluster. In parallel computing, this approach is considered suitable for data processing problems that are "embarrassingly parallel," that is, where it is relatively easy to separate the problem into a number of parallel tasks and there is no dependency or communication required between the tasks other than overall management of the tasks. These types of data processing problems are inherently adaptable to various forms of distributed computing including clusters and data grids and cloud computing.

Analytical environments are deployed in different architectural models. Even on parallel platforms, many databases are built on a shared everything approach in which the persistent storage and memory components are all shared by the different processing units.

Parallel architectures are classified by what shared resources each processor can directly access. One typically distinguishes shared memory, shared disk, and shared nothing architectures (as depicted in Figure 9.3).

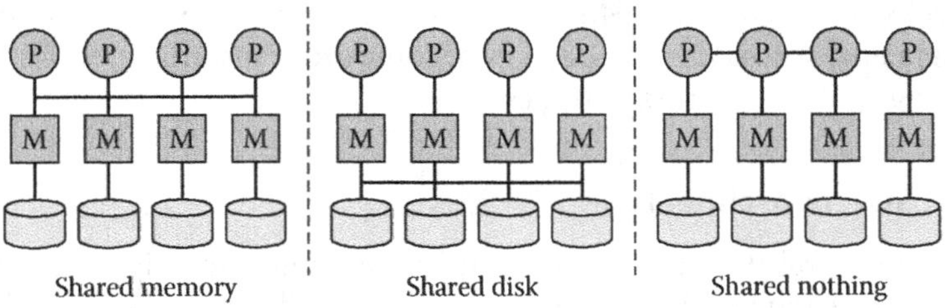

FIGURE 9.3
Parallel architectures.

1. In a shared memory system, all processors have direct access to all memory via a shared bus. Typical examples are the common symmetric multiprocessor systems, where each processor core can access the complete memory via the shared memory bus. To preserve the abstraction, processor caches, buffering a subset of the data closer to the processor for fast access, have to be kept consistent with specialized protocols. Because disks are typically accessed via the memory, all processes also have access to all disks.
2. In a shared disk architecture, all processes have their own private memory, but all disks are shared. A cluster of computers connected to a SAN is a representative for this architecture.
3. In a shared nothing architecture, each processor has its private memory and private disk. The data is distributed across all disks, and each processor is responsible only for the data on its own connected memory and disks. To operate on data that spans the different memories or disks, the processors have to explicitly send data to other processors. If a processor fails, data held by its memory and disks is unavailable. Therefore, the shared nothing architecture requires special considerations to prevent data loss.

When scaling out the system, the two main bottlenecks are typically the bandwidth of the shared medium and the overhead of maintaining a consistent view of the shared data in the presence of cache hierarchies. For that reason, the shared nothing architecture is considered the most scalable one, because it has no shared medium and no shared data. While it is often argued that shared disk architectures have certain advantages for transaction processing, the shared nothing is the undisputed architecture of choice for analytical queries.

A shared-disk approach may have isolated processors, each with its own memory, but the persistent storage on disk is still shared across the system. These types of architectures are layered on top of symmetric multiprocessing (SMP) machines. While there may be applications that are suited to this approach, there are bottlenecks that exist because of the sharing, because all I/O and memory requests are transferred (and satisfied) over the same bus. As more processors are added, the synchronization and communication needs increase exponentially, and therefore the bus is less able to handle the increased need for bandwidth. This means that unless the need for bandwidth is satisfied, there will be limits to the degree of scalability.

In contrast, in a shared-nothing approach, each processor has its own dedicated disk storage. This approach, which maps nicely to an massively parallel processing (MPP) architecture, is not only more suitable to discrete allocation and distribution of the data, it enables more effective parallelization and consequently does not introduce the same kind of bus bottlenecks from which the SMP/shared-memory and shared-disk approaches suffer. Most big data appliances use a collection of computing resources, typically a combination of processing nodes and storage nodes.

9.2.2 Big Data System Architecture

A variety of system architectures have been implemented for big data and large-scale data analysis applications including parallel and distributed relational database management systems that have been available to run on shared nothing clusters of processing nodes for more than two decades. These include database systems from Teradata,

Netezza, Vertica, and Exadata/Oracle and others that provide high-performance parallel database platforms. Although these systems have the ability to run parallel applications and queries expressed in the SQL language, they are typically not general-purpose processing platforms and usually run as a back-end to a separate front-end application processing system.

Although this approach offers benefits when the data utilized is primarily structured in nature and fits easily into the constraints of a relational database, and often excels for transaction processing applications, most data growth is with data in unstructured form and new processing paradigms with more flexible data models were needed. Internet companies such as Google, Yahoo!, Microsoft, Facebook, and others required a new processing approach to effectively deal with the enormous amount of web data for applications such as search engines and social networking. In addition, many government and business organizations were overwhelmed with data that could not be effectively processed, linked, and analyzed with traditional computing approaches.

Several solutions have emerged including the MapReduce architecture pioneered by Google and now available in an open-source implementation called Hadoop used by Yahoo!, Facebook, and others (Section 10.3.1).

9.2.2.1 BASE (Basically Available, Soft State, Eventual Consistency)

BASE follows an optimistic approach accepting stale data and approximate answers while favoring availability. Some ways to achieve this are by supporting partial failures without total system failures, decoupling updates on different tables (i.e., relaxing consistency), and item potent operations that can be applied multiple times with the same result. In this sense, BASE describes more a spectrum of architectural styles than a single model. The eventual state of consistency can be provided as a result of a read-repair, where any outdated data is refreshed with the latest version of the data as a result of the system detecting stale data during a read operation. Another approach is that of weak consistency. In this case, the read operation will return the first value found, not checking for staleness. Any stale nodes discovered are simply marked for updating at some stage in the future. This is a performance-focused approach but has the associated risk that data retrieved may not be the most current. In the following sections, we will discuss several techniques for implementing services following the BASE principle.

Conventional storage techniques may not be adequate for big data and, hence, the cloud applications. To scale storage systems to cloud-scale, the basic technique is to partition and replicate the data over multiple independent storage systems. The word independent is emphasized, since it is well-known that databases can be partitioned into mutually dependent subdatabases that are automatically synchronized for reasons of performance and availability. Partitioning and replication increase the overall throughput of the system, since the total throughput of the combined system is the aggregate of the individual storage systems. To scale both the throughput and the maximum size of the data that can be stored beyond the limits of traditional database deployments, it is possible to partition the data and store each partition in its own database. For scaling the throughput only, it is possible to use replication. Partitioning and replication also increase the storage capacity of a storage system by reducing the amount of data that needs to be stored in each partition. However, this creates synchronization and consistency problems and discussion of this aspect is out of scope for this book.

The other technology for scaling storage is known by the name not only SQL(NoSQL). NoSQL was developed as a reaction to the perception that conventional databases, focused on the need to ensure data integrity for enterprise applications, were too rigid to scale to cloud levels. As an example, conventional databases enforce a schema on the data being stored, and changing the schema is not easy. However, changing the schema may be a necessity in a rapidly changing environment like the cloud. NoSQL storage systems provide more flexibility and simplicity compared to relational databases. The disadvantage, however, is greater application complexity. NoSQL systems, for example, do not enforce a rigid schema. The trade-off is that applications have to be written to deal with data records of varying formats (schema). BASE is the NoSQL operating premise, in the same way that traditional transactionally focused databases use ACID: one moves from a world of certainty in terms of data consistency to a world where all we are promised is that all copies of the data will, at some point, be the same (see Chapter 1 note on ACID page 17).

Partitioning and replication techniques used for scaling are as follows:

1. The first possible method is to store different tables in different databases (as in multidatabase systems, MDBS).
2. The second approach is to partition the data within a single table onto different databases. There are two natural ways to partition the data from within a table are to store different rows in different databases and to store different columns in different databases (more common for NoSQL databases).

9.2.2.2 *Functional Decomposition*

As stated previously, one technique for partitioning the data to be stored is to store different tables in different databases, leading to the storage of the data in a MDBS.

9.2.2.3 *Master–Slave Replication*

To increase the throughput of transactions from the database, it is possible to have multiple copies of the database. A common replication method is master–slave replication. The master and slave databases are replicas of each other. All writes go to the master and the master keeps the slaves in sync. However, reads can be distributed to any database. Since this configuration distributes the reads among multiple databases, it is a good technology for read-intensive workloads. For write-intensive workloads, it is possible to have multiple masters, but then ensuring consistency if multiple processes update different replicas simultaneously is a complex problem. Additionally, time to write increases, due to the necessity of writing to all masters and the synchronization overhead between the masters rapidly, becomes a limiting overhead.

9.2.3 Row Partitioning or Sharding

In cloud technology, sharding is used to refer to the technique of partitioning a table among multiple independent databases by row. However, partitioning of data by row in relational databases is not new and is referred to as horizontal partitioning in parallel database technology. The distinction between sharding and horizontal partitioning is that horizontal partitioning is done transparently to the application by the database, whereas sharding is explicit partitioning done by the application. However, the two techniques have started converging, since traditional database vendors have started offering support for more sophisticated partitioning strategies. Since sharding is similar to horizontal partitioning, we first discuss different horizontal partitioning techniques. It can be seen that a good sharding technique depends on both the organization of the data and the type of queries expected.

The different techniques of sharding are as follows:

1. Round-robin partitioning: The round-robin method distributes the rows in a round-robin fashion over different databases. In the example, we could partition the transaction table into multiple databases so that the first transaction is stored in the first database, the second in the second database, and so on. The advantage of round-robin partitioning is its simplicity. However, it also suffers from the disadvantage of losing associations (say) during a query, unless all databases are queried. Hash partitioning and range partitioning do not suffer from the disadvantage of losing record associations.
2. Hash partitioning method: In this method, the value of a selected attribute is hashed to find the database into which the tuple should be stored. If queries are frequently made on an attribute (say Customer_Id, then associations can be preserved by using this attribute as the attribute that is hashed, so that records with the same value of this attribute can be found in the same database.
3. Range partitioning: The range partitioning technique stores records with "similar" attributes in the same database. For example, the range of Customer_Id could be partitioned between different databases. Again, if the attributes chosen for grouping are those on which queries are frequently made, record association is preserved and it is not necessary to merge results from different databases. Range partitioning can be susceptible to load imbalance, unless the partitioning is chosen carefully. It is possible to choose the partitions so that there is an imbalance in the amount of data stored in the partitions (data skew) or in the execution of queries across partitions (execution skew). These problems are less likely in round robin and hash partitioning, since they tend to uniformly distribute the data over the partitions.

Thus, hash partitioning is particularly well suited to large-scale systems. Round robin simplifies a uniform distribution of records but does not facilitate the restriction of operations to single partitions. While range partitioning does supports this, it requires knowledge about the data distribution in order to properly adjust the ranges.

9.2.4 Row versus Column-Oriented Data Layouts

Most traditional database systems employ a row-oriented layout, in which all the values associated with a specific row are laid out consecutively in memory. That layout may work well for transaction processing applications that focus on updating specific records associated with a limited number of transactions (or transaction steps) at a time. These are manifested as algorithmic scans performed using multiway joins; accessing whole rows at a time when only the values of a smaller set of columns are needed may flood the network with extraneous data that is not immediately needed and ultimately will increase the execution time.

Big data analytics applications scan, aggregate, and summarize over massive datasets. Analytical applications and queries will only need to access the data elements needed to satisfy join conditions. With row-oriented layouts, the entire record must be read in order to access the required attributes, with significantly more data read than is needed to satisfy the request. Also, the row-oriented layout is often misaligned with the characteristics of the different types of memory systems (core, cache, disk, etc.), leading to increased access latencies. Subsequently, row-oriented data layouts will not enable the types of joins or aggregations typical of analytic queries to execute with the anticipated level of performance.

Hence, a number of appliances for big data use a database management system that uses an alternate, columnar layout for data that can help to reduce the negative performance impacts of data latency that plague databases with a row-oriented data layout. The values for each column can be stored separately, and because of this, for any query, the system is able to selectively access the specific column values requested to evaluate the join conditions. Instead of requiring separate indexes to tune queries, the data values themselves within each column form the index. This speeds up data access while reducing the overall database footprint, while dramatically improving query performance. The simplicity of the columnar approach provides many benefits, especially for those seeking a high-performance environment to meet the growing needs of extremely large analytic datasets.

9.2.5 NoSQL Data Management

NoSQL or "not only SQL" suggests environments that combine traditional SQL (or SQL-like query languages) with alternative means of querying and access. NoSQL data systems hold out the promise of greater flexibility in database management while reducing the dependence on more formal database administration. NoSQL databases have more relaxed modeling constraints, which may benefit both the application developer and the end-user analysts when their interactive analyses are not throttled by the need to cast each query in terms of a relational table-based environment.

Different NoSQL frameworks are optimized for different types of analyses. For example, some are implemented as key_value stores, which nicely align to certain big data programming models, while another emerging model is a graph database, in which a graph abstraction is implemented to embed both semantics and connectivity within its structure. In fact, the general concepts for NoSQL include schemaless modeling in which the semantics of the data are embedded within a flexible connectivity and storage model; this provides for automatic distribution of data and elasticity with respect to the use of computing, storage, and network bandwidth in ways that do not force specific binding of data to be persistently stored in particular physical locations. NoSQL databases also provide for integrated data caching that helps reduce data access latency and speed performance.

A relatively simple type of NoSQL data store is a key_value store, a schemaless model in which distinct character strings called keys are associated with values (or sets of values, or even more complex entity objects)—not unlike hash table data structure. If you want to associate multiple values with a single key, you need to consider the representations of the objects and how they are associated with the key. For example, you may want to associate a list of attributes with a single key, which may suggest that the value stored with the key is yet another key_value store object itself.

> The key_value store does not impose any constraints about data typing or data structure—the value associated with the key is the value, and it is up to the consuming business applications to assert expectations about the data values and their semantics and interpretation. This demonstrates the schemaless property of the model.

Key_value stores are essentially very long, and presumably thin tables (in that there are not many columns associated with each row). The table's rows can be sorted by the key value to simplify finding the key during a query. Alternatively, the keys can be hashed using a hash function that maps the key to a particular location (sometimes called a "bucket") in the table. The representation can grow indefinitely, which makes it good for storing large amounts of data that can be accessed relatively quickly, as well as allows massive amounts of indexed data values to be appended to the same key_value table, which can then be sharded or distributed across the storage nodes. Under the right conditions, the table is distributed in a way that is aligned with the way the keys are organized, so that the hashing function that is used to determine where any specific key exists in the table can also be used to determine which node holds that key's bucket (i.e., the portion of the table holding that key).

NoSQL data management environments are engineered for the following two key criteria:

1. Fast accessibility, whether that means inserting data into the model or pulling it out via some query or access method.
2. Scalability for volume, so as to support the accumulation and management of massive amounts of data.

The different approaches are amenable to extensibility, scalability, and distribution and these characteristics blend nicely with programming models (like MapReduce) with straightforward creation and execution of many parallel processing threads. Distributing a tabular data store or a key_value store allows many queries/accesses to be performed simultaneously, especially when the hashing of the keys maps to different data storage nodes. Employing different data allocation strategies will allow the tables to grow indefinitely without requiring significant rebalancing. In other words, these data organizations are designed for high-performance computing of reporting and analysis.

> The model will not inherently provide any kind of traditional database capabilities (such as atomicity of transactions, or consistency when multiple transactions are executed simultaneously)—those capabilities must be provided by the application itself.

9.2.6 In-Memory Computing

The idea of running databases in memory was used by business intelligence (BI) product company QlikView. In-memory allows the processing of massive quantities of data in main memory to provide immediate results from analysis and transaction. The data to be processed is ideally real-time data or as close to real time as is technically possible. Data in main memory (RAM) can be accessed 100,000 times faster than data on a hard disk; this can dramatically decrease access time to retrieve data and make it available for the purpose of reporting, analytics solutions, or other applications.

The medium used by a database to store data, that is, RAM is divided into pages. In-memory databases save changed pages in savepoints, which are asynchronously written to persistent storage in regular intervals. Each committed transaction generates a log entry that is written to nonvolatile storage—this log is written synchronously. In other words, a transaction does not return before the corresponding log entry has been written to persistent storage—in order to meet the durability requirement that was described earlier—thus ensuring that in-memory databases meet (and pass) the ACID test. After a power failure, the database pages are restored from the savepoints; the database logs are applied to restore the changes that were not captured in the savepoints. This ensures that the database can be restored in memory to exactly the same state as before the power failure.

9.2.7 Developing Big Data Applications

For most big data appliances, the ability to achieve scalability to accommodate growing data volumes is predicated on multiprocessing—distributing the computation across the collection of computing nodes in ways that are aligned with the distribution of data across the storage nodes. One of the key objectives of using a multiprocessing nodes environment is to speed application execution by breaking up large "chunks" of work into much smaller ones that can be farmed out to a pool of available processing nodes. In the best of all possible worlds, the datasets to be consumed and analyzed are also distributed across a pool of storage nodes. As long as there are no dependencies forcing any one specific task to wait to begin until another specific one ends, these smaller tasks can be executed at the same time, that is, "task parallelism." More than just scalability, it is the concept of "automated scalability" that has generated the present surge of interest in big data analytics (with corresponding optimization of costs).

A good development framework will simplify the process of developing, executing, testing, and debugging new application code, and this framework should include the following:

1. A programming model and development tools
2. Facility for program loading, execution, and for process and thread scheduling
3. System configuration and management tools

The context for all of these framework components is tightly coupled with the key characteristics of a big data application—algorithms that take advantage of running lots of tasks in parallel on many computing nodes to analyze lots of data distributed among many storage nodes. Typically, a big data platform will consist of a collection (or a "pool") of processing nodes; the optimal performances can be achieved when all the processing nodes are kept busy, and that means maintaining a healthy allocation of tasks to idle nodes within the pool. Any big application that is to be developed must map to this context, and that is where the programming model comes in. The programming model essentially describes two aspects of application execution within a parallel environment:

- How an application is coded?
- How that code maps to the parallel environment?

MapReduce programming model is a combination of the familiar procedural/imperative approaches used by Java or C++ programmers embedded within what is effectively a functional language programming model such as the one used within languages like Lisp and APL. The similarity is based on MapReduce's dependence on two basic operations that are applied to sets or lists of data value pairs:

1. Map, which describes the computation or analysis applied to a set of input key-value pairs to produce a set of intermediate key-value pairs.
2. Reduce, in which the set of values associated with the intermediate key-value pairs output by the Map operation are combined to provide the results.

A MapReduce application is envisioned as a series of basic operations applied in a sequence to small sets of many (millions, billions, or even more) data items. These data items are logically organized in a way that enables the MapReduce execution model to allocate tasks that can be executed in parallel.

> Combining both data and computational independence means that both the data and the computations can be distributed across multiple storage and processing units and automatically parallelized. This parallelizability allows the programmer to exploit scalable massively parallel processing resources for increased processing speed and performance.

9.3 Aadhaar Project

Aadhaar project undertaken by the Unique Identification Authority of India (UIDAI) has the mission of identifying 1.2 billion citizens of India uniquely and reliably to build the largest biometric identity repository in the world (while eliminating duplication and fake identities) and provide an online, anytime anywhere, multifactor authentication service. This makes possible to identify any individual and get it authenticated at any time, from any place in India, in less than a second.

The UIDAI project is a Hadoop-based program that is well into production. At the time of this writing, over 700 million people have been enrolled and their identity information has been verified. The target is to reach a total of at least 1 billion enrolments during 2015. Currently the enrolment rate is about 10 million people every 10 days, so the project is well positioned to meet that target.

In India, there is no social security card, and much of the population lacks a passport. Literacy rates are relatively low, and the population is scattered across hundreds of thousands of villages. Without adequately verifiable identification, it has been difficult for many citizens to set up a bank account or otherwise participate in a modern economy.

For India's poorer citizens, this problem has even more dire consequences. The government has extensive programs to provide widespread relief for the poor—for example, through grain subsidies to those who are underfed and through government-sponsored work programs for the unemployed. Yet many who need help do not have access to benefit programs, in part because of the inability to verify who they are and whether they qualify for the programs. In addition, there is a huge level of so-called "leakage" of government aid that disappears to apparent fraud. For example, it has been estimated that over 50% of funds intended to provide grain to the poor goes missing, and that fraudulent claims for "ghost workers" siphon off much of the aid intended to create work for the poor.

There are clearly immense benefits from a mechanism that uniquely identifies a person and ensures instant identity verification. The need to prove one's identity only once will bring down transaction costs. A clear identity number can transform the delivery of social welfare programs by making them more inclusive of those communities now cut off from such benefits due to their lack of identification. It also enables the government to shift from indirect to direct benefit delivery by directly reaching out to the intended beneficiaries. A single universal identity number is also useful in eliminating fraud and duplicate identities, since individuals can no longer be able to represent themselves differently to different agencies. This results in significant savings to the state exchequer.

Aadhaar is in the process of creating the largest biometric database in the world, one that can be leveraged to authenticate identities for each citizen, even on site in rural villages. A wide range of mobile devices from cell phones to microscanners can be used to enroll people and to authenticate their identities when a transaction is requested. People will be able to make payments at remote sites via micro-ATMs. Aadhaar ID authentication will be used to verify qualification for relief food deliveries and to provide pension payments for the elderly. Implementation of this massive digital identification system is expected to save the equivalent of millions and perhaps billions of dollars each year by thwarting efforts at fraud. While the UIDAI project will have broad benefits for the Indian society as a whole, the greatest impact will be for the poorest people.

All application components are built using open source components and open standards. Aadhaar software currently runs across two of the data centers within India managed by UIDAI and handles 1 million enrolments a day and at the peak doing about 600 trillion biometric matches a day. Current system already has about 4 PB (4,000 terabytes) of raw data and continues grow as new enrolments come in. Aadhaar Authentication service is built to handle 100 million authentications a day across both the data centers in an active-active fashion and is benchmarked to provide sub-second response time. Central to Aadhaar system is its biometric subsystem that performs de-duplication and authentication in an accurate way.

Figure 9.4 presents the solution architecture for the Aadhaar project.

Application modules are built on common technology platform that contains frameworks for persistence, security, messaging, etc. The Platform standardizes on a technology stack based on open standards and using open source where prudent. A list of extensively used open source technology stacks is as follows:

- Spring Framework—Application container for all components and runtime
- Spring Batch—Runtime for various batch jobs
- Spring Security—For all application security needs
- Mule ESB—Runtime for loosely coupled SEDA stages of enrolment flow
- RabbitMQ—Messaging middleware
- Hadoop Stack—HDFS, Hive, HBase, Pig, and Zookeeper
- Pentaho—Open source BI Solution
- Quartz—Scheduling of batch jobs
- MongoDB—NoSQL Document Database
- MySQL—RDBMS for storing relational data
- Apache Solr—Index for full text search
- Apache Tomcat—Web container
- Liferay—Portal framework
- Several other open source libraries for random number generation, hashing, advanced data structures, HTML UI components, and others.

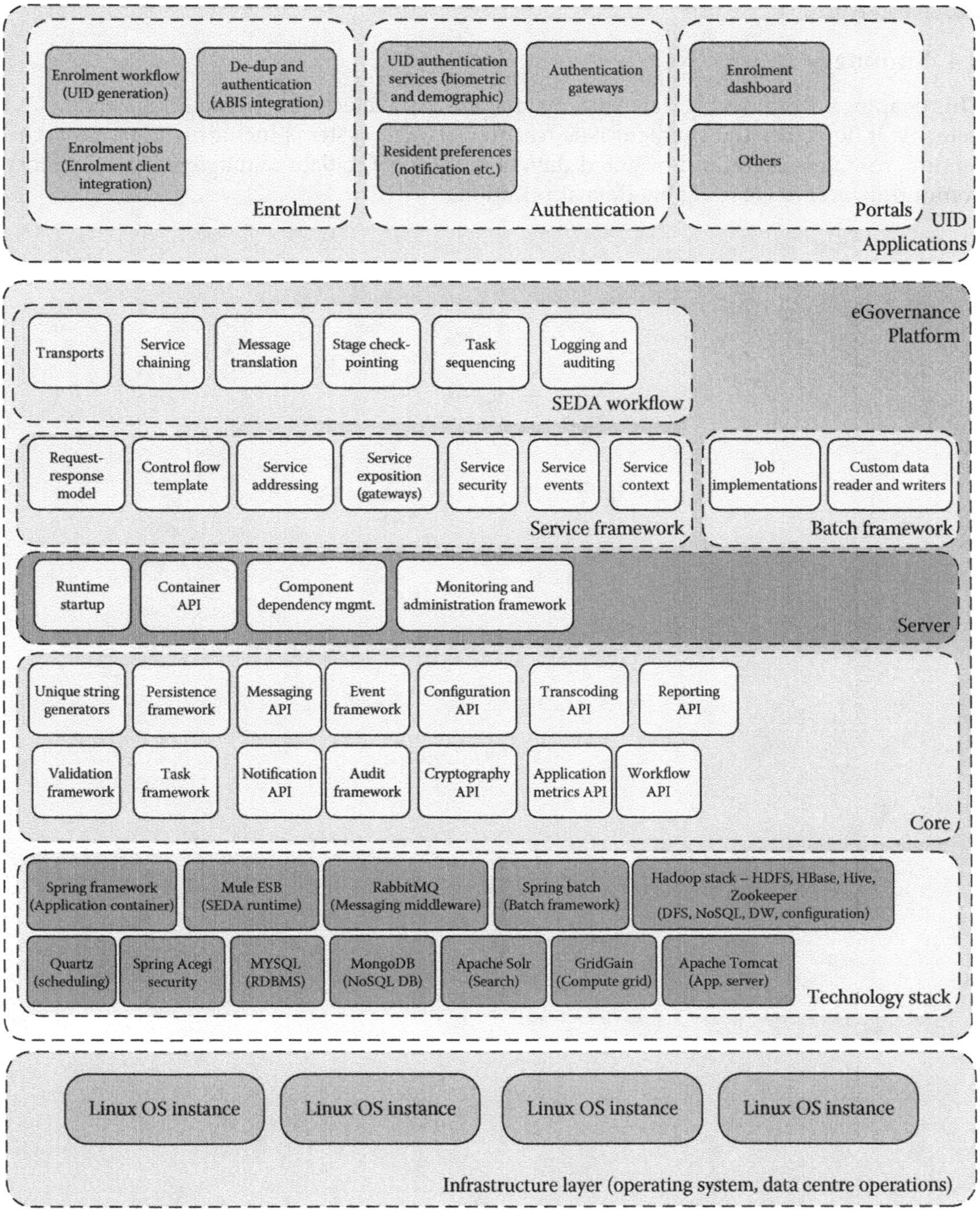

FIGURE 9.4
The solution architecture for the Aadhaar project.

9.4 Summary

This chapter introduces big data systems that are associated with big volume, variety, and velocity. It describes the characteristic features of such systems including big data architecture, row versus column-oriented data layouts, NoSQL data management, in-memory computing, and developing big data applications.

10

Big Data Technologies

Relational databases and data warehouses are necessary to run corporate businesses. They were designed for specific functionality in which they excel. Hadoop was not designed to replace them. Hadoop adds additional capabilities and features that together with relational databases and data warehouses are defining the next evolution of enterprise data platforms. Previously, it was believed that you could have speed, reliability, and price, but not all three at the same time. Hadoop changes that because with Hadoop you can have speed, reliability, and optimal price (commodity hardware) at the same time.

Hadoop is a software solution where all the components are designed from the ground up to be an extremely parallel high-performance platform that can store large volumes of information cost effectively. It handles very large ingestion rates, easily works with structured, semistructured, and unstructured data, eliminates the business data latency problem, is extremely low cost in relation to traditional systems, has a very low entry cost point, and is linearly scalable in cost effective increments. A Hadoop cluster can be purchased with a small capitalization expenditure (CAPEX) and run under a greatly reduced operational expenditure (OPEX) when compared to proprietary vertically scalable platforms.

Hadoop greatly reduces the cost of managing terabytes to petabytes of data and provides a distributed processing framework to finish the tasks as fast as it can by utilizing commodity hardware. It essentially is a Swiss army knife for big data projects because of the vast array of data access tools it exposes to various users—analysts, data scientists, and many more. Batch processing in Hadoop is an old news but still important. The advent of interactive and real time data processing is now a reality and critical for organizations. Fast data that allows decisions in near-real time can be just as important as big data capabilities.

10.1 Functional Programming Paradigm

The functional programming paradigm treats computation as the evaluation of mathematical functions with zero (or minimal) maintenance of states or data updates. As opposed to procedural programming in languages, such as C or Java, it emphasizes that the application be written completely as functions that do not save any state. Such functions are called pure functions. This is the first similarity with MapReduce abstraction. All input and output values are passed as parameters and the map and reduce functions are not expected to save state. However, the values can be input and output from a file system or a database to ensure persistence of the computed data. Programs written using pure functions eliminate side effects. So, the output of a pure function depends solely on the inputs provided to it. Calling a pure function twice with the same value for an argument will give the same result both times. Lisp is one such popular functional programming language in which two powerful recursion schemes—called map and reduce—enable powerful decomposition and reuse of code.

10.1.1 Parallel Architectures and Computing Models

MapReduce provides a parallel execution platform for data parallel applications. The following two sections describe core concepts involved in understanding such systems.

A variant of SIMD is called single program, multiple data (SPMD) model, in which the same program executes on multiple compute processes. While SIMD can achieve the same result as SPMD, SIMD systems typically execute in lock step with a central controlling authority for program execution. As can be seen, when multiple instances of the map function are executed in parallel, they work on different data streams using the same map function. In essence, though the underlying hardware can be a MIMD machine (a compute cluster), the MapReduce platform follows a SPMD model to reduce programming effort. Of course, while this holds for simple use cases, a complex application may involve multiple phases—each of which is solved with MapReduce—in which case the platform will be a combination of SPMD and MIMD.

10.1.2 Data Parallelism versus Task Parallelism

Data parallelism is a way of performing parallel execution of an application on multiple processors. It focuses on distributing data across different nodes in the parallel execution environment and enabling simultaneous sub-computations on these distributed data across the different compute nodes. This is typically achieved in SIMD mode (single instruction, multiple data mode) and can have either a single controller controlling the parallel data operations or multiple threads working in the same way on the individual compute nodes (SPMD). In contrast, task parallelism focuses on distributing parallel execution threads across parallel computing nodes. These threads may execute the same or different threads and exchange messages through shared memory or explicit communication messages, as per the parallel algorithm. In the most general case, each of the threads of a task-parallel system can be performing completely different tasks, but co-ordinating to solve a specific problem. In the most simplistic case, all threads can be executing the same program and, based on their node IDs, differentiating to perform any variation in task-responsibility. Most common Task-Parallel algorithms follow the Master–Worker model, where there is a single master and multiple workers. The master distributes the computation to different workers based on scheduling rules and other task-allocation strategies. MapReduce falls under the category of data parallel SPMD architectures.

Owing to the use of functional programming paradigm, the individual mapper processes that process the split data are not aware of (or dependent on) the results of other mapper processes. Also, since the order of execution of the mapper function does not matter, one can reorder or parallelize the execution. Thus, this inherent parallelism enables the mapper function to scale and execute on multiple nodes in parallel. Along the same lines, the reduce functions also run in parallel, and each instance works on a different output key. All the values are processed independently, again facilitating implicit data parallelism. The extent of parallel execution is determined by the number of map and reduce tasks configured at the time of job submission.

10.2 Google MapReduce

The MapReduce architecture and programming model pioneered by Google is an example of a modern systems architecture designed for processing and analyzing large data sets and is being used successfully by Google in many applications to process massive amounts of raw web data. The MapReduce system runs on top of the Google File System, within which data are loaded, they are partitioned into chunks, and each chunk is replicated. Data processing is co-located with data storage: When a file needs to be processed, the job scheduler consults a storage metadata service to get the host node for each chunk and then schedules a *map* process on that node, so that data locality is exploited efficiently.

> Google engineers designed MapReduce to solve a specific practical problem. Therefore, it was designed as a programming model combined with the implementation of that model—in essence, a reference implementation. The reference implementation was used to demonstrate the practicality and effectiveness of the concept and to help ensure that this model would be widely adopted by the computer industry. Over the years, other implementations of MapReduce have been created and are available as both open source and commercial products.

The MapReduce architecture allows programmers to use a functional programming style to create a map function that processes a key-value pair associated with the input data to generate a set of intermediate key-value pairs and a reduce function that merges all intermediate values associated with the same intermediate key.

Users define a map and a reduce function as follows:

1. The map function processes a (key, value) pair and returns a list of intermediate (key, value) pairs:

   ```
   map (in_key, in_value) → list(out_key, intermediate_value).
   ```

2. The reduce function merges all intermediate values having the same intermediate key:

   ```
   reduce (out_key, list(intermediate_value)) → list(out_value).
   ```

The former processes an input key-value pair, producing a set of intermediate pairs. The latter is in charge of combining all the intermediate values related to a particular key, outputting a set of merged output values (usually just one). MapReduce is often explained illustrating a possible solution to the problem of counting the number of occurrences of each word in a large collection of documents. The following pseudocode refers to the functions that need to be implemented.

```
map(String input_key, String input_value):
// input_key: document name
// input_value: document contents
for each word w in input_value:
EmitIntermediate(w, "1");
```

```
reduce(String output_key,
Iterator intermediate_values):
// output_key: a word
// output_values: a list of counts
int result = 0;
for each v in intermediate_values:
result += ParseInt(v);
Emit(AsString(result));
```

The map function emits in output each word together with an associated count of occurrences (in this simple example, just one). The reduce function provides the required result by summing all the counts emitted for a specific word. MapReduce implementations (e.g., Google App Engine and Hadoop) then automatically parallelize and execute the program on a large cluster of commodity machines. The runtime system takes care of the details of partitioning the input data, scheduling the program's execution across a set of machines, handling machine failures, and managing required inter-machine communication.

The programming model for MapReduce architecture is a simple abstraction where the computation takes a set of input key-value pairs associated with the input data and produces a set of output key-value pairs. The overall model for this process is shown in Figure 10.1. In the Map phase, the input data is partitioned into input splits and assigned to Map tasks associated with processing nodes in the cluster. The Map task typically executes on the same node that contains its assigned partition of data in the cluster. These Map tasks perform user-specified computations on each input key-value pair from the partition of input data assigned to the task and generates a set of intermediate results for each key. The shuffle and sort phase then takes the intermediate data generated by each Map task, sorts this data with intermediate data from other nodes, divides this data into regions to be processed by the reduce tasks, and distributes this data as needed to nodes where the Reduce tasks will execute. All Map tasks must complete prior to the shuffle and sort and reduce phases. The number of Reduce tasks does not need to be the same as the number of

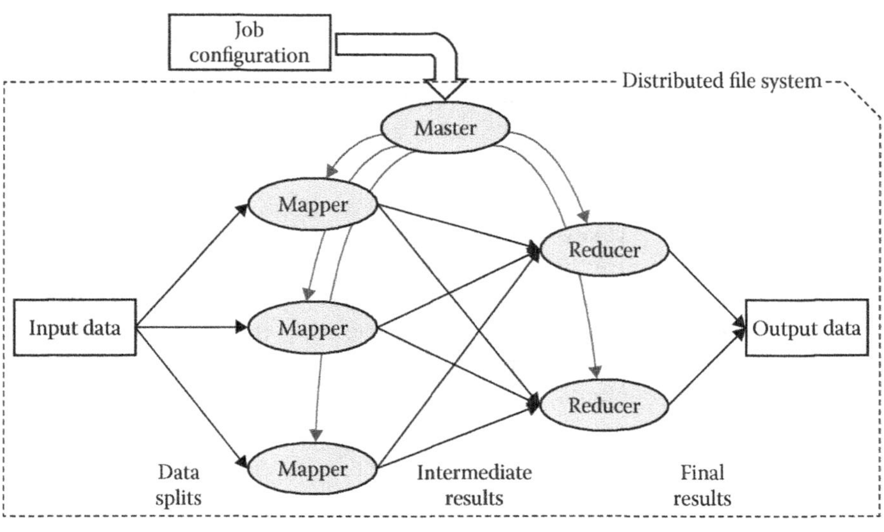

FIGURE 10.1
Execution phases in a generic MapReduce application.

Map tasks. The Reduce tasks perform additional user-specified operations on the intermediate data, possibly merging values associated with a key to a smaller set of values to produce the output data. For more complex data processing procedures, multiple MapReduce calls may be linked together in sequence.

The MapReduce programs can be used to compute derived data from documents, such as inverted indexes, and the processing is automatically parallelized by the system that executes on large clusters of commodity type machines, highly scalable to thousands of machines. Since the system automatically takes care of details such as partitioning the input data, scheduling and executing tasks across a processing cluster, and managing the communications between nodes, programmers with no experience in parallel programming can easily use a large distributed processing environment.

10.2.1 Google File System

Google File System (GFS) is the storage infrastructure that supports the execution of distributed applications in Google's computing cloud. GFS was designed to be a high-performance, scalable distributed file system for very large data files and data-intensive applications providing fault tolerance and running on clusters of commodity hardware. GFS is oriented to very large files, dividing and storing them in fixed-size chunks of 64 MB by default that are managed by nodes in the cluster called chunk servers. Each GFS consists of a single master node that acts as a name server and multiple nodes in the cluster that act as chunk servers using a commodity Linux-based machine (node in a cluster) running a user-level server process. Chunks are stored in plain Linux files that are extended only as needed and replicated on multiple nodes to provide high availability and improve performance.

GFS has been designed with the following assumptions:

- The system is built on top of commodity hardware that often fails.
- The system stores a modest number of large files; multi-GB files are common and should be treated efficiently, and small files must be supported, but there is no need to optimize for that.
- The workloads primarily consist of two kinds of reads: large streaming reads and small random reads.
- The workloads have also many large sequential writes that append data to files.
- High sustained bandwidth is more important than low latency.

The architecture of the file system is organized into a single master, which contains the metadata of the entire file system, and a collection of chunk servers, which provide storage space. From a logical point of view, the system is composed of a collection of software daemons that implement either the master server or the chunk server. A file is a collection of chunks for which the size can be configured at the file system level. Chunks are replicated on multiple nodes to tolerate failures. Clients look up the master server and identify the specific chunk of a file they want to access. Once the chunk is identified, the interaction happens between the client and the chunk server. Applications interact through the file system with a specific interface supporting the usual operations for file creation, deletion, read, and write. The interface also supports snapshots and records append operations that are frequently performed by applications. GFS is conceived considering the fact that failures in a large distributed infrastructure are common rather than a rarity; therefore, specific attention is given to the implementation of a highly available, lightweight, and fault-tolerant infrastructure. The potential single point of failure of the single-master architecture has been addressed by giving the possibility of replicating the master node on any other node belonging to the infrastructure.

10.2.2 Google Bigtable

Bigtable is the distributed storage system designed to scale up to petabytes of data across thousands of servers. Bigtable provides storage support for several Google applications that expose different types of workload: from throughput-oriented batch-processing jobs to latency-sensitive serving of data to end users. Bigtable's key design goals are wide applicability, scalability, high performance, and high availability. To achieve these goals, Bigtable organizes the data storage in tables, the rows of which are distributed over the distributed file system supporting the middleware, which is the Google File System. From a logical perspective, a table can be defined as a multidimensional sorted map indexed by a key that is represented by a string of arbitrary length. A table is organized into rows and columns; columns can be grouped in column family, which allows specific optimization for better access control, the storage and the indexing of data. A simple data access model constitutes the interface for client applications that can address data at the granularity level of the single column of a row. Moreover, each column value is stored in multiple versions that can be automatically time-stamped by Bigtable or by client applications.

Google's Bigtable solution's objective was to develop a relatively simple storage management system that could provide fast access to petabytes of data, potentially redundantly distributed across thousands of machines. Physically, Bigtable resembles a B-tree index-organized table in which branch and leaf nodes are distributed across multiple machines. Like a B-tree, nodes split as they grow, and—because nodes are distributed—this allows for high scalability across large numbers of machines. Data elements in Bigtable are identified by a primary key, column name, and, optionally, a timestamp. Lookups via primary key are predictable and relatively fast. Bigtable provides the data storage mechanism for Google App Engine.

Data is stored in Bigtable as a sparse, distributed, persistent multidimensional sorted map, which is indexed by a row key, column key, and a timestamp. Rows in a Bigtable are maintained in order by the row key, and row ranges become the unit of distribution and load balancing called a tablet. Each cell of data in a Bigtable can contain multiple instances indexed by the timestamp. Bigtable uses GFS to store both data and log files. The API for Bigtable is flexible, providing data management functions, such as creating and deleting tables, and data manipulation functions by the row key, including operations to read, write, and modify data. Index information for Bigtables utilizes tablet information stored in structures similar to a B+Tree. MapReduce applications can be used with Bigtable to process and transform data. Google has implemented many large-scale applications (e.g., Google Earth) that utilize Bigtable for storage. Table 10.1 lists several MapReduce implementations, while Table 10.2 gives a comparisons of Google, Hadoop and Disco MapReduce implementations.

TABLE 10.1
MapReduce Cloud Implementations

Owner	Imp Name and Website	Start Time	Last Release	Distribution Model
Google	Google MapReduce, http://labs.google.com/papers/inapreduce.html	2004		Internal use by Google
Apache	Hadoop, http://hadoop.apache.org/	2004	Hadoop0.20.0, April 22, 2009	Open source
GridGain	GridGain http://www.gridgain.com.	2005	GridGain 2.1.1, February 26, 2009	Open source
Nokia	Disco http://discoproject.org/	2008	Disco 0.2.3, September 9, 2009	Open source
Geni.com	SkyNet, http://skynet.rubyforge.org	2007	Skynet 0.9.3, May 31, 2008	Open source
Manjrasoft	MapReduce.net (optional service of Aneka), http://www.manjrasoft.com products.html	2008	Aneka 1.0, March 27, 2009	Commercial

TABLE 10.2
Comparison of MapReduce Implementations

	Google MapReduce	Hadoop	Disco
Focus	Data intensive	Data intensive	Data intensive
Architecture	Master-slave	Master-slave	Master-slave
Platform	Linux	Cross-platform	Linux, Mac OS X
Storage system	GFS	HDFS, CloudStore, S3	GlusterFS
Implementation technology	C++	JAVA	Erlang
Programming environment	JAVA and Python	J JAVA shell utilities using Hadoop streaming, C++ using Hadoop pipes	Python
Deployment	Deployed on Google clusters	Private and public cloud (EC2)	Private and public cloud (EC2)
Some users and applications	Google	Baidu, NetSeer, A9.com, Facebook	Nokia Research Center

10.3 Yahoo!'s Vision of Big Data Computing

As digital information began to increase over the past decade, organizations tried different approaches to solve these problems. At first, the focus was placed on providing individual machines more storage, processing power, and memory—only to quickly find that analytical techniques on single machines failed to scale. Over time, many realized the potential of distributed systems (distributing tasks over multiple machines), but data analytic solutions were often complicated, error-prone, or simply not fast enough.

In 2002, while developing a project called Nutch (a search engine project focused on crawling, indexing, and searching Internet web pages), Doug Cutting and Mike Cafarella were struggling with a solution for processing a vast amount of information. To meet the storage and processing demands for Nutch, they realized that there would be the need of a reliable distributed computing approach that would scale to the demand of the vast amount of website data that the tool would be collecting. A year later, Google published papers on the GFS and MapReduce, an algorithm and distributed programming platform for processing large data sets; they utilized large numbers of commodity servers and built GFS and MapReduce in a way that assumed hardware failures would be commonplace and were simply something that the software needed to deal with.

Hadoop was modeled after two papers produced by Google, one of the many companies to have these kinds of data-intensive processing problems. The first, presented in 2003, describes a pragmatic, scalable, distributed file system optimized for storing enormous data sets called the Google Filesystem, or GFS. In addition to simple storage, GFS was built to support large-scale, data-intensive, distributed processing applications. The following year, another paper, titled "Map-Reduce: Simplified Data Processing on Large Clusters," was presented, defining a programming model and accompanying framework that provided automatic parallelization, fault tolerance, and the scale to process hundreds of terabytes of data in a single job over thousands of machines. When paired, these two systems could be used to build large data processing clusters on relatively inexpensive commodity machines. These papers directly inspired the development of Hadoop Distributed File System and Hadoop MapReduce, respectively.

10.3.1 Apache Hadoop

In 2006, after struggling with the same "big data" challenges related to indexing massive amounts of information for its search engine, and after watching the progress of the Nutch project, Yahoo! hired Doug Cutting and decided to adopt Hadoop as its distributed framework for solving its search engine challenges. Yahoo! spun out the storage and processing parts of Nutch to form Hadoop as an open source Apache project, and the Nutch web crawler remained its own separate project. Shortly thereafter, Yahoo! began rolling out Hadoop as a means to power analytics for various production applications. The platform was so effective that Yahoo! merged its search and advertising into one unit to better leverage Hadoop technology.

In the past 10 years, Hadoop has evolved from its search engine-related origins to one of the most popular general-purpose computing platforms for solving big data challenges. It is rapidly becoming the foundation for the next generation of data-based applications. It is predicted that Hadoop will be driving a big data market that should hit more than $23 billion by 2016. Since the launch of the first Hadoop-centered company, Cloudera, in 2008, dozens of Hadoop-based start-ups have attracted hundreds of millions of dollars in venture capital investment. Simply put, organizations have found that Hadoop offers a proven approach to big data analytics.

Apache Hadoop has revolutionized data management and processing. Hadoop's technical capabilities have made it possible for organizations across a range of industries to solve problems that were previously impractical. These capabilities include the following:

1. Scalable processing of massive amounts of data on commodity hardware
2. Flexibility for data processing, regardless of the format and structure (or lack of structure) of the data

Enterprises are using Hadoop for resolving business problems:

- Content optimization and engagement—Companies are focusing on optimizing content for rendering on different devices supporting different content formats. Many media companies require that a large amount of content be processed in different formats. Also, content engagement models must be mapped for feedback and enhancements.
- Enhancing fraud detection for banks and credit card companies—Companies are utilizing Hadoop to detect transaction fraud. By providing analytics on large clusters of commodity hardware, banks are using Hadoop, applying analytic models to a full set of transactions for their clients, and providing near-real-time fraud-in-progress detection.
- Shopping pattern analysis for retail product placement—Businesses in the retail industry are using Hadoop to determine products most appropriate to sell in a particular store based on the store's location and the shopping patterns of the population around it.
- Network analytics and mediation—Real-time analytics on a large amount of data generated in the form of usage transaction data, network performance data, cell-site information, device-level data, and other forms of back-office data is allowing companies to reduce operational expenses and enhance the user experience on networks.
- Traffic pattern recognition for urban development—Urban development often relies on traffic patterns to determine requirements for road network expansion. By monitoring traffic during different times of the day and discovering patterns, urban developers can determine traffic bottlenecks, which allow them to decide whether additional streets/street lanes are required to avoid traffic congestions during peak hours.
- Social media marketing analysis—Companies are currently using Hadoop for brand management, marketing campaigns, and brand protection. By monitoring, collecting, and aggregating data from various Internet sources, such as blogs, boards, news feeds, tweets, and social media, companies are using Hadoop to extract and aggregate information about their products, services, and competitors, discovering patterns and revealing upcoming trends important for understanding their business.

10.3.1.1 Components of Hadoop Ecosystem

The Apache Hadoop project develops open source software for reliable, scalable, distributed computing. Hadoop includes the following components:

- Hadoop Common: The common utilities that support the other Hadoop subprojects
- Avro: A data serialization system that provides dynamic integration with scripting languages
- Cassandra: A scalable multi-master database with no single point of failure
- Chukwa: A data collection system for managing large distributed systems
- HBase: A scalable, distributed database that supports structured data storage for large tables
- HDFS: A distributed file system that provides high-throughput access to application data

- Hive: A data warehouse infrastructure that provides data summarization and ad hoc querying
- MapReduce: A software framework for distributed processing of large data sets on compute clusters
- Mahout: A scalable machine learning and data mining library
- Pig: A high-level dataflow language and execution framework for parallel computation
- ZooKeeper: A high-performance coordination service for distributed applications

Like the Google implementation, the Hadoop MapReduce architecture creates fixed-size input splits from the input data and assign the splits to Map tasks. The local output from the Map tasks is copied to Reduce nodes, where it is sorted and merged for processing by Reduce tasks that produce the final output.

The Hadoop MapReduce architecture is functionally similar to the Google implementation except that the base programming language for Hadoop is Java instead of C++. The implementation is intended to execute on clusters of commodity processors utilizing Linux as the operating system environment, but can also be run on a single system as a learning environment. Hadoop clusters also utilize the "shared nothing" distributed processing paradigm linking individual systems with local processor, memory, and disk resources using high-speed communications switching capabilities typically in rack-mounted configurations. The flexibility of Hadoop configurations allows small clusters to be created for testing and development using desktop systems or any system running Unix/Linux providing a JVM environment; however, production clusters typically use homogeneous rack-mounted processors in a data center environment.

10.3.1.2 Principles and Patterns Underlying the Hadoop Ecosystem

Hadoop is different from previous distributed approaches in the following ways:

- Data is distributed in advance.
- Data is replicated throughout a cluster of computers for reliability and availability.
- Data processing tries to occur where the data is stored, thus eliminating bandwidth bottlenecks.

In addition, Hadoop provides a simple programming approach that abstracts the complexity evident in previous distributed implementations. As a result, Hadoop provides a powerful mechanism for data analytics, which consists of the following:

1. Vast amount of storage—Hadoop enables applications to work with thousands of computers and petabytes of data. Over the past decade, computer professionals have realized that low-cost "commodity" systems can be used together for high-performance computing applications that once could be handled only by supercomputers. Hundreds of "small" computers may be configured in a cluster to obtain aggregate computing power that can exceed by far that of single supercomputer at a cheaper price. Hadoop can leverage clusters in excess of thousands of machines, providing huge storage and processing power at a price that an enterprise can afford.

2. Distributed processing with fast data access—Hadoop clusters provide the capability to efficiently store vast amounts of data while providing fast data access. Prior to Hadoop, parallel computation applications experienced difficulty distributing execution between machines that were available on the cluster. This was because the cluster execution model creates demand for shared data storage with very high I/O performance. Hadoop moves execution toward the data. Moving the applications to the data alleviates many of the high-performance challenges. In addition, Hadoop applications are typically organized in a way that they process data sequentially. This avoids random data access (disk seek operations), further decreasing I/O load.
3. Reliability, failover, and scalability—In the past, implementers of parallel applications struggled to deal with the issue of reliability when it came to moving to a cluster of machines. Although the reliability of an individual machine is fairly high, the probability of failure grows as the size of the cluster grows. It will not be uncommon to have daily failures in a large (thousands of machines) cluster. Because of the way that Hadoop was designed and implemented, a failure (or set of failures) will not create inconsistent results. Hadoop detects failures and retries execution (by utilizing different nodes). Moreover, the scalability support built into Hadoop's implementation allows for seamlessly bringing additional (repaired) servers into a cluster, and leveraging them for both data storage and execution.

10.3.1.3 Storage and Processing Strategies

A computation task has four characteristic dimensions as follows:

- Computation—transforming information to produce new information
- Database Access—access to reference information needed by the computation
- Database Storage—long-term storage of information (needed for later access)
- Networking—delivering questions and answers

The ratios among these quantities and their relative costs are pivotal: it is fine to send a GB over the network if it saves years of computation, but it is not economical to send a kilobyte question if the answer could be computed locally in a second. Consequently, on-demand computing is only economical for very CPU-intensive (100,000 instructions per byte or a CPU day-per gigabyte of network traffic) applications; for most other applications, preprovisioned computing is likely to be more economical.

Within the Hadoop ecosystem, the primary components responsible for storage and processing are HDFS and MapReduce respectively. A typical Hadoop workflow consists of loading data into the HDFS and processing using the MapReduce API or several tools that rely on MapReduce as an execution framework; both of these are direct implementations of Google's own GFS and MapReduce technologies. Both HDFS and MapReduce exhibit common architectural principles like:

1. Both are designed to run on clusters of commodity servers (i.e., low to medium specification servers)
2 Both have an architecture where a software cluster sits on the physical servers and manages aspects such as application load balancing and fault tolerance, without relying on high-end hardware to deliver these capabilities

3. Both scale their capacity by adding more servers (scale-out) as opposed to the previous models of using larger hardware (scale-up)
4. Both have mechanisms to detect and work around failures
5. Both provide most of their services transparently, allowing the user to concentrate on the problem at hand

Characteristics of HDFS file system are as follows:

- HDFS stores files in blocks that are typically at least 64 or 128 Mb in size, much larger than the 4–32 kb seen in most conventional file systems.
- HDFS is optimized for throughput over latency; it is very efficient at streaming reads of large files but poor when seeking for many small ones.
- HDFS is optimized for workloads that are generally write-once and read-many.
- HDFS uses replication for handling disk failures rather than by having physical redundancies in disk arrays or similar strategies,. Each of the blocks comprising a file is stored on multiple nodes within the cluster, and a service called the NameNode constantly monitors to ensure that failures have not dropped any block below the desired replication factor. If this does happen, then it schedules the making of another copy within the cluster.

Hadoop provides a standard specification (that is, interface) for the map and reduce phases, and the implementation of these are often referred to as mappers and reducers. A typical MapReduce application will comprise a number of mappers and reducers, and it is not unusual for several of these to be extremely simple. The developer focuses on expressing the transformation between the source and the resultant data, and the Hadoop framework manages all aspects of job execution and coordination.

MapReduce is an API, an execution engine, and a processing paradigm; it provides a series of transformations from a source into a result data set. In the simplest case, the input data is fed through a map function and the resultant temporary data is then fed through a reduce function. MapReduce works best on semistructured or unstructured data. Instead of data conforming to rigid schemas, the requirement is instead that the data can be provided to the map function as a series of key-value pairs. The output of the map function is a set of other key-value pairs, and the reduce function performs aggregation to collect the final set of results.

The most common deployment model for Hadoop sees the HDFS and MapReduce clusters deployed on the same set of servers. Each host that contains data and the HDFS component to manage the data also hosts a MapReduce component that can schedule and execute data processing. When a job is submitted to Hadoop, it can use the locality optimization to schedule data on the hosts where data resides as much as possible, thus minimizing network traffic and maximizing performance.

10.3.2 Hadoop 2 alias YARN

Introduction of Hadoop 2 has had a very different effect on the two primary components of Hadoop, namely, HDFS storage, and MapReduce processing.

10.3.2.1 HDFS Storage

The HDFS in Hadoop 2 is more resilient and can be more easily integrated into existing workflows and processes.

HDFS deploys a master-slave model; this model works well and has been scaled to clusters with tens of thousands of nodes at companies such as Yahoo! However, though it is scalable, there is a resiliency risk; if the NameNode becomes unavailable, then the entire cluster is rendered effectively unusable. No HDFS operations can be performed, and since the vast majority of installations use HDFS as the storage layer for services, such as MapReduce, they also become unavailable even if they are still running without problems.

The slave nodes (called DataNodes) hold the actual file system data. In particular, each host running a DataNode will typically have one or more disks onto which files containing the data for each HDFS block are written. The DataNode itself has no understanding of the overall file system; its role is to store, serve, and ensure the integrity of the data for which it is responsible. The master node (called the NameNode) is responsible for knowing which of the DataNodes holds which block and how these blocks are structured to form the file system. When a client looks at the file system and wishes to retrieve a file, it is via a request to the NameNode that the list of required blocks is retrieved.

The NameNode stores the file system metadata to a persistent file on its local file system. If the NameNode host crashes in a way that this data is not recoverable, then all data on the cluster is effectively lost forever. The data will still exist on the various DataNodes, but the mapping of which blocks comprise which files is lost. On this account, in Hadoop 1, the best practice was to have the NameNode synchronously write its file system metadata to both local disks and at least one remote network volume (typically via NFS).

In Hadoop 2, NameNode High Availability (HA) is one of the major features that provides both a standby NameNode that can be automatically promoted to service all requests should the active NameNode fail, but also builds additional resilience for the critical file system metadata on top of this mechanism.

10.3.2.2 MapReduce Processing

MapReduce in Hadoop 1 not only provided the framework for processing, but it also manages the allocation of this computation across the cluster; it not only directs data to and between the specific map and reduce tasks but also determines where each task would run, and managed the full job life cycle, monitoring the health of each task and node, rescheduling if any of them failed, and so on. From the user's perspective, the actual scale of the data and cluster for computation is transparent, and aside from affecting the time taken to process the job, it does not change the interface with which to interact with the system.

MapReduce's batch processing model was ill-suited to problem domains where faster response times were required. For instance, Hive which provides a SQL-like interface onto HDFS data, actually converted the statements into MapReduce jobs that are then typically executed in a batch processing mode.

In Hadoop 2, there is a focus on enabling different processing models on the Hadoop platform. The role of job scheduling and resource management is separated from that of executing the actual application, and is implemented by YARN. YARN is responsible for managing the cluster resources, and so MapReduce exists as an application that runs atop the YARN framework. Both semantically and practically, the MapReduce interface in Hadoop 2 is completely compatible with that in Hadoop 1, but effectively, MapReduce has become a hosted application on the YARN framework.

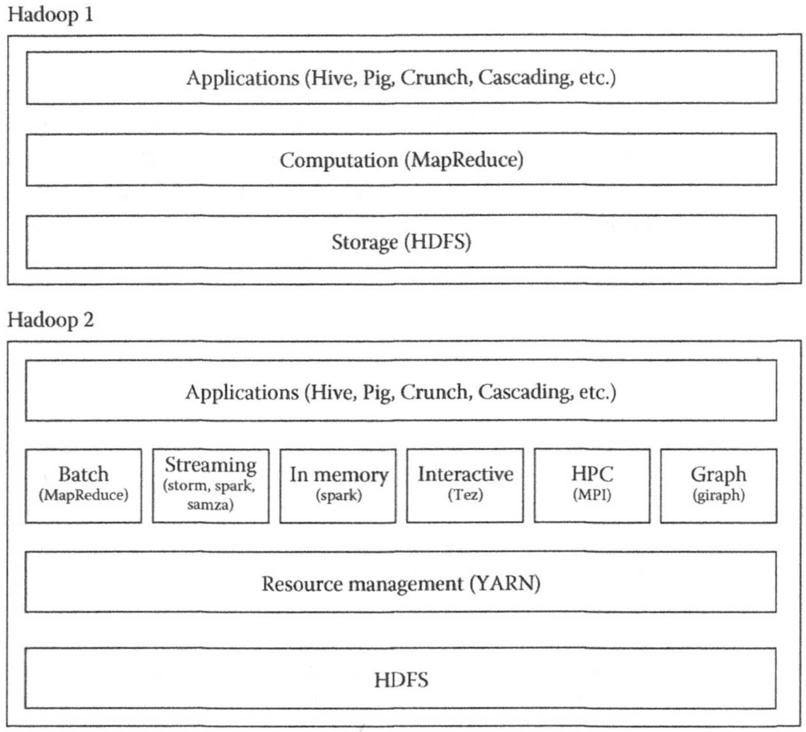

FIGURE 10.2
Comparing the architecture of Hadoop 1 and Hadoop 2.

The significance of this split is that other applications can be written that provide processing models more focused on the actual problem domain and can offload all the resource management and scheduling responsibilities to YARN. The latest versions of many different execution engines have been ported onto YARN, either in a production-ready or experimental state, and it has shown that the approach can allow a single Hadoop cluster to run everything from batch-oriented MapReduce jobs through fast-response SQL queries to continuous data streaming and even to implement models such as graph processing and the Message Passing Interface (MPI) from the High-Performance Computing (HPC) world. Figure 10.2 compares the architecture of Hadoop 1 and Hadoop 2.

10.4 Hadoop Distribution

Since 2008, there have been a number of Hadoop distributions offered by different companies excelling in some or other area. Selection of an appropriate distribution should be based on various criteria such as

1. Performance: The ability of the cluster to ingest input data and emit output data at a quick rate becomes very important for low-latency analytics. This input–output cost forms an integral part of the data processing workflow. Scaling up hardware is

one way to achieve low latency independent of the Hadoop distribution. However, this approach will be expensive and saturate out quickly. Architecturally, low I/O latency can be achieved in different ways:

a. Some distributions reduce the number of intermediate data-staging layers between the data source or the data sink and Hadoop cluster.
b. Some distributions provide streaming writes into the Hadoop cluster in an attempt to reduce intermediate staging layers. Operators used for filtering, compressing, and lightweight data processing can be plugged into the streaming layer to preprocess the data before it flows into storage.
c. Some vendors optimize their distributions for particular hardware, increasing job performance per node. The Apache Hadoop distribution is written in Java, a language that runs in its own virtual machine. Though this increases application portability, it comes with overheads such as an extra layer of indirection during execution by means of byte-code interpretation and background garbage collection; it is not as fast as an application compiled directly for a target hardware.
d. Some distributions optimize features such as compression and decompression for certain hardware types.

2. Scaling: Over time, data outgrows the physical capacity of the compute and storage resources provisioned by an organization. Scaling can be done vertically or horizontally: vertical scaling or scaling up is tightly bound to hardware advancements and is expensive; lack of elasticity is another downside with vertical scaling. Horizontal scaling or scaling out is a preferred mode of scaling the compute and storage.

   Scaling costs will depend on the existing architecture and how it complements and complies with the Hadoop distribution that is being evaluated. Scaling out should be limited to addition of more nodes and disks to the cluster network, with minimal configuration changes. However, distributions might impose different degrees of difficulty, both in terms of effort and cost on scaling a Hadoop cluster. Scaling out might mean heavy administrative and deployment costs, rewriting a lot of the application's code, or a combination of both.

3. Reliability: A distribution focusing on reliability provides high availability of its components out of the box. Any distributed system is subject to partial failures. Failures can stem from hardware, software, or network issues, and have a smaller mean time when running on commodity hardware. Dealing with these failures without disrupting services or compromising data integrity is the primary goal of any highly available and consistent system.

   Distributions that reduce manual tasks for cluster administrators are more reliable; human intervention is directly correlated to higher error rates. Failovers are critical periods for systems as they operate with lower degrees of redundancy; any error during these periods can be disastrous for the application. Lower is the recovery time from failure and better is the availability of the system. Hence, automated failover handling usually means the system can recover and run in a short period of time.

   Eliminating Single Point of Failures (SPOF) ensures availability; the usual means of eliminating SPOFs is to increase the redundancy of components. Apache Hadoop 1 had a single NameNode; consequently, any failure to the NameNode's hardware meant the entire cluster becoming unusable. With Hadoop 2 there is the concept of a secondary NameNode and hot standbys that can be used to restore the name node in the event of NameNode failure.

The integrity of data also needs to be maintained during normal operations and when failures are encountered. Integrity of data can be ensured by measures like data checksums for error detection and possible recovery, data replication, data mirroring, snapshots, and so on. Replication ensures data availability coupled with rack-aware smart placement of data and handling Mirroring helps recovery from site failures by asynchronous replication across the Internet. Snapshotting aids disaster recovery and also facilitates offline access to data without disrupting production.

4. Manageability: Capabilities of Hadoop management tools are key differentiators when choosing an appropriate distribution for an enterprise. Management tools need to provide centralized cluster administration, resource management, configuration management, and user management. Job scheduling, automatic software upgrades, user quotas, and centralized troubleshooting are other desirable features. Deploying and managing the Apache Hadoop open source distribution requires internal understanding of the source code and configuration.

There are number of distributions of Hadoop available to prospective users.

Different computational frameworks and resource management solutions are available in Hadoop. The foundation of Hadoop is the two core frameworks YARN and HDFS. These two frameworks deal with storage and processing:

- YARN, which stands for Yet Another Resource Negotiator, is the foundation for distributed processing in Hadoop. YARN can be considered a distributed data operating system because it is responsible for controlling the allocation of compute resources across a Hadoop platform. YARN greatly increases the scale-out capability of Hadoop by allowing applications with different runtime characteristics to run with a single resource management model for the distributed cluster. Without a single resource management model it was not possible to control how applications with different runtime characteristics used hardware resources. This often required separate clusters for Hadoop, NoSQL, Spark, and so on. Users did not want large-batch processes to take away resources from other processes that need to return data in near time. If required, YARN allows different frameworks, such as Hadoop, NoSQL, and Spark, to run under a single resource management model.
- Hadoop Distributed File System (HDFS) is a distributed file system that spreads data blocks across the storage defined for the Hadoop cluster. Data are usually distributed in 64MB or 128MB–1GB block sizes. The data has three replicas (default) for high availability. The Hadoop distributed file system (HDFS) is a distributed file system that spreads blocks for a file across multiple disks on separate servers. Spreading the blocks across the disks enables HDFS to leverage the throughput and input or output operations per second (IOPS) that all the disks can generate. Each block has three replicas (default) for high availability. HDFS can work with different types of storage, but for performance, local disks are recommended. Just a bunch of disks (JBOD) minimizes the overhead that can occur with RAID, SAN, and NFS systems.

10.4.1 Cloudera Distribution of Hadoop (CDH)

Cloudera was formed in March 2009 with a primary objective of providing Apache Hadoop software, support, services, and training for enterprise-class deployment of Hadoop and its ecosystem components. The software suite is branded as Cloudera Distribution of Hadoop (CDH). The company being one of the Apache Software Foundation sponsors pushes most enhancements it makes during support and servicing of Hadoop deployments upstream back into Apache Hadoop.

CDH is in its fifth major version right now and is considered a mature Hadoop distribution. The paid version of CDH comes with a proprietary management software, Cloudera Manager.

10.4.2 MapR

MapR was also founded in 2009 with a mission to bring enterprise-grade Hadoop. The Hadoop distribution they provide has significant proprietary code when compared to Apache Hadoop. There are a handful of components where they guarantee compatibility with existing Apache Hadoop projects. Key proprietary code for the MapR distribution is the replacement of HDFS with a POSIX-compatible NFS. Another key feature is the capability of taking snapshots.

MapR comes with its own management console. The different grades of the product are named as M3, M5, and M7. M5 is a standard commercial distribution from the company, M3 is a free version without high availability, and M7 is a paid version with a rewritten HBase API.

10.4.3 Hortonworks Data Platform (HDP)

The Yahoo! Hadoop team spurned off to form Hortonworks in June, 2011, a company with objectives similar to Cloudera. Their distribution is branded as Hortonworks Data Platform (HDP). The HDP suite's Hadoop and other software are completely free, with paid support and training. Hortonworks also pushes enhancements upstream, back to Apache Hadoop.

HDP is in its second major version currently and is considered the rising star in Hadoop distributions. It comes with a free and open source management software called Ambari.

10.4.4 Pivotal HD

Greenplum is a marquee parallel data store from EMC. EMC integrated Greenplum within Hadoop, giving way to an advanced Hadoop distribution called Pivotal HD. This move alleviated the need to import and export data between stores such as Greenplum and HDFS, bringing down both costs and latency.

The HAWQ technology provided by Pivotal HD allows efficient and low-latency query execution on data stored in HDFS. The HAWQ technology has been found to give 100 times more improvement on certain MapReduce workloads when compared to Apache Hadoop. HAWQ also provides SQL processing in Hadoop, increasing its popularity among users who are familiar with SQL.

10.5 Storage and Processing Strategies

10.5.1 Characteristics of Big Data Storage Methods

1. Data is distributed across several nodes: Because big data refers to much larger data sets, the data would be distributed across several nodes each being a commodity machine with a typical storage capacity of 2–4 Tb. Even with smaller sized data sets this distribution is beneficial because
   - Each data block is replicated across more than one node (the default Hadoop replication factor is 3) rendering the overall system resilient to failure.
   - Because of the prevailing parallel processing method, several nodes participate in the data processing resulting in a 5–10 times improvement in performance.
2. Applications (along with dependent libraries) are moved to the processing nodes loaded with data: Unlike the conventional 3-tier architecture where the data is transported to the centralized application tier for processing, big data cannot handle this network overhead. Moving terabytes of data to the application tier will saturate the networks and introduce considerable inefficiencies, possibly leading to system failure.
3. Data is processed local to the nodes: Since data is distributed across several nodes and applications are moved to these processing nodes, it is evident that data gets processed local or as close as possible to the data as possible. Assimilating the results of such node-local task being small compared with the overall volume of raw data itself processed across all of these node-local tasks, the consequent network overhead is manageable.
4. Sequential reads preferred over random reads: Unlike the conventional relational database management system (RDBMS) systems that are majorly random access oriented, big data systems prefer sequential oriented access to the benefit of throughput for the overall system.

10.5.2 Characteristics of Big Data Processing Methods

1. Massively parallel processing (MPP) database systems: MPP systems employ some application-specific pre-defined form of splitting or partitioning of data (across the nodes) based on values contained in a column or a set of columns, for instance, sales for different countries. While such an approach is not applicable for ad hoc queries, it is beneficial only when the manner of the distribution of data is consistent with the manner the data is accessed for processing. To address this limitation, it is common for such systems to store the data multiple times, split by different criteria. Depending on the query, the appropriate data set is accessed.
2. In-memory database systems: An in-memory database is like an in-memory MPP database with a SQL interface. From an operational perspective, in-memory database systems are identical to MPP systems with each node having a significant amount of memory, and most of the data is preloaded into this memory. SAP HANA operates on this principle. One of the major disadvantages of the commercial implementations of in-memory databases is that there is a considerable hardware and software lock-in; consequently, they also tend usually to be expensive.

3. Bulk synchronous parallel (BSP) systems: BSP system is composed of a list of processes (identical to the map processes) that synchronize on a barrier, send data to the Master node, and exchange relevant information. Once the iteration is completed, the Master node will indicate to each processing node to resume the next iteration. Synchronizing on a barrier is a commonly used concept in parallel programming. It is used when many threads are responsible for performing their own tasks, but need to agree on a checkpoint before proceeding. This pattern is needed when all threads need to have completed a task up to a certain point before the decision is made to proceed or abort with respect to the rest of the computation (in parallel or in sequence).
4. MapReduce systems: MapReduce system needs the user to define a map process and a reduce process. When Hadoop is being used to implement MapReduce, the data is typically distributed in 64–128 Mb blocks, and each block is replicated twice (a replication factor of 3 is the default in Hadoop). In the example of computing sales for the year 2000 and ordered by country, the entire sales data would be loaded into the HDFS as blocks (64–128 Mb in size). When the MapReduce process is launched, the system would first transfer all the application libraries (comprising the user-defined map and reduce processes) to each node. Each node will schedule a map task that sweeps the blocks comprising the sales data file. Each Mapper (on the respective node) will read records of the block and filter out the records for the year 2014. Each Mapper will then output a record comprising key-value pair. Key will be the country and value will be the sales number from the given record if the sales record is for the year 2014.

Finally, a configurable number of Reducers will receive the key-value pairs from each of the Mappers. Keys will be assigned to specific Reducers to ensure that a given key is received by one and only one Reducer. Each Reducer will then add up the sales value number for all the key-value pairs received. The data format received by the Reducer is key (country), and a list of values for that key (sales records for the year 2014). The output is written back to the HDFS. The client will then sort the result by states after reading it from the HDFS. The last step can be delegated to the Reducer because the Reducer receives its assigned keys in the sorted order. In this example, we need to restrict the number of Reducers to one to achieve this, however. Because communication between Mappers and Reducers causes network I/O, it can lead to bottlenecks.

MapReduce job terminate at the end of its processing cycle.

10.6 NoSQL Databases

NoSQL databases have been classified into four subcategories:

- Column family stores: An extension of the key-value architecture with columns and column families, the overall goal was to process distributed data over a pool of infrastructure; for example, HBase and Cassandra.
- Key-value pairs: This model is implemented using a hash table where there is a unique key and a pointer to a particular item of data creating a key-value pair; for example, Voldemort.

- Document databases: This class of databases is modeled after Lotus Notes and similar to key-value stores (K-V Stores). The data is stored as a document and is represented in JSON or XML formats. The biggest design feature is the flexibility to list multiple levels of key-value pairs; for example, Riak and CouchDB.
- Graph databases: Based on the graph theory, this class of database supports the scalability across a cluster of machines. The complexity of representation for extremely complex sets of documents is evolving; for example, Neo4j.

10.6.1 Column-Oriented Stores or Databases

HadoopHBase is the distributed database that supports the storage needs of the Hadoop distributed programming platform. HBase is designed by taking inspiration from Google Bigtable; its main goal is to offer real-time read/write operations for tables with billions of rows and millions of columns by leveraging clusters of commodity hardware. The internal architecture and logic model of HBase is very similar to Google Bigtable, and the entire system is backed by the HDFS, which mimics the structure and services of GFS.

10.6.2 Key-Value Stores (K-V Stores) or Databases

Apache Cassandra is a distributed object store form an aging large amounts of structured data spread across many commodity servers. The system is designed to avoid a single point of failure and offer a highly reliable service. Cassandra was initially developed by Facebook; now it is part of the Apache incubator initiative. Facebook in the initial years had used a leading commercial database solution for their internal architecture in conjunction with some Hadoop. Eventually the tsunami of users led the company to start thinking in terms of unlimited scalability and focus on availability and distribution. The nature of the data and its producers and consumers did not mandate consistency but needed unlimited availability and scalable performance. The team at Facebook built an architecture that combines the data model approaches of BigTable and the infrastructure approaches of Dynamo with scalability and performance capabilities, named Cassandra. Cassandra is often referred to as hybrid architecture since it combines the column-oriented data model from BigTable with HadoopMapReduce jobs, and it implements the patterns from Dynamo like eventually consistent, gossip protocols, a master–master way of serving both read and write requests. Cassandra supports a full replication model based on NoSQL architectures.

The Cassandra team had a few design goals to meet, considering the architecture at the time of first development and deployment was primarily being done at Facebook. The goals included

- High availability
- Eventual consistency
- Incremental scalability
- Optimistic replication
- Tunable trade-offs between consistency, durability, and latency
- Low cost of ownership
- Minimal administration

Amazon Dynamo is the distributed key-value store that supports the management of information of several of the business services offered by Amazon Inc. The main goal of Dynamo is to provide an incrementally scalable and highly available storage system. This goal helps in achieving reliability at a massive scale, where thousands of servers and network components build an infrastructure serving 10 million requests per day. Dynamo provides a simplified interface based on get/put semantics, where objects are stored and retrieved with a unique identifier (key). The main goal of achieving an extremely reliable infrastructure has imposed some constraints on the properties of these systems. For example, ACID properties on data have been sacrificed in favor of a more reliable and efficient infrastructure. This creates what it is called an eventually consistent model (i.e., in the long term all the users will see the same data).

10.6.3 Document-Oriented Databases

Document-oriented databases or document databases can be defined as a schemaless and flexible model of storing data as documents, rather than relational structures. The document will contain all the data it needs to answer specific query questions. Benefits of this model include

- Ability to store dynamic data in unstructured, semi-structured, or structured formats.
- Ability to create persisted views from a base document and store the same for analysis.
- Ability to store and process large data sets.

The design features of document-oriented databases include

- Schema free—there is no restriction on the structure and format of how the data needs to be stored. This flexibility allows an evolving system to add more data and allows the existing data to be retained in the current structure.
- Document store—objects can be serialized and stored in a document, and there is no relational integrity to enforce and follow.
- Ease of creation and maintenance—a simple creation of the document allows complex objects to be created once and there is minimal maintenance once the document is created.
- No relationship enforcement—documents are independent of each other and there is no foreign key relationship to worry about when executing queries. The effects of concurrency and performance issues related to the same are not a bother here.
- Open formats—documents are described using JSON, XML, or some derivative, making the process standard and clean from the start.
- Built-in versioning—documents can get large and messy with versions. To avoid conflicts and keep processing efficiencies, versioning is implemented by most solutions available today.

Document databases express the data as files in JSON or XML formats. This allows the same document to be parsed for multiple contexts and the results scrapped and added to the next iteration of the database data.

Apache CouchDB and MongoDB are two examples of document stores. Both provide a schema-less store whereby the primary objects are documents organized into a collection of key-value fields. The value of each field can be of type string, integer, float, date, or an array of values. The databases expose a RESTful interface and represent data in JSON format. Both allow querying and indexing data by using the MapReduce programming model, expose JavaScript as a base language for data querying and manipulation rather than SQL, and support large files as documents. From an infrastructure point of view, the two systems support data replication and high availability. CouchDB ensures ACID properties on data. MongoDB supports sharding, which is the ability to distribute the content of a collection among different nodes.

10.6.4 Graph Stores or Databases

Social media and the emergence of Facebook, LinkedIn, and Twitter have accelerated the emergence of the most complex NoSQL database, the graph database. The graph database is oriented toward modeling and deploying data that is graphical by construct. For example, to represent a person and their friends in a social network, we can either write code to convert the social graph into key-value pairs on a Dynamo or Cassandra, or simply convert them into a node-edge model in a graph database, where managing the relationship representation is much more simplified.

A graph database represents each object as a node and the relationships as an edge. This means person is a node and household is a node, and the relationship between them is an edge. Like the classic ER model for RDBMS, we need to create an attribute model for a graph database. We can start by taking the highest level in a hierarchy as a root node (similar to an entity) and connect each attribute as its sub-node. To represent different levels of the hierarchy we can add a subcategory or sub-reference and create another list of attributes at that level. This creates a natural traversal model like a tree traversal, which is similar to traversing a graph. Depending on the cyclic property of the graph, we can have a balanced or skewed model. Some of the most evolved graph databases include Neo4j, infiniteGraph, GraphDB, and AllegroGraph.

10.6.5 Comparison of NoSQL Databases

1. Column-based databases allow for rapid location and return of data from one particular attribute. They are potentially very slow with writing; however, data may need to be shuffled around to allow a new data item to be inserted. As a rough guide then, traditional transactionally orientated databases will probably fair better in an RDBMS. Column based will probably thrive in areas where speed of access to non-volatile data is important, for example, in some decision support applications. You only need to review marketing material from commercial contenders, like Ingres Vectorwise, to see that business analytics is seen as the key market and speed of data access the main product differentiator.
2. If you do not need large and complex data structures and can always access your data using a known key, then key-value stores have a performance advantage over most RDBMS. Oracle has a feature within their RDBMS that allows you to de fine a table at an index-organized table (IOT), and this works in a similar way. However, you do still have the overhead of consistency checking, and these IOTs

are often just a small part of a larger schema. RDBMS have a reputation for poor scaling in distributed systems, and this is where key-value stores can be a distinct advantage.

3. Document-centric databases are good where the data is difficult to structure. Web pages and blog entries are two oft-quoted examples. Unlike RDBMS, which impose structure by their very nature, document-centric databases allow free-form data to be stored. The onus is then on the data retriever to make sense of the data that is stored.

10.7 Summary

This chapter presented an overview of technologies on which big data computing depends: Hadoop MapReduce and NoSQL. The chapter discusses the functional programming paradigm followed by the Google MapReduce algorithm and its reference implementation. In the later part of the chapter, it provides a brief on the various types of NoSQL databases including column oriented stores, key-value stores, document oriented databases, and graph stores.

11

Big Data NoSQL Databases

A NoSQL database provides a mechanism for storage and retrieval of data that employs less constrained consistency models than traditional relational databases. Motivations for this approach include simplicity of design, horizontal scaling, and finer control over availability. NoSQL databases are often highly optimized key-value stores intended for simple retrieval and appending operations, with the goal being significant performance benefits in terms of latency and throughput. NoSQL databases are finding significant and growing industry use in big data and real time web applications. NoSQL systems are also referred to as "not only SQL" to emphasize that they may in fact allow SQL-like query languages to be used.

The term NoSQL is more of an approach or way to address data management versus being a rigid definition. Different types of NoSQL databases exist, and they often share certain characteristics, but are optimized for specific types of data, which then require different capabilities and features. NoSQL may mean not only SQL, or it may mean "No" SQL. When using Apache Hive to run SQL in NoSQL databases, those queries are converted to MapReduce(2) and run as a batch operation to process large volumes of data in parallel. A "No" SQL database may use APIs or JavaScript to access data versus traditional SQL. APIs can also be used to access the data in NoSQL to process interactive and real time queries.

When accessing big data, there is a demand for databases that are nonrelational and that are designed to work with semistructured, unstructured, and structured data. A nonrelational database provides a flexible data model, layout, and format. Predefined schemas are not required for NoSQL databases. NoSQL databases have traditionally been nonrelational databases that are distributed and designed to scale to very large sizes. NoSQL databases are designed to address the challenges of big data.

NoSQL databases are very scalable, have high availability, and provide a high level of parallelization for processing large volumes of data quickly. NoSQL databases have different characteristics and features. For example, they can be key-value based, column-based, document-based, or graph-based. NoSQL data stores may be optimized for key or value, columnar, document-oriented, XML, graph, and object data structures. Each NoSQL database can emphasize different areas of the CAP theorem (Brewer theorem).

The CAP theorem effectively states that distributed databases can have consistency, availability, and partition (CAP) tolerance, but not all three at the same time. In other words, the Cap theorem states that a database can excel in only two of the following areas: consistency (all DataNodes observe the same data at the same time), availability (every request for data will get a response of success or failure), and partition tolerance (the data platform will continue to run even if parts of the system are not available).

Choosing a NoSQL database requires choosing what the CAP priorities are. If the data are distributed and replicated, and nodes or networks between the nodes go down, a decision must be made between data consistency (having the current version of the data) and availability. NoSQL databases can address this with an eventual consistency model

(Cassandra). Eventual consistency means a DataNode is always available to handle data requests, but at a point in time the data may be inconsistent but still relatively accurate.

NoSQL databases choose their priority for CAP tolerance. For instance,

- HBase and Accumulo are consistent and partition tolerant.
- CouchDB is partition tolerant and available.
- Neo4j is available and consistent.

Choosing the correct NoSQL database requires understanding factors such as the requirements, SLAs (latency), initial size and growth projections, costs, feature or functionality, and concurrency. It's also important to understand that NoSQL databases have their own defaults and may have the capability of changing their priorities for CAP. It is also important to understand the roadmap of these NoSQL databases because they are evolving quickly.

NoSQL databases are not designed to replace the traditional RDBMS or data warehouses. It's important to understand that Hadoop is not a database, it is a data platform. Relational databases and data warehouses have a foundation of the relational model, use schema-on-write, and have features, tools, and ecosystems focused for types of operations different than Hadoop or NoSQL databases. It is not that there cannot be an overlap between relational databases, data warehouses, Hadoop, and NoSQL databases, especially as Hadoop and NoSQL evolve. But each was designed for a specific core purpose. NoSQL databases are becoming part of the enterprise data platform for organizations and providing functionality that traditional systems do not handle well, either because of the size, complexity of data, or the volume of data being ingested.

NoSQL systems have been divided into four major categories, namely, Column Databases, Key-Value Databases, Document Databases, and Graph Databases

1. Column Databases: These systems partition a table by column into column families, where each column family is stored in its own files. They also allow versioning of data values. Column-oriented data stores are used when key-value data stores reach their limits because you want to store a very large number of records with a very large amount of information that goes beyond the simple nature of the key-value store.

   The main benefit of using columnar databases is that you can quickly access a large amount of data. A row in an RDBMS is a continuous disk entry and multiple rows are stored in different disk locations, which makes them more difficult to access; in contrast, in columnar databases, all cells that are part of a column are stored continuously. As an example, consider performing a lookup for all blog titles in an RDBMS. For tackling millions of records common on the web, it might be costly in terms of disk entries, whereas in columnar databases, such a search would represent only one access.

   Such databases are very handy for retrieving large amounts of data from a specific family, but the tradeoff is that they lack flexibility. The most used columnar database is Google Cloud BigTable, especially Apache HBase and Cassandra.

One of the other benefits of columnar databases is ease of scaling because data are stored in columns; these columns are highly scalable in terms of the amount of information they can store. This is why they are used mainly for keeping nonvolatile, long-living information and in scaling use cases.

2. Key-Value Databases: These systems have a simple data model based on fast access by the key to the value associated with the key; the value can be a record or an object or a document or even have a more complex data structure.

   Key-value databases are the easiest NoSQL databases to understand. These data stores basically act like a dictionary and work by matching a key to a value. They are often used for high-performance use cases in which basic information needs to be stored—for example, when session information may need to be written and retrieved very quickly. These data stores really perform well and are efficient for this kind of use case; they are also usually highly scalable. Key-value data stores can also be used in a queuing context to ensure that data would not be lost, such as inlogging architecture or search engine indexing architecture use cases.

   Redis and Riak KV are the most famous key-value data stores; Redis is more widely used and has an in-memory K-V store with optional persistence. Redis is often used in web applications to store session-related data, such as node or PHP web applications; it can serve thousands of session retrievals per second without altering the performance.

3. Document Databases: These systems store data in the form of documents using well-known formats such as JavaScript Object Notation (JSON). Documents are accessible via their document id, but can also be accessed rapidly using other indexes.

   Columnar databases are not the best for structuring data that contain deeper nesting structures—that is where document-oriented data stores come into play. Data are indeed stored into key-value pairs, but these are all compressed into what is called a document. This document relies on a structure or encoding such as XML, but most of the time, it relies on JavaScript Object Notation (JSON).

   Document-oriented databases are used whenever there is a need to nest information. For instance, for representing an account in your application may have the following information:

   - Basic information: first name, last name, birthday, profile picture, URL, creation date, and so on
   - Additional information: address, authentication method (password, Facebook, etc.), interests, and so on

   NoSQL document stores are often used in web applications because representing an object with nested object is fairly easy; moreover, integrating with front-end JavaScript technology is seamless because both technologies work with JSON.

   Although document databases are more useful structurally and for representing data, they also have their downside. They basically need to acquire the whole document—for example, when they are reading for a specific field—and this can dramatically affect performance.

   Famous NoSQL document databases are MongoDB, Couchbase, and Apache CouchDB.

4. Graph Databases: Data are represented as graphs, and related nodes can be found by traversing the edges using path expressions. Graph databases are really different from other types of databases discussed above. They use a different paradigm to represent the data—a tree-like structure with nodes and edges that are connected to each other through paths called relations.

Those databases rise with social networks, for instance, to represent a user's friend network, their friends' relationships, and so on. With the other types of data stores, it is possible to store a friend's relationship to a user in a document, but still, it can then be really complex to store friends' relationships; it is better to use a graph database and create nodes for each friend, connect them through relationships, and browse the graph depending on the need and scope of the query.

> NoSQL systems are interchangeably referred as NoSQL data stores or NoSQL databases (to highlight their similarities to the role and functions performed by traditional databases). This should not lead to any confusion because the author believes that, at any point, the context will clarify which aspect is relevant and is being referred to.

The most famous graph database is Neo4j, and it is used for use cases that have to do with complex relationship information, such as connections between entities and others entities that are related to them, but it is also used in classification use cases.

11.1 Characteristics of NoSQL Systems

This subsection discusses characteristics of NoSQL systems.

11.1.1 NoSQL Characteristics Related to Distributed Systems and Distributed Databases

The below section makes a reference to the characteristics of distributed systems and distributed databases discussed in Chapter 6.

1. Availability, Replication, and Eventual Consistency: Many applications that use NoSQL systems require continuous system availability. To accomplish this, data are replicated over two or more nodes in a transparent manner, so that if one node fails, the data are still available on other nodes. Replication improves data availability and can also improve read performance, because read requests can often be serviced from any of the replicated data nodes. However, write performance becomes more cumbersome because an update must be applied to every copy of the replicated data items; this can slow down write performance if serializable consistency is required (see Chapter 9, Section 9.2.2.1,"BASE (Basically Available,

Soft state, Eventual consistency)"). Many NoSQL applications do not require serializable consistency, so more relaxed forms of consistency known as eventual consistency are used.

2. Replication: Two major replication models are used in NoSQL systems: master–slave and master–master replication:
   a. The master–slave replication requires one copy to be the master copy; all write operations must be applied to the master copy and then propagated to the slave copies, usually using eventual consistency, that is, the slave copies will eventually be the same as the master copy. For read, the master–slave paradigm can be configured in various ways. One configuration requires all reads to also be at the master copy, so this would be similar to the primary site or primary copy methods of distributed concurrency control, with similar advantages and disadvantages. Another configuration would allow reads at the slave copies but would not guarantee that the values are the latest writes, since writes to the slave nodes can be done after they are applied to the master copy.
   b. The master–master replication allows reads and writes at any of the replicas but may not guarantee that reads at nodes that store different copies see the same values. Different users may write the same data item concurrently at different nodes of the system, so the values of the item will be temporarily inconsistent. A reconciliation method to resolve conflicting write operations of the same data item at different nodes must be implemented as part of the master–master replication scheme.
3. Sharding of Files: In many NoSQL applications, files (or collections of data objects) can have many millions of records (or documents or objects), and these records can be accessed concurrently by thousands of users. So, it is not practical to store the whole file in one node. Sharding or horizontal partitioning (see Chapter 9, Section 9.2.2.3 "Master–Slave Replication") of the file records is often employed in NoSQL systems. This serves to distribute the load of accessing the file records to multiple nodes. The combination of sharding the file records and replicating the shards works in tandem to improve load balancing as well as data availability.
4. High-Performance Data Access: High-performance data access: In many NoSQL applications, it is necessary to find individual records or objects (data items) from among the millions of data records or objects in a file. The majority of accesses to an object will be by providing the key value rather than by using complex query conditions. The object key is similar to the concept of object id. To achieve this, most systems use one of two techniques: hashing or range partitioning on object keys:
   a. Hashing, a hash function h(K) is applied to the key K, and the location of the object with key K is determined by the value of h(K).
   b. Range partitioning, the location is determined via a range of key values; for example, location i would hold the objects whose key values K are in the range Kimin ≤ K ≤ Kimax. In applications that require range queries, where multiple objects within a range of key values are retrieved, range partitioning is preferred. Other indexes can also be used to locate objects based on attribute conditions different from the key K.
5. Scalability: There are two kinds of scalability in distributed systems: scale-up and scale-out (see Chapter 9, Section 9.2.1, "Processing Approach"). Scale-up scalability, on the other hand, refers to expanding the storage and computing power of existing

nodes. In NoSQL systems, scale-out scalability is employed while the system is operational, so techniques for distributing the existing data among new nodes without interrupting system operation are necessary. In NoSQL systems, scale-out scalability is generally used, where the distributed system is expanded by adding more nodes for data storage and processing as the volume of data grows.

11.1.2 NoSQL Characteristics Related to Data Models and Query Languages

1. Not Requiring a Schema: The flexibility of not requiring a schema is achieved in many NoSQL systems by allowing semistructured, self-describing data (see Chapter 14, Section 14.1, "Big Data Systems Development Management"). The users can specify a partial schema in some systems to improve storage efficiency, but it is not required to have a schema in most of the NoSQL systems. As there may not be a schema to specify constraints, any constraints on the data would have to be programmed in the application programs that access the data items. There are various languages for describing semistructured data, such as JavaScript Object Notation (JSON) and Extensible Markup Language (XML). JSON is used in several NoSQL systems, but other methods for describing semistructured data can also be used. We will discuss JSON in Section 11.8 when we present document-based NoSQL systems.
2. Less Powerful Query Languages: Many applications that use NoSQL systems may not require a powerful query language such as SQL, because search (read) queries in these systems often locate single objects in a single file based on their object keys. NoSQL systems typically provide a set of functions and operations as a programming application programming interface (API), so reading and writing the data objects are accomplished by calling the appropriate operations by the programmer. In many cases, the operations are called CRUD operations, for create, read, update, and delete. In other cases, they are known as SCRUD because of an added Search (or Find) operation.

   Some NoSQL systems also provide a high-level query language, but it may not have the full power of SQL; only a subset of SQL querying capabilities would be provided. In particular, many NoSQL systems do not provide join operations as part of the query language itself; the joins need to be implemented in the application programs (see Chapter 12, Section 12.1.2, "MapReduce Enhancements and Extensions").
3. Versioning: Some NoSQL systems provide storage of multiple versions of the data items, with the timestamps of when the data version was created. We will discuss this aspect in Section 11.6 when we present column-based NoSQL systems.

11.2 Column Databases

A category of NoSQL systems is known as column-based or wide-column systems. The Google distributed storage system for big data, known as BigTable, is a well-known example of this class of NoSQL systems, and it is used in many Google applications that require large amounts of data storage, such as Gmail. Big-Table uses the Google File System (GFS) for data storage and distribution. An open source system known as Apache HBase is somewhat similar to Google Big-Table, but it typically uses Hadoop Distributed File System (HDFS) for data storage. HDFS is used in many cloud computing applications, as we shall discuss in Chapter 12. HBase can also use Amazon's Simple Storage System (known as S3) for data storage.

A column, which has a name and a value, is a basic unit of storage in a column family database. A set of columns makes up a row: rows can have identical columns, or they can have different columns. A set of related columns can be grouped together in collections called column families. Column family databases are designed for rows with varying number of columns; column families can support even millions of columns. Column families are organized into groups of data items that are frequently used together. Column families for a single row may or may not be near each other when stored on a disk, but columns within a column family are stored together in persistent storage, making it more likely that reading a single block can satisfy a query.

> Columnar databases are similar to relational databases in that both use rows and columns; however, there are also significant differences in their respective data models and implementation details.

For a column database, a keyspace is the top-level data structure in that all other data structures are contained within a keyspace; typically, there is one keyspace for every application. Column families are stored in a keyspace. Each row in a column family is uniquely identified by a row key, thus making a column family analogous to a table in a relational database. However, data in relational database tables is not necessarily maintained in a predefined order, and rows in relational tables are not versioned the way they are in column family databases.

Tables in relational databases have a relatively fixed structure, and the relational database management system can take advantage of that structure when optimizing the layout of data on drives when storing data for write operations and when retrieving data for read operations. Columns in a relational database table are not as dynamic as in column family databases—adding a column in a relational database requires changing its schema definition; adding a column in a column family database merely requires making a reference to it from a client application, for example, inserting a value to a column name. Unlike a relational database table, the set of columns in a column family can vary from one row to another. Column databases do not require a fixed schema—developers can add columns as needed.

Similarly, in relational databases, data about an object can be stored in multiple tables. For example, a supplier might have name, address, and contact information in one table; a list of past purchase orders in another table; and a payment history in another. To reference data from all three tables at once requires a join operation between all these tables. Columnar databases are typically denormalized or structured so that all relevant information about an object exists in a single row.

Query languages for column family databases may look similar to SQL. The query language can support

- SQL-like terms such as INSERT, UPDATE, DELETE, and SELECT
- Column family-specific operations such as CREATE COLUMNFAMILY

11.2.1 Cassandra

Cassandra is a distributed, open source data model that handles petabytes of data distributed across several commodity servers. The robust support, high data availability, and no single point of failure by Cassandra are guaranteed by the fact that the data clusters span multiple data centers. The system offers master-less and peer-peer asynchronous replicas; the peer-peer clustering (same role for each node) helps achieve low latency, high throughput, and no single point of failure.

In the data model, the rows are partitioned into tables; the very first column of the table forms the primary key, also known as the partition key. Cassandra does not support joins and subqueries, but encourages denormalization for achieving high data availability. The Cassandra data model believes in parallel data operation that results in high throughput and low latency, and adopts data replication strategy to ensure high availability for writing too. Unlike in relational data models, in Cassandra, the data are duplicated on multiple peer nodes, enabling reliability and fault tolerance.

In Cassandra, whenever a write operation occurs, the data are stored in the form of a structure in the memory called as memtable. The same data are also appended to the commit log on the hard disk that provides configurable durability. Each and every write on a Cassandra node is also received by the commit log, and these durable writes are permanent and survive even after a hardware failure; the durable write, set to true, is advisable to avoid the risk of losing data. Though customizable, the right amount of memory is dynamically allocated by the Cassandra system and a configurable threshold is set. During the writing operation, when the contents exceed the limit of memtable, the data, including indexes, are queued, ready to be flushed to Sorted String Tables (SSTables) on disk through sequential I/O.

The Cassandra model comes equipped with an SQL-like language called Cassandra Query Language (CQL) to query data.

11.2.1.1 Cassandra Features

The basic unit of storage in Cassandra is a column. A Cassandra column consists of a name-value pair, where the name also behaves as the key; each of these key-value pairs is a single column and is always stored with a timestamp value. The timestamp is used to expire data, resolve write conflicts, deal with stale data, and do other things. Once the column data are no longer used, the space can be reclaimed later during a compaction phase.

Cassandra puts the standard and super column families into keyspaces. A keyspace is similar to a database in RDBMS where all column families related to the application are stored.

1. *Consistency:* Upon receipt of a write, the data are first recorded in a commit log and then written to an in-memory structure known as memtable. A write operation is considered successful once it is written to the commit log and the memtable. Writes are batched in memory and periodically written out to structures known as SSTable. SSTables are not written to again after they are flushed; if there are changes to the data, a new SSTable is written. Unused SSTables are reclaimed by compactation.

    a. *Using Consistency Level ONE read operations*: If we have a consistency setting of ONE as the default for all read operations, then upon a read request, Cassandra returns the data from the first replica, even if the data are stale. If the data are stale, subsequent reads will get the latest (newest) data; this process is known as read repair. The low consistency level is good to use for indifference to staleness of data or for high read performance requirements.

Write operations: Cassandra would write to a node's commit log and return a response to the client. The consistency of ONE is good to use for indifference to loss of writes (which may happen if the node goes down before the write is replicated to other nodes) or for very high write performance requirements and also do not mind if some writes are lost.

b. *Using Consistency Level QUORUM:* Using the QUORUM consistency setting for both read and write operations ensures that the majority of the nodes respond to the read and the column with the newest timestamp is returned back to the client, while the replicas that do not have the newest data are repaired via the read repair operations. During write operations, the QUORUM consistency setting means that the write has to propagate to the majority of the nodes before it is considered successful and the client is notified.

c. *Using Consistency Level ALL:* Using ALL as consistency level means that all nodes will have to respond to reads or writes, which will make the cluster not tolerant to faults—even when one node is down, the write or read is blocked and reported as a failure. It is essential to tune the consistency levels as the application requirements change.

2. *Transactions:* A write is atomic at the row level, which means inserting or updating columns for a given row key will be treated as a single write and will either succeed or fail. Writes are first written to commit logs and memtables and are considered good only when the write to commit log and memtable is successful. If a node goes down, the commit log is used to apply changes to the node, just like the redo log in Oracle.
3. *Availability:* Cassandra is, by design, highly available, since there is no master in the cluster and every node is a peer in the cluster. The availability of a cluster can be increased by reducing the consistency level of the requests. Availability is governed by the $(R + W) > N$ formula, where W is the minimum number of nodes where the write must be successfully written, R is the minimum number of nodes that must respond successfully to a read, and N is the number of nodes participating in the replication of data. You can tune the availability by changing the R and W values for a fixed value of N.
4. *Query:* When designing the data model in Cassandra, as it does not have a rich query language, it is advised to make the columns and column families optimized for reading the data. As data are inserted in the column families, data in each row are sorted by column names. If we have a column that is retrieved much more often than other columns, it is better performance-wise to use that value for the row key instead.
5. *Scaling:* Scaling an existing Cassandra cluster is a matter of adding more nodes. As no single node is a master, when we add nodes to the cluster, we are improving the capacity of the cluster to support more writes and reads. This type of horizontal scaling allows you to have maximum uptime as the cluster keeps serving requests from the clients while new nodes are being added to the cluster.

11.2.2 Google BigTable

BigTable, primarily used by Google for various important projects, is envisioned as a distributed storage system, designed to manage petabytes of data, distributed across several thousand commodity servers allowing for even further horizontal scaling. At the hardware level, these thousand commodity servers are grouped under the distributed clusters, which, in turn, are connected through the central switch. Each cluster is constituted by various racks and a rack can, in turn, consist of several commodity computing machines that communicate to each other though the rack switches. In fact, these are the switches that are connected to the central switch to help in interrack or intercluster communications.

The BigTable efficiently deals with latency and data size issues. It is a compressed, proprietary high-performance storage system, underpinned by the Google File System (GFS) for log and data files storage, and Google SSTable (String Sorted Table) that stores the BigTable data internally. SSTable offers a persistent, immutable ordered map with keys and values as byte strings, with key being the primary source for searching. The SSTable is a collection of blocks of typical (though configurable) size of 64 kb. Unlike a relational database, it is a sparse, multidimensional sorted map, indexed by a row key, a column key, and a timestamp. The map stores each value as an uninterrupted array of bytes.

In the BigTable data model, there is no support for Atomicity, Consistency, Isolation, and Durability (ACID) transactions across row keys. As the BigTable data model is not relational in nature, it does not support *join* operations and there is no SQL-type language support also. This may pose challenges to those users who largely rely on SQL-like languages for data manipulation. In the BigTable data model, at the fundamental hardware level, interrack communication is less efficient than in intrarack communication, that is communication within a rack through the rack switches.

In a write operation, a valid transaction is logged into the tablet log. The commit is the group commit to improve the throughput. On the commit moment of the transaction, the data are inserted into the memory table (memtable). During the write operation, the size of the memtable continues to grow, and once it reaches the threshold, the current memtable freezes and a new memtable is generated. The former is converted into an SSTable and finally written into GFS. In a read operation, the SSTables and the memtable form an efficient merged view and the valid read operation is performed on it.

> One of the main differences that distinguish column-based systems from key-value stores (see Section 11.3) is the nature of the key. In column-based systems such as HBase, the key is multidimensional and so has several components: typically, a combination of table name, row key, column, and timestamp. The column is typically composed of two components: column family and column qualifier.

11.2.3 HBase

11.2.3.1 HBase Data Model and Versioning

1. *HBase Data Model:* The data model in HBase organizes data using the concepts of namespaces, tables, column families, column qualifiers, columns, rows, and datacells. A column is identified by a combination of (column family:column

qualifier). Data are stored in a self-describing form by associating columns with data values, where data values are strings. HBase also stores multiple versions of a data item, with a timestamp associated with each version, so versions and timestamps are also part of the HBase data model (this is similar to the concept of attribute versioning in temporal databases). As with other NoSQL systems, unique keys are associated with stored data items for fast access, but the keys identify cells in the storage system. Because the focus is on high performance when storing huge amounts of data, the data model includes some storage-related concepts.

a. *Tables and rows*: Data in HBase is stored in tables, and each table has a table name. Data in a table are stored as self-describing rows. Each row has a unique row key, and row keys are strings that must have the property that they can be lexicographically ordered, that is characters that do not have a lexicographic order in the character set cannot be used as part of a row key.

> The use of the words table, row, and column is not identical to their use in relational databases, but the uses are related.

b. *Column families, column qualifiers, and columns:* A table is associated with one or more column families. Each column family will have a name, and the column families associated with a table must be specified when the table is created and cannot be changed later.

> The concept of column family is somewhat similar to vertical partitioning, because columns (attributes) that are accessed together because they belong to the same column family are stored in the same files. Each column family of a table is stored in its own files using the HDFS file system.

While creating a table, the table name is followed by the names of the column families associated with the table.

creating a table:

```
create 'EMPLOYEE', 'Name', 'Address', 'Details'
```

When the data are loaded into a table, each column family can be associated with many column qualifiers, but the column qualifiers are not specified as part of creating a table. So the column qualifiers make the model a self-describing data model because the qualifiers can be dynamically specified as new rows are created and inserted into the table.

A column is specified by a combination of ColumnFamily:ColumnQualifier. Basically, column families are a way of grouping together related columns (attributes in relational terminology) for storage purposes, except that the column qualifier names are not specified during table creation. Rather, they are specified when the data are created and stored in rows, so the data are self describing since any column qualifier name can be used in a new row of data.

```
put 'EMPLOYEE', 'row1', 'Name:Fname', 'Amitabh'
put 'EMPLOYEE', 'row1', 'Name:Lname', 'Bacchan'
put 'EMPLOYEE', 'row1', 'Name:Nickname', 'Amit'
put 'EMPLOYEE', 'row1', 'Details:Job', 'Engineer'
put 'EMPLOYEE', 'row1', 'Details:Review', 'Good'
put 'EMPLOYEE', 'row2', 'Name:Fname', 'Hema'
put 'EMPLOYEE', 'row2', 'Name:Lname', 'Malini'
put 'EMPLOYEE', 'row2', 'Name:Mname', 'S'
put 'EMPLOYEE', 'row2', 'Details:Job', 'DBA'
put 'EMPLOYEE', 'row2', 'Details:Supervisor', 'Prakash Padukone'
put 'EMPLOYEE', 'row3', 'Name:Fname', 'Prakash'
put 'EMPLOYEE', 'row3', 'Name:Minit', 'M'
put 'EMPLOYEE', 'row3', 'Name:Lname', 'Padukone'
put 'EMPLOYEE', 'row3', 'Name:Suffix', 'Mr.'
put 'EMPLOYEE', 'row3', 'Details:Job', 'CEO'
put 'EMPLOYEE', 'row3', 'Details:Salary', '3,100,000'
```

However, it is important that the application programmers know which column qualifiers belong to each column family, even though they have the flexibility to create new column qualifiers on the fly when new data rows are created.

c. *Versions and timestamps*: HBase can keep several versions of a data item, along with the timestamp associated with each version. The timestamp is a long integer number that represents the system time when the version was created, so newer versions have larger timestamp values. HBase uses midnight "January 1, 1970 UTC" as timestamp value zero, and uses a long integer that measures the number of milliseconds since that time as the system timestamp value (this is similar to the value returned by the Java utilityjava.util.Date.getTime() and is also used in MongoDB).

   It is also possible for the user to define the timestamp value explicitly in a date format rather than using the system-generated timestamp.

d. *Cells:* A cell holds a basic data item in HBase. The key (address) of a cell is specified by a combination of (table, rowid, column family, column qualifier, timestamp). If the timestamp is left out, the latest version of the item is retrieved unless a default number of versions is specified, say the last three versions. The default number of versions to be retrieved, as well as the default number of versions that the system needs to keep, are parameters that can be specified during table creation.

e. *Namespaces:* A namespace is a collection of tables. A namespace basically specifies a collection of one or more tables that are typically used together by user applications, and it corresponds to a database that contains a collection of tables in relational terminology.

11.2.3.2 HBase CRUD Operations

HBase has low-level CRUD (create, read, update, delete) operations, as in many of the NoSQL systems. The formats of some of the basic CRUD operations in HBase are illustrated below.

```
Creating a table: create <tablename>, <column family>, <column family>, …
Inserting Data: put <tablename>, <rowid>, <column family>:<column
qualifier>, <value>
Reading Data (all data in a table): scan <tablename>
Retrieve Data (one item): get <tablename>,<rowid>
```

HBase only provides low-level CRUD operations. It is the responsibility of the application programs to implement more complex operations, such as

- The *join* operation between rows in different tables.
- The *create* operation creates a new table and specifies one or more column families associated with that table, but it does not specify the column qualifiers, as we discussed earlier.
- The *put* operation is used for inserting new data or new versions of existing data items.
- The *get* operation is for retrieving the data associated with a single row in a table, and the scan operation retrieves all the rows.

11.2.3.3 HBase Storage and Distributed System Concepts

Each HBase table is divided into a number of regions, where each region will hold a range of the row keys in the table; this is why the row keys must be lexicographically ordered. Each region will have a number of stores, where each column family is assigned to one store within the region. Regions are assigned to region servers (storage nodes) for storage. A master server (master node) is responsible for monitoring the region servers and for splitting a table into regions and assigning regions to region servers.

HBase is built on top of both HDFS and Zookeeper.

- HBase uses the Apache Zookeeper open source system for services related to managing the naming, distribution, and synchronization of the HBase data on the distributed HBase server nodes, as well as for coordination and replication services. Zookeeper can itself have several replicas on several nodes for availability, and it keeps the data it needs in main memory to speed access to the master servers and region servers.
- HBase also uses Apache Hadoop Distributed File System (HDFS) for distributed file services.

11.3 Key-Value Databases

A key-value data store is a more complex variation on the array data structure. The main characteristic of key-value stores is the fact that every value (data item) must be associated with a unique key, and that retrieving the value by supplying the key must be very fast.

Key-value pair databases are modeled on two components: keys and values; keys are identifiers associated with corresponding values. A namespace is a collection of identifiers; keys must be unique within a namespace. If a namespace corresponds to an entire database, all keys in the database must be unique. Some key-value databases provide for different namespaces within a database by setting up separate data structures or buckets for separate collections of identifiers.

Values can be as simple as a string, such as a name, number, or more complex values, such as images or binary objects, and so on. Because key-value databases allow virtually any data type in values, it is up to the programmer to determine the range of valid values and enforce those choices as required.

Key-value databases share three essential features as follows:

- Simplicity: Key-value databases work with a simple data model; it allows addition of attributes when needed.
- Speed: With a simple associative array data structure and design features to optimize performance, key-value databases can deliver high-throughput, data-intensive operations.
- Scalability: It is the capability to add or remove servers from a cluster of servers as needed to accommodate the load on the system.

Key-value pair databases are the simplest form of NoSQL databases.

11.3.1 Riak

Riak is a key-value open source NoSQL data model that has been developed by Basho Technologies. The model is considered a fine implementation of Amazon's Dynamo principles and distributes the data through nodes by employing the consistent hashing in an ordinary key-value system into buckets, simply the namespaces. Riak consists of the supported client libraries for several programming languages such as Erlang, Java, PHP, Python, Ruby, and C/C++. that help in setting or retrieving the value of the key, the most prominent operations a user performs with Riak. The model has received wide acceptance in companies such as AT&T, AOL, and Ask.com.

Similar to other efficient NoSQL data models, Riak also has the potential fault-tolerant availability and by default replicates the key-value store at three places across the nodes of the cluster. In unfavorable circumstances such hardware failure, the node outage will not completely shut down the write operation, rather its master-less peer-to-peer architecture allows a neighboring node (beyond default three) to respond to the write operation at that moment, and the data can be read back later.

11.3.1.1 Riak Features

1. *Consistency:* In distributed key-value store implementations such as Riak, the eventually consistent model of consistency is implemented. Since the value may have already been replicated to other nodes, Riak has two ways of resolving update conflicts: either the newest write wins and the older writes lose, or both (all) values are returned, allowing the client to resolve the conflict.
2. *Transactions:* Riak uses the concept of quorum implemented by using the W value—replication factor—during the write API call. Consider a Riak cluster with a replication factor of 5 and suppose we supply the W value of 3. When writing, the write is

reported as successful only when it is written and reported as a success on at least three of the nodes. This allows Riak to have write tolerance; in our example, with N equal to 5 and with a W value of 3, the cluster can tolerate N–W = 2 nodes being down for write operations, though we would still have lost some data on those nodes for read.

3. *Query*: Key-value stores can query by the key.
4. *Scaling:* Many key-value stores scale by using sharding: the value of the key determines on which node the key is stored.

11.3.2 Amazon Dynamo

Amazon runs a worldwide e-commerce platform that serves tens of millions customers at peak times using tens of thousands of servers located in many data centers around the world. Reliability is one of the most important requirements because even the slightest outage has significant financial consequences and impacts customer trust; there are strict operational requirements on Amazon's platform in terms of performance, reliability, and efficiency, and to support Amazon's continuous growth, the platform needs to be highly scalable.

The Dynamo system is a highly available and scalable distributed key-value-based data store built for supporting Amazon's internal applications. Dynamo is used to manage the state of services that have very high reliability requirements and need tight control over the tradeoffs among availability, consistency, cost effectiveness, and performance. There are many services on Amazon's platform that need only primary-key access to a data store. The customary use of relational databases would lead to inefficiencies and limit the ability to scale and provide high availability. Dynamo provides a simple primary-key-only interface to meet the requirements of these applications. The query model of the Dynamo system relies on simple read and write operations to a data item that is uniquely identified by a key. State is stored as binary objects (blobs) identified by unique keys. No operations span multiple data items.

Dynamo's partitioning scheme relies on a variant of consistent hashing mechanisms to distribute the load across multiple storage hosts. In this mechanism, the output range of a hash function is treated as a fixed circular space or ring (i.e., the largest hash value wraps around to the smallest hash value). Each node in the system is assigned a random value within this space, which represents its position on the ring. Each data item identified by a key is assigned to a node by hashing the data item's key to yield its position on the ring and then walking the ring clockwise to find the first node with a position larger than the item's position.

In the Dynamo system, each data item is replicated at N hosts, where N is a parameter configured per instance. Each key K is assigned to a coordinator node. The coordinator is in charge of the replication of the data items that fall within its range. In addition to locally storing each key within its range, the coordinator replicates these keys at the (N – 1) clockwise successor nodes in the ring. This results in a system where each node is responsible for the region of the ring between it and its Nth predecessor. Node B replicates the key K at nodes C and D in addition to storing it locally. Node D will store the keys that fall in the ranges (A, B), (B, C), and (C, D).

The list of nodes that are responsible for storing a particular key is called the preference list. The system is designed so that every node in the system can determine which nodes should be in this list for any particular key. Thus, each node becomes responsible for the region in the ring between it and its predecessor node on the ring. The principle advantage of consistent hashing is that departure or arrival of a node affects only its immediate neighbors and other nodes remain unaffected.

11.3.2.1 DynamoDB Data Model

The basic data model in DynamoDB uses the concepts of tables, items, and attributes. A table in DynamoDB does not have a schema; it holds a collection of self-describing items. Each item will consist of a number of (attribute, value) pairs, and attribute values can be single-valued or multivalued. So basically, a table will hold a collection of items, and each item is a self-describing record (or object). DynamoDB also allows the user to specify the items in JSON format, and the system will convert them to the internal storage format of DynamoDB.

When a table is created, it is required to specify a table name and a primary key; the primary key will be used to rapidly locate the items in the table. Thus, the primary key is the key and the item is the value for the DynamoDB key-value store. The primary key attribute must exist in every item in the table.

The primary key can be one of the following two types:

1. A single attribute: The DynamoDB system will use this attribute to build a hash index on the items in the table. This is called a hash type primary key. The items are not ordered in storage on the value of the hash attribute.
2. A pair of attributes: This is called a hash and range type primary key. The primary key will be a pair of attributes (A, B): attribute A will be used for hashing, and because there will be multiple items with the same value of A, the B values will be used for ordering the records with the same A value. A table with this type of key can have additional secondary indexes defined on its attributes. For example, if we want to store multiple versions of some type of items in a table, we could use ItemID as hash and Date or Timestamp as range in a hash, and range type as the primary key.

11.4 Document Databases

Document-based or document-oriented NoSQL systems typically store data as collections of similar documents. The individual documents somewhat resemble "complex objects" or XML documents, but a major difference between document-based systems versus object and object-relational systems, and XML is that there is no requirement to specify a schema—rather, the documents are specified as self-describing data. Although the documents in a collection should be similar, they can have different data elements (attributes), and new documents can have new data elements that do not exist in any of the current documents in the collection. The system basically extracts the data element names from the self-describing documents in the collection, and the user can request that the system create indexes on some of the data elements. Documents can be specified in various formats, such as XML (Kale 2015). A popular language to specify documents in NoSQL systems is JavaScript Object Notation (JSON).

JSON, short for JavaScript Object Notation, is a lightweight computer data interchange format, easy for humans to read and write, and, at the same time, easy for machines to parse and generate. Another key feature of JSON is that it is completely language independent. Programming in JSON does not raise any challenge for programmers experienced with the C family of languages.

Though XML is a widely adopted data exchange format, there are several reasons for preferring JSON to XML:

- Data entities exchanged with JSON are typed, while XML data are typeless (some of the built-in data types available in JSON are string, number, array, and Boolean); XML data, on the other hand, are all strings.
- JSON is lighter and faster than XML as on-the-wire data format.
- JSON integrates natively with JavaScript, a very popular programming language used to develop applications on the client side; consequently, JSON objects can be directly interpreted in JavaScript code, while XML data need to be parsed and assigned to variables through the tedious usage of Document Object Model APIs (DOM APIs).

JSON is built on two structures:

1. A collection of name/value pairs. In various languages, this is realized as an object, record, structure, dictionary, hash table, keyed list, or associative array.
2. An ordered list of values. In most languages, this is realized as an array, vector, list, or sequence.

Document databases use a key-value approach to storing data but with important differences from key-value databases: a document database stores values as semistructured documents, typically in a standard format such as JavaScript Object Notation (JSON) or Extensible Markup Language (XML). Instead of storing each attribute of an entity with a separate key, document databases store multiple attributes in a single document.

Document here does not refer to word processing or other office productivity files, it specifically refers to data structures that are stored as strings or binary representations of strings.

Unlike relational databases, document databases do not necessitate defining a fixed schema before adding data to the database—adding a document to the database automatically creates the underlying data structures needed to support the document. The lack of a fixed schema gives developers more flexibility with document databases than they have with relational databases. Documents can also have embedded documents and lists of multiple values within a document, which effectively eliminates the need for joining documents the way you join tables in a relational database.

Partitioning, which refers to splitting a document database and distributing different parts of the database to different servers, is of two types:

- Vertical partitioning: It is the process of improving database performance by separating columns of a relational table into multiple separate tables or documents into multiple separate collections; this technique is particularly useful when you have some columns or documents that are accessed more frequently than others.
- Horizontal partitioning: It is the process of improving database performance by rows in a relational database or dividing a database by documents in a document database with the separate parts or shards being stored shard-wise on separate servers. Sharding is done based upon range of values or a hash function or a list of values.

Document databases provide application programming interfaces (APIs) or query languages that enable you to retrieve documents based on attribute values. They offer support for querying structures with multiple attributes, like relational databases, but offer more flexibility with regard to variation in the attributes used by each document.

Document databases are probably the most popular type of NoSQL database.

11.4.1 CouchDB

Cluster of Unreliable Commodity Hardware Data Base (CouchDB) is an open source, NoSQL, web-inclined database that uses JSON to store the data and relies on JavaScript as its query language. It uses HTTP for data access and merits with multimaster replication. CouchDB does not use tables at all for data storage or relationship management; rather it is a collection of independent documents, maintaining their self-contained schemas and data, which form the database. In CouchDB, multiversion concurrency control helps avoiding locks during write operation and document metadata holds the revision information and any offline data updates are merged and stale ones are deleted. CouchDB is equipped with a built-in administration web interface, called Futon.

11.4.2 MongoDB

MongoDB (term extracted from the word humongous) is an open source, document-oriented NoSQL database. It enables master–slave replication:

- Master performs reads and writes.
- Slave copies the data received from master, performs the read operation, and backs up the data. Slaves do not participate in write operations but may select an alternate master in case the current master fails.

Unlike the traditional relational databases, MongoDB uses a binary format of JSON-like documents and dynamic schemas. MongoDB enables flexible schemas and common fields of various documents in a collection can have disparate types of the data.

The query system of MongoDB can return particular fields and query set compass search by fields, range queries, regular expression search, and so on, and may also include user-defined complex JavaScript functions.

The latest release of the data model is equipped with more advanced concepts such as sharding that address the scaling issues, and the replica sets that assist in automatic failover and recovery. Sharding can be understood as a process that addresses the demand of the data growth by storing data records across multiple machines without any downtime. Each shard (server) functions as an independent database and all the shards collectively form a single logical database. Each config server possesses the metadata about the cluster such as information about the shard and data chunks on the shard. For protection and safety, there exist multiple config servers, such that if one of these servers goes down, another takes charge without any interruption in shard functioning. Mongod is the key database process and represents one shard. In a replica set, one of the mongod processes serves as the master and if it goes down, another is delegated for carrying out the master's responsibilities: Mongos intermediates as a routing process between the client and the sharded database.

11.4.2.1 MongoDB Features

1. *Consistency:* Consistency in the MongoDB database is configured by using the replica sets and choosing to wait for the writes to be replicated to all the slaves or a given number of slaves. Every write can specify the number of servers the write has to be propagated to before it returns as successful.
2. *Transactions:* In traditional RDBMS, transactions mean modifying the database with insert, update, or delete commands over different tables and then deciding to keep the changes or not by using commit or rollback. These constructs are generally not available in NoSQL solutions—a write either succeeds or fails. Transactions at the single-document level are known as "atomic" transactions.

   By default, all writes are reported as successful. A finer control over the write can be achieved by using the WriteConcern parameter. We ensure that order is written to more than one node before it is reported successful by using WriteConcern. REPLICAS_SAFE. Different levels of WriteConcern let you choose the safety level during writes; for example, when writing log entries, you can use the lowest level of safety, WriteConcern.NONE.
3. *Availability:* MongoDB implements replication, providing high availability using replica sets. In a replica set, there are two or more nodes participating in an asynchronous master–slave replication. The replica-set nodes elect the master, or primary, among themselves. Assuming all the nodes have equal voting rights, some nodes can be favored for being closer to the other servers, for having more RAM, and so on; users can affect this by assigning a priority—a number between 0 and 1,000—to a node.

   All requests go to the master node, and the data are replicated to the slave nodes. If the master node goes down, the remaining nodes in the replica set vote among themselves to elect a new master; all future requests are routed to the new master, and the slave nodes start getting data from the new master. When the node that had failed comes back online, it joins in as a slave and catches up with the rest of the nodes by pulling all the data it needs to get current.
4. *Query:* One of the good features of document databases, as compared to key-value stores, is that we can query the data inside the document without having to retrieve the whole document by its key and then introspect the document. This feature brings these databases closer to the RDBMS query model.

MongoDB has a query language that is expressed via JSON and has constructs such as $query for the where clause, $orderby for sorting the data, or $explain to show the execution plan of the query. There are many more constructs such as these that can be combined to create a MongoDB query.

5. *Scaling:* Scaling implies adding nodes or changing data storage without simply migrating the database to a bigger box. Scaling for heavy-read loads can be achieved by adding more read slaves, so that all the reads can be directed to the slaves. Given a heavy-read application, with our three-node replica-set cluster, we can add more read capacity to the cluster as the read load increases just by adding more slave nodes to the replica set to execute reads with the slaveOk flag. When a new node is added, it will sync up with the existing nodes, join the replica set as a secondary node, and start serving read requests. An advantage of this setup is that we do not have to restart any other nodes, and there is no downtime for the application either.

11.4.2.2 MongoDB Data Model

MongoDB documents are stored in Binary JSON (BSON) format, which is a variation of JSON with some additional data types and is more efficient for storage than JSON. Individual documents are stored in a collection. The operation createCollection is used to create each collection.

For example, the following command can be used to create a collection called project to hold PROJECTobjects from the CLIENT database.

```
db.createCollection("project", {capped : true, size : 1500000, max : 600})
```

This second command will create another document collection called worker to hold information about the EMPLOYEEs who work on each project.

```
db.createCollection("worker", {capped : true, size : 5242880, max : 2000})
```

Each document in a collection has a unique ObjectId field, called _id, which is automatically indexed in the collection unless the user explicitly requests no index for the _id field. The value of ObjectId

1. Can be specified by the user: User-generated ObjectsIds can have any value specified by the user as long as it uniquely identifies the document and so these Ids are similar to primary keys in relational systems.
2. Can be system generated if the user does not specify an _id field for a particular document. System-generated ObjectIds have a specific format, which combines the timestamp when the object is created (4 bytes, in an internal MongoDB format), the node id (3 bytes), the process id (2 bytes), and a counter (3 bytes) into a 16-byte Id value.

A collection does not have a schema. The structure of the data fields in documents is chosen based on how documents will be accessed and used, and the user can choose a normalized design (similar to normalized relational tuples) or a denormalized design (similar to XML documents or complex objects). Interdocument references can be specified by storing in one document the ObjectId or ObjectIds of other related documents.

The _id values are user defined, and the documents whose _id starts with P (for project) will be stored in the "project" collection, whereas those whose _id starts with W (for worker) will be stored in the "worker" collection.

The workers' information is embedded in the project document; so there is no need for the "worker" collection:

```
{
_id: "P1",
Pname: "ProductL",
Plocation: "Pune",
Workers: [
{ Ename: "Amitabh Bacchan",
Hours: 32.5
},
{ Ename: "Priyanka Chopra",
Hours: 20.0
}
]
};
```

This is known as the denormalized pattern, which is similar to creating a complex object or an XML document.

Another option is where worker references are embedded in the project document, but the worker documents themselves are stored in a separate "worker" collection:

```
{
_id: "P1",
Pname: "ProductL",
Plocation: "Pune",
WorkerIds: ["W1", "W2"]
}

{ _id: "W1",
Ename: "Amitabh Bacchan",
Hours: 32.5
}

{ _id: "W2",
Ename: "Priyanka Chopra",
Hours: 20.0
}
```

A third option is to use a normalized design, similar to First Normal Form (1NF) relations:

```
{
_id: "P1",
Pname: "ProductL",
Plocation: "Pune"
}

{ _id: "W1",
Ename: "Amitabh Bacchan",
ProjectId: "P1",
Hours: 32.5
}
```

```
{ _id: "W2",
Ename: "PriyankaBacchan",
ProjectId: "P1",
Hours: 20.0
}
```

The choice of which design option to use depends on how the data will be accessed.

11.4.2.3 MongoDB CRUD Operations

MongoDb has several CRUD operations, where CRUD stands for create, read, update, delete. Documents can be created and inserted into their collections using the insert operation, whose format is

```
db.<collection_name>.insert(<document(s)>)
```

The parameters of the insert operation can include either a single document or an array of documents, as shown below:

```
db.project.insert( { _id: "P1", Pname: "ProductL", Plocation: "Pune" } )
db.worker.insert( [ { _id: "W1", Ename: "Amitabh Bacchan", ProjectId: "P1",
Hours: 32.5 },
{ _id: "W2", Ename: "Priyanka Chopra", ProjectId: "P1",
Hours: 20.0 } ] )
```

The delete operation is called remove, and the format is

```
db.<collection_name>.remove(<condition>)
```

The documents to be removed from the collection are specified by a Boolean condition on some of the fields in the collection documents.

There is also an update operation, which has a condition to select certain documents, and a $set clause to specify the update. It is also possible to use the update operation to replace an existing document with another one but keep the same ObjectId.

For read queries, the main command is called find, and the format is: db.<collection_name>.find(<condition>)

General Boolean conditions can be specified as <condition>, and the documents in the collection that return true are selected for the query result.

11.4.2.4 MongoDB Distributed Systems Characteristics

Most MongoDB updates are atomic if they refer to a single document, but MongoDB also provides a pattern for specifying transactions on multiple documents. Since MongoDB is a distributed system, the two-phase commit method is used to ensure atomicity and consistency of multidocument transactions.

1. *MongoDB Replication:* The concept of "replica set" is used in MongoDB to create multiple copies of the same data set on different nodes in the distributed system, and it uses a variation of the master–slave approach for replication.

   All write operations must be applied to the primary copy and then propagated to the secondaries. For read operations, the user can choose the particular read preference for their application. The default read preference processes all reads at the primary copy, so all read and write operations are performed at the primary node. In this case, secondary copies are mainly to make sure that the system continues operation if the primary fails, and MongoDB can ensure that every read request gets the latest document value. To increase read performance, it is possible to set the read preference so that read requests can be processed at any replica (primary or secondary); however, a read at a secondary is not guaranteed to get the latest version of a document because there can be a delay in propagating writes from the primary to the secondaries.

2. *Sharding in MongoDB:* When a collection holds a very large number of documents or requires a large storage space, storing all the documents in one node can lead to performance problems, particularly if there are many user operations accessing the documents concurrently using various CRUD operations. Sharding or horizontal partitioning of the documents in the collection divides the documents into disjoint partitions known as shards. This allows the system to add more nodes as needed by a process known as horizontal or scaling-out of the distributed system, and to store the shards of the collection on different nodes to achieve load balancing. Each node will process only those operations pertaining to the documents in the shard stored at that node. Also, each shard will contain fewer documents than if the entire collection were stored at one node, thus further improving performance.

The user must specify a particular document field to be used as the basis for partitioning the documents into shards. The partitioning field—known as the shard key in MongoDB—must have two characteristics:

- It must exist in every document in the collection.
- It must have an index.

The ObjectId can be used as the partitioning filed, but any other field possessing these two characteristics can also be used as the basis for sharding.

The values of the shard key are divided into chunks, and the documents are partitioned based on the chunks of shard key either through

1. Hash partitioning: Hash partitioning applies a hash function h(K) to each shard key K, and the partitioning of keys into chunks is based on the hash values. If most searches retrieve one document at a time, hash partitioning may be preferable because it randomizes the distribution of shard key values into chunks.
2. Range partitioning: In general, if range queries are commonly applied to a collection (for example, retrieving all documents whose shard key value is between 200 and 400), then range partitioning is preferred because each range query will typically be submitted to a single node that contains all the required documents in one shard.

When sharding is used, MongoDB queries are submitted to a module called the query router, which keeps track of which nodes contain which shards based on the particular partitioning method used on the shard keys. The query (CRUD operation) will be routed to the nodes that contain the shards that hold the documents that the query is requesting.

If the system cannot determine which shards hold the required documents, the query will be submitted to all the nodes that hold shards of the collection.

Sharding and replication are used together; sharding focuses on improving performance via load balancing and horizontal scalability, whereas replication focuses on ensuring system availability when certain nodes fail in the distributed system.

11.5 Graph Databases

A graph database uses structures called nodes and relationships (or edges or link or arc). A node or vertex is an object that has an identifier and a set of attributes; a relationship is a link between two nodes that contains attributes about that relation. For instance, a node could be a city, and a relationship between cities could be used to store information about the distance and travel time between cities. Much like nodes, relationships have properties; weight of relationship represents some value about the relationship. A common problem encountered when working with graphs is to find the least-weighted path between two vertices. The weight can represent cost of using the edge, time required to traverse the edge, or some other metric that you are trying to minimize.

> Graph theory is not related to the study of charts and other visualizations sometimes referred to as graphs. Graph databases get their name from a branch of mathematics called graph theory. Graph theory is the study of objects represented by vertices and relations between them represented by edges.

Both nodes and relationships can have complex structures. There are two types of relationships: directed and undirected. Directed edges have a direction. A path through a graph is a set of vertices along with the edges between those vertices; paths are important because they capture information about how vertices in a graph are related. If edges are directed, the path is a directed path. If the graph is undirected, the paths in it are undirected paths.

Graph databases are designed to model adjacency between objects; every node in the database contains pointers to adjacent objects in the database. This allows for fast operations that require following paths through a graph. Graph databases allow for more efficient querying when paths through graphs are involved.

Many application areas are efficiently modeled as graphs and, in those cases, a graph database may streamline application development and minimize the amount of code you would have to write.

Graph databases are the most specialized of the four types of NoSQL databases.

11.5.1 OrientDB

OrientDB is an open source graph-document NoSQL data model. It largely extends the graph data model but combines the features of both document and graph data models up to a certain extents. At the data level for the schema-less content, it is document based in nature, whereas to traverse the relationship, it is graph oriented, and therefore, fully supports schema-less, schema-full, or schema-mixed data. The database is completely distributed in nature and can be spanned across several servers. It supports the state of the art multimaster replication distributed system. It is a fully ACID-compliant data model and also offers role-based security profile to the users. This database engine is light weighted, written in Java, and hence, is portable in nature, platform independent, and can run on Windows, Linux, etc. One of the salient features of OrientDB is its fast indexing system for lookups and insertion, and that is based on MVRB-Tree algorithm, originated from Red-Black Tree and B+ Tree.

OrientDB relies on SQL for basic operations and uses some graph operator extensions to avoid SQL joins in order to deal with relationships in data; graph traversal language is used as the query processing language and can loosely be termed as OrientDB's SQL. OrientDB has out-of-the-box supports for web such as HTTP, RESTful, and JSON without any external intermediaries.

11.5.2 Neo4j

Neo4j is being considered as the world's leading graph data model and is a potential member of the NoSQL family. It is an open source, robust, disk-based graph data model that fully supports ACID transactions and is implemented in Java. The graph nature of Neo4j imparts it with agility and speediness in comparison to relational databases for a similar set of operations. It is significantly faster and outperforms the former with greater than 1000x performance for several potentially important real-time scenarios.

Similar to an ordinary property (simple key-value pairs) graph, the Neo4j graph data model consists of nodes and edges where every node represents an entity, and an edge between two nodes corresponds to the relationship between those attached entities. As location has become an important aspect of data today, most of the applications have to deal with the highly associated data, forming a network (or graph); social networking sites are the obvious examples of such applications. Unlike relational database models, which require upfront schemas that restrict the absorption of the agile and ad hoc data, Neo4j is a schema-less data model that works on a bottom-up approach that allows easy expansion of the database to enable ad hoc and dynamic data.

Neo4j has its own declarative and expressive query language, called Cypher, which has pattern-matching capabilities among the nodes and relationship during the data mining and data updating. Cypher is extremely useful when it comes to creating, updating, or removal of nodes, properties, and relationships in the graph. Simplicity is one of the salient features of Cypher, evolving as a humane query language, and is designed for not only developers but for the naïve users also, who write the ad hoc queries.

11.5.2.1 Neo4j Features

1. *Consistency:* Since graph databases are operating on connected nodes, most graph database solutions usually do not support distributing the nodes on different servers. Within a single server, data are always consistent, especially in Neo4i, which is fully ACID compliant. When running Neo4j in a cluster, a write to the master is eventually synchronized to the slaves, while slaves are always available for read. Writes to slaves are allowed and are immediately synchronized to the

master; other slaves will not be synchronized immediately, though they will have to wait for the data to propagate from the master.

2. *Transactions:* Though Neo4j is ACID compliant, the way of managing transactions differs from the standard way of doing transactions in an RDBMS.
3. *Availability:* Neo4j achieves high availability by providing for replicated slaves. These slaves can also handle writes: when they are written to, they synchronize the write to the current master, and the write is committed first at the master and then at the slave. Other slaves will eventually get the update.
4. *Query:* Neo4j allows you to query the graph for properties of the nodes, traverse the graph, or navigate the nodes' relationships using language bindings. Properties of a node can be indexed using the indexing service. Similarly, properties of relationships or edges can be indexed, so a node or edge can be found by the value. Indexes should be queried to find the starting node to begin a traversal. Neo4j uses Lucene as its indexing service.

   Graph databases are really powerful when you want to traverse the graphs at any depth and specify a starting node for the traversal. This is especially useful when you are trying to find nodes that are related to the starting node at more than one level down. As the depth of the graph increases, it makes more sense to traverse the relationships by using a Traverser where you can specify that you are looking for INCOMING, OUTGOING, or BOTH types of relationships. You can also make the traverser go top-down or sideways on the graph by using order values of BREADTH_FIRST or DEPTH_FIRST.
5. *Scaling:* With graph databases, sharding is difficult, as graph databases are not aggregate oriented but relationship oriented. Since any given node can be related to any other node, storing-related nodes on the same server are better for graph traversal. Since traversing a graph when the nodes are on different machines is not good for performance, graph database scaling can be achieved by using some common techniques:

   - We can add enough RAM to the server so that the working set of nodes and relationships is held entirely in memory. This technique is helpful only if the dataset that we are working with fit in a realistic amount of RAM.
   - We can improve the read scaling of the database by adding more slaves with read-only access to the data, with all the writes going to the master. This pattern of writing once and reading from many servers is useful when the dataset is large enough to not fit in a single machine's RAM, but small enough to be replicated across multiple machines. Slaves can also contribute to availability and read scaling, as they can be configured to never become a master, remaining always read-only.
   - When the dataset size makes replication impractical, we can shard the data from the application side using domain-specific knowledge.

11.5.2.2 Neo4j Data Model

The data model in Neo4j organizes data using the concepts of nodes and relationships. Both nodes and relationships can have properties that store the data items associated with nodes and relationships. Nodes can have labels; a node can have zero, one, or several labels.

The nodes that have the same label are grouped into a collection that identifies a subset of the nodes in the database graph for querying purposes. Relationships are directed; each relationship has a start node and an end node as well as a relationship type, which serves a role similar to that of a node label by identifying similar relationships that have the same relationship type. Properties can be specified via a map pattern, which is made of one or more "name:value" pairs enclosed in curly brackets; for example {Lname: 'Bacchan', Fname : 'Amitabh', Minit : 'B'}.

There are various ways in which nodes and relationships can be created—for example, by calling appropriate Neo4j operations from various Neo4j APIs. We will just show the high-level syntax for creating nodes and relationships; to do so, we will use the Neo4j CREATE command, which is part of the high-level declarative query language Cypher. Neo4j has many options and variations for creating nodes and relationships using various scripting interfaces, but a full discussion is outside the scope of our presentation.

1. Indexing and node identifiers: When a node is created, the Neo4j system creates an internal, unique, system-defined identifier for each node. To retrieve individual nodes using other properties of the nodes efficiently, the user can create indexes for the collection of nodes that have a particular label. Typically, one or more of the properties of the nodes in that collection can be indexed. For example, Empid can be used to index nodes with the EMPLOYEE label, Dno to index the nodes with the DEPARTMENT label, and Pno to index the nodes with the PROJECT label.
2. Optional schema: A schema is optional in Neo4j. Graphs can be created and used without a schema, but in Neo4j version 2.0, a few schema-related functions were added. The main features related to schema creation involve creating indexes and constraints based on the labels and properties. For example, it is possible to create the equivalent of a key constraint on a property of a label, so all nodes in the collection of nodes associated with the label must have unique values for that property.

11.6 Summary

This chapter introduces NoSQL database vendor products. It introduces the characteristics and examples of NoSQL databases, namely, column, key-value, document, and graph databases. The chapter provides a snapshot overview of column databases (Cassandra, Google BigTable, and HBase), key-value databases (Riak, Amazon Dynamo), document databases (CouchDB, MongoDB), and graph databases (OrientDB, Neo4j).

12

Big Data Development with Hadoop

A Hadoop distribution is made of a number of separate frameworks that are designed to work together. The frameworks are extensible as well as the Hadoop framework platform. Hadoop has evolved to support fast data as well as big data. Big data was initially about large batch processing of data. Now organizations also need to make business decisions real time or near real time as the data arrives. Fast data involves the capability to act on the data as it arrives. Hadoop's flexible framework architecture supports the processing of data with different run-time characteristics.

A software framework is an abstraction in which software providing generic functionality can be selectively changed by additional user-written code, thus providing application-specific software. A software framework is a universal and reusable software platform to develop applications, products, and solutions. Software frameworks include support programs, compilers, code libraries, tool sets, and application programming interfaces (APIs) that bring together all the different components to enable development of a project or solution.

Frameworks contain the following key distinguishing features that separate them from normal libraries:

- *Inversion of control*: In a framework, unlike in libraries or normal user applications, the overall program's flow of control is not dictated by the caller but by the framework.
- *Default behavior*: A framework has a default behavior. This default behavior must be some useful behavior and not a series of no-ops.
- *Non-modifiable framework code*: The framework code, in general, is not supposed to be modified, excepting extensibility. Users can extend the framework but should not modify its code.
- *Extensibility*: A framework can be extended by the user usually by selective overriding or specialized by user code to provide specific functionality.

The main daemons for Hadoop frameworks are Java applications that run in JVMs. There are also separate frameworks that are not part of a standard distribution that can be added to Hadoop to add additional functionality. Popular open source frameworks can be added to new Hadoop distributions. The significance of using Java for these core essentials is its property of *write once and run everywhere*: Java enables portability. The current release of Hadoop is a single merged Java code set for both Linux and Windows.

A Hadoop cluster is made up of a number of daemons and software processes that work together to provide a complete solution to meet today's data needs. The Hadoop master and worker daemons all run as Java processes in their individual JVMs. Like any high-performance computing environment, tuning of the JVMs and their garbage collection is important.

There are three types of Hadoop processes:

1. *Master servers*: Primary management daemons coordinate with slave servers.
   - Master servers manage the framework for which they are responsible. The master servers include the following:
   - *NameNode*: Responsible for all I/O and storage metadata.
   - *ResourceManager*: The scheduler responsible for all processing.
   - *Zookeeper processes*: Provides coordination service.
   - *Standby NameNode*: Provides failover capability for the NameNode.
   - *Secondary NameNode*: Cleans out the edit logs of the NameNodes metadata if a standby NameNode is not used. The cluster can have a standby NameNode (HA) or a secondary NameNode (clean edit.log) but not both. If there is a standby NameNode, it will clean the edit.log, so a secondary NameNode is not needed.
   - *Backup NameNode*: Similar to the secondary NameNode, it receives journal streams of file system edits from the NameNode as opposed to downloading fsimage or edit files. This stream is persisted to disk and to memory immediately.
   - *Secondary ResourceManager*: Provides failover capability for the resource manager.
   - Ozzie server: Schedules jobs and manages the workflow of jobs submitted.
   - *HiveServer2*: Provides the JDBC or ODBC interface for Hive queries.
   - *HBase Master(s)*: Manages the HBase environment.
   - *Ambari server*: Used for provisioning, managing, and monitoring a Hadoop cluster.
   - *Ganglia server*: Manages the Ganglia environment that collects.
   - *Nagios server*: Collects information for alerts.
   - *JobHistoryServer*: Collects and manages job history for MapReduce jobs.
   - *WebHCatServer*: Processes HTTP requests for running YARN applications such as MapReduce, Hive, and Pig, as well as HCatalog DDL commands.
2. *Slave servers*: Responsible for all data storage and computational activities. I/O operations occur on the data nodes where the slave server processes run.

   All data are stored on the worker nodes (slave servers). Typically, data processing occurs on the worker nodes. The worker node servers are also referred to as slave servers or DataNodes. DataNode is the term most commonly used. A slave server can contain a DataNode, NodeManager, or both.

   Slave servers include the following:
   - *DataNodes*: Handle all I/O locally on their own nodes. These are slave servers for the name nod.
   - *NodeManagers*: Manage all YARN processes running on their slave servers. These are slave servers for the resource manager.
   - *HBase region servers*: Responsible for all local processing of HBase applications. These are slave servers for the HBase masters. These processes run on the DataNodes.
   - Different frameworks such as Storm, Kafka, Spark, Accumulo, and Cassandra.

These frameworks can have different processes that may be running in the Hadoop cluster or in a different cluster. Each framework has separate processes for its operations.

3. *Clients*: Responsible for launching applications.
    - Clients run the applications in the cluster.
    - Hadoop client launches Tez and MapReduce applications.
    - Pig client launches Pig scripts. Converts to Tez or MapReduce.
    - Hive client launches Hive SQL statements. Converts to Tez or MapReduce.

Master servers manage the Hadoop services or frameworks. DataNode servers handle all the HDFS storage activity. NodeManager servers handle all the computational tasks. Traditionally, each worker (data) node runs one DataNode process and one NodeManager process. Client processes launch the applications. Examples include the Hadoop, Pig, and Hive clients. Third-party software can also be running on the client nodes.

Master servers and slave servers are daemons that stay up and running all the time. A client process runs until the job it initiated is complete, but newer architectures supported by virtualization enable these functions to be separated into different virtual machines on the same physical host. This enables secure multitenancy and more effective elasticity.

The Hadoop execution environment supports a constellation of distributed data processing capabilities that are designed to run using the Hadoop MapReduce architecture. Several of these have become official Hadoop subprojects within the Apache Software Foundation. These include a distributed file system called Hadoop Distributed File System (HDFS), which is analogous to GFS in the Google MapReduce implementation. HBase is a distributed column-oriented database that provides similar random access read/write capabilities as and is modeled after Bigtable implemented by Google. HBase is not relational and does not support SQL, but provides a Java API and a command-line shell for table management. Hive is a data warehouse system built on top of Hadoop that provides SQL-like query capabilities for data summarization, ad hoc queries, and analysis of large datasets. Other Apache-sanctioned projects for Hadoop include Pig—a high-level data-flow language and execution framework for parallel computation, and ZooKeeper—a high-performance coordination service for distributed applications.

The Hadoop ecosystem is constituted of:

- HDFS: A distributed file system that provides high-throughput access to application data
- MapReduce: A software framework for distributed processing of large data sets on compute clusters
- HBase: A scalable, distributed database that supports structured data storage for large tables
- ZooKeeper: A high-performance coordination service for distributed applications

- Oozie: A scalable workflow system that is used to coordinate the execution of multiple MapReduce jobs
- Pig: A high-level dataflow language and execution framework for parallel computation
- Hive: A data warehouse infrastructure that provides data summarization and ad hoc querying
- Mahout: A scalable machine learning and data mining library

The Hadoop ecosystem also contains several frameworks for integration with the rest of the enterprise:

- Sqoop: A connectivity tool for moving data between relational databases and data warehouses, and Hadoop
- Flume: A distributed, reliable, and highly available service for efficiently collecting, aggregating, and moving large amounts of data from individual machines to HDFS

Hadoop's ecosystem is growing beyond the core components listed above to provide newer capabilities and components, such as the following:

- Mahout: A machine-learning and data-mining library that provides MapReduce implementations for popular algorithms used for clustering, regression testing, and statistical modeling
- BigTop: A formal process and framework for packaging and interoperability testing of Hadoop's subprojects and related components
- Whirr: A set of libraries that allows users to easily spin up Hadoop clusters on top of Amazon EC2, Rackspace, or any virtual infrastructure
- Ambari: A project aimed at simplifying Hadoop management by providing support for provisioning, managing, and monitoring Hadoop clusters . Figure 12.1 shows an overview of the Hadoop ecosystem.

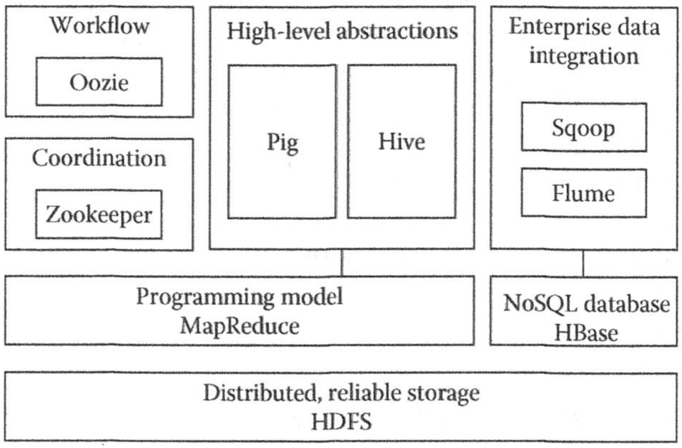

FIGURE 12.1
Hadoop ecosystem.

> The various capabilities and components described here may refer to different distributions without specifically identifying them; this should not be cause for any confusion since this section aims to provide a general overview of the various aspects of Hadoop distributions.

TABLE 12.1

Hadoop Ecosystem Classification by Timescale and General Purpose of Usage

	Purpose			
Timescale	**Ingest**	**Process**	**Persist**	**Extract**
Batch	Flume, Sqoop, Kafka, NFS	Hive, Pig	Files	NFS, Teradata, and other connectors
Ad hoc	Flume, NFS	Spark Drill, Solr, Hive	File, HBase, MapR-DB	ODBC tools such as Tableau, direct web access
Streaming and Realtime	Flume, Kafka, NFS	Spark streaming, Strom, Samza	File (Few platforms) HBase, MapR-DB	HBase MapR-DB NFS

Table 12.1 classifies Hadoop tools based upon the timescale of operations and general purpose of the usage. The timescale ranges from batch, through ad hoc, to streaming and real time. Batch processing is done typically on all the data that accumulate over a period of minutes to days or even a month or longer. The emphasis in batch processing is on total throughput, and it usually does not matter how long it takes to process any single input record as long as many records are processed quickly.

In ad hoc processing, the emphasis is on a quick (in human terms) response, but the data being processed is very much like the input for a batch process in that it typically consists of all the data available or all the data for a recent time period. In fact, ad hoc processing can be thought of as batch processing that is initiated by some user action instead of being based on a schedule. Ad hoc processing is sometimes mislabeled as real time because there is a user-visible response time, but this is a serious misnomer that could lead to some confusion about which tool is appropriate to use.

With streaming or real-time processing, records are processed as they arrive or in very small batches known as micro batches. Real-time processing adds the additional constraint that records must not only be processed as they arrive, but that processing must also be completed before a prespecified deadline passes. Requiring that records be processed one at a time is more expensive than processing large batches of records since it does not allow certain economies of scale that are possible in batch processing.

General purpose of usage is spread across ingestion, data processing or transformation, persistence, and extraction. Ingestion is the process of getting data into a system with minimal processing or transformation applied during ingestion. Processing is where all significant computing and transformation is done. The most common operation in processing raw data is that it is aggregated into summaries or arranged into profiles. Data is commonly persisted after processing, but in the Hadoop systems, data is commonly persisted in nearly raw form as it is ingested before it is processed, thus enabling the retention of relatively raw data that makes it possible for error to be performed in stream processing.

Different forms of persistence lend themselves to different kinds of processing. For example, files can be used to achieve very high scan rates that are particularly useful in batch programming, while HBase are very useful in real-time or stream processing where updates may have to be made each time a record is processed.

12.1 Hadoop MapReduce

Hadoop's MapReduce computing platform consists of two components: One is JobTracker, which acts as a master in the Hadoop cluster, while the other is called TaskTrackers.

A typical activity flow in Hadoop is as follows:

1. A server, called JobTracker, accepts jobs (MapReduce programs) from clients. A job is associated with a mapper method, a reducer method, and a set of input files and output files.
2. The JobTracker contacts the Name node to get the location of the input files. The JobTracker applies appropriate scheduling algorithm to assign tasks to a set of computing nodes, called TaskTrackers. The scheduling algorithm takes data locality into account to optimize data movements.
3. The JobTracker distributes the mapper and reducer methods among the scheduled TaskTrackers. In addition to the mapper and reducer methods, the JobTtracker also distributes the job configuration so that the mapper and reducer methods run based on the provided configuration.
4. The TaskTrackers performs the assigned mapper task. The TaskTrackers reads input from data nodes and applies the given method on the input.
5. The map task creates and writes to intermediate key-value pairs to a file on the local file system of the TaskTracker.
6. The partitioner reads the results from the map task and finds an appropriate TaskTracker to run reduce task. The intermediate results emitted by map tasks are then propagated to reduce tasks.
7. The TaskTrackers that are scheduled to run reduce tasks apply operations programmed in reduce function on the data elements streamed from map tasks and emit key-value pairs as output. The output data elements are then written to HDFS.

It is important to highlight that the tasks come down to data location to perform designated operations. If there are no computing resources available at the machine where the data is located, the computation is carried out by the machine nearest to the data. In the MapReduce context such behavior is called *data locality*. Data locality improves the distributed computations by reducing the data movements in the network within the cluster.

Figure 12.2 presents the Hadoop MapReduce architecture.

12.1.1 MapReduce Processing

12.1.1.1 JobTracker

JobTracker is a server that has the implementation for necessary user interfaces needed to submit and run a *map reduce* job. Once a map reduce job is submitted to a Hadoop cluster, the JobTracker of the Hadoop cluster engineers a scheme to run the submitted job. The

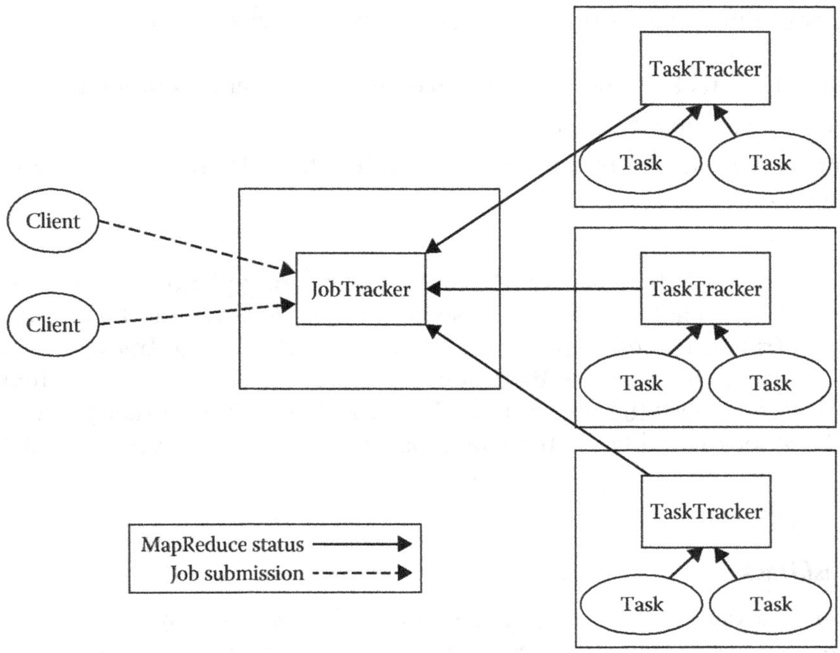

FIGURE 12.2
Hadoop MapReduce architecture.

scheme involves identifying TaskTrackers in the cluster to perform map operations, triggering the mappers on Tasktrackers, monitoring the task while it is running, etc. JobTracker runs in listening mode to take requests from clients. When a client submits a job, the jobTracker communicates with the NameNode to obtain a list of machines that carry the input data for the job. The list is used in an optimization algorithm, and the JobTracker comes up with an optimized scheme to run the job on TaskTrackers.

As mentioned earlier, the scheme attempts to reduce network bandwidth utilization within the cluster by adopting the data locality feature. By data locality, the preference in decreasing priority to run a task on a data chunk is

- The machine where the data is located
- The rack where the data is located
- A computing machine in the cluster

It is not always possible to find a node for a map task to run on local data; then, the next best possibility is to find a node in the same rack. If there is no node available on the same rack to take the task, then whatsoever machine in the cluster that can handle the task, even if not optimally, performs the task. One of the reasons a TaskTracker may not be available to take a task is that the TaskTracker may have been running the tasks up to its maximum capacity. Whenever the JobTracker identifies a TaskTracker to run a task, it monitors the task until it terminates. If a task fails on a TaskTracker, the JobTracker finds another optimal TaskTracker to handle the task. By restarting a task on another TaskTracker, the JobTracker ensures that the job does not terminate even if there is a single task that has failed even once. A job cannot be deemed to have been completed unless all the tasks of the job complete without errors.

The responsibilities of a JobTracker can be summarized as follows:

1. Manage TaskTrackers and their resources as jobs are being submitted
2. Schedule tasks among available resources
3. Monitor the tasks of jobs and restart the failed tasks for the configured number of attempts

JobTracker is the heart of MapReduce computing platform as it is the entry and exit points for clients to submit a job. However, as there is only one JobTracker process running on a Hadoop cluster, the JobTracker poses a single point of failure for the Hadoop MapReduce service because there is no alternate when the only running JobTracker shuts down. When the JobTracker fails, all the jobs running on the cluster are deemed to have been halted for the client.

12.1.1.2 TaskTracker

TaskTracker is a daemon running on the computing nodes of a Hadoop cluster. The TaskTracker receives instructions to perform map and/or reduce tasks from the JobTracker. The TaskTracker posts the available resources in the node and a heartbeat message at every specific interval of time to the JobTracker. The JobTracker performs bookkeeping of the TaskTracker and the corresponding resource, and exploits the information in job scheduling. The TaskTracker performs the assigned tasks (map, reduce) on the given data. The JobTracker tracks the TaskTrackers for the tasks that are running and instructs the TaskTrackers where to send the output data.

A TaskTracker performs a mapper method or a reduce method.

12.1.2 MapReduce Enhancements and Extensions

While the basic implementation of the MapReduce is very useful for handling data processing and data loading in a heterogeneous system with many different storage systems, this basic architecture suffers from some limitations. In this section, we present an overview of some of these limitations as also the workarounds, enhancements, and extensions to MapReduce that have been devised to address these limitations.

12.1.2.1 Supporting Iterative Processing

Many data analysis techniques (e.g., PageRank algorithm, recursive relational queries, social network analysis) require iterative computations. These techniques have a common requirement, which is that data are processed iteratively until the computation satisfies a convergence or stopping condition. The basic MapReduce framework does not directly support these iterative data analysis applications. Instead, programmers must implement iterative programs by manually issuing multiple MapReduce jobs and orchestrating their execution using a driver program. In practice, there are two key problems with manually orchestrating an iterative program in MapReduce:

1. Even though much of the data may be unchanged from iteration to iteration, the data must be reloaded and reprocessed at each iteration, wasting I/O, network bandwidth, and CPU resources.

2. The termination condition may involve the detection of when a fixpoint has been reached. This condition may itself require an extra MapReduce job on each iteration, again incurring overhead in terms of scheduling extra tasks, reading extra data from disk, and moving data across the network.

To accommodate the requirements of iterative data analysis applications, HaLoop has incorporated the following changes to the basic Hadoop MapReduce framework:

- It exposes a new application programming interface to users that simplifies the expression of iterative MapReduce programs.
- HaLoop's master node contains a new loop control module that repeatedly starts new map-reduce steps that compose the loop body until a user-specified stopping condition is met.
- It uses a new task scheduler that leverages data locality.
- It caches and indices application data on slave nodes. In principle, the TaskTracker manages not only task execution but also caches and indices on the slave node and redirects each task's cache and index accesses to the local file system.

The HaLoop system achieves this by extending the basic MapReduce framework with two main functionalities:

1. Caching the invariant data in the first iteration and then reusing them in later iterations
2. Caching the reducer outputs, which makes checking for a fixpoint more efficient, without an extra MapReduce job

HaLoop relies on the same file system and has the same task queue structure as Hadoop but the task scheduler and TaskTracker modules are modified, and the loop control, caching, and indexing modules are newly introduced to the architecture. The TaskTracker manages not only task execution but also caches and indices on the slave node, and redirects each task's cache and index accesses to the local file system.

In the MapReduce framework, each map or reduce task contains its portion of the input data and the task runs by performing the map/reduce function on its input data records where the life cycle of the task ends when the processing of all the input data records has been completed.

The iMapReduce framework supports the feature of iterative processing by keeping alive each map and reduce task during the entire iterative process. In particular, when all the input data of a persistent task are parsed and processed, the task becomes dormant, waiting for the new updated input data:

- For a map task, it waits for the results from the reduce tasks and is activated to work on the new input records when the required data from the reduce tasks arrive.
- For the reduce tasks, they wait for the map tasks' output and are activated synchronously as in MapReduce.

The iMapReduce runtime system does the termination check after each iteration. To terminate the iterations by a fixed number of iterations, the persistent map/reduce task records its iteration number and terminates itself when the number exceeds a threshold. To bound the distance between the output from two consecutive iterations, the reduce tasks can save the output from two consecutive iterations and compute the distance. If the termination condition is satisfied, the master will notify all the map and reduce tasks to terminate their execution. Jobs can terminate their iterative process in one of two ways:

1. Defining fixed number of iterations: Iterative algorithm stops after it iterates n times.
2. Bounding the distance between two consecutive iterations: Iterative algorithm stops when the distance is less than a threshold.

12.1.2.2 Join Operations

One main limitation of the MapReduce framework is that it does not support the joining of multiple data sets in one task. However, this can still be achieved with additional MapReduce steps such as the following:

1. Standard repartition join: The two input relations are dynamically partitioned on the join key and the corresponding pairs of partitions are joined using the standard partitioned sort-merge join approach.
2. Improved repartition join: One potential problem with the standard repartition join is that all the records for a given join key from both input relations have to be buffered. Therefore, when the key cardinality is small or when the data is highly skewed, all the records for a given join key may not fit in memory. The improved repartition join strategy fixes the buffering problem by introducing the following key changes:
   a. In the map function, the output key is changed to a composite of the join key and the table tag. The table tags are generated in a way that ensures records from one input relation will be sorted ahead of those from the other input relation on a given join key.
   b. The partitioning function is customized so that the hashcode is computed from just the join key part of the composite key. This way records with the same join key are still assigned to the same reduce task.
   c. As records from the smaller input are guaranteed to be ahead of those from L for a given join key, only the records from the smaller input are buffered and the records of the larger input are streamed to generate the join output.
3. Broadcast join: Instead of moving both input relations across the network as in the repartition-based joins, the broadcast join approach moves only the smaller input relation so that it avoids the preprocessing sorting requirement of both input relations and more importantly avoids the network overhead for moving the larger relation.
4. Semijoin: This join approach tries to avoid the problem of the broadcast join approach where it is possible to send many records of the smaller input relation across the network while they may not be actually referenced by any records in the other relation. It achieves this goal at the cost of an extra scan of the smaller input relation where it determines the set of unique join keys in the smaller relation, send them to the other relation to specify the list of the actual referenced join keys and then send only these records across the network for executing the real execution of the join operation.

5. Per-split semijoin: This join approach tries to improve the semijoin approach with a further step to address the fact that not every record in the filtered version of the smaller relation will join with a particular split of the larger relation. Therefore, an extra process step is executed to determine the target split(s) of each filtered join key.

Based on statistics, such as the relative data size and the fraction of the join key referenced, the tradeoffs of the join strategies can be surmised as follows:

- If data is not preprocessed, the right join strategy depends on the size of the data transferred via the network. If the network cost of broadcasting an input relation R to every node is less expensive than transferring both R and projected L, then the broadcast join algorithm should be used.
- When preprocessing is allowed, semijoin, per-split semijoin, and directed join with sufficient partitions are the best choices. Semijoin and per-split semijoin offer further flexibility since their preprocessing steps are insensitive to how the log table is organized and thus suitable for any number of reference tables. In addition, the preprocessing steps of these two algorithms are cheaper since there is no shuffling of the log data.

12.1.2.3 Data Indices

One of the main limitations of the original implementation of the MapReduce framework is that it is designed in a way that the jobs can scan the input data only in a sequential-oriented fashion. Hence, the query-processing performance of the MapReduce framework is unable to match the performance of a well-configured parallel DBMS. The Hadoop++ system aims to boost the query performance of the Hadoop system without changing any of the system internals, by injecting their changes through user-defined function (UDFs), which only affect the Hadoop system from inside without any external effect:

1. Trojan Index: The original Hadoop implementation does not provide index access due to the lack of a priori knowledge of schema and the MapReduce jobs being executed; the Hadoop++ system is based on the assumption that if we know the schema and the anticipated MapReduce jobs, then we can create appropriate indices for the Hadoop tasks. These indices are created during the data-loading time and thus have no penalty at query time.

   Each Trojan index provides an optional index access path, which can be used for selective MapReduce jobs. These indices are created by injecting appropriate UDFs inside the Hadoop implementation.

   The main features of Trojan indices can be summarized as follows:

   a. Optional access path: They provide an optional index access path that can be used for selective MapReduce jobs. However, the scan access path can still be used for other MapReduce jobs.
   b. Seamless splitting: Data indexing adds an index overhead for each data split. Therefore, the logical split includes the data as well as the index, as it automatically splits the indexed data at logical split boundaries.

c. Partial index: A Trojan index need not be built on the entire split. However, it can be built on any contiguous subset of the split as well.
d. Multiple indices: Several Trojan indices can be built on the same split. However, only one of them can be the primary index. During query processing, an appropriate index can be chosen for data access based on the logical query plan and the cost model.
e. Noninvasive: They do not change the existing Hadoop framework. The index structure is implemented by providing the right UDFs.
f. No external library or engine: Trojan indices integrate indexing capability natively into the Hadoop framework without imposing a distributed SQL query engine on top of it.

2. Trojan join: the Hadoop++ system assumes that if we know the schema and the expected workload, then we can co-partition the input data during the loading time. In particular, given any two input relations, they apply the same partitioning function on the join attributes of both the relations at data loading time and place the co-group pairs, having the same join key from the two relations, on the same split and, hence, on the same node. As a result, join operations can be then processed locally within each node at query time. Implementing the Trojan joins does not require any changes to be made to the existing implementation of the Hadoop framework. The only changes are made on the internal management of the data splitting process. In addition, Trojan indices can be freely combined with Trojan joins.

12.1.2.4 Column Storage

This is related to the design and implementation of a column-oriented and binary backend storage format for Hadoop. In general, a straightforward way to implement a column-oriented storage format for Hadoop is to store each column of the input data set in a separate file. However, this raises two main challenges:

- It requires generating roughly equal-sized splits so that a job can be effectively parallelized over the cluster.
- It needs to ensure that the corresponding values from different columns in the data set are co-located on the same node running the map task.

The first challenge can be tackled by horizontally partitioning the data set and storing each partition in a separate subdirectory. The second challenge is harder to tackle because of the default three-way block-level replication strategy of HDFS that provides fault tolerance on commodity servers but does not provide any co-location guarantees. But this can be tackled by implementing a modified HDFS block placement policy that guarantees that the files corresponding to the different columns of a split are always co-located across replicas. Hence, when reading a data set, the column input format can actually assign one or more split directories to a single split, and the column files of a split directory are scanned sequentially and the records are reassembled using values from corresponding positions in the files. A lazy record construction technique is used to mitigate the deserialization overhead in Hadoop, as well as eliminate unnecessary disk I/O. The basic idea behind lazy record construction is to deserialize only those columns of a record that are actually accessed in a map function.

Each column of the input data set can be compressed using one of the following compression schemes:

1. Compressed blocks: This scheme uses a standard compression algorithm to compress a block of contiguous column values. Multiple compressed blocks may fit into a single HDFS block. A header indicates the number of records in a compressed block and the block's size. This allows the block to be skipped if no values are accessed in it. However, when a value in the block is accessed, the entire block needs to be decompressed.
2. Dictionary compressed skip list: This scheme is tailored for map-typed columns. It takes advantage of the fact that the keys used in maps are often strings that are drawn from a limited universe. Such strings are well suited for dictionary compression. A dictionary is built of keys for each block of map values and stores the compressed keys in a map using a skip-list format. The main advantage of this scheme is that a value can be accessed without having to decompress an entire block of values.

One advantage of this approach is that adding a column to a data set is not an expensive operation. This can be done by simply placing an additional file for the new column in each of the split directories. However, a potential disadvantage of this approach is that the available parallelism may be limited for smaller data sets. Maximum parallelism is achieved for a MapReduce job when the number of splits is at least equal to the number of map tasks.

SAP HANA is an in-memory database that is delivered as an appliance and is tightly integrated with SAP BW. This data is stored in both columnar and row wise tables, making it capable to work efficiently with both type of workloads. SAP HANA stores data in a compressed format, thereby increasing the amount of data that can be stored in the database. The data loading is done through incremental updates only when the data is changed. Data can be partitioned to increase the performance and parallel capabilities. One advantage of the system which excels is that a single data store can be used for both transactional and analytical applications. There are use cases in the current organizations where the analytical decision is integrated with normal applications such as recommendation engines or personalized news feeds.

12.2 YARN

The fundamental idea of YARN (Yet Another Resource Negotiator) is to split the two major responsibilities of the Job-Tracker—resource management and job scheduling/monitoring—into separate daemons:

- A global Resource Manager
- A per-application ApplicationMaster (AM)

The Resource Manager and per-node slave, the NodeManager (NM), form the new, and generic, operating system for managing applications in a distributed manner. The Resource

Manager is the ultimate authority that arbitrates division of resources among all the applications in the system. The per-application ApplicationMaster is a framework-specific entity and is tasked with negotiating for resources from the Resource Manager and working with the NodeManager(s) to execute and monitor the component tasks.

The per-application ApplicationMaster is responsible for negotiating appropriate resource containers from the Scheduler, tracking their status, and monitoring their progress. From the system perspective, the ApplicationMaster runs as a normal container.

A container is a resource lease that has the privilege of using CPU and memory on a specific worker node. Containers are allocated to the NodeManagers for running distributed processes on the DataNodes. There is flexibility where storage and networking may be added in the future. A container is a logical definition of resources (for example, 4GB of RAM, 1 CPU core) for a specific worker node. A job may run multiple containers spread across the worker nodes in the cluster.

Application Masters can work with Node Managers to launch containers that are written in C, Java, Python, Scala, and so on. A container will have information, such as the command line to start the process or JVM in the container, defined environmental variables, security tokens, jars, libraries, data files, or any additional objects required to run the code in the container.

Following is an example for determining how many containers per node can be allocated:

# of containers = min (2*CORES, 1.8*DISKS, [Total available RAM] / MIN_CONTAINER_SIZE)

where, MIN_CONTAINER_SIZE is minimum container size in GB (RAM).

Figure 12.3 shows the YARN architecture.

The Resource Manager has a pluggable scheduler component, which is responsible for allocating resources to the various running applications subject to the familiar constraints

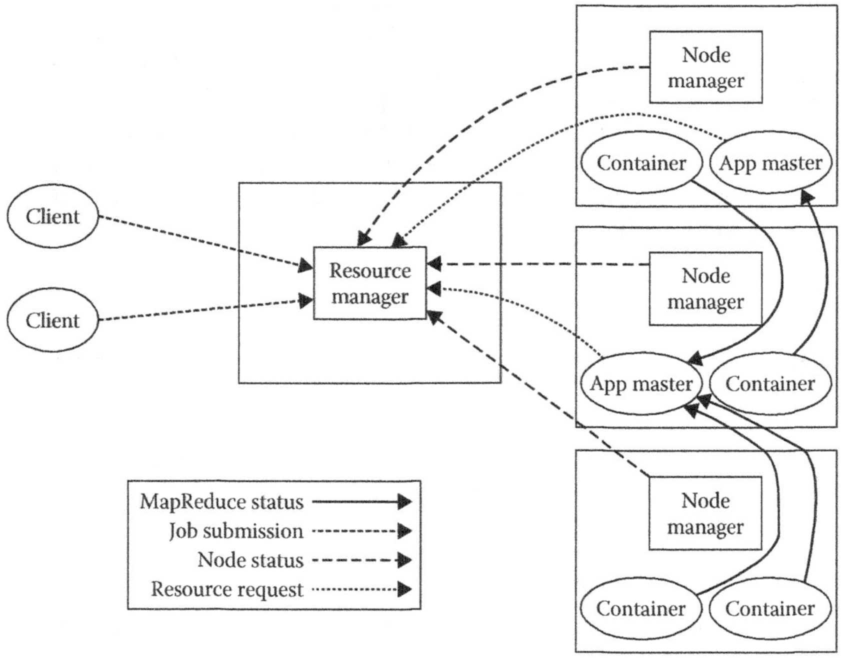

FIGURE 12.3
YARN architecture.

of capacity, queues, and other factors. The Scheduler is a pure scheduler in the sense that it performs no monitoring or tracking of status for the application, offering no guarantees on restarting tasks that are not carried out due to either application failure or hardware failure. The scheduler performs its scheduling function based on the resource requirements of an application by using the abstract notion of a resource container, which incorporates resource dimensions such as memory, CPU, disk, and network.

The NodeManager is the per-machine slave, which is responsible for launching the applications' containers, monitoring their resource usage (CPU, memory, disk, network), and reporting the same to the Resource Manager.

12.3 Hadoop Distributed File System (HDFS)

The distributed file system in Hadoop is designed to run on commodity hardware. Although it has many similarities with other distributed file systems, the differences are significant. It is highly fault tolerant and is designed to run on low-cost hardware. It also provides high throughput to stored data, and hence can be used to store and process large datasets. To enable this streaming of data, it relaxes some POSIX standards. HDFS was originally built for the Apache Nutch project and later forked in to an individual project under Apache.

HDFS, by design, is able to provide reliable storage to large datasets, allowing high-bandwidth data streaming to user applications. By distributing the storage and computation across several servers, the resource can scale up and down with demand while remaining economical.

12.3.1 Characteristics of HDFS

1. Hardware failure: Hardware failure is fairly common in clusters. A Hadoop cluster consists of thousands of machines, each of which stores a block of data. HDFS consists of a huge number of components, and with that, there is a good chance of failure among them at any point of time. The detection of these failures and the ability to recover quickly is part of the core architecture.
2. Streaming data access: Applications that run on the Hadoop HDFS need access to streaming data. These applications cannot be run on general-purpose file systems. HDFS is designed to enable large-scale batch processing, which is enabled by the high-throughput data access. Several POSIX requirements are relaxed to enable these special needs of high throughput rates.
3. Large data sets: The HDFS-based applications feed on large datasets. A typical file size is in the range of high gigabytes to low terabytes. It should provide high data bandwidth and support millions of files across hundreds of nodes in a single cluster.
4. Heterogeneous hardware and software portability: HDFS is designed to run on commodity hardware, which hosts multiple platforms. This feature helps widespread adoption of this platform for large-scale computations.
5. Simple coherency model: The write-once-read-many access model of files enables high-throughput data access as the data once written need not be changed, thus simplifying data coherency issues. A MapReduce-based application takes advantage of this model.

6. Moving compute instead of data: Any computation is efficient if it executes near the data because it avoids the network transfer bottleneck. Migrating the computation closer to the data is a cornerstone of HDFS-based programming. HDFS provides all the necessary application interfaces to move the computation close to the data prior to execution.

HDFS is analogous to GFS in the Google MapReduce implementation. A block in HDFS is equivalent to a chunk in GFS and is also very large, 64 Mb by default, but 128 Mb is used in some installations. The large block size is intended to reduce the number of seeks and improve data transfer times. Each block is an independent unit stored as a dynamically allocated file in the Linux local file system in a DataNode directory. If the node has multiple disk drives, multiple DataNode directories can be specified. An additional local file per block stores metadata for the block. HDFS also follows a master–slave architecture, which consists of a single master server that manages the distributed file system namespace and regulates access to files by clients called the NameNode. In addition, there are multiple DataNodes, one per node in the cluster, which manage the disk storage attached to the nodes and assigned to Hadoop. The NameNode determines the mapping of blocks to DataNodes. The DataNodes are responsible for serving read and write requests from file system clients such as MapReduce tasks, and they also perform block creation, deletion, and replication based on commands from the NameNode.

HDFS is a file system, and like any other file system architecture, it needs to manage consistency, recoverability, and concurrency for reliable operations. These requirements have been addressed in the architecture by creating image, journal, and checkpoint files:

1. NameNode (master node): The NameNode is a single master server that manages the file system namespace and regulates access to files by clients. Additionally, the NameNode manages all the operations such as opening, closing, moving, naming, and renaming of files and directories. It also manages the mapping of blocks to DataNodes.
2. DataNodes (slave nodes): DataNodes represent the slaves in the architecture that manage data and the storage attached to the data. A typical HDFS cluster can have thousands of DataNodes and tens of thousands of HDFS clients per cluster since each DataNode may execute multiple application tasks simultaneously. The DataNodes are responsible for managing read and write requests from the file system's clients, block maintenance, and perform replication as directed by the NameNode. The block management in HDFS is different from a normal file system. The size of the data file equals the actual length of the block. This means if a block is half full, it needs only half of the space of the full block on the local drive, thereby optimizing storage space for compactness, and there is no extra space consumed on the block unlike a regular file system.
3. Image: An image represents the metadata of the namespace (inodes and lists of blocks). On startup, the NameNode pins the entire namespace image in memory. The in-memory persistence enables the NameNode to service multiple client requests concurrently.
4. Journal: The journal represents the modification log of the image in the local host's native file system. During normal operations, each client transaction is recorded in the journal, and the journal file is flushed and synced before the

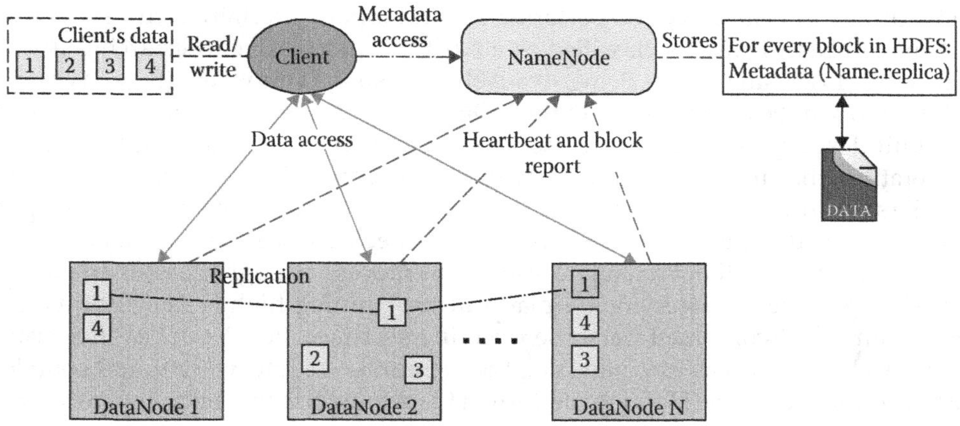

FIGURE 12.4
HDFS architecture.

acknowledgment is sent to the client. The NameNode upon startup or from a recovery can replay this journal.

5. Checkpoint: To enable recovery, the persistent record of the image is also stored in the local host's native files system and is called a checkpoint. Once the system starts up, the NameNode never modifies or updates the checkpoint file. A new checkpoint file can be created during the next startup, on a restart, or on demand when requested by the administrator or by the CheckpointNode (Figure 12.4).

The data flow in a write operation: HDFS client who wants to write some data file onto HDFS contacts NameNode for a list of DataNodes that the client can connect to and write the contents of the file. The NameNode updates its metadata of the request and responds with a block id and a DataNode details. The clients upload the content of the file to the DataNode, while DataNode copies the received content into the block specified by the NameNode . NameNode then finds another DataNode to comply with the replication factor. The NameNode instructs the DataNode to copy the block to other DataNode. The replication continues among the DataNodes until the system satisfies the replication factor.

The similar and reverse approach is involved in reading the contents of a file from HDFS. Client node, who wants to read a file, contacts NameNode for a list of DataNodes where the contents of the file reside. NameNode responds with a list of DataNodes, three DataNodes when replication factor is three. Client node chooses one from the list received and contacts the DataNodes to get served by the requested data.

12.4 HBase

HBase is an open-source, nonrelational, column-oriented, multidimensional, distributed database developed on Google's BigTable architecture. It is designed with high availability and high performance as drivers to support storage and processing of large data sets on the Hadoop framework. HBase is not a database in the purist definition of a database. It provides unlimited scalability and performance, and supports certain features of an ACID-compliant database. HBase is classified as a NoSQL database due to its architecture and design being closely aligned to Being Available and Same Everywhere (Base). Why do we need HBase when the data is stored in the HDFS file system, which is the core data storage layer within Hadoop? HBase is very useful for operations other than MapReduce execution, operations that are not easy to work with in HDFS, and when you need random access to data. First, it provides a database-style interface to Hadoop, which enables developers to deploy programs that can quickly read or write to specific subsets of data in an extremely voluminous data set, without having to search and process through the entire data set.

Second, it provides a transactional platform for running high-scale, real-time applications as an ACID-compliant database (meeting standards for Atomicity, Consistency, Isolation, and Durability) while handling the incredible volume, variety, and complexity of data encountered on the Hadoop platform. HBase supports the following properties of ACID compliance:

1. Atomicity: All mutations are atomic within a row. For example, a read or write operation will either succeed or fail.
2. Consistency: All rows returned for any execution will consist of a complete row that existed or exists in the table.
3. Isolation: The isolation level is called "read committed" in the traditional DBMS.
4. Durability: All visible data in the system is durable data. For example, to phrase durability, a read will never return data that has not been made durable on disk.

12.4.1 HBase Architecture

Data is organized in HBase as rows and columns, and tables, very similar to a database; however, here is where the similarity ends.

HBase architecture is described as follows:

1. Tables:
   a. Tables are made of rows and columns.
   b. Table cells are the intersection of row and column coordinates. Each cell is versioned by default with a timestamp. The contents of a cell are treated as an uninterpreted array of bytes.
   c. A table row has a sortable row key and an arbitrary number of columns.
2. Rows:
   a. Table row keys are also byte arrays. In this configuration, anything can serve as the row key as opposed to strongly typed data types in the traditional database.
   b. Table rows are sorted byte-ordered by row key, the table's primary key, and all table accesses are via the table primary key.
   c. Columns are grouped as families and a row can have as many columns as loaded.
3. Columns and column groups (families):
   a. In HBase, row columns are grouped into column families.
   b. All column family members will mandatorily have a common prefix; for example, the columnsperson:name and person:comments are both members of the person column family, whereasemail:identifier belongs to the email family.

c. A table's column families must be specified upfront as part of the table schema definition.
d. New column family members can be added on demand.

12.5 ZooKeeper

Apache ZooKeeper is a distributed, consensus-based coordination system used to support distributed applications. Distributed applications that require leader election, locking, group membership, service location, and configuration services can use ZooKeeper rather than reimplement the complex coordination and error handling that comes with these functions. In fact, many projects within the Hadoop ecosystem, especially HBase, use ZooKeeper for exactly this purpose.

12.6 Hive

Apache Hive is a data warehouse infrastructure built on top of Hadoop provided by Facebook. Similar to Pig, Hive was initially designed as an in-house solution for large-scale data analysis. As the company expanded, the parallel RDBMS infrastructure originally deployed at Facebook began to choke at the amount of data that had to be processed on a daily basis. Following the decision to switch to Hadoop to overcome these scalability problems in 2008, the Hive project was developed internally to provide the high-level interface required for quick adoption of the new warehouse infrastructure inside the company. Since 2009, Hive is also available for the general public as an open-source project under the Apache umbrella. Inside Facebook, Hive runs thousands of jobs per day on different Hadoop clusters, ranging from 300 nodes to 1,200 nodes, to perform a wide range of tasks including periodical reporting of click counts, ad hoc analysis, and training machine learning models for ad optimization. Other companies working with data in the petabyte magnitude like Netflix are reportedly using Hive for the analysis of website streaming logs and catalog metadata information.

The fundamental goals of designing Hive were as follows:

- Build a system for managing and querying data using structured techniques on Hadoop
- Use native MapReduce for execution at HDFS and Hadoop layers
- Use HDFS for storage of Hive data
- Store key metadata in an RDBMS
- Extend SQL interfaces, a familiar data warehousing tool in use at enterprises
- Provide high extensibility: user-defined types, user-defined functions, formats, and scripts

- Leverage extreme scalability and performance of Hadoop
- Ensure interoperability with other platforms

The main difference between Hive and the other languages discussed above comes from the fact that Hive's design is more influenced by classic relational warehousing systems, which is evident both at the data model and at the query language level. Hive thinks of its data in relational terms—data sources are stored in tables, consisting of a fixed number of rows with predefined data types. Similar to Pig and Jaql, Hive's data model provides support for semistructured and nested data in the form of complex data types such as associative arrays (maps), lists and structs, which facilitate the use of de-normalized inputs. On the other hand, Hive differs from the other higher-level languages for Hadoop in that it uses a catalog to hold metadata about its input sources. This means that the table schema must be declared and the data loaded before any queries involving the table are submitted to the system (which mirrors the standard RDBMS process). The schema definition language extends the classic DDL CREATE TABLE syntax. Currently, Hive does not provide support for updates, which means that any data load statement will enforce the removal of any old data in the specified target table or partition. The standard way to append data to an existing table in Hive is to create a new partition for each append set. Since appends in an OLAP environment are typically performed periodically in a batch manner, this strategy is a good fit for most real-world scenarios.

The Hive Query Language (HiveQL) is a SQL dialect with various syntax extensions. HiveQL supports many traditional SQL features such as from clause subqueries, various join types, group bys, and aggregations, as well as many useful built-in data processing functions that provide an intuitive syntax for writing Hive queries to all users familiar with the SQL basics. In addition, HiveQL provides native support for inline MapReduce job specification. The semantics of the mapper and the reducer are specified in external scripts, which communicate with the parent Hadoop task through the standard input and output streams (similar to the Streaming API for user-defined functions (UDFs) in Pig).

Much of Hive's performance concerns can be attributed to the use of MapReduce as Hive's execution engine (up until Hive 0.12). MapReduce is great for a good number of things, but is not a good choice for running ad hoc, interactive queries. There are a number of reasons for this, but mainly it is because MapReduce reads and writes to disk extensively, and there is a high startup cost for MapReduce jobs. Therefore, a multi join query could take minutes, not because of data size but just because of the number of read and writes to disk.

12.7 Pig

As data volumes and processing complexities increase, analyzing large data sets introduces dataflow complexities that become harder to implement in a MapReduce program. There was a need for an abstraction layer over MapReduce: a high-level language that is more user friendly, is SQL-like in terms of expressing dataflows, has the flexibility to manage multistep data transformations, and handles joins with simplicity and easy program flow. Apache Pig was the first system to provide a higher-level language on top of Hadoop. Pig started as an internal research project at Yahoo! (one of the early adopters of Hadoop), but due to its popularity, subsequently was promoted to a production level system and adopted as an open-source project by the Apache Software Foundation. Pig is widely used both inside and outside Yahoo! for a wide range of tasks including ad hoc data analytics, ETL tasks, log processing, and training collaborative filtering models for recommendation systems.

The fundamental goals of designing Pig were as follows:

- Programming flexibility: The ability to break down complex tasks comprised of multiple steps and interprocess-related data transformations should be encoded as dataflow sequences that are easy to design, develop, and maintain.
- Automatic optimization: Tasks are encoded to let the system optimize their execution automatically. This allows the user to have greater focus on program development, allowing the user to focus on semantics rather than efficiency.
- Extensibility: Users can develop user-defined functions (UDFs) for more complex processing requirements.

Pig queries are expressed in a declarative scripting language called Pig Latin, which provides SQL-like functionality tailored for big data-specific needs. Most notably from the syntax point of view, Pig Latin enforces implicit specification of the dataflow as a sequence of expressions chained together through the use of variables. This style of programming is different from SQL, where the order of computation is not reflected at the language level and is better suited to the ad hoc nature of Pig as it makes query development and maintenance easier due to the increased readability of the code.

Unlike traditional SQL systems, the data does not have to be stored in a system-specific format before it can be used by a query. Instead, the input and output formats are specified through storage functions inside the load and store expressions. In addition to ASCII and binary storage, users can implement their own storage functions to add support for other custom formats. Pig uses a dynamic type system to provide native support for nonnormalized data models. In addition to the simple data types used by relational databases, Pig defines three complex types—tuple, bag, and map—which can be nested arbitrarily to reflect the semi-structured nature of the processed data. For better support of ad hoc queries, Pig does not maintain a catalog with schema information about the source data. Instead, input schema is defined at the query level either explicitly by the user or implicitly through type inference. At the top level, all input sources are treated as bags of tuples; the tuple schema can be optionally supplied as part of the load expression.

12.8 Kafka

Apache Kafka is a robust pub-sub (publish, subscribe) framework that allows highly available, dependable message streaming. It is a paradox that a key feature of Kakfa is its small number of features. It has far fewer features and is much less configurable than Flume, which is described later. All Kafka does is store messages relatively reliably and at high volumes and rates. All computational considerations are outside of Kafka's scope. Such computation can be implemented using a variety of computational frameworks such as Spark Streaming, Apache Storm, or Apache Samza. This simplicity and focus of Kafka have helped make it very good at what it does.

12.9 Flume

Apache Flume is a streaming data collection and aggregation system designed to transport massive volumes of data into systems such as Hadoop. It supports native connectivity and support for writing directly to HDFS, and simplifies reliable, streaming data delivery from a variety of sources including RPC services, log4j appenders, syslog, and even the output from OS commands. Data can be routed, load-balanced, replicated to multiple destinations, and aggregated from thousands of hosts by a tier of agents.

Flume is a complex tool that allows processing units to be strung together to transport data, typically with the aim of doing minimal ETL on the fly and then storing in HDFS files. Flume is nominally stream based, but a de facto batch orientation is often imposed by storing data in HDFS files. If data is pushed instead into a pub-sub framework like Kafka, then true streaming operation can be achieved. Flume has limited and complex provisions for high availability and guaranteed delivery. Flume was originally limited to processing textual data arranged one record per line as is normally done in log files, and there are still echoes of this limitation in various parts of the framework. In general, the complexity of Flume makes the use of Kafka plus either Storm or Spark Streaming a preferable option.

12.10 Sqoop

Sqoop is a batch-oriented program to import data from a database or export data back to a database. Sqoop can create files in a variety of formats in a Hadoop cluster. Sqoop is a very useful tool due to the wide range of databases that it supports, but Sqoop is, by design, entirely batch oriented.

Sqoop, short for "SQL to Hadoop," performs bidirectional data transfer between Hadoop and almost any database with a JDBC driver. For even greater performance, Sqoop supports database-specific plug-ins that use native features of the RDBMS rather than incurring the overhead of JDBC. Many of these connectors are open source, while others are free or available from commercial vendors at a cost. Today, Sqoop includes native connectors (called direct support) for MySQL and PostgreSQL. Free connectors exist for Teradata, Netezza, SQL Server, and Oracle (from Quest Software), and are available for download from their respective company websites.

> An interesting alternative to using Sqoop is to use database-specific export commands to export tables directly to a cluster or import them from the cluster using NFS. A virtue of this alternative approach is that it can be very high performance since databases generally have highly optimized table export/bulk import utilities. Using database export/import utilities will not, however, provide you with the native ability to store the resulting data in an advanced format such as Parquet.

12.11 Impala

Impala is a system that is designed to scan flat files at a very high rate to compute the result of aggregation queries written in SQL. The preferred format for data to be queried by Impala is Parquet, and Impala is able to use the features of Parquet to great advantage to accelerate the scanning of large files. For the most part, Impala uses the table management capabilities of Hive to define tables and their schema. The data model used by Impala is currently very similar to the model used by relational systems.

Impala differs from most of the Hadoop ecosystem projects that existed at the time in that it is not based on MapReduce. Designed to optimize latency, its architecture is similar to that of traditional massively parallel processing (MPP) data warehouses, such as Netezza, Greenplum, and Teradata. Impala delivers query latency and concurrency similar to traditional data warehouses and significantly lower than that of Hive running on MapReduce.

To avoid creating silos of data within Hadoop, Impala uses the same SQL dialect as Hive and uses the Hive metastore. This allows users to define tables once and use them in Hive, Pig, and Impala. Similar to Hive, Impala supports both HDFS and HBase as data sources, and most of the popular data formats (delimited text, SequenceFiles, Avro, and Parquet). This allows Impala to query all data in Hadoop without requiring special transformations.

Impala has a shared nothing architecture, which allows for system-level fault tolerance and huge scalability that allows Impala to remain performant as the number of users and concurrent queries increases. Impala's architecture includes the Impala daemons ("impalad"), the "catalog service," and the "statestore." Impala daemons run on every node in the cluster, and each daemon is capable of acting as the query planner, the query coordinator, and a query execution engine. To connect to Impala, the client uses JDBC, ODBC, impala-shell, or connects directly via Apache Thrift to connect to one of the Impala daemons. All Impala daemons are identical and interchangeable, so the client will typically connect to a load balancer that will direct the connection to an active daemon. The daemon the client connects to will act as a query planner and coordinator for this query.

Note that unlike other database management systems such as an RDBMS, Impala does not have to implement the underlying data store, because this is off-loaded to HDFS and HBase. Impala also does not have to implement the table and database management solution since this is implemented by the Hive metastore. This allows Impala to focus on its core functionality, which is executing queries as fast as possible.

12.12 Drill

Apache Drill is a newly graduated top-level Apache project that offers the user an unusual level of flexibility. It provides standard SQL (not SQL-like) query capabilities that can access a surprisingly diverse range of data sources and formats, including nested formats such as Parquet and JSON. Drill queries can be schema-less, allowing flexibility in data exploration. The Drill optimizer is a sophisticated cost-based optimizer that can radically restructure queries based on characteristics of the input files. Drill also offers useful extensibility, so it is a useful tool for business analysts as well as for developers.

> Like Impala, a key focus with Drill is to make the minimum response time very short so that it can be used for interactive purposes.

12.13 Whirr

Apache Whirr was developed to simplify the creation and deployment of ephemeral clusters in cloud environments such as Amazon's AWS. Run as a command line tool either locally or within the cloud, Whirr can spin up instances, deploy Hadoop, configure the software, and tear it down on demand. Under the hood, Whirr uses the powerful jclouds library so that it is cloud provider neutral. Whirr supports both Amazon EC2 and RackspaceCloud. In addition to Hadoop, Whirr understands how to provision Apache Cassandra, Apache ZooKeeper, Apache HBase, ElasticSearch, Voldemort, and Apache Hama.

12.14 Summary

The chapter discussed the Hadoop ecosystem including Hadoop Distributed File System (HDFS), HBaseNoSQL database, Hive data warehouse solution, and the Pig query language for ad hoc analytical requirements. The chapter provides a snapshot overview of other components of the Hadoop environment, namely, Kafka, Flume, Sqoop, Whirr, Impala, and Drill.

13

Big Data Analysis Languages, Tools, and Environments

Success with Hadoop requires a new way of thinking as well as a sense of urgency. Organizations now want the capability of batch processing and interactive and real time queries with their big data platforms. This requires building the right combination of software frameworks, tools, in-memory software, distributed search, and NoSQL databases around Hadoop, and leveraging the existing software from proprietary software firms. The analytical systems that maximize business value are those systems that allow data from multiple sources of different types to be correlated to find new data patterns that provide significantly increased accuracy. The world of relational databases and data warehouses that require deleting, ignoring, aggregating, and summarizing data because of the high costs of storage is a losing formula for descriptive and predictive analytics. It is the detailed data that contains the golden information (insights) for success.

Big data platforms bring together a number of very important components required for fast and accurate analytics to address the key goals around big data, such as

- Be able to make business decisions faster than your competition with a higher degree of confidence and less risk.
- Increase the type and number of questions you can ask of your data for more business insight and value.
- Increase the level of efficiency and competitiveness of an organization.
- Create an environment that provides new business insights through data.

13.1 Spark

Spark is a fault-tolerant and distributed data analytics tool capable of implementing large-scale data intensive applications on commodity hardware. Hadoop and other technologies have already popularized acyclic data flow techniques for building data-intensive applications on commodity clusters, but these are not suitable for applications that reuse a working dataset for multiple parallel operations such as iterative machine-learning algorithms and interactive data analysis tools. Spark not only is scalable and fault-tolerant but also addresses these problems by introducing a data storage and processing abstraction called Resilient Distributed Datasets (RDDs). An RDD is a read-only distribution of objects that are partitioned across a set of machines and can be rebuilt if a partition is lost.

While Spark is a fairly new framework at the moment, it is easy to use, extendable, highly supported, well designed, and fast. Spark is expected to be eclipse MapReduce for most functionalities. Spark is already the best choice for machine-learning applications because of its ability to perform iterative operations on data cached in memory. In addition to replacing MapReduce, Spark offers SQL, graph processing, and streaming frameworks.

MapReduce revolutionized computation over huge datasets by offering a simple model for writing programs that could execute in parallel across hundreds to thousands of machines. The MapReduce engine achieves near linear scalability—as the data size increases, one can throw more computers at it and see jobs complete in the same amount of time—and is resilient to the fact that failures that occur rarely on a single machine occur all the time on clusters of thousands. It breaks up work into small tasks and can gracefully accommodate task failures without compromising the job to which they belong.

Hadoop users have a challenge in using MapReduce to address the following:

- Iterative jobs: Gradient-Descent is an excellent example of an algorithm that is repeatedly applied to the same dataset to optimize a parameter. While it is easy to represent each iteration as a MapReduce job, the data from each iteration has to be loaded from the disk, incurring a significant performance penalty.
- Interactive analytics: Interfaces such as Pig and Hive are commonly used running SQL queries on large datasets using Hadoop. Ideally this dataset is loaded into memory and queried repeatedly, but with Hadoop, every query is executed as a MapReduce job that incurs significant latency from disk read.

Distributed Shared Memory (DSM) is a mechanism by which processes can access shared data without interprocess communication. The challenges of implementing a DSM system include addressing problems such as data location, data access, sharing and locking data, and data coherence. These problems have connections with transactional models, data migrations, concurrent programming, distributed systems, etc. RDDs are an important abstraction in Spark that allows a read-only collection of objects capable of rebuilding lost partitions across clusters. These RDDs can be reused in multiple parallel operations through memory caching. RDDs use lineage information about the lost partition in the rebuilding process.

Systems such as MapReduce provide locality-aware scheduling, fault tolerance, and load-balancing features that simplify distributed programming, allowing users to analyze large datasets using commodity clusters. However, RDDs are a distributed memory abstraction that allows the users to write in-memory computations while still maintaining the advantages of current data flow systems such as MapReduce. RDD performs exceptionally well on iterative algorithms, machine learning, and interactive data mining, while the other data flows become inadequate. This is possible because RDDs provide only read-only datasets, avoiding the need to checkpoint, which is common in other shared-memory techniques.

RDDs are easy to program and capable of efficiently expressing computations. Fault tolerance is perhaps most difficult to support. Checkpointing datasets has a huge disadvantage as it would require replicating datasets across clusters. This can slow down the machines due to bandwidth restrictions and memory storage restrictions. RDDs ensure fault tolerance by supporting stages of transformation. At any point of time, a partition can be recovered by repeating the transformation steps on the parent (Lineage). RDDs are well suited for applications that require executing a single function on many data records such as graph and machine learning algorithms.

Spark maintains MapReduce's linear scalability and fault tolerance, but extends it in a few important ways. First, rather than relying on a rigid map-then-reduce format, its engine can execute a more general directed acyclic graph (DAG) of operators. This means that, in situations where MapReduce must write out intermediate results to the distributed file system, Spark can pass them directly to the next step in the pipeline.

Spark extends its predecessors (such as MapReduce) with in-memory processing. RDD enables developers to materialize any point in a processing pipeline into memory across the cluster, meaning that future steps that want to deal with the same dataset need not recompute it or reload it from disk. This capability opens up use cases that distributed processing engines could not previously approach. Spark is well suited for highly iterative algorithms that require multiple passes over a dataset, as well as reactive applications that quickly respond to user queries by scanning large in-memory datasets.

13.1.1 Spark Components

Components of Spark are as follows:

1. Driver: The driver defines RDD objects and their relationships; it is the code that includes the "main" function and defines the resilient RDDs and their transformations.
2. DAG scheduler: The DAG scheduler optimizes the code and arrives at an efficient DAG that represents the data processing steps in the application. The resulting DAG is sent to the cluster manager.

MapReduce only have two processing phases, namely, map and/or reduce; with the MapReduce framework, it is only possible to build complete applications by stringing together sets of map and reduce tasks. These complex chains of tasks are known as directed acyclic graphs, or DAGs. Thus, DAGs contain series of actions connected to each other in a workflow. Oozie actually allows users to define these workflows of MapReduce tasks in XML and use an orchestration framework to monitor their execution.

Rather than the DAG being an abstraction added externally to the model, Spark engine itself creates those complex chains of steps from the application's logic; this enables developers to express complex algorithms and data processing pipelines within the same job and allows the framework to optimize the job as a whole, leading to improved performance.

3. Cluster manager: The cluster manager is responsible for assigning specific processing tasks to workers. The cluster manager has information about the workers, assigned threads, and location of data blocks. The cluster manager is also the service that handles DAG play-back in the case of worker failure. The cluster manager can be YARN, Mesos, or Spark's cluster manager.
4. Worker: The worker receives units of work and data to manage. The worker executes its specific task without knowledge of the entire DAG, and its results are sent back to the driver application.

13.1.2 Spark Concepts

13.1.2.1 Shared Variables

Spark includes two types of variables that allow sharing information between the execution nodes, which are as follows:

- Broadcast variables: Broadcast variables are sent to all the remote execution nodes, where they can be used for data processing. This is similar to the role that configuration objects play in MapReduce.
- Accumulator variables: Accumulators are also sent to the remote execution nodes, but unlike broadcast variables, they also can be "added" by the executors. Accumulators are somewhat similar to MapReduce counters.

13.1.2.2 SparkContext

SparkContext is an object that represents the connection to a Spark cluster. It is used to create RDDs, broadcast data, and initialize accumulators.

13.1.2.3 Resilient Distributed Datasets

RDDs are collections of serializable elements that are partitioned so that they can be stored on multiple nodes. An RDD may reside in memory or on disk. Spark uses RDDs to reduce I/O and maintain the processed data set in memory while still tolerating node failures without having to restart the entire job. RDDs are typically created from either of the following:

- A Hadoop input format (e.g., a file on HDFS): Spark determines the number of partitions by the input format, very similar to the way splits are determined in MapReduce jobs.
- Transformations applied on existing RDDs: Spark can shuffle the data and repartition it to any number of partitions.

RDDs store their "lineage," that is, the set of transformations that was used to create the current state, starting from the first input format that was used to create the RDD. If the data is lost, Spark will replay the lineage to rebuild the lost RDDs so the job can continue.

13.1.2.4 Transformations

Transformations are functions that take one RDD and return another. RDDs are "immutable"; so transformations will never modify their input, and only return the modified RDD. Transformations in Spark are always "lazy" in that they do not compute their own results. Instead, calling a transformation function only creates a new RDD with this specific transformation as part of its lineage; the complete set of transformations is executed only when an "action" is called. This improves Spark's efficiency and allows it to cleverly optimize the execution graph.

> This can make debugging more challenging because exceptions are thrown when the action is called, far from the code that called the function that actually threw the exception. It is important that the exception handling code should not be placed around the action but around the function where the exception may be thrown.

There are many transformations in Spark, which are as follows:

map()

Applies a function on every element of an RDD to produce a new RDD. This is similar to the way the MapReducemap() method is applied to every element in the input data.

For example: lines.map(s=>s.length) takes an RDD of Strings ("lines") and returns an RDD with the length of the strings.

filter()

Takes a Boolean function as a parameter, executes this function on every element of the RDD, and returns a new RDD containing only the elements for which the function returned true.

For example, lines.filter(s=>(s.length>35)) returns an RDD containing only the lines with more than 35 characters.

keyBy()

Takes every element in an RDD and turns it into a key-value pair in a new RDD.

For example, lines.keyBy(s=>s.length) return, an RDD of key-value pairs with the length of the line as the key, and the line as the value.

join()

Joins two key-value RDDs by their keys.

For example, let us assume we have two RDDs: lines and more_lines. Each entry in both RDDs contains the line length as the key and the line as the value.

lines.join(more_lines) will return for each line length a pair of Strings, one from the lines RDD and one from the more_lines RDD.

Each resulting element looks like <length,<line,more_line>>.

groupByKey()

Performs a group-by operation on an RDD by the keys.

For example: lines.groupByKey() will return an RDD where each element has a length as the key and a collection of lines with that length as the value.

sort()

Performs a sort on an RDD and returns a sorted RDD.

13.1.2.5 Action

"Actions" are methods that take an RDD, perform a computation, and return the result to the driver application. Recall that transformations are "lazy" and are not executed when called. Actions trigger the computation of transformations. The result of the computation can be a collection, values printed to the screen, values saved to file, or similar. However, an action will never return an RDD.

13.1.3 Benefits of Spark

1. Interactive shell (REPL): Spark jobs can be easily deployed as an application, similar to how MapReduce jobs are executed. In addition, Spark also includes a shell called REPL (Read-Eval-Print-Loop). This allows for fast interactive experimentation

with the data and easy validation of code. REPL enables quick access to data as well as interactive queries.

2. Reduced disk I/O: MapReduce writes to the local disk at the end of the map phase and to HDFS at the end of the reduce phase. This means that while processing 1 Tb of data, the system may write 4 Tb of data to disk and send 2 Tb of data over the network. When the application is stringing multiple MapReduce jobs together, the situation is even worse. Spark's RDDs can be stored in memory and processed in multiple steps or iterations without additional I/O. Because there are no special map and reduce phases, data is typically read from disk when processing starts and written to disk only when there is a need to persist results.
3. Storage: Spark gives developers flexibility to store RDDs:
    a. In memory on a single node
    b. In memory but replicated to multiple nodes
    c. Persisted to disk

    An RDD can go through multiple stages of transformation (equivalent to multiple map and reduce phases) without storing anything to disk.
4. Multilanguage: While Spark itself is developed in Scala (see Section 13.5, "Scala"), Spark APIs are implemented for Java, Scala, and Python. This allows developers to use Spark in the language in which they are most productive. Hadoop developers often use Java APIs, whereas data scientists often prefer the Python implementation so that they can use Spark combined with Python's powerful numeric processing libraries.
5. Resource manager independence: Spark supports both YARN and Mesos as resource managers, as well as in a standalone mode. Since each resource manager has its own strengths and limitations, Spark enables developers to use resource manager(s) of their choice. This allows Spark to be enabled for changes in resource managers in future.
6. Simplicity: Spark APIs are significantly cleaner and simpler than those of MapReduce. The APIs are so usable that they obviate the need for any high-level abstractions on top of Spark like those that are essential for MapReduce, such as Hive or Pig. Consequently, Spark codes are significantly shorter than their MapReduce equivalents and are easily readable even by someone not familiar with Spark.
7. Versatility: Spark was built from the ground up to be an extensible, general-purpose parallel-processing framework. It is generic enough to support a stream-processing framework called Spark Streaming and a graph processing engine called GraphX. With this flexibility, Spark can be expected to see many new special-purpose libraries in the future.

13.2 Functional Programming

Functional Programming has its roots in the lambda calculus, originally developed in the 1930s, to explore computability. Many Functional Programming languages can thus be considered as elaborations on this lambda calculus. There have been numerous pure Functional Programming languages including Common Lisp, Clojure and Haskell. Scala allows you to write in a purely Functional Programming style or to combine functions with objects. Care needs to be taken when doing this that the principles of Functional Programming, and thus the corresponding advantages of Functional Programming, are not undermined. However, when used judiciously, functional programming can be a huge benefit for, and an enhancement to, the purely Object Oriented world.

Programming paradigms can be of two fundamental types, namely, imperative programming and functional programming. Imperative Programming is what is currently perceived as traditional programming; it is the style of programming used in languages such as C, C++, Java and C# so on. In these languages a programmer tells the computer what to do, for example, x = y + z so on. It is thus oriented around control statements, looping constructs and assignments. In contrast, functional programming aims to describe the solution.

Functional Programming is defined as a programming paradigm including a style of building the structure and elements of computer programs that treats computation as the evaluation of mathematical functions and avoids state and mutable data. The functions generate results based on input data and computations to generate a new output; they do not rely on any side effects and also do not depend on the current state of the program.

Characteristics of functional programming:

1. Functional Programming aims to avoid side effects: functions disallow any hidden side effects; only observable output allowed is the return value; only output dependency allowed are the arguments that are fully determined before any output is generated. Lack of hidden side effects evidently makes it easier to understand what the program is doing and also make comprehension, development and maintenance easier.
2. Functional Programming avoids concepts such as state. If some operation is dependent upon the state of the program or some element of a program, then its behavior may differ depending upon that state; this may make it harder to comprehend, implement, test and debug. As all of these impact on the stability and probably reliability of a system, state based operations may result in less reliable software being developed. As functions do not rely on any given state but only upon the data they are given, it results are easier to understand, implement, test and debug.
3. Functional Programming promotes declarative programming (and is in fact a subtype of declarative programming), which means that programming is oriented around expressions that describe the solution rather than focus on the imperative approach of most procedural programming languages. These languages emphasize aspects of how the solution is derived.

   For example, an imperative approach to looping through some container and printing out each result in turn would look like this:

   ```
   int sizeOfCarton = carton.length
   for (int I = 1 to sizeOfcarton) do
   element = carton.get(i)
   print(element)
   enddo
   ```

   Where as a functional programming approach would look like

   ```
   carton.foreach(print)
   ```

4. Functional Programming promotes immutable data. Immutability indicates that once created, data cannot be changed. In Scala Strings are immutable. Once you create a new string you cannot modify it. Any functions that apply to a string that would conceptually alter the contents of the string, result in a new String being generated. Scala takes this further by having a presumption of Immutability that means that by default all data holding types are immutable. This ensures that functions cannot have hidden side effects and thus simplifies programming in general.

> TheAkka Actor model builds on this approach to provide a very clean model for multiple interacting concurrent systems.

5. Functional Programming promotes recursion as a natural control structure. Functional languages tend to emphasis recursion as a way of processing structures that would use some form of looping constructs in an imperative language. While recursion is very expressive and is a great way for a programmer to write a solution to a problem, it is not as efficient at run time as looping. However, any expression that can be written as a recursive routine can also be written using looping constructs. Functional programming languages often incorporate tail end recursive optimizations to convert recursive routines into iterative ones at runtime, that is, if the last thing a routine does before it returns is to call another routine, rather than actually invoking the routine and having to set up the context for that routine, it should be possible to reuse the current context and to treat it in an iterative manner as a loop around that routine. This means that both the programmer benefits of an expressive recursive construct, and the runtime benefits of an iterative solution, can be achieved using the same source code. This option is typically not available in imperative languages.

Advantages of functional programming are as follows:

a. Good for prototyping solutions: Solutions can be created very quickly for algorithmic or behavior problems in a functional language. Thus, allowing ideas and concepts to be explored in a rapid application development style.
b. Modular Functionality: Functional Programming is modular in terms of functionality (where Object Oriented languages are modular in the dimension of components). They are thus well suited to situations where it is natural to want to reuse or componentize the behavior of a system.
c. The avoidance of state based behavior: As functions only rely on their inputs and outputs (and avoid accessing any other stored state) they exhibit a cleaner and simpler style of programming. This avoidance of state based behavior makes many difficult or challenging areas of programming simpler (such as those used in concurrency applications).
d. Additional control structures: A strong emphasis on additional control structures such as pattern matching, managing variable scope, and tail recursion optimizations.

e. Concurrency and immutable data: As functional programming systems advocate immutable data structures it is simpler to construct concurrent systems. This is because the data being exchanged and accessed is immutable. Therefore multiple executing thread or processes cannot affect each other adversely.

f. Partial Evaluation: Since functions do not have side effects, it also becomes practical to bind one or more parameters to a function at compile time and to reuse these functions with bound values as new functions that take fewer parameters.

Disadvantages of functional programming are as follows:

a. Input–output is harder in a purely functional language. Input–output flows naturally align with stream style processing, which does not neatly fit into the "data in, results out" nature of functional systems.

b. Interactive applications are harder to develop. Interactive application is constructed via "request response" cycles initiated by a user action. Again these do not naturally sit within the purely functional paradigm.

c. Not data oriented. A pure functional Language does not really align with the needs of the primarily data oriented nature of many of today's systems. Many commercial systems are oriented around the need to retrieve data from a database, manipulate it in some way and store that data back into a database: such data can be naturally (and better) represented via objects in an Object Oriented language.

d. Continuously running programs such as services or controllers may be more difficult to develop, as they are naturally based upon the idea of a continuous loop that do not naturally sit within the purely functional paradigm.

e. Functional programming languages have tended to be less efficient on current hardware platforms. This is partly because current hardware platforms are not designed with functional programming in mind and also because many of the systems previously available were focused on the academic community for whom performance was not the primary focus *per se*. However, this has changed to a large extent with Scala and the functional language Heskell.

Functional is not as prevalent as imperative programming because of many reasons:

- Programmers are less familiar with functional programming concepts and thus find it harder to pick up function oriented languages.
- Functional Programming idioms are often less intuitive to programmers than imperative programming idioms (such as lazy evaluations), which can make debugging and maintenance harder.

- Many Functional Programming languages have been viewed as exotic languages that are relevant only for academics. While this has been true of some of the older functional languages, the situation is changing with the advent of languages such as Scala.

13.3 Clojure

Clojure was forged out of a unique blend of the best features of a number of different programming languages—including various Lisp implementations, Ruby, Python, Java, Haskell, and others—Clojure provides a set of capabilities suited to address many of the most frustrating problems programmers struggle with today and those we can see barreling toward us over the horizon. And, far from requiring a sea-change to a new or unfamiliar architecture and runtime (typical of many otherwise promising languages over the years), Clojure is hosted on the Java Virtual Machine, a fact that puts to bed many of the most pressing pragmatic and legacy concerns raised when a new language is considered.

Characteristics of Clojure are as follows:

1. Clojure is hosted on the JVM: Clojure code can use any Java library, Clojure libraries can in turn be used from Java, and Clojure applications can be packaged just like any other Java application and deployed anywhere that other Java applications can be deployed: to web application servers; to desktops with Swing, SWT, or command-line interfaces; and so on. This also means that Clojure's runtime is Java's runtime, one of the most efficient and operationally reliable in the world.
2. Clojure is a Lisp: Unlike Java, Python, Ruby, C++, and other members of the Algol family of programming languages, Clojure is part of the Lisp family. However, forget everything you know (or might have heard rumored) about Lisps: Clojure retains the best of Lisp heritage, but is unburdened by the shortcomings and sometimes anachronistic aspects of many other Lisp implementations. Also, being a Lisp, Clojure has macros, an approach to metaprogramming and syntactic extension that has been the benchmark against which other such systems have been measured for decades.
3. Clojure is a functional programming language: Clojure encourages the use of first-class and higher-order functions with values and comes with its own set of efficient immutable data structures. The focus on a strong flavor of functional programming encourages the elimination of common bugs and faults due to the use of unconstrained mutable state and enables Clojure's solutions for concurrency and parallelization.
4. Clojure offers innovative solutions to the challenges inherent in concurrency and parallelization: The realities of multicore, multi-CPU, and distributed computing demand that we use languages and libraries that have been designed with these contexts in mind. Clojure's reference types enforce a clean separation of state and identity, providing defined concurrency semantics that are to manual locking and threading strategies what garbage collection is to manual memory management.
5. Clojure is a dynamic programming language: Clojure is dynamically and strongly typed (and therefore similar to Python and Ruby), yet function calls are compiled down to (fast!) Java method invocations. Clojure is also dynamic in the sense that it deeply supports updating and loading new code at runtime, either locally or remotely. This is particularly useful for enabling interactive development and debugging or even instrumenting and patching remote applications without downtime.

13.4 Python

Python is a versatile programming language that has been widely adopted across the data science sector over the last decade. Although popular programming languages like Java and C++ are better for developing standalone desktop applications, Python is terrific for processing, analyzing, and visualizing data.

We mentioned that the two most relevant Python characteristics are its ability to integrate with other languages and its mature package system that is well embodied by PyPI (the Python Package Index; https://pypi.python.org/pypi), a common repository for a majority of Python packages. The packages are strongly analytical and will offer a complete Data Science Toolbox made up of highly optimized functions for working, optimal memory configuration, ready to achieve scripting operations with optimal performance.

13.4.1 NumPy

NumPy, which is Travis Oliphant's creation, is the true analytical workhorse of the Python language. It provides the user with multidimensional arrays, along with a large set of functions to operate a multiplicity of mathematical operations on these arrays. Arrays are blocks of data arranged along multiple dimensions, which implement mathematical vectors and matrices. Arrays are useful not just for storing data, but also for fast matrix operations (vectorization), which are indispensable when you wish to solve ad hoc data science problems.

As a convention, when importing NumPy, it is aliased as np:

```
import num py as np
```

13.4.2 SciPy

SciPy completes NumPy's functionalities, offering a larger variety of scientific algorithms for linear algebra, sparse matrices, signal and image processing, optimization, fast Fourier transformation, and much more.

13.4.3 Pandas

The pandas package deals with everything that NumPy and SciPy cannot do. Thanks to its specific object data structures, Data Frames and Series, pandas allows you to handle complex tables of data of different types (which is something that NumPy's arrays cannot do) and time series. Pandas enable you to easily and smoothly load data from a variety of sources. You can then slice, dice, handle missing elements, add, rename, aggregate, reshape, and finally visualize this data at your will.

pandas is imported as pd:

```
import pandas as pd
```

13.4.4 Scikit-Learn

Scikit-learn is the core of data science operations on Python. It offers all that you may need in terms of data preprocessing, supervised and unsupervised learning, model selection, validation, and error metrics.

13.4.5 IPython

A scientific approach requires the fast experimentation of different hypotheses in are producible fashion. IPython was created by Fernando Perez in order to address the need for an interactive Python command shell (which is based on shell, web browser, and the application interface), with graphical integration, customizable commands, rich history (in the JSON format), and computational parallelism for an enhanced performance.

13.4.6 Matplotlib

Matplotlib is the library that contains all the building blocks that are required to create quality plots from arrays and to visualize them interactively.

```
import matplotlib.pyplot as plt
```

13.4.7 Stats Models

Previously part of SciKits, stats models was thought to be a complement to SciPy statistical functions. It features generalized linear models, discrete choice models, time-series analysis, and a series of descriptive statistics as well as parametric and nonparametric tests.

13.4.8 Beautiful Soup

Beautiful Soup, a creation of Leonard Richardson, is a great tool to scrap out data from HTML and XML files retrieved from the Internet. It works incredibly well, even in the case of tag soups (hence the name), which are collections of malformed, contradictory, and incorrect tags.

13.4.9 NetworkX

NetworkX is a package specialized in the creation, manipulation, analysis, and graphical representation of real-life network data (it can easily operate with graphs made up of a million nodes and edges). Besides specialized data structures for graphs and fine visualization methods (2D and 3D), it provides the user with many standard graph measures and algorithms, such as the shortest path, centrality, components, communities, clustering, and PageRank.

13.4.10 NLTK

The Natural Language Toolkit (NLTK) provides access to corpora and lexical resources and to a complete suite of functions for statistical natural language processing (NLP), ranging from tokenizers to part-of-speech taggers and from tree models to named-entity recognition. Initially, the package was created by StevenBird and Edward Loper as an NLP teaching infrastructure for CIS-530 at the University of Pennsylvania. It is a fantastic tool that you can use to prototype and build NLP systems.

13.4.11 Gensim

Gensim, programmed by Radim Řehůřek, is an open source package that is suitable for the analysis of large textual collections with the help of parallel distributable online algorithms. Among advanced functionalities, it implements Latent Semantic Analysis (LSA), topic modeling by Latent Dirichlet Allocation (LDA), and Google's word2vec, a powerful algorithm that transforms text into vector features that can be used in supervised and unsupervised machine learning.

13.4.12 PyPy

PyPy is not a package; it is an alternative implementation of Python 2.7.8 that supports most of the commonly used Python standard packages (unfortunately, NumPy is currently not fully supported). As an advantage, it offers enhanced speed and memory handling. Thus, it is very useful for heavy duty operations on large chunks of data and it should be part of your big data handling strategies.

13.5 Scala

Scala is a new programming language developed by Martin Odersky and his team at the EPFL (EcolePolytheniqueFererale de Lausanne, Lausanne, Switzerland) and now supported by Typesafe. The name Scala is derived from Sca(lable) La(nguage) and is a multiparadigm language, incorporating Object Oriented approaches with Functional Programming. Like any other object oriented language (such as Java, C# or C++) Scala can exploit inheritance, polymorphism and abstraction and encapsulation techniques. However, you can also develop solutions using purely functional programming principles in a similar manner to languages such as Haskell or Clojure; in such an approach programs are written purely in terms of functions that take inputs and generate outputs without any side effects. Thus, it is possible to combine the best of both worlds when creating a software system: you can exploit object-oriented principles to structure your solution but integrate functional aspects when appropriate.

One of the design goals of the Scala development team was to create a scalable language suitable for the construction of component based software within highly concurrent environments. This means that is has several features integrated into it that support large software developments. For example, the Actor model of concurrency greatly simplifies the development of concurrent applications. In addition the syntax reduces the amount of code that must be written by a developer (at least compared with Java).

Scala can be compiled to Java Byte Codes. This means that a Scala system can run on any environment that supports the Java Virtual Machine (JVM). There are already several languages that compile to Java Byte codes including Ada, JavaScript, Python, Ruby, Tcl and Prolog. However, this has the additional advantage that Scala can also be integrated with any existing Java code base that a project may have. It also allows Scala to exploit the huge library of Java projects available both for free and for commercial use.

Characteristics of Scala are as follows:

- Provides Object Oriented concepts including classes, objects, inheritance, and abstraction.

- Extends these (at least with reference to Java) to include Traits that represent data and behavior that can be mixed into classes and objects.
- Includes functional concepts, such as functions as first class entities in the language, as well as concepts such as partially applied functions and currying that allow new functions to be constructed from existing functions.
- Has interoperability (mostly) with Java.
- Uses statically typed variables and constants with type inference used whenever possible to avoid unnecessary repetition.

13.5.1 Scala Advantages

Scala's strong type system, preference for immutability, functional capabilities, and parallelism abstractions make it easy to write reliable programs and minimize the risk of unexpected behavior.

13.5.1.1 Interoperability with Java

Scala runs on the Java virtual machine; the Scala compiler compiles programs to Java byte code. Thus, Scala developers have access to Java libraries natively. Given the phenomenal number of applications written in Java, both open source and as part of the legacy code in organizations, the interoperability of Scala and Java helps explain the rapid popularity of Scala.

13.5.1.2 Parallelism

Parallel programming is difficult because we, as programmers, tend to think sequentially. Reasoning about the order in which different events can happen in a concurrent program is very challenging.

Scala provides several abstractions that greatly facilitate the writing of parallel code. These abstractions work by imposing constraints on the way parallelism is achieved. For instance, parallel collections force the user to phrase the computation as a sequence of operations (such as map, reduce, and filter) on collections. Actor systems require the developer to think in terms of actors that encapsulate the application state and communicate by passing messages.

13.5.1.3 Static Typing and Type Inference

Scala's static typing system is very versatile. A lot of information as to the program's behavior can be encoded in types, allowing the compiler to guarantee a certain level of correctness. This is particularly useful for code paths that are rarely used. A dynamic language cannot catch errors until a particular branch of execution runs, so a bug can persist for a long time until the program runs into it. In a statically typed language; any bug that can be caught by the compiler will be caught at compile time, before the program has even started running.

13.5.1.4 Immutability

Having immutable objects removes a common source of bugs. Knowing that some objects cannot be changed once instantiated reduces the number of places bugs can creep in. Instead of considering the lifetime of the object, we can narrow in on the constructor.

Scala encourages the use of immutable objects. In Scala, it is very easy to define an attribute as immutable:

val amountExpnd = 200

The default collections are immutable:

```
valrolIds = List("123", "456") // List is immutable
rollIds(1) = "589"             // Flag Compile-time error
```

13.5.1.5 Scala and Functional Programs

Scala encourages functional code. A lot of Scala code consists of using higher-order functions to transform collections. The developer does not have to deal with the details of iterating over the collection.

Consider the problem of locating in a list the position of occurrence of an identified element. In Scala, we first declare a new list, collection.rollWithIndex, whose elements are pairs of the collection's elements and their indexes, that is, (collection(0), 0) and (collection(1), 1).

We then tell Scala that we want to iterate over this collection, binding the currentElem variable to the current element and index to the index. We apply a filter on the iteration, selecting only those elements for which currentElem==elem. We then tell Scala to just return the index variable.

A sample occurrencesOf function would be

```
def occurrencesOf[A](elem:A, collection:List[A]):List[Int] = {
for {
(currentElem, index) <- collection.rollWithIndex
if (currentElem == elem)
} yield index
}
```

We did not need to deal with the details of the iteration process in Scala. The syntax is very declarative: we tell the compiler that we want the index of every element equal to elem in collection and let the compiler worry about how to iterate over collection.

13.5.1.6 Null Pointer Uncertainty

Scala, like other functional languages, introduces the Option[T] type to represent an attribute that might be absent. We might then write the following:

```
class User {
...
val email:Option[Email]
...
}
```

Thus, Scala goes further in achieving a higher degree of provable correctness. Never using null, we know that we will never run into null pointer exceptions. Achieving the same level of correctness in languages without Option[T] requires writing unit tests on the client code to verify that it behaves correctly when the e-mail attribute is null.

> Scala introduces many concepts such as implicits, type classes, and composition using traits that might not be familiar to programmers coming from the object-oriented world. Scala's type system is very expressive, but getting to know it well enough to use its full power takes time and requires adjusting to this new programming paradigm.

13.5.2 Scala Benefits

13.5.2.1 Increased Productivity

Having a compiler that performs a lot of type checking and works as a personal assistant is, in our opinion, a significant advantage over languages that check types dynamically at runtime, and the fact that Java is a statically typed language is probably one of the main reasons that made it so popular in the first place. The Scala compiler belongs to this category as well and goes even further by finding out many of the types automatically, often relieving the programmer from specifying these types explicitly in the code. Moreover, the compiler in your Integrated Development Environment (IDE) gives instant feedback, and therefore, increases your productivity.

13.5.2.2 Natural Evolution from Java

Scala integrates seamlessly with Java, which is a very attractive feature, to avoid reinventing the wheel. You can start running Scala today in a production environment. Large corporations such as Twitter, LinkedIn, or Foursquare (to name a few) have done that on large-scale deployments for many years now, followed recently by other big players such as Intel and Amazon. Scala compiles to Java byte code, which means that performance will be comparable. Most of the code that you are running while executing Scala program is probably Java code, the major difference being what programmers see and the advanced type checking while compiling code.

13.5.2.3 Better Fit for Asynchronous and Concurrent Code

To achieve better performance and handle more load, modern Java frameworks and libraries for web development are now tackling difficult problems that are tied to multicore architectures and the integration with unpredictable external systems. Scala's incentive to use immutable data structures and functional programming constructs as well as its support for parallel collections has a better chance to succeed in writing concurrent code that will behave correctly. Moreover, Scala's superior type system and macro support enable DSLs for trivially safe asynchronous constructs—for example, composable futures and asynchronous language extensions.

> Scala is the only language that is statically typed, runs on the JVM and is totally Java compatible, is both object-oriented and functional, and is not verbose, thereby leading to better productivity, less maintenance, and therefore more fun.

13.6 R

R is also known as GNU S, as it is basically an open source derivative and descendant of the S language. In various forms and avatars, R has been around for almost two decades now, with an ever growing library of specialized data visualization, data analysis, and data manipulation packages. With around two million users, R has one of the largest libraries of statistical algorithms and packages. While R was initially a statistical computing language, by now it has evolved into a complete analytical environment.

R is available for free download.

> Statistics are basically numbers that inform (descriptive), advise (prescriptive), or forecast (predictive). Analytics is a decision making-assistance tool. Analytics on which no decision is to be made or is being considered can be classified as purely statistical and nonanalytical. Thus the ease with which a correct decision can be made separates a good analytical platform from a not-so-good one. One way in which business analytics differs from statistical analysis is the cost of perfect information (data costs in the real world) and the opportunity cost of delayed and distorted decision making.

13.6.1 Analytical Features of R

13.6.1.1 General

1. The latest and broadest range of statistical algorithms are available in R. This is due to R's package structure in which it is rather easier for developers to create new packages than in any other comparable analytics platform.
2. It is easy to migrate from other analytical platforms to the R platform. It is relatively easy for a non-R platform user to migrate to the R platform, and there is no danger of vendor lock-in due to the GPL nature of the source code and the open community, the GPL can be seen at http://www.gnu.org/copyleft/gpl.html.
3. R offers flexible programming for your data environment. This includes packages that ensure compatibility with Java, Python, and CCC.
4. R offers the best data visualization tools in analytical software (apart from Tableau Software's latest version). The extensive data visualization available in R comprises a wide variety of customizable graphics as well as animation. The principal reason why third-party software initially started creating interfaces to R is because the graphical library of packages in R was more advanced and was acquiring more features by the day.
5. A wide range of training material in the form of books is available for the R analytical platform.
6. R's source code is designed to ensure complete custom solutions and embedding for a particular application. Open source code has the advantage of being extensively peer-reviewed in journals and the scientific literature. This means bugs will found, information about them shared, and solutions delivered transparently.

13.6.1.2 Business Dashboard and Reporting

1. R offers data visualization through ggplot, and GUIs such as Deducer, GrapheR, and Red-R can help even business analysts who know none or very little of the Rlanguage in creating a metrics dashboard.
2. For online dashboards R has packages like RWeb, RServe, and R Apachethat, in combination with data visualization packages, offer powerful dashboard capabilities. Well-known examples of these will be shown later.
3. R can also be combined with Microsoft Excel using the R Excel package to enable R capabilities for importing within Excel. Thus an Excel user with no knowledge of R can use the GUI within the R Excel plug-in to take advantage of the powerful graphical and statistical capabilities.

13.6.1.3 Data Mining

1. R has a vast array of packages covering standard regression, decision trees, association rules, cluster analysis, machine learning, neural networks, and exotic specialized algorithms like those based on chaos models.
2. R provides flexibility in tweaking a standard algorithm by allowing one to see the source code.
3. The Rattle GUI remains the standard GUI for data miners using R. This GUI offers easy access to a wide variety of data mining techniques. It was created and developed in Australia by Prof. Graham Williams. Rattle offers a very powerful and convenient free and open source alternative to data mining software.

13.6.1.4 Business Analytics

1. It has open source code for customization as per GPL and adequate intellectual protection for developers wanting to create commercial packages.
2. It also has a flexible option for enterprise users from commercial vendors like Revolution Analytics (who support 64-bit Windows and now Linux) as well as big data processing through its RevoScaleR package.
3. It has interfaces from almost all other analytical software including SAS, SPSS, JMP, Oracle Data Mining, and RapidMiner. Exist huge library of packages is available for regression, time series, finance, and modeling.
4. High-quality data visualization packages are available for use with R.
5. R is one of the few analytical platforms that work on Mac OS.

Additional analytical features of R:

1. A wide range of solutions from the R package library for statistical, analytical, data mining, dashboard, data visualization, and online applications make it the broadest analytical platform in the field.
2. Largest and fastest growing open source statistical library: The current number of statistical packages and the rate of growth at which new packages continue to be upgraded ensure the continuity of R as a long-term solution to analytical problems.

3. Extensive data visualization capabilities: These include much better animation and graphing than other software.
4. Interoperability of data: Data from various file formats as well as various databases can be used directly in R, connected via a package, or reduced to an intermediate format for importing into R.
5. Software compatibility: Official commercial interfaces to R have been developed by numerous commercial vendors including software makers who had previously thought of R as a challenger in the analytical space. Oracle, ODBC, Microsoft Excel, PostgreSQL, MySQL, SPSS, Oracle Data Miner, SAS/IML, JMP, Pentaho Kettle, and Jaspersoft BI are just a few examples of commercial software that are compatible with R usage. In terms of the basic SAS language, a WPS software reseller offers a separate add-on called the Bridge to R.
6. Multiple platforms and interfaces to input commands: R has multiple interfaces ranging from command line to numerous specialized graphical user interfaces (GUIs) for working on desktops. For clusters, cloud computing, and remote server environments, R now has extensive packages including SNOW, RApache, RMpi, R Web, and Rserve.

13.7 SAS

SAS was originally the acronym for Statistical Analysis System, which is an integrated software system that utilizes fourth-generation programming language to perform tasks like data management, report writing, statistical analysis, data warehousing, and application development. The core component of the SAS system is Base SAS software, which consists of different modules such as DATA steps, SAS Base procedures, SAS macro facility, and Output Delivery System (ODS).

The SAS system is divided into two main areas: procedures to perform an analysis and the fourth-generation language called DATA Step that allows users to manipulate data.

SAS consists of the following:

1. A data handling language (DATA step)
2. A library of prewritten procedures (PROC step)

For the context of this book, the most relevant products are SAS/STAT, SAS Enterprise Miner™ for data mining, and the SAS Text Analytics suite. SAS/STAT software, a component of the SAS System, provides comprehensive statistical tools for a wide range of statistical analyses, including analysis of variance, regression, categorical data analysis, multivariate analysis, survival analysis, psychometric analysis, cluster analysis, and nonparametric analysis. The features provided by SAS/STAT software are in addition to the features provided by Base SAS software; many data management and reporting capabilities required commonly are already part of the Base SAS software.

13.7.1 SAS DATA Step

The DATA step is your primary tool for reading and processing data in the SAS System. The DATA step provides a powerful general purpose programming language that enables you to perform all kinds of data processing tasks.

13.7.2 Base SAS Procedures

Base SAS software includes many useful SAS procedures. Base SAS procedures are documented in the SAS Procedures Guide.

The following is a list of base SAS procedures:

- CORR compute correlations
- RANK compute rankings or order statistics
- STANDARD standardize variables to a fixed mean and variance
- MEANS compute descriptive statistics and summarizing or collapsing data
- Over cross sections
- TABULATE print descriptive statistics in tabular format
- UNIVARIATE compute descriptive statistics

Other SAS software products are as follows:

1. SAS/ETS Software: SAS/ETS software provides SAS procedures for econometrics and time-series analysis. It includes capabilities for forecasting, systems modeling and simulation, seasonal adjustment, and financial analysis and reporting. In addition, SAS/ETS software includes an interactive time-series forecasting system.
2. SAS/GRAPH Software: SAS/GRAPH software includes procedures that create two- and three-dimensional high resolution color graphics plots and charts. You can generate output that graphs the relationship of data values to one another, enhance existing graphs, or simply create graphics output that is not tied to data.
3. SAS/IML Software:SAS/IML software gives you access to a powerful and flexible programming language (Interactive Matrix Language) in a dynamic, interactive environment. The fundamental object of the language is a data matrix. You can use SAS/IML software interactively (at the statement level) to see results immediately, or you can store statements in a module and execute them later. The programming is dynamic because necessary activities such as memory allocation and dimensioning of matrices are done automatically. SAS/IML software is of interest to users of SAS/STAT software because it enables you to program your methods in the SAS System.
4. SAS/INSIGHT Software: SAS/INSIGHT software is a highly interactive tool for data analysis. You can explore data through a variety of interactive graphs including bar charts, scatter plots, box plots, and three-dimensional rotating plots. You can examine distributions and perform parametric and nonparametric regression, analyze general linear models and generalized linear models, examine correlation matrixes, and perform principal component analyses. Any changes you make to your data show immediately in all graphs and analyses. You can also configure SAS/INSIGHT software to produce graphs and analyses tailored to the way you work. SAS/INSIGHT software may be of interest to users of SAS/STAT software for interactive graphical viewing of data, editing data, exploratory data analysis, and checking distributional assumptions.
5. SAS/OR Software: AS/OR software provides SAS procedures for operations research and project planning and includes a point-and-click interface to project management. Its capabilities include the following:
    a. Solving transportation problems
    b. Linear, integer, and mixed-integer programming

   c. Nonlinear programming
   d. Scheduling projects
   e. Plotting Gantt charts
   f. Drawing network diagrams
   g. Solving optimal assignment problems
   h. Network flow programming

   SAS/OR software may be of interest to users of SAS/STAT software for its mathematical programming features. In particular, the NLP procedure in SAS/OR software solves nonlinear programming problems, and it can be used for constrained and unconstrained maximization of user-defined likelihood functions.

6. SAS/QC Software:SAS/QC software provides a variety of procedures for statistical quality control and quality improvement. SAS/QC software includes procedures for Shewhart control charts:
   a. Cumulative sum control charts
   b. Moving average control charts
   c. Process capability analysis
   d. Ishikawa diagrams
   e. Pareto charts
   f. Experimental design

   SAS/QC software also includes the ADX interface for experimental design.

13.8 Summary

This chapter introduced Spark analytics tool that is suitable for iterative and interactive analytics. After an introduction to functional programming and its benefits, the chapter describes important functional languages and tool environments including Clojure, Python, Scala and R. The last part of the chapter describes the SAS analytics solution.

There are three take-aways from this chapter. First, Spark is expected to eclipse MapReduce for most functionality. Spark is already the best choice for machine-learning applications because of its ability to perform iterative operations on data cached in memory. Spark additionally offers SQL, graph processing, and streaming frameworks. Second, Scala is a scalable language suitable for the construction of component based software within highly concurrent environments. Scala is the only language that is statically typed, runs on the JVM and is totally Java compatible, is both object-oriented and functional, and is not verbose, thereby leading to better productivity and, therefore, less maintenance.

Third, Python is a versatile programming language that has been widely adopted across the data science sector over the last decade. Python is also terrific for processing, analyzing, and visualizing data.

14

Big Data DevOps Management

In large enterprises, it is typical to have hundreds of relational databases of different types and multiple data warehouses. Enterprises must be able to analyze together the data from databases, data warehouses, application servers, machine sensors, social media, and so on. Consequently, data needs be organized into repositories that can store data of all kinds, of different types, and from different sources in data refineries and data lakes. This data can be correlated using more data points for increased business value. By processing data from different sources into a single source, organizations can do a lot more descriptive and predictive analytics. Enterprises are not only wanting to predict with high degrees of accuracy but also to reduce the risk in the predictions. Organizing data pooled into a single data source or just a few data sources allows a richer set of questions to be asked of the data. Being able to add additional correlation sources increases the confidence and reduces the risk of the results of the questions.

Traditional Data warehouses are considered more rigid with schema-on-write, ACID compliance, and much less data movement. Data warehouses usually transform the data before entry using well-defined formats. Data analysts and scientists often spend 80% of their time looking at the data and 20% analyzing it. A big data platform can significantly change this ratio, allowing data insight to occur faster. Big data platforms load the data in first and then, based on the analytics and data usage, transform the data as needed.

A data lake is one way to store and process data in its native format. A data lake is a single place to pool all kinds of data and do analysis regardless of the toolset used. A data lake is a new concept where structured, semi-structured, and unstructured data can be pooled into one single repository where business users can interact with it in multiple ways for analytical purposes. A data lake is an enterprise data platform that uses software such as Hadoop and NoSQL. A data lake can run applications of different runtime characteristics. Just as a water lake does not have rigid boundaries and the shoreline of a lake undergoes changes over a period of time, a data lake is designed with inherent flexibility to support new types of data and combinations of data so it can be analyzed for new sources of insight; however, control must be exercised to ensure that only quality data or data with the potential for new insights is ingested into the data lake else it could get clogged and degenerate rapidly into a swamp.

It is highly ineffective, inefficient and expensive for enterprises to have data take a lot of hops when it goes from being stored, transformed, and then analyzed. The data lake can be used as a data ingestion, analytics, and/or compute grid. The data lake can absorb a lot of the ETL processing done by data warehouses and be used to offload data from a data warehouse. This enables a data warehouse to be right-sized and stay at a fixed size. If a data warehouse can store data for only 6 months and the volume of data keeps growing, moving the data to a data lake reduces growth pressure on the data warehouse. Letting the big data platform handle the data ingestion also frees up a lot of compute cycles to be used for analytics and not data ingestion.

A data lake enables business units to land data once in a single place. Backups, analytics, joins, security, downstream reporting, data science, and data ingestion can all be performed in one system. Hadoop's distributed file system enables it to readily store data in any form, so it can be stored in its raw data form. Hadoop is a schema-on-read platform, so a schema does not need to be applied to new data right away. Data can be integrated just-in-time when it is needed.

14.1 Big Data Systems Development Management

14.1.1 Big Data Systems Architecture

The big data systems architecture has the following major components:

1. Big data sources including sensors, web application logs, social networks, and so on.
2. Big data management including (un-)structured data, streaming data, meta data, and so on.
3. Big data analytics applications and tools including MapReduce, Scala, Spark, R, and so on.
4. Big data security infrastructure including fine-grained access control, encryption, and so on.

Figure 14.1 presents the big data systems architecture.

14.1.2 Big Data Systems Lifecycle

The big data systems lifecycle (BDSL) consists of six stages.

14.1.2.1 Data Sourcing

Data come in many forms: structured or unstructured, categorical or numeric, aggregated or transactional, longitudinal or latitudinal, and so on. In most organizations, data live both internally and externally across a variety of platforms. Data can be found in centralized data sets or data warehouses, spreadsheets, applications, service representative notes, social media feeds, third-party data sources, emails, and service calls (speech-to-text). It is not just the raw data that is important, but the variables that analysts can derive from the data.

14.1.2.2 Data Collection and Registration in a Standard Format

Data standardization requires formalization of data definitions, valid values, terminologies, and ontologies, resulting in standards for how data are captured or integrated. If data are standardized at the source, it is much easier to integrate and leverage. If not, standardization is incorporated into the data integration process. With the mass of different data from difference sources, it is unreasonable to expect all source data to be fully standardized; thus, data integration is critical.

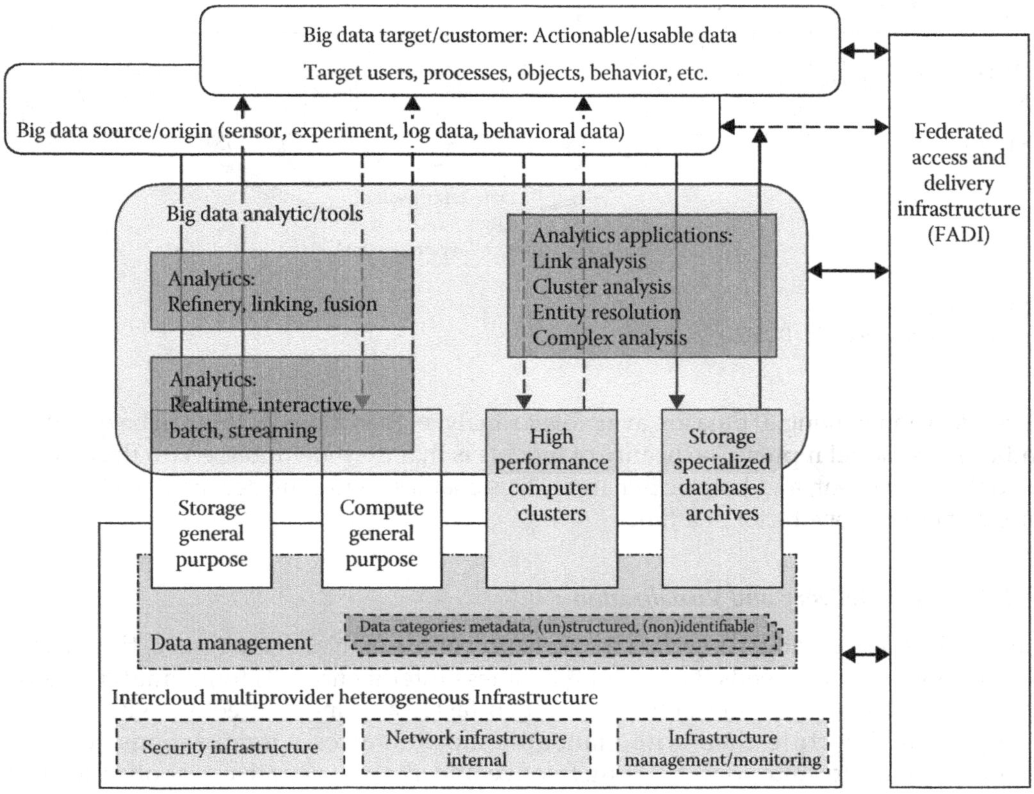

FIGURE 14.1
Big data systems architecture.

14.1.2.3 Data Filter, Enrich, and Classification

At this stage, data are parsed, collapsed, scrubbed, and manipulated. Exploratory techniques using descriptive statistics such as histograms, two-way frequencies, heat maps, and others help uncover opportunities to create new variables or reconfigure the data set. The exploration and preparation phase generates a lot of business insight, revelations, and patterns. In fact, your business stakeholders may find the output of this phase more valuable than the actual modeling results. Many analytic projects are completed at the data exploration stage. For others, a model is the end goal and they move on to the next stage of the analytic lifecycle.

14.1.2.4 Data Analytics, Modeling, and Prediction

Once a modeling data set has been created, analysts can choose from any number of applications, programming languages, and statistical modeling methodologies to start their work. In general, some problems are better suited to certain tools or techniques, but most analysts will use a wide range of methods in the model development process. As noted in the previous step, it is usually not the methodology or the software that is the differentiator, but the quality of data used as input. Models may be used to simply identify key factors in a process or may be used as a tool to enable more efficiency and automation or

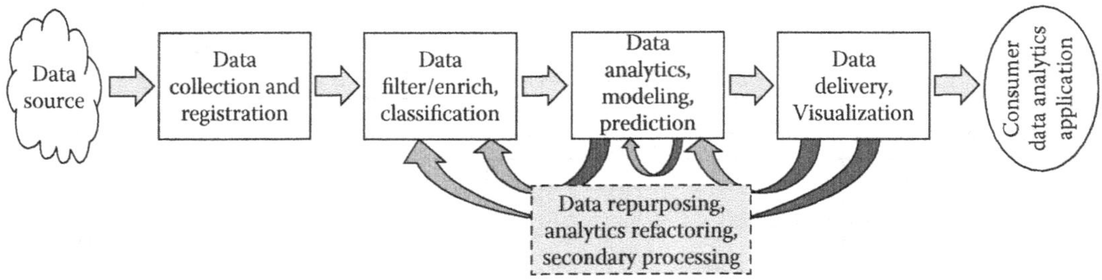

FIGURE 14.2
Big data systems lifecycle (BDSL).

better decision making. If data are available to analyze, then those factors can be quantified and used as model inputs. The beauty of models is that they are unbiased (to the extent of the data), consistent, and holistic in nature. This enables us to consider many factors, all at once rather than one factor at a time.

14.1.2.5 Data Delivery and Visualization

This is, thus, aimed at getting data to the hands of users in an easy-to-use, timely fashion, supporting their needs. Leveraging business intelligence (BI) tools, analytics tools, and portals for information delivery is much faster and more effective with a sound enterprise architecture than with standard, siloed sources. Organizations with bad data often tend to find good tools ineffective and draw a negative response to those tools. However, organizations with sound architectures of integrated data can even make moderate-to-simple tools look excellent. Many BI vendors are now focusing on that target market for their tools and are being very open with customers about the separation of tools and data.

14.1.2.6 Data Supply to Consumer Analytics Applications

Once the data is ready it can be furnished to different consumer applications dealing with sales, production, procurement, sullier management and so on. The BDSL consist of six stages as shown in Figure 14.2.

14.2 Big Data Systems Operations Management

14.2.1 Core Portfolio of Functionalities

This section discusses the functional components that have to be provided by the service provider. All the cloud service providers may not provide all of these components; on the contrary, additional components may be added if the need arises. The delivery of these functional components may be based on different optimization criteria such as cost optimization and performance optimization, and fulfill different user defined constrains like budget, performance, instance types, load balancing, instance prices, and service workload.

The following components are required:

1. Service management: This is the most critical component of the cloud service provider and performs the tasks related to service discovery, service selection (in conjunction with other functions such as semantic engine, and SLA and QoS management), service provisioning, and service de-provisioning. The allocation of services is done in a manner to preserve the on-demand and elastic nature of cloud services provisioning.
2. Metering/billing: This functionality keeps track of the services consumed, along with any aggregations and discounts, and other pricing-related information (in conjunction with rules management and monitoring engine). This module may have integration with external third-party payment gateways and will meter data from various resources and aggregate them so that they can be rated and billed.
3. Data management: It is also an important functionality dealing with data, and their storage and security (in conjunction with integration, transformation, security management, and SLA and QoS management modules).
4. Monitoring: It monitors the business activities, SLAs, holistic service status, outstanding alerts, and policy violations. This module interfaces with most other modules and provides them with relevant information.
5. Security management: It may include identity and access management functionalities for handling user roles, and access issues and security services such as authentication, authorization, auditing, encryption, wire-level security, and other conventional security measures required in a distributed environment. Privacy-related issues are also handled by this module.
6. SLA and QoS management: It makes use of metrics in the relevant areas, some of them being legal metrics, SLA, and QoS requirements pertaining to regulatory, privacy, data security, and penalties management. It also interfaces with the security management, policy management, rules management, logging/audit trails, monitoring, and performance management modules; and defines metrics for usage and assessment of charge-backs, promotions, and discount-related information management.
7. Performance management: It handles the performance-related aspects of business processes and services, and also of the underlying resources. It interfaces with certain other modules such as monitoring and support, and incident management.
8. Policy management: Policy handling including policy creation and assessment, mapping, attachment, and deployment is performed as part of this module. Policy enforcement and escalations must also be applied as appropriate as part of the functionalities of this module.
9. Self-service: It provides customers with the ability to self-register and perform self-service functions including provisioning and management tasks, and also administration. This module ties in with the security management module and may tie in with other modules such as rules management, SLA and QoS management, and policy management.
10. Support and incident management: It involves performance and utilization of diagnostic information at multiple levels to troubleshoot and resolve issues. The cloud management infrastructure must provide diagnostic capabilities for the full stack. Incident management aims to restore normal cloud operations as quickly

as possible and minimize the adverse effect on business operations. This may include resolution of the root causes of incidents and thus minimizes the adverse impact of incidents and problems on business and prevents recurrence of incidents related to these errors. If resolution is not possible, then alternative service deployment may be needed, in conjunction with the service management module.

11. Analytics: This module collects and makes use of historical data and provides analytical information for both internal usages of the cloud service provider and for the cloud users. It provides insights into business trends and user preferences, transaction visibility, business key performance indicator (KPI) monitoring, reporting functionality, and dashboards.
12. Orchestration: Business transactions are often executed by coordinating or arranging existing applications and infrastructure in the cloud to implement business processes. This involves use of technologies and tools such as ESBs, process engines, middleware, legacy, and packaged applications. Event processing may be a useful functionality to have as it provides asynchronous resource coordination and automated policy-based orchestration.
13. Transformation: Involves changing an entity in one form to another at runtime—for example, transformation of an entity from one data model to another or transformation of a message from one protocol to another.
14. Logging/audit trails: It creates logs and audit trails. The module is essential for fulfilling regulatory compliance requirements, and also for interfacing to incident management and essential for security management, SLA and QoS management, and support and incident management modules.
15. Mediation: This module helps resolve the differences between two or more systems in order to integrate them seamlessly. Mediation can happen at different levels such as security, transport, message, API, and protocol.
16. Integration: It is used to facilitate the combination or aggregation of separately produced components or services to perform a larger task, ensuring that the problems in their interactions are addressed by using some intermediary tool, say, mediation. This module is necessary for interfacing to the multiple service providers who do not follow the same standards in terms of protocols, technology, APIs, and so on.
17. Semantic engine: It is a specialized entity (could be optional) that will support the creation of a common understanding of and relationships among entities in a domain by means of creation and usage of ontologies. This module thus facilitates easier mapping and understanding of services provided by different cloud vendors and facilitates in creating ease of interoperability and common understanding among cloud services provided by different vendors.
18. Rules management: It is a support functionality that is used by many other modules to perform complex decision making and evaluation functionalities, and also to map the business requirements in a declarative, easy-to-use manner that allows easy update and changes.

14.2.1.1 Metrics for Interfacing to Cloud Service Providers

The cloud service providers provide mediation, optimization, and value-addition functionalities based on either business or technical requirements of the corresponding cloud users. It is based on these business requirements, specified by means of defined metrics, that the cloud service providers provide the best-fitting service to the users and/or perform necessary selection and filtering of the cloud service providers.

The metrics relevant for interfacing with the cloud service providers are as follows:

14.2.1.1.1 Business Metrics

1. Cost of service: It is one of the most important criteria and may be quite difficult to specify and calculate. Cost of service may be divided into one-time and ongoing fixed costs. The cost may be based on per hour/per transaction/volume of transfer, quota, time of request, availability of resources, and so on. Other criteria may be commercial versus noncommercial provider usage time, and/or cost optimization scheduling. It is one of the most important but also the most difficult parameter to monitor and regulate as it involves comparison of costing data for existing services to newly available services as well. Costing data are complicated and may involve multiple subparameters such as fixed one-time costs and variable costs depending on time and demand.
2. Regulatory-criteria-driven requirements: Regulatory requirements that need to be fulfilled by the cloud user are further taken over to the cloud service provider; examples of such data are geographical constraints such as location of data, logging, audit trails, and privacy.
3. Maximum tolerable latency: This is typically a technical metrics, but in case a business process has some specific response-time-related constraint, then it forms part of the business parameter.
4. Business SLA requirements, including availability guarantees, availability penalties, and penalty exclusions.
5. Data-related requirements, for example, data security, data location, backup, and storage.
6. Role-based access control: These are business-related access control metrics pertaining to the hierarchy of the user organization.
7. On-demand business process deployment and user or application constraint management such as management of budget and deadline.
8. Governance criteria such as quality of service, policy enforcement, and management.
9. Environmental constraints, for example, preference for green providers and incentives for green providers.

14.2.1.1.2 Technical Metrics

1. Virtual machine requirements, say, those related to central processing unit (CPU), memory, and operating system
2. Security-related requirements such as details related to encryption, digital key management, and identity and access management
3. Technical SLA requirements, including alerts and notifications when SLA terms reach a critical point
4. Maximum provisioning time

5. Redundancy and disaster recovery metrics for critical applications or functionalities
6. Environment-safety- and protection-related metrics such as carbon emission rate and CPU power efficiency

14.2.2 Characteristics of Big Data and Cloud Operations

Cloud computational resources can be scaled up and down on demand and paid for on a metered usage basis. The usage characteristics have multiple options based on a host of parameters. These options have to be evaluated on a case-by-case basis.

This ability to configure the various parameters per requirement (or changing requirement) provides tremendous advantages for clients in that they do not have to maintain internal computing systems designed for peak loads that may occur only a small percentage of the time. Though cloud offers the ability to provision massive amounts of computing power and storage, these quantities are not unlimited; like any other physical system, cloud computation must operate within physical limits imposed by practical boundary conditions. Cloud users might have to fit their applications into one set of resource usage categories defined by the cloud provider. The cloud paradigm also supports innovation in that a variety of new, advanced applications can be used in an affordable manner while reducing the total cost of ownership. Some applications that are of long duration and have stable computational requirements might be better served by in-house or leased computers and storage than by paying cloud fees over a long period of time.

The major benefits of cloud computing can be summarized as follows:

- Means to move from operating in a capital expenditure environment to an operational expenditure environment
- Ability to rapidly deploy innovative business and research applications in a cost-effective manner
- Use of virtualization to detach business services from the underlying execution infrastructure
- Capability of disaster recovery and business continuity intrinsically supported by the cloud paradigm
- Ability of the cloud provider to apply security safeguards more effectively and efficiently in a centralized environment
- Ability to select among a variety of cloud vendors that provide reliable scalable services, metered billing, and advanced development resources
- Scalable infrastructure that can rapidly provision and de-allocate substantial resources on an as-needed basis

14.2.3 Core Services

14.2.3.1 Discovery and Replication

Service discovery promotes reusability by allowing service users to find the existing services. RESTful services support discovery and reuse at design time. Replication can be used to create and maintain copies of an enterprise's data at these sites. When events affecting an enterprise's primary location occur, key application services can effectively be restarted and run at the remote location incurring no capital expenditure, only operational expenditure, until such time as the primary site is brought back online. Replication keeps all replicas as part of one atomic transaction. Replication technology is available in storage arrays and network-based appliances, and through host-based software.

14.2.3.2 Load Balancing

Load balancing prevents system bottlenecks due to unbalanced loads. It also considers implementing failover for the continuation of a service after failure of one or more of its components. This means that a load balancer provides a mechanism by which instances of applications can be provisioned and deprovisioned automatically without changing network configuration.

This is an inherited feature from grid-based computing for cloud-based platforms. Energy conservation and resource consumption are not always a focal point when discussing cloud computing; however, with proper load balancing in place, resource consumption can be kept to a minimum. This not only serves to keep costs low and enterprises greener, it also puts less stress on the hardware infrastructure of each individual component, making them potentially last longer. Load balancing also enables other important features such as scalability.

14.2.3.3 Resource Management

Cloud computing provides a way of deploying and accessing massively scalable shared resources on demand, in real time, and at affordable cost. Cloud resource management protocols deal with all kinds of homogeneous and heterogeneous resource environments. Management of virtualized resources, workload and resource scheduling, cloud resource provisioning with QoS, and scalable resource management solutions are the concerning points. Dynamic resource scheduling across a virtualized infrastructure for those environments is another issue for cloud.

14.2.3.4 Data Governance

When data begin to move out of organizations, they are vulnerable to disclosure or loss. The act of moving sensitive data outside the organizational boundaries may also violate national regulations for privacy. In Germany, passing data across national boundaries can be a federal offence. Governance in the cloud defined by *who and how* is the big challenge for enterprise clouds. Governance places a layer of processes and technology around services (location of services, service dependencies, service monitoring, service security, and so on) so that anything occurring will be quickly known. There are some questions that need to be solved before mission-critical data and functionalities can be moved outside a controllable environment.

1. Interoperability: Interoperability means easy migration and integration of applications and data between different vendors' clouds. Owing to different hypervisors (KVM, Hyper-V, ESX, ESXi), VM technologies, storage, configuring operating systems, various security standards, and management interfaces, many cloud systems are not interoperable. However, many enterprises want interoperability between their in-house infrastructure and the cloud. The issue of interoperability needs to be addressed to allow applications to be ported between clouds or to use multiple cloud infrastructures before critical business

applications are delivered from the cloud. Most clouds are completely opaque to their users. Most of the time, users are fine with this until there is an access issue. In such situations, frustration increases exponentially with time, partly because of the opacity.

2. Data migration: Data migration between data centers or cloud systems is an important concern of taxonomy. While migrating data, requisite attention should be given to aspects like no data loss, availability, scalability, cost efficiency, and load balancing. Users should be able to move their data and applications any time from one to another seamlessly, without any one vendor controlling it. Seamless transfer, as in mobile communication, is required for cloud computing to work. Many enterprises do not move their mission-critical data and applications to the cloud because of vendor lock-in, security, governance, and many more complications.

14.2.4 Management Services

The management services contain deployment, monitoring, reporting, service-level agreement, and metering billing. We discuss these in detail.

14.2.4.1 Deployment and Configuration

To reduce the complexity and administrative burden across the cloud deployment, we need the automation process lifecycle. The RightScale Cloud Management Platform addresses three stages of the cloud application deployment lifecycle, namely, design, manage, and deploy. Automated configuration and maintenance of individual or networked computers, from the policy specification, is very important in the computing arena; it improves robustness and functionalities without sacrificing the basic freedoms and self-repairing concepts. That is why, to handle complex systems such as cloud environments and data centers, we need such configuration management. Configuration management framework tools help software developers and engineers manage server and application configuration by writing code, rather than running commands by hand.

14.2.4.2 Monitoring and Reporting

Developing, testing, debugging, and studying the performance of cloud systems are quite complex. Management cost increases significantly as the number of sites increases. To address such problems, we need monitoring and reporting mechanisms. Monitoring basically monitors the SLA lifecycle. It also determines when an SLA completes and reports to the billing services. There are some services that monitor the cloud systems and produce health reports such as Hyperic HQ, which monitors SimpleDB, Simple Queue Service, and Flexible Payment Service, all offered by Amazon. It collects the matrix, and provides a rich analysis and reporting.

14.2.4.3 Service-Level Agreements (SLAs) Management

Users always want stable and reliable system service. Cloud architecture is considered highly available, up and running 24 h × 7 days. Many cloud service providers have made huge investments to make their systems reliable. However, most cloud vendors today do not provide high availability assurances. If a service goes down, for whatever reason, what can a user do? How can users access their documents stored in the cloud? In such a case, the provider should pay a fine to the user as compensation to meet SLAs. An SLA specifies the measurement, evaluation, and reporting of the agreed service-level standards such as the following:

1. How raw quality measures will be used to evaluate agreed service components?
2. How the raw quality measures will be qualified as a service quality measure?
3. How the qualified quality measures will be used to estimate the service quality levels?
4. How the results of service evaluation will be reported?
5. How disputes on service-level evaluation will be resolved?

Currently, Amazon offers a 99.9% monthly uptime percentage SLA for Simple Storage Service (Amazon S3) and credit is limited to 10%. Amazon credits 25% of charges if the availability drops below 99.0%, whereas 3Tera Virtual Private Data Center (VPDC) service will include a 99.999% availability SLA that is supposed to help assure customers about putting mission-critical apps and services in the cloud.

14.2.4.4 Metering and Billing

Transparent metering and billing will increase the trust level of users toward cloud services. Pay-as-you-go subscriptions or pay-as-you-consume models of billing and metering are popular for cloud. This service gets the status of the SLA and invokes the credit service, which debits the user credit card or account and informs the user. There are many pricing strategies such as RAM hours, CPU capacity, bandwidth (inbound/outbound data transfer), storage space (gigabytes of data), software license fee, and subscription-based pricing. There are some interesting new billing models such as GoGrid prepaid cloud hosting plan and IDC cloud billing research, which are great examples of moving cloud pricing models toward telecom models.

14.2.4.5 Authorization and Authentication

In public clouds, safeguards must be placed on machines to ensure proper authentication and authorization. Within the private cloud environment, one can track, pinpoint, control, and manage users who try to access machines with improper credentials. Single sign-on is the basic requirement for a customer who accesses multiple cloud services.

14.2.4.6 Fault Tolerance

In case of failure, there will be a hot backup instance of the application, which is ready to take over without disruption. Cloud computing outages extend into the more refined version of cloud service platforms. Some outages have been quite lengthy. For example, Microsoft Azure had an outage that lasted 22 h on March 13–14, 2008. Cloud reliance can cause significant problems if downtime and outages are removed from your control. Reliance on the cloud can cause real problems when time is money.

Google has also had numerous difficulties with its Gmail and application services. These difficulties have generated significant interest in both traditional media and the blogosphere owing to deep-seated concerns regarding service reliability. The incidents mentioned here are just the tip of the iceberg. Every year, thousands of websites struggle with unexpected downtime and hundreds of networks break or have other issues. So, the major problem for cloud computing is how to minimize outage/failover to provide reliable services. It is important to adopt the well-known Recovery-Oriented Computing (ROC) paradigm in large data centers. Google uses Google File System (GFS) or distributed disk storage; every piece of data is replicated three times. If one machine dies, a master redistributes the data to a new server.

14.2.5 Governance Services

We have seen a number of factors that need to be considered when thinking about a move to a cloud infrastructure. The number of potential issues arising from neglecting any aspect of cloud security is large, and the implications can be catastrophic. While some of the items are mostly applicable during the preparation for a switchover to cloud, many of the pertinent activities remain afterward and require careful management. It is the overall management of the business assets that should provide the focus for how security (among other things) should be considered, and this management is generally referred to as governance.

Governance is oft-talked about in the context of corporate governance, rules, practices, customs, policies, and processes, which define and steer how an organization conducts its daily business. Typically, the act of governance results in the following two key functions:

1. Providing defined chains of authority, responsibility, and communication to empower the appropriate staff to take decisions
2. Defining mechanisms for policy and control, together with the associated measurements, to facilitate roles for staff to undertake

As you would expect, corporate governance is all encompassing when it comes to the operations, strategy, and future trajectory of an organization. It has tended to have been regarded as applicable to more traditional demarcations within business, such as the accounting, sales, human resource management, or production functions, to name a few. However, as we have seen in this book, and in Chapter 10 specifically (Enterprise Cloud Computing), the opportunities created by consuming IT as a utility have the potential to completely transform how business is conducted.

As such, there is emerging recognition that the impact of IT on a business is crucial to its survival, and as more and more legislative and policy controls now assume the use of IT, the need to govern the IT function is now paramount. As we have found elsewhere in this book, cloud computing presents a convergence of the IT and business functions, and thus the governance of IT is a logical next step for organizations that choose to embrace the cloud.

14.2.5.1 Governance

The practice of IT governance needs to understand the different ways in which IT services are delivered and maintained in the presence of a cloud infrastructure. For instance, for each of the issues identified, the governance body needs to understand the implications of noncompliance with regulatory, ethical, business, and political constraints, as well as be suitably prepared for unforeseen circumstances in the future.

Management of this activity requires delegation to a body that can oversee and marshal the holistic perspective while also having the authority to intervene when required. However, it is unlikely that the governing body can understand the totality of details that increasingly complex technology involves, so consideration of the following items is needed:

1. While IT governance is concerned with the technical capabilities and requirements of technology, the adoption of cloud services, together with the associated delegation of authority (but not responsibility) to external partners, reinforces the need to understand the issues that affect the business. Governing IT that includes clouds means that an intimate understanding of the responsibility boundaries is as important as whether there is sufficient bandwidth at each point of access or not.
2. A governance perspective usefully tends to bring to the fore the potential myriad of services that may already exist. This list of services is likely to increase in the future, so it is important to empower the governing board to be able to rationalize and standardize where practicable. This in itself demands a blend of technical and business expertise that the governing board can call upon to inform its operations.
3. The pace of change is rapid, and cloud adoption will only accelerate this change. Meaningful data are required to inform the decisions taken, and therefore, it is necessary to not only understand what metrics need to be monitored and reported, but the mechanisms that do this must be automated.

IT governance should be seen as an opportunity to manage the emerging organization that aspires to align its IT and business needs to generate value. It is likely that this will require a risk-based approach to management, which of course is hugely dependent on the quality of information used to assess and monitor risk. Standards such as COBIT assist the creation of benchmarks upon which monitoring can take place, but the resulting actions that are derived from this approach should not be underestimated. How many in-house applications are subject to security auditing, for instance? What are the implications of executing tested but not audited code on public clouds?

The ability to govern effectively means that an organization must ensure that it can attribute cause to effect, be flexible in its operations, and have the capability to accurately monitor its activities.

14.2.5.2 Security

The first release of the Cloud Security Alliance (CSA) report in 2010 identified seven top threats to cloud computing:

1. Abuse of the cloud refers to the ability to conduct nefarious activities from the cloud—for instance, using multiple AWS instances or applications supported by IaaS to launch Distributed Denial-of-Service (DDoS) attacks (which prevent legitimate users from assessing cloud services) or to distribute spam and malware.
2. Shared technology considers threats due to multitenant access supported by virtualization. VMMs can have flaws allowing a guest operating system to affect the security of the platform shared with other virtual machines.

3. Insecure APIs may not protect users during a range of activities, starting with authentication and access control to monitoring and application control during runtime mode.
4. Malicious insider risk arises because the cloud service providers do not disclose their hiring standards and policies; potential harm due to this particular form of attack is quite substantial.
5. Data loss or leakage risks arise because proprietary or sensitive data may be permanently lost when cloud data replication fails and is also followed by a storage media failure; similarly, inadvertent or unauthorized access to such information by third parties can have severe consequences. Since, maintaining copies of the data outside the cloud is often unfeasible due to the sheer volume of data, both of these risks can have devastating consequences for an individual or an organization using cloud services.
6. Account or service hijacking refers to stealing of credentials and is a significant threat.
7. Unknown risk profile refers to exposure to the ignorance or underestimation of the very risks of cloud computing.

According to this report, the IaaS delivery model can be affected by all threats. PaaS can be affected by all but the shared technology, whereas SaaS is affected by all but abuse and shared technology.

14.2.5.3 Privacy

The advent of the Internet has transformed the familiar issues of security and privacy beyond recognition. This is primarily because of the following:

- Every computer can be accessed and influenced by any other computer anywhere on the Internet; this effectively eliminates the concept of locality.
- Businesses that are supported on such an extended and open IT-substrate are vulnerable to scrutiny and monitoring by interested parties.
- Browsing and visitations of websites to gather information in turn also exposes the visitor's behavior itself to interpretation and analyses.

Consumer privacy issues and concerns have a drastic effect on the enterprise's ability to market to, connect to, and create an ongoing relationship with your customers. Consumers are gravely concerned regarding the abuse of their privacy, but gathering a certain amount of information is necessary for companies to personalize and to serve their customers better. Thus, there is a need for a balance between protecting a consumer's privacy and the need for enterprises to target and personalize their offerings to the customers. In 2000, the U.S. Federal Trade Commission recommended fair information practices of notice, choice, access, and security. Enterprises need to adhere to these practices when creating and implementing their privacy policies.

Consumer-oriented commercial websites that collect personal identifying information from or about consumers online would be required to comply with the four widely accepted fair information practices:

1. Notice: Websites would be required to provide consumers clear and conspicuous notice of their information practices, including what information they collect; how they collect it (e.g., directly or through nonobvious means such as cookies); how they use it; how they provide choice, access, and security to consumers; whether they disclose the information collected to other entities; and whether other entities are collecting information through the site.
2. Choice: Websites would be required to offer consumers choices as to how their personal identifying information is used beyond the reason for which the information was provided (e.g., to consummate a transaction). Such choice would encompass both internal secondary uses (such as marketing back to consumers) and external secondary uses (such as disclosing data to other entities).
3. Access: Websites would be required to offer consumers reasonable access to the information a website has collected about them, including a reasonable opportunity to review information and to correct inaccuracies or delete information.
4. Security: Websites would be required to take reasonable steps to protect the security of the information they collect from consumers. The Commission recognizes that the implementation of these practices may vary with the nature of the information collected and the uses to which it is put, as well as with technological developments. For this reason, the Commission recommends that any legislation be phrased in general terms and be technologically neutral. Thus, the definitions of fair information practices set forth in the statute should be broad enough to provide flexibility to the implementing agency in promulgating its rules or regulations.

Third-party privacy seals are a good way to gain the trust of consumers because these third-party consumer privacy protection organizations certify the enterprise's privacy policy. There are two types of privacy seal programs. One has strict guidelines that prohibit sites from sharing consumer information they collect with other business partners or from using it for direct marketing programs. Secure Assure, which has 200 member companies, offers an audit program but requires members to adhere to a stringent privacy guideline stating that the e-business will never share a consumer's private information with a third party. Other privacy seal programs award stamps of approval to sites that simply stick to whatever privacy policy promises they have made. The oldest and most well-known privacy seal program is Electronic Frontier Foundation's TRUSTe (www.truste.org), which was started in 1997 and has more than 1,300 companies as members.

The threat to information privacy and security can never be eliminated, but controls and technologies can be applied to reduce the risks to acceptable levels. The challenges faced by various enterprises in this regard are described below.

14.2.5.4 Trust

Trust in the context of cloud computing is intimately related to the general problem of trust in online activities. The Internet offers individuals the ability to obscure or conceal their identities. The resulting anonymity reduces the cues normally used in judgments of trust. The identity is critical for developing trust relations; it allows us to base our trust on the past history of interactions with an entity. Anonymity causes mistrust because identity is associated with accountability, and, in the absence of identity, accountability cannot be enforced. The opacity extends immediately from identity to personal characteristics. It is impossible to infer whether the entity or individual we transact with is who it pretends to be, since the transactions occur between entities separated in time and distance. Finally, there are no guarantees that the entities we transact with fully understand the role they have assumed.

To compensate for the loss of clues, we need security mechanisms for access control, transparency of identity, and surveillance. The mechanisms for access control are designed to keep intruders and mischievous agents out. Identity transparency requires that the relationship between a virtual agent and a physical person be carefully checked through methods such as biometric identification. Digital signatures and digital certificates are used for identification. Credentials are used when an entity is not known. Credentials are issued by a trusted authority and describe the qualities of the entity using the credential. A Doctor of Dental Surgery diploma hanging on the wall of a dentist's office is a credential that the individual has been trained by an accredited university and hence is capable of performing a set of dental procedures; similarly, a digital signature is a credential used in many distributed applications. Surveillance could be based on intrusion detection or on logging and auditing. The first option is based on real-time monitoring, the second on offline sifting through audit records.

There are primarily two ways of determining trust, namely, policies and reputation. Policies reveal the conditions to obtain trust and the actions to take when some of the conditions are met. Policies require the verification of credentials. Reputation is a quality attributed to an entity based on a relatively long history of interactions with or possibly observations of the entity. Recommendations are based on trust decisions made by others and filtered through the perspective of the entity assessing the trust.

14.2.5.5 Security Risks

It is important to understand the risks of inadequate security so that an enterprise can make an informed judgment about what, if any, information should be trusted to the cloud.

Since the actual risks to a system are varied, an enterprise typically takes a generalized approach to security and then manages exceptions separately, for instance, identity management; it is usual for an employee to require a user identity for access to a system when on the organization's premises. But this access has a different set of potential vulnerabilities if the employee is working at home or in the field. These specific situations might not apply to the cloud provider, who will by default create security strategies that are relevant for that type of business.

The individual security mechanisms that a number of applications use may not transfer easily to a cloud environment, and therefore, a detailed understanding of the approach taken toward security is required if further, unintended vulnerabilities are not to be introduced. This situation is not new; organizations have been outsourcing data storage and telephone call centers for some time now. What is different about cloud, however, is the depth of the infrastructure that is being entrusted into the cloud. Both data storage and customer care management are discrete, vertical functions that have been devolved to third parties. The devolvement of infrastructure/applications/services is a horizontal function that contains the heart of the organization's operations.

Such is the potential complexity of the situation that enterprises adopt a risk-based approach to security. This is where controls are prioritized toward areas where security risks are the most damaging. One part of a risk-based approach is to ensure that service-level agreements (SLAs) are in place. However, SLAs are often used to protect the supplier, not the customer, again underlining the importance of understanding the security detail so that the requirements are catered for properly. So, even though you may be impressed with the physical security during the sales tour of the cloud provider's premises, it is still your responsibility to ensure that all of the other aspects of security are assured as well.

Access control is an example of perimeter security. Without an account and a password, you cannot penetrate the perimeter of the network. This assumes though that those who have an account are honest and trustworthy. Unfortunately, most breaches in security are the result of employees who have legitimate access, and they are rarely detected. These internal threats do not go away if you move to the cloud, unless the cloud provider offers a more secure service that you can use, which adds protection over and above what you are currently using.

When dealing with security, it helps to be paranoid. Migrating systems to the cloud might increase the headcount of people who have access to your data, so your security strategy must have a provision to deal with threats from the inside. While virtualization is seen as an example of a specific technology that has enabled the cloud delivery model to become workable, it also complicates the demands placed upon a security strategy as servers, storage, and even networks are now executing in virtual environments. Rather than the traditional risk of an employee divulging a password or snooping around a system, an employee of a cloud provider might only have to provide access to the virtualization layer for havoc to be wreaked. In fact, if we consider the elasticity function of a cloud resource, any hacker would have plenty of compute resource to use for nefarious purposes if granted some access to a cloud.

The provision of IT security is a challenge, and the effort required to do it can make the migration to cloud appear an attractive one if it reduces the hassle. However, the enterprise is placing trust in its provider and needs to assure itself that the provider's capabilities are at least as good as the current architecture. Another factor is that today's IT systems are complex and becoming even more intricate and bespoke. The traditional model of security is to define a hard security perimeter (usually around the data center), and monitor all inbound and outbound traffic. The problem with multitenant clouds is that all sorts of traffic will be present at the access point, and in fact another enterprise's traffic might be deemed as hostile, even though the public cloud architecture is designed to have multiple sets of data coexisting in one virtual appliance. This arrangement means that it is meaningless to have systems in place that can both monitor and proactively protect against potential breaches. The system has to be secure at the point of access.

The reality is that breaches happen, and then enterprises need to quickly plug the hole, trying to understand what went wrong afterward. In the case of serious breaches, the default behavior might be to shut a system down completely, which is massively disruptive for a business. Finally, when an enterprise is choosing a potential cloud provider, it may find it difficult to assess a candidate supplier, since they do not release details of their internal services for the purposes of maintaining security.

14.2.6 Cloud Governance, Risk, and Compliance

Cloud computing is a combination of virtualization, process automation, and dynamic response to changing application conditions. None of these, on its own, are anything more than a logical extension of existing IT; the combination, however, changes the way IT operates.

Some of the changes are as follows:

- *Dynamism*: The rapid provisioning of computing resources, as well as rapid change in application topologies as computing resources are dynamically added and subtracted in response to changing application load.

  First of all, cloud computing leverages virtualization, which breaks the association between application and physical server. Consequently, assuming security can be tied to physical resources is no longer practical. Cloud computing extends virtualization to add dynamism—the ability for applications to rapidly change deployment topology. Moreover, user self-service (NIST cloud computing characteristic number one) means that the assumptions of extended deployment timelines, with sufficient opportunity for security review and implementation prior to moving an application into production, are no longer valid.
- *Pooled resources*: Cloud computing abstracts use from assets, where use (i.e., application operation) is not associated with a particular set of computing resources, but instead is hosted in a general pool of computing resources. This means that the location of specific application components may change from time to time as loads are rebalanced within the resource pool. It also means that security measures must not be associated with specific hardware, but must instead migrate dynamically along with the application as it moves from one set of computing resources to another.

  In a pooled resource environment, no user controls the infrastructure, so the common appliance solution is not possible—after all, one user's traffic examination appliance is another user's intrusion threat. Consequently, the shared environment of cloud computing negates many traditional security practices.
- *Security deperimeterization*: Because cloud applications operate in a dynamic, shared resource pool, traditional security solutions are often unusable. Relying on a network-attached appliance to examine all network traffic is unworkable, due to restrictions imposed by cloud providers. Moreover, the ongoing opening up of applications to external parties like partners and customers also means that the traditional model of imposing strong security at the data center perimeter (i.e., relying on a restrictive firewall to prevent traffic from reaching internal resources) is unsustainable as well. The new model of security requires that each endpoint implements security measures to protect itself as appropriate.

  These changes, combined, mean that the traditional models of security, governance, and compliance all change in the world of cloud computing. In the areas of security and compliance, the cloud user and cloud provider both hold some of the responsibility. The interface between where one party's responsibility ends and the other begins may be referred to as the trust boundary. In its basic form, the trust boundary represents a demarcation line: on one side of the line, the cloud provider possesses responsibility for security measures and on the other, the cloud user possesses responsibility (see Figure 8.2). On the cloud provider's side of the trust boundary, the user is a passive assessor of what the cloud provider implements in terms of security practices. On the cloud user's side of the trust boundary, the user is an active implementer of security practices.

  The location of the trust boundary varies according to what model of cloud computing is being used: IaaS, PaaS, or SaaS. Each model has the cloud provider taking on differing levels of responsibility for the total application, and thereby affects where the trust boundary is located. The thick black zigzag line indicates where the trust boundary lies for each cloud delivery model. As an example, in a PaaS environment, the cloud provider is responsible for the security of the infrastructure and the middleware, whereas the cloud user retains responsibility for the security of the application itself. As you can see from the descriptions, this means that the cloud user would need to audit and evaluate whether the security measures of the provider in its areas of responsibility are sufficient.

Every cloud provider offers a security framework into which users integrate their application. Naturally, every provider has a somewhat different framework, so it is incumbent on users to understand the framework and ensure that they integrate with it properly. In fact, it is more than crucial. Without understanding the security framework presented by the cloud provider, it is likely that the cloud user will fail to configure its usage properly, and thereby leave security vulnerabilities that may be exploited by attackers.

Figure 8.2 is a chart of security responsibilities of each of the three cloud delivery models, along with three key areas of responsibility: infrastructure, operating system (and middleware), and application. Given below are brief descriptions of each area of responsibility:

1. *Application*: This area refers to the software used to provide the actual functionality of the application itself. Falling under this area are topics such as software component version verification, patch installation practices, application identity management, and so on.
2. *Operating system and middleware*: This area refers to software components that provide the operating environment within which the application runs. Key security issues for this area of responsibility include whether appropriate security software is installed within the OS, patch installation practices, administrative access to manage these components, and so on.
3. *Infrastructure*: This area addresses both physical security and software security. Physical security refers both to the physical infrastructure of the cloud computing environment (i.e., the data center itself) and the security practices surrounding the physical infrastructure. For example, this area covers whether the data center has redundant Internet access methods, as well as what practices are in place regarding access to the physical facility (e.g., requiring both identification documents and biometric scanning as prerequisites for entering the data center facility). Physical infrastructure would also refer to the hardware within the data center like back up generators, and so on. Finally, infrastructure also refers to the software infrastructure used to implement the cloud computing environment. Most cloud computing (though not all) uses virtualization as a foundation for the cloud computing environment, so this security area would cover the virtualization hypervisor, including security practices related to controlling access to logging into administer the virtualization, and ensuring proper security patches are installed.

14.2.6.1 Cloud Security Solutions

Here is an overview of what cloud users can and should do to minimize security risks regarding data handling by the cloud service provider (CSP). First, users should evaluate the security policies and the mechanism the CSP has in place to enforce these policies. Then users should analyze the information that would be stored and processed on the cloud. Finally, the contractual obligations should be clearly spelled out. The contract between the user and the CSP should do the following:

- State explicitly the CSP's obligations to securely handle sensitive information and its obligation to comply with privacy laws.
- Spell out CSP liabilities for mishandling sensitive information.
- Spell out CSP liabilities for data loss.
- Spell out the rules governing the ownership of the data.
- Specify the geographical regions where information and back ups can be stored.

To minimize security risks, a user may try to avoid processing sensitive data on a cloud.

14.2.6.1.1 Operating System Security

Operating system (OS) is a complex software system consisting of millions of lines of code, and it is vulnerable to a wide range of malicious attacks. An OS does not insulate completely one application from another, and once an application is compromised, the entire physical platform and all applications running on it can be affected. The platform security level is thus reduced to the security level of the most vulnerable application running on the platform. OSs provide only weak mechanisms for applications to authenticate to one another and does not have a trusted path between users and applications. These shortcomings add to the challenges of providing security in a distributed computing environment.

An OS allows multiple applications to share the hardware resources of a physical system, subject to a set of policies. A critical function of an OS is to protect applications against a wide range of malicious attacks such as unauthorized access to privileged information, tampering with executable code, and spoofing. Such attacks can now target even single-user systems such as personal computers, tablets, or smartphones. Data brought into the system may contain malicious code; this could occur via a Java applet, or data imported by a browser from a malicious website. The existence of trusted paths, mechanisms supporting user interactions with trusted software, is critical to system security. If such mechanisms do not exist, malicious software can impersonate trusted software. Some systems provide trust paths for a few functions such as log-in authentication and password changing and allow servers to authenticate their clients. A trusted-path mechanism is required to prevent malicious software invoked by an authorized application to tamper with the attributes of the object and/or with the policy rules.

A highly secure operating system is necessary but not sufficient unto itself; application-specific security is also necessary. Sometimes security implemented above the operating system is better. This is the case for electronic commerce that requires a digital signature on each transaction. Applications with special privileges that perform security-related functions are called trusted applications. Such applications should only be allowed the lowest level of privileges required to perform their functions. For example, type enforcement is a mandatory security mechanism that can be used to restrict a trusted application to the lowest level of privileges.

14.2.6.1.2 Virtual Machine (VM) Security

VM technology provides a stricter isolation of virtual machines from one another than the isolation of processes in a traditional operating system. Indeed, a VMM controls the execution of privileged operations and can thus enforce memory isolation as well as disk and network access. The VMMs are considerably less complex and better structured than traditional operating systems; thus, they are in a better position to respond to security attacks. A major challenge is that a VMM sees only raw data regarding the state of a guest operating system, whereas security services typically operate at a higher logical level, for example, at the level of a file rather than a disk block. Virtual security services are typically provided by the VMM or through a dedicated security services VM. A secure trusted computing base (TCB) is a necessary condition for security in a virtual machine environment; if the TCB is compromised, the security of the entire system is affected.

A guest OS runs on simulated hardware and the VMM has access to the state of all virtual machines operating on the same hardware. The state of a guest virtual machine can be saved, restored, cloned, and encrypted by the VMM. Not only can replication ensure reliability, it can also support security, whereas cloning could be used to recognize a malicious application by testing it on a cloned system and observing whether it behaves normally.

One of the most significant aspects of virtualization is that the complete state of an operating system running under a virtual machine is captured by the VM. This state can be saved in a file and then the file can be copied and shared. Thus, creating a VM reduces ultimately to copying a file; therefore, there will be a natural explosion in the number of VMs, and the only limitation for the number of VMs is the amount of storage space available. While traditional organizations install and maintain the same version of system software, in a virtual environment the number of different operating systems, their versions, and the patch status of each version will be very diverse, taxing the support team. A side effect of the ability to record in a file in the complete state of a VM is the possibility to roll back a VM. This opens wide the door for a new type of vulnerability caused by events recorded in the memory of an attacker.

In case of an infection, in nonvirtual environments, once it is detected, the infected systems are quarantined and then cleaned up. The systems will then behave normally until the next episode of infection occurs. However, in case of virtual environments, the infected VMs may be dormant at the time when the measures to clean up the systems are taken and then, at a later time, they could wake up and infect other systems. This scenario can repeat itself indefinitely.

Another undesirable effect of the virtual environment affects the trust. Trust is conditioned by the ability to guarantee the identity of entities involved. Each computer system in a network has a unique physical or MAC address; the uniqueness of this address guarantees that an infected or malicious system can be identified and then cleaned, shut down, or denied network access. This process breaks down for virtual systems when VMs are created dynamically. Often, to avoid name collision, a random MAC address is assigned to a new VM.

There is price to be paid for the better security provided by virtualization. This price includes higher hardware costs because a virtual system requires more resources such as CPU cycles, memory, disk, and network bandwidth, the cost of developing VMMs and modifying the host operating systems in case of paravirtualization, and the overhead of virtualization because the VMM is involved in privileged operations.

14.2.6.1.3 Security Threats from Shared VM Images

One of the major security risks, especially associated with the IaaS cloud delivery model, is the sharing of VM images like Amazon Machine Images (AMIs).

14.3 Migrating to Big Data Technologies

Prior to the popularity of relational databases, multiple data models were being used and among those, hierarchical and navigational data systems were used extensively on mainframe-based systems. Because the number of clients for these data systems were limited, they remained monolithic, and more often than not, were offered by the mainframe manufacturer and bundled with hardware.

Beginning 1980s, as the relational model was proposed and deemed suitable for a majority of data applications, it became very popular for prevalent use-cases in banking, insurance, and the financial services industry. Relational database systems became the default back-end data storage system across a variety of industries. The advent of client-server systems marked the ascendency of upfront data modelling, SQL, and formal data manipulation semantics (ACID) led to query concurrency improvements, rule-based, and cost-based query optimization, and standard access methods (ODBC and JDBC), and resulted in a plethora of visual tools for building database-backed applications and data visualizations.

The processing requirements can be classified into the following:

1. *Online Transaction Processing* (*OLTP*): Clients' access to these operational databases was a mix of CRUD primitives on either single or very few records. To provide consistency across multiple CRUD operations, a notion of transactions was introduced (where either all the operations were carried out automically or none at all). Thus, these data systems were known as OLTP (online transaction processing) systems, and their performance was measured in transactions-per-second.
2. *Online Analytical Processing* (*OLAP*): Most business intelligence (BI) and reporting workloads used very different access patterns. These queries were mostly read-only queries on a large amount of historical data. Although the operational data systems were initially used to handle both transactional and analytical workloads, they could not fulfill the low-latency transactions, and high-throughput analytics simultaneously. Thus, to serve this new class of applications, data systems specialized in OLAP (on-line analytical processing) were devised.

   Because these OLAP systems had to handle large amounts of historical data, often they were built as MPP systems on a shared-nothing distributed architecture. This created two silos of structured data in organizations—one for structured transactions and another for structured analytics. Even though both these systems were designed with relational data models in mind, often one would need to integrate multiple transactional data stores across multiple departments to provide the full historical data in the analytical data system. Thus, a notion of periodic ETL (Extract-Transform-Load) was born, which would capture data changes across multiple transactional data stores, map their relationships, and structure them into fact or dimension tables with a star schema or snowflake schema. The analytical query engines and the storage for these analytical data were quite different from their transactional counterparts, because the analytical data once stored would almost never have to change (as it was a historical record of business transactions).

3. *Semistructured and unstructured data processing*: In the world of structured operational and analytical data stores, semistructured data (such as server logs) and unstructured data (such as natural language communication in customer interactions) were either discarded, or kept in an archival store for compliance reasons. Centralized file systems became a popular choice of data stores for semistructured and unstructured historical datasets with specialized access layers (such as keyword search).

   Apache Hadoop aimed to solve the semistructured and unstructured data analytics workloads problem by providing HDFS on commodity hardware and collocating it with a batch-oriented flexible distributed data-processing paradigm called MapReduce. As the Hadoop ecosystem expanded, it was to tackle more and more data-processing workloads. Thus, there were scripting languages such as Pig, SQL-like query languages such as Hive, and a NoSQL store, HBase, that used HDFS for persistent storage. Although Apache Hadoop and associated projects have rapidly evolved to promise a unified analytics platform, the key core component of Hadoop, the HDFS, has never been designed with interactive, streaming, and transactional workloads in mind and ,thus, has become a hindrance in achieving that goal.

As a result, multiple architectures were proposed to unify multiple data-processing workloads, such as

1. *Lambda architecture*: Lambda architecture is constituted of three layers.
   - Batch layer
   - Serving layer
   - Speed layer

   All the three layers need different implementations of data-processing frameworks for the same functionality (depending on the speed and scale needed), and it is the responsibility of the implementer to transport data across these three layers. In addition, one cannot guarantee data consistency across the three layers without introducing yet another distributed transaction engine (between the data applications and the Lambda architecture).

   The primary difficulty in implementing the speed, serving, and batch layers in the same unified architecture is due to the deficiencies of the distributed file system in the Hadoop ecosystem. If we were to provide a replacement for HDFS (or if we could augment the HDFS with a storage component that can serve the speed and serving layers while keeping data consistent with HDFS for batch processing), one could truly provide a unified data-processing platform.

2. *Kappa architecture*: The Kappa architecture, introduced by the creators of Apache Kafka, relies on a distributed log as the primary source of data. A distributed log provides decoupling between data producers and data consumers. It allows different batch analytics engines and streaming analytics engines to consume data from the same data bus, thus solving the data consistency problem introduced in the Lambda architecture. But the difficulty of implementing data processing in the speed, serving, and batch layers in three different engines remains.

14.3.1 Lambda Architecture

Nathan Marz devised the term Lambda architecture as an architectural pattern that defines the interplay between batch and speed layer in order to provide low latency queries. A range of NoSQL databases are able to keep up with high update rates. Programming frameworks such as MapReduce help processing large data in batches. And Stream processing infrastructure such as Storm provide support for scalable processing of high velocity data. In practice, both technologies are required in order to design a low latency query system.

New data (A) is provided both to the batch and speed layer as depicted in Figure 14.3. The batch layer (C) stores all incoming data in its raw format as master data set (B). It is also responsible for running batch jobs that create batch views in a serving layer (D) that is optimized for efficient querying (F). The batch layer is optimized for processing large amount of data, for example, by using the MapReduce framework and may require hours to process data. Consequently, the batch view will not be updated between repeated executions of the batch jobs and the corresponding data cannot be included in the result set of a query to the serving layer.

However, the speed layer (E) addresses this information gap by providing a real-time view on the data that has arrived since the last executed batch job.

This way an application will always have up-to-date information by querying both the serving and speed layer at the same time.

14.3.1.1 Batch Processing

In order to cope with the volume challenge, NoSQL databases are gaining in popularity. Those databases can be classified according to their scalability with respect to

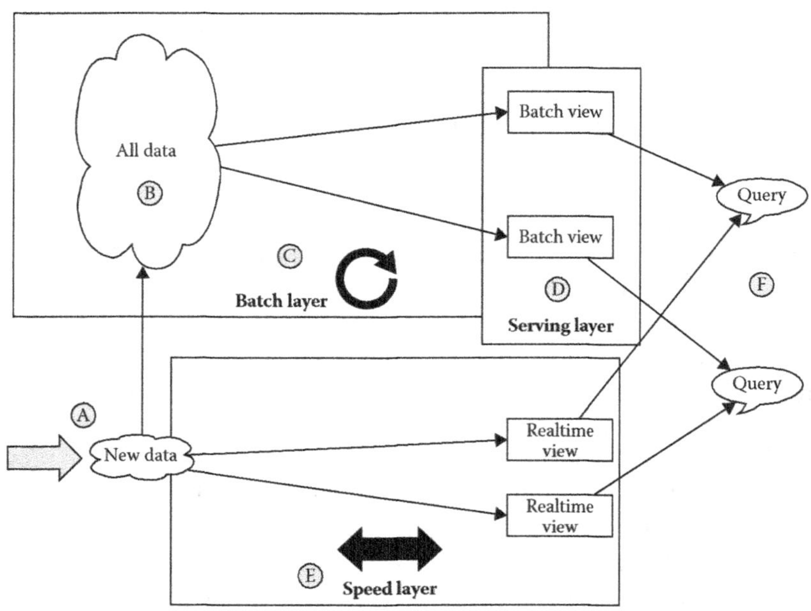

FIGURE 14.3
Lambda architecture.

data size and suitability to model complex data relationships. With decreasing ability to handle data size and increasing capability to handle complex relationships, we can distinguish between key-value stores, columnar stores, document databases, and graph databases.

Key-value stores are databases that scale easily, but are only able to capture simple relationships, that is, a key and its value. Columnar stores in contrast store data in columns and are thus better suited for queries that access only small portions of high dimensional data. Document databases are able to store even more complex data, but typically do not scale as well. Graph databases in contrast can easily model any relationship, but do not scale as easily.

14.3.1.2 Real Time Analytics

Stream processing (SP) or complex event processing systems refer to systems that are designed for executing complex logic over continuous data flows with high performance. SP engines are designed for implementing logic in the form of queries or rules over continuous data flows. Typically, they include a high level declarative language for the logic definition with explicit support for temporal constructs. The defined logic is executed by the engine using processing techniques that are optimized for continuous data flows. In contrast to batch-driven processing that is triggered on request, SP engines process incoming data continuously in an event-driven manner. Another difference with reference to batch systems is that SP engines do not persist information, that is, they operate on temporal windows or synopsis of the incoming data in-memory. Consequently the scope of this analytics is live data or data about the recent past as opposed to long-term analysis of recorded information.

The need for SP technology is rooted in various domains that required fast analysis of incoming information. Examples can be found among others in the finance domain where SP technologies are used for applications like algorithmic trading or the detection of credit card fraud. In these cases SP is very well suited due to applications requiring fast analysis of high volume data streams involving temporal patterns. For instance, a credit card fraud may be detected if multiple transactions are executed in short time from far apart locations. Other application domains for SP include fields like logistics, business process management, and security. Also, the Internet of Things (IoT) domain has sparked a range of applications that require event-driven processing and is one of the drivers for SP technology.

14.4 Summary

This chapter discussed issues related to big data development and operations management. It described the portfolio of core functionalities (including service management, metering/billing, data management, monitoring, security management, SLAs and QoS management, performance management, policy management, self-service, support and incident management, analytics, orchestration, transformation, logging/audit trails, mediation, integration, rules management, and semantic engine) and core services (including discovery and replication, load balancing, resource management, data governance), management and governance services.

Section IV

Big Data Computing Applications

15

Web Applications

Retail organizations are performing log analysis, website optimization, and customer loyalty programs by using brand and sentiment analysis and market-basket analysis. Dynamic pricing, website real time customization, and product recommendations are the results of this analysis. The finance industry is using big data for fraud pattern detection and to perform analyses for corruption, bribery, risk modeling, and trade analytics. This enables them to improve their customer risk evaluation and fraud detection, as well as to design programs for real time upsell and cross-marketing offers. Energy is doing analyses of grid failure, soil analytics, predictive mechanical failure, chemical analysis, and smart meters to name a few. Manufacturing is performing supply-chain analysis, customer-churn analysis, and part replacement, as well as layout and design of manufacturing plants and factories. Telecommunication firms use big data information for customer profiling, cell-tower analysis, optimizing customer experience, monitoring equipment status, and network analysis. This improves hardware maintenance, product recommendations, and location-based advertising. Health care uses electronic medical records (EMR) and RFID to perform hospital design, patient treatment, clinical decision support, clinical-trial analysis, and real time instrument, and patient monitoring and analysis. Government is using big data for areas such as threat identification, government program analysis, and person-of-interest discovery. It's the power of the data that is disrupting business and the IT industry.

15.1 Web-Based Applications

J2EE is the result of Sun's effort to integrate the assortment of Java technologies and API together into a cohesive Java development platform for developing complex distributed Java applications. Sun's enhancement of the *n*-tier development model for Java, combined with the introduction of specific functionalities to permit easier development of the server-side scalable Web-based enterprise applications, has led to a wide adoption of Java for Web-centric application development.

Enterprise application development entails expertise in a host of areas like interprocess communications, memory management, security issues, and database-specific access queries. J2EE provides built-in support for services in all these areas, enabling developers to focus on implementing business logic rather than intricate code that supports basic application support infrastructure.

There are numerous advantages of application development in the J2EE area:

- J2EE offers support for the componentization of enterprise applications that enable higher productivity via reusability of components, rapid development of functioning applications via prebuilt functional components, higher-quality test-driven development via pretested components, and easier maintenance via cost-effective upgrades to individual components.

- J2EE offers support for hardware and operating systems (OS) independence by enabling system services to be accessed via Java and J2EE rather than directly via APIs specific to the underlying systems.
- J2EE offers a wide range of APIs to access and integrate with third-party products in a consistent manner, including databases, mail systems, and messaging platforms.
- J2EE offers clear-cut segregation between system development, deployment, and execution, thus enabling independent development, integration, and upgradation of components.
- J2EE offers specialized components that are optimized for specific types of roles in an enterprise application such as Entity Beans for handling persistent data and Session Beans for handling processing.

All the aforementioned features make possible rapid development of complex, distributed applications by enabling developers to focus on developing business logic, implementing the system without being impacted by prior knowledge of the target execution environment(s), and creating systems that can be ported more easily between different hardware platforms and operating systems (OS).

15.2 Reference Architecture

The objective of the flexibility and reusability can be achieved primarily at two levels: application architecture level and the application component design level. The reference architecture is the vision of the application architecture that integrates common elements into a component structure modeling the current business and also positioning it to meet the challenges of the future. From a technical point of view, the architecture positions the development organization to automatically meet the benchmark requirements on time to market, flexibility, and performance.

A set of key elements drive the definition of the reference architecture that is comprised of three layers, namely, business objects, process-oriented or service-based objects, and user interface layer.

The defining elements of enterprise applications are as follows:

- Business entities are the foci of the enterprise applications. These range from top-level entities such as a customer or a supplier down to bottom-level entities such as purchase orders, sales orders, or even individual level line items of these orders. Entities participate in the business processes, have attributes or properties, have methods for responding to requests for information, and have different sets of enforceable policies or rules applicable to them. The latter include the requirement for persistence of the state of the entities as reflected in the snapshot of all attributes.
- Business processes carry out the tasks of the enterprise. They have some kind of specified workflow and essentially involve one or more business entities. They must be executed in a secure manner and also be accessible via a host of user interfaces or devices or clients.
- User interactions carry out the access and display of information related to business entities as an outcome of some business processes for scrutiny by the users of the enterprise application. This essentially involves some kind of screen flow or page navigation, attributes for presentation, user requests, or generated responses,

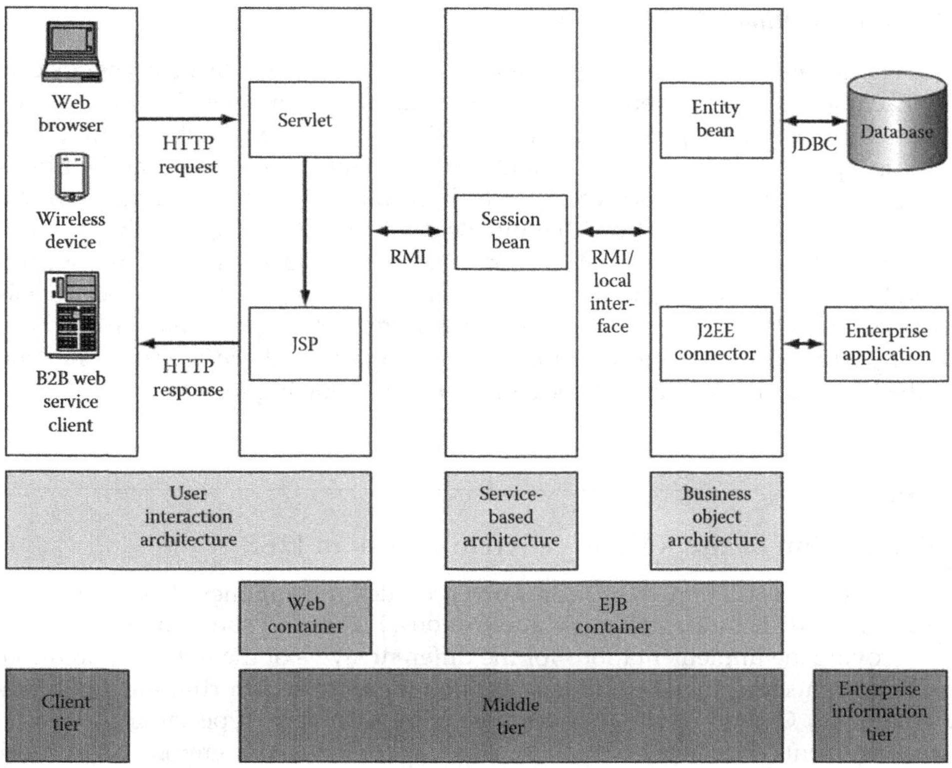

FIGURE 15.1
Enterprise application in J2EE.

that is, static or dynamic content, form-oriented processing, and error handling. The user interaction could be via a host of user interfaces or devices or clients.

Each of these elements gives rise to the three primary architecture layers of the reference architecture. These layers could reside on the same physical layer or be distributed across a network. Figure 15.1 presents the three architecture layers constituting the reference architecture.

15.2.1 User Interaction Architecture

User interactions are modeled by user interface components that comprise the User Interaction Architecture. In J2EE platform, this is typically implemented as a combination of servlets and Java Server Pages (JSP). In a web-based application, this layer would process HTML form submissions, manage state within an application, generate web-page content, and control navigation between pages. Many of the functions within this layer can be automated through configurable foundation components.

15.2.2 Service-Based Architecture

Business processes are modeled by service components that comprise the service-based architecture. In J2EE platform, this is typically implemented as a process-oriented object wrapped with a stateless Session Bean. The concept of services allows the front end to be decoupled from the back-end business object components. The service-based layer adds tremendous value in terms of flexibility, reusability, and component design.

15.2.3 Business Object Architecture

Business entities are modeled by object components that comprise the business object architecture. Each of these components manages the data and business logic associated with a particular entity, including persistence of that data into a relational database. In J2EE platform, this is typically implemented as a combination of regular Java classes and Entity Beans in J2EE application. The database access can be implemented by the container in the case of Container-Managed Persistence (CMP) Entity Beans or by the developer in the case of Bean-Managed Persistence (BMP) Entity Beans or regular Java classes. The persistence of each business object is abstracted out to the extent possible so that separate data objects, persistent frameworks, or CMP services can be used to affect the data object persistence in the database.

A major portion of the reference architecture is a generic and configurable implementation of the Model 2 architecture discussed later in the following section.

15.3 Realization of the Reference Architecture in J2EE

The Java Enterprise Edition (J2EE) platform provides a component-based approach to implement n-tier distributed enterprise applications. Figure 15.1 shows how the J2EE components provide the implementations for the different layers of the reference architecture.

The components that make up the application are executed in runtime environments called containers. Containers are used to provide infrastructure-type services such as life-cycle management, distribution, and security. Containers and components in the J2EE application are broadly divided into three tiers. The client tier is typically a web browser or alternatively Java application client. The middle tier contains two primary containers of the J2EE application, namely, web container and Enterprise JavaBeans (EJB) container. The function of the web container is to process client requests and generate corresponding responses, while the function of the EJB container is to implement the business logic of the application. The EIS tier primarily consists of data sources and a number of interfaces and APIs to access the resources and other existing or legacy applications.

15.3.1 JavaServer Pages and Java Servlets as the User Interaction Components

JSP and Java Servlets are meant to process and respond to web user request. Servlet provides a Java-centric programming approach for implementing web tier functionality. The Servlet API provides an easy-to-use set of objects that process HTTP requests and generate HTML/XML responses. JSPs provide an HTML-centric version of the Java Servlets. JSP components are document based rather than object based and possess built-in access to Servlet API request and response objects as also the user session object. JSPs also provide a powerful custom tag mechanism, enabling the encapsulation of reusable Java presentation code that can be placed directly into the JSP document.

15.3.2 Session Bean EJBs as Service-Based Components

Session Beans are meant for representing services provided to a client. Unlike Entity Beans, Session Beans do not share data across multiple clients—each user requesting a service or executing a transaction invokes a separate Session Bean to process the request. A stateless Session Bean after processing a request goes on to the next request or next client without maintaining or sharing any data. However, stateful Session Beans are often constructed for a particular client and maintain a state across method invocations for a single client until the component is removed.

15.3.3 Entity Bean EJBs as the Business Object Components

Entity Beans are meant for representing persistent data entities within an enterprise application. One of the major component services that are provided to the Entity Beans is that of Container-Managed Persistence (CMP). However, in EJB 2.0 specification, CMP is limited to one table only. Any object-relational mapping involving more than a one-to-one table-object mapping is supported only through Bean-Managed Persistence (BMP).

15.3.4 Distributed Java Components

Java Naming and Directory Interface (JNDI) enables naming and distribution of Java components within the reference architecture. JNDI can be used to store and retrieve any Java object. However, JNDI is usually used to look up for component (home or remote) interfaces to enterprise beans. The client uses JNDI to look up the corresponding EJB Home interface, which enables creation, access, or removal of instances of Session and Entity Beans. In case of local Entity Bean, a method invocation is proxied directly to the bean's implementation. While in case of remote Entity Beans, the Home interface is used to obtain access to the remote interface to invoke the exposed methods using RMI. The remote interface takes the local method call, serializes the objects that will be passed as arguments, and invokes the corresponding remote method on the distributed object. These serialized objects are converted back into normal objects to invoke the method to return the resulting value upon which the process is reversed to revert the value back to the remote interface client.

15.3.5 J2EE Access to the EIS (Enterprise Information Systems) Tier

J2EE provides a number of interfaces and APIs to access resources in the EIS tier. The use of JDBC API is encapsulated primarily in the data access layer or within the CMP classes of the Entity Bean. Data sources that map to a database are defined in JDBC, which can be looked up by a client searching for a resource using the JNDI. This enables the J2EE application server to provide connection pooling to different data resources, which should appropriately be closed as soon as the task is over to prevent bottlenecks.

The various J2EE interfaces and APIs available are as follows:

- Java Connector Architecture provides a standard way to build adapters to access existing enterprise applications.
- JavaMail API provides a standard way to access mail server applications.
- Java Message Service (JMS) provides a standard interface to enterprise messaging systems. JMS enables reliable asynchronous communication with other distributed components. JMS is used by Message-Driven Beans (MDBs) to perform asynchronous or parallel processing of messages.

15.4 Model–View–Controller Architecture

The Model 2 architecture is based on the Model–View–Controller (MVC) design pattern. A generic MVC implementation is a vital element of the reference architecture as it provides a flexible and reusable foundation for very rapid web-based application development.

The components of the MVC architecture are as follows:

- View deals with the display on the screens presented to the user
- Controller deals with the flow and processing of user actions
- Model deals with the business logic

MVC architecture modularizes and isolates screen logic, control logic, and business logic in order to achieve greater flexibility and opportunity for reuse. A critical isolation point is between the presentation objects and the application back-end objects that manage the business logic and data. This enables the user interface to affect major changes on the display screens without impacting the business logic and data components.

View does not contain the source of data and relies on the model to furnish the relevant data. When the model updates the data, it notifies as also furnishes the changed data to the view so that it can render the display to the user with the up-to-date data and correct data.

The controller channels information from the view on the user actions for processing by the business logic in the model. Controller enables an application design to flexibly handle things such as page navigation and access to the functionality provided by the application model in case of form submissions. Thus, controller provides an isolation point between the model and the view, resulting in a more loosely coupled front end and back end.

Figure 15.2 gives a complete picture of how objects in the MVC architecture are mapped to the reference architecture in J2EE.

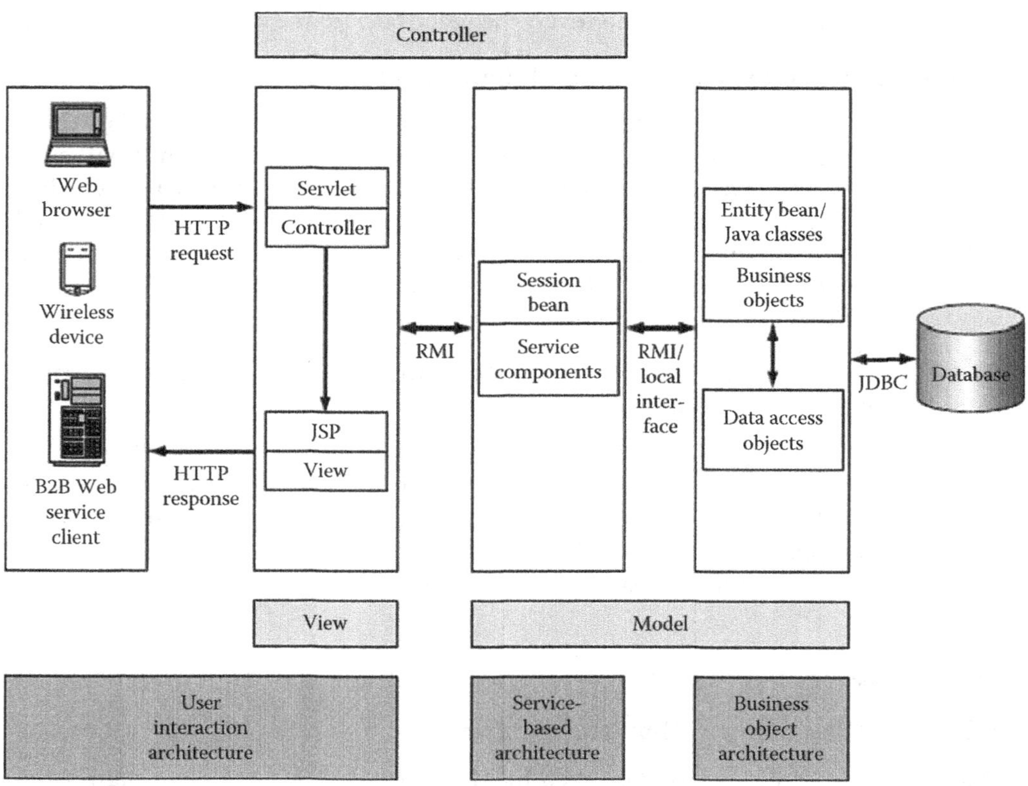

FIGURE 15.2
MVC and enterprise application architecture.

15.5 Evolution of the Web

15.5.1 Web 1.0

To start with, most websites were just a collection of static web pages. The shallow web, also known as the static web, is primarily a collection of static HTML web pages providing information about products or services offered. After a while, the web became dynamic, delivering web pages created on the fly. The ability to create web pages from the content stored on databases enabled web developers to provide customized information to visitors. These sites are known as the deep web or the dynamic web. Though a visitor to such websites gets information attuned to his or her requirements, these sites provide primarily one-way interaction and limited user interactivity. The users have no role in content generation and no means to access content without visiting the sites concerned. The shallow websites and deep websites, which have none or minimal user interaction, are now generally termed as Web 1.0.

15.5.2 Web 2.0

In the last few years, a new class of web applications, known as Web 2.0 (or Service-Oriented Applications), has emerged. These applications let people collaborate and share information online in seemingly new ways—examples include social networking sites such as myspace.com, media sharing sites such as YouTube.com, and collaborative authoring sites such as Wikipedia. These second-generation webs offer smart user interfaces and built-in facilities for users to generate and edit content presented on the web and thereby enrich the content base. Besides leveraging the users' potential in generating content, Web 2.0 applications provide facilities to keep the content under the user's own categories (tagging feature) and access it easily (web feed tool). These new version of web applications is also able to integrate multiple services under a rich user interface.

With the incorporation of new web technologies such as Asynchronous JavaScript and XML (AJAX), Ruby, blog, wiki, social bookmarking, and tagging, the web is fast becoming more dynamic and highly interactive, where users can not only pick content from a site but can also contribute to it. The web feed technology allows users to keep up with a site's latest content without having to visit it. Another feature of the new web is the proliferation of websites with APIs (application programming interfaces). An API from a web service facilitates web developers in collecting data from the service and creating new online applications based on these data.

The Web 2.0 is a collection of technologies, business strategies, and social trends. The Web 2.0 is a highly interactive, dynamic application platform than its predecessor Web 1.0.

15.5.2.1 Weblogs or Blogs

With the advent of software like Wordpress and Typepad, along with blog service companies like blogger.com, the weblog is fast becoming the communication medium of the new web. Unlike traditional Hypertext Markup Language (HTML) web pages, blogs offer the ability for the nonprogrammer to communicate on a regular basis. Traditional HTML-style pages required knowledge of style, coding, and design in order to publish content that was basically read only from the consumer's point of view. Weblogs remove much of the constraints by providing a standard user interface that does not require customization.

Weblogs originally emerged as a repository for linking but soon evolved to the ability to publish content and allow readers to become content providers. The essence of a blog can be defined by the format that includes small chunks of content referred to as posts, date stamped, maintained in the reverse chronological order, and content expanded to include links, text, and images.

The biggest advancement made with weblogs is the permanence of the content that has a unique Universal Resource Locator (URL). This allows the content to be posted along with the comments to define a permanent record of information. This is critical in that having a collaborative record that can be indexed by search engines will increase the utility and spread the information to a larger audience.

15.5.2.2 Wikis

A Wiki is a website that promotes the collaborative creation of content. Wiki pages can be edited by anyone at any time. Informational content can be created and easily organized within the wiki environment and then reorganized as required. Wikis are currently in high demand in a large variety of fields, due to their simplicity and flexibility. Documentation, reporting, project management, online glossaries, and dictionaries, discussion groups, or general information applications are just a few examples of where the end user can provide value. While stating that anyone can alter content, some large-scale wiki environments have extensive role definitions that define who can perform functions of update, restore, delete, and creation. Wikipedia, like many wiki type projects, has readers, editors, administrators, patrollers, policy makers, subject matter experts, content maintainers, software developers, and system operators. All of which create an environment open to sharing information and knowledge to a large group of users.

> The major difference between a wiki and blog is that the wiki user can alter the original content while the blog user can only add information in the form of comments.

15.5.2.3 RSS Technologies

Originally developed by Netscape, RSS was intended to publish news type information based on a subscription framework. Many Internet users have experienced the frustration of searching Internet sites for hours at a time to find relevant information. RSS is an XML-based content-syndication protocol that allows websites to share information as well as aggregate information based on the users' needs. In the simplest form, RSS shares the metadata about the content without actually delivering the entire information source. An author might publish the title, description, publish date, and copyrights to anyone that subscribes to the feed. The end user is required to have an application called an aggregator in order to receive the information. By having the RSS aggregator application, end users are not required to visit each site in order to obtain information.

From an end user perspective, the RSS technology changes the communication method from a search and discover to a notification model. Users can locate content that is pertinent to their job and subscribe to the communication that enables a much faster communication stream.

15.5.2.4 Social Tagging

Social tagging describes the collaborative activity of marking shared online content with keywords or tags as a way to organize content for future navigation, filtering, or search. Traditional information architecture utilized a central taxonomy or classification scheme in order to place in formation into specific predefined bucket or category. The assumption was that trained librarians understood more about information content and context than the average user. While this might have been true for the local library, the enormous amount of content on the Internet makes this type of system unmanageable.

Tagging offers a number of benefits to the end user community. Perhaps the most important feature to the individual is able to bookmark the information in a way that is easier for them to recall at a later date. The idea of social tagging is allowing multiple users to tag content in a way that makes sense to them, by combining these tags; users create an environment where the opinions of the majority define the appropriateness of the tags themselves. The act of creating a collection of popular tags is referred to as a folksonomy that is defined as a folk taxonomy of important and emerging content within the user community. The vocabulary problem is defined by the fact that different users define content in different ways. The disagreement can lead to missed information or inefficient user interactions.

One of the best examples of social tagging is Flickr that allows user to upload images and *tag* them with appropriate metadata keywords. Other users, who view your images, can also tag them with their concept of appropriate keywords. After a critical mass has been reached, the resulting tag collection will identify images correctly and without bias. Other sites like iStockPhoto have also utilized this technology but more along the sales channel versus the community one.

15.5.2.5 Mashups: Integrating Information

The final Web 2.0 technology describes the efforts around information integration, commonly referred to as *mashups*. These applications can be combined to deliver additional value that the individual parts could not on their own:

1. HousingMaps.com combines the Google mapping application with a real estate listing service on Craiglists.com.
2. Chicagocrime.org overlays local crime statistics on top of Google Maps so end users can see what crimes were committed recently in the neighborhood.
3. Another site synchronizes Yahoo! Inc.'s real-time traffic data with Google Maps.

Much of the work with web services will enable greater extensions of mashups and combine many different businesses and business models. Organizations, like Amazon and Microsoft, are embracing the mashup movement by offering developers easier access to their data and services. Moreover, they're programming their services so that more computing tasks, such as displaying maps onscreen, get done on the users' Personal Computers rather than on their far-flung servers.

15.5.2.6 User Contributed Content

One of the basic themes of Web 2.0 is user contributed information. The value derived from the contributed content comes not from a subject matter expert, but rather from individuals whose small contributions add up. One example of user contributed content is

TABLE 15.1

Comparison between Web 1.0 and Web 2.0

Web 1.0 Characteristics	Web 2.0 Characteristics
Static content	Dynamic content
Producer-based information	Participatory-based information
Messages pushed to consumer	Messages pulled by consumer
Institutional control	Individual enabled
Top down implementation	Bottom up implementation
Users search and browse	Users publish and subscribe
Transactional-based interactions	Relationship-based interactions
Goal of mass adoption	Goal of niche adoption
Taxonomy	Folksonomy

the product review systems like Amazon.com and reputation systems used with ebay.com. A common practice of online merchants is to enable their customers to review or to express opinions on the products they have purchased. Online reviews are a major source of information for consumers and demonstrated enormous implications for a wide range of management activities, such as brand building, customer acquisition and retention, product development, and quality assurance.

A person's reputation is a valuable piece of information that can be used when deciding whether or not to interact or do business with. A reputation system is a bidirectional medium where buyers post feedback on sellers and vice versa. For example, eBay buyers voluntarily comment on the quality of service, their satisfaction with the item traded, and promptness of shipping. Sellers comment about the prompt payment from buyers or respond to comments left by the buyer. Reputation systems may be categorized in three basic types: ranking, rating, and collaborative. Ranking systems use quantifiable measures of users' behavior to generate and rating. Rating systems use explicit evaluations given by users in order to define a measure of interest or trust. Finally, collaborative filtering systems determine the level of relationship between the two individuals before placing a weight on the information. For example, if a user has reviewed similar items in the past, then the relevancy of a new rating will be higher.

Table 15.1 presents a comparison between Web 1.0 and Web 2.0.

15.5.3 Web 3.0

In current web applications, information is presented in natural language, which humans can process easily; but computers cannot manipulate natural language information on the web meaningfully. The semantic web is an extension of the current web in which information is given a well-defined meaning, better enabling computers and universal medium for information exchange by putting documents with computer-processable meaning (semantics) on the web. Adding semantics radically changes the nature of the web—from a place where information is merely displayed to one where it is interpreted, exchanged, and processed. Associating meaning with content or establishing a layer of machine understandable data enables a higher degree of automation and more intelligent applications and also facilitates interoperable services.

Semantic web technologies will enhance Web 2.0 tools and its associated data with semantic annotations and semantic knowledge representations, thus enabling a better automatic processing of data that in turn will enhance search mechanisms, management of the tacit knowledge, and the overall efficiency of the actual KM tools. The benefits of semantic blogging, semantic wikis or semantic Wikipedia, semantic-enhanced social networks, semantic-enhanced KM and semantic-enhanced user support will increase its benefits multifold.

The ultimate goal of the semantic web is to support machine-facilitated global information exchange in a scalable, adaptable, extensible manner, so that information on the web can be used for more effective discovery, automation, integration, and reuse across various applications. The three key ingredients that constitute the semantic web and help achieve its goals are semantic markup, ontology, and intelligent software agents.

15.5.4 Mobile Web

With numerous advances in mobile computing and wireless communications and widespread adoption of mobile devices such as smart mobile, the Web is inceasingly being accessed using handheld devices. Mobile web applications could offer some additional features compared to traditional desktop web applications such as location-aware services, context-aware capabilities, and personalization.

15.5.5 The Semantic Web

While the web keeps growing at an astounding pace, most web pages are still designed for human consumption and cannot be processed by machines. Similarly, while web search engines help retrieve web pages, they do not offer support to interpret the results—for that, human intervention is still required. As the size of search results is often just too big for humans to interpret, finding relevant information on the web is not as easy as we would desire. The existing web has evolved as a medium for information exchange among people, rather than machines. As a consequence, the semantic content, that is, the meaning of the information on a web page, is coded in a way that is accessible to human beings only. Today's web may be defined as the syntactic web, where information presentation is carried out by computers, and the interpretation and identification of relevant information are delegated to human beings. With the volume of available digital data growing at an exponential rate, it is becoming virtually impossible for human beings to manage the complexity and volume of the available information. This phenomenon, often referred to as information overload, poses a serious threat to the continued usefulness of today's web.

As the volume of web resources grows exponentially, researchers from industry, government, and academia are now exploring the possibility of creating a semantic web in which meaning is made explicit, allowing machines to process and integrate web resources intelligently. Biologists use a well-defined taxonomy, the Linnaean taxonomy, adopted and shared by most of the scientific community worldwide. Likewise, computer scientists are looking for a similar model to help structure web content. In 2001, Berners-Lee, Hendler, and Lassila published a revolutionary article in Scientific American titled "The Semantic Web: A New Form of Web Content That Is Meaningful to Computers Will Unleash a Revolution of New Possibilities."

The semantic web is an extension of the current web in which information is given well-defined meaning, enabling computers and people to work in cooperation. In the lower part of the architecture, we find three building blocks that can be used to encode text (Unicode), to identify resources on the web (URIs) and to structure and exchange information (XML). Resource Description Framework (RDF) is a simple, yet powerful data model and language for describing web resources. The SPARQL Protocol and RDF Query Language (SPARQL) is the de facto standard used to query RDF data. While RDF and the RDF Schema provide a model for representing semantic web data and for structuring semantic data using simple hierarchies of classes and properties, respectively, the SPARQL language and protocol provide the means to express queries and retrieve information from across diverse semantic web data sources. The need for a new language is motivated by the different data models and semantics at the level of XML and RDF, respectively.

Ontology is a formal, explicit specification of a shared conceptualization of a particular domain—concepts are the core elements of the conceptualization corresponding to entities of the domain being described, and properties and relations are used to describe interconnections between such concepts. Web ontology language (OWL) is the standard language for representing knowledge on the web. This language was designed to be used by applications that need to process the content of information on the web instead of just presenting information to human users. Using OWL, one can explicitly represent the meaning of terms in vocabularies and the relationships between those terms. The Rule Interchange Format (RIF) is the W3C Recommendation that defines a framework to exchange rule-based languages on the web. Like OWL, RIF defines a set of languages covering various aspects of the rule layer of the semantic web.

15.5.6 Rich Internet Applications

Rich Internet applications (RIA) are web-based applications that run in a web browser and do not require software installation, but still have the features and functionality of traditional desktop applications. The term "RIA" was introduced in a Macromedia whitepaper in March 2002. RIA represents the evolution of the browser from a static request-response interface to a dynamic, asynchronous interface. Broadband proliferation, consumer demand, and enabling technologies, including the Web 2.0, are driving the proliferation of RIAs. RIAs promise a richer user experience and benefits—interactivity and usability that are lacking in many current applications. Some prime examples of RIA frameworks are Adobe's Flex and AJAX, and examples of RIA include Google's Earth, Mail, and Finance applications.

Enterprises are embracing the promises of RIAs by applying them to user tasks that demand interactivity, responsiveness, and richness. Predominant techniques such as HTML, forms, and CGI are being replaced by other programmer- or user-friendly approaches such as AJAX and web services. Building a web application using fancy technology, however, does not ensure a better user experience. To add real value, developers must address.

15.6 Web Applications

Web applications' operational environment and their development approach and the faster pace in which these applications are developed and deployed differentiate web applications from those of traditional software.

Characteristics of web applications are as follows:

- Web-based systems, in general, demand good aesthetic appeal—"look and feel"—and easy navigation.

Web-based applications demand presentation of a variety of content—text, graphics, images, audio, and/or video—and the content may also be integrated with procedural processing. Hence, their development includes the creation and management of the content and their presentation in an attractive manner, as well as a provision for subsequent content management (changes) on a continual basis after the initial development and deployment.

- Web applications are meant to be used by a vast, diverse, remote community of users who have different requirements, expectations, and skill sets. Therefore, the user interface and usability features have to meet the needs of a diverse, anonymous user community. Furthermore, the number of users accessing a web application at any time is problems—there could be a "flash crowd" triggered by major events or promotions.

  Web applications, especially those meant for a global audience, need to adhere to many different social and cultural sentiments and national standards—including multiple languages and different systems of units.
- Ramifications of failure or dissatisfaction of users of web-based applications can be much worse than conventional IT systems. Also, web applications could fail for many different reasons.
- Successfully managing the evolution, change, and newer requirements of web applications is a major technical, organizational, and management challenge. Most web applications are evolutionary in their nature, requiring (frequent) changes of content, functionality, structure, navigation, presentation, or implementation on an ongoing basis. The frequency and degree of change of information content can be quite high; they particularly evolve in terms of their requirements and functionality, especially after the system is put into use. In most web applications, frequency and degree of change are much higher than in traditional software applications, and in many applications it is not possible to specify fully their entire requirements at the beginning.
- There is a greater demand on the security of web applications; security and privacy needs of web-based systems are in general more demanding than those of traditional software.
- Web applications need to cope with a variety of display devices and formats, and support hardware, software, and networks with vastly varying access speeds.

  Proliferation of new web technologies and standards and competitive pressure to use them bring its own advantages and also additional challenges to development and maintenance of web applications.
- The evolving nature of web applications necessitates an incremental developmental process.

15.6.1 Web Applications Dimensions

15.6.1.1 Presentation

Presentation technologies have advanced over time, such as in terms of multimedia capabilities, but the core technology of the web application platform, the Hypertext Markup Language (HTML), has remained relatively stable. Consequently, application user interfaces have to be mapped to document-oriented markup code, resulting in an impedance or a gap between the design and the subsequent implementation.

The task of communicating content in an appropriate way combines both artistic visual design and engineering disciplines. Usually, based on the audience of the website, there are numerous factors to be considered. For example, in the international case, cultural differences may have to be accounted for, affecting not only languages but also for example, the perception of color schemes. Further restrictions may originate from the publishing organizations themselves that aim at reflecting the company's brand with a corresponding corporate design or legal obligations with respect to accessibility.

15.6.1.2 Dialogue

Interactive elements in web applications often appear in the shape of forms that allow users to enter data that are used as input for further processing. More generally, the dialogue concern covers not only interaction between humans and the application, but rather between arbitrary actors (including other programs) and the manipulated information space. The flow of information is governed by the web's interaction model, which, due to its distributed nature, differs considerably from other platforms. The interaction model is subject to variations, as in the context of recent trends toward more client-sided application logic and asynchronous communication between client and server like in the case of AJAX focusing on user interfaces that provide a look and feel that resembles desktop applications.

15.6.1.3 Navigation

In addition to the challenge of communicating information there exists the challenge of making it easily accessible to the user without ending in the "lost in hyperspace" syndrome. This holds true even though the web makes use of only a subset of the rich capabilities of hypertext concepts, for example, allowing only unidirectional links. Over time, a set of common usage patterns have evolved that aids them in navigating through new websites that may not have been visited before. Applied to web application development, navigation concepts can be extended for accessing not only static document content but also application functionality.

15.6.1.4 Process

The process dimensions relate to the operations performed on the information space that are generally triggered by the user via the web interface and whose execution is governed by the business policy. Particular challenges arise from scenarios with frequently changing policies, demanding agile approaches with preferably dynamic wiring between loosely coupled components. Beneath the user interface of a web application lies the implementation of the actual application logic, for which the web acts as a platform to make it available to the concerned stakeholders. In case the application is not distributed, the process dimension is hardly affected by web-specific factors, allowing for standard non-web approaches like Component-Based Software Engineering to be applied. Otherwise, service-oriented approaches account for cases where the wiring extends over components that reside on the web.

15.6.1.5 Data

Data are the content of the documents to be published; although content can be embedded in the web documents together with other dimensions like presentation or navigation, the evolution of web applications often demands a separation, using data sources such as XML files, databases, or web services. Traditional issues include the structure of the information space as well as the definition of structural linking. In the context of the dynamic nature of web applications, one can distinguish between static information that remains stable over time and dynamic information that is subject to changes. Depending on the media type being delivered, either the data can be persistent, that is, accessible independently of time, or it can be transient, that is, accessible as a flow, as in the case of a video stream. Moreover, metadata can also describe other data facilitating the usefulness of the data within the global information space established by the web. Similarly, the machine-based processing of information is further supported by semantic web approaches that apply technologies like the resource description framework (RDF) to make metadata statements (e.g., about web page content) and express the semantics about associations between arbitrary resources worldwide.

15.7 Search Analysis

Exploiting the data stored in search logs of web search engines, Intranets, and websites provides important insights into understanding the information searching habits and tactics of online searchers. Web search engine companies use search logs (also referred to as transaction logs) to investigate searching trends and effects of system improvements. This understanding can inform information system design, interface development, and information architecture construction for content collections. Search logs are an unobtrusive method of collecting significant amounts of searching data on a sizable number of system users.

A search log is an electronic record of interactions that have occurred during a searching episode between a web search engine and users searching for information on that web search engine. The users may be humans or computer programs acting on behalf of humans. Interactions are the communication exchanges that occur between users and the system initiated wither by the user or the system. Most search logs are server-side recordings of interactions; the server software application can record various types of data and interactions depending on the file format that the server software supports. The search log format is typically an extended file format, which contains data such as the client computer's Internet Protocol (IP) address, user query, search engine access time, and referrer site, among other fields.

Search Log Analysis (SLA) is defined as the use of data collected in a search log to investigate particular research questions concerning interactions among web users, the web search engine, or the web content during searching episodes. Within this interaction context, SLA could use the data in search logs to discern attributes of the search process, such as the searcher's actions on the system, the system responses, or the evaluation of results by the searcher. From this understanding, one achieves some stated objective, such as improved system design, advanced searching assistance, or better understanding of some user information searching behavior.

There are methodological issues with SLA like execution, conception, and communication. SLA can be difficult to execute due to collection, storage, and analysis problems associated with the huge volume and complexity of the dataset (i.e., significant number of variables). With complex datasets, it is sometimes difficult to develop a conceptual methodology for analyzing the dependent variables. Communication problems occur when researchers do not define terms and metrics in sufficient detail to allow other researchers to interpret and verify their results. Big data computing environment coupled with the accompanying cloud computing environment expressly address these issues.

15.7.1 SLA Process

SLA involves the following three major stages:

1. Data collection involves the process of collecting the interaction data for a given period in a search log. Search logs provide a good balance between collecting a robust set of data and unobtrusively collecting that data. Collecting data from real users pursuing needed information while interacting with real systems on the web affects the type of data that one can realistically assemble. On a real-life system, the method of data monitoring and collecting should not interfere with the information searching process. Not only a data collection method that interferes with the information searching process may unintentionally alter that process, but such an nonpermitted interference may also lead to a loss of a potential customer.

   A search log typically consists of data such as

   a. User Identification: The IP address of the customer's computer
   b. Date: The date of the interaction as recorded by the search engine server
   c. The Time: The time of the interaction as recorded by the search engine server

   Additionally, it could also consist of data such as

   a. Results Page: The code representing a set of result abstracts and URLs returned by the search engine in response to a query
   b. Language: The user preferred language of the retrieved web pages
   c. Source: The federated content collection searched
   d. Page Viewed: The URL that the searcher visited after entering the query and viewing the results page, which is also known as click-thru or click-through

2. Data preparation involves the process of cleaning and preparing the search log data for analysis. For data preparation, the focus is on importing the search log data into a relational or NoSQL database, assigning each record a primary key, cleaning the data (i.e., checking each field for bad data), and calculating standard interaction metrics that will serve as the basis for further analysis.

   Data preparation consists of steps like

   a. Cleaning data: Records in search logs can contain corrupted data. These corrupted records can be as a result of multiple reasons; but they are mostly related to errors when logging the data.

b. Parsing data: Using the three fields of The Time, User Identification, and Search URL, common to all web search logs, the chronological series of actions in a searching episode is recreated. The web query search logs usually contain queries from both human users and agents. Depending on the research objective, one may be interested in only individual human interactions, those from common user terminals, or those from agents. Depending on the search objective, one may be interested in only individual human interactions, those from common user terminals, or those from agents.

c. Normalizing searching episodes: When a searcher submits a query, then views a document, and returns to the search engine, the web server typically logs this second visit with the identical user identification and query, but with a new time (i.e., the time of the second visit). This is beneficial information in determining how many of the retrieved results pages the searcher visited from the search engine, but unfortunately, it also skews the results of the query level analysis. In order to normalize the searching episodes, one must first separate these result page requests from query submissions for each searching episode.

3. Data analysis involves the process of analyzing the prepared data. The three common levels of analysis for examining search logs:

a. Session analysis

A searching episode is defined as a series of interactions within a limited duration to address one or more information needs. This session duration is typically short, with web researchers using between 5 and 120 minutes as a cutoff; each choice of time has an impact on the results: the searcher may be multitasking within a searching episode, or the episode may be an instance of the searcher engaged in successive searching.

This session definition is similar to the definition of a unique visitor used by commercial search engines and organizations to measure website traffic. The number of queries per searcher is the session *length*. Session *duration* is the total time the user spent interacting with the search engine, including the time spent viewing the first and subsequent web documents, except the final document. Session duration can therefore be measured from the time the user submits the first query until the user departs the search engine for the last time (i.e., does not return). This viewing time of the final web document is not available since the web search engine server does not record the time stamp.

A *web document* is the web page referenced by the URL on the search engine's results page. A web document may be text or multimedia and, if viewed hierarchically, may contain a nearly unlimited number of subweb documents. A web document may also contain URLs linking to other web documents. From the results page, a searcher may click on a URL, (i.e., visit) one or more results from the listings on the result page. This is *click through analysis* and measures the page viewing behavior of web searchers.

b. Query analysis

The query level of analysis uses the query as the base metric. A query is defined as a string list of one or more terms submitted to a search engine. This is a mechanical definition as opposed to an information searching definition. The first query by a particular searcher is the *initial query*. A subsequent query by the same searcher that is different than any of the searcher's other queries is a *modified query*. There can be several occurrences of different modified queries by a particular searcher. A *unique query* refers to a query that is different from all other queries in the transaction log, regardless of the searcher. A *repeat query* is a query that appears more than once within the dataset by two or more searchers.

Query complexity examines the query syntax, including the use of advanced searching techniques such as Boolean and other query operators.

c. Term analysis

The term level of analysis naturally uses the term as the basis for analysis. A term is a string of characters separated by some delimiter such as a space or some other separator. At this level of analysis, one focuses on measures such as *term occurrence*, which is the frequency that a particular term occurs in the transaction log. High Usage Terms are those terms that occur most frequently in the dataset. *Term co-occurrence* measures the occurrence of term pairs within queries in the entire search log. One can also calculate degrees of association of term pairs using various statistical measures

The mutual information formula measures term association and does not assume mutual independence of the terms within the pair. One can calculate the mutual information statistic for all term pairs within the data set. Many times, a relatively low frequency term pair may be strongly associated (i.e., if the two terms always occur together). The mutual information statistic identifies the strength of this association:

$$I(w_1, w_2) = \ln \frac{P(w_1, w_2)}{P(w_1) * P(w_2)}$$

where $P(w_1)$, $P(w_2)$ are probabilities estimated by relative frequencies of the two words and $P(w_1, w_2)$ is the relative frequency of the word pair (ignoring the order sequence).

Relative frequencies are observed frequencies (F) normalized by the number of the queries:

$$P(w_1) = \frac{F_1}{Q'};\ P(w_1) = \frac{F_2}{Q'};\ P(w_1, w_2) = \frac{F_{12}}{Q'}$$

Both the frequency of term occurrence and the frequency of term pairs are the occurrence of the term or term pair within the set of queries. However, since a one term query cannot have a term pair, the set of queries for the frequency base differs. The number of queries for the terms is the number of nonduplicate queries in the data set.

The number of queries for term pairs is defined as

$$Q' = \sum_{n}^{m} (2n - 3)\, Qn$$

where Qn is the number of queries with n words (n > 1), and m is the maximum query length. So, queries of length one have no pairs. Queries of length two have one pair. Queries of length three have three possible pairs. Queries of length four have five possible pairs. This continues up to the queries of maximum length in the data set. The formula for queries of term pairs (Q′) account for this term pairing.

15.8 Web Analysis

Effective website management requires a way to map the behavior of the visitors to the site against the particular objectives and purpose of the site. Web analysis or Log file analysis is the study of the log files from a particular website. The purpose of log file analysis is to assess the performance of the website.

Every time a browser hits a particular web page the server computer on which the website is hosted registers and records data called log files for every action a visitor at that particular website takes. Log files data includes information on

- Who is visiting the website (the visitor's URL, or web address)
- The IP address (numeric identification) of the computer the visitor is browsing from
- The date and time of each visit
- Which pages the visitor viewed, how long the visitor viewed the site
- Other relevant data

Log files contain potentially useful information for anyone working with a website—from server administrators to designers to marketers—who needs to assess website usability and effectiveness.

1. Website administrators use the data in log files to monitor the availability of a website to make sure the site is online, available, and without technical errors that might prevent easy access and use. Administrators can also predict and plan for growth in server resources and monitor for unusual and possibly malicious activity. For example, by monitoring past web usage logs for visitor activity, a site administrator can predict future activity during holidays and other spikes in usage and plan to add more servers and bandwidth to accommodate the expected traffic. In order to watch for potential attacks on a website, administrators can also monitor web usage logs for abnormal activity on the website such as repetitive login attempts, unusually large numbers of requests from a single IP address, and so forth.
2. Marketers can use the log files to understand the effectiveness of various on- and off-line marketing efforts. By analyzing the weblogs, marketers can determine which marketing efforts are the most effective. Marketers can track the

effectiveness of online advertising, such as banner ads and other links, through the use of the referrer logs (*referring URLs*). Examination of the referring URLs indicates how visitors got to the website, showing, say, whether they typed the URL (web address) directly into their web browser or whether they clicked through from a link at another site.

Weblogs can also be used to track the amount of activity from offline advertising, such as magazine and other print ads, by utilizing a unique URL in each offline ad that is run. Unlike online advertising that shows results in log information about the referring website, offline advertising requires a way to track whether or not the ad generated a response from the viewer. One way to do this is to use the ad to drive traffic to a particular website especially established only for tracking that source.

3. Website designers use log files to assess the user experience and site usability. Understanding the user environment provides web designers with the information they need to create a successful design. While ensuring a positive user experience on a website requires more than merely good design, log files do provide readily-available information to assist with the initial design as well as continuous improvement of the website. Web designers can find useful information about
   a. The type of operating system (e.g., Windows XP or Linux)
   b. The screen settings (e.g., screen resolution)
   c. The type of browser (e.g., Internet Explorer or Mozilla) used to access the site

This information allows designers to create web pages that display well for the majority of users.

Click trail can show how a viewer navigates through the various pages of a given website; the corresponding clickstream data can show

- What products a customer looked at on an e-commerce site
- Whether the customer purchased those products
- What products a customer looked at but did not purchase
- What ads generated many click-throughs but resulted in few purchases
- And so on

By giving clues as to which website features are successful, and which are not, log files assist website designers in the process of continuous improvement by adding new features, improving on current features, or deleting unused features. Then, by monitoring the weblogs for the impact on the user reaction, and making suitable adjustments based on those reactions, the website designer can improve the overall experience for website visitors on a continuous basis.

Internet technologies relevant for Web analysis

1. proxy server is a network server which acts as an intermediary between the user's computer and the actual server on which the website resides; they are used to improve service for groups of users. First, it saves the results of all requests for a particular web page for a certain amount of time. Then, it intercepts all requests to the real server to see if it can fulfill the request itself. Say user A requests a certain web page (called Page 1); sometime later, user B requests the same page. Instead of forwarding the request to the web server where Page 1 resides, which can be a time-consuming operation, the proxy server simply returns the Page 1 that it already fetched for user A. Since the proxy server is often on the same network as the user, this is a much faster operation. If the proxy server cannot serve a stored page, then it forwards the request to the real server. Importantly, pages served by the proxy server are not logged in the log files, resulting in inaccuracies in counting site traffic.

   Major online services (such as Facebook, MSN, and Yahoo!) and other large organizations employ an array of proxy servers in which all user requests are made through a single IP address. This situation causes weblog files to significantly under-report unique visitor traffic. On the other hand, sometimes home users with an Internet Service Provider get assigned a new IP address each time they connect to the Internet. This causes the opposite effect of inflating the number of unique visits in the weblogs.
2. Firewalls: For the purpose of security rather than efficiency, acting as an intermediary device, a proxy server can also function as a firewall in an organization. Firewalls are used by organizations to protect internal users from outside threats on the Internet, or to prevent employees from accessing a specific set of websites. Firewalls hide the actual IP address for specific user computers and instead present a single generic IP address to the Internet for all its users. Hence, this contributes to under-reporting unique visitor traffic in web analytics.
3. Caching refers to the technique in which most web browser software keeps a copy of each web page, called a cache, in its memory. So, rather than requesting the same page again from the server (for example, if the user clicks the "back" button), the browser on the computer will display a copy of the page rather than make another new request to the server. Many Internet Service Providers and large organizations cache web pages in an effort to serve content more quickly and reduce bandwidth usage. As with the use of proxy servers, caching poses a problem because weblog files don't report these cached page views. Again, as a result weblog files can significantly under-report the actual visitor count.

15.8.1 Veracity of Log Files Data

Despite the wealth of useful information available in log files, the data also suffer from limitations.

15.8.1.1 Unique Visitors

One of the major sources of inaccuracy arises from the way in which unique visitors are measured. Traditional weblog reports measure unique visitors based on the IP address, or network address, recorded in the log file. Because of the nature of different Internet technologies, IP addresses do not always correspond to an individual visitor in a one-to-one relationship. In other words, there is no accurate way to identify each individual visitor. Depending on the particular situation, this causes the count of unique visitors to be either over- or under-reported.

Cookies are small bits of data that a website leaves on a visitor's hard drive after that visitor has hit a website. Then, each time the user's web browser requests a new web page from the server, the cookie on the user's hard drive can be read by the server. These cookie data benefit in several ways:

- Unique cookie gets generated for each user even if multiple viewers access the same website through the same proxy server; consequently, a unique session is recorded and a more accurate visitor count can be obtained.
- Cookies also make it possible to track users across multiple sessions (i.e., when they return to the site subsequently), thus enabling a computation of new versus returning visitors.
- Third-party cookies enable the website to assess what other sites the visitor has visited; this enables personalization of the website in terms of the content that is displayed.

Cookies are not included in normal log files. Therefore, only a web analytics solution that supports cookie tracking can utilize the benefits.

15.8.1.2 Visitor Count

Another source of inaccuracy is in visitor count data. Most weblog reports give two possible ways to count visitors—hits and unique visits. The very definition of hits is a source of unreliability. By definition, each time a web page is loaded, each element of the web page (i.e., different graphics on the same page) is counted as a separate "hit." Therefore, even with one page view, multiple hits are recorded as a function of the number of different elements on a given web page. The net result is that hits are highly inflated numbers.

In contrast, the under-reporting of visitors is a serious issue for online advertising. If the ad is cached, nobody knows that the ad was delivered. As a result, the organization delivering the ad does not get paid. Log files cannot track visitor activity from cached pages because the web server never acknowledges the request. This deficiency is remedied by using page tagging. This technique has its origins in hit counters, which like a car odometer increases by one count with each additional page view. Page tagging embeds a small piece of Javascript software code on the web page itself. Then, when the website user visits the web page, the Java code is activated by the computer user's browser software. Since page tagging is located on the web page itself rather than on the server, each time the page is viewed, it is "tagged"; while server logs cannot keep track of requests for a cached page, a "tagged" page will still acknowledge and record a visit. Moreover, rather than recording a visit in a weblog file that is harder to access, page tagging records visitor information in a database, offering increased flexibility to access the information more quickly and with more options to further manipulate the data.

15.8.1.3 Visit Duration

Weblogs do not provide an accurate way to determine visit duration. Visit duration is calculated based on the time spent between the first page request and the last page request. If the next page request never occurs, duration cannot be calculated and will be underreported. Weblogs also cannot account for the user who views a page, leaves the computer for 20 minutes, and comes back and clicks to the next page. In this situation, the visit duration would be highly inflated.

15.8.2 Web Analysis Tools

New tools in web analytics like Google Analytics provide a stronger link between online technologies and online marketing, giving marketers more essential information lacking in earlier versions of web analytics software. For many years, web analytics programs that delivered only simple measurements such as hits, visits, referrals, and search engine queries were not well linked to an organization's marketing efforts to drive online traffic. As a result, they provided very little insights to help the organization track and understand its online marketing efforts.

Trends in web analytics specifically improve both the method of data collection and the analysis of the data, providing significantly more value from a marketing perspective. These newer tools attempt to analyze the entire marketing process, from a user clicking an advertisement through to the actual sale of a product or service. This information helps to identify not merely which online advertising is driving traffic (number of clicks) to the website and which search terms lead visitors to the site, but which advertising is most effective in actually generating sales (conversion rates) and profitability. This integration of the weblog files with other measures of advertising effectiveness is critical to provide guidance into further advertising spending.

Web analytics software has the capability to perform more insightful, detailed reporting on the effectiveness of common online marketing activities such as search engine listings, pay-per-click advertising, and banner advertising. Marketing metrics to assess effectiveness can include the following:

- Cost-per-click: The total online expenditure divided by the number of click-throughs to the site.
- Conversion rate: The percentage of the total number of visitors who make a purchase, signup for a service, or complete another specific action.
- Return on marketing investment: The advertising expense divided by the total revenue generated from the advertising expense.
- Bounce rate: The number of users that visit only a single page divided by the total number of visits; one indicator of the "stickiness" of a web page.

Web 2.0 presents a challenge for measuring web activity because much of the key user activity is more complicated than simply viewing a page. Because user activity on Web 2.0 sites can involve watching a video, listening to a podcast, subscribing to real simple syndication (RSS) feeds, or creating rather than just viewing content, new metrics must be considered. For instance, web analytics of rich-media content might include, say, metrics such as the number of times a video has been played, the average duration of viewing, and completion rates. Or, in an interactive user environment, the quality of the user base may be more important than the quantity per se.

15.9 Summary

This chapter introduced the concept of a web-based application. It then sketched the reference architecture along with the realization of this architecture in J2EE. In the later part of the chapter we discuss the details and characteristics of weblog analysis. It then traces the development of web-based applications from Web 1.0 to Web 2.0 on to developments envisaged in future in Web 3.0, mobile web, semantic web, and rich internet applications.

16

Social Network Applications

Customers are sending tremendous amounts of detail through their social media activities, clickstream activity on websites, e-mail, and cell phones. This digital information can provide incredible insights into the patterns and behaviors of individuals and groups. Digital personalization is about deeper understanding and then being able to provide customized services around value choices that are relevant and dynamic across all digital channels (computer, smart phone, tablet, watch, etc.). Combining this digital information with a history of a customer's transactions and external data about other customers or groups with similar characteristics provides tremendous clarity into next likely actions of a customer or group. Someone who understands a customer's next likely actions not only has the capability of influencing the next action but can also influence the drivers of that action. This can provide a distinct competitive advantage.

A 360° view of the customer is an old term that refers to having a complete view of the customer. A 720° view refers to an additional 360° view of the customer using unstructured and semistructured data. This allows cross-silo and cross-channel analysis. Businesses such as banks, credit card companies, insurance, retail, health care, financial services, telcos, gaming, and Internet companies all need this capability.

Social computing is the use of social software, which is based on creating or recreating online social conversations and social contexts through the use of software and technology. An example of social computing is the use of email for maintaining social relationships. Social Networks (SN) are social structures made up of nodes and ties; they indicate the relationships between individuals or organisations and how they are connected through social contexts. SN operate on many levels and play an important role in solving problems, on how organisations are run and they help individuals succeed in achieving their targets and goals. Computer-based social networks enable people in different locations to interact with each other socially (e.g., chat and viewable photos) over a network. SN are very useful for visualising patterns: A social network structure is made up of nodes and ties: there may be few or many nodes in the networks or one or more different types of relations between the nodes. Building a useful understanding of a social network is to sketch a pattern of social relationships, kinships, community structure, and so forth. The use of mathematical and graphical techniques in social network analysis is important to represent the descriptions of networks compactly and more efficiently.

Social Networks operate on many different levels from families up to nations, and play a critical role in determining the way problems are solved, organisations are run and the degree to which people succeed in achieving their goals.

16.1 Networks

Networks have become the basic conceptual building blocks of the computational sciences especially triggered by the burgeoning growth of Internet and fuelled by rising significance of cloud computing, big data, mobile computing, and social networking solutions and applications.

This subsection presents a quick overview of the concept of networks and enterprises based on characteristics of networks, namely, network enterprises that are likely to swamp the business environment in the future.

16.1.1 Concept of Networks

At its most basic level, a network is any system or structure of interconnected elements that can be represented by a graph of nodes (the elements) connected by some kind of links (whatever ties them together). The nodes of a network may be anything from landmasses to cells in a body, political institutions, or people. The links between the nodes might be physical connections, biochemical interactions, relationships of power and authority, or reciprocal social ties such as friendship.

The concept of a network first arose in a field of mathematics known as graph theory, pioneered by Swiss-born mathematician Leonhard Euler in 1736. In a seminal paper, Euler solved a long-standing puzzle of geography known as the Konigsberg Bridge problem: Could someone cross each of the seven bridges of that Baltic seaport without repeating once. Euler found the solution (which was in the negative) by treating the city's islands and river banks as featureless nodes and Konigsbergs bridges as links connecting them. By reducing urban geography to a simple mathematical graph, the puzzle was easily solved, and the mathematics of networks was born.

In the mid-twentieth century, the Hungarian mathematicians Paul Erdo's and Alfred Renyi greatly expanded the theory of nodes and links in eight papers exploring the topology and behavior of randomly generated networks. In the late twentieth century, the mathematics of graph theory gave birth to a new interdisciplinary science of networks, devoted to examining the common principles of network graphs that are found across domains ranging from engineering to information science to biology to sociology.

Decades before the arrival of websites like Facebook, sociologists attempted to map the social ties within groups via the field of social network analysis. Different typologies of networks were seen to represent varying organizational structures, from the hierarchical models of companies and traditional militaries to the more distributed, centerless topologies of voluntary organizations whose numerous cells are only loosely connected to one another. Similarly, social network analysis has often focused on how and why certain innovations spread rapidly, be they new technologies (use of smartphones), new language (twitter), or new ideas (video call). In all these cases, a network model has allowed for new insights to be gained into the behavior and properties of extremely complex systems—insights that may not be visible by simply observing the actions of the individual constituent parts.

In the field of communications, networks were used to map telephone systems, with their wires (links) connecting phone lines and exchanges (the nodes). Later, these same phone networks began to link computers into the Internet. In terms of communications content (rather than communications hardware), the World Wide Web has been mapped as a network of interconnected web pages linked together by hyperlinks. Transportation systems have been mapped as networks, starting with Eulers bridges of Konigsberg, and continuing later as train networks, with stations (the nodes) linked by lines of track; road networks, with cities connected by interstate highways; and air traffic networks, with airports linked by the airline routes that crisscross our globe. In biology, network science has been used to map out the relationships of nerve cells connected by the dendrites and axons that transmit and receive their messages. Networks are used to map molecules in an organism by how they are linked through biochemical reactions. Network maps have also been applied to tracking the spread of infectious diseases, with patients representing the nodes and vectors of disease transmission being the links between them.

16.1.2 Principles of Networks

16.1.2.1 Metcalfe's Law

Robert Metcalfe, the inventor of the Ethernet and founder of 3Com, evaluated that the value of a network increases as the square of the number of users; consequently, additional users are attracted to connect to the network resulting in a virtuous cycle of positive feedback. Considering that the original observation was inspired by telephonic systems that are typically bilateral, the value associated with computer networks that admit multilateralism is manifold. Thus, for computer networks with n number of nodes allowing conversations of m users simultaneously, the value of the computer network may increase as nm! This phenomenon has important implications for corporations competing in network markets.

While in the traditional economy, value is derived from scarcity, in the network economy, critical mass supersedes scarcity as a source of value. Positive feedback works to the advantage of big networks and to the detriment of smaller networks. Consequently, the bigger networks continue to grow bigger, while the smaller networks are sucked into a vortex of negative feedback and shrink to insignificance. The classic examples of this phenomenon are Microsoft Windows rapid ascendancy to market domination against other alternatives like Apple or UNIX operating systems or the VHS versus Betamax standard battle.

16.1.2.2 Power Law

Many natural phenomena, such as the height of a species, follow the random distribution known as a bell curve: most animals grow to be quite close to the average height of their species, and those that deviate will be only slightly taller or shorter. But among phenomena that follow a power law curve, there is no clustering around the average; instead there are a few extremely high values and then many, many more increasingly small values. Power law distributions are seen in the distribution of wealth, as famously observed by Vilfredo Pareto's principle (also termed as the 80–20 rule) that 80% of the wealth is held by 20% of the population. Network enterprises (network customers) follow this kind of power law distribution as well: some enterprises (customers) are much more or less connected or active within a network than the average enterprise (customer).

16.1.2.3 Small Worlds Networks

The phenomenon of networks is pervasive, and they deeply affect all aspects of human life and relationships. Networks matter because local actions have global consequences, and the relationship between local and global dynamics depends on the network structure.

The idea of small worlds is applicable to diverse problems—community of prospects or customers, organizations, national markets, global economy, flying routes, postal services, food chains, electrical power grids, disease propagation, ecosystems, language, or firing of neurons. In 1998, Cornell mathematician Duncan Watts with his advisor, Steve Strogatz, recognized the structural similarity between graph problems describing any collection of dots connected by lines and the coordinated lightning of fireflies. The 1967 idea of sociologist Stanley Milgram states that the world's six billion people are all connected by six degrees of separation, that is, the average number of steps needed to get from one selected person to another is six.

They showed that when networks of connected dots have a degree of order to their clustering, the degree of separation is correspondingly high, but adding random links shrinks the degree of separation rapidly. Real-world networks are far from being a bunch of nodes randomly linked to each other; instead, a few well-connected hubs keep most of the networks together. They showed that networks operate on the power law, the notion that a few large interactions carry the most action or the rich get richer! This explains why the Internet is dominated by a few highly connected nodes or large hubs such as Yahoo! or Google or Amazon.com as also the dominance of Microsoft Windows on desktops. Similarly, in a separate context, a few individuals with extraordinary ability to make friendships keep the society together.

Thus, networks combine order and randomness to reveal two defining characteristics of the small worlds networks: local robustness and global accessibility. Local robustness results from the fact that excepting the hubs, malfunctioning at other smaller nodes does not disrupt or paralyze the network; it continues to function normally. However, paradoxically, the elegance and efficiency of these structures also make them vulnerable to infiltration, failures, sabotage, and, in case of the Internet, virus attacks.

16.2 Computer Networks

Two computers are said to be networked if they are able to exchange information. The connection need not be via a copper wire; fiber optics, microwaves, infrared, and communication satellites can also be used. Networks come in many sizes, shapes, and forms, as we will see later. They are usually connected together to make larger networks, with the Internet being the most well-known example of a network of networks.

Computer Network and a Distributed System: The key distinction between them is that in a distributed system, a collection of independent computers appears to its users as a single coherent system. Usually, it has a single model or paradigm that it presents to the users. Often, a layer of software on top of the operating system, called middleware, is responsible for implementing this model. A well-known example of a distributed system is the WWW. It runs on top of the Internet and presents a model in which everything looks like a document (web page). However, in a computer network, coherence, model, and software are absent. Users are exposed to the actual machines, without any attempt by the system to make the machines look and act in a coherent way. If the machines have different hardware and different operating systems, that is fully visible to the users. If a user wants to run a program on a remote machine, it entails logging onto that machine and run it there. In effect, a distributed system is a software system built on top of a network. The software gives it a high degree of cohesiveness and transparency.

Thus, the distinction between a network and a distributed system lies with the software (especially the operating system), rather than with the hardware. Nevertheless, there is considerable overlap between the two subjects. For example, both distributed systems and computer networks need to move files around. The difference lies in who invokes the movement, the system, or the user.

16.2.1 Internet

The origins of the internet can be traced to the U.S. government support of the ARPANET project. Computers in several U.S. universities were linked via packet switching, and this allowed messages to be sent between the universities that were part of the network. The use of ARPANET was limited initially to academia and to the U.S. military, and in the early years, there was little interest from industrial companies.

However, by the mid-1980s, there were over 2000 hosts on the TCP/IP-enabled network, and the ARPANET was becoming more heavily used and congested. It was decided to shut down the network by the late 1980s, and the National Science Foundation in the United States commenced work on the NSFNET. This work commenced in the mid-1980s, and the network consisted of multiple regional networks connected to a major backbone. The original links in NSFNET were 56 Kbps, but these were later updated to the faster T1 (1.544 Mbps) links. The NSFNET T1 backbone initially connected 13 sites, but this increased due to a growing interest from academic and industrial sites in the United States and from around the world. The NSF began to realize from the mid-1980s onward that the internet had significant commercial potential.

16.2.2 World Wide Web (WWW)

The WWW was invented by Tim Berners-Lee in 1990 at CERN in Geneva, Switzerland. One of the problems that scientists at CERN faced was that of keeping track of people, computers, documents, databases, and so on. This problem was more acute due to the international nature of CERN, as the center had many visiting scientists from overseas who spent several months there. Berners-Lee essentially created a system to give every page on a computer a standard address. This standard address is called the universal resource locator and is better known by its acronym URL. Each page is accessible via the hypertext transfer protocol (HTTP), and the page is formatted with the hypertext markup language (HTML). Each page is visible using a web browser.

Inventors tend to be influenced by existing inventions and especially inventions that are relevant to their areas of expertise. The internet was a key existing invention, and it allowed worldwide communication via electronic email, the transfer of files electronically via FTP, and newsgroups that allowed users to make postings on various topics. Another key invention that was relevant to Berners-Lee was that of hypertext. This was invented by Ted Nelson in the 1960s, and it allows links to be present in text. For example, a document such as a book contains a table of contents, an index, and a bibliography. These are all links to material that is either within the book itself or external to the book. The reader of a book is able to follow the link to obtain the internal or external information. The other key invention that was relevant to Berners-Lee was that of the mouse. This was invented by Doug Engelbart in the 1960s, and it allowed the cursor to be steered around the screen. The major leap that Berners-Lee made was essentially a marriage of the Internet, hypertext, and the mouse into what has become the World Wide Web.

The invention of the WWW by Berners-Lee was a revolution in the use of the Internet. Users could now surf the web: that is, hyperlink among the millions of computers in the world and obtain information easily. The WWW creates a space in which users can access information easily in any part of the world. This is done using only a web browser and simple web addresses. Browsers are used to connect to remote computers over the Internet and to request, retrieve, and display the web pages on the local machine. The user can then click on hyperlinks on web pages to access further relevant information that may be on an entirely different continent. Berners-Lee developed the first web browser called the World Wide Web browser. He also wrote the first browser program, and this allowed users to access web pages throughout the world. The invention of the WWW was announced in August 1991, and the growth of the web has been phenomenal since then.

The WWW is revolutionary in that

- No single organization is controlling the web.
- No single computer is controlling the web.
- Millions of computers are interconnected.
- It is an enormous market place of millions (billions) of users.
- The web is not located in one physical location.
- The web is a space and not a physical thing.

The WWW has been applied to many areas including the following:

- Travel industry (booking flights, train tickets, and hotels)
- E-marketing
- Portal sites (such as Yahoo! and Hotmail)
- Ordering books and CDs over the web (such as www.amazon.com)
- Recruitment services (such as www.jobserve.com)
- Internet banking
- Online casinos (for gambling)
- Newspapers and news channels
- Online shopping and shopping malls

16.3 Social Networks

The study of social networks really began to take off as an interdisciplinary specialty only after 1970, when modern discrete combinatorics (particularly graph theory) experienced rapid development and relatively powerful computers became readily available. Since then, it has found important applications in organizational behavior, interorganizational relations, the spread of contagious diseases, mental health, social support, the diffusion of information and animal social organization.

German sociologist, F. Tönnies was a major contributor to sociological theory and it was him who initially highlighted that social groups exist by containing individuals which are linked together through shared beliefs and values. E. Durkheim gave a nonindividualistic explanation of social facts arguing that social phenomena arise when interacting individuals constitute a reality that can no longer be accounted for in terms of the properties of individual actors. He distinguished between a traditional society—"mechanical solidarity"—which prevails if individual differences are minimized, and the modern society—"organic solidarity"—that develops out of cooperation between differentiated individuals with independent roles. By the turn of the twentieth century, another major German sociologist, Georg Simmel, became the first scholar to think appropriately in social network terms. Simmel produced a series of essays that pinpointed the nature of network size. He further displayed an understanding of social networking with his writings as he highlighted that social interaction existed within loosely-knit networks as opposed to groups. The next real significant growth of social networking didn't really commence until the 1930s when three main social networking traditions emerged. The first tradition to emerge was pioneered by Jacob Levy Moreno, who was recognised as one of the leading social scientists. Moreno began the systematic recording and analysis of social interaction in smaller groups such as work groups and classrooms. The second tradition was founded by a Harvard group that began to focus specifically on interpersonal relations at work. The third tradition originated from Alfred Radcliffe-Brown, an English social anthropologist.

Social groups can exist as personal and direct social ties that either link individuals who share values and beliefs or impersonal, formal, and instrumental social links. Durkheim gave a nonindividualistic explanation of social facts arguing that social phenomena arise when interacting individuals constitute a reality that can no longer be accounted for in terms of the properties of individual actors. He distinguished between a traditional society—"mechanical solidarity"—which succeeds if individual differences are lessened, and the modern society that develops out of support between differentiated individuals with independent roles. Social network analysis has emerged as a key technique in modern sociology, and has also gained a following in anthropology; biology, communication studies, economics, geography, information science, organizational studies, social psychology, and sociolinguistics.

Efforts to support social networks via computer-mediated communication were made in many early online services, including Usenet, Arpanet, listserv, and bulletin board services (BBS). Many prototypical features of social networking sites were also present in online services such as America Online, Prodigy, and CompuServe. Early social networking on the World Wide Web began in the form of generalized online communities such as the Globe.com (1995), Geocities (1994) and Tripod.com (1995). Many of these early communities focused on bringing people together to interact with each other through chat rooms, and encouraged users to share personal information and ideas via personal web pages by providing easy-to-use publishing tools and free or inexpensive web space. Some communities—such as Classmates.com took a different approach by simply having people link to each other via email addresses. In the late 1990s, user profiles became a central feature of social networking sites, allowing users to compile lists of "friends" and search for other users with similar interests.

New social networking methods were developed by the end of the 1990s, and many sites began to develop more advanced features for users to find and manage friends. Web based social networking services make it possible to connect people who share interests and activities across political, economic, and geographic borders. Through email and instant messaging, online communities are created where a gift economy and mutual unselfishness are encouraged through collaboration. Information is particularly suited to gift economy, as information is a nonrival good and can be gifted at practically no cost. The newer generation of social networking sites began to flourish with the emergence of Makeoutclub in 2000, followed by Friendster in 2002, and soon became part of the Internet mainstream. Friendster was followed by MySpace and LinkedIn a year later, and finally

Bebo and Facebook in 2004. Attesting to the rapid increase in social networking sites' popularity, by 2005, MySpace was reportedly getting more page views than Google. Facebook launched in 2004, has since become the largest social networking site in the world. Today, it is estimated that there are now over 200 active sites using a wide variety of social networking models.

Social networks differ from most other types of networks, including technological and biological networks, in two important ways. First, they have non-trivial clustering or network transitivity and second, they show positive correlations between the degrees of adjacent vertices. Social networks are often divided into groups or communities, and it has recently been suggested that this division could account for the observed clustering. Furthermore, group structure in networks can also account for degree correlations. Hence, assortativemixing in such networks with a variation in the sizes of the groups provides the predicted level and compares well with that observed in real-world networks.

A definition of social networks that is merely based on their structure: "a social network is an organized set of people that consists of two kinds of elements: human beings and the connections between them." The online social network in that case is the tool or the platform that facilitates the development and maintenance of this relationship that may stem from different needs of the participants.

The current metrics for social network analysis are as follows:

- Bridge: An edge is said to be a bridge if deleting it would cause its endpoints to lie in different components of a graph.
- Centrality: This measure gives a rough indication of the social power of a node based on how well they "connect" the network. "Betweenness," "Closeness," and "Degree" are all measures of centrality.
- Betweenness: The extent to which a node lies between other nodes in the network. This measure takes into account the connectivity of the node's neighbors, giving a higher value for nodes that bridge clusters. The measure reflects the number of people who a person is connecting indirectly through their direct links.
- Closeness: The degree an individual is near all other individuals in a network (directly or indirectly). It reflects the ability to access information through the "grapevine" of network members. Thus, closeness is the inverse of the sum of the shortest distances between each individual and every other person in the network. The shortest path may also be known as the "geodesic distance."
- Centralization: The difference between the number of links for each node divided by maximum possible sum of differences. A centralized network will have many of its links dispersed around one or a few nodes, while a decentralized network is one in which there is little variation between the number of links each node possesses.
- Clustering coefficient: A measure of the likelihood that two associates of a node are associates. A higher clustering coefficient indicates a greater "cliquishness."
- Density: The degree a respondent's ties know one another/proportion of ties among an individual's nominees. Network or global-level density is the proportion of ties in a network relative to the total number possible (sparse vs. dense networks).

- Degree: The count of the number of ties to other actors in the network.
- Cohesion: The degree to which actors are connected directly to each other by cohesive bonds. Groups are identified as "cliques" if every individual is directly tied to every other individual, "social circles" if there is less stringency of direct contact, which is imprecise, or as structurally cohesive blocks if precision is wanted.
- Eigenvector centrality: A measure of the importance of a node in a network. It assigns relative scores to all nodes in the network based on the principle that connections to nodes having a high score contribute more to the score of the node in question.
- Prestige—In a directed graph prestige is the term used to describe a node's centrality. "Degree Prestige," "Proximity Prestige," and "Status Prestige" are all measures of Prestige.
- Reach—The degree to which any member of a network can reach other members of the network.
- Structural hole—Static holes that can be strategically filled by connecting one or more links to link together other points. Linked to ideas of social capital: if you link to two people who are not linked you can control their communication.

> The most important centrality measures are: degree centrality, closeness centrality and betweenness centrality.
>
> 1. Degree centrality: Degree of a node is the number of direct connections a node has. Degree centrality is the sum of all other actors who are directly connected to ego. It signifies activity or popularity. Lots of ties coming in and lots of ties coming out of an actor would increase degree centrality.
> 2. Betweenness centrality: This type of centrality is the number of times a node connects pairs of other nodes, who otherwise would not be able to reach one another. It is a measure of the potential for control as an actor who is high in "betweenness" is able to act as a gatekeeper controlling the flow of resources (information, money, power, e.g.) between the alters that he or she connects. This measurement of centrality is purely structural measure of popularity, efficiency, and power in a network; in other words, the more connected or centralized an actor is, the more popular, efficient, or powerful he or she is.
> 3. Closeness centrality: Closeness centrality is based on the notion of distance. If an node or actor is close to all others in the network, a distance of no more than one, then it is not dependent on any other to reach everyone in the network. Closeness measures independence or efficiency. With disconnected networks, closeness centrality must be calculated for each component.

As indicated earlier, the two basic elements of SN are links and nodes. Links are connections, or ties, between individuals or groups, and, nodes are the individuals or groups involved in the network. A nodes importance in a social network refers to its centrality. Central nodes have the potential to exert influence over less central nodes. A network that possesses just a few or perhaps even one node with high centrality is a centralized network. In this type of network all nodes are directly connected to each other. Subordinate nodes direct information to the central node and the central node distributes it to all other nodes. Centralized networks are susceptible to disruption because they have few central nodes and damage to a central node could be devastating to the entire network.

Decentralized networks are those that do not possess one central hub; but rather possess several important hubs. Each node is indirectly tied to all others and therefore the network has more elasticity. Consequently, these networks are more difficult to disrupt due to their loose connections and ability to replace damaged nodes. Consequently, terror networks choose this type of structure whenever possible.

The term degrees is used in reference to the number of direct connections that a node enjoys. The node that possesses the largest number of connections is the hub of the network. The term betweenness refers to the number of groups that a node is indirectly tied to through the direct links that it possesses. Therefore, nodes with high a degree of betweenness act as liaisons or bridges to other nodes in the structure. These nodes are known as "brokers" because of the power that they wield. However, these "brokers" represent a single point of failure because if their communication flows is disrupted than they will be cut off to the nodes that it connects. Closeness measures the trail that a node would take in order to reach all other nodes in a network. A node with high closeness does not necessarily have the most direct connections; but because they are "close" to many members they maintain rapid access to most other nodes through both direct and indirect ties.

16.3.1 Popular Social Networks

This section briefly describes popular social networks like LinkedIn, Facebook, Twitter, and Google+.

16.3.1.1 LinkedIn

LinkedIn is currently considered the de facto source of professional networking. Launched in 2003, it is the largest business-oriented social network with more than 260 million users. This network allows users to find the key people they may need to make introductions into the office of the job they may desire. Users can also track friends and colleagues during times of promotion and hiring to congratulate them if they choose; this results in a complex social web of business connections. In 2008, LinkedIn introduced their mobile app as well as the ability for users to not only endorse each other but also to specifically attest to individual skills that they may hold and have listed on the site. LinkedIn now supports more than 20 languages.

Users cannot upload their resumes directly to LinkedIn. Instead, a user adds skills and work history to their profile. Other users inside that social network can verify and endorse each attribute. This essentially makes a user's presence on LinkedIn only as believable as the people they connect with.

16.3.1.2 Facebook

Facebook was created by Mark Zuckerberg at Harvard College. Launched in 2004, it grew rapidly and now has more than a billion and half users. In 2011, Facebook introduced personal timelines to complement a user's profile; timelines show chronological placement of photos, videos, links, and other updates made by a user and his or her friends. Though a user can customize their timeline as well as the kind of content and profile information that can be shared with individual users, Facebook networks rely heavily on people posting comments publically and also tagging people in photos. Tagging is a very common practice that places people and events together, though, if required, a user can always untag himself or herself.

Conceptually, timeline is a chronological representation of a person's life from birth until his or her death, or present day if you are still using Facebook. A user's life can be broken up into pieces or categories that can be more meaningfully analyzed by the algorithms run by Facebook. These categories include Work and Education, Family and Relationships, Living, Health and Wellness, and Milestones and Experiences. Each category contains four to seven subcategories. Users have granular control over who sees what content related to them, but less so about what they see in relation to other people.

Facebook is often accused of selling user information and not fully deleting accounts after users choose to remove them. Because Facebook has such a generalized privacy policy, they can get away with handling user information in almost any way that they see fit. Facebook has done many things to improve security in recent years.

Facebook has provided users with a detailed list of open sessions under their account name and given them the ability to revoke them at will. This is to say that, if an unauthorized person accesses a user's account or the user forgets to log out of a computer, they can force that particular connection to close. Location and time of access are listed for each open session, so a user can easily determine if their account is being accessed from somewhere unexpected.

When viewed through a web browser, Facebook supports https. This protocol is considered secure; however, it is not supported by mobile devices. Data transmitted by Facebook to mobile devices has been proven to be in plain text, meaning if it is intercepted it is easily human readable. However, Global Positioning System (GPS) coordinates and information about your friends require special permission. Default access granted to any Facebook app includes user ID, name, profile picture, gender, age range, locale, networks, list of friends, and any information set as public. Any of this information can be transmitted between devices at any time without a user's express permission, and, in the case of mobile devices, in plain, unencrypted text.

> Facebook has partially solved this problem by releasing a separate app for messaging. It provides more granular control for mobile device permissions, such as contact syncing and specific profile information. The only problem with this solution is that it relies on every user to not only know about and download the separate app, but to also carefully take the considerable amount of time to properly read through and set all the new permissions properly.

16.3.1.3 Twitter

Twitter's original idea was to design a system for individuals to share short SMS messages with a small group of people. Hence, tweets were designed to be short and led to the limit of 144 characters per tweet. By 2013, Twitter had 200 million users sending 500 million tweets a day.

Twitter was originally designed to work with text messages. This is why the 140 character limit was put into the original design, to comply with text message rates. Twitter's original design was to create a service that a person could send a text to, and that text would not only be available online but it would then be able to resend that text to other people using the service. Subsequently, Twitter has incorporated many different sources of media. In 2010, Twitter added facility for online video and photo viewing without redirection to third-party sites. In 2013, Twitter added its own music service as an iPhone app. Despite Twitter's continued expansion of supported content, the language used in modern tweets along with some other helpful additions has continued to adhere to the 140 character limit.

> When Twitter was first implemented, tweets were handled by a server running Ruby on Rails and stored tweets in a shared MySQL database. As the number of Twitter users grew rapidly and the number of tweets being made skyrocketed past the throughput capacity of the system, the MySQL database could not keep up resulting in read and write errors that prevented tweets from being handled properly. Eventually, Rails components were replaced with the corresponding Scala implementations leading to improvement of throughput by more than 50 times.

16.3.1.4 Google+

Google+ is the only social network to rival Facebook's user base with more than a billion users. The main feature of Google+ is circles; by being part of the same circle, people create focused social networks. Circles allow networks to center around ideas and products; circles are also the way that streaming content is shared between people. Circles generate content for users and help organize and segregate with whom information is shared. A user makes circles by placing other Google+ users into them. This is done through an interface built very similar to Gmail and Google maps.

When circles create content for a user, it is accumulated and displayed on their Stream. A user's Stream is a prioritized list of any content from that user's circles that they have decided to display. A user can control how much of a Circle's content is included in their Stream. Circles can also be shared, either with individual users or other circles. This action being a single time share means that there is no subsequent syncing after the share takes place. The lack of synchronous updates without sharing a Circle again means that it is simply very easy for others to have incorrect information about Circles that change on a regular basis. If frequent updates are made and a user wants his or her network to stay up-to-date, a user may have to share a Circle quite frequently.

Google+ Pages are essentially profiles for businesses, organizations, publications, or other entities that are not related to a single individual. They can be added to Circles like normal users and share updates to user Streams in the same way. The real distinction is that Pages do not require a legal name to be attached to the associated Google account.

Google+ has a large amount of additional services and support owing to its high level of integration with Google accounts including games, messenger, photo editing and saving, mobile upload and diagnostics, apps, calendars, and video streaming. Hangouts, which is Google's video-streaming application, is available free for use and supports up to 10 simultaneous users in a session. Hangouts can be used as a conference call solution or to create instant webcasts. Functionally, Hangouts is similar to programs like Skype

16.3.1.5 Other Social Networks

Here are some of the other notable social networks:

1. Classmates was established in 1995 by Randy Conrads as a means for class reunions, and has more than 50 million registered users. By linking together people from the same school and class year, Classmates.com provides individuals with a chance to "walk down memory lane" and get reacquainted with old classmates that have also registered with the site. With a minimum age limit of 18 years, registration is free and anyone may search the site for classmates that they may know. Purchasing a gold membership is required to communicate with other members through the site's email system. User email addresses are private, and communication for paying members is handled through a double-blind email system that ensures that only paying members can make full use of the site, allowing unlimited communication and orchestration of activities for events like reunions.
2. Friendster was launched in 2002 by Jonathan Abrams as a generic social network in Malaysia. Friendster is a social network made primarily of Asian users. Friendster was redesigned and relaunched as a gaming platform in 2011 where it would grow to its current user base of more than 115 million. Friendster filed many of the fundamental patents related to social networks. Eighteen of these patents were acquired by Facebook in 2011.
3. hi5 is a social network developed by Ramu Yalamanchi in 2003 in San Francisco, California; and was acquired by Tagged in 2011. All of the normal social network features were included like friend networks, photo sharing, profile information, and groups. In 2009, hi5 was redesigned as a purely social gaming network with a required age of 18 years for all new and existing users. Several hundred games were added, and Application Programming Interfaces (APIs) were created that include support for Facebook games. This popular change boosted hi5's user base, and at the time of acquisition its user base was more than 80 million.
4. Orkut was a social network almost identical to Facebook that was launched in 2004 and was shut down by the end of September 2014. Orkut obtained more than 100 million users, most of which were located in India and Brazil.
5. Flickr is a photo-sharing website that was created in 2004 and was acquired by Yahoo! in 2005; photos and videos can also be accessed via Flickr. It has tens of millions of members sharing billions of images.
6. YouTube is a video-sharing website that was created in 2005 and was acquired by Google in 2006. Members as well as corporations and organizations post videos of themselves as well as various events and talks. Movies and songs are also posted on this website.

16.4 Social Networks Analysis (SNA)

In social science, the structural approach that is based on the study of interaction among social actors is called social network analysis. The relationships that social network analysts study are usually those that link individual human beings, since these social scientists believe that besides individual characteristics, relational links or social structure, are necessary and indispensable to fully understand social phenomena.

Social network analysis is used to understand the social structure, which exists among entities in an organization. The defining feature of social network analysis (SNA) is its focus on the structure of relationships, ranging from causal acquaintance to close bonds. This is in contrast with other areas of the social sciences where the focus is often on the attributes of agents rather than on the relationships between them. SNA maps and measures the formal and informal relationships to understand what facilitates or impedes the knowledge flows that bind the interacting units, that is, who knows whom and who shares what information and how. Social network analysis is focused on uncovering the patterning of people's interaction. SNA is based on the intuition that these patterns are important features of the lives of the individuals who display them. The network analysts believe that how an individual lives depends in large part on how that individual is tied into larger web of social connections. Moreover, many believe that the success or failure of societies and organizations often depends on the patterning of their internal structure, which is guided by formal concept analysis, which is grounded in systematic analysis of the empirical data. With the availability of powerful computers and discrete combinatorics (especially graph theory) after 1970, the study of SNA took off as an interdisciplinary speciality; the applications are found manifolds that include organizational behavior, inter-organizational relations, the spread of contagious diseases, mental health, social support, and the diffusion of information and animal social organization. SNA software provides the researcher with data that can be analyzed to determine the centrality, betweenness, degree, and closeness of each node.

An individual's social network influences his/her social attitude and behavior. Before collecting network data typically through interviews, it must first be decided as to the kinds of networks and kinds of relations that will be studied:

1. One mode versus two mode networks: The former involve relations among a single set of similar actors, while the latter involve relations among two different sets of actors. An example of two mode network would be the analysis of a network consisting of private, for profit organizations, and their links to nonprofit agencies in a community [10]. Two mode networks are also used to investigate the relationship between a set of actors and a series of events. For example, although people may not have direct ties to each other, they may attend similar events or activities in a community and in doing so, this sets up opportunities for the formation of "weak ties."
2. Complete/whole versus ego networks: Complete/whole or sociocentric networks consist of the connections among members of a single, bounded community. Relational ties among all of the teachers in a high school is an example of whole network. Ego/Egocentric or personal networks are referred to as the ties directly connecting the focal actor, or ego to others, or ego's alters in the network, plus ego's views on the ties among his or her alters. If we asked a teacher to nominate the people he/she socializes with outside of school, and then asked that teacher to indicate who in that network socializes with the others nominated, it is a typical ego network.
   a. Egocentric network data focus on the network surrounding one node, or in other words, the single social actor. Data are on nodes that share the chosen relation(s) with the ego and on relationships between those nodes. Ego

network data can be extracted from whole network data by choosing a focal node and examining only nodes connected to this ego. Ego network data, like whole network data, can also include multiple relations; these relations can be collapsed into single networks, as when ties to people who provide companionship and emotional aid are collapsed into a single support network. Unlike whole network analyses, which commonly focus on one or a small number of networks, ego network analyses typically sample large numbers of egos and their networks.

b. Complete/whole networks focus on all social actors rather than focusing on the network surrounding any particular actor. These networks begin from a list of included actors and include data on the presence or absence of relationships between every pair of actors. When researcher adopts the whole network perspective, he/she will inquire each social actor and all other individuals to collect relational data.

Using a network perspective, Mark Granovetter put forward the theory of the "strength-of-weak-ties." Granovetter found in one study that more numerous weak ties can be important in seeking information and innovation. Because cliques have a tendency to have more homogeneous opinions and common traits, individuals in the same cliques would also know more or less what the other members know. To gain new information and opinion, people often look beyond the clique to their other friends and acquaintances.

16.5 Text Analysis

Text analysis is a new and exciting research area that tries to solve the information overload problem by using techniques from data mining, machine learning, natural language processing (NLP), information retrieval (IR), and knowledge management. Text analysis involves the preprocessing of document collections (text categorization, information extraction, term extraction), the storage of the intermediate representations, the techniques to analyze these intermediate representations (such as distribution analysis, clustering, trend analysis, and association rules), and visualization of the results. Text analysis draws on advances made in other computer science disciplines concerned with the handling of natural language because of the centrality of natural language text to its mission; text analysis exploits techniques and methodologies from the areas of information retrieval, information extraction, and corpus-based computational linguistics.

Since, text analysis derives much of its inspiration and direction from seminal research on data mining, there are many high-level architectural similarities between the two systems. For instance, text analysis adopts many of the specific types of patterns in its core knowledge discovery operations that werefirst introduced and vetted in data mining research. Further, both types of systems rely on preprocessing routines, pattern-discovery algorithms, and presentation-layer elements such as visualization tools to enhance the browsing of answer sets.

> Regarding preprocessing, because data mining assumes that data have already been stored in a structured format, much of its preprocessing focus falls on two critical tasks: Scrubbing and normalizing data creating extensive numbers of table joins.

In contrast, for text analysis systems, preprocessing operations center on the identification and extraction of representative features for natural language documents. These preprocessing operations are responsible for transforming unstructured data stored in document collections into a more explicitly structured intermediate format, which is not a concern relevant for most data mining systems.

The sheer size of document collections makes manual attempts to correlate data across documents, map complex relationships, or identify trends at best extremely labor-intensive and at worst nearly impossible to achieve. Automatic methods for identifying and exploring interdocument data relationships dramatically enhance the speed and efficiency of research activities. Indeed, in some cases, automated exploration techniques like those found in text analysis are not just a helpful adjunct but a baseline requirement for researchers to be able, in a practicable way, to recognize subtle patterns across large numbers of natural language documents. Text analysis systems, however, usually do not run their knowledge discovery algorithms on unprepared document collections. Considerable emphasis in text analysis is devoted to what are commonly referred to as preprocessing operations.

Text analysis preprocessing operations include a variety of different types of techniques culled and adapted from information retrieval, information extraction, and computational linguistics research that transform raw, unstructured, original-format content (like that which can be downloaded from document collections) into a carefully structured, intermediate data format. Knowledge discovery operations, in turn, are operated against this specially structured intermediate representation of the original document collection.

16.5.1 Defining Text Analysis

Text analysis can be broadly defined as a knowledge-intensive process in which a user interacts with a document collection over time by using a suite of analysis tools. In a manner analogous to data mining, text analysis seeks to extract useful information from data sources through the identification and exploration of interesting patterns. In the case of text analysis, however, the data sources are document collections, and interesting patterns are found not among formalized database records but in the unstructured textual data in the documents in these collections.

16.5.1.1 Document Collection

Adocument collection can be any grouping of text-based documents. Practically speaking, however, most text analysis solutions are aimed at discovering patterns across very large document collections. The number of documents in such collections can range from the many thousands to the tens of millions.

Document collections can be either static, in which case the initial complement of documents remains unchanged dynamic, which is a term applied to document collections characterized by their inclusion of new or updated documents over time.

Extremely large document collections, as well as document collections with very high rates of document change, can pose performance optimization challenges for various components of a text analysis system.

16.5.1.2 Document

A document can be very informally defined as a unit of discrete textual data within a collection that usually correlates with some real-world document such as a business report, legal memorandum, email, research paper, manuscript, article, press release, or news story. Within the context of a particular document collection, it is usually possible to represent a class of similar documents with a prototypical document. But a document can (and generally does) exist in any number or type of collections—from the very formally organized to the very ad hoc. A document can also be a member of different document collections, or different subsets of the same document collection, and can exist in these different collections at the same time.

1. Document, as a whole, is seen as a structured object.
2. Documents with extensive and consistent format elements in which field-type metadata can be inferred–such as some email, HTML web pages, PDF files, and word-processing files with heavy document templating or style-sheet constraints–are described as semistructured documents.
3. Documents that have relatively little in the way of strong typographical, layout, or markup indicators to denote structure—like most scientific research papers, business reports, legal memoranda, and news stories—are referred as free format or weakly structured documents.

Some text documents, like those generated from a WYSIWYG HTML editor, actually possess from their inception more overt types of embedded metadata in the form of formalized markup tags. However, even a rather innocuous document demonstrates a rich amount of semantic and syntactical structure, although this structure is implicit and hidden in its textual content. In addition, typographical elements such as punctuation marks, capitalization, numerics, and special characters—particularly when coupled with layout artifacts such as white spacing, carriage returns, underlining, asterisks, tables, columns, and so on—can often serve as a kind of "soft markup" language, providing clues to help identify important document subcomponents such as paragraphs, titles, publication dates, author names, table records, headers, and footnotes. Word sequence may also be a structurally meaningful dimension to a document.

16.5.1.3 Document Features

An essential task for most text analysis systems is the identification of a simplified subset of document features that can be used to represent a particular document as a whole. Such a set of features is referred as the representational model of a document; features required to represent a document collection tends to become very large effecting every aspect of a text analysis system's approach, design, and performance.

The high dimensionality of potentially representative features in document collections is a driving factor in the development of text analysis preprocessing operations aimed at creating more streamlined representational models. This high dimensionality also indirectly contributes to other conditions that separate text analysis systems from data mining systems such as greater levels of pattern overabundance and more acute requirements for postquery refinement techniques. The feature sparsity of a document collection reflects the fact that some features often appear in only a few documents, which means that the support of many patterns is quite low; furthermore, only a small percentage of all possible features for a document collection as a whole appears in any single document.

While evaluating optimal set of features for the representational model for a document collection, the tradeoff is between the following two conflicting objectives:

- To achieve the correct calibration of the volume and semantic level of features to portray the meaning of a document accurately, which tends toward evaluating relatively a larger set of features
- To identify features in a way that is most computationally efficient and practical for pattern discovery, which tends toward evaluating a smaller set of features

Commonly used document features are described below.

1. Characters: A character-level representation can include the full set of all characters for a document or some filtered subset; and, this feature space is the most complete of any representation of a real-world text document. The individual component-level letters, numerals, special characters and spaces are the building blocks of higher-level semantic features such as words, terms, and concepts. Character-based representations that include some level of positional information (e.g., bigrams or trigrams) are more useful and common. Generally, character-based representations can often be unwieldy for some types of text processing techniques because the feature space for a document is fairly unoptimized.
2. Words: Word-level features existing in the native feature space of a document. A word-level representation of a document includes a feature for each word within that document—that is the "full text," where a document is represented by a complete and unabridged set of its word-level features. However, most word-level document representations exhibit at least some minimal optimization and therefore consist of subsets of representative features devoid of items such as stop words, symbolic characters, and meaningless numerics and so on.
3. Terms: Terms are single words and multiword phrases selected directly from the corpus of a native document by means of term-extraction methodologies. Term-level features, in the sense of this definition, can only be made up of specific words and expressions found within the native document for which they are meant to be generally representative. Hence, a term-based representation of a document is necessarily composed of a subset of the terms in that document.

   Several of term-extraction methodologies can convert the raw text of a native document into a series of normalized terms—that is, sequences of one or more tokenized and lemmatized word forms associated with part-of-speech tags. Sometimes an external lexicon is also used to provide a controlled vocabulary for term normalization. Term-extraction methodologies employ various approaches for generating and filtering an abbreviated list of most meaningful candidate terms from among a set of normalized terms for the representation of a document. This culling process results in a smaller but relatively more semantically rich document representation than that found in word-level document representations.

4. Concepts: Concepts are features generated for a document by means of manual, statistical, rule-based, or hybrid categorization methodologies. Concept-level features can be manually generated for documents but are now more commonly extracted from documents using complex preprocessing routines that identify single words, multiword expressions, whole clauses, or even larger syntactical units that are then related to specific concept identifiers.

Many categorization methodologies involve a degree of cross-referencing against an external knowledge source; for some statistical methods, this source might simply be an annotated collection of training documents. For manual and rule-based categorization methods, the cross-referencing and validation of prospective concept-level features typically involve interaction with a "gold standard" such as a preexisting domain ontology, lexicon, or formal concept hierarchy—or even just the mind of a human domain expert. Unlike word- and term-level features, concept-level features can consist of words not specifically found in the native document.

Term- and concept-based representations exhibit roughly the same efficiency but are generally much more efficient than character- or word-based document models. terms and concepts reflect the features with the most condensed and expressive levels of semantic value, and there are many advantages to their use in representing documents for text analysis purposes. Term-level representations can sometimes be more easily and automatically generated from the original source text (through various term-extraction techniques) than concept-level representations, which as a practical matter have often entailed some level of human intervention.

Concept-based representations can be processed to support very sophisticated concept hierarchies, and arguably provide the best representations for leveraging the domain knowledge afforded by ontologies and knowledge bases. They are much better than any other feature set representation at handling synonymy and polysemy and are clearly best at relating a given feature to its various hyponyms and hypernyms. Possible disadvantages of using concept-level features to represent documents include the relative complexity of applying the heuristics, during preprocessing operations, required to extract and validate concept-type featuresthe domain dependence of many concepts.

There are also hybrid approaches to the generation of feature-based document representations. For instance, a particular text analysis system's preprocessing operations could first extract terms using term extraction techniques and then match or normalize these terms, or do both, by pruning them against a list of meaningful entities and topics (i.e., concepts) extracted through categorization. However, such hybrid approaches need careful planning, testing, and optimization to avoid a dramatic surge in the feature dimensionality of individual document representations without corresponding increase in system effectiveness.

16.5.1.4 Domain Knowledge

Text Analysis can leverage information from formal external knowledge sources for these domains to greatly enhance elements of their preprocessing, knowledge discovery, and presentation layer operations. A domain is defined as a specialized area of interest with dedicated ontologies, lexicons, and taxonomies of information. Domain Knowledge can be used in text analysis preprocessing operations to enhance concept extraction and validation activities; domain knowledge can play an important role in the development of more meaningful, consistent, and normalized concept hierarchies.

Advanced text analysis systems can create fuller representations of document collections by relating features by way of lexicons and ontologies in preprocessing operations and support enhanced query and refinement functionalities. Domain knowledge can be used to inform many different elements of a text analysis system:

- Domain knowledge is an important adjunct to classification and concept-extraction methodologies in preprocessing operations
- Domain knowledge can also be leveraged to enhance core mining algorithms and browsing operations.
- Domain-oriented information serves as one of the main basis for search refinement techniques.
- Domain knowledge may be used to construct meaningful constraints in knowledge discovery operations.
- Domainknowledge may also be used to formulate constraints that allow users greater flexibility when browsing large result sets.

16.5.1.5 Search for Patterns and Trends

The problem of pattern overabundance can exist in all knowledge discovery activities. It is simply aggravated when interacting with large collections of text documents, and, therefore, text analysis operations must necessarily be conceived to provide not only relevant but also manageable result sets to a user. Although text analysis preprocessing operations play the critical role of transforming unstructured content of a raw document collection into a more tractable concept-level data representation, the core functionality of a text analysis system resides in the analysis of concept co-occurrence patterns across documents in a collection. Indeed, text analysis systems rely on algorithmic and heuristic approaches to consider distributions, frequent sets, and various associations of concepts at an interdocument level in an effort to enable a user to discover the nature and relationships of concepts as reflected in the collection as a whole.

Text analysis methods—often based on large-scale, brute-force search directed at large, high-dimensionality feature sets—generally produce very large numbers of patterns. This results in an overabundance problem with respect to identified patterns that is usually much more severe than that encountered in data analysis applications aimed at structured data sources. A main operational task for text analysis systems is to enable a user to limit pattern overabundance by providing refinement capabilities that key on various specifiable measures of "interestingness" for search results. Such refinement capabilities prevent system users from getting overwhelmed by too many uninteresting results.

16.5.1.6 Results Presentation

Several types of functionality are commonly supported within the front ends of text analysis systems:

- Browsing: Most contemporary text analysis systems support browsing that is both dynamic and content-based; the browsing is guided by the actual textual content of a particular document collection and not by anticipated or rigorously prespecified structures; user browsing is usually facilitated by the graphical presentation of concept patterns in the form of a hierarchy to aid interactivity by organizing concepts for investigation.

- Navigation: Text mining systems must enable a user to move across these concepts in such a way as to always be able to choose either a "big picture" view of the collection in toto or to drill down on specific concept relationships.
- Visualization: Text analysis systems use visualization tools to facilitate navigation and exploration of concept patterns; these use various graphical approaches to express complex data relationships. While basic visualization tools generate static maps or graphs that were essentially rigid snapshots of patterns or carefully generated reports displayed on the screen or printed by an attached printer, state-of-the-art text analysis systems increasingly rely on highly interactive graphic representations of search results that permit a user to drag, pull, click, or otherwise directly interact with the graphical representation of concept patterns.
- Query: Languages have been developed to support the efficient parameterization and execution of specific types of pattern discovery queries; these are required because the presentation layer of a text analysis system really serves as the front end for the execution of the system's core knowledge discovery algorithms. Instead of limiting a user to limiting a user to run only a certain number of fixed, preprogrammed search queries, text analysis systems are increasingly designed to expose much of their search functionality to the user by opening up direct access to their query languages by means of query language interfaces or command-line query interpreters.
- Clustering: Text analysis systems enable clustering of concepts in ways that make the most cognitive sense for a particular application or task.
- Refinement constraints: Some text mining systems offer users the ability to manipulate, create, or concatenate refinement constraints to assist in producing more manageable and useful result sets for browsing.

16.6 Sentiment Analysis

Social media systems on the web have provided excellent platforms to facilitate and enable audience participation, engagement, and community, which has resulted in our new participatory culture. From reviews and blogs to YouTube, Facebook, and Twitter, people have embraced these platforms enthusiastically because they enable their users to freely and conveniently voice their opinions and communicate their views on any subject across geographic and spatial boundaries. They also allow people to easily connect with others and to share their information. This participatory web and communications revolution has transformed our everyday lives and society as a whole. It has also popularized two major research areas, namely, *social network analysis* and *sentiment analysis*.

Although social network analysis is not a new research area, as it started in the 1940s and the 1950s when management science researchers began to study social actors (people in organizations) and their interactions and relationships, social media has certainly fueled its explosive growth in the past 15 years. Sentiment analysis essentially grew out of social media on the web that has been very active since the year 2002. Apart from the availability of a large volume of opinion data in social media, opinions and sentiments also have a very wide range of applications simply because opinions are central to almost all human activities. Whenever we need to make a decision, we often seek out others' opinions. This is true not only for individuals but also for organizations. It is thus no surprise that the industry and applications surrounding sentiment analysis have flourished since around 2006.

Because a key function of social media is for people to express their views and opinions, sentiment analysis is right at the center of research and application of social media itself. It is now well recognized that, to extract and exploit information in social media, sentiment analysis is a necessary technology. One can even take a sentiment-centric view of social network analysis and, in turn, social media content analysis because the most important information that one wants to extract from the social network or social media content is what people talk about and what their opinions are. These are exactly the core tasks of sentiment analysis.

Social media also allows us to study the participants themselves. We can produce a sentiment profile of each social media participant based on his or her topical interests and opinions about these interests expressed in the users' posts, because a person's topical interests and opinions reflect the nature and preferences of the person. Such information can be used in many applications, for example, recommending products and services and determining which political candidates to vote for. Additionally, social media participants can not only post messages but also interact with one another through discussions and debates, which involve sentiments such as agreement and disagreement (or contention). Discovery of such information is also of great importance. For example, contentious social and political issues and views of opposing positions can be exploited to frame political issues and to predict election results. This necessitates highlighting another attendant problem of imposters gaming the system by posting fake or deceptive opinions to promote some target products, services, and ideological agendas. Detecting such fake or deceptive opinions is an important challenge.

16.6.1 Sentiment Analysis and Natural Language Processing (NLP)

Sentiment analysis, also called opinion mining, is the field of study that analyzes people's opinions, sentiments, appraisals, attitudes, and emotions toward entities and their attributes expressed in written text. The entities can be products, services, organizations, individuals, events, issues, or topics. The field represents a large problem space. The term *opinion* is taken to mean the whole concept of sentiment, evaluation, appraisal, or attitude and associated information, such as the opinion target and the person who holds the opinion, and the term *sentiment* is taken to mean the underlying *positive* or *negative* feeling implied by opinion. Sentiment analysis or opinion mining aims to identify positive and negative opinions or sentiments expressed or implied in text and also the targets of these opinions or sentiments.

Sentiment analysis mainly focuses on opinions that express or imply positive or negative or sentiments, also called positive or negative or neutral opinions respectively in everyday language. This type of opinion is similar to the concept of *attitude* in social psychology. Apart from sentiment and opinion, there are also the concepts of *affect*, *emotion*, and *mood*, which are psychological states of mind. Sentences expressing opinions or sentiments, being inherently subjective, are usually subjective sentences as opposed to objective sentences that state facts. However, objective sentences can imply positive or negative sentiments of their authors too, because they may describe desirable or undesirable facts.

Sentiment analysis is a semantic analysis problem, but it is highly focused and confined because a sentiment analysis system does not need to fully "understand" each sentence or document; it only needs to comprehend some aspects of it, for example, positive and negative opinions and their targets. Owing to some special characteristics of sentiment analysis, it allows much deeper language analyses to be performed to gain better insights into NLP than in the general setting because the complexity of the general setting of NLP is simply overwhelming. Although general natural language understanding is still far from us, with the concerted effort of researchers from different NLP areas, we may be able to solve the sentiment analysis problem, which, in turn, can give us critical insight into how to deal with general NLP.

The experience in the past 15 years seems to indicate that rather than being a subarea of NLP, sentiment analysis is actually more like a mini version of the full NLP or a special case of the full-fledged NLP; the reason for this is that sentiment analysis touches every core area of NLP, such as lexical semantics, co-reference resolution, word sense disambiguation, discourse analysis, information extraction, and semantic analysis.

Sentiment analysis is mainly carried out at three levels:

1. Document level: Assuming that each document expresses opinions on a single entity (e.g., a single product or service), document-level sentiment classification indicates whether a whole opinion document expresses a positive or negative sentiment. For instance, given a product review, the system determines whether the review expresses an overall positive or negative opinion about the product.
2. Sentence level: Sectence-level sentiment classification indicates whether each sentence expresses a positive, negative, or neutral opinion. This level of analysis is closely related to subjectivity classification, which distinguishes sentences that express factual information (called objective sentences) from sentences that express subjective views and opinions (called subjective sentences).
3. Aspect level: If a sentence has multiple opinions, It does not make much sense to classify this sentence as positive or negative because it is positive about one entity but negative about another. To obtain this level of fine-grained results, we need to go to the aspect level. Instead of looking at language units (documents, paragraphs, sentences, clauses, or phrases), aspect-level analysis directly looks at opinion and its target (called opinion target). Thus, the goal of this level of analysis is to discover sentiments on entities and/or their aspects. On the basis of this level of analysis, a summary of opinions about entities and their aspects can be produced.

There are two different types of opinions:

- A regular opinion expresses a sentiment about a particular entity or an aspect of the entity, for example, "Orange tastes very good" expresses a positive sentiment or opinion on the aspect taste of orange. This is the most common type of opinion.
- A comparative opinion compares multiple entities based on some of their shared aspects, for example, "Mango tastes better than orange" compares mango and orange based on their tastes (an aspect) and expresses a preference for mango.

Sentiment analysis involves addressing the problems of opinion searching and opinion summarization at appropriate levels.

Sentiment words, also called opinion words, are words in a language that indicate desirable or undesirable states. For example, good, great, and beautiful are positive sentiment words and bad, awful, and dreadful are negative sentiment words. Sentiment words and phrases are instrumental to sentiment analysis. A list of such words and phrases is called a sentiment lexicon. Sentiment analysis is usually undertaken in the context of a predefined lexicon.

Initial work in the area of sentiment analysis usually tends to focus on document- and sentence-level sentiment and subjectivity classification, which is insufficient for real-life applications. Practical applications almost always demand aspect-level analysis.

16.6.2 Applications

Individuals, organizations, and government agencies are increasingly using the content in social media for decision making. If an individual wants to buy a consumer product, he or she is no longer limited to asking his or her friends and family for opinions because there are many user reviews and discussions in public forums on the web about the product. For an organization, it may no longer be necessary to conduct surveys, opinion polls, or focus groups to gather public or consumer opinions about the organization's products and services because an abundance of such information is publicly available. Governments can also easily obtain public opinions about their policies and measure the pulses of other nations simply by monitoring their social media.

Sentiment analysis applications have spread to almost every possible domain, from consumer products, health care, tourism, hospitality, and financial services to social events and political elections. There are now hundreds of companies in this space, start-up companies and established large corporations, that have built or are in the process of building their own in-house capabilities, such as Google, Microsoft, Hewlett-Packard, Amazon, eBay, SAS, Oracle, Adobe, Bloomberg, and SAP.

A popular application of sentiment analysis is stock market prediction. The system identifies opinions from message board posts by classifying each post into one of three sentiment classes: bullish (optimistic), bearish (pessimistic), or neutral (neither bullish nor bearish). The resulting sentiments across all stocks were then aggregated and used to predict the stock Index. Instead of using bullish and bearish sentiments, an alternate approach is to identify positive and negative public moods on Twitter and used them to predict the movement of stock market indices such as the Dow Jones, S&P 500, and NASDAQ. The analysis shows that when emotions on Twitter fly high, that is, when people express a lot of hope, fear, or worry, the Dow goes down the next day. When people have less hope, fear, or worry, the Dow goes up.

16.7 Summary

This chapter discussed the social network applications of big data. It started with an introduction to the concept and principles of networks; this was followed with the description of the Internet and the World Wide Web that enabled the phenomenon of social networks and, consequently, social network analysis. After describing the social networks and discussing the characteristics of social network analysis, it focuses on text analytics as a prerequisite to sentiment analysis that is discussed in the later part of the chapter.

17

Mobile Applications

A mobile environment is different from traditional distributed environments due to its unique characteristics such as the mobility of users or computers, the limitation of computing capacity of mobile devices, and the frequent and unpredictable disconnection of wireless networks. Therefore, development of mobile systems is different from development of distributed systems. In other words, when designing a mobile system, we have to overcome challenges due to physical mobility of the clients, the portability features of mobile devices and the fact that the communication is wireless. Thus, it is important that these issues are examined carefully when considering the system requirements, in terms of both functional and nonfunctional requirements.

> Functional requirements include all the logical and specific behaviors of a system, while nonfunctional requirements concern the overall characteristics of the system-like performance, reliability, and security.

The process to identify the requirements of a mobile client-server-based system is very different from a nonmobile one. This is due to the unique characteristics of mobile environments that are the mobility of users or computers, the limitation of computing capacity of mobile devices, and the frequent and unpredictable disconnections of wireless networks.

17.1 Mobile Computing Applications

A wireless mobile application is defined as a software application, a wireless service, or a mobile service that can be either pushed to users' handheld wireless devices or downloaded and installed, over the air, on these devices.

Such applications must work within the daunting constraints of mobile devices themselves:

- Memory: Wireless devices such as cellular phones and two-way pagers have limited amounts of memory, obliging developers to consider memory management most carefully when designing application objects.
- Processing power: Wireless devices also have limited processing power (16-bit processors are typical).
- Input: Input capabilities are limited. Most cell phones provide only a one-hand keypad with 12 buttons: the 10 numerals, an asterisk (*), and a pound sign (#).

- Screen: The display might be as small as 96 pixels wide by 54 pixels high and 1 bit deep (black and white). The amount of information that can be squeezed into such a tight screen is severely limited.

The wireless environment itself imposes further constraints as follows:

1. Wireless networks are unreliable and expensive, and bandwidth is low
2. They tend to experience more network errors than wired networks
3. The very mobility of wireless devices increases the risk that a connection will be lost or degraded

In order to design and build reliable wireless applications, designers need to keep these constraints in mind and as also the impact these wireless devices with limited resources have on application design.

Wireless applications themselves can be classified into three streams:

1. Browser-based: Applications developed using a markup language. This is similar to the current desktop browser model where the device is equipped with a browser. The wireless application protocol (WAP) follows this approach.
2. Native applications: Compiled applications where the device has a runtime environment to execute applications. Highly interactive wireless applications are only possible with the latter model. Interactive applications, such as mobile computer games, are a good example. Such applications can be developed using the fast growing Java 2 Micro Edition (J2ME) platform, and they are known as MIDlets.
3. Hybrid applications: Applications that aim at incorporating the best aspects of both streams above: the browser is used to allow the user to enter URLs to download native applications from remote servers, and the runtime environment is used to let these applications run on the device.

17.1.1 Generations of Communication Systems

17.1.1.1 1st Generation: Analog

The 1st-generation analog cell phone was a rather bulky piece of equipment. This invention nonetheless was the exciting beginning to cellular technology for the consumer and business marketplace. Though the concept of "mobile" devices for voice communication was truly nothing new in early 1980s, the important technology of leveraging a distinct network of "cells" to enable wireless voice communication was a revolution. The "cell" technology works by assigning multiple base stations to a subset of users, thereby increasing the system's capacity exponentially, while reducing power requirements for the user terminals, namely, the analog cell phones. Analog networks can only carry voice and not data. So, it is impossible to send an email or any other type of data element that requires the movement of digital information.

17.1.1.2 2nd Generation: CDMA, TDMA, and GSM

The 2nd-generation (2G) of wireless and mobile phone technology gave users the capability to send and receive data in a digital format. Digital technology offers many benefits over analog by offering better service to customers (a service operator can fit more information in a transmission), much improved clarity of sound (during voice conversations), higher security, and access to future generation features.

However, it led to the creation of three mutually incompatible networks:

17.1.1.2.1 CDMA

Code Division Multiple Access (CDMA) is actually a military technology first used during World War II by the English allies to foil German attempts at jamming transmissions. Because Qualcomm Inc. created communications chips for CDMA technology, it was privy to the classified information and became the first to patent and commercialize it. CDMA is a digital cellular technology that uses spread-spectrum techniques. CDMA does not assign a specific frequency to each user; instead, every channel uses the full available spectrum. Individual conversations are encoded with a pseudorandom digital sequence. The architecture of CDMA is such that multiple conversations are transpiring at the same time, sharing the same frequency as other CDMA conversations. The CDMA systems decipher each of the conversations so that each listener understands whom he or she is listening to.

Advantages of CDMA over analog systems include the following:

- Enhanced privacy through the spreading of voice signals
- Improved coverage characteristics, allowing for fewer cell sites
- Increased talk time for portables
- Improved call quality, with better and more consistent sound compared with AMPS systems
- Capacity gains of 8–10 times that of AMPS analog systems
- Simplified system planning through the use of the same frequency in every sector of every cell

17.1.1.2.2 TDMA

Time Division Multiple Access (TDMA) was released in 1984. It uses the frequency bands available to the wireless network and divides them into time slots, with each phone user having access to one time slot at regular intervals. TDMA exists in North America at both the 800 MHz and 1900 MHz bands. Major U.S. carriers using TDMA are AT&T Wireless Services, BellSouth, and Southwestern Bell. The TDMA architecture works in a "timeslot" format. In other words, one person speaks, and another is listening. For another person to speak, a time slot (channel) must open up. Only one subscriber is assigned a channel at one time, and no other subscriber can access that same channel until the call is ended. Consequently, the total requirement for the number of channels is very high.

Advantages of TDMA include the following:

- TDMA is the most cost-effective technology for upgrading a current analog system to digital.
- TDMA is the only technology that offers an efficient utilization of hierarchical cell structures (HCSs) offering picocells, microcells, and macrocells. HCSs allow coverage for the system to be tailored to support specific traffic and service needs. By using this approach, system capacities of more than 40 times AMPS can be achieved in a cost-efficient way.

- Because of its inherent compatibility with analog systems, TDMA allows service compatibility with dual-mode handsets.
- Unlike spread-spectrum techniques such as CDMA, which can suffer from interference among the users all of whom are on the same frequency band and transmitting at the same time, TDMA's technology, which separates users in time, ensures that they will not experience interference from other simultaneous transmissions.
- TDMA provides the user with extended battery life and talk time because the mobile is only transmitting a portion of the time (from 1/3 to 1/10) of the time during conversations.
- TDMA installations offer substantial savings in base-station equipment, space, and maintenance, an important factor as cell sizes grow ever smaller. Table 17.1 shows a comparison of the various wireless networks.

17.1.1.2.3 GSM

Global System for Mobile Communications (GSM) is actually based on an improved version of TDMA technology. In 1982, the Conference of European Posts and Telecommunications (CEPT) began the process of creating a digital cellular standard that would allow users to roam from country to country in Europe. By 1987, the GSM standard was created based on a hybrid of FDMA (analog) and TDMA (digital) technologies. GSM engineers decided to use wider 200 kHz channels instead of the 30 kHz channels that TDMA used, and instead of having only three slots like TDMA, GSM channels had eight slots. This allowed for fast bit rates and more natural-sounding voice-compression algorithms. GSM is currently the only one of the three technologies that provide data services such as email, fax, Internet

TABLE 17.1

Evolution of Wireless Networks

Generation	1G	2G	2.5G	3G	4G
Starting time	1985	1992	1995	2002	2010–2012
Driven technique	Analog signal Processing	Digital signal	Packet switching	Intelligent signal processing	Intelligent software autoconfiguration
Representative standard	AMPS, TACS, NMT	GSM, TDMA	GPRS, I- Mode, HSCSD, EDGE	IMT-2000(UMTS WC DMA, CDMA2000)	OFDM, UWB
Radio frequency (Hz)	400 M–800 M	800 M–900 M	1800 M–1900 M	2G	3G–5G
Bandwidth (bps)	2.4 kbps–30 kbps	9.6 kbps–14.4 kbps	171 kbps–384 kbps	2 Mbps–5 Mbps	10 Mbps–20 Mbps
Multiaddress technique	FDMA	TDM A, CDMA	TDM A, CDMA	CDMA	FDMA, TDM A, CDMA
Cellular coverage	Large area	Medium area	Medium area	Small area	Mini area
Core networks	Telecom networks	Telecom networks	Telecom networks	Telecom networks, some IP networks	All-IP networks
Service type	Voice Mono-service Person-to-person	Voice, SMS Mono media Person-to-person	Data service	Voice, data Some multimedia Person-to-person	Multimedia Machine-to-machine

browsing, and intranet/LAN wireless access, and it is also the only service that permits users to place a call from either North America or Europe. The GSM standard was accepted in the United States in 1995. GSM-1900 cellular systems have been operating in the United States since 1996, with the first network being in the Washington, DC area. Major carriers of GSM 1900 include Pacific Bell, BellSouth, and Sprint Spectrum.

> Analog networks still exist today because digital networks like CDMA, TDMA, and GSM cannot readily communicate and interchange information directly with each other. For interchangeable communication 2G networks have to fall back on 1G analog communication.

17.1.1.3 2.5 Generation: GPRS, EDGE, and CDMA 2000

The 3rd-generation networks require a complete overhaul of the wireless network, the expense to complete the implementation is very high. The 2.5G is actually more of an intermediate solution to 3rd-generation networks. 2.5G networks provide the following additional functions:

- Speed of data access
- Identification of location of the wireless device
- Ability to access customized information based upon location
- Ability to store information such as addresses and credit card numbers within personal profiles
- Ability to facilitate mobile online shopping
- Full mobility on the Internet
- Ability to provide business users with access to intranets

2.5G networks are of the following three types:

1. GPRS: General Packet Radio Services (GPRS) enables true "always-on" capability in the wireless network. Similar to a modem dialing for service to an Internet service provider, in today's cell network, a phone call must be initiated to connect to a network. Similarly, "always-on" can be compared with broadband-wired connections such as DSL (Digital Subscriber Line) or T1 lines and faster connections. However, GPRS only enables speeds in the range of 115 kbps.
2. EDGE: Enhanced Data Rate for GSM Evolution (EDGE) can simply be termed as a faster version of the GSM wireless service. EDGE technology enables data to be delivered at rates of up to 384 kbps on broadband connections. The standard is based on the GSM standard and uses TDMA multiplexing technology. In essence, the EDGE may enable higher functionality such as the downloading of music and videos over mobile devices.
3. CDMA 2000: Code Division Multiple Access 2000 (CDMA 2000) is essentially a migration or upgrade of the CDMA standard discussed in the 2nd-generation section. CDMA 2000 is also an "always-on" technology that offers transmission speeds around 100 kbps.

17.1.1.4 3rd Generation: wCDMA, UMTS, and iMode

3G mobile communication systems support data rates of over 153.6 kbps. 3G systems provide the ability to transfer both voice data such as a phone call and nonvoice data such as uploading and downloading information, email exchange, and instant messaging. They provide better quality of experience for the users and support multimedia data transfers such as transfer of audio, video, text, and pictures.

3G enables receiving wired Internet features and services at ISDN-like speeds over a mobile handset. Examples of 3G technology include the wideband-CDMA (wCDMA) and Universal Mobile Telecommunication System (UMTS).

17.1.1.5 4th Generation

4G is a fully IP-based integrated system and the Internet work is accomplished with the union of wired and wireless networks including computers, consumer electronics, communication technology, and the capability to provide 100 Mbps and 1 Gbps, respectively, in outdoor and indoor environments with better quality of service (QoS) and improved security, facilitating any kind of services anytime, anywhere, at affordable cost and single billing.

17.1.2 Mobile Operating Systems

An Operating System (OS) is a set of programs making the link between the hardware and the software. They manage the processor, the file system, the memory, and the peripherals.

Most of these OS developed for the mobile devices adopt a layered architecture. Some of the common layers are as follows:

- The Application Suite contains the majority of the applications available in the system. Here, we can find browsers, configuration menus, the calendar, games, among others.
- The User Interface layer furnishes the graphical environment of each system.
- The Application Execution Environment offers Application Programming Interfaces (API) for the development of new applications.
- The Middleware is a transparent layer making the link to the peripherals through software libraries.
- The Kernel is the core of the operating system where, among others, we can find the hardware, memory, and file system drivers. It is also the responsible for the proper process management.

17.1.2.1 Symbian

The Symbian Foundation is a nonprofit organization that started its activity in 1998, supported by a set of manufacturers with the goal of licensing a software platform (which is based on Symbian OS) for mobile devices.

This OS supports 2G and 3G technology, communications protocols such as WAP (Wireless Application Protocol), TCP, IPv4, and IPv6. At the PAN level, Symbian OS supports irDA, Bluetooth, and USB and also provides multitask, multithread, and the ability to work with the different types of phones, either they be numeric, alpha-numeric, or touch screen. In addition to the telephony services, Symbian OS also supports others as Short

Message Service (SMS), Enhanced Messaging Service (EMS) and Multimedia Messaging Service (MMS), video conference, and the capability of switching between networks.

Navigation, agenda, email, fax, and a word processor are some of the applications developed for this OS.

17.1.2.2 BlackBerry OS

Research In Motion® (RIM) is a Canadian designer, manufacturer, and marketer of wireless solutions for the worldwide mobile communications market. Products include the BlackBerry wireless email solution, wireless handhelds, and wireless modems. RIM is the driving force behind BlackBerry smartphones and the BlackBerry solution. RIM provides a proprietary multitasking OS for the BlackBerry, which makes heavy use of specialized input devices, particularly the scroll wheel or more recently the trackball.

BlackBerry offers the best combination of mobile phone, server software, push email, and security from a single vendor. It integrates well with other platforms, it works with several carriers, and it can be deployed globally for the sales force which is on move. It is easy to manage, has a longer than usual battery life, and has a small form-factor with an easy-to-use keyboard. BlackBerry is good for access to some of the simpler applications, such as contact list, time management, and field force applications. Table 17.2 shows a comparison of the various mobile operating systems.

17.1.2.3 Google Android

Google's Android Mobile platform is the latest mobile platform on the block. This open-source development platform is built on the Linux kernel, and it includes an operating system (OS), middleware stack and a number of mobile applications. Enterprises will benefit from Android because the availability of open-source code for the entire software stack will allow the existing army of Linux developers to create special-purpose applications that will run on a variety of mobile devices.

The Android is the open-source mobile OS launched by Google. It is intuitive, user-friendly and graphically similar to the iPhone and Blackberry. Being open source, the Android applications may be cheaper and the spread of the Android possibly will increase. The Kernel is based on the Linux v 2.6 and supports 2G, 3G, Wi-Fi, IPv4, and IPv6.

TABLE 17.2

Comparison of Mobile Operating Systems

Mobile OS	Android	BlackBerry OS	iOS	Windows Phone
Provider (Major Company)	Open Handheld Alliance	RIM	Apple	Microsoft
Development Languages	Java	Java	Objective C/C++	Visual C++
Kernel Type	Linux	Unix	Hybrid	Windows CE6/7
IDEs, Libraries. Frameworks	Android SDK; ADTplug-in for Eclipse	BlackBerry JDE	iPhone SDK	Windows Phone SDK(works with VisualStudio)
Source Model	Open	Closed	Closed (open for thecore)	Closed
Initial Release	2008	1999	2007	2010
Latest version as of December 2013	4.4 KitKat	7.1	7	8
Mobile Application Store	Google Play	BlackBerry World	App Store	Windows Phone Store

At the multimedia level, Android works with OpenGL and several images, audio, and video formats. The persistence is assured with the support of the SQLite. Regarding security, the Android uses SSL and encryption algorithms.

If Android makes it into phones designed specifically for the enterprise, those products will have to include technology from the likes of Sybase, Intellisync or another such company to enable security features like remote data wipe functionality and forced password changes.

17.1.2.4 Apple iOS

iPhone OS is the Apple proprietary OS used in the Macintosh machines; an optimized version is used in the iPhone and iPod Touch.

The simplicity and robustness provided either in the menus navigation or in the application' navigation are two of the main potentialities of the OS. iPhone OS is also equipped with good quality multimedia software, including games, music, and video players. It has also a good set of tools including imaging editing and word processor.

17.1.2.5 Windows Phone

The Windows Mobile, variant of the Windows CE (also known officially as Windows Embedded Compact), was developed for the Pocket PCs at the beginning but arises by 2002 to the HTC2 mobile phones. This OS was engineered to offer data and multimedia services. By 2006, Windows Mobile becomes available for the developers community. Many new applications started using the system, turning Windows Mobile in one of the most used systems

Windows Mobile comes in two flavors. A smartphone edition is good for wireless email, calendaring, and voice notes. A Pocket PC edition adds mobile versions of Word, Excel, PowerPoint, and Outlook. Palms Treo700w, with the full functionality of the Pocket PC edition, is a better choice for sales force professionals. The main draw of the Windows Mobile operating system is its maker Microsoft. Windows Mobile also actively syncs to the Exchange and SQL servers. This augurs very well for use by the sales force. Mobile sales force solutions for Windows Mobile are available from companies like SAP, Siebel, PeopleSoft, and Salesforce.com as well as other leading solution providers.

Windows Mobile permits Bluetooth connections through the interface Winsock. It also allows 902.11x, IPv4, IPv6, VoIP (Voice over IP), GSM, and CDMA (Code Division Multiple Access) connections.

Some of the main applications available are the Pocket Outlook (adapted version of the Outlook for Desktops), Word, and Excel. It provides also Messenger, Browser, and remote desktop. The remote desktop is an easy way of access to other mobile or fixed terminals. ActiveSync application facilitates the synchronization between the mobile devices and the desktops. At the multimedia level, Windows Mobile reproduces music, video, and 3D applications. Security is also a concern, so Secure Socket Layer (SSL), Kerberos, and the use of encryption algorithms are available.

17.2 Mobile Web Services

Web services are the cornerstone toward building a global distributed information system, in which many individual applications will take part; building a powerful application whose capability is not limited to local resources will unavoidably require interacting with other partner applications through web services across the Internet. The strengths of web services come from the fact that web services use XML and related technologies connecting business applications based on various computers and locations with various languages and platforms. The counterpart of the WS in the context of mobile business processes would be Mobile Web Services (MWS).

The proposed MWS are to be the base of the communications between the Internet network and wireless devices such as mobile phones, PDAs, and so forth. The integration between wireless device applications with other applications would be a very important step toward global enterprise systems. Similar to WS, MWS is also based on the industry-standard language XML and related technologies such as SOAP, WSDL, and UDDI.

Many constraints make the implementation of WS in a mobile environment very challenging. The challenge comes from the fact that mobile devices have smaller power and capacities as follows:

- Small power limited to a few hours
- Small memory capacity
- Small processors not big enough to run larger applications
- Small screen size, especially in mobile phones, which requires developing specific websites with suitable size
- Small keypad that makes it harder to enter data
- Small hard disk
- The speed of the data communication between the device and the network, and that varies

The most popular MWS is a proxy-based system where the mobile device connects to the Internet through a proxy server. Most of the processing of the business logic of the mobile application will be performed on the proxy server that transfers the results to the mobile device that is mainly equipped with a user interface to display output on its screen. The other important advantage a proxy server provides in MWS is, instead of connecting the client application residing on the mobile device to many service providers and consuming most of the mobile processor and the bandwidth, the proxy will communicate with service providers, do some processing, and send back only the final result to the mobile device. In the realistic case where the number of mobile devices becomes in the range of tens of millions, the proxy server would be on the cloud and the service providers would be the cloud service providers.

Mobile web services use existing industry-standard XML-based web services architecture to expose mobile network services to the broadest audience of developers. Developers will be able to access and integrate mobile network services such as messaging, location-based content delivery, syndication, personalization, identification, authentication, and billing services into their applications. This will ultimately enable solutions that work seamlessly across stationary networks and mobile environments. Customers will be able to use mobile web services from multiple devices on both wired and wireless networks.

The aim of the mobile web services effort is twofold:

1. To create a new environment that enables the IT industry and the mobile industry to create products and services that meet customer needs in a way not currently possible within the existing web services practices. With web services being widely

deployed as the SOA of choice for internal processes in organizations, there is also an emerging demand for using web services enabling mobile working and e-business. By integrating web Services and mobile computing technologies, consistent business models can be enabled on a broad array of end points: not just on mobile devices operating over mobile networks but also on servers and computing infrastructure operating over the Internet. To make this integration happen at a technical level, mechanisms are required to expose and leverage existing mobile network services. Also, practices for how to integrate the various business needs of the mobile network world and their associated enablers such as security must be developed. The result is a framework, such as the Open Mobile Alliance, that demonstrates how the web service specifications can be used and combined with mobile computing technology and protocols to realize practical and interoperable solutions.

Successful mobile solutions that help architect customers' service infrastructures need to address security availability and scalability concerns both at the functional level and at the end-to-end solution level, rather than just offering fixed-point products. What is required is a standard specification and an architecture that tie together service discovery, invocation, authentication, and other necessary components—thereby adding context and value to web services. In this way, operators and enterprises will be able to leverage the unique capabilities of each component of the end-to-end network and shift the emphasis of service delivery from devices to the human user. Using a combination of wireless, broadband, and wireline devices, users can then access any service on demand, with a single identity and single set of service profiles, personalizing service delivery as dictated by the situation. There are three important requirements to accomplish user (mobile-subscriber)-focused delivery of mobile services: federated identity, policy, and federated context.

Integrating identity, policy, and context into the overall mobile services architecture enables service providers to differentiate the user from the device and deliver the right service to the right user on virtually any device:

a. Federated identity: In a mobile environment, users are not seen as individuals (e.g., mobile subscribers) to software applications and processes who are tied to a particular domain, but rather as entities that are free to traverse multiple service networks. This requirement demands a complete federated network identity model to tie the various personas of an individual without compromising privacy or loss of ownership of the associated data. The federated network identity model allows the implementation of seamless single sign-on for users interacting with applications (Nokia 2004). It also ensures that user identity, including transactional information and other personal information, is not tied to a particular device or service, but rather is free to move with the user between service providers. Furthermore, it guarantees that only appropriately authorized parties are able to access protected information.
b. Policy: User policy, including roles and access rights, is an important requirement for allowing users not only to have service access within their home network but also to move outside it and still receive the same access to services. Knowing who the user is and what role they fulfill at the moment they are using a particular service is essential to providing the right service at the right instance. The combination of federated identity and policy enables service providers and users to strike a balance between access rights and user privacy

c. Federated context: Understanding what the user is doing, what they ask, why it is being requested, where they are, and what device they are using is an essential requirement. The notion of federated context means accessing and acting upon a user's current location, availability, presence, and role, for example, at home, at work, on holiday, and other situational attributes. This requires the intelligent synthesis of information available from all parts of the end-to-end network and allows service providers and enterprises to deliver relevant and timely applications and services to end users in a personalized manner. For example, information about the location and availability of a user's device may reside on the wireless network, the user's calendar may be on the enterprise intranet, and preferences may be stored in a portal.

2. To help create web services standards that will enable new business opportunities by delivering integrated services across stationary (fixed) and wireless networks. Mobile web services use existing industry-standard XML-based web services architecture to expose mobile network services to the broadest audience of developers. Developers will be able to access and integrate mobile network services such as messaging, location-based content delivery, syndication, personalization, identification, authentication, and billing services into their applications. This will ultimately enable solutions that work seamlessly across stationary networks and mobile environments. Customers will be able to use mobile web services from multiple devices on both wired and wireless networks.

Delivering appealing, low-cost mobile data services, including ones that are based on mobile Internet browsing and mobile commerce, is proving increasingly difficult to achieve. The existing infrastructure and tools as well as the interfaces between Internet/web applications and mobile network services remain largely fragmented, characterized by tightly coupled, costly, and close alliances between value-added service providers and a complex mixture of disparate and sometimes overlapping standards (WAP, MMS, Presence, Identity, etc.) and proprietary models (e.g., propriety interfaces). This hinders interoperability solutions for the mobile sector and at the same time drives up the cost of application development and ultimately the cost of services offered to mobile users. Such problems have given rise to initiatives for standardizing mobile web services. The most important of these initiatives are the Open Mobile Alliance and the mobile web services frameworks that are examined below.

The Open Mobile Alliance (www.openmobilealliance.org). The OMA is a group of wireless vendors, IT companies, mobile operators, and application and content providers, who have come together to drive the growth of the mobile industry. The objective of OMA is to deliver open technical specifications, based on market requirements, for the mobile industry, that enable interoperable solutions across different devices, geographies, service providers, operators, and networks. OMA includes all key elements of the wireless value chain and contributes to the timely availability of mobile service enablers. For enterprises already using a multitiered network architecture based on open technologies, such as web services, which implement wireless services, OMA is a straightforward extension of existing wireline processes and infrastructures. In this way, wireless services become simply another delivery channel for communication, transactions, and other value-added services. Currently, the OMA is defining core services such as location, digital rights, and presence services and using cases involving mobile subscribers, mobile operators, and service providers; an architecture for the access and deployment of core services; and a web services framework for using secure SOAP.

The technical working groups within OMA address the need to support standardized interactions. To achieve this, the OMA is currently addressing how mobile operators can leverage web services and defines a set of common protocols, schemas, and processing rules using web services technologies that are the elements that can be used to create or interact with a number of different services. The OMA web services enabler (OWSER) specification capitalizes on all the benefits of web services technologies to simplify the task of integrators, developers, and implementers of service enablers by providing them with common mechanisms and protocols for interoperability of service enablers. Examples of functionality common across service enablers range from transport and message encoding definitions to security concerns, service discovery, charging, definition, and management of SLAs, as well as management, monitoring, and provisioning of the service enablers that exist within a service provider's network.

The OMA web service interfaces are intended to enhance a service provider's data for a particular mobile subscriber. A common scenario starts with a data request from some application (perhaps a mobile browser) to a service provider. The service provider then uses web services to interact with a subscriber's mobile operator to retrieve some relevant data about the subscriber such as location or presence. These data can be used to enhance the service provider's response to the initial request. Mobile web services are envisioned to support server-to-server, server-to-mobile terminal, mobile terminal-to-server, and mobile terminal-to-mobile terminal (or peer-to-peer) interactions.

Similarly, the objective of the mobile web services framework is to meet the requirements for bridging stationary enterprise infrastructure and the mobile world, and it enables the application of web services specifications, SOA implementations, and tools to the problem of exposing mobile network services in a commercially viable way to the mass market of developers. The focus of the work concentrates on mechanisms to orchestrate the calls to mobile web services.

The mobile web services framework places particular emphasis on core mechanisms such as security, authentication, and payment. Core security mechanisms are offered that apply WS-Security to mobile network security services, such as the use of a GSM-style SIM security device within a web services end point to provide a means for authentication. In addition, a set of core payment mechanisms within the WS architecture have been proposed that understand how to interact with the participating WS end points. It is expected that a number of services dependent on the mobile web services framework and that rely on its core mechanisms will be developed. SMS services, MMS services, and location-based services have been identified as common services that are candidates for specification activity. Specification work will include profiling and optimization of the core web services protocols so that they can easily be realized over any bearer, on any device, or both. This addresses the inefficiencies that current web services specifications exhibit when used over a narrowband and possibly intermittent bearer or when being processed by a low-performance mobile device.

17.2.1 Mobile Field Cloud Services

Companies that can outfit their employees with devices like PDAs, laptops, multifunction smartphones, or pagers will begin to bridge the costly chasm between the field and the back office. For example, transportation costs for remote employees can be significantly reduced, and productivity can be significantly improved by eliminating needless journeys back to the office to file reports, collect parts, or simply deliver purchase orders.

Wireless services are evolving toward the goal of delivering the right cloud service to whoever needs it, for example, employees, suppliers, partners, and customers, at the right place, at the right time, and on any device of their choice. The combination of wireless handheld devices and cloud service delivery technologies poses the opportunity for an entirely new paradigm of information access that in the enterprise context can substantially reduce delays in the transaction and fulfillment process and lead to improved cash flow and profitability.

A field cloud services solution automates, standardizes, and streamlines manual processes in an enterprise and helps centralize disparate systems associated with customer service life-cycle management including customer contact, scheduling and dispatching, mobile workforce communications, resource optimization, work order management, time, labor, material tracking, billing, and payroll. A field web services solution links seamlessly all elements of an enterprise's field service operation—customers, service engineers, suppliers, and the office—to the enterprise's stationary infrastructure, wireless communications, and mobile devices. Field web services provide real-time visibility and control of all calls and commitments, resources, and operations. They effectively manage business activities such as call taking and escalation, scheduling and dispatching, customer entitlements and SLAs, work orders, service contracts, time sheets, labor and equipment tracking, preinvoicing, resource utilization, reporting, and analytics.

Cloud service optimization solutions try to automatically match the most cost-effective resource with each service order based on prioritized weightings assigned to every possible schedule constraint. To accommodate evolving business priorities, most optimization solutions allow operators to reorder these weightings and to execute ad hoc what-if scenario analyses to test the financial and performance impacts of scheduling alternatives. In this way, they help enhance supply chain management by enabling real-time response to changing business conditions.

Of particular interest to field services are location-based services, notification services, and service disambiguation as these mechanisms enable developers to build more sophisticated cloud service applications by providing accessible interfaces to advanced features and intelligent mobile features:

1. Location-based services provide information specific to a location using the latest positioning technologies and are a key part of the mobile web services suite. Dispatchers can use GPS or network-based positioning information to determine the location of field workers and optimally assign tasks (push model) based on geographic proximity. Location-based services and applications enable enterprises to improve operational efficiencies by locating, tracking, and communicating with their field workforce in real time. For example, location-based services can be used to keep track of vehicles and employees, whether they are conducting service calls or delivering products. Trucks could be pulling in or out of a terminal, visiting a customer site, or picking up supplies from a manufacturing or distribution facility. With location-based services, applications can get such things such as real-time status alerts, for example, estimated time of approach, arrival, departure, duration of stop, current information on traffic, weather, and road conditions for both home-office and en route employees.

2. Notification services allow critical business to proceed uninterrupted when employees are away from their desks, by delivering notifications to their preferred mobile device. Employees can thus receive real-time notification when critical events occur, such as when incident reports are completed. The combination of location-based and notification services provides added value by enabling such services as proximity-based notification and proximity-based actuation. Proximity-based notification is a push or pull interaction model that includes targeted advertising, automatic airport check-in, and sightseeing information. Proximity-based actuation is a push–pull interaction model, whose most typical example is payment based on proximity, for example, toll watch.
3. Service instance disambiguation helps distinguish between many similar candidate service instances, which may be available inside close perimeters. For instance, there may be many on-device payment services in proximity of a single point of sale. Convenient and natural ways for identifying appropriate service instances are then required, for example, relying on closeness or pointing rather than identification by cumbersome unique names.

17.3 Context-Aware Mobile Applications

A mobile application is context aware if it uses context to provide relevant information to users or to enable services for them; relevancy depends on a user's current task (and activity) and profile (and preferences). Apart from knowing who the users are and where they are, we need to identify what they are doing, when they are doing it, and which object they focus on. The system can define user activity by taking into account various sensed parameters like location, time, and the object that they use. In outdoor applications, and depending on the mobile devices that are used, satellite-supported technologies, like GPS, or network-supported cell information, like GSM, IMTS, and WLAN, is applied. Indoor applications use RFID, IrDA, and Bluetooth technologies in order to estimate the users' position in space. While time is another significant parameter of context that can play an important role in order to extract information on user activity, the objects that are used in mobile applications are the most crucial context sources.

In mobile applications, the user can use mobile devices, like mobile phones and PDAs and objects that are enhanced with computing and communication abilities. Sensors attached to artifacts provide applications with information about what the user is utilizing. In order to present the user with the requested information in the best possible form, the system has to know the physical properties of the artifact that will be used (e.g., artifact screen's display characteristics), the types of interaction interfaces that an artifact provides to the user need to be modeled (e.g., whether artifact can be handled by both speech and touch techniques), and the system must know how it is designed. Thus, the system has to know the number of each artifact's sensors and their position in order to gradate context information with a level of certainty. Based on information on the artifact's physical properties and capabilities, the system can extract information on the services that they can provide to the user.

In the context-aware mobile applications, artifacts are considered as context providers. They allow users to access context in a high-level abstracted form, and they inform other application's artifacts so that context can be used according to the application needs.

Users are able to establish associations between the artifacts based on the context that they provide; keep in mind that the services enabled by artifacts are provided as context. Thus, users can indicate their preferences, needs, and desires to the system by determining the behavior of the application via the artifacts they create. The set of sensors attached to an artifact measure various parameters such as location, time, temperature, proximity, and motion—the raw data given by its sensors determine the low-level context of the artifact. The aggregation of such low-level context information from various homogenous and non-homogeneous sensors results into a high-level context information.

17.3.1 Ontology-Based Context Model

This ontology is divided into two layers: a common one that contains the description of the basic concepts of context-aware applications and their interrelations representing the common language among artifacts, and a private one that represents an artifact's own description as well as the new knowledge or experience acquired from its use. The common ontology defines the basic concepts of a context-aware application; such an application consists of a number of artifacts and their associations. The concept of artifact is described by its physical properties and its communication and computational capabilities; the fact that an artifact has a number of sensors and actuators attached is also defined in our ontology. Through the sensors, an artifact can perceive a set of parameters based on which the state of the artifact is defined; an artifact may also need these parameters in order to sense its interactions with other artifacts as well as with the user. The ontology also defines the interfaces via which artifacts may be accessed in order to enable the selection of the appropriate one. The common ontology represents an abstract form of the concepts represented, especially of the context parameters, as more detailed descriptions are stored into each artifact's private ontology. For instance, the private ontology of an artifact that represents a car contains a full description of the different components in a car as well as their types and their relations.

The basic goal of the proposed ontology-based context model is to support a context management process, based on a set of rules that determine the way in which a decision is made and are applied to existing knowledge represented by this ontology. The rules that can be applied during such a process belong to the following categories: rules for an artifact's state assessment that define the artifact's state based on its low- and high-level contexts, rules for local decisions that exploit an artifact's knowledge only in order to decide the artifact's reaction (like the request or the provision of a service), and finally rules for global decisions that take into account various artifacts' states and their possible reactions in order to preserve a global state defined by the user.

17.3.2 Context Support for User Interaction

The ontology-based context model that we propose empowers users to compose their own personal mobile applications. In order to compose their applications, they first have to select the artifacts that will participate and establish their associations. They set their own preferences by associating artifacts, denoting the sources of context that artifacts can exploit, and defining the interpretation of this context through rules in order to enable various services. As the context acquisition process is decoupled from the context management process, users are able to create their own mobile applications avoiding the problems emerging from the adaptation and customization of applications like disorientation and system failures.

The goal of context in computing environments is to improve interaction between users and applications. This can be achieved by exploiting context, which works like implicit commands and enables applications to react to users or surroundings without the users' explicit commands. Context can also be used to interpret explicit acts, making interaction much more efficient. Thus, context-aware computing completely redefines the basic notions of interface and interaction. In this section, we present how our ontology-based context model enables the use of context in order to assist human–computer interaction in mobile applications and to achieve the selection of the appropriate interaction technique. Mobile systems have to provide multimodal interfaces so that users can select the most suitable technique based on their context. The ontology-based context model that we presented in the previous section captures the various interfaces provided by the application's artifacts in order to support and enable such selections. Similarly, the context can determine the most appropriate interface when a service is enabled. Ubiquitous and mobile interfaces must be proactive in anticipating needs, while at the same time working as a spatial and contextual filter for information so that the user is not inundated with requests for attention.

Context can also assist designers to develop mobile applications and manage various interfaces and interaction techniques that would enable more satisfactory and faster closure of transactions. Easiness is an important requirement for mobile applications; by using context according to our approach, designers are abstracted from the difficult task of context acquisition and have merely defined how context is exploited from various artifacts by defining simple rules. Our approach presents an infrastructure capable of handling, substituting, and combining complex interfaces when necessary. The rules applied to the application's context and the reasoning process support the application's adaptation. The presented ontology-based context model is easily extended; new devices, new interfaces, and novel interaction techniques can be exploited into a mobile application by simply incorporating their descriptions in the ontology.

17.4 Mobile Web 2.0

Mobile Web 2.0 results from the convergence of the Web 2.0 services and the proliferation of web-enabled mobile devices. Web 2.0 enables to facilitate interactive information sharing, interoperability, user-centered design, and collaboration among users. This convergence is leading to a new communication paradigm, where mobile devices act not only as mere consumers of information but also as complex carriers for getting and providing information, and as platforms for novel services.

Mobile Web 2.0 represents both an opportunity for creating novel services and an extension of Web 2.0 applications to mobile devices. The management of user-generated content, of content personalization, of community and information sharing is much more challenging in a context characterized by devices with limited capabilities in terms of display, computational power, storage, and connectivity. Furthermore, novel services require support for real-time determination and communication of the user position.

Mobile Web 2.0 is constituted of the following:

1. Sharing services that are characterized by the publication of contents to be shared with other users. Sharing services offer the users the capability to store, organize, search, and manage heterogeneous contents. These contents may be rated,

commented, tagged, and shared with specified users or groups that can usually visualize the stored resources chronologically, by category, rating or tags, or via a search engine. Multimedia sharing services are related to sharing of multimedia resources, such as photos or videos. These resources are typically generated by the users that exploit the sharing service to upload and publish their own contents. Popular examples of web portals offering a multimedia sharing service include Flickr, YouTube and Mocospace.

2. Social services that refer to the management of social relationships among the users. This is constituted of services such as
   - Community management services enable registered users to maintain a list of contact details of people they know. Their key feature is the possibility to create and update a personal profile including information such as user preferences and his list of contacts. These contacts may be used in different ways depending on the purpose of the service, which may range from the creation of a personal network of business and professional contacts (e.g., Linkedln), to the management of social events (e.g., Meetup), and up to the connection with old and new friends (e.g., Facebook).
   - Blogging services enable a user to create and manage a blog, that is, a sort of personal online journal, possibly focused on a specific topic of interest. Blogs are usually created and managed by an individual or a limited group of people, namely author(s), through regular entries of heterogeneous content, including text, images, and links to other resources related to the main topic, such as other blogs, web pages, or multimedia contents. A blog is not a simple online journal, because the large majority of them allow external comments on the entries. The final effect is the creation of a discussion forum that engages readers and builds a social community around a person or a topic. Other related services may also include blogrolls (i.e., links to other blogs that the author reads) to indicate social relationships to other bloggers. Among the most popular portals that allow users to manage their own blog we cite BlogSpot, Wordpress, and so on.
   - Microblogging services is characterized by very short message exchanges among the users. Although this class of services originates from the blogging category, there are important differences between microblogging and traditional blogs, namely, the size of the exchanged messages is significantly smaller, the purpose of microblogging is to capture and communicate instantaneous thoughts or feeling of the users, and the recipient of the communication may differ from that of traditional blogs because microblogging allows authors to interact with a group of selected friends. Twitter is an example of portals providing microblogging services.
3. Location services that tailor information and contents on the basis of the user location. The knowledge of the user current location may be exploited in several ways to offer value added services.
   - People discovery services that enable locating user friends; usually these services plot the position of the user and his/her friends on a map; the geographical location of the users is uploaded to the system by means of a positioning system installed on the user mobile devices.
   - Points of interest (POIs) discovery exploits geographical information to locate POIs, such as events, restaurants, museums, and any kind of attractions that

may be useful or interesting for a user. These services offer the users a list of nearby POIs selected on the basis of their personal preferences and specifications. POIs are collected by exploiting collaborative recommendations from other users that may add a new POI by uploading its geographical location, possibly determined through a GPS positioning system installed on the mobile device. Users may also upload short descriptions, comments, tags, and images or videos depicting the place.

17.5 Mobile Analytics

The objectives of mobile analytics are twofold: prediction and description—prediction of unknown or future values of selected variables, such as interests or location of mobiles, and description in terms of human behavior patterns. Description involves gaining "insights" into mobile behaviors, whereas prediction involves improving decision making for brands, marketers, and enterprises. This can include the modeling of sales, profits, effectiveness of marketing efforts, and the popularity of apps and a mobile site. The key is to realize the data that is being aggregated and how to not only create and issue metrics on mobile activity, but more importantly, how to leverage it via the data mining of mobile devices to improve sales and revenue.

For years, retailers have been testing new marketing and media campaigns, new pricing promotions, and the merchandizing of new products with freebies and half-price deals, as well as a combination of all of these offers, in order to improve sales and revenue. With mobiles, it has become increasingly easy to generate the data and metrics for mining and precisely calibrating consumer behaviors.

Brands and companies leveraging mobile analytics can be more adept at identifying, co-opting, and shaping consumer behavior patterns to increase profits. Brands and mobile marketers that figure out how to induce new habits can enhance their bottom lines. Inducing a new habit loop can be used to introduce new products, services, and content via the offer of coupons or deals based on the location of mobiles.

17.5.1 Mobile Site Analytics

Mobile site analytics can help the brand and companies solve the mystery of how mobile consumers are engaging and interacting with their site. Without dedicated customer experience metrics, brands, marketers, and companies cannot tell whether the mobile site experience actually got better or how changes in the quality of that experience affected the site's business performance. Visitors tend to focus on three basic things when evaluating a mobile site: usefulness, ease-of-use, and how enjoyable it is. Metrics should measure these criteria with completion rates and survey questions.

17.5.2 Mobile Clustering Analysis

Clustering is the partition of a dataset into subsets of "similar" data, without using a priori knowledge about properties or existence of these subsets. For example, a clustering analysis of mobile site visitors might discover a high propensity for Android devices to make higher amounts of purchases of, say, Apple mobiles. Clusters can be mutually exclusive (disjunct) or overlapping. Clustering can lead to the autonomous discovery of typical customer profiles.

Clustering detection is the creation of models that find mobile behaviors that are similar to each other; these clumps of similarity can be discovered using SOM software to find previously unknown patterns in mobile datasets. Unlike classification software, which analyzes for predicting mobile behaviors, clustering is different in that the software is "let loose" on the data; there are no targeted variables. Instead, it is about exploratory autonomous knowledge discovery. The clustering software automatically organizes itself around the data with the objective of discovering some meaningful hidden structures and patterns of mobile behaviors. This type of clustering can be done to discover key words or mobile consumer clusters, and it is a useful first step for mining mobiles. It allows for the mapping of mobiles into distinct clusters of groups without any human bias.

Clustering is often performed as a prelude to the use of classification analysis using rule-generating or decision-tree software for modeling mobile device behaviors.

Market basket analysis using a SOM is useful in situations where the marketer or brand wants to know what items or mobile behaviors occur together or in a particular sequence or pattern. The results are informative and actionable because they can lead to the organization of offers, coupons, discounts, and the offering of new products or services that prior to the analysis were unknown.

Clustering analyses can lead to answers to such questions as why do products or services sell together, or who is buying what combinations of products or services; they can also map what purchases are made and when. Unsupervised knowledge discovery occurs when one cluster is compared to another and new insight is revealed as to why. For example, SOM software can be used to discover clusters of locations, interests, models, operating systems, mobile site visitors, and app downloads, thus enabling a marketer or developer to discover unique features of different consumer mobile groupings.

17.5.3 Mobile Text Analysis

Another technology that can be used for data mining mobile devices is text mining, which refers to the process of deriving, extracting, and organizing high-quality information from unstructured content, such as texts, emails, documents, messages, and comments. Text mining means extracting meaning from social media and customer comments about a brand or company in mobile sites and app reviews.

This is a different variation in clustering programs; text mining software is commonly used to sort through unstructured content that can reside in millions of emails, chat, web forums, texts, tweets, blogs, and so on, that daily and continuously accumulate in mobile sites and mobile servers.

Text analytics generally includes tasks such as the following:

- Categorization of taxonomies
- Clustering of concepts
- Entity and information extraction
- Sentiment analysis
- Summarization

Text analytics is important to the data mining of mobile devices because, increasingly, companies, networks, mobile sites, enterprises, and app servers are accumulating a large percentage of their data in unstructured formats, which is impossible to analyze and categorize manually. Text mining refers to the process of deriving an understanding from unstructured content through the division of clustering patterns and the extraction of categories or mobile trends using machine learning algorithms for the organization of key concepts from unstructured content.

Text mining can be used to gain new insight into unstructured content from multiple data sources, such as a social network of a mobile site or an app platform. Text analytical tools can convert unstructured content and parse it over to a structure format that is amenable to data mining of mobile devices via classification software. For example, all the daily emails or visits that a mobile site accumulates on a daily basis can be organized into several groupings, such as those mobiles seeking information, service assistance, or those complaining about specific products, services, or brands. Text mining can also be used to gauge sentiment regarding a brand or company.

Mobile marketers, developers, and brands need to consider how to incorporate time, demographics, location, interests, and other mobile available variables into their analytics models. Clustering, text, and classification software can be used to accomplish this for various marketing and brand goals. Clustering software analyses can be used to discover and monetize mobile mobs. Text software analyses can discover important brand value and sentiment information being bantered about in social networks. Finally, classification software can pinpoint important attributes about profitable and loyal mobiles. Classification often involves the use of rule-generating decision-tree programs for the segmentation of mobile data behaviors.

17.5.4 Mobile Classification Analysis

There are two major objectives to classification via the data mining of mobile devices: description and prediction. Description is an understanding of a pattern of mobiles behaviors and to gain insight—for example, what devices are the most profitable to a mobile site and app developer. Prediction, however, is the creation of models to support, improve, and automate decision making, such as what highly profitable mobiles to target in an ad marketing campaign via a mobile site or app. Both description and prediction can be accomplished using classification software, such as rule-generator and decision-tree programs. This type of data mining analysis is also known as supervised learning.

For example, a mobile analyst or marketer can take advantage of segmenting the key characteristics of mobile behaviors over time to discover hidden trends and patterns of purchasing behaviors. Machine learning technology can discover the core features of mobiles by automatically learning to recognize complex patterns and make intelligent decisions based on mobile data, such as what, when, where, and why certain mobiles have a propensity to make a purchase or download an app, while others do not. Classifying mobiles enables the positioning of the right product, service, or content to these moving devices via precise messages on a mobile site, or the targeting of an email, text, or the creation of key features to an app.

The marketer or developer will need to use classification software known as rule-generators or decision-tree programs. Decision trees are powerful classification and segmentation programs that use a tree-like graph of decisions and their possible consequences. Decision-tree programs provide a descriptive means of calculating conditional probabilities. Trained with historical data samples, these classification programs can be used to predict future mobile behaviors.

A decision tree takes as input an objective, such as what type of app to offer, described by a set of properties from historical mobile behaviors or conditions, such as geolocation, operating system, and device model. These mobile features can then be used to make a prediction, such as what type of app to offer to a specific mobile. The prediction can also be a continuous value, such as total expected coupon sales, or what price to offer for an app. When a developer or marketer needs to make a decision based on several consumer factors, such as their location, device being used and total log-in time, a decision tree can help identify which factors to consider and how each factor has historically been associated with different outcomes of that decision—such as what products or services certain mobiles are likely to purchase based on observed behavioral patterns over time.

One common advantage of using decision trees is to eliminate a high number of noisy and ineffective consumer attributes for predicting, say, "high customer loyalty" or "likely to buy" models. Developers and marketers can start with hundreds of mobile attributes from multiple data sources and, through the use of decision trees, they can eliminate many of them in order to focus simply on those with the highest information gain as they pertain to predicting high loyalty or potential revenue growth from mobile features and behaviors.

17.5.5 Mobile Streaming Analysis

The data mining of mobile devices may require the use of both deductive and inductive "streaming analytical" software that is event driven to link, monitor, and analyze mobile behaviors. These new streaming analytical software products react to mobile consumer events in real time. There are two main types of streaming analytical products:

1. There are deductive streaming programs that operate based on user-defined business rules and are used to monitor multiple streams of data, reacting to consumer events as they take place.
2. There are also inductive streaming software products that use predictive rules derived from the data itself via clustering, text, and classification algorithms. These inductive streaming products build their rules from global models involving the segmentation and analysis from multiple and distributed mobile data clouds and networks.

These deductive and inductive software products can work with different data formats, from different locations, to make real-time predictions using multiple models from massive digital data streams.

17.6 Summary

The potential of mobile experience can be judged from the fact that consumers are spending almost half of the media time available to them on mobile, the other half being spent on watching TV. Unlike print advertising, mobile marketing can be precisely calibrated to reach and persuade consumers by the data mining of their mobile devices. In short, despite the fact that mobile advertising is growing, the platform is far from getting rational levels of spending compared to other media. There is really no modeling of mobile big data taking place aside from mobile site reports and the counting of app downloads, although several companies are developing new mobile analytic strategies and tools.

18

Location-Based Systems Applications

Location-based services are services that are sensitive to and take advantage of the location of the service user. Any service that makes use of the location of the user can be called a location-based service. The location of a person can be determined using a GPS receiver or other technologies, now available in many mobile phone platforms. This positioning determination technology (PDT) is generally carried by the person, from which the location must be provided to the location-based service provider. Today, the location-based services are generally hosted in the network, which may pose performance and scalability issues.

The uptake of mobile phones with PDT capabilities continues to grow, and most mobile phone users have a phone that can be traced with good accuracy and a lower cost. This new technology has given the location-based service market a greater push.

LBS can be divided into the following four categories:

1. Business to business
2. Business to consumer
3. Consumer to business
4. Consumer to consumer

The business-to-business services include fleet tracking and courier tracking. Business-to-consumer services include pushed ads based on the location, where a user will receive ads most relevant to the location. Consumer to business services include location-based search, where a user is searching for the nearest restaurant, petrol pump, and so forth. A consumer-to-consumer service is the friend finder service where the user will be alerted if his/her friend is within a few meters (see Table 18.1).

18.1 Location-Based Systems

Since the days of the early location tracking functionalities introduced in Japan and in some U.S. networks in 2001, LBS have made considerable progress. In addition to the currently emerging satellite-based systems, such as GPS (United States), GLONASS (Russian), GALILEO (EU), and COMPASS (China), that will provide wider coverage to benefit LBS, some location information can also be derived and used from sensors, radio-frequency identification (RFID), Bluetooth, WiMax, and wireless local area networks (WLANs). These systems can be used as stand-alone or to supplement the coverage for location tracking in indoor environments, where satellite coverage is intermittent or inaccurate. Wi-Fi, especially, could be used as the basis for determining position—like an indoor form of GPS, with access points acting as satellites.

TABLE 18.1

Location-Based Services (LBS) Classification

B2B	B2C	C2C	C2B
Fleet and freight, tracking, and so on.	Discounts, ads, special events, and so on.	Find a friend, primary schools, and so on.	Find a gas station, community events, and so on.
Trigger Services	*Tracking and Monitoring*	*Location-Based Information*	*Assistance Services*
E-commerce, payment information, advertising, and so on.	Fleet management, telematics, asset tracking, and so on.	Traffic and navigation, entertainment, mapping, and so on.	Personal/vehicle emergency, roadside assistance, alarm management, and so on.
Push Services		*Pull Services*	
Travel directions, taxi hailing, m-commerce, and so on.		Zone alerts, traffic alerts, and so on.	

In the development of LBS standards, there are many organizations that play significant roles, such as the Open Mobile Alliance (OMA) and the Open Geospatial Consortium (OGC). These organizations offer various location-based protocols and standards for the development of LBS. The most important specification that OMA has come up with is the Mobile Location Protocol (MLP). MLP enables LBS applications to interoperate with a wireless network regardless of its interfaces (Global System for Mobile Communications [GSM], CDMA, etc.) and positioning methods. MLP defines a common interface that facilitates exchange of location information between the LBS application and location servers in wireless networks. It also supports the privacy of users by providing access to location information only to those who are authorized users. Hence, the OMA is the key enabler of mobile service specification standards that support the creation of interoperable end-to-end mobile services. The OGC is an international organization responsible for the development of standards for geospatial and LBS. To complement Location Interoperability Forums (LIF) advanced MLP services, the OGC has come up with OpenLS services that address geospatial interoperability issues. Key services handled by OpenLS specifications are coordinate transformation, web mapping, geography markup language (GML), geoprocessing, and web integration.

18.1.1 Sources of Location Data

Location sources can take various forms, but can be classified into two basic forms: those which determine location with respect to global coordinates, using known reference points; and those which simply determine location with respect to other nodes in the system.

18.1.1.1 Cellular Systems

A primary source of location information is gained through proximity to a sensor. The range of the sensor may vary, but if presence is detected then the located object can be said to be within that sensor's range (or cell).

In some cases, this requires contact with the sensor: pressure on a seat, etc. If cells are designed such that there is no overlap, then cell ID can translate to a region in a trivial manner. Note that the cell may broadcast its ID, or a device may broadcast a query for location information. In a system where a device will only see or be seen by one reference node (or beacon, base station) there is little difference, apart from any overheads.

> In some cases, this contact (or other very close connection) is substituted with some proxy for the located object, for example,
>
> - Terminal activity on a computer
> - Swipe cards on doors as proxies for user location
> - RFID tags as proxies for object location

As cells become more dense, so that regions usually overlap, the location can become more accurate as the intersection of cells reduces the possible region referred to. If the cells are defined as regions around the known location of reference nodes in a regular grid, then the average coordinate in each axis of the reference nodes seen at some point defines the centroid of the device to be located. As the overlap ratio of beacon range to separation increases the average error, in this centroid becomes a smaller multiple of the beacon separation. In real-world situations, the movement of beacon position and range due to the environmental changes means that a regular grid may not be seen, but geometric intersection of known (or expected) signal patterns can still be used to identify a region that contains the device to be located. Where cells overlap there is a greater possibility of beacons or query responses overlapping, although timing for stationary beacon may be easier than the response to a query from a device with an unknown location.

Some location systems require inputs from multiple sources in order to arrive at a location, by triangulation or trilateration, for example, GPS, ultrasonic systems with a mesh of sensors in the room and use of signal strength from multiple wireless network base stations. Here geometry is applied so that multiple distance (trilateration) or angle measurements (triangulation) from beacons, which do not map into a single plane, are combined to find the place of intersection. In general, using distance measurements requires (at least) D + 1 measurements, that is, three measurements for 2D and four measurements for 3D. Where the system implies extra information about the relative location of object of interest and transmitters is known, this number can be reduced; for example, in GPS satellites are above the receiver. Using angular measurements is similar, but the distance separating two sources is usually required; sometimes a constant reference such as magnetic north is used. In both cases, installation-specific knowledge can be applied to simplify the problem.

> Distance is rarely measured directly, with a tape measure, but through other measures such as time of flight and signal attenuation. These measures can sometimes be had with little cost due to existing infrastructure, for example 802.11 base stations, but can require calibration to the local environment. Time of flight either requires precisely synchronised clocks (rather hard to achieve in practise); or two signals, commonly RF and audio, so that time of flight is determined from the difference.

18.1.1.2 Multireference Point Systems

18.1.1.2.1 Global Positioning System (GPS)

It uses highly accurate atomic clocks on satellites to transmit a time signal, which also send data on their orbits ("ephemeris") to allow calculation of time of flight and approximate data on other satellite positions to aid signal acquisition ("almanac"). This orbit means that each satellite moves across the sky when seen from a stationary point on the Earth's surface, requiring a receiver to scan for new signals but providing robustness against individual satellite failure and ensuring satellites are distributed across the sky to facilitate global coverage and accuracy. At least four satellites must be visible to achieve an accurate 3D location plus time, from a constellation of at least 24 satellites in medium Earth orbit.

A message from an individual satellite is encoded using Code Division Multiple Access (CDMA), allowing all satellites to share a frequency band. This message is decoded and arrival time recorded using an internal clock at the receiver. This clock is not synchronized with the satellite clock, so cannot by itself compute a distance. However, the difference in time of flight between satellites together with ephemeris can be used to compute an initial distance estimate. Due to the very short times small timing errors imply large positioning errors and the distance calculation must include corrections for relativistic effects. This distance describes a sphere in space centered on the satellite (although it is assumed the receiver is below the orbit, so a full sphere is not required).

As additional satellite signals are decoded, additional spheres can be described. Receiver position is computed from the intersection of the spheres. This requires that the satellites are not lying on the same plane as each other; but their number and orbits help to ensure this condition is met. A fourth satellite signal is usually used to correct the GPS receiver's internal clock, by measuring the distance from its sphere to the 3-satellite position estimate. With an accurate clock a new estimate of time of flight, and hence distance to satellite, can be produced. This computation is typically an iterative estimation, improving the local clock accuracy and acquiring additional signals to refine the accuracy of the distance estimates and hence reducing the error in the position estimate. During initial signal acquisition movement makes this refinement of timing rather difficult and leads to delays in achieving an accurate estimate of location. The principle of lateration used in GPS is illustrated in Figure 18.1 that illustrates of two possible intersecting points from signals emanating from three satellites.

There is some inherent uncertainty in GPS data, arising from various factors including the following:

- Satellite clock accuracy causing drift over time, this is frequently updated.
- Accuracy of the measured signal delay limiting resolution.
- Accuracy of the model of real satellite position for calculating signal delay, this is frequently updated.
- Atmospheric variation, which is the least easy to model and predict the effect on signal time of flight.
- Selective availability, introducing deliberate errors of up to 100 m into the signal for military purposes, can be corrected for using differential GPS.

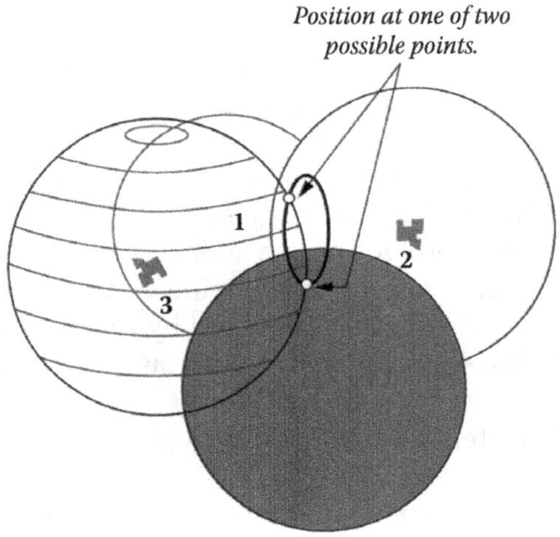

FIGURE 18.1
Principle of lateration.

18.1.1.3 Tagging

Location can be determined by systems with tags in two ways:

- By fixing tags at known locations, when a tag is scanned the scanner must be within scanning range (which depends on the technology) of the tag's location.
- By having tags report to some infrastructure cellular or triangulation techniques can be applied.

Tag systems are characterized by the following:

1. The cost and integration involved in deploying the tags and the cost and integration involved in reading tags. There may be setup costs for a system where tags refer to an infrastructure.
2. The behavior mode of the tag-reader system, including whether the reading of a tag is automatic or manually triggered; and whether the reading is an entry or trigger event or a state of presence.
3. The range that a reader can read a tag over. This may be variable for a given technology, influenced by tag and reader design, available power, and the environment.
4. The "location" of the tag may be fixed, for example, tags to identify rooms and bus stops, or the tag may be attached to a mobile object, in which case the location only describes proximity rather than absolute position.
5. The tags may be unique, for example, Bluetooth tags with a MAC address; the tag may have duplicates, for example, identifying a shop by brand not location: or a given location may have multiple tags, for example, at different entrances or identifying different properties of the place. Where tags are intended to be unique, one should consider whether security or functionality issues arise from forgery or accidental reuse or tag repositioning.

18.1.1.3.1 Bar Codes

Bar codes are commonly found on printed product packaging and provide a simple optical ID system. The tag can encode numbers, alphanumeric codes, 8-bit binary, or kanji. The code can be read from any angle, is somewhat damage resistant, and the detail required depends on the amount of data being encoded. To deploy codes requires some software to encode the data into a black and white image and a printer or display. To read the code requires a simple camera and software—as available with any smart phone. The reading of such a code is a one way process; the tag being unaware unless it is displayed by a device that is informed of any data access triggered by the encoded data. Lighting conditions (bright lights and darkness) can interfere with tag reading, particularly with glossy weatherproofing.

Bar code systems are characterized by the following:

- Cameras are built into many consumer devices, where these already exist, the cost of reading approaches zero. The monetary and power cost for additional tags is low for printed tags, higher for active displays.
- Reading a tag is typically manually triggered, as the device often has other purposes and required re-enabling after a read, but this behavior could be changed. The reading of a tag is typically an event.
- The tags are easily duplicated, and a given location may have multiple tags, if there is space to display them.
- The range depends on lighting, printer size, and camera quality, but is usually under a meter in practical applications.

18.1.1.3.2 Bluetooth

Bluetooth-enabled devices can be used as a form of tagging. To act as a tag a device needs to have its Bluetooth switched on and discoverable. To act as a reader, a device needs to scan for other Bluetooth devices. The tag data can simply be the tag's unique Bluetooth address, which tells the reader little about the device but is easy to acquire and could be correlated with other data. In this case, the tag is not aware of the reader detecting it, and, where tags are in fact personal devices, it may give rise to privacy concerns—particularly where the device has been given a personal name, or where the readers store scans and correlate with other data (a network of readers in other locations, very particular reader locations, video observations, etc.).

Bluetooth systems are characterized by the following:

- Bluetooth circuits are built into many consumer devices, where these already exist, the cost approaches zero. The cost for additional tags is low. The energy cost of tag beacons and reader scanning can be quite high, if mobile phone battery life with Bluetooth on.
- Once switched on and properly coded, the scanning can be automatic, frequent, registers presence, and is invisible to the human observer—although each of these properties can be modified in code and/or device configuration.
- The tags are generally unique, but a given location may have multiple tags.
- The range depends on power and antenna design for both reader and tag. A typical configuration would allow detection over 5–10 m, although longer range devices may extend this and substantial walls and metal structures may reduce it.

18.1.1.3.3 Radio Frequency ID (RFID)

Radio Frequency ID (RFID) tags are widely used in warehouse, retail, library and transport situations, supporting theft detection, stock identification, and tracking and account identity for payment. The tag data depends on the design of the tag, and can range from a simple numeric ID (used in a similar way to a bar-code for stock control), to more complex structured records. The tag computation may range from unauthenticated, unencrypted data exchange on demand, to protocols which require an identifier and provide simple encryption; some protocols may also record tag reading events or cause tag data to be changed. The modification of tag data increases the need for security provision but allows the tag system to function where access to a database indexed by tag data is problematic. The main barrier to invisible tag reading is the need to camouflage long-range antennas; and as possession of tagged objects could reveal quite personal data, their use has been somewhat limited.

Reading is contact-less, using radio (unlike a smartcard), with range depending on available power and antenna design that typically spans from a few centimeters to a meter. A tag consists of an aerial and some small memory and/or computing capacity plus two-way radio interface circuitry, typically printed on a label or embedded in a card. A wide range of radio frequencies and protocols (both standard and proprietary) are in use, with the choice affecting tag and reader size, power consumption, range, and data transfer speed. Different systems also have differing abilities to handle reading multiple in-range tags simultaneously. The tag and aerial are often several centimeters across; corresponding miniaturization is conditioned by the antenna design necessary for a desired range. It is possible to embed a power source into a tag, but passive-RFIDs are the norm wherein power is extracted from the radio signal of the reader in order to power the tag while it is being read.

RFID systems are characterized by the following:

- The marginal cost of a tag is very low and they are widely used as disposable labels for low-value goods. The costs of tag producing/writing hardware are higher. Reader costs are moderate, often requiring integration with other systems. Power costs of reading are significant, but passive RFID has no routine maintenance cost.
- Once switched on and properly coded the scanning is automatic, frequent, registers presence and is invisible to the human observer. Modifying this behavior is hard as the tags and scanner are less likely to be easily user programmable and incorporate displays than in the Bluetooth case.
- The tags may be unique where suitable security provisions have been made but for simpler technology should be treated as duplicatable, a given location may have multiple tags and it may be possible to read them all in one scan.
- Tag range is from mm to a few meters, generally requiring clear air.

18.1.2 Mobility Data

The number of mobile phone users worldwide was estimated about 2 billion in 2015. While the location technologies, such as GSM and UMTS, currently used by wireless phone operators are capable of providing an increasingly better estimate of a user's location, the integration of various positioning technologies is progressing rapidly:

1. GPS-equipped mobile devices can transmit their trajectories to some service provider.

2. Wi-Fi and Bluetooth devices can be a source of data for indoor positioning.
3. Wi-Max can be a source of data for outdoor positioning.

As computing and communication devices are all pervasive, it renders possible sensing of all human activity merely as a side effect of the ubiquitous services provided to all mobile users. Thus, the wireless phone network, designed to provide mobile communication, can also become an infrastructure to gather mobility data, if used to record the location of its users at different times.

We have today a chance of collecting and storing mobility data of unprecedented quantity, quality and timeliness at a very low cost: in principle, a dream for traffic engineers and urban planners, compelled until yesterday to gather data of limited size and precision only through highly expensive means such as field experiments, surveys to discover travelling habits of commuting workers and ad hoc sensors placed on streets.

18.1.2.1 Mobility Data Mining

The way people live and move, and, their everyday actions and activities leave digital traces in the information systems of the organizations that provide services through the wireless networks for mobile communication. Because of the increasing pervasiveness and positioning accuracy that can be achieved, the potential value of these traces in recording the human activities in an area is increasing tremendously every day.

Each time a mobile phone is used on a given network, the phone company records real-time data about it, including time and cell location. Source data are positioning logs from mobile cellular phones, reporting user's locations with reference to the cells in the GSM network; these mobility data come as streams of raw log entries recording:

- Users entering a cell—(userID, time, cellID, in)
- Users exiting a cell—(userID, time, cellID, out)
- User's absolute position, in the case of GPS/Galileo equipped devices
- User's position within a cell—(userID, time, cellID, X, Y) as a future norm

The location tracking process entailing the analysis of mobility with reference to a particular geographical location at appropriate scales and granularity would entail the following steps:

18.1.2.1.1 Trajectory Reconstruction

The stream of raw mobility data has to be processed to reconstruct trajectories of individual moving objects. The reconstruction accuracy of trajectories, as well as their level of spatiotemporal granularity, depends on the quality of the log entries, since the precision of the position may range from the granularity of a cell of varying size to the relative (approximated) position within a cell. Sophisticated reconstruction of trajectories from raw mobility data needs to be undertaken to take into account the spatial and temporal imperfections in the reconstruction process.

Each moving object trajectory is typically represented as a set of localization points of the tracked device, called sampling. This representation has intrinsic imperfection mainly due to:

1. The sampling rate and involves the trajectory reconstruction process that approximates the movement of the objects between two localization points.
2. The measurement error of the tracking device. For example, a GPS-enabled device introduces a measurement error of a few meters, whereas the imprecision introduced in a GSM/UMTS network is the dimension of a cell, which could be from less than hundred meters in urban settings to a few kilo meters in rural areas.

The resulting trajectories are stored into appropriate repositories, such as a trajectory database (such as moving object databases) or data warehouse. The management and querying of large volumes of mobility data and reconstructed trajectories also pose specific problems that can now be addressed by big data computing technologies.

18.1.2.1.2 Trajectory Mapping

Spatiotemporal data mining methods are needed to extract useful patterns out of trajectories including

1. Frequent patterns, the discovery of frequently followed (sub)paths or trajectories. Such information can be useful in urban planning, for example, by spotlighting frequently followed inefficient vehicle paths, which can be the result of a mistake in the road planning (Figure 18.2a).
2. Classification, the discovery of behavior rules, aimed at explaining the behavior of current users and predicting that of future ones. Urban traffic simulations are a straightforward example of application for this kind of knowledge, since a classification model can represent a sophisticated alternative to the simple ad hoc behavior rules, provided by domain experts, on which actual simulators are based (Figure 18.2b).
3. Clustering, the discovery of groups of "similar" trajectories, together with a summary of each group. Knowing which are the main routes (represented by clusters) followed by people or vehicles during the day can represent precious information for mobility analysis. For example, trajectory clusters may highlight the presence of important routes not adequately covered by the public transportation service (Figure 18.2c).

18.1.2.1.3 Trajectory Visualization

Trajectory maps are usually devoid of the corresponding geographical information. Once suitable methods for interpreting and delivering geographic knowledge on trajectories are available, several application scenarios become possible. For instance, trajectory visualization can enable to support and improve decision making in mobility-related issues including

- Timely detecting problems that emerge from the movement behavior
- Timely detecting changes that occur in the movement behavior

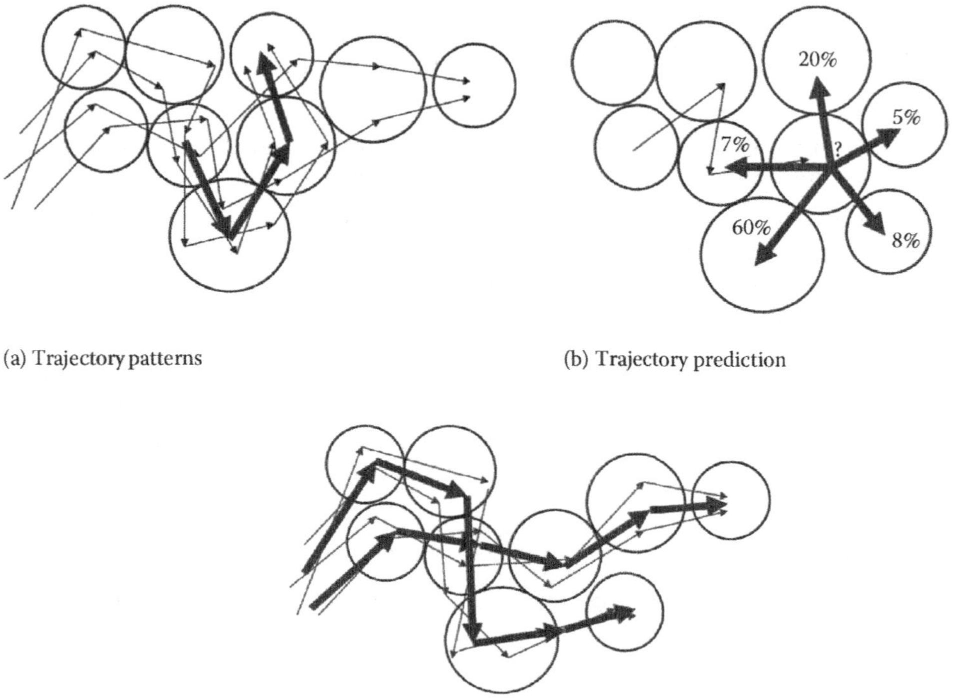

(a) Trajectory patterns

(b) Trajectory prediction

(c) Trajectory clustering

FIGURE 18.2
Trajectory mapping.

- Localizing new services in our towns
- Forecasting traffic-related phenomena
- Organizing postal and logistics systems
- Planning traffic and public mobility systems in metropolitan areas
- Planning physical communication networks, such as new roads or railways

18.2 Location-Based Services

Location-Based Services (LBS) can be defined as services that depend on and are enhanced by positional information of mobile devices. An LBS is a mobile information service that extends spatial and temporal information processing capability to end users via Internet and wireless communications. LBS are applications that take a user's location into account in order to deliver a service. From a value chain perspective, LBS are services that increase location information value to users through specific services. Therefore, an LBS can be further defined as a value-added service offered in a wireless environment that exploits mobile terminal location position information.

Based on the information delivery method, we identify three basic types of LBS: pull, push, and tracking services. In the case of a pull service, the user issues a request in order to be automatically positioned and to access the LBS he or she wants. A use-case scenario demonstrating a pull service is the following. A tourist roams in a foreign city and wants to receive information about the nearest restaurants to his or her current location. Using a mobile device, the tourist issues an appropriate request (e.g., via short message service (SMS) or wireless application protocol (WAP)), and the network locates his or her current position and responds with a list of restaurants located near it. On the contrary, in the case of a push service, the request is issued by the service provider and not the user. A representative example of push services is location-based advertising, which informs users about products of their interest located at nearby stores. In this service, users submit their shopping preference profiles to the service provider and allow the provider to locate and contact them with advertisements, discounts, and/or e-coupons for products of interest at nearby stores. So, in this case, the service provider is the one who pushes information to the user. Finally, in a tracking service, the basic idea is that someone (user or service) issues a request to locate other mobile stations (users, vehicles, fleets, etc.).

LBS can be classified as follows:

1. Emergency services: The ability to locate an individual who is either unaware of his or her exact location or is not able to reveal it because of an emergency situation. This requires the system to automatically determine the mobile users' exact location after receiving an emergency call and to transfer the location information to the emergency assistance agency.
2. Tracking services: Applicable on the personal and the corporate level to monitor the exact whereabouts of a person or property. One popular business application is fleet management, which refers to tracking and managing vehicles so that companies know where their goods are at any time so that they can thereby organize their business. These kinds of applications can also be used by companies in order to locate and manage their working team; this is known as field management. Other applications are those used for product tracking within a supply chain.
3. Navigation services: Navigation services are based on a mobile user's need for directions within their current geographical location. The ability of a mobile network to locate the exact position of a mobile user can be manifested in a series of navigation-based services. In navigation services, the system needs to determine the position by direction prediction and routing calculation, which is based on the destination and relevant information displayed. In addition, services can be provided to allow mobile users to locate friends, family, workers, or other members of a particular group in order to improve communication.
4. Information services: Information services generally refer to the digital distribution of content to mobile terminal devices based on their location, time specificity, and user behavior. Mobile users can be provided with a wide range of localized information such as landmarks, restaurants, theaters, and public transportation options.

   The following services can be identified within this category:

   a. Travel services that can be provided to tourists moving around in a foreign city, such as guided tours, notification about nearby places of interest, and transportation services.

b. Mobile yellow pages that provide a mobile user, upon request, with information regarding nearby facilities.
c. Infotainment services such as information about location-specific multimedia content and community events.

5. Advertising services: Wireless advertising refers to advertising and marketing activities that deliver advertisements to mobile devices using wireless networks and mobile advertising solutions to promote the sales of goods and services or to build brand awareness. Typical LBS advertising takes the form of mobile banners, short message service (SMS) messages, and proximity triggered advertisements, but its intrusive nature is a big challenge.

LBS are the key enabler for a plethora of applications across different domains ranging from tracking and navigation systems to directory services, entertainment to emergency services, and various mobile commerce applications. Some LBS examples and their quality of service (QoS) requirements are presented in Table 18.2. QoS requirements of LBS can be expressed from the following aspects: location accuracy required, response time, and reliability of operation. These attributes could offer some guidance to network designers and operators on the need for applications and the functionalities required in location-aware network infrastructure.

TABLE 18.2

LBS Quality of Service (QOS) Requirements

Location-Based Services	Applications	Quality of Service
Emergency services	• Police and fire response • Search and rescue missions • Roadside assistance • Emergency medical/ambulance	Location accuracy of a few meters Response time of a few seconds Need for very high reliability (Goal should be 100%)
Tracking and navigation services	• Tracking of children or locating lost pets • Locating friends in a particular area • Tracking stolen vehicles or asset tracking • Dynamic navigational guidance • Voice-enabled route description	Location accuracy of a few meters Response time of a few seconds Need for very high reliability (Goal should be 100%)
Information/directory services	• Guided tours, notification about nearby places of interest, transportation services • Dynamic yellow pages that automatically inform user of location of nearest facilities, hospitals, restaurants, etc. • Location multimedia content, community events	Location accuracy of tens of meters Response time of a few seconds Need for high reliability (98%–99%)
Advertising services	• Wireless coupon presentation, targeted and customized ads • Marketing promotions and alerts • Customer notification and identification in the neighborhood store	Location accuracy of meters Response time of a minute Need for high reliability (98%–99%)

18.2.1 LBS Characteristics

Key characteristics of LBS are as follows:

1. Person-Oriented LBS
    a. Consists of applications where a service is user based.
    b. User typically controls how location information is collected and used.
2. Device-Oriented LBS
    a. Applications are external to the user.
    b. Person or device located is not controlling the service.
3. Push- versus Pull-Based Applications
    a. Push-based: information is delivered to the mobile terminal (end user) automatically when certain event occurs.
    b. Pull-based: Mobile terminal (end user) initiates the request.
4. Direct versus Indirect User Profile
    a. Based on how the user profile is collected—directly from the user during the set up phase, by tracking the user's behavior pattern, or from third parties.
    b. Security and privacy issues become critical to maintain user trust and to avoid fraudulent activities.
5. Availability of User Profile Information
    a. Profile information requested on the fly or already available to the LBS.
6. Mobility and Interaction
    a. Range of mobility scenarios exist based on combinations of mobility of users and network components.
    b. Level and type of interactions depend the mobility scenario.
7. State of Interaction
    a. Stateless interaction: Each request is an independent transaction unrelated to the previous request.
    b. Stateful interaction: LBS preserves the state across service requests (beneficial for forecasting future transactions, requests, and behavior).
8. Static versus Dynamic Source of Information
    a. Static: Data about historical buildings and landmarks, places of attraction, hotels and restaurants, maps.
    b. Dynamic: Information that changes with time (weather, traffic, and road conditions).
9. Sources of Location Information
    a. Location information provided by the user or the network infrastructure or by a third party.
10. Accuracy of Location Information
    a. Depending on the positioning technology used in the network infrastructure, different accuracy of localization request of mobile terminals may result.

18.2.2 LBS Positioning Technologies

LBS provide users with information about geographical location; they require specific infrastructure for positioning the mobile terminal. Positioning means the determination of the location of the object in a reference system. The reference system can be a coordinate or an address system, an aerial division or a route system. Geocoding is a process used for associating the object to a general coordinate system if some other system, such as an address, is used as a reference system.

From a technological point of view, LBS are split into two major categories depending on the approach for positioning used to locate the mobile stations, namely, the handset-based approach and the network-based approach. The former approach requires the mobile device to actively participate in the determination of its position, while the latter relies solely on the positioning capabilities of elements belonging to the mobile network. What distinguish them from one another are the accuracy they provide and the cost of their implementation. The most popular network-based positioning techniques are cell-global-identity (CGI) methods, timing advance (TA), uplink time of arrival (TOA), and angle of arrival (AOA), while the most popular handset-based positioning techniques are observed time difference of arrival (OTDOA), enhanced observed time difference (E-OTD), and Assisted Global Positioning System (A-GPS).

The technologies offering positioning for mobile terminals in LBS can be roughly classified as outdoor and indoor technologies, depending on what they are targeted for. Different positioning techniques vary due to their features—such as accuracy, reliability, and time to fix.

1. Indoor localization technique: In indoor environments, the GPS signal cannot be used because inside the buildings the signal power gets attenuated. Location-sensing systems relying on standard wireless networking hardware measure signal intensity and attenuation to determine user location. For short-range positioning technologies, location identification relies on the cooperation between the moving target object and a fixed reference point. Some popular technologies for indoor environments are introduced as follows. Popular indoor localization technologies include ultrasound, infrared, RF identification, Bluetooth and Wireless Local Area Network (WLAN).
2. Outdoor localization technique: For outdoor environments, the technologies used to determine location information can be divided into three categories: network-based technologies, handset-based technologies, and the hybrid systems. Network-based technologies depend on the ability of a mobile device to receive signals from a mobile network covering the area of presence, and these usually perform well in densely populated environments. Handset-based technologies do not need mobile network coverage to work but do require hardware or software computing capability in the handset to determine its position. The most common application of handset-based technologies is GPS. Hybrid systems are those that incorporate a combination of network- and handset-based technologies.

The accuracy provided by some of these techniques in different coverage areas of the mobile network is presented in Tables 18.3 and 18.4.

TABLE 18.3

Location Enablement Technologies

Technology	Description	Advantages	Disadvantages
Network based			
Cell of origin (COO)	Information generated about the cell occupied by a user	RF technology Inexpensive—uses existing network No handset modification Fast implementation No consumer behavior change	Low resolution
Angle of Arrival (AOA)	Measures angle of signal from mobile device to cell towers Minimum of two cell sites required	FF technology No handset modification No consumer behavior change	Expensive network modifications required Resistance toward more antennas in neighborhoods Line-of-sight constraint Medium resolution (not less than 150 m)
Time Distance of Arrival (TDOA)	Triangulates at least three stations to measure and compare arrival time of signal from a user	RF technology No handset modification No consumer behavior change	Line-of-sight constraint Expensive Medium resolution Appropriate for CDMA
Enhanced cell ID (E-CID)	Software-based solution that compares list of cell sites available to user and checks for overlaps	RF technology Line of sight not required Moderate cost to upgrade	Works only with GSM Some modification required in handset and network
Handset based			
Global Positioning System (GPS)	Radio navigation system comprising low-orbit satellites. Triangulation by measuring the time to communicate with three satellites	FF technology Very accurate, 1–5 m, 95% precision Not dependent on network	Line-of-sight issues Significant handset Handset modification May require consumer behavior change modifications
Hybrid technology			
Enhanced observed time difference (E-OTD)	Similar to TDOA, but handset calculates the location	RF technology Accuracy of 50–125 m Some behavior change	Suited for GSM only Network and handset modification Cell coverage necessary
Assisted Global Positioning System (A-GPS)	Processing done by network while using the satellites	RF technology Moderate modification to handset Line-of-sight constraint reduced	Significant changes to network

18.2.3 LBS System Architecture

Location information is usually provided in terms of a latitude/longitude pair that is sent to an application in a server or back to the mobile device, which is then transmitted with some additional identification information to an application in a server that may reside inside or outside the wireless network. The location information can be tied to a location

TABLE 18.4

Accuracy and TIFF for Several Location Techniques

Technique	Network Impact	Terminal Impact	Accuracy	TTFF
Cell ID	None	None	250 m–20 km	<1 s
Signal strength	None	None	100 m–10 km	<1 s
TOA/TDOA	Medium	Low/medium	40–150 m	<1 s
AOA/DOA	High	None	50–150 m	<1 s
Fingerprint	High	None	50–150 m	Seconds
GPS	Low	Very high	3–50 m	Seconds
Hybrid systems	Depends on the techniques hybridized	Depends on the techniques hybridized	3–100 m	Seconds
Ultrawide baud	Dedicated infrastructure	Very high	10–50 cm	<1 s

database server that could interest users and that will then send a related message to the user about restaurants or hotels.

A reference LBS architecture consists of four major entities:

1. Mobile devices
2. Positioning systems
3. Communication networks
4. Service providers

Users use their mobile devices (e.g., smartphones) to send queries to LBS servers. The locations in the queries are obtained via positioning systems such as GPS. The queries, as well as their responses from the LBS servers, are transmitted via communication Unlike geographic information systems (GISs), which are usually desktop or client/server applications with a limited number of users, LBS have to provide access and information to dozens of users with mobile terminals.

The following capabilities of LBS usually exceed the general requirements of static GISs use

- Current: Support the delivery of real-time, dynamic information
- Device: Availability from any device and from any location
- High performance: Delivering answers in a sub second if querying information from Internet and databases
- Scalable architecture: Support thousands of concurrent users and terabytes of data:
- Reliable: Capable of delivering up to 99.999% uptime
- Secure: Manage the underlying database locking and security services
- Interoperable: Integrated with e-business applications such as customer relationship management, billing, personalization, and wireless positioning gateways
- Open: Support common standards and protocols, such as HTTP, Wireless Application Protocol (WAP), Wireless Markup Language (WML), Extensible Markup Language (XML), Multimedia Markup Language (MML)

18.2.4 LBS System Components

LBS is an intersection of the three technologies, namely, new information and communication technologies (NICTSs) such as the mobile telecommunication system and handheld devices, the Internet, and Geographic information systems (GIS) with spatial databases.

LBS gives the possibility of a two-way communication and interaction. Therefore, the user tells the service provider his/her actual context, like the kind of information he needs, his/her preferences, and his/her position. This helps the provider of such location services to deliver information tailored to the user needs. If the user wants to use a location-based service, different infrastructure elements are necessary.

Here are the basic components in LBS:

1. Mobile devices: A tool for the user to request the needed information. The results can be given by speech, using pictures, text, and so on. Possible devices are PDAs, mobile phones, laptops, and so on, but the device can also be a navigation unit of car or a toll box for road pricing in a truck.
2. Communication network: The second component is the mobile network, which transfers the user data and service request from the mobile terminal to the service provider and then the requested information back to the user.
3. Positioning determination technology (PDT) component: For the processing of a service, the user position usually has to be determined. The user position can be obtained either by using the mobile communication network or by using the Global Positioning System (GPS). Further possibilities to determine the position are WLAN stations, active badges, or radio beacons. The latter positioning methods can be especially used for indoor navigation, like in a museum. If the position is not determined automatically, it can be also specified manually by the user.
4. Service and application provider: The service provider offers a number of different services to the user and is responsible for the service request processing. Such services offer the calculation of the position, finding a route, searching yellow pages with respect to position, or searching specific information on objects of the user interest (e.g., a bird in wild life park).
5. Data and content provider: Service providers will usually not store and maintain all the information that can be requested by users. Therefore, geographic base data and location information data will usually be requested from the maintaining authority (e.g., mapping agencies) or business and industry partners (e.g., yellow pages, traffic companies).

18.2.5 LBS System Challenges

Despite the appealing idea of using user location information to provide highly personalized and intelligent services, there are certain challenges that should be addressed in order for LBS to succeed.

We can divide these challenges into three categories:

1. Technological challenge for LBS is the capability to create easy-to-use and satisfying services. There is much talk concerning what would be the most suitable user interface and type of service (pull or push) in terms of user satisfaction. For example, in the case of push-based services, a user is not required to manually issue

queries in order to get the information he or she seeks. The system automatically informs him or her based on the current location and a list of preferences listed in the user's profile. The problem is that in this way, user intent cannot be perfectly captured and the user may be frequently disturbed by out-of-context information. So, despite the easiness of usage (no or minimal interface), user satisfaction is not assured. On the other hand, in pull-based LBS, in which clients have to poll the server for updates, the users may experience difficulties in using these services because cell phones, PDAs, and wearable computers are less suitable for browsing and query-based information retrieval due to their limited input device capabilities. All these restrictions along with the unpredictability in mobile environments (disconnections, frequent context differentiations, etc.) have to be taken very carefully into account when designing LBS.

Some of the implied requirements are the following:

a. A less intensive use of the mobile network and a minimal volume of transmitted data.
b. The possibility of offline operation.
c. Simple and user-friendly interfaces and limited and well-specified amounts of presented information content.

Therefore, it becomes apparent that LBS will not succeed in attracting users without implementing sophisticated techniques based on carefully designed interfaces and/or detailed knowledge of customer profiles, needs, and preferences. So, given existing technical limitations such as device capabilities and access speeds combined with human limitations such as reduced consideration sets and the need for speed and convenience, in order for LBS to succeed, they will need to deliver relevant, targeted, and timely information to consumers at the time and place of their choice.

Also, from a database perspective, LBS raise critical challenges such as spatial and temporal query processing because the continuous movement of users or objects leads to the need for fast and frequent or continuous updates to the databases.

Some of the most important database research challenges brought to the surface by LBS are the following:

a. Support for nonstandard-dimension hierarchies: In LBS, the geographical area may be divided into multidimensional regions following the pattern of network coverage. Until now, geographical area representation models used by data warehouses were in the form of completely balanced trees (strict hierarchies), which cannot capture irregularities like those that frequently occur in mobile networks (e.g., the same region covered by more than one base station).
b. Support for imprecision and varying precision: Varying precision means that the location of the same user may be pinpointed with different accuracies depending on the positioning technology used while he or she is roaming from network to network. Imprecision means that the location data for the trace of a specific user may be incomplete (e.g., a user may have gone out of the network coverage or may have switched off the device for some time). So, varying precision and imprecision should be carefully handled by employing intelligent query-processing techniques, especially for queries on complete user traces.

   c. Support for movement constraints and transportation networks: Most of the time, users move on certain routes as defined by transportation networks (e.g., railways, roads), and their movement is blocked depending on the morphology of the land (e.g., mountains). The incorporation of such constraints into query resolution may offer increased positioning accuracy to LBS despite the potentially low-accuracy positioning technology used.
   d. Support for spatial data mining on vehicle movement.
   e. Support for continuous location change in query-processing techniques.
2. Ethical challenges: From an ethical point of view, a critical challenge is to protect user privacy. LBS can potentially intrude on customer privacy. The adoption of LBS is highly dependent on the successful confrontation of digital frauds, attempts of intrusion in customer databases with sensitive data and profiles, and the threat of unauthorized or uncontrolled resale of location information. It has also been shown that a privacy-intruding service (e.g., an always-on tracking service), despite its usability, is not desirable by users since it does not allow them to switch it off whenever they want. So, when designing an LBS and in order for the service to be adopted, the provider should take into account very seriously the user's concerns on privacy.
3. Business challenges: Capitalizing on the promise of LBS requires developing sustainable and viable business models for offering such services. Unfortunately, until today, there has been little effort on developing a framework with which to identify the most appropriate business models for the large variety of LBS. The major obstacle for this arises from the fact that there is a multitude of players participating in the provision of such services forming a complex value network.

The main categories under which these players are grouped are the following:

- Application developers and content providers
- Service providers and network providers
- Hardware manufacturers

The roles of all these different actors or players are many times conflicting if not competitive, and fairness in revenue sharing is viewed differently by each actor. In this context, it is difficult to determine which activities should be performed by which actor (e.g., should the network operator develop its own services or outsource them to more focused application providers) or to identify which actor should be the dominant one in the business model (i.e., the operator providing access to its customer base, the content or service provider offering the actual service, or the location technology vendor offering the enabling positioning equipment).

18.3 Location-Based Social Networks

Location-based social networking (LBSN) refers to a type of social networks with embedded geographical properties which is usually generated by using the general location-based services. Location-based services, for example, Foursquare, Yelp, and Facebook Places, have emerged in recent years and become increasingly popular since 2010. Generally, LBSNs consist of social connections among users and "location-based" context including geographical check-in POIs, check-in time stamps, and user/location-associated content (e.g., descriptions, tips, pictures, and videos). Such elements reflect aspects of human mobility in a "W4" (i.e., who, when, where, and what) information layout, corresponding to four distinct information layers.

LBSN sites allow a user to "check in" at a real-world point of interest (POI, e.g., a hotel, restaurant, and theater), leave tips toward the POI, and share the check-in with their online friends. Location-based social networking services maintain a large POI database and allow a user to "check-in" at a POI with his/her smartphone regarding his/her current physical location. The user can also leave tips and share "check-in" experience with his/her online friends, along with creating the opportunity to make new friends.

> The "check-in," recognized as a location-tagging function, has been considered a distinguishing feature between location-based social networks and general social networks (GSNs). With the rapid development of mobile technologies, it can be expected that in future LBSN may eventually be integrated into a location-based feature of a general social network.

Electronic check-in action bridges the gap between real world and online social networks, resulting in a new type of social networks, namely location-based social networks (LBSNs). Compared to traditional GPS data, location-based social networks data contains unique properties with abundant heterogeneous information to reveal human mobility, that is, "when and where a user (who) has been to for what," corresponding to an unprecedented opportunity to better understand human mobility from spatial, temporal, social, and content aspects.

In traditional cellphone-based GPS data, users' geographical movements are automatically tracked and recorded by the service provider according to a predefined time interval (usually within 10 min). The increasing use of mobile devices has led to the availability of big mobile data. Thus, one can easily obtain a long trajectory with massive GPS points from a single user. However, studies on such data are still limited to the small number of participant users. Location-based social networking services provide semantic indications on check-in locations. Traditional cellphone data stores GPS trajectories in terms of longitude and latitude, and there is generally no mapping between a GPS position to a specific location (i.e., a POI). For example, it is not easy to figure out whether a GPS point corresponds to a restaurant, theater, or just point on highway. Although there are location databases available aimed at generating such correlations, residual uncertainty remains with regard to the actual visit or otherwise at a location.

In contrast, location-based social networks adopt a user-driven check-in strategy, that is, the user decides whether or not to check-in at a specific place based on his/her own choices. Data generated on LBSNs being user-driven obviates any residual ambiguity regarding the actual visit or otherwise for at a location. When a user plans to check-in, LBSN services provide him with nearby POIs according to the user's current position. The user selects the correct one and performs a check-in action by clicking the "check-in" button for the location. Each location in LBSN is associated with textual descriptions such as tags, categories, and names. The user can also provide additional content of the location in terms of tips and comments.

The mining and understanding of human mobility can further lead to effective approaches to improve current location-based services from mobile marketing to recommender systems, providing users more convenient and engaging life experience than before. Analyzing LBSN data can reveal representative tasks of mining human mobility on location-based social networks, including capturing user mobility patterns to understand

1. When and where a user commonly goes (location prediction)?
2. Exploiting user preferences and location profiles to investigate where and when a user wants to explore (location recommendation)?
3. Studying a user's check-in activity in terms of why a user goes to a certain location?

The increasing use of location-based social networking services generates large-scale data with geographical distance between users and their social networks. The study on geo-social metrics reveals that

- Users who live close to each other have a higher probability of creating friendship links than those who are distanced
- Users in the same social cluster show short geographical distances.

By comparing location-based social networks (like Brightkite and Foursquare) with content-based social networks (LiveJournal and Twitter), it is seen that people within a social cluster on LBSNs tend to have smaller geographical distance than online social networks that focus on content producing and sharing. As expected, probability of a social tie between two users is roughly a function of the geographical distance between them. Thus, a user is more likely to befriend other users who are geographically close, for example, coworkers, colleagues. Likewise, a user may check-in at a location due to the influence from his/her friends, such as following friends' suggestions to visit a restaurant, going out with friends for shopping.

> The study on LBSN data and cell phone data highlights that long-distance travel is more influenced by social friendship while short-range human movement is not influenced by social networks!

18.4 Summary

This chapter describes location-based services (LBS) including characteristics, positioning technologies, system architecture, components, and challenges. The later part of the chapter discusses discovering spatial mobility patterns through the use of calls data. Mobile services and applications have the potential to be the killer apps for the coming boom in the m-business.

19

Context-Aware Applications

Most mobile applications are location-aware systems. Specifically, tourist guides are based on users' locations in order to supply more information on the city attraction closer to them or the museum exhibit they are seeing. Nevertheless, recent years have seen many mobile applications trying to exploit information that characterizes the current situation of users, places, and objects in order to improve the services provided.

The principle of context-aware applications (CAA) can be explained using the metaphor of the Global Positioning System (GPS). In aircraft navigation, for example, a GPS receiver derives the speed and direction of an aircraft by recording over time the coordinates of longitude, latitude, and altitude. This contextual data is then used to derive the distance to the destination, communicate progress to date, and calculate the optimum flight path.

For a GPS-based application to be used successfully, the following activities are a prerequisite:

1. The region in focus must have been GPS-mapped accurately.
2. The GPS map must be superimposed with the relevant information regarding existing landmarks, points of civic and official significance, and, facilities and service points of interest in the past to the people—this is the context in this metaphor.
3. There must be a system available to ascertain the latest position as per the GPS.
4. The latest reported position must be mapped and transcribed onto the GPS-based map of the region.
5. This latest position relative to the context (described in the second activity) is used as the point of reference for future recommendation(s) and action(s).

It should be noted that the initial baseline of the context (described in the second activity) is compiled and collated separately and then uploaded into the system to be accessible by the CAA. However, with passage of time, this baseline gets added further with the details of each subsequent transaction.

> We can also imagine an equivalent of the Global Positioning System for calibrating the performance of enterprises. The coordinates of longitude, latitude, and altitude might be replaced by ones of resource used, process performed, and product produced. If we designed a GPS for an enterprise, we could measure its performance (e.g., cost or quality) in the context of the resource used, the process performed, and the product delivered as compared with its own performance in the past (last month or one year back) or in particular cases that of another target organization. Such an approach could help us specify our targets, communicate our performance, and signal our strategy.

Most of the current context-aware systems have been built in an ad hoc approach and are deeply influenced by the underlying technology infrastructure utilized to capture the context. To ease the development of context-aware ubicomp (ubiquitous computing) and mobile applications, it is necessary to provide universal models and mechanisms to manage context. Even though significant efforts have been devoted to research methods and models for capturing, representing, interpreting, and exploiting context information, we are still not close to enabling an implicit and intuitive awareness of context nor efficient adaptation to behavior at the standards of human communication practice.

Context information can be a decisive factor in mobile applications in terms of selecting the appropriate interaction technique. Designing interactions among users and devices, as well as among devices themselves, is critical in mobile applications. Multiplicity of devices and services calls for systems that can provide various interaction techniques and the ability to switch to the most suitable one according to the user's needs and desires. Current mobile systems are not efficiently adaptable to the user's needs. The majority of ubicomp and mobile applications try to incorporate the user's profile and desires into the system's infrastructure either manually or automatically observing their habits and history. According to our perspective, the key point is to give them the ability to create their own mobile applications instead of just customizing the ones provided.

Thus, mobile applications can be used not only for locating users and providing them with suitable information but also for

- Providing them with a tool necessary for composing and creating their own mobile applications.
- Supporting the system's selection of appropriate interaction techniques.
- Selecting recommendation(s) and consequent action(s) conforming with the situational constraints judged via the business logic and other constraints sensed via the context.
- Enabling successful closure of the interaction (answering to a query, qualifying an objection, closing an order, etc.).

19.1 Context-Aware Applications

Context is understood as "the location and identities of nearby people and objects, and changes to those objects." Initially, the term context was equivalent to the location and identity of users and objects. Very soon, though, the term expanded to include a more refined view of the environment assuming either three major components—computing, user, and physical environment—or four major dimensions—system, infrastructure, domain, and physical context. The interaction between the user and application was added by Dey (2001); according to him, a context is "any information that can be used to characterize the situation of an entity." An entity should be treated as anything relevant to the interaction between a user and an application, such as a person, a place, or an object, including the user and the application themselves and, by extension, the environment the user and applications are embedded in. Thus, a system is context-aware if it uses context to provide relevant information and/or services to the user, where relevancy depends on the user's task.

Context-aware features include using context to

1. Present information and services to a user.
2. Automatically execute a service for a user.
3. Tag information to support later retrieval.

In supporting these features, context-aware applications can utilize numerous different kinds of information sources. Often, this information comes from sensors, whether they are software sensors detecting information about the networked, or virtual, world or hardware sensors detecting information about the physical world. Sensor data can be used to recognize the usage situation, for instance, from illumination, temperature, noise level, and device movements. A context-aware application can make adaptive decisions based on the context of interaction in order to modulate the information presented to the user or to carry out semantic transformation on the data, like converting text to speech for an audio device. The promise and purpose of context awareness are to allow computing systems to take action autonomously and enable systems to sense the situation and act appropriately. For example, in context-aware mobile applications, location is the most commonly used variable in context recognition as it is relatively easy to detect. User activity is much more difficult to identify than location, but some aspects of this activity can be detected by placing sensors in the environment.

Location is the most commonly used piece of context information, and several different location detection techniques have been utilized in context-awareness research. The Global Positioning System (GPS) is a commonly used technology when outdoors utilized, for example, in car navigation systems. Network cellular ID can be used to determine location with mobile phones. Measuring the relative signal strengths of Bluetooth and WLAN hotspots and using the hotspots as beacons are the frequently used techniques for outdoor and indoor positioning. Other methods used indoors include ultrasonic or infrared-based location detection. Other commonly used forms of context are time of day, day of week, identity of the user, proximity to other devices and people, and actions of the user.

Context-aware device behavior may not rely purely on the physical environment. While sensors have been used to directly provide this physical context information, sensor data often need to be interpreted to aid in the understanding of the user's goals. Information about a user's goals, preferences, and social context can be used for determining context-aware device behavior as well. Knowledge about a user's goals helps prioritize the device actions and select the most relevant information sources. A user's personal preferences can offer useful information for profiling or personalizing services or refining information retrieval. The user may also have preferences about the quality of service issues such as cost efficiency, data connection speed, and reliability, which relate closely to mobile connectivity issues dealing with handovers and alternative data transfer mediums.

Finally, social context forms an important type of context as mobile devices are commonly used to support communication between two people and used in the presence of other people.

Challenges of context-aware systems include the following:

- A main issue regarding context-aware computing is the fear that control may be taken away from the user. Apart from control issues, privacy and security issues arise. The main parameters of context are user location and activity, which users consider as part of their privacy. Users are especially reluctant to exploit context-aware systems, when they know that private information may be disclosed to others.

- There is a gap between how people understand context and what systems consider as context. The environment in which people live and work is very complex; the ability to recognize the context and determine the appropriate action requires considerable intelligence.
- A context-aware system cannot decide with certainty which actions the user may want to be executed; as the human context is inaccessible to sensors, we cannot model it with certainty.
- A context-aware system cannot be developed to be so robust that it will rarely fail, as ambiguous and uncertain scenarios will always occur and even for simple operations exceptions may exist.
- A context-aware system can add more and more rules to support the decision-making process; unfortunately, this may lead to large and complex systems that are difficult to understand and use.
- A context-aware application is based on context information that may be imperfect. The ambiguity over the context soundness arises due to the speed at which the context information changes and the accuracy and reliability of the producers of the context, like sensors.
- It is a challenge for context-aware systems to handle context, which may be nonaccurate or ambiguous, in an appropriate manner—more information is not necessarily more helpful; context information is useful only when it can be usefully interpreted.

19.1.1 Types of Context-Awareness

The type of context-awareness determines the type of contexts required.

The various types of context-awareness are

1. Selection of information that can be used as context: Here the selection of the context is based on the proximity of the service required. It could also just be the information needed rather than a choice of service. For example, nurses at a nearby location or restaurants of choice in the proximity or printers in the vicinity are presented and the user chooses one of them.
2. Automatic reconfiguration of the context: The system automatically reconfigures itself on the basis of the context of the user. For example, on recognizing the context of the user, when the user is in a cinema theater, a mobile phone goes on silent mode and calls may be diverted to one's secretary without the need for one to select this service. It is a system-level technique that creates an automatic binding to an available resource on the basis of the current context. It could also be a process of adding/removing components or altering connections on the basis of the context. There is also a possibility that the results of an application are modified on the basis of the context, as one has seen typically in object-oriented systems.
3. Automatic triggering of action on the basis of context: Applications that execute commands for the user on the basis of the available context use context-triggered actions. They may be in the form of simple if–then rules that specify how context-aware systems should adapt.
4. Tagging of context for future use: Once the context has been identified, it can be tagged for future use. A wide spectrum of applications can use such a tagged context.

19.1.2 Types of Contexts

Various kinds of context can be examined. Context information may be permanent or temporary in nature, static or dynamic, and may be manually entered or automatically captured.

On the basis of the types of sensors, categories of context can be grouped as follows:

1. Location-based context: Information in this category includes that related to location, physical environment (light conditions, noise levels, traffic conditions, or temperature), and situation (in the canteen, in a conference, in a meeting, or in a movie theater). The initial context-aware applications were built using these contexts as these were minimal and measurable, and could be used in available systems without much difficulty.
2. Time-based context: Date and time-based information (day, week, time, or season) that can be easily collected from the clock built into mobile devices. This context is useful in many applications such as healthcare applications where reminders can be given for dispensing medication at appropriate times and also requesting stocks at regular intervals.
3. Application-based context: This type of context generates application- and server-specific information. This information can be used by any service. For example, the traffic density at various locations on a particular route can be used for suggesting alternative routes when there is a traffic jam on a subscriber's route.
4. Network/device-based context: These consist of network and device parameters and variables. One possible application would be to look at the available bandwidth and reconfigure the information/services that are triggered, for instance, bandwidth utilization while using multiple applications on a mobile device.
5. User state-based context: Information in this category includes the user's biological and emotional state, which can be collected by using the physiological sensors mentioned previously. This context can be extremely useful in emergency situations. For example, alterations in dosage/timing of automatically dispensed medications (e.g., insulin), on the basis of the user's condition, can be an excellent application for saving lives.
6. Context history: To give the user the experience of "ecstasy," the history of the user as well as the contextual information can be used for creating user profiles. These would be extremely useful in many applications. The limitations of memory and processing power will need to be addressed before this type of context becomes widely used.

The context can also be bundled in two categories of "physical context" and "logical" context. The physical context, such as location, time, temperature, and so on, would be more directly obtainable, whereas the logical context is a little more difficult to gather as it needs certain processing before one can use it, for example, preferences of the user, relationships, privileges, and so on. Most work has been in the area of physical context processing.

19.1.3 Context Acquisition

As the need for context has become clear, the next issue to be addressed is how to incorporate this context information in system design. There are two standard ways of obtaining information: one is to pull the required/desired information from the environment and the second is to have the context pushed:

1. Pulling the context: This type of information becomes available to the application only when it is requested for. An obvious advantage is that the user will have complete control over the context information requested. Also, "requesting" a certain context, as per the need of the application, could be built into the application. The user then has to be aware of the needs of the application and has to "work" to incorporate the context. If the application is going to automatically pull out the required context information, the bandwidth limitation and costs will come into the picture. In case the required bandwidth is not available, the application may suffer. Also, if the context does not change as frequently as the frequency of "pull" then one will be wasting the bandwidth, without real use. In times of emergencies such as earthquakes or other natural disasters, a large number of consumers may pull out the same information from a supplier, causing severe scalability problems.
2. Getting the context pushed: The other alternative is similar to a "broadcast" facility in networks. The context information will keep getting pushed out at regular intervals to all the users. This simplifies the life of the user (and complexity of application development), in the sense that now the user/application is relieved of the job of getting the contextual information. The utility of the context information is not known unless the user has specifically subscribed for it. It could be possible that a particular context information is irrelevant to a particular user/application. In that case, it is waste of expensive resources in mobile networks. Also, there would be additional need for buffering this context in order to process and check its utility. This increases the cost of the component.

The best approach would then be to combine both these approaches to address all the issues such as bandwidth limitation, cost, frequency of pull, and the utility of context information. The application would request for certain specialized context information (pull) and there could be some information that could keep getting pushed out at regular intervals.

19.1.4 Context Models

Contextual information can be provided to/obtained by the application in two ways:

- The user feeds the information classified as profiled information.
- Meaningful information is extracted from raw data collected by the sensors, that is, data need to be modeled to reflect the physical entities for interpretation.

Evaluation of the context implies the verification of proposed information generated by modules against a specific context. There are different ways in which context data are modeled; these context data models specify the way in which data structures are defined for representing and exchanging the desired context with the system.

1. Key structure models: The simplest of data structures, the value of context information (location information, sound level, etc.) is provided to an application as an environment variable. This model is most widely used in various service frameworks and quite frequently in distributed service frameworks. In such frameworks, the services themselves are usually described with a list of simple attributes in a key-value manner. For instance, the context vocabulary may contain (Temperature, Cold) or (Temperature, Hot) where the environment variable is "temperature" and the context is "cold" or "hot." The service discovery procedure used then operates an exact matching algorithm on these attributes. Note that key-value pairs are easy to manage but lack the capabilities of sophisticated structuring for enabling efficient context retrieval algorithms. Additional attributes such as timestamp, source, and confidence in the accuracy of the context are also of great importance.
2. Graphical models: The current generic graphical language UML used to represent objects and their interactions is found to be suitable to model the context in multiple scenarios. Another modeling approach can be extended to the object role modeling included in the context.
3. Markup scheme models: Once systems became web-based, it became natural to represent context as a data structure consisting of a hierarchical context and markup tags (e.g., location: state, city, street, building, and so on). Profiles contain typical markup scheme models. This XML-based language or encoding in RDF/S allows accounting for contextual information and dependencies when defining interaction patterns on a limited scale. Owing to the fact that no design criteria and only parts of the language are available to the public, the actual appropriateness and capabilities of this context modeling approach remains unknown.
4. Object-oriented models: Use of object-oriented techniques to model the context gives it all the capabilities of object orientation such as encapsulation, polymorphism, and abstraction. Existing approaches use various objects to represent different types of context. They encapsulate the details of context processing and representation. Access to them is only through well-defined interfaces. An example is the use of objects to represent various inputs from a sensor and the processing of that information necessary to represent the context can be the methods defined for the particular object.
5. Logic-based models: It is suitable to use a logic-based system when the contextual information shows a high degree of formality. These systems manage the facts, expressions, and rules used to define the context model. They permit not only updating or deleting existing facts/rules but also the addition of new ones.
6. Ontology-based models: The nature of context-aware service demands that the context information should be modeled in a platform-independent manner and should support interoperation. Thus, use of ontology in a context model at a semantic level and establishing a common understanding of terms are imperative. The description of the concepts and the relationships between them can be represented as ontologies. This would enable context sharing, reasoning, and reusing in such environments. The simplicity of representation, flexibility, extensibility, genericity, formal expressiveness of ontology, and the possibility of applying the ontology reasoning technique have made these models the most promising instrument in multiple current frameworks for modeling contextual information.

19.1.5 Generic Context-Aware Application Architecture

A generic architecture for a context-aware application will include the following components:

1. Context providers/acquirers: These are sensors or devices responsible for collecting context. These sensors could be physical sensors (such as photodiodes, temperature sensors, and GPS), virtual sensors (use of retrieved electronic calendars as estimators for position parameters), or logical sensors (some combination of physical and virtual sensor data).
2. Context aggregator: This is a module that will take inputs from various context providers/acquirers, aggregate the context, and provide it to a context interpreter. To perform the aggregation, a set of statistical models may be required along with some learning techniques. This layer may be merged in the context of inferencer/interpreter in some simple models. However, this extra layer of abstraction will enhance encapsulation and ease the development process and the flexibility available to the developer. Also, it will help improve network performance when the aggregator can be accessed remotely. Then, the client application will not need to access multiple context providers, thus reducing the network traffic.
3. Context interpreter/Inferencer: This module, using the inference engine, provides a "why" to the context. Gathered/interpreted context will be evaluated on the basis of the need of the application.
4. Context processor: This module, based on the repositories and aggregated, interpreted context, generates a list of services required to provide a specific service. The simplest of the models will have the context processing logic embedded in identifying the required service. However, separating the context logic module from other components and the architecture from supporting service providers will make context processing more generic and also dynamic.
5. Service fetcher: A network may be used to fetch the desired service; the levels of abstraction and object orientation enhance network performance.
6. Service disburser: This is a component for deploying the required/desired service on the mobile device on the basis of the context.

The functions of components 4, 5, and 6 may be carried out by the server, the network, and the actual mobile device, respectively.

19.1.6 Illustrative Context-Aware Applications

Context-aware applications can be classified into the following five categories:

1. Location-aware applications: These are applications where the context is basically obtained from the location and the application set provided is also about the location or the services relevant to that location. These applications use either pull or push techniques to gather context and may be made to respond in a specific way on the basis of the context.
2. Time-aware applications: These are applications where the context is basically obtained from time and date, and they also respond to the time of day or the season. This type of context is relatively easy to obtain, from the clock embedded in the device and the simple temperature sensor, and so on.

3. Device-aware applications: In these applications, the context is basically dependent on various devices or the state of the network and other devices that will share the context collected by them.
4. Personalized applications: In these applications, the user specifies limits on the contexts that devices should respond to. This means that the user will have to manually customize the conditions that the application is expected to respond to.
5. Adaptable applications: These applications/services automatically reconfigure themselves on the basis of the context in the environment and respond to the changing context. These types of systems are still in the development stage. A category of these applications respond dynamically to the emotional and physical state of the user along with the environment.

19.2 Decision Pattern as Context

This chapter discusses location-based services applications as a particular example of context-aware applications. But, context-aware applications can significantly enhance the efficiency and effectiveness of even routinely occurring transactions. This is because most end-user applications' effectiveness and performance can be enhanced by transforming them from a bare transaction to a transaction clothed by a surround of a context formed as an aggregate of all relevant decision patterns utilized in the past.

The decision patterns contributing to a transaction's context include the following:

- Characteristic and sundry details associated with the transaction under consideration
- Profiles of similar or proximate transactions in the immediately prior week or month or six months or last year or last season
- Profiles of similar or proximate transactions in the same or adjacent or other geographical regions
- Profiles of similar or proximate transactions in same or adjacent or other product groups or customer groups

To generate the context, the relevant decision patterns can either be discerned or discovered by mining the relevant pools or streams of primarily the transaction data. Or they could be augmented or substituted by conjecturing or formulating decision patterns that explain the existence of these characteristic pattern(s) (in the pools or streams of primarily the transaction data). In the next subsection we look at function-specific decision patterns with particular focus on financial decision patterns.

> Thus, generation of context itself is critically dependent on employing big data and mobilized applications, which in turn needs cloud computing as a prerequisite.

19.2.1 Concept of Patterns

The concept of patterns used in this book originated from the area of real architecture. Alexander gathered architectural knowledge and best practices regarding building structures in a pattern format. This knowledge was obtained from years of practical experience. A pattern according to Alexander is structured text that follows a well-defined format and captures nuggets of advice on how to deal with recurring problems in a specific domain. It advises the architect on how to create building architectures, defines the important design decisions, and covers limitations to consider. Patterns can be very generic documents, but may also include concrete measurements and plans. Their application to a certain problem is, however, always a manual task that is performed by the architect. Therefore, each application of a pattern will result in a differently looking building, but all applications of the pattern will share a common set of desired properties. For instance, there are patterns describing how eating tables should be sized so that people can move around the table freely, get seated comfortably, find enough room for plates and food, while still being able to communicate and talk during meals without feeling too distant from people seated across the table. While the properties of the table are easy to enforce once concrete distances and sizes are specified, they are extremely hard to determine theoretically or by pure computation using a building's blueprint.

In building architecture, pattern-based descriptions of best practices and design decisions proved especially useful, because many desirable properties of houses, public environments, cities, streets, and others, are not formally measurable. They are perceived by humans and, thus, cannot be computed or predicted in a formal way. Therefore, best practices and well-perceived architectural styles capture a lot of implicit knowledge how people using and living in buildings perceive their structure, functionality, and general feel. Especially, the indifferent emotion that buildings trigger, such as awe, comfort, coziness, power, and cleanness, are hard to measure or explain and are also referred to as the quality without a name or the inner beauty of a building. How certain objectives can be realized in architecture is, thus, found only through practical experience, which is then captured by patterns. For example, there are patterns describing how lighting in a room should be realized so that people feel comfortable and positive. Architects capture their knowledge gathered from existing buildings and feedback they received from users in patterns describing well-perceived building design. In this scope, each pattern describes one architectural solution for an architectural problem. It does so in an abstract format that allows the implementation in various ways. Architectural patterns, thus, capture the essential properties required for the successful design of a certain building area or function while leaving large degrees of freedom to architects.

Multiple patterns are connected and interrelated resulting in a pattern language. This concept of links between patterns is used to point to related patterns. For example, an architect reviewing patterns describing different roof types can be pointed to patterns describing different solutions for windows in these roofs and may be advised that some window solutions, thus, the patterns describing them cannot be combined with a certain roof pattern. For example, a flat rooftop cannot be combined with windows that have to be mounted vertically. Also, a pattern language uses these links to guide an architect through the design of buildings, streets, cities, and others, by describing the order in which patterns have to be considered. For example, the size of the ground on which a building is created may limit the general architecture patterns that should be selected first. After this, the number of floors, the aforementioned roofing style, and others, can be considered.

19.2.1.1 Patterns in Information Technology (IT) Solutions

In a similar way, the pattern-based approach has been used in IT to capture best practices in how applications and systems of applications should be designed. Examples are patterns for fault-tolerant software, general-application architectures, object-oriented programming, enterprise applications, or message-based application integration. Again, these patterns are abstract and independent of the programming language or runtime infrastructure used to form timeless knowledge that can be applied in various IT environments. In the domain of IT solutions, the desirable properties are portability, manageability, flexibility to make changes, and so on. The properties of IT solutions become apparent over time while an application is productively used, evolves to meet new requirements, has to cope with failures, or has to be updated to newer versions. During this lifecycle of an application, designers can reflect on the IT solution to determine whether it was well designed to meet such challenges.

19.2.2 Domain-Specific Decision Patterns

In the following, we discuss as illustrations, decision patterns for two domains or functional areas, namely, finance and customer relationship management (CRM). While the former is a formalized area to a large degree because of the statutory and regulatory requirements, the latter is defined and fine-tuned, across an extended period of operational experience, by the specific requirements of the business, offerings, and geographic region(s) in which the company operates.

19.2.2.1 Financial Decision Patterns

Financial management focuses on both the acquisition of financial resources on as favorable terms as possible and the utilization of the assets that those financial resources have been used to purchase, as well as looking at the interaction between these two activities. Financial planning and control is an essential part of the overall financial management process. Establishment of precisely what the financial constraints are and how the proposed operating plans will impact them are a central part of the finance function. This is generally undertaken by the development of suitable aggregate decision patterns like financial plans that outline the financial outcomes that are necessary for the organization to meet its commitments. Financial control can then be seen as the process by which such plans are monitored and necessary corrective action proposed when significant deviations are detected.

Financial plans are constituted of three decision patterns:

1. Cash flow planning: This is required to ensure that cash is available to meet the payments the organization is obliged to meet. Failure to manage cash flows will result in technical insolvency (the inability to meet payments when they are legally required to be made). Ratios are a set of powerful tools to report these matters. For focusing on cash flows and liquidity, a range of ratios based on working capital are appropriate; each of these ratios addresses a different aspect of the cash collection and payment cycle.

   The five key ratios that are commonly calculated are as follows:

   - Current ratio, equal to current assets divided by current liabilities
   - Quick ratio (or acid test), equal to quick assets (current assets less inventories) divided by current liabilities

- Inventory turnover period, equal to inventories divided by cost of sales, with the result being expressed in terms of days or months
- Debtors to sales ratio, with the result again being expressed as an average collection period
- Creditors to purchases ratio, again expressed as the average payment period

There are conventional values for each of these ratios (for example, the current ratio often has a standard value of 2.0 mentioned, although this has fallen substantially in recent years because of improvements in the techniques of working capital management, and the quick ratio a value of 1.0), but in fact these values vary widely across firms and industries. More generally helpful is a comparison with industry norms and an examination of the changes in the values of these ratios over time that will assist in the assessment of whether any financial difficulties may be arising.

2. Profitability: This is the need to acquire resources (usually from revenues acquired by selling goods and services) at a greater rate than using them (usually represented by the costs of making payments to suppliers, employees, and others). Although, over the life of an enterprise, total net cash flow and total profit are essentially equal, in the short term, they can be very different. In fact, one of the major causes of failure for new small business enterprises is not that they are unprofitable but that the growth of profitable activity has outstripped the cash necessary to resource it. The major difference between profit and cash flow is in the acquisition of capital assets (i.e., equipment that are bought and paid for immediately, but that have likely benefits stretching over a considerable future period) and timing differences between payments and receipts (requiring the provision of working capital).

   For focusing on longer-term profitability with short-term cash flows, profit to sales ratios can be calculated (although different ratios can be calculated depending whether profit is measured before or after interest payments and taxation). Value added (sales revenues less the cost of bought-in supplies) ratios can also be used to give insight into operational efficiencies.
3. Assets: Assets entail the acquisition and, therefore, the provision of finance for their purchase. In accounting terms, the focus of attention is on the balance sheet, rather than the profit and loss (P/L) account or the cash flow statement.

For focusing on the raising of capital as well as its uses, a further set of ratios based on financial structure can be employed. For example, the ratio of debt to equity capital (gearing or leverage) is an indication of the risk associated with a company's equity earnings (because debt interest is deducted from profit before obtaining profit distributable to shareholders). It is often stated that fixed assets should be funded from capital raised on a long-term basis, while working capital should fund only short-term needs.

It is necessary to be aware that some very successful companies flout this rule to a considerable extent. For example, most supermarket chains fund their stores (fixed assets) out of working capital because they sell their inventories for cash several times before they have to pay for them—typical inventory turnover is three weeks, whereas it is not uncommon for credit to be granted for three months by their suppliers.

There is, therefore, no definitive set of financial ratios that can be said to measure the performance of a business entity. Rather, a set of measures can be devised to assess different aspects of financial performance from different perspectives. Although some of these measures can be calculated externally, being derived from annual financial reports, and can be used to assess the same aspect of financial performance across different companies, care needs to be taken to ensure that the same accounting principles have been used to produce the accounting numbers in each case. It is not uncommon for creative accounting to occur so that acceptable results can be reported. This draws attention especially to the interface between management accounting (which is intended to be useful in internal decision making and control) and financial accounting (which is a major mechanism by which external stakeholders, especially shareholders, may hold managers accountable for their oversight).

> Financial scandals, such as Enron and WorldCom have highlighted that a considerable amount of such manipulation is possible palpably within generally acceptable accounting principles (GAAPs). There is clear evidence that financial numbers alone are insufficient to reveal the overall financial condition of an enterprise. Part of the cause has been the rules-based approach of U.S. financial reporting, in contrast to the principles-based approach adopted in United Kingdom. One result of the reforms that have followed these scandals has been a greater emphasis on operating information. In addition, legislation such as the Sarbanes–Oxley Act (SOX) in the United States has required a much greater disclosure of the potential risks surrounding an enterprise, reflected internally by a much greater emphasis on risk management and the maintenance of risk registers.

The finance function serves a boundary role; it is an intermediary between the internal operations of an organization and the key external stakeholders who provide the necessary financial resources to keep the organization viable. Decision patterns like financial ratios allow internal financial managers to keep track of a company's financial performance (perhaps in comparison with that of its major competitors), and to adjust the activities of the company, both operating and financial, so as to stay within acceptable bounds. A virtuous circle can be constructed whereby net cash inflows are sufficient to pay adequate returns to financiers and also contribute toward new investment; given sound profitability, the financiers will usually be willing to make additional investment to finance growth and expansion beyond that possible with purely internal finance. Conversely, a vicious cycle can develop when inadequate cash flows preclude adequate new investment, causing a decline in profitability, and so the company becomes unable to sustain itself.

19.2.2.2 CRM Decision Patterns

This section describes an overview of the statistical models-based decision patterns used in CRM applications as the guiding concept for profitable customer management. The primary objectives of these systems are to acquire profitable customers, retain profitable customers, prevent profitable customers from migrating to competition, and winning back lost profitable customers. These four objectives collectively lead to increasing the profitability of an organization.

CRM strategies spanning the full customer lifecycle are constituted of four decision patterns or models:

1. Customer acquisition: This involves decisions on identifying the right customers to acquire, forecasting the number of new customers, the response of promotional campaigns, and so on. The objectives of customer acquisition modeling includes identifying the right customers to acquire, predicting whether customers will respond to company promotion campaigns, forecasting the number of new customers, and examining the short- and long-run effects of marketing and other business variables on customer acquisition.

   This is a conscious move from mass marketing of products to one that is focused on the end consumer. This is a direct result of increases in data collection and storage capabilities that have uncovered layer upon layer of customer differentiation. Differentiating and segmenting with regards to demographic, psychographic, or purchasing power-related characteristics became more affordable and possible, and eventually became necessary in order to keep up with competing firms. Although segment-level acquisition did not take this theory to the extent that one-to-one customer acquisition has, it reinforced a growing trend of subsets or groups of customers within a larger target market. Being able to collect, store, and analyze customer data in more practical, affordable, and detailed ways has made all of this possible. As firms have become more capable and committed with data analyses, offerings have become more specific, thus increasing the amount of choice for customers. This has in turn spurred customers to expect more choice and customization in their purchases. This continuous firm–customer interaction has consistently shaped segment-level marketing practices in the process to better understand customers.

   The customer acquisition decision patterns would incorporate the following:

   - Differences between customers acquired through promotions and those acquired through regular means
   - Effect of marketing activities and shipping and transportation costs on acquisition
   - Impact of the depth of price promotions
   - Differences in the impact of marketing-induced and word-of-mouth customer
   - Acquisition on customer equity

2. Customer retention: This involves decisions on who will buy, what the customers will buy, when they will buy, and how much they will buy, and so on. During a customer's tenure with the firm, the firm would be interested in retaining the customer for a longer period of time. This calls for investigating the role of trust and commitment with the firm, metrics for customer satisfaction, and the role of loyalty and reward programs, among others. The objective of customer retention modeling includes examining the factors influencing customer retention, predicting customers' propensity to stay with the company or terminate the relationship, and predicting the duration of the customer–company relationship. Customer retention strategies are used both in contractual (where customers are bound by contracts, such as cell (mobile) phone subscription or magazine subscription) and noncontractual settings (where customers are not bound by contracts, such as grocery purchases or apparel purchases).

Who to retain can often be a difficult question to answer. This is because the cost of retaining some customers can exceed their future profitability and thus make them unprofitable customers. When to engage in the process of customer retention is also an important component. As a result, firms must monitor their acquired customers appropriately to ensure that their loyalty is sustained for a long period of time. Finally, identifying how much to spend on a customer is arguably the most important piece of the customer retention puzzle. It is very easy for firms to overcommunicate with a customer and spend more on his/her retention than the customer will ultimately give back to the firm in value.

The customer retention decision patterns would incorporate the following:

- Explaining customer retention or defection
- Predicting the continued use of the service relationship through the customer's expected future use and overall satisfaction with the service
- Renewal of contracts using dynamic modeling
- Modeling the probability of a member lapsing at a specific time using survival analysis
- Use of loyalty and reward programs for retention
- Assessing the impact of a reward program and other elements of the marketing mix

3. Customer attrition or churn: This involves decisions on whether the customer will churn or not, and, if so, what will be the probability of the customer churning, and when. The objective of customer attrition modeling includes churn with time-varying covariates, mediation effects of customer status and partial defection on customer churn, churn using two cost-sensitive classifiers, dynamic churn using time-varying covariates, factors inducing service switching, antecedents of switching behavior, and impact of price reductions on switching behavior.

   Engaging in active monitoring of acquired and retained customers is the most crucial step in being able to determine which customers are likely to churn. Determining who is likely to churn is an essential step. This is possible by monitoring customer purchase behavior, attitudinal response, and other metrics that help identify customers who feel underappreciated or underserved. Customers who are likely to churn do demonstrate symptoms of their dissatisfaction, such as fewer purchases, lower response to marketing communications, longer time between purchases, and so on. The collection of customer data is therefore crucial in being able to identify and capture such symptoms and that would help in analyzing the retention behavior and the choice of communication medium. Understanding who to save among those customers who are identified as being in the churn phase is again a question of cost vs. future profitability.

   The customer attrition decision patterns would incorporate

   - When are the customers likely to defect
   - Can we predict the time of churn for each customer
   - When should we intervene and save the customers from churning
   - How much do we spend on churn prevention with respect to a particular customer

4. Customer win-back: This involves decisions on reacquiring the customer after the customer has terminated the relationship with the firm. The objective of customer win-back modeling includes customer lifetime value, optimal pricing strategies for recapture of lost customers, and the perceived value of a win-back offer.

   Identifying the right customers to win back depends on factors such as the interests of the customers to reconsider their choice of quitting, the product categories that would interest the customers, and the stage of customer life cycle and so on. If understanding what to offer customers in winning them back is an important step in the win-back process, measuring the cost of win-back is as important as determining who to win back and what to offer them. The cost of win-back, much like the cost of retention or churn, must be juxtaposed with the customer's future profitability and value to the firm.

19.3 Context-Aware Mobile Services

Advances in mobility and wireless communications have increased the use of smart mobile applications. Many of the smart applications are now looking at the cloud-computing paradigm as an enabler to exploit its raw computing power, memory, and storage resources to overcome the resource limitations of mobile devices. Single monolithic applications for the mobile have now evolved toward a distributed loosely coupled composition of services where some of the service components are still running on the mobile but where others are running in the cloud.

As many of the applications try to become smarter, they aim to understand and anticipate the situation of their users by alerting them in time, or adapting their behavior according to the new context, and this without any intervention of their users. As such, context management becomes an integral part of the mobile cloud applications, with some of these tasks running on the mobile (e.g., context sensing and simple processing) and other computationally more expensive context management tasks being outsourced and taking place remotely on the cloud infrastructure (e.g., pattern detection, reasoning, and learning). For some tasks, the decision of what to do where is not always so clear-cut. This decision depends on various overhead trade-offs, including the quality of service (QoS) and the quality of experience (QoE). These trade-offs involve computation, communication, storage, energy consumption, availability, and connectivity, as well as user preferences with respect to privacy and security for sensitive data.

19.3.1 Limitations of Existing Infrastructure

19.3.1.1 Limited Capability of Mobile Devices

The first limitation arises due to the physical limitations of mobile devices. This relates to the limited memory of a mobile device, the display space, and the processing power of a device. Although the processing power has improved, the display space is still a limitation. The effective use of display space is a challenge in itself. The information given in the limited space needs to be optimized. In spite of the sufficient memory, if the data are not indexed and properly maintained, retrieval times can be a problem, taking away from the user's feeling of comfort and confidence.

19.3.1.2 Limited Sensor Capability

An important aspect from the providers' point of view is to be able to collate the heterogeneous data from various sensors in real time. The delayed response of the sensors can be a bottleneck in identifying the location of the user, as the context may change, especially when one is working with mobile devices. The context information collected, if dependent on sensors, also faces another difficulty. If the user switches off one of the sensors, then the context information may not be accurate. Also, the inaccuracy of the sensor data is likely to give wrong responses. Incorporation of multiple sensors creates an ambiguous situation regarding the context to be extracted. However, in recent decades, there have been reports of a few successful attempts in the development of several context-aware devices.

19.3.1.3 Restrictive Network Bandwidth

Another limitation is network bandwidth; the speed at which information moves over the network is limited by the bandwidth. A situation where the user is video streaming certain information or authentication of certain information is required from the server; the limited bandwidth in such a case can make the application absolutely nonproductive. Also, as the user is mobile, (s)he may be using various connections, such as the wireless local area network (LAN) or Bluetooth or infrared connectivity, at different locations. Services can be disconnected when the user moves from one cell to another and switching takes place. If the context data are being sent to the server for processing owing to limited processing capabilities of mobile devices, this disconnection (permanent connections are not guaranteed) can create problems leading to dissatisfaction.

19.3.1.4 Trust and Security Requirements

The last category of limitation arises from privacy and security requirements of users. Intuitively, we understand that the user is generally not comfortable with someone "watching over the shoulders" every activity and location of the user. The findings reported indicate that the user is not comfortable with generalized services and prefers personalized service; thus, the user would be more comfortable with an SMS going to people in their friend's list about their availability in a particular locality. So if the provider gives an option of filtering services (of course, there would be a cost associated depending on requirement), it would be beneficial and desired by the user.

19.3.1.5 Rapidly Changing Context

Another limitation is the problem arising as a result of rapid changes in the context and correct interpretation using the received heterogeneous data. When the user is stationary or in a static environment, like sitting on a computer at home and working with specific software or browsing the Internet, providing context-aware services is less challenging. When the user is mobile, the context is changing rapidly. To interpret this context, alignment to the requirement of the user with respect to that context and providing the required services/information will require extremely fast processing to be of any use. Also, the heterogeneous nature of the data gathered by the sensors can lead to ambiguity and complexity of interpretation. The interpretation of certain relative terms like angry or hungry, far and near, can change with situation and application. For example, a "loud voice" needs to be interpreted differently in the conference room, meeting room, or on the road. The "racing pulse" sensed by the pulse sensor when a person is stationary and the person is running is to be interpreted differently on the basis of the activity of the person. The device also needs to work with averages or some predecided computations in case the observations of the sensors vary rapidly. Techniques are required that can help predict the difficulties with perception and interpretation at design time.

19.3.2 Types of Sensors

The entire spectrum of context-aware systems is dependent on sensors that will convey the context to the application.

The most commonly used sensors can be classified into three categories:

1. Motion/location sensors: These sensors assist in finding the location and motion of the user. These are also known as orientation sensors. They include accelerometers, cameras, ambient noise detectors, GPS receivers, RFID readers, ultrasonic range finders, infrared sensors, and so on.
2. Environmental sensors: These allow the device to sense the environmental factor as the name suggests. These may include ambient temperature sensor, humidity sensor, barometer, and so on.
3. Physiological sensors: These sensors include skin temperature sensors, skin resistance sensors, grip sensors, pulse sensors, and so on.

The most commonly used are GPS receivers for location identification (outdoors), RFID or ultrasonic range finders, and infrared sensors (indoors). Accelerometers are most popular for gauging motion (sitting, walking, climbing, and so on) as they are inexpensive and also small enough to be embedded in mobile devices without making them bulky. Microphones and cameras help identify the ambient location on the basis of noise levels (recognizing speaking or talking). These are incorporated in most mobile devices available currently in the market. Light and temperature sensors are also used to determine a user's environmental context.

The actual sensors included will be on the basis of the applications and the services the provider chooses to incorporate in the device. The number of sensors used by providers in mobile devices will decide the size of such devices. The more the number of sensors, the bulkier the size, reducing its popularity.

19.3.3 Context-Aware Mobile Applications

The mobile cloud-computing paradigm from a context-aware perspective can be regarded as finding effective ways to make cloud services, being utilized in mobile applications, aware of the context of their customers and applications. To ease the development of context-aware applications, it is paramount to decouple the application logic and its adaptation logic from context acquisition and inference, and at the same time, it is equally important to provide efficient and effective ways to utilize the acquired context. That is why writing scalable and robust smart applications for mobile devices in the cloud environment not only involves being mindful of the architecture of both the cloud services and the management of the context information but also about the communication and coordination between all the parties involved that drive the smart adaptive behavior of the application.

Context awareness requires an effective approach to cater for getting the right information at the right time to make the correct decisions for changing or optimizing its behavior. Context awareness can be regarded as the dynamic adaptation of these applications according to the continuously changing context of the user, the communication network, the physical environment, and the device itself. For instance, if a user wants to download and play a video in his mobile device, a context-aware video playing application on the mobile device may automatically select the appropriate variant according to its available bandwidth, memory and battery power and display size of the device and if necessary offload the transcoding of the original video to this variant to the cloud. This way, the mobile device gets a suitable video stream with respect to its own capabilities and resource availability.

Context awareness usually involves three basic steps:

1. Discovery: This involves the identification of entities that are relevant for the application's tasks. In the first step, a context-aware application has to discover and explore its environment in order to get information to work with. In the above example, it means contextual information not only about resources on its own device but also about other networks, computational facilities, and displays in the neighborhood.
2. Selection: A context-aware application has to filter the information that was discovered according to its specific needs. Information about displays that are located on the floor below is irrelevant. This selection process can be fairly complex as it may require complex filtering techniques to decide which sensor or device is offering relevant information.
3. Use: The application uses the discovered and selected information to make the right decision or change its configuration or behavior. Context can be utilized in many ways:
    - Contextual information display: The context can be presented to the user. A simple example is finding the closest Mexican restaurant to your current location.
    - Contextual augmentation: Augmentation will associate the metadata about the captured context, for example, showing on a map all the shops that sell a particular item, with nearby parking facilities and that will still be open for at least half an hour by the time you reach the shop.
    - Contextual mediation: This use case focuses on getting relevant context information to the entities that need it (but they might not be able to sense it themselves). For example, remote applications might optimize their services or functionality to best meet the needs and limits arising from the local and evolving context of interaction.
    - Context-aware configuration: This use of context defines the rules for the actions to be performed in a given context, for example, choosing a nearby printer or relocating the display to another screen.
    - Context-triggered actions: This context-aware behavior will initiate certain steps when certain contextual conditions are met, for example, turning on the silent mode of the mobile and hiding the notifications if the user is in a meeting.

19.3.3.1 Context-Awareness Management Framework

Context-awareness refers to the capability of an application or a service being aware of its physical environment or situation (e.g., context) and to respond proactively and intelligently based on this awareness. Context-awareness is considered to be the cornerstone technique for developing pervasive computing applications that are flexible, adaptable, and capable of acting autonomously on behalf of the user. The context-aware process adaptation as the action that modifies the process in a way that causes process behavior to evolve according to the evolution of business and users' requirements, and the context considered relevant to that process. To this end, process modeling must be flexible enough to deal with constant changes—both at the business level (e.g., evolving business rules) and the technical level (e.g., contextual information and platform upgrades).

The flexibility could be provided or addressed by incorporating variabilities into the system; such variabilities must enable the possibilities to infer or interpret different context information from different perspectives. However, while doing this, the design of the process core should be decoupled from the design of the adaptation logic, which can contribute significantly in easing the process design and rapid prototyping. This framework must enable capturing the variability in the service-based process in a logical form by introducing the notion of context fragments and context primitives. This would enable the ultimate flexibility to automatically generate and deploy a customized process based on the context. Above all, to ease the development of such applications efficiently and effectively, it is necessary to decouple the application from context acquisition and representation, and at the same time provide universal models and mechanisms to manage context. This last requirement arises from the fact that generic and dynamically manageable context models can be reused by different applications and ease context sharing between systems.

Variability management techniques from software product line (SPL) can be applied to handle context variabilities for customization and adaptation wherein context modeling can be treated as feature modeling in SPL. Thus, the feature model of the system context will be considered as a composition of segmented context features models, each of which models a part of the whole context. Based on the context feature model, specific context—member of a product line—can be constructed by composing features from the context information. Feature models are less powerful than ontologies, and are more appropriate for expressing a subset of what ontologies can express, but they can be deployed to represent the context information from the requirements perspective. In ontology modeling, a concept is described by adding its details and implicitly defining in a bottom-up fashion the scope of the concept through these details. Whereas, in feature modeling, a concept is described by first setting its scope and hierarchically adding its details in a top-down fashion. Thus, features allow the context modeler to devise in a top-down fashion, generic, and reusable context features, which can be shared among all applications that need to use this context. The relationship between context and features expresses the context variability from an application point of view.

A software product line (SPL) is a set of software-intensive systems sharing a common, managed set of features that satisfy specific needs of a particular market or mission, and that are developed from a common set of core assets in a prescribed way. Feature modeling is a domain modeling technique; modeling product family as a hierarchy of features, their similarities, differences, and relationships among them. Feature models can be used for modeling common and variable requirements of products in a SPL, scoping SPLs, and product configuration, and derivation.

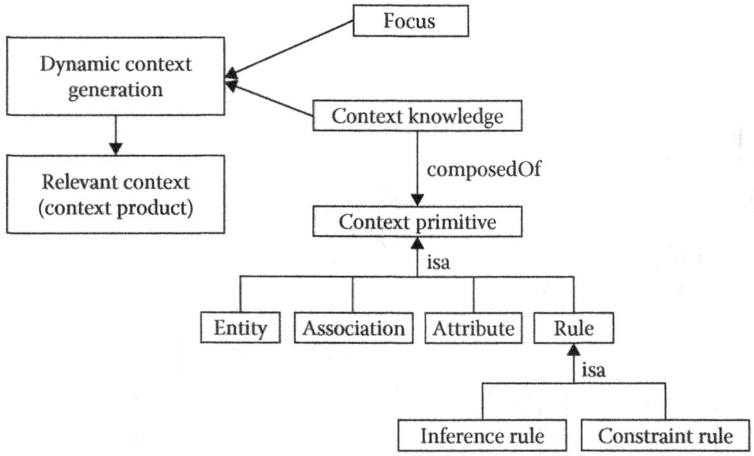

FIGURE 19.1
Context definition.

Given a focus, context knowledge is composed of a set of small pieces termed as context primitives (CP). CP refers to a piece of contextual knowledge such as entity, entity attribute, relationship between two entities, their constraints, or inference rules—used to define context situations and infer new knowledge—that can be used to define the context. Given a focus, a relevant subset of CPs can be used to generate the current context (see Figure 19.1). Each context feature corresponds to a specific set of context primitives. The focus is a concept representing the point of view the application is interested in looking at the current context. Each focus corresponds to a specific set of context features. Given a focus, a relevant subset of these pieces will be used to generate a per-application customized contextual knowledge. Obviously, considering only the relevant context primitives will improve the reasoning performance and reduce response time, which is a vital issue in a pervasive environment. Thus, a feature is a set of context primitives that is relevant to some stakeholder from a specific "focus" point of view.

Figure 19.2 depicts the conceptual metamodel. The concepts of the conceptual metamodel were identified and grouped into two different sections: the context related concepts (white) and the context feature concepts (shaded). The main construct for representing context knowledge is the ContextPrimitive, which represents the base context constructs (primitives) mentioned above: entity classes, entity attributes, entity associations, and rules. Two types of rules could be identified:

1. Consistency rules provide a mechanism for context consistency by specifying conditions that must be held in the context information.
2. Inference rules used to generate new context information after reasoning on the existing one.

Further modeling constructs are axioms that add additional facts about the entities and attributes. These are specialization and equivalence relationships that may be specified between two entity classes, two attribute classes, or two association classes.

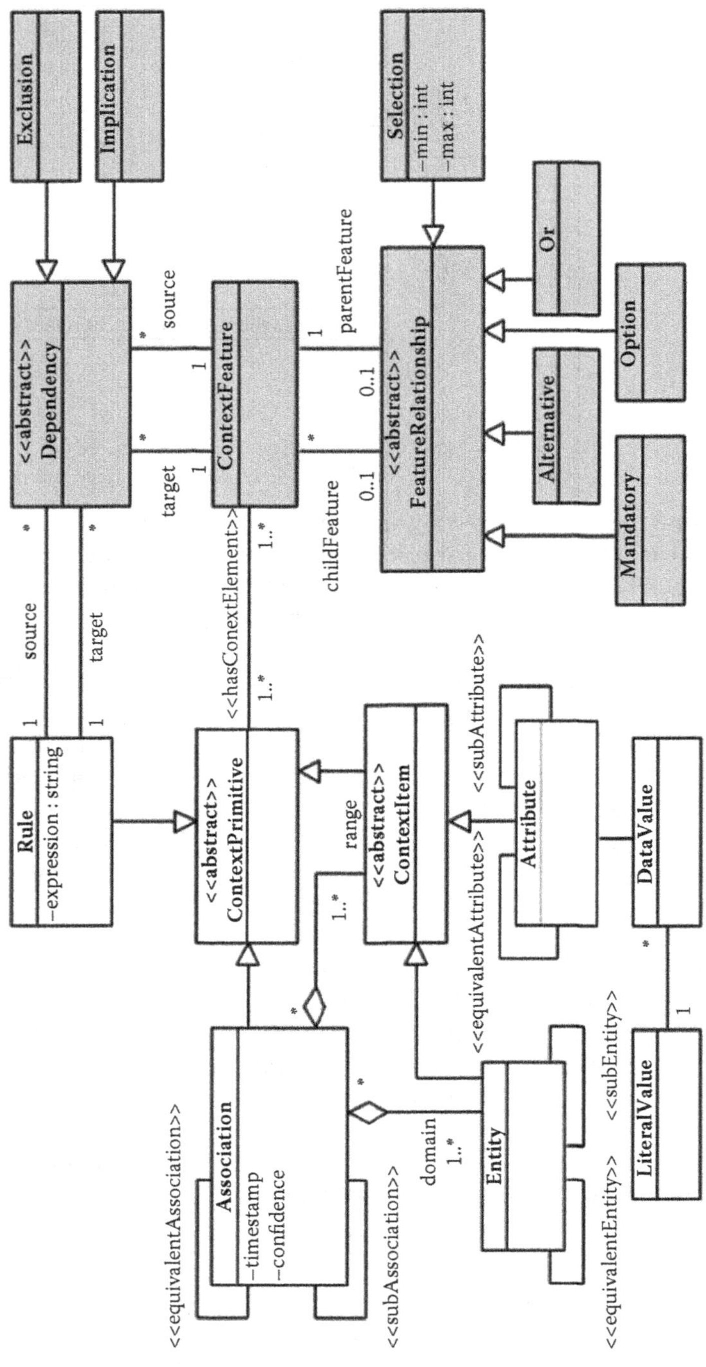

FIGURE 19.2
Conceptual metamodel of a context.

19.4 Summary

Considering the tremendous growth in mobile-based and sensor-based services and applications, context-aware applications are envisaged to emerge as an area with high-growth business potential in the future. None of these services and applications will be viable without being enabled by cloud computing, big data and Internet of Things (IoT). This chapter introduces the fundamentals of context-aware systems with specific context of the mobile-based application that is presently witnessing the highest growth in the consumer market space.

Epilogue: Internet of Things

The combination of the Internet and emerging technologies, such as near-field communications, real-time localization, and embedded sensors, transform everyday objects into smart objects capable of understanding and reacting to their environment. Advances in sensing and computing capabilities are making it possible to embed increasing computing power in small devices. This has enabled the sensing devices not just to passively capture data at very high resolution but also to take sophisticated actions in response. Such objects enable new computing applications and are at the base of the vision of a global infrastructure of networked physical objects known today as the Internet of Things (IoT). The IoT refers to the ever-growing network of physical objects that feature an IP address for Internet connectivity and the communication that occurs between these objects and other Internet-enabled devices and systems. These objects include various sensors, indicators, or actuators and can both transmit the collected sensor data to other networked devices and be controlled from another device. There has been a huge increase in commercial availability of such devices recently, encompassing everything from security systems to media players and speakers, car equipment, appliances, thermostats, light bulbs, locks, weather stations, etc.

Consequently, devices all the way from heavy assets such as aircraft engines to wearables such as health monitors can not only generate massive amounts of data but can draw back on aggregate analytics to *improve* their performance over time. Big data analytics has been identified as a key enabler for the IoT. The amount of data around us is growing exponentially, and the leaps in storage and computational power in the past decade underpin the unique selling proposition of big data of being able to provide better insights into various business processes or everyday life in a way that was not possible in the past. By analyzing large data sets and discovering relationships across structured and unstructured datasets, it is the driving force behind business analytics and advocated as a significant opportunity to boost innovation, production, and competition.

The increasing volume, variety, velocity, and veracity of data produced by the IoT will continue to fuel the explosion of data for the foreseeable future. With estimates ranging from 16 to 50 billion Internet connected devices by 2020, the hardest challenge for large-scale, context-aware applications and smart environments is to tap into disparate and ever growing data streams originating from everyday devices and to extract hidden but relevant and meaningful information and hard-to-detect behavioral patterns out of it. To reap the full benefits, any successful solution to build context-aware data-intensive applications and services must be able to make this valuable or important information transparent and available at a much higher frequency to substantially improve the decision making and prediction capabilities of the applications and services.

Just like the Internet and Web connects humans, the Internet of Things (IoT) is a revolutionary way of architecting and implementing systems and services based on evolutionary changes. The Internet as we know it is transforming radically, from an academic network in the 1980s and early 1990s to a mass-market, consumer-oriented network. Now, it is set to become fully pervasive, connected, interactive, and intelligent. Real-time communication is possible not only by humans but also by *things* at any time and from anywhere.

It is quite likely that sooner or later the majority of items connected to the Internet will not be humans, but things. IoT will primarily expand communication from the 7 billion people around the world to the estimated 50–70 billion machines. This would result in a world where everything is connected and can be accessed from anywhere—this has a potential of connecting 100 trillion things that are deemed to exist on Earth. With the advent of IoT, the physical world itself will become a connected information system. In the world of the IoT, sensors and actuators embedded in physical objects are linked through wired and wireless networks that connect the Internet. These information systems churn out huge volumes of data that flow to computers for analysis. When objects can both sense the environment and communicate, they become tools for understanding the complexity of the real world and responding to it swiftly.

Internet of Things (IoT) can be defined as the network formed by things or objects having identities and virtual personalities that interact using intelligent interfaces to connect and communicate with the users, social and environmental contexts. IoT is also referred as pervasive or ubiquitous computing systems. The goal of IoT is to achieve pervasive IoT connectivity and grand integration and to provide secure, fast, and personalized functionalities and services such as monitoring, sensing, tracking, locating, alerting, scheduling, controlling, protecting, logging, auditing, planning, maintenance, upgrading, data mining, trending, reporting, decision support, dashboard, and back-office applications.

IoT would be closely associated with environmental, societal, and economic issues such as climate change, environment protection, energy saving, and globalization. For these reasons, the IoT would be increasingly used in a large number of sectors such as healthcare, energy and environment, safety and security, transportation, logistics, and manufacturing.

Major IoT applications in various sectors are as follows:

- Energy and Power: Supply/Alternatives/Demand. Turbines, generators, meters, substations, and switches
- Healthcare: Care/Personal/Research. Medical devices, imaging, diagnostics, monitor, and surgical equipment
- Buildings: Institutional/Commercial/Industrial/Home. HVAC, fire and safety, security, elevators, access control systems, and lighting
- Industrial: Process Industries/Forming/Converting/Discrete Assembly/Distribution/Supply Chain. Pumps, valves, vessels, tanks, automation and control equipment, capital equipment, and pipelines
- Retail: Stores/Hospitality/Services. Point-of-sale terminals, vending machines, RFID tags, scanners and registers, lighting, and refrigeration systems
- Security and Infrastructure: Homeland Security/Emergency Services/National and Regional Defense. GPS, radar systems, environmental sensors, vehicles, weaponry, and fencing
- Transportation: On-Road Vehicles/Off-Road Vehicles/Nonvehicular/Transport Infrastructure. Commercial vehicles, airplanes, trains, ships, signage, tolls, RF tags, parking meters, surveillance cameras, and tracking systems
- Information Technology and Network Infrastructure: Enterprise/Data Centers. Switches, servers, and storage
- Resources: Agriculture/Mining/Oil/Gas/Water. Mining equipment, drilling equipment, pipelines, and agricultural equipment
- Consumer/Professional: Appliances/White Goods/Office Equipment/Home Electronics. M2M devices, gadgets, smartphones, tablet PCs, and home gateways

In terms of the type of technological artifacts involved, IoT applications can be subdivided into four categories:

1. The Internet of Devices: Machine-to-Machine (M2M): M2M refers to technologies that allow both wireless and wired devices to communicate with each other or, in most cases, a centralized server. An M2M system uses devices (such as sensors or meters) to capture events (such as temperature or inventory level), which are relayed through a network (wireless, wired, or hybrid) to an application (software program) that translates the captured events into meaningful information. M2M communication is a relatively new business concept, born from the original telemetry technology, utilizing similar technologies but modern versions.
2. The Internet of Objects: Radio-frequency identification (RFID): RFID uses radio waves to transfer data from an electronic tag attached to an object to a central system through a reader for the purpose of identifying and tracking the object.
3. The Internet of Transducers and Wireless Sensor Networks (WSN): WSN consists of spatially distributed autonomous sensors to monitor physical or environmental conditions, such as temperature, sound, vibration, pressure, motion, and pollutants, and to cooperatively pass their data through the network to a main location. More modern networks are bidirectional, becoming wireless sensor and actuator networks (WSANs) enabling the control of sensor activities.
4. The Internet of Controllers: Supervisory Control and Data Acquisition (SCADA): SCADA is an autonomous system based on closed-loop control theory or a smart system or a cyber physical system (CPS) that connects, monitors, and controls equipment via the network (mostly wired short-range networks, sometimes wireless or hybrid) in a facility such as a plant or a building.

References

Albright, S. C. and W. L. Winston. *Business Analytics: Data Analysis and Decision Making* (Cengage Learning, 5th ed., 2015).

Alexandre, T. *Scala for Java Developers* (Packt Publishers, 2014).

Andrews, G. R. *Foundations of Multithreaded, Parallel, and Distributed Programming* (Addison-Wesley, 1999).

Berman, J. J. *Principles of Big Data: Preparing, Sharing and Analyzing Complex Information* (Morgan Kaufman, 2013).

Berners-Lee, T., O. Lassila, and J. Hendler. The semantic web: A new form of web content that is meaningful to computers will unleash a revolution of new possibilities. *Scientific American,* 284(5), 34–43, 2001.

Bessis, N. and C. Dobre. *Big Data and Internet of Things: A Roadmap for Smart Environments* (Springer, 2014).

Blazewicz, L. et al. *Handbook on Data Management in Information Systems* (Springer, 2003).

Burgess, M. *In Search of Certainty: The Science of Our Information Infrastructure* (CreateSpace, 2013).

Chin, A. and D. Zhang (Eds.). *Mobile Social Networking: An Innovative Approach* (Springer, 2014).

Cioffi-Revilla, C. *Introduction to Computational Social Science: Principles and Applications* (Springer, 2014).

Coulouris, G., J. Dollimore, T. Kindberg, and G. Blair. *Distributed Systems: Concept and Design* (Boston, MA: Addison-Wesley, 2011).

Dey, A. K. Understanding and using context. *Personal and Ubiquitous Computing Journal*, 1, 4–7, 2001.

Domingue, J., D. Fensel, and J. A. Hendler (Eds.). *Handbook of Semantic Web Technologies* (Springer, 2011).

Elmasri, R. and S. B. Navathe. *Fundamentals of Database Systems* (Pearson, 2016).

Firtman, M. *High Performance Mobile Web* (O'Reilly, 2010).

Frampton, M. *Big Data Made Easy: A Working Guide to the Complete Hadoop* (Apress, 2014).

Gorton, I. and D. K. Gracio (Eds.). *Data Intensive Computing: Architectures, Algorithms and Applications* (Cambridge University Press, 2013).

Grover, M., T. Malaska, J. Seidman, and G. Shapira. *Hadoop Application Architectures: Designing Real World Big Data Applications* (O'Rielly, 2015).

Hillard, R. *Information Driven Business: How to Manage Data and Information for Maximum Advantage* (Wiley, 2010).

Hwang, K. et al. *Distributed and Cloud Computing: From Parallel Processing to the Internet of Things* (Morgan-Kaufmann, 2011).

Isson, J. P. and J. S. Harriott. *Win with Advanced Business Analytics: Creating Business Value from Your Data* (Wiley, 2013).

Kale, V. *Guide to Cloud Computing for Business and Technology Managers: From Distributed Computing to Cloudware Applications* (London: Auerbach Publication, 2015).

Knight, J. *Fundamentals of Dependable Computing for Software Engineers* (CRC Press, 2012).

Linoff, G. S. and M. J. A. Berry. *Data Mining Techniques: For Marketing, Sales and Customer Relationship Management* (Wiley, 3rd ed., 2011).

Loke, S. *Context-Aware Pervasive Systems: Architectures for a New Breed of Applications* (Boca Raton, FL: Auerbach Publications, 2006).

Marinescu, D. *Cloud Computing: Theory and Practice* (Boston, MA: Morgan Kaufmann, 2013).

McGovern, J., O. Sims, A. Jain, and M. Little. *Enterprise Service Oriented Architectures: Concepts, Challenges, Recommendations* (Dordrecht, the Netherlands: Springer, 2006).

McWherter, J. and S. Gowell. *Professional Mobile Application Development* (Wiley, 2012).

Mehta, N. *Mobile Web Development: Building Mobile Websites, SMS and MMS Messaging, Mobile Payments, and Automated Voice Call Systems with XHTML MP, WCSS, and Mobile AJAX* (Packt Publishing, 2008).

Pacheco, P. *An Introduction to Parallel Programming* (Amsterdam, the Netherlands: Morgan Kaufmann, 2011).

Palfrey, J. and U. Gasser. *Interop: The Promise and Perils of Highly Interconnected Systems* (Basic Books, 2012).

Pankratius, V., A. Adl-Tabatabai, and W. Tichy (Eds.). *Fundamentals of Multicore Software Development* (CRC Press, 2012).

Pentreath, N. *Create Scalable Machine Learning Applications to Power a Modern Data-driven Business Using Spark* (Packt Publishing, 2015).

Plattner, H. *A Course in In-Memory Data Management: The Inner Mechanics of In-Memory Databases* (Springer, 2013).

Ponniah, P. *Data Warehouse Fundamentals: A Comprehensive Guide for IT Professionals* (Wiley, 2001).

Provost, F. and F. Fawcett. *Data Science for Business* (O'Reilly, 2013).

Rauber, T. and G. Runger. *Parallel Programming for Multicore and Cluster Systems* (Springer, 2nd ed., 2013).

Revesz, P. *Introduction to Databases: From Biological to Spatio-Temporal* (Springer, 2010).

Sakr, S. *Big Data 2.0 Processing Systems: A Survey* (Springer, 2016).

Scoble, R. and S. Israel. *Age of Context: Mobile, Sensors, Data and the Future of Privacy* (Patrick Brewester, 2014).

Siegel, E. *Predictive Analytics: The Power to Predict Who Will Click, Buy, Lie, or Die* (Wiley, 2013).

Sottile, M. J., T. G. Mattson, and C. R. Rasmussen. *Introduction to Concurrency in Programming Languages* (CRC Press, 2009).

Stocker, R. and T. Bossomaier. *Networks in Society: Links and Language* (Pan Stanford Publishing, 2013).

Xu, G., Y. Zhang, and L. Li. *Web Mining and Social Networking: Techniques and Applications* (Springer, 2011).

Yang, L., A. Waluyo, J. Ma, L. Tan, and B. Srinivasan. *Mobile Intelligence* (Hoboken, NJ: Wiley, 2010).

Yin, Y. et al. *Data Mining: Concepts, Methods and Applications in Management and Engineering Design* (Springer, 2011).

Index

Note: Page numbers followed by f and t refer to figures and tables, respectively.

B

C

I

J

P

X

Y

Z